◆FOURTH EDITION◆

Purchasing for Food Service Managers

by

M.C. Warfel, B.S.
formerly with James Madison University
and a vice president, Sheraton Corporation

and

Marion L. Cremer, R.D., Ph.D.
Professor Emeritus, Ohio State University, Columbus

Fourth Edition Revised by
Marion L. Cremer
and
Richard J. Hug, M.B.A.

Contributing Author for Computer Technology,
Kimberly J. Harris, Ed.D.

McCutchan Publishing Corporation
P.O. Box 774, 2940 San Pablo Ave., Berkeley, CA 94702

**In memory of
M.C. Warfel**

ISBN 0-8211-2275-4
Library of Congress Catalog Card Number 00-106702

First edition published 1985; second edition, 1990; third edition, 1996

Printed in the United States of America

Preface

The authors analyze the subject of food and beverage purchasing and present it to the student as experienced food and beverage managers would. Purchasing is not an isolated function. It operates in the midst of and in cooperation with all the other functions of a complete food and beverage operation. Consequently, successful interaction by the buyers with those responsible for the conduct of the other departments is a subject of study in this volume. Likewise, the relationships of the buyer and the vendors is a key to productive buying—it too deserves and is given in-depth commentary.

The "Guides to Purchasing Food" and "The Big Four: Basic Complement Manual for a Hotel or Restaurant" in the Appendix will be of use to you as a student and as you are on the job in the food service industry.

A note of interest in the education field: more people are training for the food service industry in educational institutions than ever before. There are an increasing number of job opportunities for graduates of these institutions.

We hope that you find this book most helpful as well as interesting as you pursue your future in one of the most rewarding commercial professions.

We would like to express our thanks to John McCutchan, the publisher, and Kim Sharrar, the editor of this volume.

Contents

Exhibits

Part I
BASIC PRINCIPLES AND FUNCTIONS OF PURCHASING

1 Food Purchasing Dynamics

Purpose: To survey developments in agriculture, food processing, food marketing, food regulation, and the food service industry over time to provide a basis for understanding the broad scope of the purchasing function and the knowledge needed by competent buyers.

INTRODUCTION

The business of food purchasing in the food service industry is dynamic because of its integral involvement with constantly changing political, social, and economic systems and systems of agriculture, food processing, food marketing, and food regulation throughout the world. For example, the end of the Cold War with the former Soviet Union and the enactment of trade agreements, such as the North American Free Trade Agreement (NAFTA), have opened societies, expanded markets, furthered business opportunity, and complicated regulation.

Ramifications of change are seen in U.S.-based (chain) restaurants found throughout the world; in increased amounts of imported foods available in U.S. markets; in various kinds of fresh food available throughout the year; in food quality and safety control problems increased due to expanded territory and increased amounts of food; in food safety being the top interest of restaurant customers; and in a completely revised regulatory system to ensure the safety of meat, fish, and poultry products. Finally, societal developments such as consumer interest in healthful foods and the development of biotechnology in agricultural science is leading to a new generation or revolution in the types of foods available in the next century. Consequently, food buyers are challenged to evaluate these products and provide them to food service customers.

Thus, developments in various types of systems will be reviewed in historical perspective in this chapter to provide a comprehensive view of food purchasing today. The student should understand that though change is constant and the future dynamic, many developments, institutions, or cultural features of the past still exist and are used in food purchasing today.

AGRICULTURE

Agriculture and fishing are the basic sources of all foods, and, consequently, are of fundamental importance to the food service industry. Agriculture encompasses the developmental phases of mechanization, application of science, business specialization, and world marketing.

Mechanization began with the U.S. Industrial Revolution, when the invention of power-driven machines triggered the establishment of American industry. Beginning in the late 1800's, many people left family farms to work in factories, and the use of machines greatly increased farm productivity. The main result of these changes was mass production of food and a larger market for this food.

Science has increased food production, changed food quality characteristics, and improved the keeping quality of food. Increased production is due to the use of fertilizers, pesticides, hormones, and breeding. Food quality characteristics are particularly affected by plant and animal breeding through normal processes or the applications of biotechnology.

Plants and animals can be bred to possess particular physical and chemical characteristics for a purpose or to thrive in particular soil and weather conditions. Also, plants naturally have chemical characteristics directly related to soil composition, and breeders work to capitalize on traits for growth in particular soils. For example, breeds of wheat have been developed that grow well in the weather and soil of Canada and in North Dakota and South Dakota in the United States. These wheats have high protein content and make good bread or pastas but poor cakes and cookies. Breeds that grow well in Ohio and the eastern United States will naturally contain more starch and less protein, which makes excellent cakes and cookies but very poor quality bread. Another example is in cattle being bred to have good conformation (shape) for high meat yield in relation to bone.

Because scientific alterations in the chemical and physical properties of foods may result in differences that cannot be seen, as in flour, foods must be evaluated for their use in recipes or operational situations to determine if the quality is right for a particular use. The food buyer must remember that there can be "more than meets the eye."

Breeding with biotechnology is a major consideration for product development in the twenty-first century. It has already resulted in a tomato, called "Flavr Savr," that has been modified genetically to permit vine ripening for superior flavor without the problem of deterioration during harvesting and marketing. Also (though presently not directly related to the food supply), is the fact that sheep have been cloned. Advances in food science will lead to further development of foods with improved sensory quality characteristics and those, called nutraceuticals or functional foods, that contribute to improved health.

Another development of science is the use of controlled atmosphere storage in warehouses and the use of packing materials containing chemicals that preserve food and improve the keeping qualities of fresh fruits and vegetables. While products can be kept fresh in a controlled gaseous atmosphere for a long time, these products may deteriorate rapidly when removed from storage. Further, in products such as apples, desirable volatile flavor components characteristic of the food may be lost to the controlled atmosphere. For this reason, it is very important that purchasers know the extent and kind of storage. Another function of controlled atmosphere is for ripening foods such as bananas. Green bananas must be ripened with the appropriate temperature and humidity or they will readily rot. Knowledge of the sophistication of dealers' ripening facilities is extremely important because if the early stages of ripening are not done right, somewhat green bananas will not ripen acceptably. The development of biotechnology may make use of controlled atmosphere obsolete because fresh fruits and vegetables are being bred to have improved keeping quality.

A "food revolution" based on science and technology has been projected[1] for

---

[1] Cain, Herman. "The Food Revolution," *Restaurants USA* 19:5 (May 1999): 51.

the future. Food service buyers and managers must welcome the opportunity to evaluate these products, adapt to change, and incorporate them in food service operations where appropriate.

Business in agriculture today means farm management by specialists and production contracting. Agriculture has evolved from yesterday's family members or hired hands doing all the activities related to the production of various crops and animals on individual farms to today's farm managers contracting for specialists (when, for example, a very large specialized piece of farm equipment is needed) to perform all phases of crop or animal product production. This includes leasing land, planting, cultivating, crop dusting with airplanes, harvesting either mechanically or with migrant workers, storage, or marketing.

Production contracting is a second facet of agricultural business. Today, contracts are made for food products to be produced according to buyers' specifications rather than for growers to produce food products and hope for a market. For producers, price is assured and a market is guaranteed, and most of the risk in agricultural production is eliminated. Buyers have an assured source of supply, a guaranteed price, and food with desired characteristics. In these kinds of agreements, insurance should be purchased to provide protection during production, and the time when ownership is passed from seller to buyer should be precisely established. This is important for determining ownership in case of loss due to disaster.

Examples of contract buying and selling are for a food processor to contract for a number of acres to be planted with tomatoes to make catsup, a food service operator who serves mostly chicken to contract for a number of heads of chicken to be produced, or a food service operator whose main product is French fries

to contract for potatoes. Contracts may be very specific, noting the variety of fruit or vegetable desired, such as tomatoes or potatoes; breed of chicken; use of fertilizers and pesticides (including the amount of any pesticide residue that may remain); and time of harvesting or slaughter. Contract buying and selling minimizes risk, stabilizes price, and allows both buyers and sellers to plan for profitable operation. Without contracting, neither agricultural producers nor buyers have price protection in case of good or poor production due to weather or growing conditions.

Worldwide production and marketing makes a wide variety of fresh foods available throughout the year, increases the extent of potential variation in food characteristics, and dilutes the effect of U.S. regulatory control. These effects enhance the food buyer's options but increase the complexity of purchasing. Grapes, melons, tomatoes, or other fruits imported from South America and available in U.S. markets in the winter are attractive. However, these foods may not bear a U.S. grade to assure quality and may be inadequately inspected for contaminants. To obtain proper quality, buyers may need to visit wholesale markets to make selections.

Fishing is an important part of agriculture, and the supply and safety of fish have changed drastically over time. In the early history of the United States, fish were plentiful in all of the coastal waters and in inland lakes and other streams. The price of fish was low. Pollution, overfishing, and dams are but three of the factors that have reduced the fish population, caused some scarcity, higher prices, and some concern for the safety of fish products. Further, demand has increased because of consumer interest in fish as a low-fat food, and foreign interests have complicated the market. Initially, foreign fishing vessels were considered to encroach on the waters of the United States until a fishing limit was established. Now, U.S. waters are not so attractive, and much of the fish used in the United States is imported.

Recently, changes have occurred in the U.S. fishing industry. Due to concern for microbial safety, new regulations have been enacted that require inspection of fish (both foreign and domestic) according to Hazard Analysis Critical Control Point (HACCP) procedures (Exhibit 1.1; Chapter 3). This change is important in ensuring fish safety to buyers, since fish inspection was lacking except for canned or frozen U.S. graded products. Another change is the introduction of fish farming. This can increase the supply of some items, particularly shrimp, and perhaps help to control cost.

Although environmental problems, safety, high demand, some scarcity, and relatively high price are still issues in the purchase of fish; some progress has been made.

FOOD PROCESSING

Beginning at the time of the Industrial Revolution, the food processing industry developed in response to the need to preserve the food resulting from increased agricultural production. Food preservation, originally done by farm families for their own use, has developed to a large-scale industrial level.

Preservation techniques, including canning, freezing, drying, jelly making, pickling, curing, and radiation, have been developed over time with a view to improving the sensory quality of food and assuring food safety by maintaining chemical and microbiological quality. However, processing that assures microbial and chemical safety can greatly affect sensory quality. Following are descriptions of a few basic processes that will provide some understanding of their effects.

In *canning*, high temperature short time (HTST) and aseptic methods have been developed to shorten processing time and reduce product damage from excessive heat.

Commercial *freezing* was a major advance over canning because quality was not adversely affected by heat. The commercial freezing process was developed by Clarence Birdseye. He began marketing the frozen food through a company he established in 1924, which later became known as General Foods. The type of freezing he developed was "contact plate freezing," where food is frozen in packages (boxes) sandwiched between giant supercooled steel plates. Other forms are "immersion freezing," where food is immersed in a supercooled sugar or salt solution or liquid nitrogen and units are individually quick frozen (IQF), and "fluidized bed freezing," in which food is frozen when supercooled air or other gas is blown through a metal, meshlike conveyor belt on which the food travels. Immersion freezing is used for whole turkeys and chickens packaged in shrink wrap, which adheres during freezing, and sometimes for fruits and vegetables, such as corn, peas, strawberries, blueberries, or cherries individually quick frozen in individual units. Fluidized bed-type freezing is used for individually quick freezing many kinds of food, but particularly for individually quick freezing vegetables. Whether food is frozen in solid blocks or individual units is important knowledge for any food buyer, who must consider how the food will be used. For example, peas frozen solid in a 30-pound block are impractical to use if only small amounts are cooked at a time, but peas individually quick frozen can be removed in the quantity needed at one time.

Drying techniques include drying in the sun; drum drying, where food is applied to a hot metal drum; spray drying, where food material is sprayed into heated air;

foam drying, where a gas is applied to aerate or make food foamy and porous during the drying process, which occurs as the food moves on a conveyor; and freeze drying, where water is evaporated from frozen food. Different drying techniques affect the textural and flavor characteristics of food. For example, drum-dried milk, coffee, or potatoes will have hard particles and may have a scorched flavor from the heat of the drum. Spray- or foam-dried products will not be so damaged by heat and will have particles that are more easily dissolved in water or will produce a fluffier texture (particularly relevant to mashed potatoes) when rehydrated. Freeze drying will produce much less damage from heat and loss of volatile components, as with coffee, because water is evaporated with food frozen rather than hot. Freeze drying is done by sublimation (applying heat to frozen food). Food is first frozen and then heat is applied to evaporate moisture, as when the sun hits an icy window and removes moisture.

Radiation processing involves ionic (nuclear) and non-ionic (microwave) types. Microwave processing is sometimes used for partially cooking frozen fried chicken products and for potato chips. When partially cooked with microwave, chicken can be quickly cooked and then appropriately browned by deep-fat frying at the point of service. Potato chips can be processed by being fried to an appropriate light brown color and then further crisped by dehydration with microwave heat.

The technology of ionic radiation (also known as "irradiation") for food preservation has been developed and ready for commercialization since the early 1950s. However, the Food Additives Amendment (1958) to the Federal Food, Drug, and Cosmetic Act delayed commercialization of the process. Now, based on consumer and regulatory concerns for food safety, the process has come to the forefront as

a mechanism for control of microbial hazards in the food supply. This is manifested in the U.S. Food and Drug Administration's recent (1997) approval of irradiation for red meats, changes in requirements for labeling irradiated foods made by the Food and Drug Administration Modernization Act of 1997, and endorsement of meat irradiation by the National Restaurant Association.

Other foods previously approved for irradiation are wheat and wheat flour (insect disinfestation); white potatoes (sprout inhibition); pork (*Trichinella spiralis* control); fruit (disinfestation, ripening delay); fresh vegetables (disinfestation); and herbs, spices, vegetable seasonings, and fresh and frozen poultry (microbial control); animal feed and pet food (*Salmonella* control); and frozen packaged meats for National Aeronautics and Space Administration space flight programs (food sterilization). That irradiated foods are safe for humans and animals and that irradiation is effective in destroying microorganisms have been definitely established. However, the process is not widely used except for spices and in foods for immune system compromised patients in hospitals. In considering the purchase of irradiated foods, buyers should be aware of the fact that the sensory quality of meat, in particular, may be reduced because changes in color and flavor (rancidity) are produced by oxidative reactions. Also, there may be some consumer reluctance to accept these products.

Preparing *specialty products* such as cheese and other diary items, pickles, sauerkraut, jams, jellies, sauces such as Tabasco or Worcestershire, ham, alcoholic beverages, and convenience foods are specialized operations related to particular industries. Products may be distinguished by art in formulation as well as by science in preparation. Buyers probably will make purchases based on taste testing and operational preferences.

Food buyers generally need to know about food processing procedures in order to acquire the best food for particular purposes and also to understand the potential for defects in food purchases. Buyers should consider visiting plants to see first hand the different production processes.

FOOD LAW

The development of food law has been closely aligned with the development of food processing and increased agricultural production. Statutes have established standards not only for chemical and microbiological safety to protect the public health but also to facilitate trade through commercial standards and to protect the public from product fraud. The food buyer must know today's laws in order to communicate and to understand the extent of quality assurance provided.

Exhibit 1.1 is a synopsis of significant legal developments that provides insight into the effects of law on food purchasing. The exhibit shows that the legal system evolved to provide continuously more protection until a very high level of quality assurance and safety was attained. Then shortly before the time of publication of the last edition of this book, occurrences in the food service industry caused concern. These included outbreaks of severe illness related to contaminated hamburger, increased amounts of imported foods, lack of required seafood inspection, huge volumes of food processed, and reduced governmental expenditures for inspection.

Since 1990, as indicated in the exhibit (1.1), there have been several pieces of legislation that are significant bases for again building legitimate confidence in the wholesomeness of food in the United States. These include totally revised systems for microbial control or inspection of meat and poultry, called Hazard Analy-

sis and Critical Control Points (HACCP) and regulatory rules that require that all fish (both foreign and domestic) sold in interstate commerce be evaluated for wholesomeness according to Hazard Analysis and Critical Control Point plans. Other legislation was enacted to improve the regulatory control of pesticide residues on food and to provide for and ensure safe use of dietary substances that are added to foods to promote health or increase dietary intake.

Although major steps have been taken to improve the system of safety assurance through regulatory processes, the systems as presently developed are not infallible and new developments arise as control problems are identified. Thus the food buyer should take nothing for granted, but must inspect suppliers' facilities, review quality control processing records, and have strict requirements for the microbial as well as the sensory quality characteristics of foods purchased. Further, food buyers should advocate for regulatory developments that will meet the food service industry's needs.

FOOD MARKETING

Developments in food marketing closely parallel developments in agriculture and food processing, and may be summarized as follows:

1. Food produced and used on family farms
2. Animals, fruits, and vegetables transported for sale at large central markets through assemblers, wholesalers, or brokers
3. Food processing industry development—leading to processed food marketing by manufacturers' representatives, brokers, and wholesalers—increasing the number of middlemen involved in bringing food to consumers
4. Large buyers going directly to pro-

1878 ... A commission of agriculture published results of food examinations showing chemicals in food. Congress was alarmed and legal remedies began.

1879 ... Congress requested a department to examine food.

1883 ... Harvey Wiley was appointed Chief Chemist in the Department of Agriculture.

1897 ... The Tea Importation Act was passed to provide inspection of tea and prevent contaminated tea from entering the market.

1902 ... Wiley's "Poison Squads" found sulfur dioxide, formaldehyde, and nitrates in food. Fifty people died from eating vanilla checked for flavor but not safety.

Congress made an appropriation to establish pure food standards.

Congress passed the Sherman Act, which prohibited false branding of food and dairy products.

1906 ... The Food and Drug Act—Pure Food Law—was passed to prevent food adulteration and mislabeling.

1907 ... The Federal Meat Inspection Act was passed to ensure wholesomeness of meat.

1913 ... The Gould Amendment to the Federal Food and Drug Act was enacted to require net weight declaration on packages .

1924 ... A Model Milk Ordinance was developed by the U S. Public Health Service to ensure wholesomeness of milk.

1930 ... The McNary-Mapes Amendment was made to the Federal Food and Drug Act to provide standards of quality and fill of container.

1934 ... The Seafood Amendment to the Federal Food and Drug Act was passed to provide for seafood inspection.

1938 ... Previous legislation was incorporated into a new act, the Federal Food, Drug, and Cosmetic Act, which is currently the primary statute governing all foods except meat and poultry

(1954) Miller Pesticide Chemicals Amendment

(1958) Food Additives Amendment

(1960) Color Additives

1946 ... The Agricultural Marketing Act was enacted to provide grade standards to indicate differences in quality above a minimum level.

1947 ... The Poultry Products Inspection Act provided for inspection for wholesomeness.

1966 ... The Fair Packaging and Labeling Act made requirements for labeling quantity contents of packages.

1967 ... The Wholesome Meat Act Amendment to the Federal Meat Inspection Act required state meat inspection for wholesomeness equal to federal standards and provided Standards of Identity for meat.

1968 ... The Wholesome Poultry Products Inspection Act made poultry inspection mandatory within states as well as in interstate commerce and provided Standards of Identity.

1973 ... Provisions for nutrition labeling were made through the Federal Food, Drug, and Cosmetic Act. Nutrition labeling was required for any product about which a nutrition claim was made.

1990 ... The Nutrition Labeling and Education Act was enacted to encourage a particular way of eating—that is, to reduce fat and salt and encourage consumption of fiber. This act mandated nutrition labeling of most processed foods, completely changed requirements for labeling, and negated most of the provisions for nutrition labeling made in 1973.

1993 ... Regulatory proposals have been made for mandatory nutrition labeling of restaurant foods.

The Food and Drug Administration has proposed revised rules for seafood inspection.

The adequacy of the meat and poultry inspection systems to ensure safety are being considered due in part to several deaths from hamburgers eaten in a restaurant chain operation.

Controversy exists about use of milk from cows given hormones.

Opening of world trade, increased production, and lack of regulatory resources to ensure adequate inspection for microbial and chemical safety pose problems.

1994 ... Due to wide use of vitamins, minerals, herbs and other botanicals, and amino acids and other dietary substances to increase total dietary intake, the Dietary Supplement Health and Education Act (amended the Federal Food, Drug, and Cosmetic Act) was passed to protect consumers' right of access, ensure safety, and incorporate these products in the regulatory system.

1995 ... Regulatory "rule" enacted to ensure safety of fish by requiring all persons selling fish in interstate commerce to identify and control hazards through closely monitored Hazard Analysis Critical Control Point (HACCP) procedures.

1996 ... Food Quality Protection Act passed to improve regulatory control of pesticide residues, exclude pesticides from food additives regulations, and make known to consumers actions taken against particular chemicals and the foods on which they are used — partially based on incidence of illness due to Alar on apples.

1996 ... Pathogen Reduction; Hazard Analysis and Critical Control Point (HACCP) systems regulatory rule passed to totally revamp the U.S. meat and poultry inspection system, based on severe illness and deaths attributable to microbial contamination of meat.

1997 ... Food and Drug Modernization Act passed for faster marketing of safe and effective new drugs, prompter provision of valid nutrition and health claim information on food product labels, and revision of regulations for labeling irradiated foods.

Exhibit 1-1. Legal developments related to food purchasing.

cessors or agricultural producers and eliminating middlemen

5. Increasing sales in world markets

These stages in the development of food marketing are still sources for purchasing food. Today, a food buyer can choose to purchase from a roadside market, from wholesalers or brokers of various individual commodities in cities or central areas throughout the United States, from manufacturers' representatives who directly represent processors and may have offices close to large cities or buying areas, directly from an agricultural producer, through wholesalers or brokers who are importers, or directly from foreign or U.S. corporate producers throughout the world.

Food marketing has come full circle. Food was initially produced, sold, or used by individual farm units. Now, the trend is to eliminate middlemen and again go directly back to producers when purchasing, which increases the food buyer's options.

FOOD SERVICE

The food service industry has become an important economic entity in the past thirty years as the United States has moved from an agrarian to an industrial to a world economy and people eat away from home more often. In 1999, food service industry sales were projected to be $400 billion and to reach $577 billion by the year 2010.[2] About 46 percent of all adults eat out on a typical day, and the food service industry is a nationally important retail employer, with 10.2 million employees and employment expected to reach 12.0 million by the year 2006.[3] Eating and drinking places ranked third among private sector industries in total employment in 1997. Exhibit 1–2 shows a timeline in food service development in relation to national economic and social development to show the integral involvement of and relationships between food service business and world economic and societal events.

The food service industry has developed in relation to the national economy, social legislation, war, and world political events. For example, restaurateurs came together in 1919 to found the National Restaurant Association because of threatened strikes and high food prices. In the same year, the Prohibition Amendment was enacted as a major piece of social legislation. Restaurant sales fell substantially, because the amendment prohibited sale of alcoholic beverages. In reaction, restaurateurs began to promote the sale of food; thus legislation spurred the development of food as an important business entity.

Restaurants, as with other businesses, have thrived or have been constrained by, respectively, high and low points in the national economy. The Great Depression reduced business in restaurants, and afterwards general business expansion carried into the food service industry. The food service industry has grown through the nation's economic ups and downs, which indicates the increasing importance of food service in meeting fundamental needs.

The basic organization for managing hotels, institutions, restaurants, and other public food services began to emerge about 1935. The positions of food and beverage manager, restaurant manager, food and beverage controller, and independent purchasing agent were established, and the responsibilities of each were outlined. Regardless of the type of food service operation, it seemed best to separate purchasing from day-to-day operations, making it an independent

[2] "Foodservice Trends—A Guide to Success in 2010," *Restaurants USA* 19...8 (September 1999): 38–44.

[3] "1999 National Restaurant Association Restaurant Industry Pocket Factbook," *Restaurants USA* 18:11 (December 1998): 14.

arm of management, usually under the control of the accounting department. This is the organizational pattern that is in common use today.

The food service industry has been directly involved with labor, civil rights, environmental, and, currently, health care legislation. Legislation has a great effect on food service businesses because profit margins are low in relation to unit sales, large numbers of people are employed, and food meets fundamental needs. Equal access and service in restaurants was a focus early in the civil rights movement and continues to be important. Restaurants have a social responsibility both for access and for the microbial and chemical safety of food. In current times, issues of health and safety are major societal concerns, and food service operators as major providers of food must address those concerns.

Implications for Purchasing

The food service industry has changed in relation to developments in other industries, which in turn have affected how food is purchased. When restaurants were relatively small independent units, food was purchased from local wholesalers or producers. Dairy products were generally purchased from a local dairy and bread from a local bakery. Other foods were brought by truck or rail to local wholesalers and made available for sale. As the food service industry grew and other industries developed, buyers went to increasingly large centers to buy food. Fresh foods became readily available by air transport. Then, to meet high volume and specialized needs, buyers went to growers and processors to purchase by contract for the supply and quality desired. Finally, today's food buyer must deal with cosmopolitan markets, tastes, and foods, as world cultures are increasingly mixed.

World marketing enhances opportunity, but buying can be more difficult. Standards may be lacking or inadequately applied, and a larger supply makes finding the correct quality more difficult. World expansion of food service operations has produced a problem in determining how to supply food for worldwide operations—that is, should food be grown and processed at the site or shipped from the United States? Choosing to produce foods at a distant site creates in effect a complete evolution in development, as food service operators become managers of agriculture and food processing.

Social issues in food purchasing include microbial safety, the quality and consumer acceptability of irradiated foods, foods produced with techniques of biotechnology, and the nutrient content (and possible nutrition labeling) of foods served in restaurants. Microbial safety concerns attach to products such as fresh meat, fish, fruits, and vegetables. Recently, severe illness and deaths have resulted from consumption of foods contaminated by special strains of the *E. coli* and *Listeria* microorganisms. To assure safety, buyers may need to write specifications for microbial content, take special care to know about the sources of fresh foods, and conduct sanitation inspections of the food supply operations.

In terms of consumer acceptability, buyers should be particularly cautious when purchasing foods produced through biotechnology or those that are irradiated. Products must be approved as safe and may have advantages for purchase, but consumers may be adamantly unaccepting. Buyers might avoid the use of specially produced and processed foods until products gain acceptance in retail markets.

Mandatory nutrition labeling of all processed foods was put into effect on May 9, 1994, and is a current regulatory consideration for food service. For pur-

Decade	Restaurant Development	Dates	National Development	Dates
			Hall of Machines featured at Philadelphia Exposition	1876
1910–1920	Restaurant operations increased to meet needs of people working in factories rather than at home or on farms		Country changing from an agrarian to an industrial economy	
			Social reformers being heard	
	High food prices and threats of strikes by restaurant employees		World War I ended 1918	
	Restaurateurs primarily independent operators			
	National Restaurant Association founded in Kansas City	1919	Volstead Act to enforce the 18th Amendment to the Constitution — Prohibition — prohibiting the manufacture, transportation, and sale of beverage alcohol	1919
1920–1930	Development of Howard Johnson franchises, White Castle (5¢) hamburgers, and Marriott's A&W root beer operations		National economic development after World War I; economic depression at the end of the decade	
1930–1940	Difficult times economically despite development of options in serving alcoholic beverages at the end of Prohibition		Economic depression — "The Great Depression"; notorious time of gangsters; repeal of Prohibition by 21st Amendment to Constitution	1933
			Social Security Act	1935
			Wages and Hours Act (also called the Fair Labor Standards Act)	1938
			World War II began	1939
1940–1950	Food and gasoline shortages due to rationing; labor shortage caused by men at war and women working in defense industries; demand for restaurant food greatly increased; Education Department established by National Restaurant Association		Japanese bomb Pearl Harbor, December 7	1941
			Atomic bomb tested by exploding in New Mexico; bombs dropped on Hiroshima and Nagasaki; World War II ended	1945
1950–1960	High demand for restaurant food; rapid expansion of all food service segments; restaurants promote carryout food to eat while viewing television; the National Restaurant Association supports use of credit cards to increase sales		Economic boom	
			Korean War	1950–1953
			Television developed and increasingly important; credit cards developed as an important entity	
			"Sputnik" put into orbit by Soviet Union to begin era of space exploration; science education a U.S. national priority	1957

	Food service development		National developments
1960–1970			
	Food service industry recognized as important economic entity due to expansion and increased sales; limited menu—fast food concept becomes important; chain operations developed		
1961	McDonald's name purchased from McDonald brothers by Ray Kroc	1963	John F. Kennedy assassinated
1965	McDonald's makes over-the-counter stock offering; Howard Johnson's, Big Boy drive-ins, ARA (Automatic Retailers of America), F. W. Woolworth, and McDonald's rival the U.S. government school lunch and military food service in volume of sales	1965	Congress enacts Medicare
1966	McDonald's listed on New York Stock Exchange		
1967	Company mergers begin including Stouffer's with Litton Industries, Pillsbury with Burger King, and Baskin Robbins with TWA-Hilton; KFC (Kentucky Fried Chicken) grows by $101 million in one year		
1968	Restaurant stock values increase 75 percent; stocks of forty-nine companies increase over 165 percent	1969	Apollo 11 puts man on moon
1970–1980			
1970	International expansion becomes important; computer becomes integrally involved in operations; contract food service evolves in response to more expansion of government supported school food service	1970	Growth and development of computer use; student riots
1971	KFC opens first Tokyo outlet		
1971	Financial successes, losses, and mergers or spin-offs prevalent; Holiday Inns become first billion dollar food service-lodging operation		
1972	General Foods writes off $47 million loss on Burger Chef	1972	Pet writes off $5 million loss on Schrafft's and Stuckey's; military food purchases drop 30 percent due to scaledown of Vietnam War
1973	Litton sells Stouffer's to Nestle	1973	Rose v. Wade abortion case; cease-fire signed in January to begin total withdrawal of all U.S. troops

Exhibit 1-2. Time line of restaurant food service development and related national developments

Decade	Restaurant Development	Dates	National Development	Dates
	McDonald's is the first largest and KFC the second largest food service operations; for the first time, private operations surpass the U.S. Army and school food service in volume	1974	"Watergate" scandal	1974
			Fall of Saigon and end of Vietnam War	1975
	Salad bars become important	1977	U.S. hostages seized in Iran	1979
1980–1990	Food service industry continues to expand and develop; consumer interest in convenience, home-related activities, quality with good value, healthful foods, and cosmopolitan tastes lead to development of carry-out food service; menus emphasizing broiled or baked foods, fresh fruits and vegetables, chicken, and fish; restaurants featuring ethnic or national foods such as Chinese, Mexican, Italian; and special consideration of quality and price		Favorable economic climate for business and economy supported by high amounts of consumer debt	
			Education becomes major political issue	
			U.S. hostages released from Iran	1981
			U.S. a debtor nation	1985
			Challenger shuttle explodes on take-off	1986
	Continued international development		Increasing interest in children, including abortion rights; social issues continue to be important	
1990–2000	Continued but modest growth from decline in 1988		Persian Gulf War begins	1990
	Demand for food consumed off premises and at quick service restaurants high compared to higher-check, up-scale and mid-scale operations or for food eaten on premises		Persian Gulf War ends; civil rights issues are a major focus; coup fails to remove Mikhail Gorbachev; Soviet Union dissolved and Commonwealth of independent states formed	1991
	Food away from home a routine occurrence rather than a luxury and almost half of all adults patronizing food service operations on a typical day	1992	Business recession; low inflation; low interest rates; millions of jobs lost through corporate restructuring, plant closings, company failures, and military base closings; poor job market for managers and some professionals; decline in private sector gross hourly wage	
	Food service industry sales projected at $275.1 billion; sales at fast food restaurants ($86 billion) expected to exceed sales at full-service restaurants ($85.5 billion) for the first time; food service share of food dollar is 43.1 percent; food service industry the largest retail employer; with over 9 million persons employed		Signs of slow economic recovery; low inflation rate; low but rising interest rates; value-conscious consumers due to decreasing real wages, unemployment, and economic uncertainty	1994
	"Total Quality Management" to improve efficiency and meet consumer demand for high quality and good value; focus on engineering to provide quality with efficiency; changes in restaurant sales closely related to sales in disposable incomes		Health care, crime, economic wellbeing, and civil rights major issues; major concern for food safety and genetically engineered foods	
			Deadline (May 8) for implementation of Nutrition Labeling of all processed foods according to Nutrition Labeling and Information Act of 1990	

Date	Event
	Food safety a primary concern; health-related food service expanding
	National Restaurant Association views mandated employer paid health insurance a threat to the industry; consideration of pending issues in nutrition labeling of restaurant foods; consideration of new FDA Sanitation Code
	Travel-related expenditure on food service expected to grow 5.7 percent and exceed $80 billion
	Advancing sales and menu prices but stable or lower wholesale food prices; increasing labor cost and labor shortage; interest in foreign expansion into the Pacific Rim and Southeast Asia
1997–1998	In response to robust economy, restaurant customer counts rose 3 percent and the average check rose 4 percent in two consecutive years, to the highest levels in a decade, with rises of 5 percent in midscale and 6 percent in upscale operations
1995	FDA releases new food code for food service sanitation, "FDA Food Code 1993"
1994 continued	
1995	Real growth in gross domestic product (GDP) with low rate of inflation but low growth in wage rates, fluctuating employment, and consumer sense of economic insecurity; U.S. military forces sent to Bosnia
	Very high public concern for microbial safety in food—particularly related to *E. coli*—and healthful foods, including supplements
	November elections give Republicans control of both houses of Congress for the first time in 40 years
1994–1999	At various times, U.S. militarily involved in peacekeeping, humanitarian, or democratic activities throughout the world, including Somalia, the Balkans, Haiti, Korea, and Iraq
1994–1995	O.J. Simpson trial—sometimes called the "trial of the century"—with Simpson acquitted of criminal acts
1995 (April 9)	Deadliest terrorist attack ever to occur in the United States with car bomb blowing up Alfred Murrah Federal Building in Oklahoma City
1995	Dow posts 33.5 percent gain for year
1996	Dow posts 26 percent gain for year
1996–1999	Strong economic growth, low inflation rate, relatively full employment
1997–1999	Unemployment falls below 5.0 percent
1997 (Aug. 31)	Diana, Princess of Wales, killed in Paris car crash
1997 (July 1)	Hong Kong restored to Chinese rule after 150 years as a British colony
1997	Dow up 1,459.98 points for year to close at 7,908.25, a 22.6 percent gain

Exhibit 1-2 (continued)

Decade	Restaurant Development	Dates	National Development	Dates
	Relatively full employment produces grave shortage of restaurant workers, particularly those of high skill	1998–1999	"Y2K" computer glitches a major concern and focus of much work as the year 2000 approaches	1997–1999
			President Clinton impeached in U.S. House of Representatives but not removed from office by U.S. Senate	1998–1999
	Restaurants expanding by diversification in purchasing other chains	1999	Unemployment rate at 4.2 percent, a 29 year low	1999 (June)
			Dow closes above 11,000	1999 (May 7)
	McDonald's purchases Donato's Pizza	1999 (May)	Dow closes above 11,000	1999 (May-Sept.)
	Warren Buffett purchases Allied Domecq PLC, which owns Dunkin' Donuts, Baskin Robbins, Togo's, pubs and restaurants across Britain, and some of the world's best known brands of liquor including Ballantine's, Teacher's Beefeater, Kahlua, Courvoisier, Tequila, Sauga, Canadian Club, Harvey's Bristol Cream, and Tia Maria	1999 (Summer)	Dow at all time high (11,186.41)	1999 July 16
			Dow below 11,000	1999 (Sept.-Nov. 6)
			Unemployment rate at 4.1 percent	1999 (Nov. 6)
			Dow closes above 11,000	1999 (Nov. 18)
2000–2010	Foodservice industry sales projected to be $577 billion by 2010		The extent of the continuation of a boom economy unpredictable	
	Computer technology increasingly applied to the performance of functions in the foodservice industry		Continued advances in computer technology and telecommunications that will change the way of life in the 21st century	
	Use of improved foods with healthful (nutraceuticals or functional foods) characteristics in the foodservice industry		Continued development of agriculture, food science, and technology that results in engineered foods that are more healthful (nutraceuticals or functional foods), safer, and have longer shelf life and improved flavor	
	Increasing development of restaurant chains throughout the world		Increase in worldwide interdependence and a world order	

Exhibit 1-2 (continued)

poses of providing nutrition labeling, buyers should specifically request processors to supply nutrient content information or labeling, since the Nutrition Labeling and Information Act does not require nutrient labeling for wholesale packages. If buyers require nutrition labeling from suppliers, food service operators can then use this information without doing a separate analysis.

In 1999, food and drink purchases by foodservice operators are expected to exceed \$114.0 billion.[4] Expenditures of this size mean the food buyer has an immense legal and business responsibility to assure proper supply, quality, price, and contract negotiation.

Large operators have learned that food buying is not just a matter of "making a phone call" and that millions of dollars are lost through inept purchasing. The demand for trained and competent food buyers has grown with the size of the industry. The job is not simple and requires a wide range of knowledge in many areas. Good food buyers, like many types of professional people, must be trained. That is the purpose of this book. It behooves all food buyers, as well as those who participate in the education and training of food buyers, to learn as much as possible about every facet of their chosen specialty.

Purchasing, as a function of food service operations, has developed and grown in complexity along with the food service industry. In the early years of the food service industry, buying food was typically the responsibility of whoever was doing the preparation. Today, professional buying as a separate occupation is essential to keeping up with current technology and handling the high volume of purchasing transactions with huge expen-

ditures that are associated with buying food in a greatly expanded food service industry operating world wide.

REFERENCES

Associated Press. "On the Street," *The Columbus Dispatch* (Columbus, Ohio), November 6, 1999, sec. G, p. 3.

Austin, Kim. "FDA Releases New Food Code," *Restaurants USA* 14:4 (April 1994): 7.

Cain, Herman. "The Food Revolution," *Restaurants USA* 19:5 (May 1999): 51.

Chapdelaine, Stephen. "1994 Travel-Related Foodservice Spending to Exceed \$80 Billion," *Restaurants USA* 14:5 (May 1994): 44–47.

Gebolys, Debbie. "McDonald's Set to Acquire a Slice of Pizza Market," *The Columbus Dispatch* (Columbus, Ohio), May 6, 1999.

Hasler, Clare M. "Functional Foods: Their Role in Disease Prevention and Health Promotion," *Food Technology*, 52:11 (November 1998): 63–70.

McDaniel, Lynda. "The New Crop of Nutraceuticals," *Restaurants USA* 19:5 (May 1999): 23–26.

National Restaurant Association. *Restaurant Industry Operations Report '87.* Washington, D.C.: National Restaurant Association and Laventhal and Horvath, 1987.

National Restaurant Association. *Restaurant Industry Operations Report '90.* Washington, D.C.: National Restaurant Association and Laventhal and Horvath, 1990.

Nelson, Marilyn K. "Celebrating 75 Years," *Restaurants USA* 14:2 (February 1994): 22–34.

Obenauer, Irina. "1998 Crest Annual Report," *Restaurants USA* 19:4 (April 1999): 44–46.

Olson, Dennis G. "Irradiation of Food," A scientific status summary, *Food Technology* 52: 1 (January 1998): 56–62.

Sloan, A. Elizabeth. "The New Market: Foods for the Not-So-Healthy," *Food Technology* 53: 2 (February 1999): 54–60.

Strauss, W., and Howe, Neil. *Generations—The History of America's Future—1584 to 2069.* New York: William Morrow and Company, Inc., 1991.

———. "Foodservice Trends—A Guide to Success in 2010," *Restaurants USA* 19: 8 (September 1999): 38–44.

---

[4] "1999 National Restaurant Association Industry Pocket Factbook" in *Restaurants USA* 18: 11 (December, 1998): 14.

————. "Money and Investing" section, *The Wall Street Journal*, October 22, 1999, sec. C, p. 1.

————. *The New American Desk Encyclopedia.* New York: Signet, the Penguin Group by arrangement with Concord Reference Books, Inc., 1993.

————. "Position of the American Dietetic Association: Functional Foods," *Journal of the American Dietetic Association* 99: 10 (October 1999): 1278–1285.

————. "U.S. Jobless Rate Dips to 4.2 percent," *The Columbus Dispatch* (Columbus, Ohio), June 5, 1999, sec. G, p. 1.

————. *World Almanac and Book of Facts 1999.* Mahwah, New Jersey: PRIMEDIA Reference Inc., 1998.

————. *World Almanac and Book of Facts 1998.* Mahwah, New Jersey: K-111 Reference Corporation, 1997.

————. "35th Annual Top 400 Restaurant Concepts," *Restaurants and Institutions* 109: 19 (July 15, 1999): total issue.

————. "The 400: Food & Finance," *Restaurants & Institutions* 103: 17 (July 15, 1993): total issue.

————. "The 400: Food & Finance," *Restaurants & Institutions* 99: 18 (July 10, 1993): total issue.

————. "1996 Foodservice Industry Forecast," *Restaurants USA* 15:11 (December, 1995): 15–38.

————. "1999 National Restaurant Association Restaurant Industry Pocket Factbook," *Restaurants USA* 18: 11 (December 1998): 14.

————. "1999 Restaurant Industry Forecast," *Restaurants USA* 18: 11 (December 1998): F13-F28.

2 Markets and Their Functions

Purpose: To acquaint prospective food and beverage buyers with the types and functions of the several food markets, the various methods of buying, and the contributions of the different people involved in the buying process.

INTRODUCTION

Food buyers in a hotel or restaurant must be ever aware that the success of the functions of preparation, presentation, and selling, which result in customer satisfaction, depends on starting with the proper product—the procuring of which is the buyer's responsibility.

To establish a successful buying program, a study must be made, much like a feasibility search made before building a restaurant, auto repair shop, or clothing boutique. If the buyer is selecting merchandise for a property in a small Midwestern or Southern town, the plan and buying program will have to be considerably different from those developed for downtown Chicago or Miami. If the property is in an isolated area, the timing of purchases will be a prime consideration because of possible difficulties and delays in deliveries. The buying plan must take these factors into account. A good food buyer will work with all available tools. The buyer will make the most of the particular market rather than fight it and try to change it.

THE FUNCTIONS OF THE MARKET

The first thing a buyer must understand is the functions of the market, which include the following:

1. The market exchanges information between seller and buyer.
2. The market provides for exchange of ownership after a sale from seller to buyer.
3. The market provides for the movement and physical exchange of the goods sold by the seller and received by the buyer.
4. The market provides a physical location for carrying out the business of the market.

These four functions are summarized below.

Exchange of Information

The market allows for the exchange of information about factors that range from weather and world trade conditions to the availability and quality of supplies from different parts of the country, the prices being asked, and the types of packaging available. Practically every line of merchandise has a trade association that has been formed to promote sales and regulate quality and to see that the product meets the consumer's needs. The buyer orders the product that meets his specifications and the seller agrees to fulfill the order.

Exchange of Ownership

The market provides ways and means for a buyer to make purchases from a purveyor. In this process of exchange, deals are made over the telephone, by mailgram, by fax, by e-mail, or through a third person. It is becoming increasingly common for orders, especially for supplies, to be made through a broker's or a manufacturer's website. Ultimately, the transaction must be put down on paper before it is legal. Let a buyer or seller "renege" on his agreement or fail to meet payment deadlines, and he or she will be out of business.

Moving Goods from Seller to Buyer

The many ways of moving goods to the buyer from the seller include piggyback railroad transportation, refrigerated railroad cars, short- and long-haul trucking, refrigerated trucks, and, in recent years, air transportation, both refrigerated and nonrefrigerated. Improvement in packaging and faster transportation schedules have opened up worldwide markets, making exotic foods available from almost anywhere. If a buyer really wants a 25-pound green truffle from France or a shipment of kiwi fruit from New Zealand, the items, the transportation, and the means of purchase are available. All it takes is the money.

THE BUSINESS OF THE MARKET

The business of the market includes bookkeeping, payment of bills, extension of credit, collection of late payments, transfer of documents and public relations. The various associations in the market ensure that each of their clients is given the best of public relations, as well as help in promoting new products. The public relations duties of the market also cover the important responsibility of helping to direct consumer demand during periods of shortages due to crop failure, foreign market fluctuations, transportation breakdowns, and strikes.

Markets Available

Primary markets are the basic sources of supply. Such sources include the fresh-seafood markets along the coasts, the meat markets throughout the Midwest and Southeast, the fruit and vegetable producing areas in Florida and California, the poultry market in the Del Marva area, and, of course, the vast array of canned and frozen food processors all over the country.

The *secondary markets,* usually located in the user's area, are better known as purveyors or wholesalers. Full-service wholesalers handle all of the items normally offered in their trade, while specialty wholesalers handle only three or four items within a particular line. The secondary markets have the responsibility of buying in large quantities from the primary markets and redistributing to local purchasers in smaller quantities.

Secondary markets have traditionally been divided into thirteen basic product lines:

1. Fresh and frozen meats
2. Fresh and frozen poultry
3. Fresh and frozen seafood
4. Fresh fruits and produce
5. Coffee and spices
6. Frozen fruits and vegetables
7. Canned goods and groceries
8. Convenience foods and convenience entrees
9. Milk and cream
10. Butter and eggs
11. Ethnic foods and exotic foods
12. Flours and cereals
13. Oils and shortening

Eight years ago, the average hotel and restaurant bought their food supplies from ten different dealers within a market group. The average is now down to five and one-half dealers in each market. This change has been due to more binding specifications adopted by the trade, the growth of the one-stop buying system, and the desire on the part of the user to cut down on delivery and bookkeeping costs. With the addition of computer use, there is no question that the number of markets used by the average purchasing agent will shrink even further.

The third type of market available to the food buyer is the *local market,* which offers great opportunities for savings on seasonal foods and delivery costs. Farmers' markets, for example, are still very popular because food service operators know they can get fresh merchandise of excellent quality if they go to the market and pick it up themselves. In the fishing areas along the coasts, it is common practice for many of the food service operators to make a daily pilgrimage to the fish markets and pick up their fresh supplies.

Small restaurant operators have also discovered the value of buying their food supplies at nearby supermarkets. Not only are the prices right, but the quality is generally good, and the operator can buy only what is currently needed. By paying cash and buying in portion counts only, the small operator may find this form of purchasing an effective method of cost accounting.

Some operators who have to stay in the low-price market have found that working out a deal with the local supermarket to buy up merchandise not in demand by the customer is good business. This practice enables them to stay in business when they cannot afford to go through regular supply sources.

FOOD AGENTS

Some food processors are big enough that they can afford to have their own sales representatives out in the field selling their product directly to large users and various wholesalers. Most food processors, however, have to depend on agents. Occasionally the food buyer will meet these people and should know what their responsibilities are. There are four types of food service agents.

1. *Brokers:* Food brokers are in business for themselves, and they usually represent small businesses. Sometimes brokers have just an office with a secretary and telephone service. In other cases, the staff, including office personnel and salespeople, can total several hundred. Brokers do *not* buy any merchandise for resale. Their job is strictly to get commitments from manufacturers and to seek buyers, such as the armed forces, wholesalers, or, in some cases, large quantity chain buyers.

2. *Commission agents or houses:* Even though the duties of commission houses are the same as those of brokers, there is one major difference—commission houses *buy* their merchandise and then, with a guaranteed source of supply, sell the merchandise for what they can get. Commission houses take greater risks than brokers; as a result, their markup is a little higher. Where brokers are satisfied with a 3 to 5 percent markup, commission houses normally charge 10 to 12 percent.

3. *Manufacturers' agents:* Many food manufacturers have manufacturers' agents, sometimes called *missionary* people, special salespersons on the payroll of the manufacturer who go out into the market and promote the manufacturers' products. They usually do this when a new product is put on the market or a drive is put on to improve the use of some regular market item. "Missionaries" sell products on a commission basis and may charge 10 to 20 percent, depending on how difficult their product is to sell.

4. *Special sales "reps":* These specialty salespeople are, like manufacturers' agents, direct representatives of manufacturers, but generally they represent what might be known as "boutique" salespeople. Since their line of goods is limited, actual sales are more difficult; consequently, their commissions are high. For this reason, the purchasing agent should be very cautious when dealing with manufacturing agents or special sales "reps."

5. *Food purchasing service:* This service assembles a group of independent restaurants or hotel food operations of moderate volume that alone do not have the advantage of volume buying into a group that together has considerable clout in negotiating favorable prices with purveyors. The organizers do the purchasing for the represented properties for a fee, usually 2 or 3 percent of the total purchases made. For a property to participate in such a service, it must adhere to certain minimum delivery schedules and make prompt payments for merchandise.

WHOLESALERS

The great bulk of food service supply is done through the local wholesaler, whose basic job, as we have pointed out, is to buy food in large quantities, warehouse it, and redistribute it in smaller quantities to local consumers. Full-service wholesalers generally have a wide variety of stock and prices. This group is now adopting the one-stop buying system, frequently offering all of the other lines necessary in the food service business, such as china, glass, silver, paper supplies, throwaways, single-service plastics, cleaning supplies, kitchen equipment, and utensils. Some have added menu making and even room-supply items through contracts with furniture manufacturers.

Limited-Function Wholesalers

This group of people is often called "wagon jobbers." As a rule, they operate out of a supply truck that calls on the operator on a daily basis and fills in the needs and makes sales from stock carried in the truck. Many dairy dealers; bakery goods suppliers; bread dealers; coffee, tea, and spice dealers fall into this category. These dealers generally maintain a par stock in the user's storerooms, and, theoretically, add the new stock to the rear. However, experience has shown that this is not necessarily true. The buyer is warned to beware of this type of wholesaler, as slippages can occur very quickly without constant vigilance on the part of the receiving clerk.

Some users buy in quantities that make it worthwhile to buy in drop shipments. These drop shipments are generally made in full truckload or partial truckload lots. A full truckload is generally 44,000 pounds, and some drop-shipment wholesalers arrange for four drop shipments in an area, which means that the buyer has to buy in lots of only 10,000 pounds and up to make a savings. The drop-shipment purchase eliminates the necessity for the wholesaler to warehouse, redistribute, deliver, and bill in smaller quantities; in some instances, the savings can be substantial.

Prime Supply Wholesalers

Given the growth of one-stop buying and the increase of chain-operated buying services, naturally there has been an increase in purveyors who specialize in a complete line of food service and hospitality industry supplies, including food and beverage supplies, linens, china, glassware, decorative materials, furniture, kitchen equipment, pots and pans, uniforms, cleaning supplies, and about anything that you would possibly need in the food service industry. Some of these suppliers have gone so far as to offer legal services as well as operating consulting services, employee training, and payroll controls. Beverage supplies such as liquor, wines, and beers and ales are ruled out of this type of service by laws regulating the distribution of liquor supplies to the hospitality industry.

Franchise operators cannot be forced to buy from the franchisor. Companies such as Holiday Inn, Sheraton, Hilton, and Weston, to name a few, have found that it is very beneficial to both the franchisor and franchisee to have a source of supply that will benefit both parties and make it easy for the franchisee to get necessary supplies at a reasonable price with minimal problems.

FACTORS AFFECTING THE FOOD SERVICE MARKETS

Many factors, from storms to strikes, can disrupt the flow of goods to markets. A good buyer will be aware of these possibilities and will have set up a contingency plan for any occurrence that might interrupt the flow of supplies. It is also up to the management of each food service operation to have worked out a similar plan with the buyer and other department heads. This might mean keeping some reserve stock on hand and rotating it from time to time to insure freshness or making changes in the menu structure and even in the type of food and beverage service given in the dining rooms. In extreme situations, it has been necessary for management to completely shut down food service operations and wait out the emergency.

Let's look at some of the factors that can affect food service supply.

International

War has by far the most catastrophic effect on the food market. If there is political conflict in the areas from which food is being purchased, the buyer must make sure that any supplies coming from the countries involved are stored locally in sufficient quantities to cover the needs of the operation. Strikes, revolutions, and changes in government can occur overnight, and the results of political elections can be short-

ages and transportation problems. Crop failures or unusual weather can also affect the availability of supplies.

The foregoing are some of the major problems that have beset the world market in the last few years, but we should not forget what happens when a group of people attempt to control a supply. OPEC is one prime example, and we recall the periodic "frosts" in South America that affected the supply and price of coffee. Such manipulations of the market can easily backfire, as illustrated when Zanzibar successfully cornered the natural vanilla bean market. The price was raised tenfold overnight, and Zanzibar has not yet been able to sell the hoard. That many such shortages are contrived is proven by the latest coffee "frost" in Brazil, where movies were taken of tons of coffee being bulldozed into the Amazon River despite the claim of a coffee bean shortage.

The United States Market

Of several dozen factors that can affect the U.S. market for food supplies, the most troublesome are the weather (drought or excessive rain), strikes, recessions, and changes in the economic climate. The latter may include changes in government policies concerning exports and imports, tariffs, money supply subsidies for certain crops, and entitlement programs. Of the foregoing, strikes and weather are the two factors that the food buyer should be especially prepared for. The other factors are slower in creating problems for the food buyer.

Local and Regional Food Service Markets

Omitting local strikes, which can occur overnight, the majority of the other factors affecting local markets are more likely to create a nuisance than a crisis. Finding sources of supply near an operation can guard against such disruptions. Delivery schedules are another factor that should be taken into consideration, as well as the available facilities for storing supplies at the site of the hotel or restaurant.

Some of the other factors that should be kept in mind by the buyer are management's policies regarding the inventory and stockpiling of supplies. The buyer must also know the amount of money available for stockpiling, as well as the purchasing power of the operation. The latter includes credit rating. A good business relationship between the staff members of the hotel or restaurant and the personnel of the supplier is crucial in a shortage.

A buyer is in a poor situation if located in an area where there is only one dealer to supply the different classes of food service supplies needed. Unless adequate arrangements have been worked out with the dealer in advance and extra effort made to maintain a good relationship, the buyer could find supplies cut off. As we have pointed out, the food buyer may need to use the supermarkets and the farmers' markets as a contingency plan to cover shortages.

Rungis—The World's Largest Market

The one market that has contributed the most to international food variety displays, however, is the pride of France, the Rungis.

Some readers may have been to Paris and remember Les Halles. As Les Halles grew, transportation and vendor space became such a problem that a new market was needed. Thus the Rungis was built, close to major thoroughfares and several miles out of town.

The Rungis—the world's largest food market, located south of Paris, France—has 1,500 acres of vendor stations, and all the products are delivered there fresh every day. Exhibit 2-1 is from the pamphlet given to new vendors and visitors to this renowned market. It explains that Rungis encom-

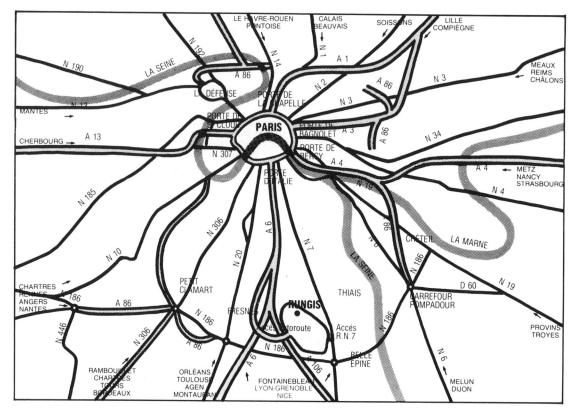

Exhibit 2-1. Map showing Rungis food market in relation to urban centers and highways

passes 874 grocers, 857 producers of grocery items, 16,000 employees, 25,000 purchasers, 18,000 small vendor wagons, and 727,000 large trucks and other transport vehicles. The Rungis sold 2,254,458 tons of merchandise in 1986, and in 1985 there were 39,800 couriers who brought global market news and made financial exchanges just for those purchasers sending in orders. The pamphlet further explains where each type of vendor is located within the market's realms and also comments that 60 percent of all of France's fruit and produce is exchanged in this market. (See Exhibit 2-2.)

In this unique distribution center, all products must be completely turned over (sold) within twenty-four hours of delivery, and therefore, Rungis operates twenty-four hours a day. The fishmongers arrive at 3 A.M., followed by the meat and dairy suppliers, the vegetable producers, and then the flower salespeople. Sales continue throughout the day, and the delivery schedules are set up for the purchasers. This market is open to professionals only, so the prices are wholesale and apply only to commercial food service businesses. The Rungis is located just 13 kilometers south of Paris from the site of the Notre Dame. (See Exhibit 2-1.)

Local Strikes

A common problem for the food buyer in obtaining supplies is a local truckers' strike or a strike affecting any segment of the food-handling system of the market. The prudent food buyer will keep informed of the possibility of local strikes. Extra supplies can be accumulated, but to cope with an extended breakdown of the supply system, a long-term contingency plan should be worked out with management.

Exhibit 2-2. An aerial view of the Rungis

3 Food Laws and the Food Buyer

Purpose: To identify and explain the statutes which are the basis for determining the characteristics of foods sold in the United States.

INTRODUCTION

Writing contracts for food, selecting food with particular characteristics, and trusting in the wholesomeness of food depend on basic federal laws that provide standards. The most important of these are (1) the Federal Food, Drug, and Cosmetic Act of 1938, as amended: (2) the Federal Meat Inspection Act, 1907, as amended by the Wholesome Meat Act, 1967; (3) the Poultry Products Inspection Act as amended by the Wholesome Poultry Products Act, 1968; (4) the Agricultural Marketing Act, 1946; (5) the Fair Packaging and Labeling Act, 1966; (6) the Egg Products Inspection Act, 1970; (7) the Filled Milk Act, 1923; (8) the definition of butter by act of Congress, 1923; (9) the Standard Milk Ordinance, 1924, and subsequent editions; (10) the Federal Import Milk Act, 1927; and (11) the Tea Importation Act, 1897.

Important amendments to the Federal Food, Drug, and Cosmetic Act are (1) the Food Additives Amendment, 1958; (2) the Color Additives Amendment, 1960; (3) the Pesticide Chemicals Act, 1954, as amended by (4) the Federal Insecticide, Fungicide, and Rodenticide Act; and (5) the Federal Environmental Pesticide Control Act, 1972. Recent amendments are (1) the Nutrition Labeling and Education Act, 1990; (2) the Dietary Supplement Health and Education Act, 1994; (3) the Food Quality Protection Act, 1996 (also amended the Federal Insecticide, Fungicide and Rodenticide Act); (4) the Food and Drug Administration Modernization Act, 1997, and (5) enactment of the new rule, "Procedures for the Safe and Sanitary Processing and Importing of Fish and Fishery Products," 1995, that *requires* the inspection of fish by using Hazard Analysis Critical Control Point (HACCP) procedures.

The Wholesome Meat Act and the Wholesome Poultry Products Act have recently (1996) been revised to incorporate regulatory "rules" that make drastic and fundamental changes in the procedures for inspecting or assuring the safety of meat and poultry products. These new regulations are called Pathogen Reduction, Hazard Analysis, and Critical Control Point (HACCP) Systems.

An overview of the provisions of these various federal laws, the responsible agencies, and the principal commodities affected is presented in Exhibits 3-1 through 3-14. Knowledge of the standards and procedures incorporated is essential to

Principal Provisions	Principal Commodities Affected	Federal Regulatory Authority
Standards of Identity	Processed (canned and frozen) fruits and vegetables	Food and Drug Administration (FDA), Department of Health and Human Services (DHHS)
	Acidified foods (pH 4.6 or less), i.e., pickles or pickled products, carbonated beverages, salad dressings, jellies, and similar products	
	Cocoa or chocolate products	
	Smoked and smoke-flavored fish	
	Frozen and breaded shrimp	
	Milk and cream	
	Cheeses and related cheese products	
	Frozen desserts	
	Bakery products	
	Cereal flours and related products	
	Macaroni and noodle products	
	Canned fruits	
	Canned fruit juices	
	Fruit butters, jellies, preserves, and related products	
	Fruit pies (frozen cherry)	
	Canned vegetables	
	Canned vegetable juices (tomato)	
	Frozen vegetables	
	Processed (frozen or dried) egg products	
	Nuts and nut products (peanut butter)	
	Nonalcoholic beverages (carbonated)	
	Margarine	
	Sweeteners and table syrups	
	Food dressing (salad dressings) and flavorings	
	Bottled water	
Standards of quality	Principally processed fruits and vegetables	
Standards of fill of container	Principally processed (canned) fruits and vegetables	
Prohibited acts and penalties Misbranding foods Includes dietary foods and nutrition labeling Adulterating food	Basically all commodities except meat and poultry products	
Seafood inspection	Iced, frozen, or canned shrimp, canned oysters, or other canned fish product	

Exhibit 3-1. The Federal Food, Drug, and Cosmetic Act, 1938: Provisions, commodities affected, and regulatory authority

negotiating food purchases, specifying the food quality characteristics desired, and assuring the safety of foods served to food service consumers.

Laws are revised or written continuously to meet changing societal needs. For example, meat inspection regulations (HACCP) have been written in response to outbreaks of *E. coli* food poisoning; regulations related to dietary supplements have been enacted because of consumer or societal interest in these products; the Food Quality Protection Act has resulted from consumer and regulatory concern about pesticides in food; the HACCP regulations for fish arose due to concern for pathogenic microorganisms and sanitary practices; and the Food and Drug Modernization Act makes agency regulatory procedures up to date, better organized, and more efficient in meeting consumer needs.

A food buyer must know the current legislation in order to avoid breaking the law, to know the protection provided, and to effectively serve customers and meet their interests.

THE FEDERAL FOOD, DRUG, AND COSMETIC ACT

The Federal Food, Drug, and Cosmetic Act, as amended (Exhibit 3-1), applies to all food commodities except meat and poultry. The principal provisions concern definitions of foods in terms of standards of identity, standards of quality, standards for fill of container, prohibitions against adulterated food, and definitions of misbranding related to labeling.

Standards of Identity

Standards of identity enable food buyers, in either wholesale or retail markets, to identify food products and characteristics by a legal name, such as *canned tomatoes, skim milk, flour,* or *fruit jelly.* Legal names are given based on definitions or specifications of ingredients that can (optional ingredients) and must be present and the manner of product preparation.

Statements of ingredients may specify the scientific name (genus and species), and the varietal color and size. "Manner of preparation" includes (1) the processing procedures that are necessary to ensure safety, (2) form, or style of the product, and (3) the packing medium. Examples of styles or forms of products include halves, slices, diced, whole, irregular slices, French cut, julienne, cream style, whole kernel, cut, or short cut. Packing mediums may be water, heavy syrup, light syrup, fruit juice, fruit juice with water, or water with salt.

Standards of identity are extremely important to food buyers, because the names provide the basis for identifying, defining, and writing specifications for the food items desired.

Standards of Quality

Legal standards of quality are based on product defects. These standards are not as numerous as standards of identity. Essentially, they have been established only for canned fruits and vegetables. Defects include extraneous material such as leaves, stems, or fruit pits that may be in canned food; color characteristics related to brightness or bruising of fruit; and characteristics of product workmanship, such as precision in cutting peach or pear halves in the center of the fruit.

Standards of quality are minimum standards. Products that don't meet these standards may be wholesome food but must be labeled "below minimum standard of quality" and the reason, such as excess pits, indicated on the label. Quality above the minimum standard may be indicated by U.S. Quality Grade Standards provided through the Agricultural Marketing Act. Together, these standards provide a basis for economically buying food with the characteristics needed for a particular purpose.

Standards of "Fill of Container"

Standards of "fill of container" are specific legal standards that have been established for some but not all processed (canned) fruit and vegetable commodities and do not refer to filling of containers in general. These standards are of limited usefulness in food buying, because although the standards are written for specific commodities, they may provide only a general indication of a container's contents. For example, for canned peaches the container must be filled with the maximum quantity of peaches in relation to juice or other packing medium that can be effectively sealed in a can and processed with heat to prevent spoilage and crushing or breaking the peaches.

Other standards may merely indicate that a can must be 90 percent full. For a product such as canned tomatoes, the standard may be quite effective and useful, because both the juice and whole tomato product are generally eaten. For a commodity such as canned peach halves, when a specific number of halves of peaches is desired, the legal standard provides no indication of number.

Prohibited Acts

The manufacture, shipment, or receipt of food that may be unwholesome (adulterated) for any reason, misbranded, or falsely represented in any way is prohibited under the Federal Food and Drug Cosmetic Act. These prohibitions provide the basis for confidence in safety and proper representation of products. Specifically, prohibited actions are

1. Introduction into interstate commerce of any food, drug, device, or cosmetic that is adulterated or misbranded
2. Manufacture in any territory of any food that is misbranded or adulterated
3. Receipt or accepting an offer for delivery of adulterated or misbranded goods either as a gift or for payment
4. Introduction or receipt in interstate commerce of any food that may be injurious to health because of contamination with microorganisms
5. Refusal to permit access to records and inspection of a facility
6. Giving a false guarantee of merchandise, or forging, counterfeiting, simulating, or falsely representing a product

Adulterated Food

Food is considered to be adulterated

1. If the food contains a poisonous or other substance that may be harmful to health or an added chemical that is not used in accordance with any federal law; has incorporated any filthy, putrid, or decomposed substance; has been prepared, packed, or held under unsanitary conditions where it may have been contaminated by filth; or contains any part of a diseased animal or animal that has died for reasons other than slaughter.
2. If the food container is composed of any poisonous or harmful substance.
3. If a valuable constituent (ingredient) has been omitted or substituted, or another substance has been added to make the product interior, particularly as related to the legal name and the standard of identity, or to increase weight or bulk.
4. If damage or inferiority has been concealed in any manner.
5. If it is a dietary supplement or contains a dietary ingredient that presents a significant risk of illness or injury under conditions of recommended use; it is a new dietary ingredient not yet proven safe; it is a substance the Secretary declares poses an imminent hazard to public health; or it contains a dietary ingredient that makes it adulterated as for number 1 above.

Misbranding

A food product is "misbranded" in terms of the Federal Food, Drug, and Cosmetic Act, as amended, in any of the following circumstances:

1. The labeling is false or misleading in any particular.
2. The product is offered for sale under the name of another food.
3. The product is an imitation of another, and the word "imitation" does not appear conspicuously on the label.
4. The container is filled, formed, or made to be misleading.
5. The name and business address of the manufacturer, distributor, or packer does not appear on the label.
6. The quantity of product, in weight, measure, or numerical count, is not indicated.
7. Any word, statement or information

required by the act does not appear on the label in the required manner or cannot be read by the average person under normal conditions of purchase or use.

8. The product does not conform to an established standard of identity, standard of quality, or standard of fill of container or is not appropriately labeled for a product that is below minimum standard of quality or fill of container.

9. The label does not indicate the optional ingredients included in a product with a standard of identity.

10. Ingredients are not properly listed for a product that has no standard of identity.

11. A nutritional or special dietary claim is made, and the requirements for nutritional labeling are not appropriately met.

12. The food contains artificial coloring, flavoring, or chemical preservatives and is not appropriately labeled.

13. The food is a raw agricultural commodity to which a chemical pesticide has been added after harvest and has not been labeled accordingly.

14. The product contains saccharin or a color additive and is not appropriately labeled.

Amendments to the Federal Food, Drug, and Cosmetic Act

The *Food and Color Additives Amendments* to the Federal Food, Drug, and Cosmetic Act and the Pesticide Chemicals Act (Miller Act) as amended (see Exhibit 3-2) are the major pieces of legislation used to control the kind and amounts of chemical substances that may be added to food.

In the food and color additives amendments substances that are considered food or color additives are defined and provisions are made for indicating their presence in food products. Subsequent testing and regulation of chemical substances has given consumers added assurance of safety. Related requirements that were made for labeling of added artificial colors or flavors are useful to buyers in obtaining the color and flavor characteristics desired in food.

The Pesticide Chemicals Amendment (Miller Act) of 1954, which was incorporated into the Federal Food, Drug, and Cosmetic Act, provided for controlling the use of pesticides on raw agricultural com-

Pesticide Chemicals Amendment (Miller Act), 1954, as amended by the Federal Insecticide, Fungicide, and Rodenticide Act, and the Environmental Pesticide Control Act, 1972

Principal Provisions	Principal Commodities Affected	Federal Regulatory Authority
Establishment of control on residues of chemical pesticides left on fresh fruits and vegetables	Fresh fruits and vegetables	Environmental Protection Agency (EPA) since 1970 (formerly USDA, DHHS)

Food Additives Amendment, 1958

Principal Provisions	Principal Commodities Affected	Federal Regulatory Authority
Definition of food additives (including chemical and ionic radiation), conditions of safe use and substances prohibited from use	All food, including human food; substances migrating to food from food contact articles used in processing or packaging; pet food; animal feed; alcoholic beverages; chewing gum; fresh, canned, or frozen meat, poultry, fish, and dairy products; and other food products	FDA, DHHS

Exhibit 3-2. Major amendments to the Federal Food, Drug, and Cosmetic Act, 1938: Provisions, commodities affected, and regulatory authority

Color Additives Amendment, 1960

Principal Provisions	Principal Commodities Affected	Federal Regulatory Authority
Approval, listing and certification, with safe dilutents or without dilutents, of chemical coloring agents that become a part of food	All food, including human and animal	FDA, DHHS

Nutrition Labeling and Education Act, 1990

Principal Provisions	Principal Commodities Affected	Federal Regulatory Authority
Mandatory labeling of all processed foods (including meat and poultry) and most other foods	All processed foods except infant formulas and medical foods; voluntary compliance recommended for the 20 most commonly consumed varieties of fruits and vegetables and the 20 most commonly consumed species of fish	FDA, DHHS, principally; also, Food Safety and Inspection Service (FSIS) Meat and Poultry Inspection, USDA
Voluntary nutrition guidelines for labeling each of the 20 kinds of fruits, vegetables, and fish most frequently consumed in a year		
New nutrient standards, called Reference Daily Intakes (RDI), Daily Reference Values (DRV) and Daily Values to replace the U.S. Recommended Dietary Allowances (U.S. RDA)		
Required labeling of all food ingredients, including those with legal Standards of Identity		
New labeling format requirements		
Definitions for descriptors such as "light," "reduced," and "high," which are used in labeling foods for special dietary applications		

Dietary Supplement Health and Education Act, 1994, Amendment

Principal Provisions	Principal Commodities Affected	Federal Regulatory Authority
Protection of consumer right of access to *safe* dietary supplements that promote wellness; and provision of a basis for an integrated policy in regulating these products, including conforming (other laws) amendments	Products, *intended to supplement* the diet, that contain a vitamin, a mineral, an herb or other botanical, an amino acid, a dietary substance used to increase total dietary intake, or a concentrate, metabolite, constituent, or combination of these substances	FDA, DHHS
Definition of safe use based on law for "adulterated" food and placement of responsibility for assuring safety on the Secretary of Health and Human Services		
Stipulations for labeling related to statements being "false or misleading"; requirements for claiming a benefit related to a disease; nutrition labeling; requirements for supplement labeling		
Requirements for using "new dietary ingredients" and "good manufacturing practices"		
Establishment of a "Commission on Dietary Supplement Labels"		

Exhibit 3.2, continued

Food Quality Protection Act, 1996[1]

Principal Provisions	Principal Commodities Affected	Federal Regulatory Authority
Revision of the Federal Insecticide, Fungicide, and Rodenticide Act (FIFRA) and the Federal Food, Drug, and Cosmetic Act (FFDCA) to improve the regulatory control of pesticide residues in foods	Raw agricultural commodities and processed foods (fruits and vegetables, primarily)	"Administrator" of the U.S. Environmental Protection Agency, primarily; also, FDA, USDA
Requirement that the Environmental Protection Agency, which has responsibility for registering (licensing) chemical pesticides in terms of safe use under FIFRA, review within ten years (after 1996) all tolerances and exemptions for pesticide residues on fresh and processed food		
Exclusion of pesticide chemicals from "food additive" regulations and expansion of the law (FFDCA) regarding "tolerances and exemptions" (related to adulterated food) to establish a single new standard for all pesticide residues in food		
Requirement that within two years (after 1996), the Administrator (Food Quality Protection Act) will publish and distribute for display in grocery stores, in a form understandable to consumers, a discussion of risks and benefits of pesticide chemicals; actions taken against particular chemicals and the foods on which they have been used; and recommendations to consumers for reducing dietary exposure to pesticide chemical residues		

[1]Amends the Federal Insecticide, Fungicide, and Rodenticide Act as well as Federal Food, Drug, and Cosmetic Act

Food and Drug Administration Modernization Act, 1997

Principal Provisions	Principal Commodities Affected	Federal Regulatory Authority
Facilitation of the regulatory processes related to the approval, development, and marketing of safe and effective new drugs, and new or improved medical devices; and for food, prompt provision of valid nutrition and health claim information on food product labels, revision of labeling regulations for irradiated (ionic) foods, and revision of regulations for decorations on glass and ceramic wear and for food contact surfaces	Drugs; medical devices; and foods for which health benefits or nutritional content claims are made or foods treated with ionic radiation	FDA, DHHS

Exhibit 3.2, continued

modities and for residual amounts of these chemicals that are permissible in foods. In 1970, the power to administer and enforce the regulation of pesticide chemicals was transferred to the administrator of the Environmental Protection Agency.

The Nutrition Labeling and Education Act of 1990 (Exhibit 3-2) amended the Federal Food, Drug and Cosmetic Act to prescribe nutrition labeling and permit alteration in Standards of Identity to encourage a way of eating considered healthy for the general population. Implementation, effective May 9, 1994, requires food processing companies to analyze nutrient content of products and present nutrition facts or claims in a particular manner. Provision to alter Standards of Identity provides opportunity to develop and market foods that are lower in fat, calories, or some other substance. The Act does not apply to wholesale packages for restaurants or institutions but provides for expanding the kinds of products and product information that is available. Data may be used by dietitians in making nutrient calculations or by commercial food service operators who wish to market foods low in calories or some other substance. Further information on the Nutrition Labeling and Education Act is provided in Chapter 21 of this text.

The Dietary Supplement Health and Education Act, the Food Quality Protection Act, and the *Food and Drug Modernization Act Amendments* (Exhibit 3-2) are important for showing marketplace factors of which the food buyer needs to be aware. Buyers need to know that supplements are vitamins, minerals, herbs or other botanicals (generally concentrated), amino acids, or other dietary substances meant to *supplement* the diet. Supplements are distinct from food additives, drugs, or foods generally on the market. These products are commonly available (grocery stores), and the law will not preclude but protect their continued availability. Sup-

plements are extremely popular with consumers, as indicated by sales of at least four billion dollars (1993–1994)[1].

The *Food Quality Protection Act* is highly important to buyers because it regulates the pesticide chemicals in foods. The incident of food poisoning from the chemical Alar (used on apples) is an example of the problems that can arise. An important provision of this law is that the Administrator publish a discussion of the risks and benefits of pesticide chemicals and the actions that have been taken against *particular chemicals* along with the foods on which they have been used. Buyers should obtain this information to be aware of possible or likely hazards associated with particular commodities and thus help to assure the safety of *fresh* foods served to foodservice customers.

The *Food and Drug Administration Modernization Act* is designed to improve regulatory procedures. As applied to food, it incorporates revisions regarding nutrition and health claim information labeling, size of labels for products treated with ionic radiation, and the time frame for disapproval of china with lead- and cadmium-based enamels on the rims or lips. Buyers may wish to give consideration to the type of decorations on glassware products and the status of regulatory approval before making these purchases.

Federal Food, Drug, and Cosmetic Act Rule Change

The new Food and Drug Administration (FDA) "rule," *Procedures for the Safe and Sanitary Processing and Importing of Fish and Fishery Products* (21 CFR, Parts 123 and 1240) has been developed under the section of the Federal Food, Drug, and Cosmetic Act (Section 401) that deals with "adulterated food." The new regulation (Exhibit 3-3) requires that all fish processors (foreign and domes-

---

[1] The Dietary Supplement Health and Education Act, 1994

Principal Provisions	Principal Commodities	Federal Regulatory Authority
Requirements that (1) every processor engaged in commercial, custom, or institutional processing of fish or fishery products for interstate commerce in the United States or a foreign country *conduct* or have conducted for it *a hazard analysis* to determine if there are any food safety hazards that are reasonably likely to occur for each fish or fish product processed, and (2) *develop and implement a written* Hazard Analysis Critical Control Point (HACCP) plan to control the hazards identified. Hazards include natural toxins, microorganisms, chemicals, pesticides, drug residues, decomposition, parasites, and physical conditions in plants. *Processing includes* handling, storing, preparing, heading, eviscerating, shucking, freezing, dockside unloading and changing into different market forms.	Fish (fresh and frozen) sold in interstate commerce, including fresh or saltwater finfish; shellfish, including mollusks (oysters, clams, mussels, scallops), and crustaceans (lobsters, crabs); and other aquatic animal life such as alligators, frogs, water turtles, jellyfish, sea cucumbers, sea urchins, and fish roe	FDA, DHHS

Exhibit 3-3. Procedures for the safe and sanitary processing and importing of fish and fishery products, regulatory rule, 1995: Provisions, commodities affected, and regulatory authority

tic) who sell fish in interstate commerce develop detailed Hazard Analysis Critical Control Point (HACCP) plans to identify the risks for each species of fish processed and the controls to be applied that will control or eliminate the risk. Plans and facilities are monitored by the Food and Drug Administration. A processor is any person engaged in custom, commercial, or institutional processing of fresh fish. Processing includes handling, storing, preparing, heading, eviscerating, shucking, and freezing. The regulation does not apply to procedures on harvest (fishing) vessels or to the operation of retail establishments.

The new "rule" for assuring the safety of fish is extremely important to commercial and retail buyers, because prior to this, little legal protection of consumer health was provided. Inspecting fresh fish for wholesomeness was available (at a requester's expense) but was not required unless the product was federally graded

and U.S. grade certification was applied (at a requester's expense).

Fair Packaging and Labeling Act

The Fair Packaging and Labeling Act (Exhibit 3-4) was enacted to require that packages and labels provide an accurate representation of the quantity of contents in containers and permit value comparisons of products.

A principal provision of this act was to expand the kinds of commodities covered by the labeling requirements already incorporated in the Federal Food, Drug, and Cosmetic Act. The act covers "consumer commodities," which include retail items (such as soap and toothpaste) for personal care or household use, in addition to products covered under the Federal Food, Drug, and Cosmetic Act. The regulatory authority for food, drugs, and cosmetics rests with the Department of Health and Human Services; and for other commodities, with

Principal Provisions	Principal Commodities Affected	Federal Regulatory Authority
Accurate labeling and representation of quantities of products in packages	All consumer commodities sold through retail sales, except meat, poultry, and alcoholic beverages	FDA, DHHS for commodities covered under the Federal Food, Drug, and Cosmetic Act
Precise requirements for placement, form, and language to be used in statements of quantity	Consumer commodities not covered by the Federal Food, Drug, and Cosmetic Act	Federal Trade Commission, Department of Commerce for commodities that are not included in the Federal Food, Drug, and Cosmetic Act
Prohibitions against packaging, labeling, or transporting any consumer commodity that is incorrectly represented		

Exhibit 3-4. Fair Packaging and Labeling Act, 1966: Provisions, commodities affected, and regulatory authority

the Federal Trade Commission. This act does not apply to meat and poultry products, because their sale is regulated by the U.S. Department of Agriculture (USDA) under different laws.

Requirements for labeling of products include the name of the commodity; the name, place of business, and address of the manufacturer, packer, or distributor; the net quantity of contents with precise requirements of the manner for making statements of quantity; and appropriate size of lettering and positions for placement of information.

Wholesome Meat Act Amendment

The Wholesome Meat Act Amendment (1967) to the Federal Meat Inspection Act (Exhibit 3-5) essentially made the same provisions for meat as the Federal Food, Drug, and Cosmetic Act made for other foods. These included prohibitions against adulterated food and misbranding and the establishment of legal standards of identity for various meat products. Standards of identity include fresh ground meat products,

luncheon-type meats, and various canned or frozen items.

The act also made inspection of meat, in federal standards, mandatory and placed the regulatory authority for meat and meat products in the USDA. Previously, federal inspection was not required unless the meat or meat product moved in interstate commerce.

Wholesome Poultry Products Act Amendment

The Wholesome Poultry Products Amendment to the Poultry Products Inspection Act (Exhibit 3-6) made provisions for poultry that were similar to those made for meat by the Wholesome Meat Act Amendment. These include mandatory federal inspection for disease or tumors whether the poultry moves in intra- or interstate commerce; definitions of class, such as fryer or roaster, and definitions of cut, such as breast quarter; labeling requirements; and prohibition of adulteration and misbranding.

Principal Provisions	Principal Commodities Affected	Federal Regulatory Authority
Mandatory meat inspection according to federal standards	Meat and meat products, including carcass, fresh cuts, and various processed products, including ground, canned or frozen entrees, and luncheon meat	Food Safety and Inspection Service, Meat and Poultry Inspection, USDA
Prohibition against adulteration		
Manner of disposal of diseased or adulterated meat or carcasses		
Prohibition of misbranding		
Definitions and standards of identity or composition		

Exhibit 3-5. The Federal Meat Inspection Act, as amended by the Wholesome Meat Act, 1967; Provisions, commodities affected, and regulatory authority

Principal Provisions	Principal Commodities Affected	Federal Regulatory Authority
Mandatory poultry products inspection according to federal standards Prohibition of adulteration Requirements for labeling and prohibition of misbranding Definitions and standards of identity or composition, including various forms of canned and frozen products, and standards for kinds, classes, and cuts of raw poultry	Poultry and poultry products, including carcasses, parts, and various kinds of canned or frozen products	Food Safety and Inspection Service, Meat and Poultry Inspection, USDA

Exhibit 3-6. Poultry Products Inspection Act, 1957, as amended by the Wholesome Poultry Products Act, 1968: Provisions, commodities affected, and regulatory authority

Meat and Poultry Inspection Rule Change

The U.S. Department of Agriculture has established a new (1996) system of meat and poultry inspection by a regulatory "rule," "Pathogen Reduction; Hazard Analysis and Critical Control Point (HACCP) Systems (9 CFR, Part 304 et al.). The new regulatory "rule" (Exhibit 3-7) is based on requirements for inspection to ensure wholesomeness and safety. These were previously established in the Wholesome Meat Act and the Wholesome Poultry Products Act. The new system has been developed because outbreaks of food-based illness, particularly from *E. coli*, have shown the old system of managing inspection was inadequate. This was done mainly with inspectors in slaughter and processing establishments. The new rule requires (Exhibit 3-6) that all establishments develop detailed HACCP plans that identify hazards that exist in any stage of operation and the controls that will be exercised. Also, microbial evaluation for *E. coli* is required and standards for *Salmonella* reduction must be met. Records, plants, and procedures are monitored by the Food Safety Inspection Service (FSIS) in the U.S. Department of Agriculture.

Food buyers need to be aware of the revised system and the way it functions to determine if there are other controls needed to assure the safety of meat and poultry products served to food service customers. In purchasing it is important to remember that severe illness resulted from *E. coli* in hamburger served at a major chain restaurant.

EGG PRODUCTS INSPECTION ACT

The development of the market for processed egg products led to the Egg Products Inspection Act (Exhibit 3-8). Standards for sanitation and wholesomeness of products are the principal focus. These apply to eggs that are removed from the shells and are pasteurized, frozen, dried, or processed in some other way.

AGRICULTURAL MARKETING ACT

The Agricultural Marketing Act (Exhibit 3-9) provides authority for establishing quality grades and inspection service for a wide variety of commodities. Through these standards, quality above the minimum standards established for foods covered under the various other federal laws may be indicated.

Grade standards are extremely useful in

Principal Provisions	Principal Commodities Affected	Federal Regulatory Authority

Reformed system of inspection (HACCP), for meat and poultry products, to reduce the occurrence and numbers of pathogenic microorganisms and the incidences of food-borne disease associated with these products, through requiring
1. each establishment to develop and implement written sanitation standard operating procedures (SOP's);
2. regular microbial testing (*E. coli*) to verify process controls for prevention and removal of fecal contamination and associated bacteria;
3. the Food Safety and Inspection Service (FSIS) to establish pathogen reduction performance standards for *Salmonella* that slaughter houses and establishments producing raw *ground* products must meet;
4. all meat and poultry establishments to develop and implement a system of preventive controls designed to improve the safety of their products including
  a. conduct of a hazard analysis of each process to identify and list the safety hazards reasonably likely to occur and the preventive measures necessary to control the hazards
  b. identification of the "critical control points" (CCP) in each process, that is, a point, step, or procedure where a control can be applied and a hazard can be prevented, eliminated, or reduced to an acceptable level
  c. establishing a "*critical limit*" maximum or minimum value (e.g. temperature) to which a CCP must be controlled to prevent, eliminate, or reduce to an acceptable level any hazards identified
  d. establishing the measurements or observations that must be made to assess whether CCPs are within established critical limits
  e. prescribing the corrective action to be taken when monitoring shows deviation from a critical limit at a critical control point
  f. developing an effective record-keeping system that documents the entire HACCP system process
  g. systematic verification, by operating establishments and the U.S.D.A. Food Safety and Inspection Service, to determine if HACCP systems are in compliance with HACCP plans and if any change is needed to assure food safety objectives
 	
Broadened rule of the FSIS to extend regulatory influence beyond slaughter and processing establishments to include hazards during transportation, distribution, and retail, restaurant, or foodservice sale of meat
	Meat and poultry products including slaughter for all species, raw ground meat or poultry, raw product (not ground), shelf-stable nonheat-treated products (e.g. jerky), shelf-stable heat-treated products (e.g. edible fats), heat-treated sterile products (e.g. canned soup), fully cooked nonshelf-stable products (e.g. canned hams that must be refrigerated), not fully cooked heat-treated products (e.g. charmarked beef patties), and nonshelf-stable products with secondary inhibitors (e.g. fermented sausage)	Food Safety and Inspection Service (FSIS), USDA

Exhibit 3-7. Pathogen Reduction; Hazard Analysis and Critical Control Point (HACCP) Systems, regulatory rule, 1996 (regulatory rule for the modernization of meat and poultry inspection): Provisions, commodities affected, and regulatory authority

Principal Provisions	Principal Commodities Affected	Federal Regulatory Authority
Mandatory "continuous" inspection of egg products during processing	Egg products (processed) for human food, including dried, frozen, or liquid	Agricultural Marketing Service, USDA
Requirements for processing procedures and facilities for breaking of eggs, filtering, mixing, blending, pasteurizing, stabilizing, cooling, freezing, drying, and packaging		
Prohibitions against adulteration and requirements for labeling		

Exhibit 3-8. Egg Products Inspection Act, 1970: Provisions, commodities affected, and regulatory authority

Principal Provisions	Principal Commodities Affected	Federal Regulatory Authority
U.S. Grade Standards	Fresh fruits and vegetables Rabbits Meat Poultry (chicken, turkey, ducks, guineas, and pigeons) Eggs (shell) Cheese (colby, cheddar, Swiss, Emmentaler) Butter Dry milk (various kinds) Dry whey Grain and related commodities Honey and syrups or molasses Processed fruits and vegetables (canned, frozen, dried, including dates, raisins, prunes) Fruit juices Jams and jellies Pickles and olives Sauerkraut Olive oil Peanut butter Potatoes, peeled Cherries, sulfured	Agricultural Marketing Service, USDA
Inspection and Grading Service	All commodities listed above	
	Fish (fresh and frozen) of various forms and species, Crustacean shellfish products (shrimp), molluscan shellfish products (scallops)	National Marine Fisheries Service, National Oceanic and Atmospheric Administration, Department of Commerce

Exhibit 3-9. Agricultural Marketing Act, 1946: Provisions, commodities affected, and authority

selecting food for particular needs. For example, substantial differences in both quality and price occur in beef that is graded "Prime," "Choice," or "Good," or in poultry that is graded "A," "B," or "C," or in fruits or vegetables that are "Fancy" or "Number 1."

Commodity processors, growers, or producers are not required by this law to inspect and label products for grade, but if a quality grade is indicated, the product must meet the standards for that grade. A product that does not meet a U.S. standard for grade is considered "misbranded" under the federal law applicable to the particular commodity.

Buyers are wise to take advantage of grade standards to select and write specifications for food products and of the inspection service to require processors or other vendors from whom food is purchased to provide certification of grade. This is done by official labeling, inspection, or certification of products or certification that a product meets a particular specification.

Principal Provisions	Principal Commodities Affected	Federal Regulatory Authority
Definition of "butter" as a food product made exclusively from milk or cream or both, with or without common salt, with or without coloring matter, with no less than 80 percent, by weight, of milk fat, and without chemical additives or artificial flavor. Provision for butter to be examined for use of dirty cream or milk and for mold indicating the use of decomposed cream.	Butter	FDA, DHHS

Exhibit 3-10. Definition of butter by Act of Congress, March 4, 1923

Principal Provisions	Principal Commodities Affected	Federal Regulatory Authority
Definition of "filled milk" as milk or cream or skim milk, in any form, including condensed, evaporated, concentrated, powdered, or dried, to which fat of any kind *other than milk fat* is added, substituted, or blended in any way. Declaration that "filled milk" is "adulterated," "injurious to the public health" and a "fraud upon the public." Made the manufacture and shipment of "filled milk" unlawful.	Milk Cream	FDA, DHHS

Exhibit 3-11. Filled Milk Act, 1923: Provisions, commodities affected, and authority

LAWS FOR DAIRY PRODUCTS

In the years 1923, 1924, and 1927, several pieces of legislation were passed to protect the integrity and wholesomeness of dairy products and to require that they be made wholly from milk or cream.

Definition of Butter

"Butter" was defined by an act of Congress in 1923 (Exhibit 3-10, so that similar products made with vegetable oils could not be misrepresented. Provision for the sale of "margarine" or "oleomargarine," prepared from fat other than cream, was made by Congress in 1950 by an amendment to the Federal Trade Commission Act, as amended, and by the Federal Food, Drug, and Cosmetic Act, as amended. This legislation provided definitions and legal standards of identity, requirements for appropriate labeling, and specifications for packaging.

Filled Milk Act

The Filled Milk Act (Exhibit 3-11) made illegal the addition of fats such as corn oil or palm oil to products marketed as milk or cream. However, in today's markets many creamlike products are available for sale. In terms of labeling requirements under the Federal Food, Drug, and Cosmetic Act, these products may be sold if they are appropriately labeled as "imitation" or if the product is given a new or fanciful name, such as "whipped topping" or "nondairy creamer."

Milk Ordinance

The first Model Milk Ordinance (Exhibit 3-12) was established in 1924 by the U.S. Public Health Service. Numerous editions and revisions of the original ordinance have been published since that time to provide a standard for Grade A pasteurized milk. The standard for Grade A milk is a standard for sanitation and wholesomeness. Unlike other

Principal Provisions	Principal Commodities Affected	Federal Regulatory Authority
Sanitation standards for U.S. Grade A Pasteurized Milk and milk products	Milk Cream	FDA, DHHS
Standards for and inspection of dairy farms, milking barns, and milk plants in terms of construction and equipment		
Requirements for pasteurization, aseptic processing, packaging, transportation, and marketing		
Standards and sampling for microbiological quality and chemical residues		
Temperature standards		

Exhibit 3-12. U.S. Public Health Service—Food and Drug Administration Grade A Pasteurized Milk Ordinance

grade standards, the grade does not indicate differences in quality characteristics.

The Pasteurized Milk Ordinance is a model that is used as a standard in the voluntary Cooperative State–Public Health Service Program for Certification of Interstate Milk Shippers, in which all fifty states participate. Although no federal agency has authority to require use of the model ordinance in its entirety, adoption by states, counties, or municipalities that do have legal authority is recommended. Mislabeled or adulterated products are prohibited under the Federal Food, Drug, and Cosmetic Act, administered by the Food and Drug Administration (FDA).

The ordinance relates to sanitation and provides the following: prohibitions on the sale of adulterated and misbranded products; bases for regulating the inspection of dairy farms and milk plants; processes for pasteurization, aseptic processing, and pack-aging; provisions for the distribution and sale of milk products; and requirements for construction of farms and dairy plants. Standards of identity for various milk products are in Title 21 of the *Code of Federal Regulations* as a part of the Federal Food, Drug, and Cosmetic Act.

Federal Import Milk Act

Protection from foreign competition and assurance of the sanitary quality of imported milk was provided in the Federal Import Milk Act (Exhibit 3-13).

TEA IMPORTATION ACT

The Tea Importation Act (Exhibit 3-14) significantly contributed to assuring the purity and sanitary quality of various teas imported into the United States. The provisions are unique in requiring actual sample standards of various teas from different parts of the world.

Principal Provisions	Principal Commodities Affected	Federal Regulatory Authority
Requirement of a permit to import milk in order to promote the dairy industry in the United States	Milk Cream	FDA, DHHS
Definition of milk or cream that is unfit for importation in terms of substance or conditions related to the public health		
Provisions for inspection to insure that milk and cream are produced and handled to comply with health standards		

Exhibit 3-13. Federal Import Milk Act, 1927: Provisions, commodities affected, and authority

Principal Provisions	Principal Commodities Affected	Federal Regulatory Authority
Board of experts to provide standard samples of tea to the secretary and customhouses at ports of entry into the U.S., including New York, Chicago, and San Francisco	Tea	Secretary, DHHS
Uniform standards of purity, quality, and fitness for consumption of all kinds of teas imported into the United States		
Prohibition of importing into the United States any tea that is inferior (in purity, quality, and fitness for consumption) to the standards established by the board of experts		
Tea·Examiners Board of Tea Appeals as a mechanism for protesting the rulings of examiners		

Exhibit 3-14. Tea Importation Act, 1897: Provisions and authority

MISCELLANEOUS STANDARDS

Other standards that are not related to those presented in the exhibits are important in selecting food and beverages or for general information. These include standards for beer, distilled spirits and wine, standards for grinds of coffee, and international standards for food.

Beer, Distilled Spirits, Wine

The Federal Alcohol Administration Act, administered through the U.S. Bureau of Alcohol, Tobacco and Firearms in the Department of the Treasury, is the basis for marketing alcoholic beverages in the United States. The law provides definitions and standards of identity for various kinds of alcoholic beverages, bases for taxation, requirements for labeling, and conditions for importation.

Definitions and standards of identity provide legal requirements for ingredients that must be used in preparing the products and for the alcohol content of finished beverages. Requirements for preparation may also be included. Definitions and standards of identity have been established for the following products: grape wine, table wine, dessert wine, sparkling grape wine, champagne, crackling wine, carbonated grape wine, citrus wine, fruit wine, wine from other agricultural products (such as raisins and rice), neutral spirits (vodka), whiskeys of various kinds, gin, brandies of various kinds, blended apple jack, rum, tequila, cordials and liqueurs, flavored rum, vodka and whiskey, and beer. These definitions and standards provide the basis for distinguishing among various products available.

Grinds for Coffee

Standard grinds for coffee, designated as "regular," "drip," or "fine," have been established at the National Bureau of Standards in the Department of Commerce. The standards are based on the percentage of particles that will pass through a mesh screen of a particular size.

International Standards

The regulatory provisions and agencies cited in Exhibits 3-1 through 3-12 generally are in effect for both imported and domestic products, particularly for standards related to the wholesomeness of food. A set of standards, called Codex Alimentarius Food Standards, is also available. These are international standards that are established by the Codex Alimentarius Commission established through the United Nations. Codex Alimentarius standards are reviewed through the U.S. Food and Drug Administration for acceptance without change, acceptance with change, or nonacceptance, based on appropriate publication and review according to established procedures. Accepted food quality standards are equal to those for the same products produced in the United States.

CONCLUSION

The average person is generally unfamiliar with the provisions of the food laws presented in this chapter, even though they profoundly affect the substances that are the basis for life and health. The law may appear complicated and confusing because of its parallel development with the food industry, changes in society, and reorganizations of the federal government. However, some knowledge is essential for effective food buying.

An overview of food law is provided in this chapter to give a professional food buyer a real concept of the overall provisions of the law and a basis for understanding the factors in purchase of various commodities, as the details are presented in subsequent chapters of this book.

REFERENCES

Code of Federal Regulations, Animals and Animal Products, Title 9, Part 200 to End. Washington, D.C.: U.S. Government Printing Office, 1999.

Code of Federal Regulations, Food and Drugs, Title 21, Parts 1–99. Washington, D.C.: U.S. Government Printing Office, 1988.

Code of Federal Regulations, Food and Drugs, Title 21, Parts 100–169. Washington, D.C.: U.S. Government Printing Office, 1999.

Code of Federal Regulations, Food and Drugs, Title 21, Parts 170–199. Washington, D.C.: U.S. Government Printing Office, 1999.

Code of Federal Regulations, Alcohol, Tobacco Products and Firearms, Title 27, Parts 1–199. Washington, D.C.: U.S. Government Printing Office, 1987.

Code of Federal Regulations, Alcohol, Tobacco Products and Firearms, Title 27, Parts 200– End. Washington, D.C.: U.S. Government Printing Office, 1987.

Code of Federal Regulations, Wildlife and Fisheries, Title 50, Parts 200–599. Washington, D.C.: U.S. Government Printing Office, 1987.

Compilation of Selected Acts within the Jurisdiction of the Committee on Energy and Commerce, Vol. I: *Health Law*. Washington, D.C.: U.S. Government Printing Office, February 1987.

Compilation of Selected Acts within the Jurisdiction of the Committee on Energy and Commerce, Vol. 2: *Food, Drug, and Related Law*. Washington, D.C.: U.S. Government Printing Office, February 1987.

Dietary Supplement Health and Education Act of 1994, Public Law 103–417. Oct. 25, 1994, 21 USC 301 *et seq.*

Federal Register of Wednesday, January 6, 1993 (58 FR 467-2964). Washington, D.C.: U.S. Government Printing Office.

Federal Register of Thursday, July 19, 1990 (55 FR 29339-29552). Washington, D.C.: U.S. Government Printing Office.

Federal Register of Monday, December 18, 1995, Part II. 60 FR 65197-65202. *Department of Health and Human Services, Food and Drug Administration, Procedures for the Safe and Sanitary Processing and Importing of Fish and Fishery Products; Final Rule; Code of Federal Regulations Title 21*, Parts 123 and 1240. Washington, D.C.: U.S. Government Printing Office.

Federal Register of Thursday, July 25, 1996, Part II. 61 FR 38806-38989. *Department of Agriculture, Food Safety and Inspection Service, Pathogen Reduction; Hazard Analysis and Critical Control Point (HACCP) Systems; Final Rule; Code of Federal Regulations, Title 9*, Parts 304, 308, 310, 320, 327, 381, 416, 417. Washington, D.C.: U.S. Government Printing Office.

Food and Drug Administration Acts. HHS Publication No. (FDA) 80-1051. Washington, D.C.: U.S. Government Printing Office, 1980.

Food and Drug Modernization Act of 1997, Public Law 105–115, Nov. 21. 1997, 21 USC 300 *et seq.*

Food Quality Protection Act of 1996, Public Law 104–170, Aug. 3, 1996, 7 USC, *136 et seq.*

Nutrition Labeling and Education Act of 1990, 21 U.S.C. 301.

PMO Grade A Pasteurized Milk Ordinance, Public Health Service, Food and Drug Administration, Publication No. 229, Washington, D.C.: Public Health Service—Food and Drug Administration, Milk Safety Branch HFF-346.

Requirements of Laws and Regulations Enforced by the U.S. Food and Drug Administration. HEW Publication No. (FDA) 79-1042. Washington, D.C.: U.S. Government Printing Office.

The Almanac of the Canning, Freezing, Preserving Industries. Westminister, Md.: Edward E. Judge & Sons, 1998.

4 The Purchasing Department in the Food Service Industry

Purpose: To provide an overview of the purchasing department and the buyer's relationship to the general organization of a food service operation.

INTRODUCTION

The food purchasing department in any food service operation directs its efforts to the same end—that of providing a specified quality product for the best price. But because there are so many types and sizes of food service operations, the purchasing department of any one operation must be adapted to account for different budget and personnel limitations. Even though there is a commonly used general organizational plan in the food service industry, we find almost as many variations as there are types and sizes of operations within the industry. Consider purchasing for these different operations: a freestanding restaurant with 65 seats, a 500-bed hospital, a school district, and a 700-store hamburger chain. Each is considered a food service operation, but obviously the purchasing methods and general organizational plans must vary.

ORGANIZATION IN THE FOOD SERVICE INDUSTRY

The general scheme of organization is that management is responsible for the overall operation, with four areas of operational activities under management: purchasing material and supplies, preparing the product for sale, selling the product, and policing the entire operation through a continuous review of the costs. How skillfully management operates the four different divisions and how expertly it coordinates the activities of the divisions are the keys to a successful operation. A successful operation produces the quality of product desired at the budgeted profit. One of the best illustrations of the division of operational responsibility can be found in a typical family-owned Chinese restaurant. In this instance, the father is generally the cook in charge of preparation; the mother is the bookkeeper and cashier; the daughter is in charge of dining room service; the son is the bartender; Uncle Harry is in charge of purchasing, and everyone watches Uncle Harry.

THE PLACE OF THE FOOD PURCHASING DEPARTMENT

Hotels

A few years ago the typical metropolitan hotel had from 300 to 500 rooms, and, in a few instances, some chain hotels reached 700 to 800 rooms. Economy of operation then forced new metropolitan hotels to the point where any hotel with fewer than 1,000 rooms was considered economically unsound. Naturally there are exceptions—some hotels of 2,000 or more rooms are able to operate at a profit largely because of revenues obtained from housing large conventions, with attendant food and beverage sales.

Experience has shown that a certain type of organization seems to produce the best results for a medium- to large-size hotel, and it is the one generally used. Exhibit 4-1 shows how the organization is set up, how the various operating departments relate to each other, and how management communicates with each of the many departments.

The four general divisions of operations can be traced. The procurement department, the food production department, the sales department, and the controller's department are all set up as separate spheres of operation, and the heads report to the general manager of the hotel. The controller's department is in a position to exert cost controls throughout the entire operation and is directly responsible for receiving all supplies into the hotel, for the functioning of the food and beverage cost control office, and for supervising all checkers and cashiers who handle funds throughout the entire house.

Motor Inns

Although there are many chain-operated motor inns in North America, most are privately owned or are members of a franchised organization. The actual operation of even a franchised motor inn can be, and generally is, largely the responsibility of the owner. In spite of the relatively small size of a motor inn and its food and beverage department, the organizational patterns show only minor variations from those of a hotel. An organizational chart for a motor inn is depicted in Exhibit 4-2. Note that the food and beverage department is set up in terms of four operational areas: purchasing, preparation, sales, and control.

The purchasing agent buys all of the food and beverage supplies, as well as the general operating supplies. The storage and issuing of food and beverage supplies is also the responsibility of purchasing. The chef and head bartender are responsible for the preparation of food and beverages, respectively. The sales department, which has responsibility for banquets and dining rooms, is under the direction of a catering manager. The independent control function is under the direction of a controller responsible for food and beverage control, revenue control, receiving, inventory, and the direction and control of persons handling money. Overall responsibility is the function of the general manager or innkeeper, as he or she is designated on the chart.

This organizational chart is satisfactory for a motor inn with 200 to 400 rooms. Even if there are only 100 rooms, with a proportionately smaller organization, it is possible to keep the four areas of operation separate. This is generally accomplished by having the innkeeper take over the responsibility for purchasing; the chef, for production and storage; a dining room hostess, for catering and bar service; a bookkeeper, for control. What better opportunity is there for controlling costs in a motor inn with 100 to 150 rooms than for the manager to do the purchasing?

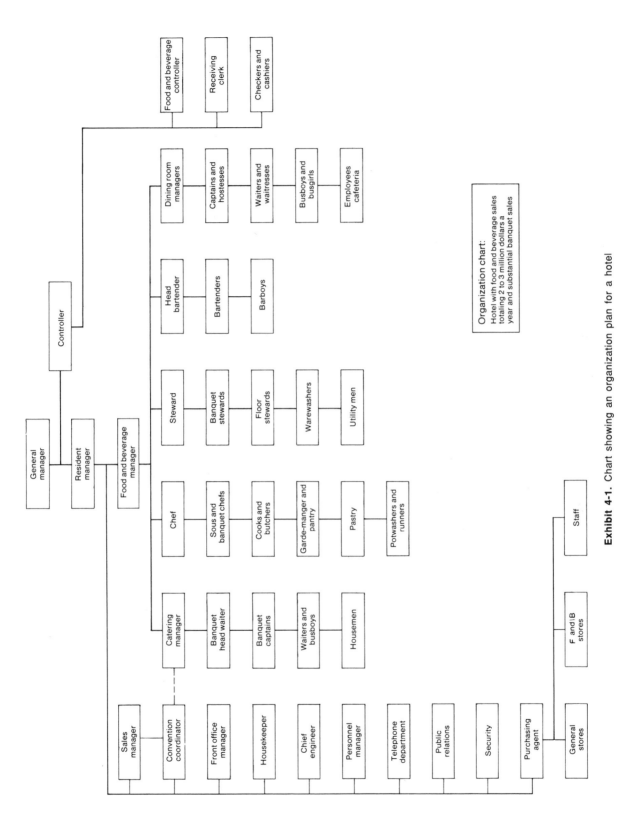

Exhibit 4-1. Chart showing an organization plan for a hotel

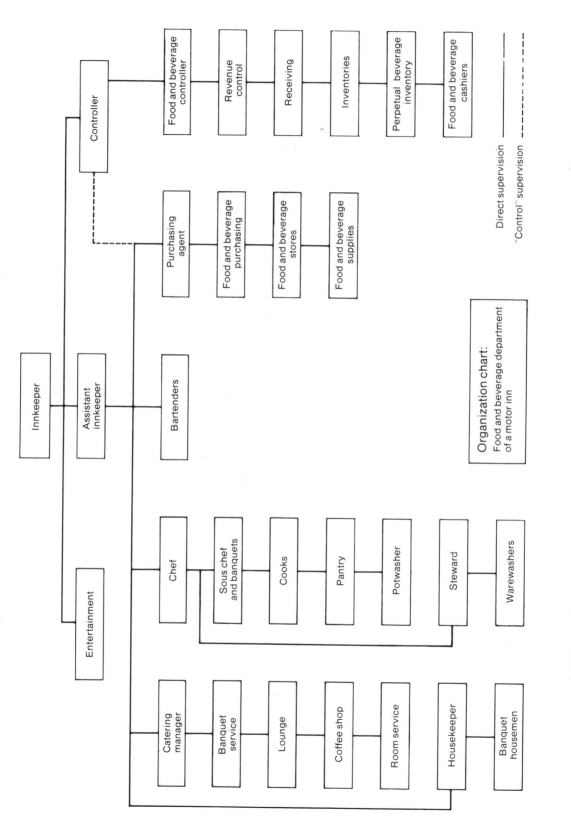

Exhibit 4-2. Chart showing an organization plan for the food and beverage department in a franchised motor inn

Institutions

The quick-service restaurants, with a sales volume of nearly $110 million annually, and full-dining restaurants, with an annual sales volume of close to $100 million, each experience more volume than the entire institutions segment, whose annual sales volume is about $85 million. Growth in the commercial operations segment during the past five years has been slightly more than 40 percent. The institutional operations segment reported growth during this same period of less than 25 percent. There were substantial gains in the corrections institutions and elder care, but the gains were offset by a decline in military feeding.

One of the larger-volume segments of the institutional operations is hospitals, which garner about 15 percent of the total volume. Exhibit 4-3 shows an organizational chart for the dietary department of a medium- to large-size hospital. Since the last edition of this text, the changes in operations that were underway at that time have accelerated along with changes characteristic of the health-care industry. The operation of the dietary departments in a considerable number of hospitals has been contracted with catering firms. The merger of several hospitals has given rise to centralization of the food preparation, where both regular and dietary foods are prepared at one hospital and transported to the "satellite" hospitals. As these food operations become larger, there is a drift away from the use of convenience foods in favor of total preparation.

The organizational chart in Exhibit 4-4 shows the controller's department, the dietary manager, and the purchasing department as the three operational activities. This is true of most medium- to large-size hospitals. However, a sales department, or a sales manager under the dietary manager, exists in a number of hospitals that cater functions in the hospitals facilities or outside as a profit center to supplement income.

Government Institutions

These operations usually have a separate purchasing department that uses the formal bid contract and specification system of buying. The different types of buying are explained fully in Chapter 6, "The Mechanics of Buying." In government, as in private industry, purchasing is under the scrutiny of a controller or other prescribed control departments.

WHY A SEPARATE PURCHASING DEPARTMENT?

One decision facing many people in the food service industry today concerns whether or not to set up a separate food purchasing department. Following are the principal arguments against and for a separate department.

Arguments Against a Separate Department

1. It is not cost effective except in the very large operations.
2. Each department is better equipped to do its own buying.
   a. They know better what is needed and the amounts needed.
   b. They are more familiar with specifications.
3. A separate department creates an atmosphere of distrust and misunderstanding.
4. The different departments must make the decisions on what and how much is needed.
5. A separate department will not be interested in prompt delivery because it is not involved in the problems of the overall operation.
6. Each department must draw up elaborate specifications to guide the independent buyer.

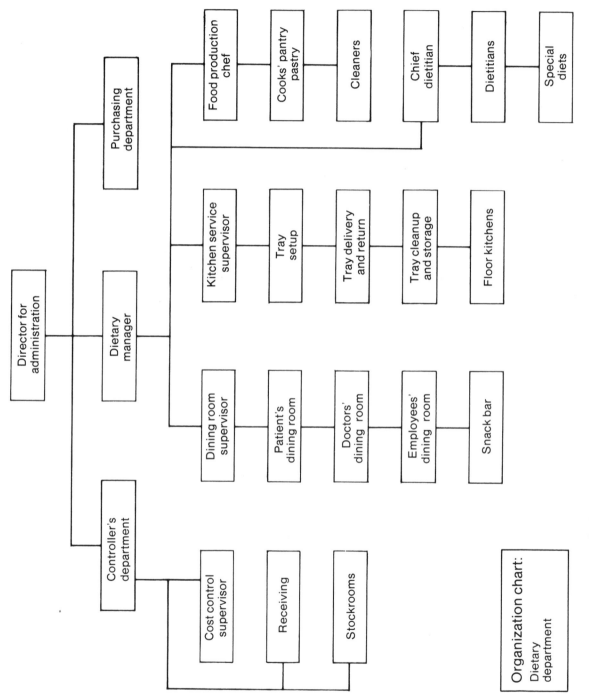

Exhibit 4-3. Chart showing an organization plan for the dietary department in a hospital

Arguments for a Separate Department

1. The extensive use of computers in the purchasing operation and in the food and beverage purveyors' operations has considerably complicated purchasing operations, technologically considered, and adds to the importance of a limited number of persons in information exchanges between buyers and sellers.
2. Department heads have a full schedule without the burden of purchasing.
3. One person handling all purchasing sets up a better condition for response to management.
4. A trained professional buyer can adapt to buy any type of product.
5. Regardless of who does the buying, specifications should be set up by a committee with members who can provide the several types of information needed—costs, availability of products, quality, and market for products.
6. Professional buyers develop innovative ideas for getting good prices and reliable sources of supply.

Unless some new element enters the purchasing field of the food service industry, the trend is definitely toward separate purchasing departments. It is interesting that even in smaller motels and motor inns, the managers of the operation have taken over the food purchasing function, as well as purchasing for all other departments. This represents a variation of the idea of a separate purchasing department.

FUNCTIONS OF A FOOD PURCHASING DEPARTMENT

The first responsibility is to buy the food supplies needed to carry on the operation. In addition to this fundamental function, the department or food purchaser provides information to the chef and catering manager on the cost and availability of products and special buys that may be of advantage, and on shortages that are forecast due to weather, strikes, or other conditions. Information from the purchasing department is necessary to the menu-writing team, and is essential in the preparation of the annual budget, especially monthly revisions. Both the secondary function of providing information and the primary responsibility of the purchasing department should be carried out in such a manner that the operation makes a profit.

5 The Food Service Purchasing Agent

Purpose: To examine the job requirements of the purchasing agent, to consider the type of person needed to fill the position, and to suggest ways to organize the job.

INTRODUCTION

The job of purchasing agent is difficult and demanding. It requires a great deal of detailed product knowledge, not only of food and beverages, but also of china, glassware, and other supplies. In addition to product knowledge, the purchasing agent must have good communications skills in order to gain the cooperation of other department heads and be able to deal with food service managers, chefs, catering managers, dietitians, and purveyors. The buyer must be able to understand salespeople and learn from them while maintaining their respect. The objective of this chapter is to examine the job requirements, to consider the type of person needed to fill the job, and to suggest ways to organize the job so that the position and the person will be as productive as possible.

JOB DESCRIPTION

The first requirement for any job is a clear, detailed written statement of what the job entails and what is expected of the person filling it. Personnel people maintain that the main reason good employees fail on the job is because they do not understand what the boss expects. It is amazing how many executives or employees in such key positions as department heads find no job description available when they start in a new position and no one to accept the responsibility for preparing one.

A good job description not only helps the food buyer; it also helps clarify the responsibilities of those who work with him or her, and they are less likely to interfere with the purchasing function at the expense of their own jobs. The job description enables a boss to rate the performance of the food buyer fairly and comprehensively, and it helps the food buyer evaluate his or her own performance.

A food scientist might describe a food buyer as "the link in the world food distribution system where the flow of goods moves from the supply chain to the production process and on to the end user." The food operator, on the other hand, would probably describe the buyer as "the guy that gets what we want, when we want it, and at the best possible price." Both definitions are correct, but the second one leaves nothing to the imagination.

No one job description is perfect for all food buying jobs. The following job description, although it is designed for a food buyer in a hotel, could be modified for use in many large- or medium-size food service organizations.

JOB DESCRIPTION FOR THE FOOD BUYER WITH STOREROOM RESPONSIBILITY

I. Basic responsibility
  A. For purchasing, storage, and issuance of food (or other items designated by management)
  B. For security, cleanliness, and maintenance in all food and beverage supply storage areas

II. Organizational relationships
  A. Reports to: General manager
  B. Supervises: Purchasing office staff
    Supply storage personnel
  C. Functional relationships
    1. With food and beverage manager regarding department requirements
    2. With chef regarding food and menus
    3. With receiving clerk regarding receiving of food, beverages, and other supplies and regarding training and policing in receiving
    4. With catering manager regarding group meals
    5. With dining room managers regarding their suggestions for food and beverage supplies
    6. With controller and food and beverage controller regarding cost controls
    7. With kitchen stewards regarding food and beverage supplies
    8. With staff planner regarding scheduling
  D. Lateral supervision
    1. From general manager directly, or from resident manager or senior assistant manager in general manager's absence
    2. From food and beverage manager and controller as their responsibilities relate to purchasing
    3. From senior department heads, but only in terms of suggestions and requests for purchases
  E. Authority
    1. Under the supervision of the general manager, makes decisions for the purchasing department in order to achieve an efficient overall operation
    2. Has final approval of quality, price, quantity, and source of supply in keeping with house policy and purchase specifications

III. Functions and duties
  A. Purchases food, beverages, and other supplies, either on own responsibility or after consultation with chef or other department heads
  B. Visits
    1. Markets to select and stamp meats for aging and to mark other products of specific nature and quality for delivery
    2. Purveyors to inspect product quality and to keep up to date on available quality and seasonal products
  C. Solicits and analyzes bids, places orders, and makes contracts with the approval of management

D. Selects purveyors on the basis of their ability to deliver specified quality merchandise at competitive prices, with the approval of management

E. Monitors receiving procedures and assists in training receiving personnel

F. Acts as chairperson of testing committee and carries out a continuous program of product testing

G. Inspects supply storerooms for
1. Sanitation
2. Orderliness
3. Condition of stock
4. Rotation of supplies
5. Maintenance of parts
6. Security measures

H. Carries out internal accounting control procedures regarding purchasing, storing, and issuing of food and beverage supplies, in conjunction with food and beverage controller

I. Reviews and approves invoices as to prices paid, quantities ordered, and quality of merchandise received

J. Employs, trains, directs, and discharges purchasing office staff and supply storage personnel

K. Maintains reasonable, regular visiting hours for salespeople

L. Maintains a constant search for new and better supplies and for opportunities to economize

M. Maintains a good working relationship with other department heads and personnel throughout operations and solicits opinions and suggestions from others regarding operation of the purchasing department

N. Develops computer relationships with purveyors to facilitate placing of orders by computer

IV. Requirements
A. Personal
1. Must have a cooperative attitude toward own job and other personnel
2. Should have a "Let's try it and see" approach to problems
3. Must have integrity and be completely honest
4. Must possess a "curiosity factor" that pushes one to do things
5. Must be an aggressive bargainer, but must not demand the impossible; an ability to recognize the "bottom price" is essential
6. Must have the ability to resist flattery and avoid the "God Syndrome" (self-importance)
7. Should be in good health with normal living habits
8. Must inspire job loyalty in associates and staff
9. Must be able to do a good public relations job for the employer

B. Experience and training
1. Must read, write, and communicate well
2. Should have at least two years in college or in a technical trade school
3. Should have at least five years of experience in the back of the house, with at least one year of experience in food purchasing
4. Must be thoroughly acquainted with food, beverages, supply products, specifications and the market
5. Should have some training in business law
6. Must be computer literate.

FINDING A GOOD BUYER

A job can be set up with operating manuals, specification lists, checklists, internal controls, management supervision, and outside advisory services. But, if the food buyer is wrong for the job, whether the reason is personal, lack of experience, or poor technique, the job will not be as well done as it should be.

The Search

A good buyer can frequently be promoted from within the organization, unless it is a new operation. If an organization has been established for some time and there is no such person, management should realize that their policy regarding training needs revision. One of the marks of good management is to see that there is a backup person ready to step into all key department jobs.

One of the easiest ways to get a good food buyer is to determine who is doing the best job for a successful food operation in the area. The offer of a higher salary or an increase in benefits might persuade that person to make a move. Sometimes a change in management creates a situation where an outstanding employee will entertain a bid from another company.

Another good place to look is among people working immediately under successful buyers. If such a person has been on the job for a while, he or she has usually been well trained and is probably looking for advancement. If advancement appears to be blocked in the present job, that person might entertain an outside offer.

Accounting firms and operational consultants to the food industry can generally be depended on for an unbiased recommendation. They are also helpful in checking the background of an applicant.

The Candidate

Such considerations as personality and character are probably as important as experience and formal training for the job when weighing a candidate for the position of food buyer. Anyone who is interested and has the basic qualifications can learn the trade, but personal attitudes and habits are not likely to change much.

The good buyer should view the job as a game that must be played according to accepted rules—and won for the benefit of management. If management does not benefit, a new player will be introduced.

The buyer must have self-control and be slow to anger. On many occasions the buyer may be criticized or harassed by people seeking favors. One way to maintain control in difficult situations is not to get so personally involved in a problem that one's judgment is affected. A good sense of humor is a real asset, for it can relieve a tense situation and permit a graceful retreat.

Any candidate for a position of trust in any part of the food service industry should be checked for any record of excessive use of alcohol, the use of drugs, or involvement in any payoff or kickbacks. It is not difficult for investigating companies to pinpoint any discrepancies in a candidate's background.

Qualifications

Although the most important requirements for a professional food buyer are those reflected in personality and character, education and experience cannot be ignored. A top food buyer needs at least two years in college or in a technical school, plus at least five years of back-of-the-house experience and a minimum of one year as a buyer or as an assistant buyer in a large, first-class operation, whether it be institution, hotel, or restaurant.

Back-of-the-house experience covers all

phases of the food operation: catering manager, restaurant manager, food and beverage controller, receiving clerk, storeroom manager, steward, cook, and even warewasher. Often, a young chef or sous chef eager to get into management will accept a food buying job as part of his or her training and development.

A good buyer has to know all of the sources of supply in the immediate community, and should also know the supply situation in nearby communities.

The buyer must have a thorough knowledge of current packaging, grading, sizes, and sectional and seasonal products. He or she should have experience in making butcher and taste tests in order to set up purchase specifications.

An experienced food buyer knows that there is no point in trying to change the marketing system. A *professional* food buyer understands completely how the market works and knows how to make it work to the company's advantage.

THE PURCHASING AGENT AND THE MENU-WRITING TEAM

One of the principal duties of the purchasing department is to research market conditions and prices. For any food operation this research and the resulting contribution the purchasing agent can make to the menu-writing process are vital. Much of the operation's cost efficiency will depend on the accuracy of this market research.

A few years ago, when hotels had print shops, the menus for the hotel restaurants were printed daily. Cyclical menus were used with day-to-day adjustments to take advantage of favorable market prices. High printing costs have led to discontinuing that process. Most restaurants, whether in a hotel or free standing, now use a two- or three-week cycle. The layout of the menus allows for the insertion of a limited number of items, which might change daily. The entire format of the menu is reconsidered every three months. Hotels and restaurants with banquet business can use the market information provided by the purchasing agent to great advantage, since banquet menus are generally priced at the time the customer requests the banquet services. The banquet manager can also help customers make economical choices of foods if the manager is kept current on the market prices and availability of items. The purchasing agent will advise which foods are in short supply or out of season, of poor quality, or overpriced.

FOOD BUYING AS A PROFESSION

The buyer who approaches the job professionally, whether buying food or other supplies, is constantly on the alert to find a better way to do the necessary tasks. A professional buyer constantly studies the market and reads newspapers, magazines, and other literature pertaining to products. He or she visits market sources on a regular basis, checks the quality and availability of products on the market, and anticipates market changes and trends. A good buyer is willing to learn and be educated by people in the market who, as a rule, know more about the products than a buyer does. A curious buyer looks for new purchasing techniques—this is what makes the work satisfying and challenging.

Keeping up with the Profession

Often, after several years of hard work, a food buyer may begin to feel complacent about his or her achievements. Such an attitude can be fatal. A buyer should constantly make self-evaluations to be sure that he or she is doing everything possible to protect the buyer's own job, to lay the groundwork for future promotion, and to increase the buyer's own sense of worth. The buyer must keep up with the world and look toward tomorrow.

6 The Mechanics of Buying

Purpose: To present a review and discussion of the various factors involved in the mechanics of food and beverage buying in the food service industry.

INTRODUCTION

There are many different types of food service operations, and variations in purchasing systems are necessary for each type. However, certain basic concepts are required for all plans. In this chapter, we discuss the basics that are vital to a controlled money-saving system. This simple, topical outline is followed in the discussions.

1. A step-by-step food and beverage plan
2. The ABCs of food buying
   a. What and how much to buy
   b. Where to buy
   c. How to buy
3. Managing the purchasing office
4. Computer application

The first three steps include what must be known to pursue a successful food purchasing program regardless of the type of food purchasing program followed. For large properties today, it should come as no surprise that the use of a computer can improve the execution time and accuracy of the many *quantifiable* steps in buying. After establishing the compatibility of purchase specifications (see Chapter 7) with the several purveyors, products can be computer coded with purveyors, and much information, such as price quotations, daily price changes, and the placing of orders can be done without verbal contact between buyer and seller.

STEP-BY-STEP FOOD AND BEVERAGE PURCHASING PLAN

The Basic Plan

1. Establish the responsibility of management and publish a functional organizational plan showing responsibility for the entire purchasing procedure.
   a. Management should approve sources of supply.
   b. Management should retain final decisions on all quality questions, subject to advice from the food and beverage manager, chef, and purchasing agent.
2. Prepare an adequate set of purchase specifications based on tests. Tests should be conducted by a commit-

tee representing management and the several food departments. The specifications should be approved by management and made the basis for quality control.

3. The several departments should use purchase requests approved by management for all supplies other than daily food item purchases. The purchasing department should issue a completed purchase order on the basis of the purchase requests received showing items, amounts, prices, and suppliers.

4. The purchasing department should maintain a complete record of all price quotations, contracts, and purchases made.

5. Quantities to be purchased must be based on needs. Storerooms for dry stores should be set up with minimum and maximum par stocks and purchases made to maintain the pars. Perishables should be purchased to meet variations in volume and type of business. Daily sales history records plus expected banquets should be the basis for determining amounts.

THE ABCS OF FOOD BUYING

What and How Much to Buy

It is unfair to expect a food buyer to know exactly what is needed by operating departments and how much of it to buy. In fact, it would be unwise for the buyer to ignore the chef and other operating department heads.

In setting up a new operation, the purchasing agent should meet with the chef, catering manager, and storeroom manager and develop a commodity list, while considering the needs of the menus. Specifications are then agreed on (see Chapter 7). The commodity list should be broken down into staples and perishables. Staples are normally considered grocery storeroom items, and as mentioned above, minimum and maximum par stocks should be established.

The two categories of perishable items are fresh and frozen. Fresh perishables should be purchased as needed, based on specific intended use. Either they back up the daily menu, or they are for use at a function or a special event. Par stocks can be set up for frozen items, and purchases are based on maintaining the pars.

In some operations the chef is expected to submit a daily list of all perishables to be delivered for an immediate specified use. Usually the chef works up a list of requirements only for meats, poultry, and fish. The storeroom manager normally maintains the proper quantities of fresh fruits and vegetables by referring to banquet menus or a list of special requirements that can then be added to the average daily use of these items.

The food and beverage controller can be very helpful in determining requirements for the amount of perishables needed to serve a given number of covers, that is, persons to be served. These amounts are generally figured in terms of pounds or units necessary to serve one hundred covers in dining rooms or for banquets. By making periodic tests, the food and beverage controller works with the food and beverage manager and the chef to estimate just how much of the many key items is needed to provide for the estimated number of covers required for the various food services, banquets, parties, and special diets.

The key to controlling food costs is to establish a relationship between pounds or units of food purchased to serve an accurately estimated number of persons on a day-to-day basis.

Portion cost factors (see Appendix I, Table 1) are used by the food and beverage controller in costing menus. They can also be used to find out how much to buy for a certain number of people.

First find the portion cost factor for the size portion being served. The portion cost factor multiplied by the number of covers to be served equals the poundage necessary to buy to serve this number of people. *For example*, to serve 125 people 6-ounce portions of pot roast made from roast-ready top round, multiply the cost factor (.68) by the number of people to be served (125): .68 x 125 = 85. So, 85 pounds are needed. The weight specification for roast-ready top round is 19 to 23 pounds. Thus, four top rounds will be required to serve the party of 125.

Where to Buy

Before a decision is made concerning where to buy, a market search should be made. Much depends on the country, or the part of the country, where the operation is located, what supplies are available, and the season of the year.

Location, which influences the quantities of food that must be purchased and stored, helps to determine mini-maxi limits. It also affects delivery schedules, and, since the cost of delivery is rising, limited delivery schedules worked out with suppliers could result in greater discounts, better quotations, or lower average unit delivery costs.

Other considerations are the amount of storage area available for the operation and whether or not there is a dependable source of energy for refrigeration and the maintenance of equipment or a reliable alternate source of power, such as a diesel generator or a standby steam-driven generator fired by coal, or, in some parts of the world, by wood, for emergencies.

In deciding whether to buy locally, other questions arise. Are local suppliers large enough to carry adequate stocks? Are there enough local food purveyors to permit the buyer to get truly competitive prices? During particular times of the year, it should be recognized that the local farmers' market can be one of the best sources for certain perishables. Not only do you save money,

but there is also an opportunity to improve relations with local people and to support the local economy. If an operation is close to a large metropolitan area, it should be recognized that large purveyors will make deliveries as far as a hundred miles from their base of operations, often delivering merchandise at considerably lower cost than if it is purchased locally.

Today, there is also the matter of contracts. Many large companies distribute nationally by working out satisfactory arrangements for the delivery of merchandise on a national or long-term basis.

From Whom to Buy

In Chapter 2 there was a general discussion of functions, including the supply function, of the market and of some of the functionaries who operate in it. It is important that the food buyer have a clear understanding of the respective functions of the suppliers with whom he does business.

In the case of meat, a *packer* may slaughter, clean, store, and sell. Today, some so-called packers buy animals from slaughterhouses (abattoirs) that specialize in killing and cleaning carcasses of meat animals. A *processor* generally turns raw food into finished products through canning, mixing, baking, or some other means. Sometimes packers process such items as hams, bacon, sausage, corned beef, or tongues, and often, shortening and oil. Some large packers—for example, Swift, Armour, and Cudahy—do more processing and marketing than killing and breaking. Companies such as Iowa Beef Processors, Missouri Packing Company, Monfort, Oscar Mayer, Excel, Litvak, Spencer Packing, and a host of others engage in the killing, breaking, and marketing of boxed, ready-for-use meats and in sideline feedlot operations, bagging fertilizers for the garden and recycling food dropped in the feedlot in a pelletized form for cattle and pets. Chicken feathers have also proved to be an important commodity in the manufacturing of pet food.

A *breaker* is a company that specializes in buying carload lots of meat carcasses and "breaks" them into wholesale cuts that are then sold to meat supply houses, chain stores, grocery stores, and fabricators. The *fabricator,* who buys wholesale cuts of meat, makes them up on a custom order basis for wholesalers and processors or sells them directly to a user who pays his or her account on a weekly basis.

Dealers, purveyors, suppliers, and *wholesalers* perform similar services, and the titles are used interchangeably. They deal directly with the buyer, either by means of a house account (no salesperson) or through a salesperson. Most dealers specialize in a single item or a group of related items. In smaller communities, a supply house sometimes acts as a general supplier (a one-stop supply service).

Salespeople, the backbone of the food supply business, are probably the hardest working, least appreciated members of the marketing system. A commission house generally sells, on a commission basis, to purveyors or wholesalers who in turn sell to the food buyer. Most commission houses specialize in certain foods and seldom sell direct to a user, except for large accounts and food processors. *Agents* generally buy or sell specialized items on a paper basis. They accept carload lots of lettuce, for example, from a cooperative in California and sell it, for a commission, in the best market while the goods are still en route. Sometimes a commission house speculates by buying a lot of merchandise and selling it at a profit or a loss.

A *broker* is a salesperson who represents a manufacturer or a group of manufacturers by setting up a distribution point and selling, on a commission basis, to a regular food supply house. *Missionary salespeople* go out from headquarters to open up new accounts, to research and overcome resistance to a product, to introduce new products, or to start a new sales campaign, among other activities.

With all of these steps in the food supply line, it is a wonder that food does not cost more. Today, a quantity food buyer must investigate every legal and ethical way to "buypass" any step in the distribution chain. This is not easy because, even if a purveyor would benefit, he is not anxious to tamper with a "safe" situation.

Selecting Suppliers. The selection of suppliers is one of the most important decisions that management must make in setting up and operating any type of food operation, whether it be food processing, a hotel, a restaurant, a hospital or some other institution, or a catering service. Good management works with the food buyer and the testing committee before approving a list of purveyors. Management is stressed because the final decision as to who the supplier will be belongs to management alone.

The testing committee, which includes the production manager, the chef, the food and beverage manager, and other operating department heads, should also be concerned with which suppliers are chosen to furnish food to the operation. Through decisions as to what brand names or qualities are to be used in the operation, the committee influences selection, for its recommendations are reflected in the specifications. The wise food buyer is glad that he does not have the final say in selecting purveyors.

Before any selection is made, the reputations of the purveyors available in the area should be thoroughly investigated. One of the best ways to judge a purveyor is to find out who his customers are. If the operations he services have good reputations and competent management personnel, the chances are that the purveyor is reliable. A few telephone calls to other institutions or to hotel, restaurant, and food managers in the area, the local Better Business Bureau, the Chamber of Commerce, local trade associations, and local bankers often provide helpful information, and confidential reports can be obtained from companies that specialize in such activities. If the potential volume of business to be done is large, a complete, independent report on the reputation of the purveyor might be worthwhile.

Management can, in addition, visit the purveyor's premises with the food buyer, so that both can assess the size and the quality of the operation. By inspecting the quantities on hand and the quality of the merchandise, one can make a considered judgment as to whether a business association would be beneficial. The general manager can use a first visit to make clear to the purveyor that, if he is selected, his performance will be judged solely on the quality of merchandise delivered, the service rendered, and the prices quoted in competition with other dealers.

How to Buy

Too many people buy food by sitting down with a list of needed items, phoning familiar dealers, placing an order, and asking the dealer to rush the order. There is little or no attempt to compare prices from different sources, but the buyer is secure in the knowledge that the dealers will give good service, that they will be nice to him around the holidays, and that the merchandise will be of good quality. As long as it gets the job done, everyone is satisfied, the operation shows a profit, and the manager goes along with it to keep peace, this type of buying continues. Of course, the fact that it costs anywhere from 10 to 20 percent more than it should is played down.

Other buyers meticulously call various purveyors and haggle over every price quotation before recording it on the daily market list. After several hours of telephoning, such a buyer goes over the quotation list and circles the prices he is willing to pay, thereby choosing his suppliers. The telephone is again used to place orders, and the supplies are delivered the next day. If this is the purchasing method, the receiving clerk or the food buyer should check deliveries as meticulously as prices were checked. This type of one-track buying also can cost a company

money because no one system of buying suffices for all of the various kinds of merchandise used in a food service operation.

The professional food buyer uses different systems of buying, with different, detailed procedures, for different kinds of merchandise. A good buyer will also change the system from time to time to meet market conditions, to take advantage of dips in the market, and to flatten out purchase costs when uptrends are expected in the market. The good buyer also continues to add new purveyors to his list and drops those who are not interested enough in the account to perform satisfactorily. Even though all the purveyors might be making an effort to keep the account, a good buyer gives some "vacations" to purveyors, but rotates the "vacations" so that no conscientious purveyor is eliminated from the list.

Purchasing Systems

The purchasing systems most commonly used in the food industry today are as follows:

1. Open market buying
2. One-stop buying
3. Fixed markup over daily trade quotation
4. Buy and hold
5. Formal written bid system
6. Drop shipments from national purveyors
7. Prime supplier program
8. Cost-plus from best competitive dealers

The following examination of each system includes discussion of both its good and bad points. There are other systems and variations of systems that might be preferable to those listed, depending on circumstances. The personalities involved, the type of operation, distance from market sources, available transportation, the local and international political situation, availability of funds, and the season of the year—all influence the system used.

Open Market Buying. Open market

buying, quotation buying, competitive market buying, or whatever the name, is the most popular means of buying food in the industry today. The system is basically one of ordering needed food supplies from a selected list of dealers based on either daily, weekly, or monthly price quotations. The quotations are based on a set of specifications in the hands of each dealer, and every day the buyer asks various dealers to quote a price for the quantities needed that particular day.

Even though the buyer may have been given a weekly list of prices on certain perishables, experience has shown that, because prices fluctuate on perishables, it is best to get a quotation for specific purchases. Because of the many grocery items involved, the average buyer does use the dealer's monthly price submissions as the basis for deciding what to buy from each dealer. This system of buying simplifies controlling food costs, as it permits the chef, the kitchen supervising dietitian, the food production manager, or the restaurant manager to decide daily what and how much of various food items should be purchased. The food buyer then makes the actual purchase.

Large institutions, food processors, and hotel and restaurant operations normally prepare a special purchase request listing items generally needed in their particular operation. This saves time in writing, serves as a reminder of items needed, and reduces mistakes to a minimum.

For smaller, perhaps average-sized food operations, probably the easiest and simplest way for the chef or those responsible for suggesting what to buy is to use a copy of the regular food requisition, listing the items and the amounts needed. The pantry, the butcher shop, and the pastry department could do the same, with the approval of the chef, and pass on requests to the food buyer. An example of such a form is shown in Exhibit 6-1. In larger, formalized operations, a form similar to a steward's daily market quotation list (see Exhibit 6-2) is used to indicate quantities

required. The list is then passed on to the food buyer as a formal request for purchase. A previously prepared and duplicated list of grocery items can also be used by the storeroom attendant to indicate his requirements and can then be passed on to the purchasing department. In lieu of individual, formalized lists, standard forms are available from hotel stationery supply houses.

When the food buyer has received requests for purchase, he records them on a custom or a standard steward's daily market and quotation list (see Exhibit 6-3) in the quantities needed. Then he calls various dealers to get current quotations. Even though purveyors have a set of purchase specifications, it is good business for the food buyer to repeat basic specifications so that there is no cause for misunderstanding on the part of the purveyor.

After the market and quotation sheet is complete and the dealer is selected, orders are placed by telephone. Generally, the sheet is made out in duplicate. A copy is retained in the purchasing office, and the original is sent to the receiving department to verify delivery and from there to the chef or to the food and beverage manager for their information.

The open market system of buying is best on a year-round basis for the average food operation. It does, however, have certain shortcomings, and other forms of buying, properly pursued, may prove more beneficial.

One of the main objections to open market buying is that the buyer is limited to the stock available on the market. The purchase procedure, since it is completed in one day, does not give the buyer a chance to negotiate or take advantage of seasonal trends, and, unless the chef and others are familiar with the best buys in the market, they may request items out of season that are extremely expensive.

Another fault is that the system permits those purveyors being called regularly for price quotations to agree on prices. It is not unusual for a group of purveyors to take

Form 489   **FOOD REQUISITION**   S. L. 100 PADS 9/73

№ 6253

Date _____

	ARTICLE	QUAN.	PRICE	AMOUNT

_____   _____
Department Head

Exhibit 6-1. Form used to requisition food, items not listed

advantage of a buyer by getting together to apportion the business from a particular operation. They can then arrange bids or prices that enable them to divide the business at prices very advantageous to themselves.

A buyer may combat this practice by introducing new dealers from time to time.

UNIFOOD CORPORATION				HOTEL	DATE		
BEEF				**PROVISIONS**			
Rib CH 34-40, 10x9				Bacon, Canadian 5-8			
Rib CHOP 3x4 #107				Bacon, Sli. 18-20			
Rib CH RR 19-22 #109				Bacon, Sli. 20-24			
Strip CH 9" Bl				Sli. Dried Beef			
Strip CH #180				Bologna			
Tender, Long 8-9				Brisket, Corned 12-14			
Tender, Short 5½-6				Brisket, Fresh 12-14			
Tender, Peeled				Cooked Corned Beef			
Knuckleface, Tied				Frankfurts 8/1			
Top Rnd. CH Bnls 20/22				Frankfurts 10/1			
Bottom Rnd. Bnls 25/28				Frankfurts, Cktl.			
Round, S. S. CH				Ham B & R 10-12			
Chuck, Sq. Bnls. CH				Ham, RTE 12-14			
Top Sir. Butt CH 12/14				Ham, RTE 10-12			
Top Sir. Butt PR 12/14				Ham, "Cure 81"			
Hamburger Meat, Sher.				Ham, Danish Pear			
Patties, 4 oz.				Ham, Dom. Pear			
Patties, 5 oz.				Ham, Danish Pull.			
Patties, 8 oz.				Ham, Dom. Pullman			
Flank Steak 2-3				Ham, Prosciutto Bnls.			
Short Ribs, 10 oz.				Ham, Virginia			
Steer Livers 8-10				Ham, Fresh			
Sirloin Steaks				Knockwurst 7/1			
Sirloin Flanks				Liverwurst			
Tenderloin Steaks				Oxtails			
Rump Steaks 8 oz.				Pastrami			
Swiss Steaks 4 oz.				Pigs Knuckles			
Rib Cap Meat				Port Butts CT Bnls.			
Beef Bones				Pork Loins, Fresh			
				Pork Loins, Smkd.			
VEAL				Pork, Salt			
Veal Legs Sgl. 25/28				Pork Shoulders			
Veal Loins, Dbl.				Pork Tenders 3/4-1			
Veal Loins, Dbl. Bnls.				Salami, Genoa			
Veal Racks, Dbl.				Salami, Cooked			
Veal Shoulders				Sausage Link, 12 lb.			
Calves Liver 2-3				Sausage Link, Ckt.			
Sweetbreads				Sausage, Ital. Swt.			
Veal Cutlets, Leg				Sausage, Meat			
Cutlets, Breaded				Spareribs, 3 dn.			
Veal Tops				Sweetbreads			
				Tongue, Smkt. 4-5			
LAMB				Tripe, H.C.			
Lamb Legs, Sgl.							
Lamb Back, 16-18							
Lamb Rack, 6-8							
Lamb Loins							
Lamb Chucks (Fores)							
Lamb Chucks, Bnls.							
POULTRY				**POULTRY**			
Broilers, 2 1/4 lb.				Cornish Hens 14-16 oz.			
Broilers, 2 1/2 lb.				Breast Kiev 7 oz.			
Broilers 3 1/2 lb.				Breast Cor. Bleu, 7 oz.			
Roasters, 4 lb.				Duck Breast, 2 lb.			
Fowl, 6-6½ lb.				Chic Livers, lb.			
Ducks, 4-5				Chic Breast, 8 oz.			
Turkeys, 22-24				Chic Breast, 10 oz.			
Turkey Breast, 8-10				Chic Legs, 8 oz.			
Turkey Breast, 14 lb.				Giblets, lb.			
Turkey Breast, Cooked							

Exhibit 6-2. Form used to requisition food, items listed (Courtesy: Sheraton Corporation of America, Boston, Massachusetts)

Visiting the market at least once a week enables him to examine what is available from other dealers and the prices for the current week, which leads to another shortcoming in this system of buying. Unless the food buyer has an assistant or a clerk to take care of all the paperwork, he may be too tied down to visit the market.

One-Stop Buying. For years the idea of a one-stop buying and delivery service has intrigued both enterprising purveyors and forward-looking food buyers, especially in relation to large-institution and chain food operations. The idea made little progress until rising delivery costs made the concept more attractive in 1974.

The first company to offer this service in any depth was known as Foodco. The company started in New York about 1960, and it was made up of a number of purveyors who had been supplying hotels with meats, fish, produce, canned goods, groceries, butter, and eggs. They decided that a buyer would prefer to make one telephone call and purchase most of the items he needed. The overhead, delivery costs, and selling and billing costs would be less than they were for several individual houses, and kickbacks could be eliminated. There would also be better control over quality. The savings realized could be passed on, at least in part, to the food buyer. Foodco launched the project with much enthusiasm and managed to stay in business for a number of years before the company had to be rescued by a large insurance company. The insurance company apparently found a way to make the system work profitably. One reason Foodco had difficulty was because the company refused to make or take payoffs.

There is always resistance to changing any system that is familiar and seems to work, and the established system tried to discredit the whole idea of one-stop buying. Local purveyors saw it as a threat to specialized businesses, and unions saw it as a threat to the job security of members. It was even rumored in New York City that, if Foodco succeeded, chefs in the city would ask for $10,000 more a year, and they would still lose money. Various chefs' organizations in the area strongly opposed this unfair allegation.

Top management in the institutional and hotel and restaurant fields was also reluctant to support the one-stop system. Although it seemed to be a good idea, there was fear of antagonizing the system that controlled all of food buying in the New York metropolitan area at that time. The institutional trade was, however, the first to venture into one-stop buying, and the idea is now winning acceptance in the hotel and restaurant trade. Mounting delivery charges will make one-stop buying increasingly practical.

It is a well-known "secret" that the average markup on meat, produce, fish, and almost any other commodity is from 15 percent to 25 percent over cost. Cost to the average purveyor means everything, including depreciation, business expense, and any personal living expenses that the Internal Revenue Service will allow. At first, the one-stop buying idea was to offer a service at a true 10 percent to 12 percent markup over cost before selling expense and delivery costs and, naturally, without any business promotion costs. At first, this markup was impossibly low because of high overhead in terms of salaries and high initial costs involved with warehousing, delivery, billing, and all of the unexpected routine work. These problems have been overcome, and the system has proved feasible. According to large food buyers, the one-stop system is actually saving 10 percent to 12 percent over the cost of using the individual purveyor system for food buying.

The Future of One-Stop Buying. Over 65 percent of the meals eaten away from home are purchased or eaten in institutional food services, and almost 80 percent of the food used in institutional food service is of the convenience type. So, quite obviously, the

FORM 1291   COPYRIGHT 1968

AMERICAN HOTEL REGISTER CO., 226 W. ONTARIO ST., CHICAGO, ILL. 60610

Inventory and Quotation List

ARTICLE	QTY. ON HAND	QTY. NEEDED	QUOTATIONS			ARTICLE	QTY. ON HAND	QTY. NEEDED	QUOTATIONS			ARTICLE	QTY. ON HAND	QTY. NEEDED	QUOTATIONS		
BEEF						**PORK (Cont.)**						**SHELL FISH**					
Brisket						Ham, Corned						Abalone					
Chipped Beef						Ham, Fresh						Clams					
Chuck						Ham, Polish											
Corned Beef						Ham, Smoked											
						Ham, Virginia						Crabs					
Fillets						Ham, Westphalia											
Foreshank																	
Flank												Crawfish					
Ground Beef						Head Cheese						Lobster					
Kidney						Hock											
Liver						Lard											
Loin, Short						Loin						Mussels					
Ox Tails						Phila. Scrapple						Oysters					
Ribs						Pig's Feet											
Round						Pig's Head											
Rump						Pig's Knuckles						Scallops					
Shank												Shrimp					
Short Plate						Pig, Suckling											
Sirloin																	
Smoked Beef						Salt Pork						Turtle					
Tongues						Sausage, Country											
Tongues, Smoked						Sausage, Frankfurter						**FISH**					
Tripe						Sausage, Meat						Bass, Black					
												Bass, Sea					
												Bass, Striped					
												Bloaters					
												Blowfish					
						Shoulder, Corned						Bluefish					
VEAL						Shoulder, Fresh						Bonito					
Brains												Carp					
Breast						Spare Ribs						Catfish					
Flank						Tenderloin						Cod					
Foreshank						Tongues											
Hindshank																	
Kidney																	
Leg												Eel					
Liver												Finnan Haddie					
Loin						**POULTRY**						Flounder					
Rib						Capons											
Shoulder						Chicken						Fluke					
Sweetbreads						Chicken, Roast						Frog's Legs					
						Chicken, Broiler						Haddock					
												Halibut					
						Cocks											
MUTTON						Duck						Herring					
Fore Quarters												Herring, Kippered					
Hind Saddle						Ducklings						Kingfish					
Kidney						Geese						Mackerel					
Leg						Gosling											
Rack						Guinea Hens											
Shoulder						Guinea Squab						Octopus					
						Pigeon						Perch					
						Squab						Pickerel					
						Turkey, Roasting						Pike					
						Turkey, Spring						Pompano					
LAMB												Red Snapper					
Breast												Salmon					

Exhibit 6-3. Inventory and quotation list for fresh and refrigerated items (Courtesy: American Hotel Register Company, Chicago, Illinois)

# of Fresh and Refrigerated Items

DATE _____

ARTICLE	QTY ON HAND	QTY NEEDED	QUOTATIONS	ARTICLE	QTY ON HAND	QTY NEEDED	QUOTATIONS	ARTICLE	QTY ON HAND	QTY NEEDED	QUOTATIONS
VEGETABLES				**VEGETABLES (Cont.)**				**CHEESE**			
Artichokes				Tomatoes				American			
Asparagus											
Asparagus Tips								Bel Paese			
								Bleu			
Beans, Green				Turnips, White				Brick			
Beans, Lima				Turnips, Yellow				Brie			
Beans, Wax				Watercress				Camembert			
								Cheddar			
Beets											
Beet Tops								Cheshire			
Broccoli								Cottage			
Brussels Sprouts								Cream			
Cabbage, Green											
Cabbage, Red				**FRUIT**							
Carrots				Apples, Baking				Edam			
				Apples, Cooking				Feta			
Cauliflower				Apples, Crab				Gouda			
Celery				Apples, Table				Liderkranz			
Celery Knobs				Apricots				Longhorn			
Chervil				Avocados				Monterey Jack			
Chickory				Bananas				Mozzarella			
Chives				Blackberries				Muenster			
Corn				Blueberries				Parmesan			
				Cantaloupe				Port du Salut			
Cranberries								Romano			
Cucumber				Cherries				Roquefort			
Dandelion								Swiss, Emmanthal			
Egg Plant								Swiss, Gruyere			
Endive				Chestnuts				Tilsit			
Escarole				Coconuts							
Estragon				Currants							
Garlic				Dates							
Horseradish				Figs							
Kale				Gooseberries							
Kohlrabi				Grapes				**DAIRY PRODUCTS**			
Leeks								Butter, Cooking			
Lentils								Butter, Prints			
Lettuce								Butter, Sweet			
				Grapefruit							
								Buttermilk			
Marjoram				Guava				Cream			
Mint				Honeydew Melons				Half-and-Half			
Mushrooms				Huckleberries				Margarine			
				Kumquats							
Okra				Lemons				Milk, homogenized			
Onions				Limes				Milk, skim			
Bermuda				Mangos				Milk, 2%			
Red				Muskmelons				Milk, whole			
Scallions				Nectarines							
Spanish				Oranges				Sour Cream			
White								Whipping Cream			
Yellow								Yogurt			
				Peaches							
Oyster Plant											
Parsley								**MISCELLANEOUS**			
Parsnips				Pears							
Peas											

future for one-stop buying is extremely bright.

Keep in mind that a sharp line divides purchasing for the hospitality industry and purchasing for the institutional food service. The hospitality food service is an innovative business; growth and profits depend on being more innovative, cost conscious, and sales minded than the competition. The goal in this industry is to augment the hotel service in which one operates or to attract business from one's competition. The customers in the hospitality industry have free choice to go where they wish. There is an old proverb in the restaurant game: "Every day is a new day, and what's new for today?"

Institutional operations have a more captive audience, and their goal is to furnish the maximum amount and quality of food allowed by the budget, which is set by management or ownership. The circumstances under which institutional food service operates are considerably different from those in the hospitality trade. Management likes satisfied, happy employees; school supervisors want happy, satisfied students; politicians don't want to hear complaints from their constituents; hospital management doesn't want to hear complaints from patients or the doctors; and no one wants to read about a revolt in a penal institution because of the "lousy food service."

Today, with the advanced techniques in the processing of food and the improved quality of convenience food, good food can be served in the institutional trade at reasonable prices to meet a budget. In fact, if this is *not* being done in some institutions, there is room for investigation, because this goal is being achieved in practically all institutional operations throughout the country.

Prime Supplier Program. Currently, the largest food distributors in the country all generally use one-stop buying. However, they are upgrading the procedure with a new name—the "prime supplier program" (which the dealers feel is more sophisticated than the old "one-stop buying").

A prime supplier offers a complete line of food supplies for food preparation and, in many cases, a complete line of equipment to complete a kitchen and the entire equipment list for food service. Some prime suppliers are also now offering consulting service to help their clients with operating procedures, cost controls, public relations, sales technique, specification preparation, recipe preparation, job training, and payroll control. In fact, they offer a complete line of management, assistance, and consulting to their clients. Some of these services are free, and others are charged at a rate high enough to cover expenses and a small profit to the account. Mainly, however, these services are offered to get and keep clients for the supplier's food service operation.

Most prime supplier programs include a complete line of fresh meats, fruits and vegetables, frozen foods, canned foods, dry groceries, with the exception of coffee, fresh dairy supplies, ice cream, fresh seafood, and fresh bread. One list in this program, referred to as the "basic 400," is a list of food items that are regularly used in a large institutional food service. The list does not include truffles, imported caviar, or smoked reed birds from India, but it does include just about everything else available in the United States to supply the hospitality trade as well as the institutional trade. The list included in this chapter as an example from the prime supplier program is backed by a complete set of specifications, with computerized descriptions of packaging, to expedite fast delivery and to avoid misunderstandings between buyer and seller.

The way these programs work varies according to circumstances. For example, where is the central purchasing office? How far is the operation from the supplier's headquarters? Is there a good backup local market that can furnish all the fresh supplies on a variable basis? And what type of institutional operation is involved?

Benefits of the Prime Supplier Program. What benefits are claimed by the larger prime supplier companies? We have checked out claims with some of their customers, and we find that the following claims of benefits are reasonable and are being fulfilled:

1. Money can be saved by achieving better prices and reduced record-keeping.
2. Product consistency is improved by this because the program distributor knows the needed volume and prepares better for it than by using the open-market buying method.
3. Appreciable time is saved in price shopping, multiple receiving, returns, credits, accounting procedures, and payment of bills.
4. There is greater consistency in the end product because the supply is consistent and the staff gain expertise in using a consistent product.
5. This program relieves great pressure on the purchasing department from other departments wishing to gain benefits from the purchasing cycle, from individual members of the organization, and from city, state, and the federal government.

For the past ten years a "coupon craze" has been going on in the country, but this idea of marketing has hardly been touched in the wholesale trade. Some prime suppliers are working as go-betweens between the food processing industry and the institutional buyer to obtain volume-priced discounts that can be worked out with the cooperation of the distributor. Of course, the food distributor claims that the profit margin is far greater for food distribution, and the food processor denies this. Regardless of claims, the idea is working and substantial credits are going directly into the corporation accounts rather than getting lost in slippage along the line. One institutional food buyer has managed to get a flat 12 percent rebate from certain food processors by concentrating orders into monthly deliveries and paying the account on a weekly basis. Even in the hospitality field it is possible to get an addi-

tional 2–3 percent discount for paying on a weekly basis.

One of the most significant benefits that emerges from this program is that the program is carried out on a long-term basis, which can benefit the buyer, the distributor, and the processor alike. The contracts generally run three months, six months, or a year, which give all three parties a chance to adjust cost savings to the consumer's benefit.

Another benefit that can be substantial is that the contract details are generally worked out by the top management of the users' operation, the distributorship, and the processor. Thus the chances of slippage are reduced to almost zero, which is not so certain if the negotiations are carried out on a lower level of responsibility.

This type of buying has been carried out in almost all other lines of business for years. The food supply business is finally joining in, and it is reaping considerable benefits.

Fixed Markups. In the fixed-markup system, the buyer negotiates a fixed markup over current market price for items listed in daily market reports. Sometimes the price is tied to the market as reported in the daily newspaper, in the Urner Barry market report, *Producers Price-Current,* in one of the USDA bulletins, or in *Fresh Fruit and Vegetables Market News,* which is published in various metropolitan areas. This type of activity is pretty much restricted to butter, eggs, turkeys, turkey parts, broilers, ducks, poultry parts, and some game items.

Dealers willing to work on this basis normally do not become involved unless the volume of business is substantial. This system has worked well, especially for those who buy for large institutions or large food-processing companies. Buying in carload lots generally means a price from 1 cent to 3 cents a pound over the top spot market as reported in the market reporting ser ice for turkeys, poultry, ducks, and poultry parts. Butter can generally be purchased from 5 cents to 7 cents a pound over the top side of the spot market, and fresh eggs will be priced from 4 cents to 8 cents over, depending on whether the eggs are Midwestern mixed or extra large double A Eastern whites. The markup for frozen eggs can be as low as 2 cents to 3 cents a pound over the top spot market.

Such arrangements are generally made for a period of three to six months, and, if both parties are satisfied, a renewal can easily be negotiated. Buyers who work out these arrangements are under pressure to divide this business up for one reason or another. A fair buyer will keep a record of the prices that he pays under this type of arrangement and give 80 percent to 85 percent of the business to the dealer with whom he has negotiated it, buying the other 15 percent on a daily quotation basis in order to determine whether he is making money by such an arrangement.

Where records have been kept, it has been found that the buyer can save from 3 percent to 5 percent over the year by negotiated markup over cost as against daily price quotation buying. Usually a purveyor in this line has to get from 15 percent to 25 percent markup over costs to run his business, and, of this amount, as much as a quarter or a third, or 5 percent to 8 percent, has to be set aside for promotion and selling costs. Most dealers would be willing to eliminate this selling cost if they could be assured of a sufficient volume of business from a negotiated markup over costs. The 5 percent to 8 percent is the food buyer's possible savings.

There is always the danger that such an arrangement will be exploited by a dishonest buyer or purveyor who cheats the boss through collusion on fixing the price. The simplicity of the system and the ease of checking the cost price and negotiated markup by any auditor seem, however, to discourage manipulation, and many of the best buyers do use this system to their advantage.

Exhibit 6-4 shows a sample of the *Producer's Price-Current* and a market report from a metropolitan daily newspaper.

Most such market reports are put out by the Associated Press, and they are the same in all publications for each area throughout the country. It does not make much difference what source is used as a base, so long as it remains constant over the period of the arrangement.

Buy and Hold. A buyer who uses the buy-and-hold system must represent a large user, or there is no advantage. The system takes advantage of seasonal fluctuations in the market. At certain periods of the year, as at harvesttime, an excess of supply drives a price down so that a buyer with some money can make substantial savings by eliminating the middleman. The food buyer deals with the producer—frozen food manufacturer, canner, shrimp packer, production line meat fabricator, or large local purveyor—who has access to a lot of stock or has overbought and wants to reduce his inventory.

Usually the buyer has to pay cash for the amount of stock that he buys, and there are always problems involving storage, delivery, insurance, and losses through spoilage. In noninflationary times there is always the specter that the bottom will fall out of the market, leaving the buyer sitting there holding the bag.

Large chain operators, especially in certain fast food operations, take advantage of this type of buying. Buyers for large processors of convenience foods use it regularly. Even some large hotel and restaurant chains have found it worthwhile to follow the buy-and-hold method of food purchasing on occasion.

Some items that lend themselves to this type of buying are green headless shrimp or processed shrimp, lobster tails, any type of frozen fish, any cut of fabricated meat that can be used frozen, canned tomatoes and canned fruits, frozen fruits and vegetables (particularly peas, green beans, asparagus, and orange juice, and, for a certain type of chain operator, blueberries, cherries, apples, peaches, and other fruits for use in a pastry department).

The Urner Barry Market UB

Producers' Price-Current

ESTABLISHED 1858 - MORE THAN A CENTURY OF MARKET REPORTING SERVICE

PUBLISHED DAILY EXCEPT SATURDAYS, SUNDAYS AND HOLIDAYS BY URNER BARRY PUBLICATIONS, INC.
34 EXCHANGE PLACE, JERSEY CITY, N. J. 07302 • N. J. PHONE 201 432 7777 • N. Y. PHONE: 212 349 0240 • WIRE: JGC • TELETYPE: 710-730-5370
Second Class Postage Paid at Jersey City, N. J. Copyright 1974 By Urner Barry Publications Inc

No. 103 THURSDAY, MAY 30, 1974

BUTTER

URNER BARRY QUOTATIONS

Based on extensive country-wide trade reports and other terminal market wholesale transactions.

TRUCKLOTS BULK Deliv. East (Spot Mkt.)	SALT	SALES FROM WAREHOUSE 1 Pound Solids	1 Pound Quarters
62.00	.....93 Score (AA)....	65.50-67.25	69.50-71.75
61.50	.....92 Score (A)......	64.25-66.00	68.25-70.50
60.00	.....90 Score (B)......	63.25-65.00	67.25-69.50

MIDWEST

LOADS & POOL LOADS DELIVERED

93 Score	92 Score	90 Score
59.75-60.00	59.25-59.50	57.25-57.50

IMPORTED

LOADS & POOL LOADS

Finest	1 st's	2nds
–	–	–

CHEESE

CHEDDARS - Whole Milk - lbs.

	Ex Sharp	Sharp	Medium	Mild
Blocks	$ .98-1.05	$ .92-1.02	$ .87- .90	$ .79- .83
Daisies	-	-	.88- .96	.86- .92
Splits	1.01-1.08	.95-1.05	.88- .94	.84- .87
Midgets	1.03-1.05	.97-1.07	.90- .96	.86- .92
Flats	1.00-1.06	.97-1.04	-	-

5 lb. Loaf - Processed –
Known Brands .725- .840
Other Brands .745- .765

Muenster...... .785-.860

OTHER VARIETIES

SWISS - Cuts

DOMESTIC	
Grade A.........	$1.05-1.11
Grade B.........	1.01-1.08
Grade C.........	.95-1.03
IMPORTED –	
Austria.........	1.03-1.09
Denmark.......	1.05-1.10
Finland........	1.06-1.10
Switzerland...	1.28-1.32
French.........	-

FLUID MILK

TRUCKLOTS DELIVERED MET. NEW YORK
Bottling quality per 40 quart unit $ -

CONDENSED SKIM MILK

DELIVERED METROPOLITAN NEW YORK
Per lb. Solids (SNF) in tanklots ¢61.00-63.00

FLUID CREAM

CLASS II or MANUFACTURING
SPOT SALES DELIVERED MET. NEW YORK
Butterfat per lb in tanklots ¢.7800-.8175
Per 40 qt unit in tanklots $25.75-27.00

SPOT SALES DELIVERED PHILADELPHIA
Butterfat per lb in tanklots ¢.7900-.8200
Per 40 qt unit in tanklots $26.05-27.05

SPOT SALES DELIVERED BOSTON
Butterfat per lb in tanklots ¢.7800-.8200
Per 40 qt unit in tanklots $25.75-27.05

BOSTON EQUIVALENT PRICE
May 19-25.............. $26.843

FLUID MILK & CREAM

Milk production trends upward and is at or near "peak" levels. This combined with poor bottling sales results in a very ample supply. Diversions to manufacture are heavy and these

Fats & Oils

MARGARINE
Less Carlots
Sales by First Receiver - Cents per lb.-

Vegetable Oil, 1 lb. Solids	37.00-38.00
Vegetable Oil, 1 lb. Quarters	38.00-39.00
Animal - Vegetable, 1 lb. solids	32.00-33.00
1 lb. Quarters.................	33.00-34.00

Trucklots - Delivered East - Cents per lb -
Vegetable Oil, 1 lb. Solids 35.00-
Vegetable Oil, 1 lb Quarters 36.00-

SOYBEAN OIL FUTURES

Chicago Board of Trade futures trading for previous day.

Deliv.	Open	High	Low	Close	Prev Close
July	27.20	28.05	27.20	28.05	27.10
Aug	26.10	26.85	26.10	26.85	25.90
Sept	25.15	25.88	25.15	25.88	24.90
Oct	24.15	24.80	24.10	24.80	23.80
Dec	22.90	23.60	22.90	23.60	22.65
Jan	22.15	22.75	22.15	22.65	22.00
Mar	21.95	22.40	21.90	22.35	21.70

POULTRY S

Carlot turkey marke creased selling pressu and consumer sizes of to what improved for the but with available stock tone is highly unsettle is true on the consumer

Mid-sizes of toms are light offerings. Demand tious. Heavier weights hands.

Canner packs irregu selling pressure builds

Iced chickens full ste prices are asked for ne mand is sharply impro feature sales noted. port a firm undertone.

Fowl and roasters is clearing the limited s

D.P.S.C.Purchases at C Turkeys Boneless Expor Domestic Cent. 63.83

WEDNESDAY, MAY 29, 1974

FRESH VEGETABLES

ARRIGULA	
Local bchd 20-24s	2 50-3 00
Local lugs 20s	3 50-4 00
ARTICHOKES	
Bibb-	
Local W/bu cr	2 00-2 50
MUSHROOMS bkt-	
Pa med-lg	2 50-3 00
Pa med-lg fair	2 00-2 25
Pa sm-med	2 00-2 25
Pa sm-med fair	-1 75

NC green bu bsk
NC bu b
NC yell bskt
NC yel b
SC green

Commodity Markets

July 10, 1975

THE WASHINGTON POST
Friday, July 11, 1975 D 11

Chicago Board of Trade

CHICAGO (AP) — Wheat, soybean and soybean oil futures soared to daily allowable limits on the Chicago Board of Trade Thursday, but fell back at the close under the liquidation.

Wheat and soybeans have advanced 20 cents a bushel around noon and oil was up 100 points, or 1 cent a pound. Corn was then just short of its 10 cent a bushel limit at about 8 cents higher while oats were up 5½ cents. Profit taking then took over and prices eased a little in the wheat, soybean and oil pits and closed mixed in corn and oats.

Some validity was given to reports that Russian agents were in the United States to buy grain. Senator Jackson of Washington said that this was so. Another report, unofficial, had Russians buying 200 million bushels of wheat and 80 million bushels of corn.

Trade was mixed in the major pits but sellers were very scarce throughout the day.

As the Russian buying gave prices a lift, the specter of a bearish government report dealing with small grain production, issued after the close, hung over the pits. Record production was expected in corn, wheat and soybeans but world needs for soybeans and products might not be met and trade bought these commodity futures.

Iced broilers closed steady to about ½ cent a pound higher after a lightly traded session. Domestic gold was about $1 to $1.50 lower.

At the close, wheat futures were 11½ to 17 cents a bushel higher, July 3.43½; soybeans were 8 to 14 higher, July 5.56; corn was 2 lower to ½ higher.

	Open	High	Low	Close	Prev Close
WHEAT (5,000 bu)					
Jul	3.35	3.52	3.32	3.43½	3.32
Sep	3.41	3.58½	3.39	3.51¼	3.38¼

Gold Trading

Here is the gold futures trading for Thursday, July 10, 1975:

Chicago Board of Trade
3 1-kilogram bars contracts

	Open	High	Low	Close	Prv Close
Jul	164.50	164.50	164.50	164.50	166.00
Aug	—	—	—	165.50n	166.90
Sep	166.90	167.70	165.80	166.60	168.20
Nov	169.70	170.70	169.20	169.50	171.00
Jan	173.00	173.20	172.00	172.30	173.90
Mar	175.70	175.70	174.80	175.50	176.80
May	—	—	—	178.20n	179.60
Jul	—	—	—	180.90n	182.90

529 volume 3,435 contracts.

Chicago Mercantile Exchange
100-Troy ounce contracts

Sep	166.60	167.60	165.90	166.50	168.00
Dec	170.70	171.70	170.10	170.50	172.00
Mar	175.30	175.90	174.40	174.80 —	—
Jun	179.40	180.10	178.30	179.10a	180.10
Sep	183.10	183.70b	182.70	182.70	184.00

Sales: Sep 1,565; Dec 345; March 52; June 36; Sep 3.

New York Commodity Exchange
100 troy ounce contracts

Jul	164.60	164.60	164.60	164.50s	166.00
Aug	165.90	165.90	164.60	165.30s	166.90
Oct	168.00	168.00	167.40	168.00s	169.50
Dec	171.10	171.30	170.10	170.70s	172.20
Feb	173.90				
.30	173.30	173.60s	175.00		
Apr	176.30	177.40	176.10	176.40s	177.80
Jun	179.50	179.90	179.30	179.20s	180.60
Aug	182.50	182.50	182.50	182.00s	183.40
Oct	184.20	184.20	184.20	184.80s	186.20

Sales: 2,323.
s-settling.

New York Mercantile Exchange
1 kilogram contracts

Jul	164.40	164.40	164.40	164.40	166.00
Aug	166.20	166.20	166.00	165.40a	166.60
Sep	167.60	167.60	166.20	166.20	168.00
Dec	171.00	171.00	171.00	171.00	172.20
Jan	173.60	173.60	[illegible]	[illegible]	[illegible]

Mercantile Futures

CHICAGO (AP) — Futures trading on the Chicago Mercantile Exchange Thursday:

	Open	High	Low	Close	Prev Close
LIVE BEEF CATTLE (40,000 lbs)					
Aug	46.30	47.30	46.10	47.20	45.75
Oct	41.25	42.55	41.20	42.05	40.90
Dec	39.75	41.12	39.75	40.95	39.55
Feb	49.40	40.42	39.40	40.00	39.25
Apr	39.25	39.95b	39.20	39.60	38.95
Jun	39.40	40.50	39.35	40.50	39.40

Sales: Aug 5,260; Oct 3,072; Dec 1,407; Feb 672; April 80; June 14.
Open interest: Aug 15,196; Oct 9,688; Dec 5,246; Feb 3,475; April 381; June 20.

FEEDER CATTLE (42,000 lbs)					
Aug	34.00	34.30	33.75	34.25a	33.95
Sep	34.00	33.40	32.80	33.40	32.35
Oct	32.60	33.40	32.60	33.07	32.50
Nov	33.00	33.25b	32.60	33.20	32.50
Mar	—	—	—	—	33.40

Sales: Aug 20; Sep 14; Oct 157; Nov 44; March 0.
Open interest: Aug 211; Sep 141; Oct 1,299; Nov 277; March 49.

LIVE HOGS (30,000 lbs)					
Jul	55.80	56.80	55.50	56.80b	55.35
Aug	52.20	53.50	52.20	53.50b	51.95
Oct	46.90	47.82	46.60	47.65	46.30
Dec	46.70	47.65	46.45	47.65	46.20
Feb	45.35	46.62	45.35	46.62	45.10
Apr	42.30	43.25	42.25	43.25	42.25
Jun	43.00	43.80	42.70	43.60b	42.70
Jul	42.55	43.70b	42.55	43.70b	42.45

Sales: July 918; Aug 1,932; Oct 1,050; Dec 940; Feb 436; April 159; June 59; July 8.
Open interest: July 1,701; Aug 4,594; Oct 3,186; Dec 5,782; Feb 3,357; April 827; June 318; July 45.

SHELL EGGS (22,500 doz)					
Jul	—	—	—	43.60n	43.60
Aug	46.20	46.95	46.20	46.75	45.75
Sep	53.75	54.65	53.55	54.40	53.40
Oct	53.00	53.25	53.00	53.25	52.75
Nov	56.95	57.75b	56.30	57.50a	56.95

Government Securities

Treasury Bills

Due	Bid	Ask	Yld	Due	Bid	Ask	Yld
—1975—				11- 6	6.26	6.08	6.29
7-17	6.06	5.28	5.35	11-13	6.26	6.08	6.30
7-24	5.96	5.36	5.44	11-18	6.27	6.11	6.34
7-29	5.96	5.30	5.38	11-20	6.31	6.13	6.36
7-31	5.89	5.35	5.44	11-28	6.29	6.11	6.35
8- 7	5.87	5.37	5.46	12- 4	6.30	6.14	6.39
8-14	5.87	5.45	5.55	12-11	6.30	6.14	6.39
8-21	5.90	5.54	5.65	12-16	6.30	6.10	6.36
8-26	5.91	5.55	5.66	12-18	6.30	6.10	6.36
8-28	5.93	5.63	5.75	12-26	6.28	6.14	6.39
9- 4	5.95	5.73	5.86	—1976—			
9-11	5.95	5.75	5.88	1- 2	6.41	6.27	6.56
9-18	5.95	5.75	5.89	1- 8	6.38	6.32	6.62
9-23	5.92	5.70	5.84	1-13	6.41	6.21	6.50
9-25	5.96	5.80	5.95	1-31	6.53	6.37	6.68
10- 2	6.03	5.89	6.05	2-10	6.49	6.31	6.62
10- 9	6.04	5.96	6.13	3- 9	6.51	6.33	6.67
10-16	6.15	5.96	6.17	4- 6	6.53	6.41	6.77
10-21	6.17	6.01	6.20	5- 4	6.57	6.37	6.75
10-23	6.21	5.95	6.24	6- 1	6.58	6.40	6.81
10-30	6.21	6.05	6.25	6-29	6.51	6.45	6.89

Treasury Bonds and Notes

NEW YORK (AP)—Closing Over-the-Counter U.S. Treasury Bonds for Thursday.

Rate	Mat.	date	Bid	Asked	Bid Chg	Yld
5⅞	Aug	1975 n	99.29	99.31	—.1	6.08
8⅜	Sep	1975 n	100.12	100.16	....	5.86
7	Nov	1975 n	100.4	100.8	—.1	6.17
7	Dec	1975 n	100.6	100.10	....	6.29
5⅞	Feb	1976 n	99.13	98.17	+.1	6.70
6¼	Feb	1976 n	99.18	99.26	—.2	6.58
8	Mar	1976 n	100.25	100.29	+.1	6.69
5¾	May	1976 n	99.2	99.6	....	6.76
6½	May	1976 n	99.22	99.26		6.73

Exhibit 6-4. Examples of market reports (Courtesy: Urner Barry Publications, Inc., Jersey City, New Jersey; Associated Press, New York, New York)

A large buyer also keeps constant check on the futures market and judges his buying to take advantage of long-term trends. If a drought is forecast, if a revolution in a coffee country seems imminent, if an unseasonal frost hits some area of the country, if it appears that a huge grain deal will be negotiated with a foreign country, then the large-quantity buyer steps in and protects himself for a reasonable period of time with a large buy-and-hold order.

Smaller buyers can take advantage of such a program by taking into consideration the two times of the year when meat prices are traditionally low and the two times of the year when meat prices are traditionally high. By buying, freezing, and holding certain items, it is possible for them to realize a considerable savings.

Beef prices, which are low about the middle of January, continue low through February. Then they start rising until after Easter and through May. They tend to stay high over the summer and start down again in the fall until, in November, they are generally at their lowest level. Right after Thanksgiving, however, the price of beef starts a rapid rise for the holidays and reaches a peak just before the Christmas-New Year season that holds until about the middle of January, when they again drop.

Most large chain hotel and restaurant operators lay in a supply of heavy beef items such as ribs, strips, filets, and top butts during the early part of November to avoid paying the premium price over the holidays. During the past few years, these savings have amounted to as much as 75 cents a pound, especially on strips and filets.

Formal Written Bid. In the institutional field, in the food manufacturing and processing field, and especially in government procurement systems, the formal written bid is the key to practically all food buying. This system ensures a steady flow of merchandise at a nonfluctuating price, and it conforms with the requirements of most governmental agencies at both the national and local levels.

The formal bid system is easy to police, which goes far toward solving the problem of questionable ethics, and the possibility of misunderstandings as to quality, price, delivery, and packaging is practically eliminated. On the whole, this has proved to be an excellent system. There are, however, two basic problems. The system is rather cumbersome, and whatever purchasing is done has to be planned well in advance so that the buyer has a chance to get the bid forms out and the suppliers have a chance to line up stock and suggest a fair price. The bid system is fine for canned goods, frozen products, smoked meats, and other staple items. It is not practical for perishable items because market prices fluctuate from day to day.

This system, designed to ensure honesty in the purchasing system, does discourage petty manipulation, but it lends itself to larger manipulation, especially if the purchasing department and purchasing agent are open to political pressure. Because bids cannot be sent out to every dealer in the area who handles the type of merchandise required, there is generally a selected list of approved purveyors to whom requests for bids are sent. The names appearing on the list of approved dealers and who approves the dealers on the list are important decisions. It is not difficult to imagine what would happen to a large supplier if, during a drive for campaign funds, he did not make a substantial contribution to the potential winning candidate for a sensitive political office. All other dealers in the area expecting an opportunity to bid on supplies, since they are subject to the same pressure, would also contribute. Contributions are generally made to both party candidates and sometimes even to a third-party candidate who might possibly be elected to an office of power. Since this cost must be added to the cost of doing business, the bids are generally higher than they would be if political considerations were not a factor.

Sometimes formalized bids call for a supply of merchandise over a period of time at prices that fluctuate with the market. Without a provision allowing for flexibility, the prices submitted by all dealers must again be higher than they would be if the dealer could manipulate prices in accord with the market.

Most bids are, however, for a specific quantity of merchandise that the buyer withdraws and uses within a set period of time. A bid can be written so that the buyer pays for all at the time of purchase, or it can be paid for as it is withdrawn, with a suitable arrangement to cover the cost of storage and the cost of carrying the inventory in storage.

Many different forms are used in the written bidding system, but all of them are basically invitations to bid with the conditions of the bid clearly specified. Attached to the invitation is a listing of the merchandise needed, the quantities involved, and any conditions related to supply and fluctuations in the market. Any invitation to bid generally includes a copy of the purchase specifications set forth by the buyer so that there is no confusion over what is wanted by the buyer.

A typical request for bid appears in Exhibit 6-5. Generally, the bids are to be sent in by a specified date, and they are to be sealed. More often than not, the bids are reviewed by a committee rather than one person. In some cases the identity of the bidder is disguised so that the committee doing the reviewing and decision making cannot identify the successful bidder; thus, personalities have no effect on the decisions of the committee. After the identity of the successful bidder is revealed, a purchase order (see Exhibit 6-6) is issued to him. This is the formal closing of the deal and covers the various legal aspects involved. In this system withdrawal of stock, as needed, is authorized by the issue of a purchase order that refers to the accepted master bid.

This system is complete and effective, and it has the benefit of thoroughness, complete legality, and the almost total elimination of misunderstandings.

Drop Shipments. Some large grocery houses and food processors, in order to secure a greater share of the market for their products, have devised a national marketing system. It can be helpful, from an economic standpoint, for the large-quantity food buyer.

National distributors tend to have knowledgeable salesmen. They know their business, they know their products, and their ethics are almost always above reproach. Such companies cannot afford any hanky-panky over the small markups that they receive, and they cannot be subject to the whims of an excitable food buyer or chef. They simply avoid these situations.

The salespeople work out delivery schedules with large-quantity buyers so that the maximum drop shipment can be made direct from a trailer truck. The price schedule is related to the size of the shipment: the larger the shipment, the better the price that the buyer gets. Shipments are programmed. Deliveries are made to certain areas on certain days of the week, and the record of the trucking concerns has been very good.

Savings run, in many instances, as high as 10 to 15 percent against the average local purveyor's price, and, in some instances, the savings can run as high as 25 percent. This type of buying lends itself to such items as canned tomatoes, canned fruits, cooking oil, salad oil, shortening for frying or pastry, mayonnaise, tomato juice, ketchup, olives, pickles—almost any type of item handled by a national grocery house. This system has not worked for meats, poultry, or other perishable items, or for commodities subject to wide price fluctuations.

Cost-Plus Buying. On first inspection, cost-plus buying appears to flaunt every rule

SUBMIT BIDS TO:

Florida International University
Purchasing Services
PC Bldg., Room 519
University Park
Miami, Florida 33199
(305) 348-2161
FAX: (305) 348-3600

FLORIDA INTERNATIONAL UNIVERSITY

INVITATION TO BID

Bidder Acknowledgment

BIDS WILL BE OPENED

and may not be withdrawn within 45 days after such date and time.

BID NO.

MAILING DATE:	PURCHASING AGENT	BID TITLE

All awards made as a result of this bid shall conform to applicable Florida Statutes.

DELIVERY WILL BE _____ DAYS after receipt of Purchase Order

VENDOR NAME

REASON FOR NO BID

VENDOR MAILING ADDRESS

F.E.I.D. NO:

| AREA CODE | TELEPHONE NUMBER |
| | TOLL-FREE NUMBER |

Certified or cashier's check is attached, when required, in the amount of: $

I certify that this bid is made without prior understanding, agreement, or connection with any corporation, firm, or person submitting a bid for the same materials, supplies, or equipment, and is in all respects fair and without collusion or fraud. I agree to abide by all conditions of this bid and certify that I am authorized to sign this bid for the bidder.

AUTHORIZED SIGNATURE (MANUAL)

AUTHORIZED SIGNATURE (TYPED) TITLE

GENERAL CONDITIONS

BIDDER: To ensure acceptance of the bid, follow these instructions.

SEALED BIDS: All bid sheets and this form must be executed and submitted in a sealed envelope.(DO NOT INCLUDE MORE THAN ONE BID PER ENVELOPE).The face of the envelope shall contain, in addition to the above address, the date and time of the bid opening and the bid number. All bids are subject to the conditions specified herein. Those Which do not comply with these conditions are subject to rejection.

1. **EXECUTION OF BID:** Bid must contain a manual signature of authorized representative in the space provided above. Bid must be typed or printed in ink. Use of erasable ink is not permitted. All corrections made by bidder to this bid must be initialed.
2. **NO BID:** If not submitting a bid, respond by returning this form, marking it "NO BID", and explain the reason in the space provided above. Failure to respond 3 times in succession without justification shall be cause for removal of the supplier's name from the bid mailing list. NOTE: To qualify as a respondent, bidder must submit a "NO BID", and it must be received no later than the stated bid opening date and hour.
3. **BID OPENING:** Shall be public on the date and at the time specified on the bid form. It is the bidder's responsibility to assure that their bid is delivered at the proper time and place of the bid opening. Bids which for any reason are not so delivered, will not be considered. NOTE: Bid tabulations will be furnished upon written request with an enclosed, self-addressed, stamped envelope. Bid files may be examined during normal working hours by appointment.
4. **PRICES, TERMS, AND PAYMENT:** Firm prices shall be bid and include all packing, handling, shipping charges, and delivery to the destination shown herein. Bidder is requested to offer cash discount for prompt invoice payment.
   (a) **TAXES:** The State of Florida does not pay Federal Excise and Sales taxes on direct purchases of tangible personal property. See exemption number on face of purchase order. This exemption does not apply to purchases of tangible personal property made by contractors who use the tangible personal property in the performance of contracts for the improvement of state-owned real property as defined in Chapter 192, F.S.
   (b) **DISCOUNTS:** Bidders are encouraged to reflect cash discounts in the unit prices quoted; however, bidders may offer a cash discount for prompt payment. Discounts shall not be considered in determining the lowest net cost for bid evaluation purposes.
   (c) **MISTAKES:** Bidders are expected to examine the specifications, delivery schedule, bid prices, extensions, and all instructions pertaining to supplies and services. Failure to do so will be at bidder's risk. In case of mistake in extension, the unit price will govern.
   (d) **CONDITION AND PACKAGING:** It is understood and agreed that any item offered and shipped as a result of this bid shall be a new current standard production model available at the time of this bid. All containers shall be suitable for storage or shipment, and all prices shall include standard commercial packaging.
   (e) **SAFETY STANDARDS:** Unless otherwise stipulated in the bid, all manufactured items and fabricated assemblies shall comply with applicable requirements of Occupational Safety and Health Act and any standards thereunder.

(f) **PAYMENT:** Payment will be made by the buyer after the items awarded to a vendor have been received, inspected and found to comply with award specifications, free of damage or defect and properly invoiced. All invoices shall bear the purchase order number. An original and three (3) copies of the invoice shall be submitted. Failure to follow these instructions may result in delay of processing invoices for payment. The purchase order number must appear on bills of lading, packages, cases, delivery.lists, and correspondence.

5. **DELIVERY:** Unless actual date of delivery is specified (or if specified delivery cannot be met), show number of days required to make delivery after receipt of purchase order in space provided. Delivery time may become a basis for making an award (see Special Conditions).

6. **MANUFACTURERS' NAMES AND APPROVED EQUIVALENTS:** Any manufacturers' names, trade names, brand names, information, and/or catalog numbers listed in a specification are for information and not intended to limit competition. If bids are based on equivalent products, indicate on the bid form the manufacturers' name and number. Bidder shall submit with his proposal cuts sketches, and descriptive literature, and/or complete specifications. Reference to literature submitted with a previous bid will not satisfy this provision. The bidder shall also explain in detail the reason(s) why the proposed equivalent will meet the specifications and not be considered an exception thereto. Bids which do not comply with these requirements are subject to rejection. Bids lacking any written indication of intent to quote an alternate brand will be received and considered in complete compliance with the specifications as listed on the bid form.

7. **INTERPRETATIONS:** Any questions concerning conditions and specifications shall be directed to this office. Inquiries must reference the date of bid opening and bid number. Failure to comply with this condition will result in bidder waiving his right to dispute the bid conditions and specifications

8. **CONFLICT OF INTEREST:** The award hereunder is subject to the provisions of Chapter 112, Florida Statutes. All bidders must disclose with their bid the name of any officer, director, or agent who is also an employee of the State of Florida, or any of its agencies. Further, all bidders must disclose the name of any State employee who owns, directly or indirectly, an interest of the five percent or more in the bidder's firm or any of its branches.

9. **AWARDS:** As the best interest of FIU may require, the right is reserved to make award(s) by individual item, group of items, all or none or a combination thereof; to reject any and all bids or waive any minor irregularity or technicality in bids received. When it is determined there is competition to the lowest responsive bidder, then other bids may not be evaluated. Bidders are cautioned to make no assumptions unless their bid has been evaluated as being responsive.

10. **ADDITIONAL QUANTITIES:** For a period not exceeding ninety (90) days from the date of acceptance of this offer by FIU, the right is reserved to acquire additional quantities up to but not exceeding those shown on bid or $10,000 for commodities at the prices in this invitation. If additional quantities are not acceptable the bid sheets must be noted "BID IS FOR SPECIFIED QUANTITY ONLY."

11. **SERVICE AND WARRANTY:** Unless otherwise specified the bidder shall define any warranty service and replacements that will be provided during and subsequent to this contract. Bidders must explain on an attached sheet to what extent warranty and service facilities are provided.

Exhibit 6-5. Form used by all state agencies in Florida to request bids, with name of agency appearing in the top, left corner (Courtesy: Florida International University, Miami)

12. **SAMPLES:** Samples of items, when called for, must be furnished free of expense, on or before bid opening, time and date, and if not destroyed may upon request be returned at the bidders expense. Each individual sample must be labeled with bidder's name, manufacturers' brand name and number, bid number and item reference. Request for return of samples shall be accompanied by instructions which include shipping authorization and name of carrier and must be received with your bid. If instructions are not received within this time, the commodities shall be disposed of by FIU.

13. **INSPECTION, ACCEPTANCE, AND TITLE:** Inspection and acceptance will be at destination unless otherwise provided. Title and risk of loss or damage to all items shall be the responsibility of the contract supplier until acceptance by the ordering agency, unless loss or damage results from negligence by FIU.

14. **DISPUTES:** In case of any doubt or difference of opinion as to the items to be furnished hereunder, the decision of the buyer shall be final and binding on both parties.

15. **GOVERNMENTAL RESTRICTION:** In the event any governmental restrictions may be imposed which would necessitate alteration of the material, quality, workmanship, or performance of the items offered in this proposal prior to their delivery, it shall be the responsibility of the successful bidder to notify FIU at once, indicating in his letter the specific regulation which required an alteration. FIU reserves the right to accept any such alteration, including any price adjustments occasioned thereby, or to cancel the contract at no expense to FIU.

16. **LEGAL REQUIREMENTS:** Applicable provisions of all Federal, State, county, and local laws, and of all ordinances, rules, and regulations shall govern development submittal and evaluation of all bids received in response hereto and shall govern any and all claims and disputes which may arise between person(s) submitting a bid response hereto and FIU by and through its officers, employees, and authorized representatives, or any other person, natural or otherwise; and lack of knowledge by any bidder shall not constitute a cognizable defense against the legal affect thereof.

17. **PATENTS AND ROYALTIES:** The bidder, without exception, shall indemnify and save harmless FIU and its employees from liability of any nature or kind, including cost and expenses for or on account of any copyrighted, patented or unpatented invention, process, or article manufactured or used in the performance of the contract, including its use by FIU. If the bidder uses any design, device or materials covered by letters, patent or copyright, it is mutually agreed and understood without exception that the bid prices shall include all royalties or cost arising from the use of such design, device, or materials in any way involved in the work.

18. **ADVERTISING:** In submitting a bid, bidder agrees not to use the results therefrom as a part of any commercial advertising.

19. **ASSIGNMENT:** Any Purchase Order issued pursuant to this bid invitation and the monies which may become due hereunder are not assignable except with the prior written approval of FIU.

20. **PUBLIC PRINTING (APPLIES ONLY TO PRINTING CONTRACTS):**
    (a) **PREFERENCE GIVEN PRINTING WITHIN THE STATE:** FIU shall give preference to bidders located within the state when awarding contracts to have materials printed, whenever such printing can be done at no greater expense than, and at a level of quality comparable to that obtainable from a bidder out side the state.
    (b) **CONTRACTS SUBLET:** In accordance to Class B Printing Laws and Regulations, "Printing shall be awarded only to printing firms. No contract shall be awarded to any broker, agent, or independent contract or offering to provide printing manufactured by other firms or persons."
    (c) **DISQUALIFICATION OF BIDDER:** More than one bid from an individual, firm, partnership, corporation, or association under the same or different names will not be considered. Reasonable grounds for believing that a bidder is involved in more than one proposal for the same work will be cause for rejection of all proposals in which such bidders are believed to be involved. Any or all proposals will be rejected if there is reason to believe that collusion exists between bidders. Proposals in which the prices obviously are unbalanced will be subject to rejection.
    (d) **TRADE CUSTOMS:** Current trade customs of the printing industry are recognized unless expected by Special Conditions or Specifications herein .
    (e) **COMMUNICATIONS:** It is expected that all materials and proofs will be picked up and delivered by the printer or his representative, unless otherwise specified. Upon request, materials will be forwarded by registered mail.
    (f) **RETURN OF MATERIALS:** All copy, photos, artwork, and other materials supplied by the purchaser must be handled carefully and returned in good condition upon completion of the job. Such return is a condition of the contract and payment will not be made until return is effected.

21. **LIABILITY:** The seller agrees to indemnify, and save FIU its officers, agents and employees harmless from any and all judgements, orders, awards, costs, and expense including attorneys' fees, and all claims on account of damages to property, including loss of use thereof, or bodily injury (including death) which may be hereafter sustained by the seller, its employees, its subcontractors, or FIU employees, or third persons, arising out of or in connection with this contract and which are determined by a court of competent jurisdiction to be a legal liability of the seller.

22. **FACILITIES:** The University reserves the right to inspect the bidder's facilities at any time with prior notice.

23. **ANTI-DISCRIMINATION CLAUSE:** The Bidder shall comply with the provisions of Executive Order 11246, September 24,1965, and the rules, regulations, and relevant Orders of the Secretary of Labor.

NOTE: ANY AND ALL CONDITIONS ATTACHED HERETO WHICH VARY FROM THESE GENERAL CONDITIONS SHALL HAVE PRECEDENCE.

laid down for buying procedures. In the hands of the right food buyer and at times when the volume of business is substantial, however, there is potential for significant savings. This system is used by large chain food operators and those in the institutional field. The chief difference between this system and one-stop buying is that the cost-plus plan can be worked out with the individual dealer who specializes in just one or two items such as beef, seafood, or frozen fruits and vegetables, fats, oil, dressings, and grocery items. Records of companies using the cost-plus system prove that they save, on a yearly basis, 10 percent to 12 percent on the purchase prices of commodities bought in this manner as against open market buying.

A buyer agrees with a purveyor to buy as much as 75 percent to 85 percent of the buyer's need for a particular classification of food from the dealer for a period of time based on a fixed markup over the dealer's cost. This might seem to be risky at first. Because the arrangement can be made for as little as thirty days or as much as six months, depending upon the situation, however, the whole arrangement can be open to bid among different dealers. An agreement can also be cancelled on short-term notice if something goes wrong. These arrangements are not new. Institutional food buying has been working for years on a negotiated markup over cost with food purveyors, but the same system has only recently been tried in the hotel and restaurant business.

Such a plan works only when the volume of business is large and deliveries are restricted, preferably to one location. If the arrangement involves meat, for example, the fewer items the buyer needs, the easier it is to control the procedure and the more accurate the costs.

The amount of markup over cost is not difficult to arrive at because this can be either the result of a bid or the result of negotiations. Purveyors normally operate on a 15 percent to 25 percent markup over their true cost, and, even for better customers with good credit and large orders, the markup over true cost is generally around 15 percent to 18 percent. When a customer has a poor credit rating, volume is small, or there are kickbacks, the markup can rise as high as 30 percent or more over cost.

Often a purveyor, when approached by a food buyer, will be skeptical of cost-plus purchasing, especially if he is one of the regular suppliers. The purveyor understands that such an arrangement cuts into the profit margin, but he must also realize that it is better to make a small markup doing a large volume of business than it is to lose the account. Most purveyors try to avoid the issue by saying that it is impossible to know costs closely enough to be able to work fairly with such an arrangement.

This is only a ploy. Every dealer who has been in business longer than a month knows exactly what his costs are. It is only a matter of laying it out on the table and arriving at a definition of cost with the buyer.

True cost generally works out to be the cost of material to the purveyor plus any costs of fabrication, change in packaging, or loss because of required trim, cooking, or shrinkage from aging. This is the true material cost to the purveyor, and it does not include any overhead, salespeople's salaries, delivery, cost of billing, promotion, taxes, or other nuisance charges, which are borne by the purveyor from his "markup over cost." If the purveyor receives 10 percent over cost, he stands to make about 5 percent profit before income taxes, which is better than average in the food business.

A workable markup over cost varies with the type of food being purchased. There are instances where meats, because of location, have to be purchased in the frozen state. In such instances markup over true cost from 8 percent to 10 percent can be obtained as against the normal markup of 15 percent to 20 percent on fresh, chilled meats. There are other instances where both the food buyer and the purveyor are satisfied with a markup of only 6 percent over cost in frozen fish, poultry, and ready-to-cook poultry items. Another arrangement of this type that has been used is based on a 10-cents-per-pound markup over cost on all items costing over $1.00 per pound and 5 cents per pound on any item merely transferred from the purveyor's source of supply to the food buyer in its original box or shape. This arrangement has been successfully worked out with several meat dealers who receive 10 cents per pound over cost for fabricated and aged meats, and 5 cents per pound on items such as boxed bacon, hams, and packaged corned beef. In grocery houses a markup of 8 percent to 10 percent over cost seems to work.

The highly perishable nature of fresh produce makes it difficult for a purveyor to know true cost on any particular item. Also, the volume of business in produce is generally not so great that it is worth the time and effort required to work out a cost system.

Summary. The systems of food buying outlined above cover current methods widely used to purchase food supplies, whether for the small "mom and pop" restaurant or the large food processing company with worldwide distribution. Variations of every system are in use, and, as was pointed out earlier, no one system can or should be utilized to the exclusion of all the other systems.

The good and bad points of each system, as they apply to an individual situation, must be weighed by management and the food buyer so that the operation gains maximum benefit.

Visiting the Market

Regardless of the system used for buying food, a good buyer makes it his business to visit the market. He checks prices, the quality of perishables, and the availability of supply. It is also his opportunity to learn from dealers the expected long-term market trend as well as that for the immediate future. By knowing what is available in good supply on the market and what will be arriving in plentiful supply or "gathering short," the food buyer can relay this information to the chef or food service manager and to the food director so that menus can be planned to take advantage of market trends.

One of the things a good buyer should do on regular visits to the market is personally to select and stamp for delivery as many items as possible, especially heavy beef items such as ribs, strips, filets, rounds, legs of veal, lamb legs and racks, some fish items, and even cases of melons and hampers of vegetables that lend themselves to individual selection and stamping.

When one buys meat for aging, it is imperative that the buyer put his stamp on it before it goes into cryovac. When a buyer goes to the market, he can look for good buys, and he has first selection of quality. Today, with the rather wide latitude in grading beef, a buyer has an obligation to select and stamp his purchase of major meat items. There are five different yield grades and three different levels of U.S. Choice grade on the market. The best meat goes to the person in the market.

Sometimes there are three or four "marks" for honeydews or cantaloupes and eight or ten different labels for citrus fruits. The only way to know which is best is to go to the market and cut and taste.

Formerly a buyer would go to the market as early as 4:00 or 5:00 A.M. to get the pick of the market, but eventually everyone agreed to open the wholesale (suppliers) market at 6:00 A.M. Commission houses (those that sell to wholesalers) and auctions still keep early hours. In some areas these markets open the night before so that wholesalers can be stocked by 6:00 A.M. the next day.

Going to the market is not only worthwhile; it is fun! If a food buyer fails to see the advantage of frequent visits for his own edification, thereby sharpening the tools of his trade, it may be because of the burden of office work or a lack of initiative. Whatever the reason, such a buyer often does an inadequate job of buying. He also acquires the reputation of being a telephone order clerk, instead of a professional food buyer.

MANAGING THE OFFICE

Management

The location of the food buyer's office is important. Unless it is a corporate buying office, with headquarters located in a remote city, the best location is on the premises of the operation involved. It should be adjacent to the storeroom and as near the receiving area as practical. If the buyer is responsible for the operation of food and beverage storerooms, his office should also allow him full view of the storerooms and access to them.

The office and furnishings have to be adequate and in keeping with the image that the operation is trying to project. The buyer who is expected to do a prestigious negotiating job for hundreds of thousands of dollars worth of merchandise should have a suitably attractive and comfortable office. Even if the buyer has only a few thousand dollars worth of merchandise to buy each week, he is at least entitled to privacy and some comfort.

The office should be divided into a reception area, where salespeople can wait in reasonable comfort, an area for assistant buyers if the operation is sufficiently large, and a private area where the buyer can carry on discussions with salespeople without being overheard. Recording equipment, if it is used to tape discussions related to contracts and quality as an aid to memory, should be in full view of everyone in the office, and the practice should be agreed to by both parties.

There should be a regular schedule of visiting hours for sales representatives. Usually one morning a week, from 8:00 until 12:00, is adequate for seeing salespeople, but, if the buyer has time, two mornings a week should be worked into the schedule. The best single morning seems to be Wednesday. If two mornings can be set aside, however, the best ones appear to be Tuesday and Thursday.

The food buyer intent on doing a good job also finds that it usually takes two visits to the market every week to keep abreast of market conditions. He can go either by himself or with a food production manager, a chef, the receiving clerk, or, on occasion, the general manager or the food and beverage manager.

The actual placing of telephone orders and the routine solicitation of quotes should be delegated to a capable assistant. If the buyer himself has to spend much time making telephone calls, getting quotations, and placing orders, he does not have time to analyze the market, to explore ways of improving buying procedures, or to take advantage of market trends.

If a buying office is only large enough to support one buyer plus an assistant-secretary, as much detail as possible should be assigned to the secretary or, in some instances, to the head storeroom person. Using the head storeroom person to assist in purchasing procedures equips him to serve as a potential backup for the food buyer.

Records

Every transaction performed by a food buyer or his staff should be recorded in a systematic manner so that, at any time, any question regarding the conduct of the office can be answered in writing.

Requests for merchandise from the various departments should be signed by the proper department head and filed. Any quotation received from any dealer should be recorded on a properly authorized form or filed for ready reference. Every order placed should have a purchase order number or be duly recorded in an order book showing who was given the order, the item and the quantity ordered, and the price in reference to a specification. There should be a detailed description of any cost-plus contract or any arrangement made on a long-term basis, showing competitive prices secured, before signing a cost-plus contract or making a long-term purchase.

One weak point often found in a purchasing office is poor communications between that office and the receiving department. If the two offices are adjacent, a copy of the quotation sheet used for determining orders can be given to the receiving clerk so that he can anticipate and check in the orders for the day. Many orders, such as those for bread and milk, are made by telephone. Others are based on long-term contracts. They are not shown on daily or weekly quotation sheets. In this case, the purchase book, which is filled out when the purchase is made, should be set up so that a copy can be taken from the book and sent to the receiving clerk's office.

Another weak point is the lack of a formalized method of recording grocery quotations. The good buyer will make sure that he has a properly organized quotation book to back up every purchase of groceries. It should show items, dealers, and current competitive prices in order that there can be no argument about what is proper and what is not. As much as 15 percent of the total dollar purchase can be in grocery items, and, with as many as four hundred or five hundred items in use, there must be a good, systematic way of recording quotations for easy reference. Otherwise, money may be lost to the operation because the buyer is unaware that the price quoted by one dealer is 25 cents or 30 cents a case less than that quoted by another dealer.

Procedures should be established so that each day the invoices from the receiving department, plus the original copy of the receiving sheet, come to the buyer's office for approval of price and quantity after the invoices are compared with the orders placed. After approval by the buyer, these records are then passed on to the accounting department.

The buyer should have at hand a complete list of discounts and credits; thus, he can make sure that any invoice showing regular prices bears a discount notation. Then the accounting department will be sure to pick up the credit.

FINANCIAL ASPECTS OF PURCHASING

The Cost of Money

Every purveyor or salesperson hopes to sell large orders of everything because it means more commissions and bigger profits. A food buyer who succumbs to this type of selling soon finds himself in trouble. Large quantities of dead stock in a storeroom or items that do not turn over in sixty to ninety days should cause concern.

Although there should be an immediate use for merchandise purchased, this does not mean that food must be bought on a hand-to-mouth or day-to-day basis. Delivery and the cost of handling bills often exceed the cost of having some money tied up for a reasonable period of time. Buying canned goods weekly on a rotating month's supply can save in terms of transportation costs and cost per unit. A wise buyer knows how to use his buying power. He saves money by buying large quantities of merchandise but only when this is feasible.

Because of rising delivery costs, food buyers have found that weekly or semiweekly deliveries of even such items as dairy products, meats, and produce are satisfactory as well as profitable. Money costs approximately 1 percent a month and, if a food buyer can get a 10 percent discount by buying a six-month supply of a nonperishable item, he would not be doing his job if he did not make the purchase and realize the savings. A 4 percent net savings on a cost of 6 percent means a return on a cost of over 120 percent a year that can be realized if there is storage space and if the company can secure financing.

During an inflationary period, it is always good business to make sure that every possible way has been explored to get merchandise on hand, as long as it is nonperishable, to circumvent the inflationary trend. This has not been as much of a problem in the United States as it has been in other countries, where inflation is one of the biggest problems of the food buyer and management. In some areas inflation has made it expedient to buy an entire year's supply of canned goods and groceries and to make a year's commitment, if possible, on such items as liquors, soap powders, paper supplies, china, glass, silver, linen, and practically everything else a food operation requires.

Paying Bills

One of the best tools a food buyer has is his operation's good credit rating. It seems to be the nature of the food business that many operations are marginal. A poor credit rating means the buyer has to pay higher prices and will invariably get some lower-quality merchandise.

Most prices are quoted on a thirty-day credit basis with a ten-day grace period. This means a buyer can order for a period of one month or thirty days on credit, but he must have the bill paid by the end of the tenth of the following month. The dealer must get his bills out on the first or second of the month, and he can expect payment by the tenth or the eleventh of that month.

When a company is unable to pay bills on a thirty-day basis and goes to sixty or ninety days, purveyors either have to borrow money to pay their bills, or they have to assign the account to a factor who charges as much as 25 percent to 35 percent yearly. This cost must be borne by the buyer, for it is included in the price of the goods purchased. Paying food bills on time is vital, even though some other bills have to be postponed.

Some dealers, because of their financial setup, have to factor their bills every week, and, if a buyer is in a position to work with the dealer and pay on a weekly basis, the chances are he can get some substantial discounts, averaging anywhere from 2 percent to 5 percent, for weekly payment of bills. Every food buyer and management should look into this possibility if they are in a position to take advantage of such a situation.

WORKING WITH SALESPEOPLE

Advice for Food Buyers

It does not take long for a good food buyer to learn that the salespeople or purveyors he contacts know much more about their own products than he will probably ever know. The average salesperson or purveyor constantly works with the same few items, whereas the buyer works with hundreds. The buyer cannot hope to know as much about each product, and it would be foolish to try. The smart buyer quickly adopts a friendly attitude toward salespeople and purveyors so that he can use their knowledge to his own advantage.

This is not to advocate personal involvement of the buyer with salespeople or purveyors. A friendly business relationship, based on fairness and mutual cooperation, can exist without the buyer's showing the slightest favoritism, practicing any dishonesty, or earning any justifiable criticism. It is better to conduct business in a relaxed, friendly atmosphere than in a tense, highly competitive one.

Even though purveyors and salespeople are highly competitive, they will, when necessary, function as a group to deal with an unsatisfactory or unfair situation created by a food buyer or a group of buyers. More than one buyer has been forced to leave a business because a group of purveyors joined forces against him and kept him from doing a satisfactory job. This situation occurs more often in smaller communities where the market is rather limited and the number of purveyors is small and becomes a close-knit group. It is wise, therefore, to stay on friendly business terms with purveyors.

Salespeople can, if they are so inclined, help the buyer, whether he is just starting on the job or has been doing it for a long time. The salesperson not only educates the buyer in terms of his own products; he also keeps him abreast of the activity of competitors and up to date on market trends. A salesperson can also use his influence to see that orders are given a bit of extra care. When a salesperson is on good terms with the buyer, delivery service always seems to be a little better, and, if there is an emergency (and there always are in the food business), a salesperson can have deliveries made on weekends, even if he has to make them himself.

The one time a food buyer inevitably needs a friend is during a strike. There is no friend like the salesperson, who will, somehow or other, find a way to get deliveries to the buyer, often at considerable expense to himself. In strike situations the salesperson may risk his own well-being to help a buyer who has treated him fairly.

A purveyor and his salespeople also spend money. Buyers for hospitals, other institutions, and charitable organizations that depend largely on financial contributions from the public must keep in mind that many purveyors have funds for such purposes, and they are more likely to make a liberal contribution if their representatives have been treated with consideration.

What, then, constitutes "fair," "proper," and "considerate" treatment? Salespeople are human beings, and they should be accorded respect and courtesy at all times. This means that they are entitled to present their product to the food buyer, and they should have his full attention. Lack of attention is not only unfair; it is rude.

The practice of having regular visiting hours for salespeople is also considerate, and a good buyer makes sure each salesperson has approximately the same amount of time.

There should be no obvious preferential treatment for any sales representative.

Salespeople should also, if possible, be provided with a suitable place to wait. In many operations the buyer's office is in the lower level of a building. It is not unusual for six or eight salespeople to be standing in a hot, dirty, ill-lighted hallway, waiting their turn to see the buyer. Perhaps nothing can be done about the location of the buyer's office, but the area in which the salespeople wait could be clean, freshly painted, bright, and well ventilated, with some seating provided.

Sometimes a salesperson must prove himself to his boss. The best way to do this is to show the boss that he can call the buyer and make an appointment for himself and his boss. This happens only occasionally, but it means a great deal to the salesperson if the buyer cooperates. The small favor is often repaid many times over by the salesperson.

The wise buyer listens to rumors from salespeople and immediately puts them out of his mind. He never betrays the confidence of a salesperson by divulging a price or telling a trade secret.

The buyer should immediately make clear that he is a one-price buyer, that he wishes to hear only the salesperson's "lowball" price, and that there will be no opportunity to quote a second price if the first one is too high. The sale is made or lost on the first quote. The buyer who haggles over prices, going from one dealer to another in search of a lower price, can never be sure that he settled for the lowest one. Perhaps, because of lack of confidence on the part of the dealers, he was given too high a price in the beginning.

If any food buyer is to last in the business, he must avoid the reputation of being a chiseler. Certainly he must try to get the bottom price for the quantity and quality of merchandise needed, but he must also recognize when that point has been reached.

Salespeople and purveyors should not be imposed upon. It is important that a buyer never ask a personal favor that is not connected with business and that he keep emergency orders to a minimum.

The biggest concern of any salesperson is to retain an account, even though the volume of business is small. He should be assured that the buyer will use his product as long as the salesperson produces, that the account will not be lost through capriciousness on the part of the buyer or anyone else in the organization who might have an ulterior motive. With such assurance, the salesperson will go out of his way to support the account.

Being a salesperson is not easy. Selling is a tough job, both physically and emotionally. It is difficult to make a call, regardless of the weather or any other problem, only to be turned down by a buyer. Any doubts about the hardships of selling would be dispelled by Arthur Miller's *Death of a Salesman*. It takes an exceptional person to sell. It may even take more expertise than to buy. The buyer holds the power of decision, whereas the salesperson has only his own personality, his products and his knowledge of them, and his ability to convince the buyer. However he does it, short of dishonesty, it is the salesperson's job to get his product into use. It is unfortunate that many salespeople become overzealous in their attempt to succeed.

If a salesperson tries to buy his way into an account by going behind the buyer's back, then the salesperson has asked for rough treatment, and the buyer should dismiss him. A salesperson who does not know his product and "trade puffs" should also be discouraged.

What the Salespeople Think of You

Recently we attended a series of divisional sales meetings of one of the largest food distributors in the country, and we certainly got an education in sales and personnel management. Every purchasing agent, if he or she has never had the experience of selling, should at least make arrangements to accompany a salesperson on a series of sales calls to see what a salesperson must go through.

What are the salesperson's pet peeves? Here is what these salespeople answered, loud and clear:

1. Purchasing agents who do not know their products and refuse to listen and learn are a number one peeve.
2. Egotistical purchasing agents are out, too. Salespeople can take the weather, back doors, and dirty offices, but none enjoy trying to work with an "uppity" buyer who has developed the habit of "talking down" to people.
3. A "two-price" purchasing agent is "the pits." A buyer who will take a salesperson's quote and shop it around to get a lower price is soon a "marked man" in the trade.
4. A purchasing agent who is a gossip or "talker" is not popular with salespeople.
5. Purchasing agents that think all purveyors and salespeople are "crooks, liars, and cheats" seldom if ever hear of any good deals. In case of strikes or shortages, these buyers get little help, and no picket lines are crossed to help them.
6. An emergency order buyer is costly to his or her employer, and to the purveyor, and to the salespeople. This careless habit can cause work schedule problems within an operation; such facts are always "directed" to management's attention.
7. Salespeople just do not like to be used. A buyer who is always asking for favors seldom receives them for long. Requests for free tickets, car rides, card games, golf games, and tournaments turn a good salesperson off.
8. Salespeople like and will help a buyer whose "word you can put in the bank" and whose forgetful memory is remarkably beneficial.

9. Profanity, sex, and dirty jokes soon mark a buyer as a source of danger.

Advice for Salespeople

What, in the opinion of a food buyer, is the mark of a good salesperson? What should the salesperson do to make a sale?

The answer to the first question is that a good salesperson comes to the buyer with a thorough knowledge of his product and what his product can do for the buyer. If a salesperson calls on a buyer without even knowing whether the buyer can use the product, he is wasting his own and the buyer's time. A salesperson should also try to determine whether a buyer is having a problem with some product or a line of products. If so, he may be able to offer a similar product. And, any salesperson who tells a buyer that he should be using his products, rather than those of a competitor, implies that the buyer is not very smart if he is not using them—often the kiss of death for a salesperson.

As to what motivates the purchasing of products, most buyers will say, first, that they need the product, and, second, that they have confidence in the salesperson because of his knowledge of the product and what it can do. The best advice that can be given a salesperson is to do his homework well. He should find out what the buyer needs and try to fill those needs. Price is usually not a consideration in placing first orders or in securing an account.

A fast-talking, fast-joking salesperson seldom wins the confidence of a good food buyer. If a salesperson's feelings are easily hurt or if he is self-conscious for any reason, he has probably chosen the wrong occupation.

THE FOOD BUYER AND THE LAW

Under ordinary circumstances, the food buyer can carry on his activities for years and never require a legal settlement of a disagreement or a misunderstanding. As long as the buyer is dealing with local purveyors and deliveries are made in the dealer's trucks directly to the receiving department of the buyer's company within a day or two of when the order was placed, there is little risk of disagreement or need to resort to the law. Today, however, legal actions are becoming more common, and the professional food buyer should have a working knowledge of the law as it applies to his activities. Perhaps the most important thing for the buyer to know is when he needs help from a lawyer to avoid trouble and costly litigation.

The first line of defense for a food buyer is the purchase specifications worked out with the testing committee, approved by management, and distributed to all purveyors with whom he does business. These specifications protect both buyer and seller from misunderstandings about what is desired by the buyer.

There is more chance of trouble when merchandise has to travel a considerable distance by common carrier and in sufficient quantities that it requires the use of public storage. Another source of trouble is the contract covering an extended period of time. Perhaps by intent, but more often because the situation has changed, it becomes impossible to carry out the terms of the contract.

Purchase Orders

If a purchase involves more than one delivery, the food buyer should make sure that a formal purchase order (see Exhibit 6-6) is issued to the purveyor. It should make clear the specifications of the product and all of the conditions involving payment. One of the most important parts of any written contract or purchase order is the method of payment. It should make clear who pays how much for what and when.

Not only should the purchase order spell out the specifications—price, manner of shipment, and quantities involved—and method of payment, but it should also clearly state who is responsible for insurance, timing of the delivery, follow-up, transportation schedules, claims, and so forth. A purchase order made out in this manner clearly defines when the title to the goods passes from the seller to the buyer, which is necessary information in every transaction of buying and selling. If there should be loss while the goods are being transported, it is necessary to know the legal owner of the merchandise at the time the loss occurred.

If the order, which is actually a sales contract, whether written or verbal, states that the merchandise is to be delivered to the buyer's place of business, there is no question as to who is responsible for any losses. If the seller fails to deliver on time, the buyer has at least a basis to claim damages, providing he actually suffered damages because the merchandise was not delivered as ordered and agreed upon.

If the merchandise was ordered FOB (free on board) from the city of the seller to a local carrier, it is the responsibility of the buyer, who actually took possession of the merchandise when it was delivered to the carrier, to file a claim with the carrier for adjustment or damages in case of loss.

Sometimes merchandise is purchased FAS (free alongside ship), which is basically the same as FOB except that, when the merchandise arrives at the port of destination, an additional carrier is involved. If the shipment is warehoused and later delivered from the warehouse to the ship, this involves a number of carriers and conditions. Because the title to such merchandise passes to the buyer when it is delivered alongside ship, it becomes the responsibility of the buyer to make sure that his shipment is insured, either by his own company or that of the various carriers involved. Losses from overseas shipments are notoriously high. It is largely because of these high losses that the idea of containerized shipments of all classes of food merchandise has won support, and the need to consolidate different classifications of food into a single shipment has encouraged the use of one-stop buying for overseas and off-mainland shipments.

A buyer can choose another procedure. He can purchase under a contract that has a CIF (cost, insurance, and freight) destination point stipulation. This means that the seller has to arrange for shipment of the merchandise and to pay the cost of transportation to the point of delivery, and any freight costs involved from the point of disembarkation. This plan is usually used to cover overseas shipment. All necessary papers are sent ahead to the buyer, and, when the merchandise arrives at the port, the buyer arranges for his own transportation and pickup at dockside. He is free of any charges and losses up to the time he actually takes physical possession of the merchandise.

Speculative Buying

When a buyer wants to procure a large quantity of a certain item, there can be cost savings if the merchandise is purchased at the source during the height of the harvest season, with storage in the buyer's city and deliveries spaced according to the buyer's needs.

The help of an experienced lawyer is necessary in preparing the contract for such a purchase. Provisions must be made for payment direct to the packer, generally in advance of any shipments from him. The specifications must be extremely clear as to amounts, prices, delivery schedules, and quality. Provisions concerning transportation must clearly state who is responsible for arranging the details as well as insurance and transportation costs. Details include where and how the merchandise is to be stored, who has title to the merchandise, and cost of storage (which can run as high as 2 cents to 3 cents a pound per month, plus 1 cent or 2 cents a pound for being placed in storage, plus an additional 1 cent or 2 cents a pound to get it out of storage). Finally, the terms

PURCHASE ORDER

BILL TO

S A M P L E

VENDOR

DO

NOT

USE

SHIP TO

Attention:

PURCHASE ORDER NO.
REQUISITION NO.
PROJECT NO.

THESE NUMBERS MUST BE SHOWN ON ALL PACKAGES, SHIPPING PAPERS, INVOICES, CORRESPONDENCE ETC.

PURCHASE ORDER DATE

All invoices must be submitted ATTENTION ACCOUNTS PAYABLE bill to above address in duplicate. Failure to comply may result in delay of payment.

Shipping & Handling Instructions

1. All orders must be acknowledged within 7 days of receipt of order.

2. All acknowledgements must state a shipping date, or the shipping date specified herein shall control.

3. Ship the least expensive method of parcel post, UPS, REA, Truck or Rail. Air freight may only be used if indicated in the ship via column.

4. You must use your name as the shipper on all orders.

5. Ship from the F.O.B. point indicated.

6. Ship transportation prepaid or collect as indicated in the 'ship via' column. If shipment is transportation prepaid, you must pay the carrier and you must bill us on your invoice. No other method is permitted.

7. All bills of lading, packing lists, pieces invoices and other documents must state our purchase order number.

These instructions must be followed. Any changes require our approval in writing.

SHIP DATE	REQ. AT SHIP TO	F.O.B.	CONTRACT #	SHIP VIA	TERMS

ITEM	QUANTITY	UNIT	CATALOG NO.	DESCRIPTION	UNIT COST	EXTENSION
				TOTAL		
		SPECIAL INSTRUCTIONS			

Authorized Signatures:

_____ _____ _____
Hotel Controller   Hotel General Manager   Purchasing Agent

_____ _____ _____
Date   Date   Date

PRINTED IN USA #573R

PURCHASING

Exhibit 6-6. Form used to order merchandise

concerning pickup and delivery to the buyer's operation have to be clearly set forth.

A prospective buyer should remember that some deterioration in the quality of merchandise is normal; it occurs between the time merchandise is packed and the time it is unpacked in the buyer's storeroom or kitchen. If the merchandise is not usable on delivery, the question of responsibility arises. When the litigation is over, it is usually determined that the buyer is responsible for the loss as it is almost impossible to determine when deterioration began in such items as shrimp, seafood, chickens, hams or bacon, canned goods, and frozen fruits and vegetables.

Contracts: The Promises People Live By

A contract is a legally enforceable agreement between two or more persons involving mutual promises to do or not to do something. Whether it is implied or specific, it always involves an offer, consideration, and acceptance. Harry Sherman, a leading economist, in his book, *The Promises Men Live By,* remarks on the extraordinary number of times that people do things or fail to do things because they count on someone else to do something or not to do something. He also brings out the fact that many activities involve promises that are actually legal contracts, but they are never put in writing.

Just going into a restaurant and sitting down is an implied contract with the restaurant owner that you are there to buy food or beverages and to receive service and that you will pay for this service. When a person checks in to a hotel, there is an implied contract that he desires the services of the hotel and that he is in a position to pay for those services. He also implies that he will conduct himself in accord with the rules of the hotel and of the commonweal. Businesspeople make contracts that are never recorded merely by meeting people on the street and discussing business deals with them, or they

make telephone calls or write letters—all of which involve an implied contract.

Oral and Written Contracts. Remember that an oral contract, made in good faith, is legally binding and enforceable by law. Of course, neither all oral nor all written contracts are enforceable. Some, both oral and written, are illegal or against public policy or unenforceable because one of the parties is not competent to make a contract. If, for example, a seller is selling stolen merchandise, and the buyer, upon learning this, refuses to accept it or pay for it, the seller would then have no redress against the buyer. If a seller contracts to sell certain merchandise to a buyer and then fails to deliver because the producer failed to deliver to the seller, the buyer clearly cannot force the seller to produce the merchandise. The buyer does, however, have the right to sue the seller for damages as a result of nondelivery of the merchandise. The seller then has the option of trying to collect damages from the producer if the producer is in a position to pay damages or can even be located.

Expressed and Implied Contracts. Most contracts for the sale of merchandise are spelled out so that there is no question that they are expressed contracts. Even if a contract does not explicitly state everything regarding the merchandise, there is always an implied contract that the merchandise will be of the actual quality necessary to perform the intended function under ordinary circumstances.

The question of quality may arise because the person making the complaint has "exquisite" or "extraordinary" taste. The courts must then determine what the ordinary person would feel about the quality of the product. A food buyer should keep this in mind when he rejects a shipment because, in his opinion, the quality is not exactly right.

Other forms of contracts in which a food buyer might become involved are unilateral or bilateral contracts and voidable and unenforceable contracts. He might also be concerned with the legal capacity of parties (minors and incompetents) to make contracts, responsibility of partnerships, individuals, and legal corporations, assignment of contracts, inability to perform, rescinding of contracts, cancellation and surrender of contracts, substitution of new contracts, and breach of contract. If a food buyer is not careful, he might fall into these legal traps.

When this does occur, he should seek professional help immediately.

The best protections a food buyer can have, again, are a good set of specifications, which is in the hands of the purveyors with whom he does business, and a written purchase order spelling out details of the transaction such as quality, price, length of contract, shipping instructions, and any other considerations that apply to the order.

7 Purchase Specifications and Testing

Purpose: First, to provide an understanding of purchasing specifications—what information is required, why specifications are necessary, and how to formulate a set of specifications. Second, to consider the procedures a testing committee follows and the decisions it makes.

INTRODUCTION

Specifications are important because they spell out standards, and thus facilitate communication between the supplier and the buyer. Variances in food quality, price, packaging, fabrication, and the like make it absolutely necessary to have precise, detailed descriptions of products.

Although it is best to build a set of specifications around standard meat cuts, product packaging, counts, weights, and the like, it is necessary to tailor specifications to the individual conditions of the food operation to be served. The points to be considered are fully discussed in this chapter.

SPECIFICATIONS

The U.S. government defines a specification as a "statement of particulars in specific terms." Authors of textbooks furnish as many definitions as there are textbooks. A simple definition is "a description of an item stated in such a way that the exact requirements can be understood by both buyer and seller." The basic requirement for effective purchasing specifications is that they have the approval and support of management and that they be used.

Specifications must comply with current standards, which may be set by the federal government, by state government, or by marketing associations such as the National Association of Hotel and Restaurant Meat Purveyors, which publishes the *Meat Buyer's Guide to Standardized Meat Cuts*.

Specifications should be the result of a carefully conceived and implemented testing plan that involves the important decision makers in the food department. Testing should be done regularly at a specified time. At each meeting, the program for the next meeting must be outlined so that everyone who attends can come prepared to discuss the products involved.

The writers of specifications should cover the essential information with a minimum amount of detailed description but enough to give a precise understanding. Simpler items sometimes require a more detailed and lengthy description than more expensive and familiar items because of the nature of the items involved. Although a specification should be concise, it is better to have too much information rather than too little, to avoid any misunderstanding. The terms used should be commonly accepted in the trade.

Certain information should be included in all specifications:

1. The common or usual trade name of the product
2. The recognized federal, trade, or commonly accepted local grade
3. The unit or container on which the price is quoted
4. The name and size of the basic container

Additional information often needed includes the following:

1. The count and size of items or units in the container
2. The weight ranges
3. Minimum and maximum trims
4. The type of processing and packaging
5. The degree of ripeness
6. Additional information that would eliminate any possibility of misunderstanding

Purveyors should be given a complete set of specifications for products the purchaser might buy, and they should be notified in writing that these specifications must be adhered to and that only the testing committee and management can change them. A set of specifications must also be given to the receiving clerk as a guide to inspecting incoming merchandise—effective buying by specification requires receiving by specification as well.

An explanation of the ten items of information to be included in specifications follows.

Common or Trade Name

The common or trade name of an item is usually simple, but the names of some items, especially certain cuts of beef, differ in various parts of the country. A spec writer has to recognize this. For example:

- On the west coast there is a long tenderloin known as a "Special K," whereas on the east coast the nearest thing to this cut is a "Silverskin tender," listed in the *Meat Buyer's Guide* as "Specification #190 Full Tenderloin Special."
- A Pullman ham is square; other canned hams are pear shaped.
- A lamb rack, hotel style, could well be a bracelet of lamb elsewhere.
- Lemon sole is lemon sole in Boston, but it is Boston sole in New York City. Boston sole in Boston can be called yellowtail or dab.

Federal, Trade, or Commonly Recognized Local Grades

It has been accepted in the food service business that if it can be eaten, the USDA has a grade for it. This is a fairly accurate statement, for U.S. grading standards are probably the best in the world, followed closely by those of Canada and Australia.

A more complete listing and discussion of the federal, state, and local grading systems, packaging, terminology, laws, and characteristics of food products are found in Chapters 13, 14, 15, 16, 18, 19, and 20. Chapter 17 addresses convenience foods, which also must be purchased according to appropriate specifications.

The Unit or Container on Which Price Is Quoted

This refers to whether the unit is a pound, liter, bushel, carton, box, crate, bunch, piece, case, barrel, hogshead, gallon, or any other unit in common use.

The Name and Size of the Basic Container

The size of the container could be a case holding six #10 cans, four single gallons, or twenty-four #2 cans, a 50-pound bag of carrots or cabbage, a 30-pound can of frozen apples, a 30-pound lug of tomatos, a 28-pound hamper of string beans, or a 52-gallon barrel of vinegar.

Count or Size of Units in the Container

Inclusion of the count or size of units in specifications is usually essential. Some examples are: 18- to 20-slice pound of bacon, 23-size grapefruit, 90-count Idaho potatoes, and 30 to 35 count for a #10 can of Bartlett pears. The chapters in this text (in the Part "Food Commodities") previously referred to deal extensively with this topic.

Weight Ranges

This refers primarily to cuts of meat and sizes of poultry. Such a specification can also refer to the weight of the individual item, as in the case of melons, or the weights of bags of carrots or cabbages. In order to check "overrun," containers of ice cream should be weighed in the receiving process.

Minimum or Maximum Trim

Practically every government or trade standard specifies trim. The maximum length of trim, from the end of the eye of the meat on a strip loin is, for example, particularly important because of the price of the item. The yield grade determining the allowable thickness of the fat covering on meats is also important.

Processing

Usually the name of the item indicates whether it is fresh, frozen, dehydrated, canned, corned, or packed in a certain way. The desired state of processing should be made clear in the specifications to avoid cheaper substitutions by unscrupulous dealers. The difference in the price between certain fresh fish and frozen fish can be as much as 100 percent.

Degree of Ripeness

To avoid spoilage losses, most dealers prefer to sell perishable fruits and produce, such as tomatoes, in the "hard ripe" stage. The dealer thereby reduces labor costs and passes any losses to the customer. Too often the "customer" then serves green tomatoes, peaches, melons, pears, and avocados to the guests who, if they knew, would prefer to patronize a restaurant where the specifications say "ready for use upon delivery."

Additional Information Required

Many subjects fall into this category. For examples:

- Particular brand names—Primex shortening, Butterball turkeys, Plume de Veau veal, Dickinson jellies, Orchid grapefruit
- Should butter be sweetened or unsweetened, and should it be packed in prints, boxes, or chips?
- The fat content of ground beef
- The drained weight of fruits in fresh fruit sections

SETTING UP A LIST OF SPECIFICATIONS

Before a list of specifications can be drawn up, the buyer and others involved must do considerable research to do the job effectively. Some of the factors to consider are discussed below.

Type of Operation

Specifications will vary considerably among different operations, whether it is an industrial feeding service, a private hospital, a luxury hotel, or a motor inn, for both type and quality of items. A buyer must also know the expected volume of business, the expected costs, and the expected ratio of profit to sales in a commercial enterprise.

The Organizational and Physical Setup of the Operation

The person responsible for preparing the specifications must know with whom he or she will work—food manager, chef, food and beverage controller, and catering manager. Sometimes all of these persons are needed to make up an effective testing committee.

The physical setup of the food facilities influences specifications. The amount of storage space, including dry storage and refrigerator and freezer space, the kitchen equipment (are there, for example, potato peelers?), the number of stations in the kitchen (are there a bake and pastry shop and a butcher shop?) all bear on the type of product to be purchased. Of course, the first consideration is the size and type of restaurant.

Market Conditions

Distance to market sources and the commodities available in the market area are important. Delivery schedules and delivery facilities should be scrutinized carefully. Another factor concerned with the market is the credit rating available to the food buyer. Purveyors sometimes have very strict credit rules.

Menus

This must be the first consideration when specifications are formulated. Sometimes, in new operations, prepared menus are not available. Sample menus from similar operations can help. If sample menus are not available, a prototype or a series of menu outlines should be furnished by management.

Items Needed

When a food buyer is setting up specifications for a new facility, there is seldom a testing committee already in operation. The buyer should thus understand that any preliminary list of items needed will be subject to approval and correction by a testing committee when one is formed. Perhaps the quickest and best way to formulate a list is for the food buyer to obtain lists of items available from various purveyors representing the different food delivery services in the area and then to review them with the chef, the food service manager, and steward or storeroom manager and have those affected indicate the items that are to be used in food preparation and service.

Borrowing Specifications

In a new operation, the food buyer or purchasing agent should design a good set of specifications for that particular facility, but often simply does not have time to do so. Perhaps the most practical thing to do in such a situation is to determine who has the best operation of the same type in the area and ask to borrow its list. If this is not feasible, a dealer might have a set of specifications. It is important to pick the best competitor in the area since one of the probable reasons for its success is its list of specifications.

Preparing Individual Specifications

It is still best, of course, to prepare an individual set of specifications based on the requirements of the particular establishment. This might initially appear to be a formidable task because in the day-to-day operation of a food service operation some four or five hundred items are generally used. Since most food items are already covered by standards set by individual companies, trade groups, or government agencies, however, only a few items must be tested to turn those standards into specifications for an establishment. Testing generally involves the selection of standards already established by the government or by trade practices.

There is help available for anyone charged with the responsibility for assembling a set of specifications. The best and most complete source of information is government publications. Standards produced by the USDA cover nearly every item from fresh meats to canned goods and groceries currently available in the United States and often throughout the world (see Appendix I).

Trade publications sponsored by such groups as the National Association of Meat Purveyors and publications of manufacturers such as Blue Goose, Inc., include specifications. Finally, commercial publishers have put out volumes that are helpful in drawing up specifications.

IRRADIATION OF FOOD

At the present time, irradiation of food must be considered in discussing purchasing specifications because certain products, including poultry, pork, grains, produce, spices, and flavorings, have been approved for irradiation because the process, while not mandatory, is effective in controlling foodborne illness.

Scientific research on the relationship of salmonella poisoning and poultry indicates that tainted poultry feed introduces the salmonella germ into poultry; consequently, the FDA has approved the irradiation of poultry feed. Poultry products had been previously approved for irradiation. The FDA is now studying petitions submitted by the National Fisheries Institute for approval of using irradiation on seafood and shellfish.

A buyer must specify that irradiated poultry products, for example, are desired. It becomes part of the poultry purchasing specifications as are weight and whether or not the item should be eviscerated and ice packed. Irradiated foods can be easily identified when received because by law they must be labeled with the international "radura" symbol, which signifies irradiation. The symbol consists of simple green petals (representing the food) in a

broken circle (representing the rays from the energy source). In the United States, this symbol must be accompanied by the words, "treated by irradiation" or "treated with radiation." (See Exhibit 7–1.) Exhibit 7–2 shows the symbol as it is used by a distributor of irradiated products.

In addition to eliminating insects, fungi, and bacteria that cause illness, irradiation makes it possible to keep food longer and in better condition. Irradiated strawberries will last for more than two weeks at 38°F without molding, and potatoes and onions will not sprout for weeks even if not refrigerated. When irradiated, fruit like peaches and man-

Exhibit 7-1. The radura symbol

Exhibit 7-2. A label showing irradiated food

goes can be harvested after they have fully ripened and are at their height of flavor, and have as long a market life as do unirradiated less ripe fruit; only with irradiation can such items be shipped without danger of spoilage during normal transit. Irradiation has many other applications. For example, the meat and poultry eaten by the astronauts in the U.S. space program are irradiated to preserve them without refrigeration.

The irradiation process is not new. The *Kiplinger Agriculture Letter* calls it a decades-old method for preserving food whose time is about to come. Irradiation has been used extensively for years in the cosmetics industry to rid the ingredients of harmful substances. It is used to sterilize packaging material, particularly orange juice, creamers, and milk cartons to retard growth of harmful bacteria. It is used in making nonstick cookware coatings, purifying wool, bonding carpet to backing and paper to plastic, and making automobile tires more durable. Currently the only widespread use of irradiation of food in the United States has been to kill insects or bacteria on spices and seasonings, even though it has been legal since 1986 for use on other foods such as fresh fruits and vegetables. Until recently, it was not economically feasible to site a plant where a critical mass of potential business was present. Various clearances for the use of irradiation in processing some fifty food items has been given in thirty-six countries around the world including Canada, the United Kingdom, France, Germany, Japan, Norway, and Finland, where lifestyles are similar to ours in the United States. Twenty-four other countries are in the development stage of planning irradiation use. Canada and Mexico are also moving in the direction of commercialization of food irradiation, having researched it for many years on their own.

Food irradiation has been endorsed by such diverse bodies as the World Health Organization, the U.S. Department of Agriculture (USDA), the National Food Processors Association, the U.S. Public Health Service, the American Medical Association, the American Council on Science and Health, several university-based food research institutes, and the Food and Drug Administration (FDA).

The use of irradiation is limited in the United States because in addition to the traditionally slow movement of government to approve products and services, several consumer groups oppose its use and seem to command more attention than the seriousness of their claims warrants. A group called Food and Water, Inc., headquartered in Marshfield, Vermont, is the leading opponent of the irradiation of foods, and the group has been opposed by most food scientists. Irradiation can be compared to pasteurization as a food process. When pasteurization was introduced, consumers similarly protested that milk lost its nutritional value when heated to 145°F. Politicians passed laws prohibiting the sale of pasteurized milk. We know now that pasteurization is one of the great advances in food science. It not only makes food safer, but also extends the time that food can be transported or stored without spoiling and reduces the costs for the health care industry. With concerted educational programs, the irradiation of food will similarly gain acceptance.

How Food Irradiation Works

Food irradiation is a physical means of food treatment comparable to heat pasteurization, canning, or freezing. The process involves exposing food, either packaged or in bulk, to one of three types of ionizing energy: gamma rays, machine-generated electrons, or X-rays. This is done in a special processing room or chamber for a specified duration. The most common source of gamma rays for food processing is the radioisotope cobalt-60. Food is treated by cobalt-60 gamma rays in a facility known as an irradiator. Exhibit 7–3 is a diagram of an irradiator.

Gamma energy is electromagnetic radiation of very short wavelength. This form of energy is used for a wide range of purposes; for example, to cook food in microwave ovens and to X-ray luggage.

The principal concerns about irradiating food are possible radioactivity, nutritional loss, safety of workers in a plant using the process, possible exposure to radiation during transport of the cobalt-60 pencils from the manufacturer, and possible exposure to radiation for persons living next to an irradiation processing plant.

With respect to concerns about radio-activity, since the energy used in irradiation is not strong enough to change the atoms of the food, and since the food never actually touches the radioactive source, the food cannot become radio-active. As for concerns about nutrition, even when higher doses of irradiation are used to extend shelflife or control harmful bacteria, nutritional losses are less than or about the same as losses due to cooking and freezing. And when lower doses of irradiation are used, nutrient losses are either not measurable or insignificant. The fact is, all forms of food processing—cooking, freezing, canning, and even storage—lower the amounts of some nutrients.

A tour through an irradiation plant

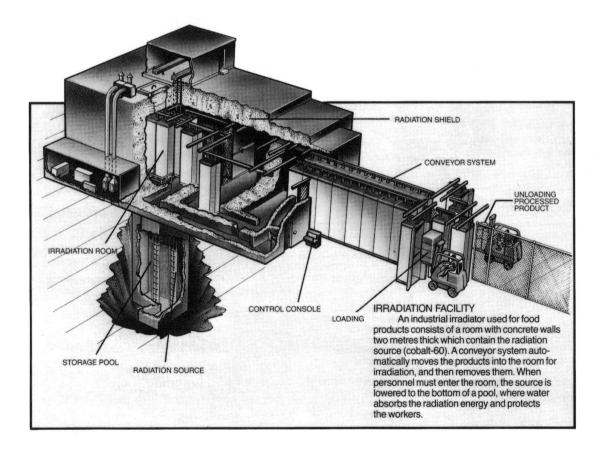

RADIATION SHIELD

CONVEYOR SYSTEM

UNLOADING PROCESSED PRODUCT

IRRADIATION ROOM

CONTROL CONSOLE

LOADING

STORAGE POOL

RADIATION SOURCE

IRRADIATION FACILITY
An industrial irradiator used for food products consists of a room with concrete walls two metres thick which contain the radiation source (cobalt-60). A conveyor system automatically moves the products into the room for irradiation, and then removes them. When personnel must enter the room, the source is lowered to the bottom of a pool, where water absorbs the radiation energy and protects the workers.

Exhibit 7-3. A food irradiation facility   (Illustration provided courtesy of Nordion International Inc. All rights reserved ©.)

reveals that the irradiating process is relatively simple compared to the complexity of the safety system. The irradiation cell has six-foot thick, steel-reinforced concrete walls that fortify the 30-foot x 30-foot x 30-foot cell where the irradiation takes place. The floor is a thick slab of concrete wrapped around a square, stainless-steel-lined pool of water 28 feet deep in which the racks of cobalt-60 pencils are stored. Six feet of water creates a biological shield similar to six feet of concrete. The radioisotope cobalt-60 pencils, the source of radiation, are raised into the concrete cell to expose the packages of food stacked on pallets in 14-foot high stainless steel carriers for the duration of the irradiation. The concrete walls that form the entrance (exit) of the cell are a maze with more right-angle turns than gamma rays can handle. Each surface hit by gamma rays absorbs 99 percent of the energy hitting it. After the third absorption ("bounce"), the remaining energy is harmless. There are a series of seven safety steps to put the process in operation. The single operator remains outside the cell to perform these steps. The irradiation process is immediately stopped automatically if any intrusion into the cell is attempted. Inadvertent or intentional entry cannot be made with the rack in an operating position.

Transport safety is assured by the U.S. Department of Transportation requirements that cobalt-60 be moved in lead-lined casks that have been drop-tested to remain intact in impacts far greater than the impact of a crash on the highway. These casks are moved on normal flatbed vehicles, whether they are being delivered to food irradiators, to hospitals, or to irradiation processors of medical supplies.

The last of the principal concerns mentioned above is the safety from radiation of the persons living next to an irradiation processing plant. Irradiation facilities must include many safety features to prevent environmental as well as worker exposure. A food irradiation plant is not a nuclear reactor—there is no chance of meltdown. If there were ever a leak of cobalt-60 from its double-welded stainless steel pencils, it would sink to the bottom of the storage pool of water and remain there—purifying the water—until it was recaptured into a lead-lined cask. Cobalt-60 is not water soluble, so there is no environmental contamination risk. The use and transportation of radioactive materials—including the equipment and the facilities in which they are used—is closely monitored by the Nuclear Regulatory Commission, state agencies, and the Department of Transportation. In the United States, the irradiation processing of food is also monitored by the USDA, FDA, and state food safety inspectors.

A PRACTICAL TESTING PROGRAM

The old army saying "Your way, the Army way, and the Right way" states the philosophy for the testing program discussed here.

Because any testing program is built around a testing committee, the first consideration is the purpose or mission of the program and the committee. Activities of the program and the committee cover most phases of the procuring, processing, preparing, and serving of food, but this wide range of activities can be reduced to three basic functions: to assist in setting up purchase specifications based on house requirements; to assist in making "buy-or-make decisions"; and to maintain a continuous testing program to monitor costs, quality, taste, and presentation of food used and served in the operation.

Composition of the Committee

The testing committee in a typical, large, commercial hotel will be used to demonstrate the organization and activities of such a committee. It can be easily adapted to practically any type of large food operation.

The top decision maker of any operation should be the executive chairman of the testing committee. This would mean the general manager of a hotel, restaurant, or motor inn, the director of a dietary department in a hospital, the general manager of an institutional food service, or any other person in a position to back up decisions of the food testing committee.

The regular chairman of the committee should be the food service manager of the hotel or his counterpart in other operations. In Holiday Inns, for example, the assistant innkeeper is often in charge of the food and beverage department. In some companies the resident manager is the active supervisor of the department, and in still others the executive-assistant manager for food and beverage operations is responsible.

The executive secretary of the committee (not the secretary who keeps the notes) does most of the research and work, and this position should be filled by the company's purchasing agent or food buyer. The balance of the committee consists of persons from the various departments, for they are more likely to reflect the taste and wishes of the general public than a committee made up entirely of persons in the food production department.

Certainly the committee should include the production manager, the chef, the steward, the catering manager, a dining room manager, if available, the food and beverage controller, the receiving clerk, the head stockroom person, the housekeeper, the senior room clerk, the public relations manager, and, on a rotating basis, the sous chef, the bell captain, a room clerk, a cook, a pantry person, a butcher if one is used, and a guest of the hotel who volunteers to serve, if this can be arranged.

Basic Requirements of the Program

If a testing program, backed by a testing committee, is to prove effective and worth the time and expense involved, there are a few basic requirements or ground rules that should be observed throughout the program. The most important one, perhaps, is that the findings and decisions of the committee must be accepted by all committee members and by management. Management must then see that the decisions are enforced. Complete written minutes of all committee meetings should be kept and signed by management.

Testing should be done in a suitable environment. An adequate test kitchen is rarely available, and the tendency is to meet in a kitchen where it is convenient to cook or cut up some item. This is, of course, wrong. Participating members cannot help but be distracted; there are too many comments from persons who are not involved; and, because the facilities are uncomfortable, there is a tendency to rush decisions. An operation large enough to support such a program generally has at least one banquet kitchen that can be set up as a suitable test kitchen. An employees' cafeteria can often be used in the afternoon. And, when butcher tests are being made, the butcher shop is an ideal place for the committee to meet.

Many large food-processing corporations have complete test kitchens with both gas and electric ranges, fluorescent and incandescent lighting, and even provision for ultraviolet lights to disguise the appearance of food when making taste tests. Although such an elaborate testing environment may be necessary for large institutional food-processing companies, it is not necessary for the average hotel, hospital, or restaurant.

The committee should meet regularly, with provision for special meetings when a question arises that needs immediate action. If a department head who is a member of the committee is unavailable, there should be an alternate who can attend the meeting and has the power to vote.

Testing should be done on a blind basis and should be carried out in accord with specific procedures. There are three stages: the first should be restricted to selection of quality; the second, to price; the third, to identifying the product and supplier if necessary.

During the first stage when the quality or the appearance of a prepared dish is being considered, the committee should conduct the procedure in silence so that no one will influence another person's thinking. Unless strict silence is maintained, an aggressive person in a responsible position could influence the activities of the committee, thereby making the committee's activities useless and the specifications worthless. If an employee with special interests has a chance to offer a comment in a testing committee meeting, he is in a position to pursue questionable activities. Nor should anyone know the cost of products being tested until after quality selection has been made. The price often reveals the source.

A committee should not limit itself to just one selection. There are often two or three products of equal quality or of a quality suitable for the needs of the operation. By providing the purchasing department with an alternative, the food buyer can "shop" within a quality and a price range. The voting of the committee should be a matter of record, and voting procedures should be set.

Other requirements should be kept in mind by the testing committee. Any samples should resemble each other as closely as possible (aging in beef, cut and trim on meats, size of boxes or cans, method of cooking). Samples should also be selected from regular stock, and no purveyor should be informed that a test is planned or be permitted to send in a special sample. If new products are to be tested, it is advisable for the food buyer either to buy samples from a retail outlet, obtain them from another hotel or operation, or go to the purveyor's place of business and pick samples at random.

Samples should be identified by code numbers or letters, and only the buyer and the committee chairman should be able to identify them. It is preferable for the buyer not to vote or express an opinion, and the chairman should not open the identification envelopes until at least a quality standard has been established. An important decision should never be based on a single test; a series of tests is needed to arrive at a fair decision.

"Make-or-Buy" Decisions

These decisions represent one of the most important responsibilities of the testing committee. Whether to make a food item or to buy it prepared and whether to buy primal cuts of meat and butcher them or to buy precuts may depend on a number of factors. The decision is occasionally determined by the physical setup of the kitchen and storage areas or by the type and nature of the food service. The decision may also depend on either economic or quality considerations, though one is frequently sacrificed for the other. The following questions must be asked in order for decisions to be made.

Will the Customer Buy It? If the quality of a prepared item is not up to the standards of the operation, then the answer is obvious. Often, however, there is so little difference between the item to be made and the item already made that the decision requires very objective thinking by committee members. If the vote of the committee results in a tie, management has to decide.

Will Labor Costs Really Be Reduced? One case where a wrong decision was based on faulty research has already been cited in this chapter. Many similar decisions have been made without full consideration of contributing circumstances.

Some time can be saved in buying a product that is already prepared, but it is not a saving unless it is reflected on the time card. If an employee cannot be eliminated, overtime cannot be reduced, or the saved time cannot be used to improve quality or relieve another department, thus resulting in improved sales and profits, there is no saving.

Sometimes a decision has to be made as to whether to open or close a butcher shop, a pastry shop, or a bakeshop. With delivery costs soaring, some operators have decided to reopen pastry shops and bakeshops and to expand their butcher shops. Within today's market, any full-menu operation in a hotel or restaurant doing $2.5 million in gross business (or an institution doing an equal volume of business) can support a bakeshop as well as a pastry shop. When sales reach $1.5 million, management should take a hard look at the possibility of opening or closing butcher and pastry shops. This seems to be the point at which a decision is required.

Institutional operations, which are often smaller and have limited menus, have generally found it impractical to operate their own butcher shops. They find that it is more to their advantage to purchase prefabricated, fresh meats.

Are Food Costs Really Being Controlled? There are many who claim it is easier to control food costs by using "prefab" meats and "prepared" foods. It goes without saying that this makes it easier to determine portion costs and to control portion sales—on paper. It must be recognized, however, that the use of such products also makes it easier to pilfer. Loss from pilferage can exceed the savings involved. According to some successful hotel operators, whenever controlled tests have been made during the past thirty years food costs have gone up from two to four points as a result of the introduction of prefab, preprepared, or preportioned foods.

Another consideration intrudes at this point. Most authorities on personnel and production standards claim that, as far as can be determined, one-half of the average employee's time on duty is nonproductive. Even if this claim is only half true, the possibilities for savings and increased production based on this nonproductive time might reduce the number of previously prepared items needed. The next question, then, is: "How good is the control system?" That is management's problem, not the testing committee's.

Is the Merchandising Plan Well Developed? There are instances where the merchandising plan affects a food operation. Sometimes a pastry shop or a butcher shop operates far below capacity and at a loss because neither the menu nor the menu merchandising promotes the products of those departments. In properties doing a large banquet business, for example, it is often easier for the banquet manager to sell an "Ice Cream Bombe, Fantasia" than an "Angel Cake with Fresh Strawberries."

For years the Plaza Hotel in New York City featured a "Stuffed Breast of Capon a la Plaza" (made from a whole chicken) that cost the hotel just half the price of a prefab product, and they had the legs at no cost for other dishes. Employees often appreciate a freshly made chicken potpie instead of leftover roast, and potpie costs much less than pot roast.

Butcher Test Card

"Make-or-buy" decisions have to be based on recorded butcher and cooking loss tests, plus consideration of the labor and merchandising aspects. It is fortunate that the procedures and records used in making such tests are fairly well standardized and followed.

Large operators often have their own testing records, but all establishments need certain basic information. The sample shown in Exhibit 7-4 is a typical butcher and cooking loss test card. Providing the information on this card is the food and beverage controller's responsibility, but the testing committee should insist that the tests be made and the results recorded.

Sample Specifications

Excerpts from a set of specifications now in use in a large chain food operation are shown in Exhibit 7-5. Many of the points shown there have been discussed throughout this chapter.

Score Sheets

Score sheets for taste tests (see Exhibit 7-6) should provide room for comments that can be used by the scorer to support his vote. This forces the committee member to give full attention to the test so that he can support his opinion. Analysis of the comments is often revealing and more useful than the arithmetical score.

Some Facts Based on an Actual Testing Program

From an actual series of fifty tests on various food items, the following interesting facts and perhaps a valuable lesson were learned:

1. Only two times out of fifty was the highest-priced item judged to be of the best quality.
2. In eighteen times out of fifty the lowest-priced item in the test was judged to be of the best quality.
3. At no time was the lowest-priced item judged to be last in quality.
4. At no time was it impossible to accept as an alternate a nearly equal item, and thirty-five times out of fifty it was possible to accept a third alternate item as being of nearly equal quality.
5. At no time did any one product receive all first-place votes.
6. The average saving in purchase price between the product selected and the highest-priced item in each category was 28 percent.

Testing, it would appear, is worthwhile.

BUTCHER TEST CARD

Item_____ _____Grade_____Date_____

Pieces_____Weighing_____lbs._____oz.   Average weight_____

Total cost $_____at $_____per_____Supplier_____Hotel_____

Breakdown	No.	Weight		Ratio to total weight	Value per pound	Total value	Cost of each		Portion		Cost factor per	
		lb.	oz.				lb.	oz.	Size	Cost	Pound	Portion
Total												

Item   Portion size   Portion cost factor

COOKING LOSS

Cooked_____Hours_____Minutes at_____Degrees

_____Hours_____Minutes at_____Degrees

Breakdown	No.	Weight		Ratio to total weight	Value per pound	Total value	Cost of each		Portion		Cost factor per	
		lb.	oz.				lb.	oz.	Size	Cost	Pound	Portion
Original weight												
Trimmed weight												
Loss in trimming												
Cooked weight												
Loss in cooking												
Bones and trim												
Loss in slicing												
Salable meat												
Salable meat												
Remarks:												

Item   Portion size   Portion cost factor

Exhibit 7-4. Butcher test card: (a) Front, uncooked item; (b) Back, cooked item (Courtesy: Sheraton Corporation of America, Boston, Massachusetts)

FOOD PURCHASE AND RECEIVING SPECIFICATIONS

Company: _____   Date: _____

Item	Unit	Trade specs.	U.S. Grade	Detailed requirements	Weight or count	Required per 100 portions
BEEF						
Rib, roast ready	lb.	#109	Choice	Top half of grade, cryovac aged three weeks from date of kill, three-inch trim on loin end, four-inch trim on chuck end, no fat over one-inch	20-22 lbs.	150 lbs.
Rib-eye roll, boneless	lb.	#112	Choice	Top half of grade, three weeks aged, all outside fat removed except one grade stamp	10-12 lbs.	50 lbs.
Strip loin—boneless, short cut	lb.	#180	Choice	Top half of grade, cryovac aged three weeks from date of kill, three-inch trim at rib end, two-inch trim at butt end, no fat over one inch, average 1/2 inch	12-14 lbs.	100 lbs.
Strip loin—boneless, steak ready	lb.	#180 Modified	Choice	Same as #180 above except trim one inch from eye of meat	10-12 lbs.	85 lbs.
Top sirloin, butt, boneless	lb.	#184	Choice	Top half of grade, cryovac aged four weeks from date of kill, one inch maximum fat, cut western style	12-14 lbs.	75 lbs.
Full tenderloin, regular	lb.	#189	Steer	Fat not to exceed 3/4 inch at gland, tenderloin to be 1/4 naked, no scores over 1/2 inch, must be three inches minimum at center of cut	7-8 lbs.	50 lbs.
Short loin, regular	lb.	#173	Choice	Top third of grade, dry aged three weeks from date of kill, soft bone cut with no cartilage from hip, fat covering not to exceed one inch, flank not to be over six inches from eye of meat	36-38 lbs.	150 lbs.
Full tenderloin special (also known as silver skin)	lb.	#190	Steer	Same as #189 above except all fat removed leaving silver skin	5-6 lbs.	40 lbs.
Square-cut chuck boneless clod cut	lb.	#116	Choice	Lean, fat not to exceed one inch at any surface, fresh cut	58-65 lbs.	50 lbs.
Round-rump and shank off	lb.	#164	Prime	Must be aged three weeks minimum, fat not to exceed one inch at any surface, cut through round bone posterior to ball joint	60-75 lbs.	60 lbs.
Round inside—top round boneless	lb.	#168	Prime	Must be aged three weeks minimum, fat not to exceed one inch at any surface	22-25 lbs.	50 lbs.

(handwritten note: IMPS — near Trade specs. column)

Item	Unit	Spec	Grade	Description	Weight	Quantity
Round bottom—gooseneck boneless	lb.	#170	Choice	Must be aged three weeks maximum, fat not to exceed one inch at any surface, top 1/2 of grade	25-30 lbs.	50 lbs.
Corned brisket—deckle off boneless	lb.	—	Choice	Lean-cured kosher-style brisket, to be trimmed to specification, cryovac packaged	12-14 lbs.	60 lbs.
Ground beef special	lb.	#137	—	25 percent trimmable fat, ground twice, final grind 1/2 to 3/16 inch holes in plate, no bull, stag, cow, or variety meats, no additives, fresh-ground on day of delivery	—	40 lbs.
POULTRY						
Chickens, broilers	lb.	Fresh	A	Eviscerated, no necks or giblets, White Cross preferred, ice packed	2, 2½, or 3 lbs.	50 birds
Chickens, roasting	lb.	Fresh	A	Eviscerated, no necks or giblets, White Cross preferred, ice packed	4, 4½, or 5 lbs.	100 lbs.
Fowl, stewing	lb.	Fresh	A	Eviscerated, White Rocks preferred, ice packed	5-6 lbs.	75 lbs.
Turkeys, toms, roasting	lb.	Fresh or frozen	A	Eviscerated, Beltsville or Wagon strain, northern-raised birds preferred, cryovac wrapped, box packed	22-24 lbs. 24-26 lbs.	75 lbs. 70 lbs.
Duckling	lb.	Frozen	A	Eviscerated, Peking strain, no necks or giblets, cryovac wrapped, box packed	4½-5 lbs.	50 birds
Turkeys, hens, roasting	lb.	Fresh or frozen	A	Same specs as turkeys, toms, roasting	10-12 lbs. 12-14 lbs.	75 lbs.
EGGS						
Boiling, white	Doz.	Extra large	AA	Clean, not oiled, white or cream-colored shells, 30 dozen, cardboard cases	54 lbs., gross 48 lbs., net	½ case
Cooking, white	Doz.	Large	A	Clean, not oiled, white shells only, cardboard cases, 30 dozen	52 lbs., gross 46 lbs., net	½ case
Bakers, mixed	Doz.	Large	A	Clean, mixed colors permitted, no cracks or checks, 30 dozen, wood or cardboard cases	52 lbs., gross 46 lbs., net	½ case

Exhibit 7-5. Table showing food purchasing and receiving specifications, by item

Item	Unit	Trade specs.	U.S. Grade	Detailed requirements	Weight or count	Required per 100 portions
FRESH VEGETABLES						
Asparagus—jumbo	Crate	Fancy	Fancy	Loose or bunch as specified, fresh, 90 percent all green stems, crisp, no spreading tips, 5/8 inch minimum diameter per spear	35 lbs., gross 30 lbs., net	2 crates
String beans	Hamper	Fancy	Fancy	Round, uniform size, clean, fresh, crisp, tender, dark green color, free of leaves and stems, length of beans four inches to six inches	35 lbs., gross 28 lbs., net	1 hamper
Onions, Spanish	Bag	#1	#1	Mature, firm, uniform shape and size, free from damage or decay, three inches minimum diameter	50 lbs., net	Cooking or slicing, 10 lbs.
Potatoes, baking	Box	Fancy	Fancy	Idaho Russets when available, Russet Burbanks and Norgold Russets acceptable, packed 70-80-90 as specified, uniform in size and shape, free of cuts, dirt, and decay	Box filled, count not to vary over 3 percent as ordered, minimum 55 inches gross	100 potatoes
Tomatoes, fresh	Lug	Fancy	#1	Firm ripe, good red color, uniform size, color, and condition, free of scab, nailhead, bruises, and rots, order by size 5 x 6, 6 x 6, or 6 x 7	33 lbs., gross 30 lbs., net	1 lug for salads
Lettuce, iceberg	Carton	Fancy	#1	California or Arizona lettuce preferred, heads to be fresh, firm, and green, free from decay, burn, mildew, dirt, and burst, wrapper leaves not to exceed eight, twenty-four heads per carton	43 lbs., gross 40 lbs., net	1 carton for salads
CANNED GOODS						
Green beans	Case	Fancy	A	Blue Lake variety preferred, cut or whole as ordered, whole beans No. 2 sieve	6 No. 10 per case or 24 No. 2½	4 No. 10 or 20 No. 2½
Carrots, whole	Case	Fancy	A	Specify 100 or 125 count or 200 or 250 count per No. 10 can, good color, no broken or blemished carrots, water and light sugar pack	6 No. 10 per case	4 No. 10
Tomatoes, cooking	Case	Extra-standard	B	Jersey, Michigan, or midwestern pack preferred, minimum drained weight per No. 10 can, 63.5-68 oz., tomatoes to be 70 percent whole	6 No. 10 per case	6 No. 10 or for cooking

Item	Unit	Grade		Specification		
Tomato juice	Case	Fancy	A	Fancy California tomato juice preferred, Sacramento brand where available, red, heavy, sweet juice specified	12 No. 5 per case	10 No. 5
Green olives (queen)	Case	Fancy	A	Fancy Spanish queen olive desired (colossal—80/90 per kilo, 200/225 per kilo, jumbo—100/110 per kilo, 250/275 per gallon), minimum drained weight per gallon, 86 oz., packed stuffed, whole, or pitted as ordered	6 gallons per case	2 gallons 3 gallons
Peaches, yellow cling	Case	Choice	Choice	Specify halves, quarters, or sliced, packed in medium syrup, size 30 to 35 in No. 10 can, full pack with minimum of syrup	6 No. 10 per case	6 No. 10

Exhibit 7-5 (continued)

TASTE TEST—SCORE SHEET

Product: _____   Date: _____

Item	First (5 points)	Second (3 points)	Third (2 points)	Fourth (1 point)	Remarks	Total points
A						
B						
C						
D						
E						
F						
G						
H						
I						
J						
K						
L						
M						
N						

Grading to be based on flavor, tenderness, color, shrinkage, aroma, juiciness, and general appearance.

Additional remarks: _____

_____

_____

Signature

Exhibit 7-6. Score sheet for taste test

Part II
COST CONTROL AS RELATED TO PURCHASING

8 Receiving: A Hidden Hard Spot

Purpose: To explain the organization and functioning of the receiving department in a food service organization. Consideration is given to the receiving clerk's job; the forms, tools, and procedures used; and controls available for the receiving system.

INTRODUCTION

The functions of the receiving department are of critical importance in terms of both cost and quality control. It is through the receiving department that the operator accepts legal ownership and physical possession of the goods. Competent management and conscientious employees can, of course, catch and rectify mistakes made in receiving, but such mistakes should be caught at this point, so it is essential that the receiving department develop sound operating procedures and practices.

Receiving can be considered the reverse side of the purchasing coin. As indicated in Chapter 6, "The Mechanics of Buying," many of the items that make up the purchasing procedure can be programmed for computer use. The close relationship between purchasing and receiving would seem to indicate that the receivers must be trained to check in computerized purchases and pass them on to a computerized storeroom and the programmed issuing function. Chapter 11, "The Computer and the Purchasing Agent," explains the procedural steps in receiving under these conditions.

WHAT IS A "HARD SPOT"?

In the corporate vernacular, a hard spot is an opportunity for a profit that has been overlooked. This definition certainly justifies the title of this chapter.

It has long been recognized in the food business that the receiving clerk is often overworked, poorly trained, unappreciated, and underpaid. Often many millions of dollars worth of merchandise pass through the hands of a receiving clerk, whose job it is to see that it is accounted for and that it meets all specifications. That person is probably the sole judge of 90 percent of the merchandise delivered. In large operations purchasing several million dollars worth of food per year, the receiving of merchandise is often left to a storeroom clerk, a timekeeper, or a kitchen steward, and sometimes to the food buyer. Under such circumstances, there is no way that a satisfactory receiving job can be done.

Even when a receiving department is properly set up under the control and supervision of the accounting department, the receiving department is often left to fend for itself. Too often the receiving clerk is given a few directions and then practically forgotten by the controller, which means that he is often adopted by the food and beverage controller, the kitchen manager, the chef, the steward, or some other interested party.

In terms of the food purchasing function in the food business, it is said that a good food buyer constitutes the head, while a good set of specifications is the backbone. It should also be recognized that the receiving clerk serves as the arms and the legs and that he must be ambitious, honest, and alert. Because of this, it should also be recognized that the person should be well trained and well paid.

When a scandal related to purchasing erupts in some food department, it appears that the trouble generally starts in the receiving department. The findings of outside investigators generally show that, where there are problems involving the receiving function, receiving clerks are somewhat vague as to who their boss is and are poorly supervised; the receiving office is poorly located in relation to the storeroom and receiving dock; scales are inadequate; there are no written instructions as to how the department should be operated; accounting forms are inadequate; and there is no backing from management.

Merchandise enters the food operation through the receiving department so that is where short weights begin, poor quality is passed, double billing is made, prices are inflated, excessive trims and mislabeled merchandise are accepted, substitutes for size and quality are passed, spoiled merchandise is dumped, inflated orders are accepted, home deliveries start—any of which could encourage a series of nonviolent crimes. Investigations have shown that food costs can rise by as many as five or six points because of practices that start in a receiving department. That is where small things begin and grow to serious proportions.

A GOOD RECEIVING SYSTEM

Before any receiving system can be set up, management has to outline a plan that suits the operation involved. It should be patterned after a system that has proved satisfactory elsewhere in the food industry, and then it should be followed by all involved. Unless the plan is written out in sufficient detail to establish responsibility for each part and unless there is a time schedule for the completion of the plan, there is little chance for success. If management cannot handle such an assignment, outside professional assistance should be sought. The major concerns are:

1. proper organizational relationships among the receiving department, the accounting department, and operations;
2. adequate facilities and proper tools in a convenient location;
3. the need for a competent, trained receiving clerk adequately compensated; and
4. continuous checks by those within the house and outsiders on receiving.

The receiving of all food, beverages, and operating supplies is traditionally the responsibility of the accounting department under the controller. The receiving clerk should be a recognized member of the accounting department, directly responsible to the controller and assisted by the food and beverage manager. It is imperative that management support the independence of the receiving clerk's office. The prerogatives of the receiving clerk with relationship to the food buyer, the chef, the food and beverage manager, and other department heads should be clearly spelled out in the organization chart and in the operating manual covering the operation.

A receiving clerk cannot be any better than the controller to whom he reports. Many controllers are not particularly interested in the food business, and they do not take the time to give the proper backing and supervision to the receiving clerk. This minimizes the effectiveness of the receiving department. Some controllers arrive at their office around 9:00 A.M. or even 10:00 A.M., but they work later in the evening. By the time he arrives, three-fourths of the merchandise going through the receiving department is already checked in and is in the storeroom.

Facilities

Location. The receiving clerk's office and receiving area should be located as near as possible to the receiving dock and adjacent to the storeroom and the food and beverage control office. The receiving office should not be either in the storeroom or in the food control office; it should be located adjacent to them. The front of the receiving clerk's office should be glass in order that, as he works at his desk, he can see all of the activity at the entrance to the storeroom. And all of the merchandise coming in or leaving the property should pass his office. There should be enough space outside the office so that merchandise does not pile up, thereby making the receiving function a rush job.

Equipment. In larger operations the receiving clerk should be provided with adequate scales built into the floor. They facilitate loading and unloading. There should also be a small platform scale, perhaps table mounted, for weighing smaller items.

For the average-sized operation there are varied sizes and types of scales designed to serve specific needs. These range from the plan "balance arm" platform model to the sophisticated automatic recording ones with ounce calibrations and fluid recording. Some scales can even be programmed into a central, in-house computer, complete with scanner, but such equipment would only be needed in a large warehouse operation.

The office and receiving area should be well lit and should meet the sanitary requirements of the Occupational Safety and Health Act (see Chapter 3), and both the office and its contents should be adequately secured.

The receiving office should be equipped with such other "tools of the trade" as rulers and other measuring devices; receiving sheets; receiving tickets and dispenser; credit memo forms; forms for goods received without invoice; an operation manual for the receiving department; a complete set of receiving specifications (duplicating the purchasing specifications); instant-reading thermometers; strap cutters, crate hammers, small crowbars, a cardboard box cutter, and a sharp knife or two for cutting merchandise for inspection; and adequate filing cabinets.

THE RECEIVING CLERK

What kind of person usually takes a position as a receiving clerk? A young, ambitious person might use the position to gain experience needed to take on a better job, or a semiretired or a handicapped person proud of being able to work can often perform the tasks. Then there are the "sharpies" looking for a place to "make a fast buck" and move on; the lazy incompetents who do only what they must to hold a job; and others who might or might not be capable of doing the job, depending upon the amount of training and supervision needed and provided.

The personnel department should take the initiative in locating and screening applicants for the position, checking qualifications and experience. Then the applicant should be approved by the controller, the personnel department, and the operation manager. If an applicant has had good experience and is unemployed for no clear reason, one should be wary. A good receiving clerk with a good record is seldom available through the open job market.

The best way to find a good candidate is often by promotion from within the present storeroom staff, the food and beverage control staff, the accounting office, or the steward's department. Sometimes a cook who has had institutional training is interested in obtaining managerial experience to further his career, and he is willing to start in the receiving department.

One successful chain food operator has a policy of paying key department heads 25 percent more than the normal rate. This includes the receiving clerk. The policy has apparently paid off many times.

Even if a receiving clerk is experienced in food operations and has a good background in food receiving, management should provide for a continuous training program. Some large food operations have a program whereby certain positions are rotated on a periodic basis. This plan works quite well when there is adequate supervision.

Continuous Training

Once a receiving clerk has been given a set of purchase specifications that he can use for receiving, he should understand that these specifications cannot be changed by any one individual unless such a change has been passed by the purchasing committee and approved by management. Because he is involved with the food buyer, the food production manager, the chef, storeroom personnel, and the food and beverage controller, the receiving clerk might find that these people will contribute to his training and knowledge.

Because the quality of fresh foods varies so much from week to week, the food buyer should, on a regular basis, take the receiving clerk to the market to round out his training. It is a good idea to include the chef on occasion. Then food buyer, chef, and receiving clerk look at

the same merchandise at the same time and agree on the quality that is acceptable. If the food buyer does not ask the receiving clerk to accompany him, the controller should suggest to the general manager that the food buyer do so. One very wise food buyer invites the receiving clerk to sit with him while he meets with salespeople. It is well known that salespeople are among the best trainers in the business, whether the training be good or bad.

THE RECEIVING OPERATION

The hours that the receiving operation is open and manned should be coordinated with delivery practices. In downtown areas of big cities, where traffic is heavy, it might be necessary to open the receiving department at 6:00 A.M., and all receiving, other than emergency deliveries, is generally completed by 3:00 P.M. In suburban areas, on the other hand, delivery trucks might not arrive until midmorning. There is no point in having the receiving dock open if no deliveries are expected.

The food buyer should cooperate with the receiving clerk and the various dealers to work out a schedule of deliveries that is satisfactory to both the dealer and the receiver. Because of high delivery costs and the prospect of higher ones, the food buyer may be able to realize substantial savings just by establishing economical delivery schedules with purveyors. The advisability of having deliveries every other day, twice a week, or weekly has already been reviewed in Chapter 6, along with possibilities for savings in the monthly purchasing of canned goods and other food supplies.

Saturday and Sunday deliveries should be made only if there is a real emergency. When there are many such emergencies, the controller and management should investigate. Either someone is not determining the needs of the operation in a systematic manner, or someone is intentionally bypassing normal purchasing and receiving procedures.

Even if there is a regular schedule for the receiving office to be open and for most deliveries to be made, some deliveries may be made before the receiving office is open. The receiving clerk should work out specific instructions for that person in the food department who will be signing for such deliveries and checking on the shipment. Someone in a position of responsibility should check periodically to determine how well this early morning or late evening receiving is being executed.

The set of purchasing specifications that also serves as receiving specifications should be posted behind glass so that every page can be seen by everyone involved, including deliverypeople, the receiving clerk, or anyone working with the receiving clerk who performs the receiving functions. If the receiving clerk is referring to the specifications on a regular basis, truck drivers notice this and report the fact back to the dealers, which is exactly the intent of a good receiving department.

When there is a blind receiving system, deliverypeople bring only a list of the items in the shipment. The receiving clerk must then count and weigh everything that comes in to complete the receiving sheet. The theory is that the invoice, with the dealer's weights and prices, is sent to the accounting department, where it is matched with the prices quoted to the food buyer and the receiving tickets. If everything matches, monthly statements can be paid after management approves them. Some receiving systems even include scales that stamp weights on delivery slips. Computerized scales and scanners are also being used in the receiving function. Blind receiving has not proved practical because it is difficult to match invoices with delivery slips, and extra staff is needed to compare the various records.

A receiving clerk should be in a position to accept or reject merchandise on the spot. If there are any weight shortages or there is a disagreement on count or specification, he should be able to adjust the delivery slip or invoice at once or reject questionable items. Most satisfactory receiving systems in use today require that the deliveryperson bring an invoice with merchandise so that it can be checked for accuracy at the time of delivery. Any variations can be handled either with a credit memorandum or a statement of goods received without invoice.

FORMS IN USE

Receiving Sheets and Tickets

A properly organized receiving department for any type of operation, including a food service, should be charged with receiving all merchandise that enters the building. One point of entry makes it easier to check everything into the building, keep the proper control records, and see that all merchandise meets the specifications and matches the orders, that invoices are complete, and that pricing is accurate.

In some operations where highly technical merchandise is delivered, it is sometimes preferable to set up a food and beverage receiving point near the food and beverage storeroom and another receiving point near the engineering department, medical storeroom, or housekeeping department. Regardless of where the receiving point is located and what is received at any one point, there are certain basic requirements for good receiving that must be met to avoid possible losses. This chapter, which deals with the receiving of food and food supplies, also shows how the receiving of beverages fits.

Everything that passes through the receiving department in a day should be listed on a receiving sheet on which are recorded the activities of the department. These records can always be used as the basis for establishing accounting controls needed to safeguard a company's assets.

There does not appear to be a single form of receiving record that is really adequate for writing up food and beverage items and other food department supplies, such as soap powders, paper supplies, china, glass, silver, pots and pans, and some three hundred to four hundred other items used in the operation of the food department. The three forms in general use today have been utilized for some time, and they comprise the receiving clerk's daily report (Exhibit 8-1), which is used for all incoming food. Miscellaneous supplies can be written up either on the regular receiving sheet or on a receiving ticket, and a copy then attached to the delivery slip or invoice that accompanies the incoming merchandise.

A separate sheet is generally used for the receiving of alcoholic beverages because many states require certain information regarding the purchasing and receiving of them. It is best to record this information for the accounting department on what is commonly known as the beverage receiving clerk's daily report (Exhibit 8-2) at the point where the beverages enter the operation.

A receiving sheet (see Exhibit 8-3) should be written up in detail so that there is no question as to what came into the operation, what goods were received without invoice, what credits were taken for any merchandise that did not arrive according to the invoice, and what merchandise was taken out through the receiving department. Some receiving clerks merely write down the name of the dealer and the total of the bill on the receiving sheets "to save time" but, for all practical purposes, this type of entry is useless.

After the receiving sheet has been completed, showing dealers, items, quantities, prices, and extensions, the columns should be totaled and the sheets signed by the receiving clerk each day. The receiving sheet is normally prepared in duplicate. The original, with copies of all invoices, credit memorandums, and lists of goods received without invoice, is sent first to the food and beverage control office, then to the food buyer, the general manager, and on to the controller for payment. The copy is retained in the receiving department. In larger operations it has proved helpful to prepare it in triplicate, with one copy being forwarded to the general manager's office and on to the controller, the second being kept at the receiving point, and a third copy being used by the food and beverage controller.

Individual receiving tickets are useful when there are only a few large shipments of supplies, but the difficulty of handling the many separate pieces of paper that would be required for receiving food makes this system impractical.

Receiving Stamps

Each invoice attached to the original of the receiving sheet should be stamped with a receiving stamp that has space for the date, the initials of the persons approving price, quantity, quality, and extensions, the controller's initials, and the general manager's final approval for payment.

The receiving stamp should be set up to show the following:

Date _____

Received by _____

Weight and count OK _____

Prices OK _____

Quality OK _____

Food and beverage control OK _____

General manager OK _____

This may seem to be a lot of work, but if

SCA-251 PRINTED IN U.S.A.

RECEIVING CLERK'S DAILY REPORT

NO. _____

DATE _____

Purveyor	QUAN.	UNIT	DESCRIPTION	✓	UNIT PRICE	AMOUNT	TOTAL AMOUNT	PURCHASE JOURNAL DISTRIBUTION		
								FOOD DIRECT	FOOD STORES	SUNDRIES

SIGNATURE _____

Exhibit 8-1. Form for receiving clerk's daily report

BEVERAGE RECEIVING CLERK'S DAILY REPORT

No. ______

DATE ______

	QUAN.	UNIT	DESCRIPTION	✓	UNIT PRICE	AMOUNT	AMOUNT TOTAL	CHAMPAGNE & WINE	LIQUOR	BEER	BEER CONTAINER	MINERAL	MINERAL CONTAINER	OTHERS

PRINTED IN U.S.A.

______ SIGNATURE

Exhibit 8-2. Form for beverage receiving clerk's daily report

RETURN TO
ACCOUNTING DEPT

RECEIVING RECORD

No. 55006 _____   Date_____

Received from_____

Address_____

Order No._____ Complete **Partial**		**Delivered to**_____**Dept.**	

No.	DESCRIPTION	Via	Freight _____ Parcel Post Express City	Prepaid C.O.D.
			Charges	$
			Total	$
			Weight	

Receiving Clerk _____

Quantity	ARTICLES	Amount
	1	

Counted, inspected and received in stock _____19 ____

By_____**Department Clerk**

7/64E 0-325451-T

Exhibit 8-3. Form for recording merchandise received

<table>
<tr><td colspan="8">HOTEL_____
CITY_____ DATE_____
NOTICE OF ERROR CORRECTION

PURVEYOR_____
SHIPPER_____
    ATTENTION:
    CORRECTIONS HAVE BEEN MADE ON YOUR INVOICE AS SHOWN BELOW.

INVOICE NO._____   DATE_____</td></tr>
</table>

ITEM	REASON FOR CORRECTION	UNIT PRICE	YOUR BILLING	CORRECTED BILLING	DIF-FERENCE
	KINDLY ADJUST YOUR RECORDS ACCORDINGLY. HOTEL_____ BY_____ TITLE_____		TOTAL CORRECTIONS TOTAL YOUR INVOICE OUR CORRECTED TOTAL		
SCA 315	PRINTED IN U.S.A.				

Exhibit 8-4. Form used for correcting an invoice

approvals are not obtained on a regular daily basis, a control system eventually breaks down, with resulting operational losses.

It is important that the general manager of the operation get the receiving sheet and invoices every day so that he is aware of what is being purchased. A good general manager can spot irregularities, excess purchases, changes in cost prices that necessitate menu changes or changes in dealers, and many other variants from the norm.

Credit Memorandums

Most good receiving systems provide for the use of a credit memorandum (see Exhibit 8-4) when merchandise is returned, when credit is taken for a short weight or count, when a price is corrected, or when salvage, such as grease, bones, or egg cartons, is sold. Some receiving clerks merely make a notation on the invoice, but this system breaks down when there is no invoice or the deliveryman does not turn in the corrected delivery slip.

The credit memorandum is generally prepared in duplicate, with the original going back to the purveyor via the deliveryman and the copy being sent on with the invoices to the controller after being noted on the receiving sheet.

Goods Received Without Invoice

To avoid the complications and disagreements that arise when merchandise is received without an invoice, the receiving clerk should fill out a goods received without invoice (GRWI) form (see Exhibit 8-5). The form is generally made up in duplicate, with the original going to the accounting department after being noted on the receiving sheet and the

SHERATON CORPORATION OF AMERICA

GOODS RECEIVED WITHOUT INVOICE

No

RECEIVED FROM:_____

_____   DATE_____

QUANTITY	ITEM	UNIT PRICE	AMOUNT

Signature

SCA-314   Printed in U.S.A.

Exhibit 8-5. Form indicating goods received without an invoice   (Courtesy: Sheraton Corporation of America, Boston, Massachusetts)

duplicate remaining with the receiving clerk.

When the invoice arrives, the accounting department, having been forewarned, sends the invoice to the receiving clerk, who attaches the duplicate GRWI to the invoice, writes the invoice up completely on the receiving sheet, and sends the invoice, plus the duplicate GRWI form, through the regular channels for payment.

FUNCTIONS OF THE DEPARTMENT

Weighing, Counting, and Measuring

These functions are the most important activities of the receiving department and the main reason for having an independent department. The words seem simple, but this is where questionable practices carried on by smart dealers are begun and the worth of a good receiving clerk is demonstrated.

The following are good rules for any receiving clerk to follow:

1. Remove the paper or containers from turkeys, meats, and other wrapped items or take a standard allowance that is agreeable to the purveyors.

2. Never accept weights stamped on a box or container if it can be opened and weighed or counted.

3. Check the weights of such incoming merchandise as eggs, oranges, lemons, lettuce, tomatoes, butter, and coffee against the weights that

appear in the receiving specifications.

4. Weigh containers of frozen foods on a spot-check basis.

5. Count or weigh bags containing such items as carrots, beets, cabbage, potatoes, dry beans, rice, and flour to determine whether the weights match the invoices.

6. Check individual weights of melons to see if they meet the specifications.

7. Count baking potatoes, melons, tomatoes, grapefruit, lemons, oranges, apples, and any other items sold by size or count.

8. When weighing large quantities of like items such as hams, ribs, strips, top butts, and poultry, weigh the total gross and then spot-check individual items to see that weight ranges are according to specifications.

9. If using meat tags, average individual weights for the shipment to save time.

10. Keep a ruler tied to the scale for checking length and trim of meats so that when the receiving clerk finds excess trim and the dealer says that the meat stretched in handling, even though it has a bone in it, the company will know enough to get a new dealer.

11. Weigh sealed cases since a case can be opened and two or three bottles or cans removed without leaving a mark on the case, or the count could have been short when the case was originally closed.

Judging Quality

The judging of quality at the receiving point is the most difficult part of the receiving clerk's work. More disagreements arise over quality than any other single phase of the receiving procedure.

For many years, the kitchen manager,

chef, or a food and beverage manager passed on the quality of merchandise. This practically eliminated any need for an independent receiving department. In an efficient department, however, a receiving clerk is trained by the food buyer, in cooperation with the chef, to reflect the opinion of the food buyer, the food and beverage manager, and the chef in judging quality. If there is a real question as to the quality of some product, the problem should be referred to the purchasing committee for final decision, subject to the general manager's approval. The smart receiving clerk calls for help when there is a doubt in his mind, and it is this sharing of decision making with others that builds confidence in his decisions and avoids many problems.

A Few Points to Remember

Deliverypeople have eyes and ears, and they report back to the dealer everything that the receiving clerk does. If the receiving clerk knows his business, properly weighs and counts the merchandise, observes the quality of the merchandise, and checks the bottom layers of packages containing such items as lettuce and tomatoes for quality, then dealers are not going to take many chances and try to pass short weights or poor-quality merchandise. If, on the other hand, the receiving clerk just waves the delivery in, as often happens, then the dealers know that the receiving is carelessly handled and can take advantage.

Deliverypeople usually try to hurry the receiving clerk. Sometimes this is a deliberate attempt to confuse the receiving clerk so that he will overlook some short weights or other discrepancies. In other instances, it is simply because there is a parking problem or the deliveryperson is faced with a heavy schedule. The receiving clerk occasionally must help the deliveryperson by setting merchandise aside to be checked thoroughly later. This is risky, but, if necessary, it can be done, and purveyors will accept credits taken under such circumstances.

When first-of-the month deliveries are made for groceries and other items bought in large quantities, it is only fair for the food buyer to work out a delivery schedule with purveyors to avoid undue delays at the receiving dock. There is no reason why large deliveries must be made on the first of the month; they can be spaced out through the month by design.

Emergency delivery costs are high. The receiving clerk should advise the controller and management if the number of emergency deliveries exceeds one or two a day.

The strict maintenance and constant use of various accounting forms in the receiving department are what make the receiving process work. If corners are cut there, the effectiveness of the department will suffer.

The receiving clerk should be of such stature and the receiving system should be so efficient that the receiving clerk should feel free at all times to discuss anything questionable with the controller. He should also be in position to request to talk with both the general manager and the controller if the need arises.

CONTROLS IN THE SYSTEM

No system of any kind has ever been devised that has been able to eliminate completely the part played by human error. Someone has to police the receiving system, or the system, somewhere along the line, breaks down. Any receiving system, the manner in which the system functions, and the policing of the system are the unqualified responsibility of the accounting department and the controller.

The receiving clerk and the food and beverage controller are both part of the accounting department. In order to avoid the charge of collusion, however, the receiving clerk should not report directly to the food and beverage controller. The food and beverage controller should be in a position to observe the functioning of the receiving system. If the receiving clerk is not performing his job satisfactorily, the food and beverage controller should report his observations to the receiving clerk and the controller. In this manner, an independent person other than the controller, who might not have adequate time or perhaps training in receiving, is checking on the receiving clerk, thereby eliminating a possible weakness in the system.

By freeing the food and beverage controller of responsibility for receiving, that person is in a position to act as a controller. If he were responsible for the receiving clerk, he would be part of the operation and should not be performing a control function. Many controllers have, unfortunately, given this responsibility to the food and beverage controller with some rather disastrous results. Even though accounting department employees are supposed to be trustworthy and are thoroughly investigated, they are human. It is very easy for a receiving clerk and a food and beverage controller to join forces, to the detriment of the company.

In a well-managed and disciplined operation, the receiving department and the receiving clerk work under the scrutiny of a good food buyer. Any reputable chef also continuously checks on the receiving department to be sure that sloppy practices do not affect the cost or quality of food that he is to prepare, and a good controller manages to find time to spend a few minutes with the receiving clerk and at the receiving dock every normal working day. The dedicated, outstanding controller finds some time to be at the receiving dock at odd hours and on days not normally regarded as working days. It is unfortunate that many controllers are prone to work from 9:00 A.M. to 5:00 P.M., five days a week. Such a schedule does not allow much time for checking on the receiving department, and such people are not ideal controllers. They are more bookkeepers with the title of controller.

The director of food services in a hospital or an institution, a general manager of a hotel, a food and beverage director in a hotel, or a manager of a restaurant is always a busy person in any operation. He should, however, find time daily or at odd intervals to observe how the receiving department is operating.

According to a leading security service manager who specializes in this phase of the food industry, whenever a breakdown in the purchasing system occurs it generally starts with poor receiving practices. Perhaps there is an adequate system, but there is no one policing the system.

In large operations, regardless of whether they are hospitals, institutional food services, or hotels, it is always good to have outside auditors do spot checks of the receiving function from time to time on a nonregular schedule. Accounting companies that offer these services have qualified, trained personnel who in one day can measure the efficiency of a receiving department. This surprise check is a valuable, relatively inexpensive management tool. One of the best-organized and carefully hidden systems devised to steal from a large chain hotel company was uncovered when the president of the company engaged a spot-check service from an outside auditing firm to look at the receiving department, as he said later, "just for the hell of it."

Another part of a good receiving system is the use of a visitor's logbook at the receiving office. Good management encourages the controller, the chef, the food-purchasing agent, the head storeroom person, the food and beverage director, and even the catering manager to visit the receiving dock if for no other reason than to show the receiving clerk that he is being watched and that his work is appreciated. There

should be a logbook in the receiving office, and the receiving clerk should insist that all visitors sign in, with the date and time of their visit. Management can then review the logbook from time to time. If the visits by responsible people are frequent, then the manager has just one more good management tool working for him.

In small operations, where buying, receiving, storing, and issuing are done by one employee and any independent checking is done by the controller and manager or perhaps even by the senior room clerk, the logbook system is even more essential.

THE ROLE OF GOVERNMENT

Some of the problems involved in food purchasing, transportation, and receiving are discussed in Chapter 10. Because of the existence of these problems and efforts to solve them, many institutions and large companies, especially companies operating outside the United States, turned to the government for help. In addition to establishing complete grade standards, the government has set up an acceptance service within the USDA concerned with meats and meat products. This service is designed to assure purchasers that available products comply with detailed specifications approved by the USDA. After bids have been submitted by purveyors and accepted by a buyer, a grader from the Department of Agriculture inspects the beef or any other meats or meat products to ascertain whether the products comply with the specifications. If they do comply, an inspector accepts them, and the federal grader certifies that they have been accepted. The containers are then marked and sealed so that the purchaser receiving the merchandise can be reasonably sure that the products being received are the products shipped and that the products comply with government standards.

The cost of this service is normally

nominal. It generally averages less than two or three cents per pound depending on the size of the shipment, and this is generally offset by peace of mind where the exporting or shipping of large quantities of meat from one area to another is concerned.

In certain parts of the world, primarily the United States, Canada, and Europe, there are accredited and, in some cases, licensed accounting firms, consultants, and sanitarians who act as independent receiving agents or spot-receiving agents for companies that need this type of service.

These people are generally highly trained, competent, and, on the whole, conscientious and honest. They help to maintain standards when they might not otherwise be maintained.

Why, one might ask, if there is a professional food buyer involved in the buying process, is it necessary to hire specialists to check on food buyers or other persons involved? The answer, which goes back to the weaknesses of "human nature," is the main concern of Chapter 10.

9 The Storeroom: A Place to Make Money

Purpose: To provide an understanding of how a storeroom is organized and operated.

INTRODUCTION

The storeroom is a place to make money by saving money—by reducing costs through efficient management of materials. A typical food service operation has a considerable amount of cash tied up in food, beverages, and various supplies. A well-organized and properly operated storeroom is an essential part of good management.

BASIC FUNCTIONS

The storeroom has three basic functions of equal importance: supply, control, and safekeeping of inventory. Each is briefly explained next, and the different facets of each function are explained in detail throughout this chapter. How the computer can aid in the execution of these functions is explained in Chapter 11.

Supply

This function, when it is efficiently handled, is the means of supplying an operation with what is needed, when it is needed, and in the amount needed. It resembles the purchasing phase of the operation, and the two activities are interrelated. A reserve stock of nonperishable goods kept in a storeroom helps maintain price levels by making it unnecessary for the food buyer to purchase under the pressure of need. If sufficient space is available for storage, a good buyer can always negotiate for better prices on large-quantity deliveries and avoid purchasing when a commodity is in short supply.

Delivery schedules were not a great problem in the past. There was no shortage of fuel to move trucks at low cost. That cost factor is becoming increasingly important. In the 1960's the average delivery to a food operation in a metropolitan area cost $5.00. By 1970 this had increased to $15.00 per delivery, and the current average cost per delivery is approximately $30.00 and headed toward $50.00. A well-run storeroom with sufficient space available can operate with weekly and monthly deliveries on many items, greatly reducing delivery charges.

Control

This function and the safekeeping of inventory somewhat overlap, but they are distinct in that control is primarily concerned with (1) the *cost of merchandise* as it moves from the receiving department into the storeroom, (2) amounts on hand at any given time during and accounting period, and (3) the cost of the merchandise as it moves from the storeroom into the preparation departments. To efficiently operate controls, management must consider the character of the personnel, the scheduled hours of operation, the requisitioning system, inventory taking, and security. These concerns are explained in detail in the section "The Storeroom Operation."

Safekeeping of Inventory

This function is devoted to care of the *physical condition of the merchandise* while it is located in the storeroom. To execute this function profitably, the storeroom layout must be adequate for frozen, refrigerated, and dry storage from the standpoints of location, space, and equipment. Other considerations include temperature controls, rotation of stock, a sanitary program, and security. These safeguards are explained in detail in this chapter.

THE STOREROOM OPERATION

As in all other operating departments, the general manager of any food operation or facility has the final responsibility for operating the storeroom. It is his responsibility to set up a proper organization or to see that one is set up, to see that written instructions cover all phases of storeroom operations, to see that the department manager is suitable, and to see that proper controls are provided and maintained and that proper inspections of the storage areas are made. If the general manager cannot do all of this personally, he should delegate the responsibility for working with the storeroom staff to other department heads.

If the food buyer or purchasing agent has an office in the storeroom or nearby, he is generally in charge of the storeroom, the wine cellar, and general food stores. If that person is not located nearby, it is best to appoint a storeroom manager who reports to the food and beverage manager or someone responsible for the overall operation of the food and beverage department. Pricing of requisitions can be the responsibility of the storeroom manager, but the controller should see that the pricing is accurate. Actual control should, however, be exercised through the food and beverage manager, who would then be responsible for setting up the proper systems of issuing, planning for the security of the storeroom, securing the keys, and seeing that properly authorized signatures appear on all issues from the storeroom. An ambitious controller occasionally takes over the operation of the storeroom, but this is poor policy for the controller is then responsible for both operation and control. Over an extended period of time this could lead to a conflict of interest. It is independent control that ensures against losses.

The controller is responsible for setting up the control system over storeroom operations, for supervising the system, and for taking independent, month-end inventories. Taking these inventories is the sole responsibility of the controller's office unless the controller delegates it to the food and beverage controller in cooperation with the storeroom manager. Such an arrangement is satisfactory, providing the controller or another capable person from the accounting department is present and verifies the quantities of the month-end food and beverage inventories.

Personnel

Anyone who works in the storeroom should be thoroughly screened by the personnel department, investigated by a security service, and bonded against any form of thievery or shortages in the storeroom. Upgrading job titles for positions in the storeroom seems to have a beneficial effect on storeroom operations. One suggestion has been to call the head storeroom person a storeroom manager and the other people who work with him storeroom attendants or food supply clerks.

Schedules

Storeroom hours depend on a number of circumstances. Since the storeroom must be open to receive incoming merchandise, the location of the food operation in relation to the market influences when the storeroom opens in the morning. Normally, milk, bread, and some produce deliveries start arriving at about 6:00 A.M. Most storerooms, therefore, open at that hour six days a week since there are milk and bread deliveries on Saturday. If the food operation is some distance from the market area, deliveries do not arrive until 8:00 or 9:00 A.M. In that case, the storeroom can open as late as 8:00 A.M. Because deliveries are not usually made on Sunday, it should be possible to arrange for the kitchen to requisition supplies on Saturday for use on Sunday; then the storeroom can be closed.

Most food storerooms in large operations remain open from 6:00 A.M. to 8:00 or 9:00 P.M., requiring two shifts. When storerooms are open so long each day and so many days of the week, it is usually for the purpose of servicing departments that are continually running out of supplies—a bad habit that should not be encouraged. Careful planning on the part of kitchen and storeroom management to schedule issues to the various kitchen departments can usually eliminate the need for such long hours of operation, in which case the following schedule might prove more effective:

Monday through Saturday: 6:00 A.M. to 2:00 P.M., closed 2:00 P.M. to 4:00 P.M., reopened 4:00 P.M. to 7:00 P.M.
Sundays and holidays: 6:00 A.M. to 2:00 P.M., closed the rest of the day.

The two-hour break in the afternoon should be used for cleanup and arranging and taking inventory of the stock as a basis for the next day's ordering.

Well-managed kitchens and storerooms have an ordering schedule that requires each kitchen department to submit a daily requisition. If the requisitions are submitted to the chef in the afternoon, he can review them, make necessary changes, and approve them. In late afternoon the storeroom personnel fill all of the various orders and place them on a truck or trucks for delivery or pickup the first thing in the morning. Not only does this increase the degree of control over the issue of merchandise, but it also reduces the food supplies in the kitchen at night, when losses are more likely to occur.

Equipment

Shelving. The equipment needed to operate a good-sized storeroom is rather simple and inexpensive after refrigeration is installed in the necessary areas (see Exhibit 9-1). Perhaps the most immediate need is adequate shelving (see Exhibit 9-2).

The shelves should be 18 inches to 20 inches deep, and there should be 16 inches to 18 inches between them. The bottom shelf should be at least 6 inches off the floor to permit air circulation and cleaning. The top shelf should not be more than 6½ feet from the floor for ease in loading and unloading.

All shelving must meet local sanitary codes where the operation is located and the sanitary codes set by the Occupational Safety and Health Act (see Chapter 3). Some shelving should be of the modular type for easy arrangement or rearrangement. The best shelving is made of stainless steel, but, because it is extremely expensive, manufacturers have produced shelving made of alternative materials for the refrigerated area and for other storeroom areas.

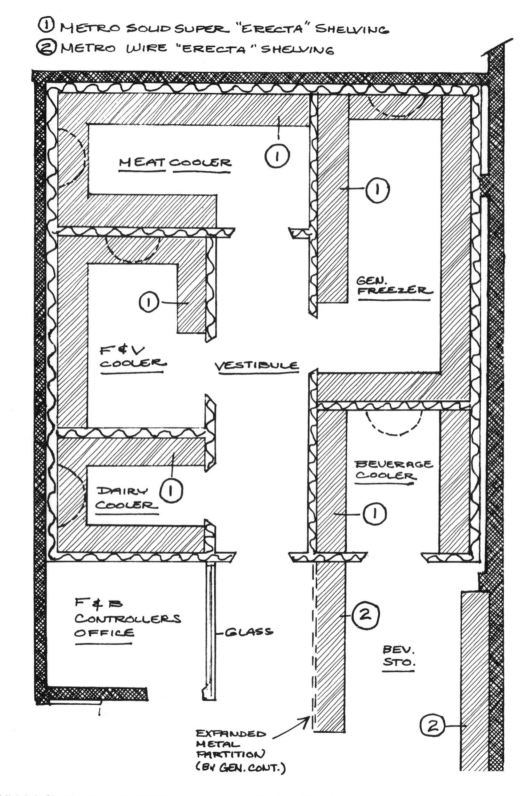

Exhibit 9-1. Sketched layout for refrigerated storage area (Courtesy: Sheraton Supply Company, Boston, Massachusetts)

Exhibit 9-2. Various types of shelving for storage (Courtesy: Seco, Washington, Missouri; Metropolitan Wire Goods Corporation, Wilkes-Barre, Pennsylvania)

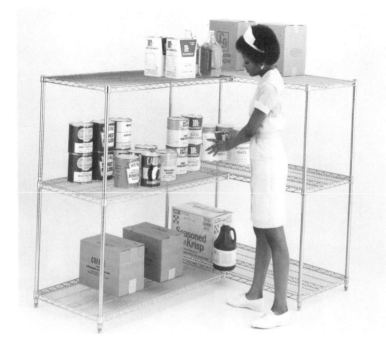

Exhibit 9-2. *(continued)*

For refrigerated areas, vinyl-coated, louvered shelving is acceptable, as is the old standby, galvanized, slotted metal shelving. The use of perforated or slotted shelving in the refrigerated area has the advantage of allowing better air circulation than solid shelving. Some manufacturers have introduced "embossed" shelves with raised ridges that allow air to circulate around the pans without any foreign materials dropping into the food below (which is why most sanitary codes require that any food be covered during storage in the refrigerator).

A very good shelving for the dry storage area, whether it be food, liquor, or other supplies, is made of chrome-plated wire. It is available under a variety of trade names. This shelving is strong, lightweight, and can be put up and taken down easily. It is, however, unsatisfactory for refrigerating and freezing areas because it tends to rust under damp conditions. Some operators have turned to solid painted metal shelving for dry storage areas, but it requires painting about every three years to control rust on worn surfaces. In areas where sanitary codes permit, for supplies other than food, wooden shelving is satisfactory, provided it is tight, well painted, and free from breaks where vermin can hide.

Solid metal or wooden shelving is good for storing liquor, but vinyl-coated, louvered, or flat shelving is best for storing refrigerated wines. There is also a vinyl-coated, honeycomb shelving for storing refrigerated wines in a horizontal position to keep the corks moist.

Kitchen architects or kitchen equipment contractors often fill the storeroom with too much shelving. Not only does this cost more than it should, but it interferes with storeroom operations. It is advisable, in fact, not to equip over 50 percent of the area with shelving. Some merchandise can be stored in cases, with only the top case being open. This reduces labor costs and facilitates taking inventory. It also contributes in a small way to better security.

Pallets or Dunnage Racks. Nothing should be stored directly on the floor of either the storeroom or the refrigerated areas. It is usually a sanitary code violation to do so. Pallets or dunnage racks (Exhibit 9-3) of lightweight materials can be used to keep stored items off the floor. Wooden skids are also satisfactory and relatively inexpensive.

Trucks. If the storeroom is large enough, an electric motorized truck can be used to move skids and dunnage racks, or a motorized forklift truck with a small turning radius is ideal. (See Exhibit 9-4.) A few metal hand trucks should also be available for moving storeroom stock, as should two- or three-deck trucks for use by purveyors, even though most deliverymen have their own small hand trucks.

One type of truck, often overlooked or forgotten entirely in setting up a storeroom area, is the small two-deck delivery truck (Exhibit 9-5) used by a storeroom man to deliver merchandise to the kitchen or used by the runner from the kitchen in picking up his stock. In hotel operations room service tables are generally pressed into service, but they are fragile and expensive. The price for not having proper storeroom delivery trucks is high.

Scales. Even though the receiving area is equipped with large floor-type scales (see Exhibit 8-1), the storeroom should be equipped with a floor scale capable of weighing up to approximately two hundred pounds. It does not necessarily have to be embedded in the floor. In addition, the storeroom should have a table-model scale that can be used for checking smaller weights and weighing small quantities of bulk merchandise that is to be rebagged and issued to the kitchen. This type of scale is also important in operations that utilize the central ingredient room concept where no one has access to the store-

Exhibit 9-3. Pallets or dunnage racks used to keep stored items off the floor (Courtesy: Servolift Eastern Steel Rack Corporation, Boston, Massachusetts)

Exhibit 9-4. Motorized vehicles for storeroom work (Courtesy: Clark Equipment Company, Battle Creek, Michigan)

Exhibit 9-5. Three-deck hand truck for storeroom deliveries (Courtesy: Seco, Washington, Missouri)

room except those who weigh out all ingredients for recipes—a system that is gaining acceptance in large hospitals today.

Other Equipment. The storeroom manager should be provided with a suitable desk, a chair, a file case, and a small cabinet where he can lock up small, valuable merchandise that might otherwise be lost. There should be a work table with a stainless steel top where merchandise can be examined and where large, bulky packages can be broken down into smaller portions for use in the kitchen.

Storeroom personnel should be issued uniforms to improve the appearance of the area, to provide better sanitation, and to upgrade the job. Freezer coats are necessary for individuals working in the freezer area.

FOOD STORAGE AREAS

Basic Requirements

The average storeroom operation falls into the same category as the receiving operation. It is a busy place where valuable merchandise is received, stored, and dispensed, but no one seems to know or to care much about what goes on there unless things go very wrong. When that happens, however, there are reverberations.

Often food storage areas are inadequately planned when the initial layout is made, and they are invariably the first places to suffer when funds are allocated. If the usual pattern is followed, the storage area is usurped for engineering needs, for housekeeping supplies, and for paper and cleaning supplies, leaving about half the space that is needed for food and liquor. Sometimes the various storage areas for the food department are far apart, even on different floors. Under such circumstances, it is little wonder that there is less control over the merchandise. Those responsible for setting up a storeroom and planning storeroom areas should give consideration to location and size.

Location. The storeroom should be between the kitchen and the receiving area. Because of building layouts, however, this is often difficult to achieve. If the kitchen or kitchens are located on different floors, it is preferable to have the storeroom next to the receiving area to facilitate delivery of supplies to the storeroom after the shipment has been checked through the receiving area. Once the merchandise is in the house, various departments may pick up their supplies from the storeroom as needed.

In the past, storerooms have usually been located in the first or second basement of a building, but new building codes are forcing architects to relocate storerooms on street and upper-floor levels so that there is light and ventilation. Backed-up sewer lines have caused problems, especially in areas where there is danger of flood, another reason why storage areas should be located on upper floors.

Size. There is a direct relationship between size of storeroom area required and type of operation, between size of operation and proximity to supply sources. An operation in a large school, which uses mainly convenience foods, requires larger freezer and canned goods storage areas than a full-service restaurant or hotel using large quantities of fresh meats, poultry, and produce. A resort hotel in the Caribbean requires about twice the usual amount of space for canned and frozen items, and the storage area needed for fresh produce and dairy products is determined in accordance with local laws.

In the initial planning stage, the planner must make an educated guess as to what the requirements will be many years in the future. Once the walls are finished, there is little chance that the storage area will ever be made larger, though it can easily be made smaller.

Space Requirements. Every kitchen architect has a schedule showing space allocations for storage that he uses in kitchen planning, and the standards are changed to fit the needs of the operation being planned. How skillfully these adaptations are made depends largely upon the ability of management and the kitchen architect to determine the future needs of the operation.

Whether the requirements are based on cubic feet per hundred covers served per day, the dollar volume of business, or the size of the kitchen area and, thereby, the dining area, the final decisions are always tied to the volume of business expected and the distance to and adequacy of the market to be used.

One system commonly used to determine the amount of storage and refrigerated space required for a proposed hotel or motel operation is an average percentage allotment of the total space to be provided for the entire operation. The total space includes dining area, banquet service, bar (if a part of the setup), and back of the house. Some adjustments have to be made for a bar, cocktail lounge, and banquet service in a hotel serving liquor that are unnecessary in a large commercial or institutional food service. Because any plan is affected by location, distance from market, type of business, personnel involved, and other factors, professional help is needed in designing and planning any food operation.

To illustrate this system of space allocation, assume the following circumstances:

Facility	Number of seats		Square feet per seat		Square feet in area
Coffee shop	125	x	12	=	1,500
Dining room	150	x	20	=	3,000
Subtotal					4,500
Employees' cafeteria	60	x	15	=	900
Bar and lounge	125	x	20	=	2,500
Ballroom	600	x	12	=	7,200
Private dining rooms	200	x	15	=	3,000
Subtotal					13,600
Divided by a use factor of 6 (rounded)					2,300
Total determining area (4,500 + 2,300)					6,800
Multiplied by allocation for back of the house (2) to get total basis for storage area					13,600
Multiplied by 10 percent to determine size of storage area					1,360

Exhibit 9-6. Working out the formula for space requirements in a food service facility

Area	Allocation (percent)		Storage area (square feet)		Allocation (square feet)
Dry storage (including liquors and mineral waters)	50	x	1,360	=	680
Freezer	15	x	1,360	=	204
Meat refrigeration	10	x	1,360	=	136
Fruits and vegetables	8	x	1,360	=	109
Dairy	5	x	1,360	=	68
Liquor refrigeration	5	x	1,360	=	68
Vestibule outside refrigerated area	7	x	1,360	=	95
TOTAL	100				1,360

Exhibit 9-7. Allocation of storage area in a food service facility

125-seat coffee shop
150-seat dining room
 60-seat employees' cafeteria
125-seat bar and lounge
600-seat ballroom
200-seat accommodations in private dining
  rooms
kitchen, with pastry shop
storerooms, no butcher shop

A rule of thumb is that storage area should constitute 10 to 12 percent of the square foot area of the entire facility. Because of the limited food service in the bar and lounge and some function areas, a lower percentage of storage and refrigerated area is needed there. For determining the correct amount of space, the following formula is useful:

Total dining area plus ⅛ of bar and function room area multiplied by 2 (to allow for back of house) and the result multiplied by 10 percent. (See Exhibit 9-6.)

The space thus determined is the total space required for storage, including dry, refrigerated, and freezer. Space is further allocated (see Exhibit 9-7) as:

	Percent
Dry storage (including liquors and mineral waters)	50
Freezer	15
Meat refrigeration	10
Fruits and vegetables	8
Dairy	5
Liquor refrigeration	5
Vestibule outside refrigerated area	7
TOTAL	100

This somewhat detailed treatment of the storage areas has been included to emphasize the many facets that must be considered in designing those areas. The ability and the judgment of architect and management are as clearly reflected in well-planned storage areas as they are throughout the rest of the establishment. No one method or formula covers all of the many types of food service operations found throughout the world. Ultimately space requirements should be based on the type of food service, purchasing and inventory policies, the menu, the availability of production and service personnel, and the location of the establishment and the effectiveness of distribution systems.

Temperature Ranges

The following is a list of temperature ranges for various storage areas normally provided in temperate zones:

Storage areas	Temperature Range Fahrenheit	Celsius
Nonrefrigerated		
Dry grocery storage	50°-70°	10°-22°
Liquor storage, whiskeys	50°-70°	10°-22°
Wine storage, red	50°-70°	10°-22°
Wine storage, white	50°-70°	10°-22°
Beer storage	50°-70°	10°-22°
Mineral waters	50°-70°	10°-22°
Refrigerated		
Vestibule	50°-60°	10°-15°
Meats	30°-35°	0°-2°
Poultry	30°-35°	0°-2°
Fish and seafood	30°-35°	0°-2°
Smoked meats	30°-35°	0°-2°
Dairy products	30°-35°	0°-2°
Butter and eggs	30°-35°	0°-2°
Fresh fruits and vegetables	36°-40°	2°-4°
Delicatessen	36°-40°	2°-4°
Wine storage, white	40°-45°	3°-5°
Beer and mineral waters	40°-45°	3°-5°
Freezer storage	0°-(-)10°	(-)18°-(-)24°

Where dry storeroom temperatures exceed 70°F, it is necessary to air-condition the storeroom to prevent excessive losses from spoilage of wines, beers, and canned goods. Cereal grains and flour should be stored where the temperature can be kept below 65°F to prevent growth of weevils.

Storage Times

The length of time for safe storage of frozen foods depends on the storage temperature and how well it is maintained, the nature of the items stored, and the manner in which the items are packaged. Fluctuating temperatures reduce the life expectancy of frozen foods, and small packages are more susceptible to freezer burn and dehydration than larger, well-packaged items. Some foods such as pork, especially hams and bacon, do not freeze well because of the soft content.

Once a frozen packaged item has been thawed, it should not be refrozen unless necessary because there is deterioration in quality. Any refrozen item, even though packaged, should not be kept over thirty days. The following storage time limits, although they are not maximum, are considered safe.

Frozen item	Safe storage time limits*
Raw beef, lamb, veal	Up to 1 year
Cooked beef, lamb, veal	Up to 3 months
Pork, fresh	Up to 6 months
Pork, cooked, smoked	Up to 1 month
Sausages, smoked	Up to 1 month
Raw poultry, fish	Up to 6 months
Cooked poultry, fish	Up to 3 months
Chopped meats, any	Up to 3 months
Fruits and vegetables	Up to 1 year
Cooked fruits and vegetables	Up to 3 months
Ice cream	Up to 6 weeks
Frozen entrées	Up to 3 months
Sandwiches	Up to 2 weeks

*0°-(-)10°F. or (-)18°-(-)24°C.

Refrigerated item	Safe storage time limits
Meats, fish, poultry	
Beef, aging (cryovac)	1 month
Beef, other	10 days
Lamb	1 week
Veal	1 week
Pork	5 days
Poultry	3 days
Smoked meats	10 days
Fish and seafood	3 days
Dairy products	
Butter	10 days
Eggs	5 days
Milk and cream	3 days
Smoked meats	10 days
Cheese, hard	30 days
Cheese, soft	10 days
Cheese, cottage	3 days
Fruits	
Apples, oranges, grapefruit, lemons, limes	1 month
Pears, peaches, apricots, pineapples, grapes, plums, cherries, nectarines	2 weeks
Grapefruit, oranges, pineapple, and mixed fruit sections in gallons	1 week
Berries	
Strawberries, raspberries, blackberries	48 hours
Blueberries	72 hours
Cranberries	1 month
Melons, ripe	
Cantaloupes, Crenshaw, Spanish, Persian, honeydew, Rockport, muskmelon	1 week
Watermelon	2 weeks
Avocado, papaya	1 week

Vegetables	
Onions (dry storage)	3 months
Peas, stringbeans, peppers, lima beans, broccoli, cauliflower, eggplant, asparagus, sprouts, summer squash, cucumbers, radishes, parsley, cress	10 days
Spinach, chard	72 hours
Corn	48 hours
Beets, carrots	1 month
Lettuce, escarole, romaine, endive, chicory, celery	10 days
Tomatoes, ripe	1 week
Mushrooms	3 days
Peeled potatoes	3 days

Vestibule storage	
Bananas	72 hours
Sweet potatoes	10 days
Potatoes, sack	1 month
Mayonnaise	2 months
Salad dressings	2 months
Oils and shortening	3 months
Dry beans, rice, cereal, grains	2 months

Canned goods and groceries

Most items can be kept six months but not over a year. Canned fish and seafood, canned meats, stews, and hash should not be kept longer than three months.

Storage Areas

The following paragraphs discuss specialized storage areas and how they are used.

Dry Storage Area. This general area should be separated further into storage of dry foods, liquor, mineral water, cleaning supplies, and, in some instances, operating equipment such as pots and pans, china, glass, silver and paper supplies, and cooperage supplies. Sometimes accounting supplies are kept in a locked area in the food storeroom, to which only the controller has the key.

It is unfortunate that the food storeroom often becomes a catchall for old accounting records, old menu stock, broken equipment, and other junk when no one has authorized proper disposal of such items. Management could well authorize the head storekeeper to sell as salvage or throw out anything not belonging in the area that has been there for 120 days.

Refrigerated Area. Such an area is generally divided to accommodate fresh meats and poultry, fresh fruits and vegetables, and dairy products. In larger storage facilities the refrigerated area is sometimes separated further, allotting areas to smoked meats, delicatessen items, and a fish box.

Freezer Area. This was formerly a small box at the back of the meat area, but, with the increased use of frozen merchandise, a separate freezer for storing meats, fruits. vegetables, and other convenience foods is needed. A well-designed freezer area has one section for meats and poultry, another for fruits, vegetables, and seafood, and a third for frozen convenience foods of various types.

Vestibule. In any well-planned food storeroom all of the refrigeration and freezer areas open into a vestibule that in turn opens into the storeroom proper. This vestibule helps to reduce loss of refrigerated air and to maintain steady refrigerator temperatures and reduces the amount of outside air entering the freezer and refrigeration areas. It can also be used for the storage of such items as bananas, lemons, sweet potatoes, avocados, grapefruit, oranges, potatoes, onions, and other items not normally refrigerated.

Exhibit 9-1 shows an actual layout of the refrigerated area of a storeroom. In this particular layout, management placed the food and beverage controller's office in the food and beverage storeroom as a means of strengthening internal control. The purchasing office and the receiving office were located at the receiving dock three floors below, along with the storeroom and the production kitchen. The storeroom attendant had a work table, a scale, a desk, and a file for his records and packaging activities.

Commissary Area. In larger, newer storeroom setups, provision has been made for a small butcher shop and a salad and vegetable preparation area so that the storeroom acts as a commissary for the preparation and distribution of these items to the using kitchens throughout the operation. There are fewer distractions in the storeroom, and the output per person per hour increases so much that there is no question of the value of this arrangement.

One very large hotel, which does over $5 million worth of business per year, found it possible to reduce its butcher shop crew from six people to two when the butcher shop was moved to the storeroom area.

Another large hotel, which takes in $8 million in annual food revenue, found that one butcher working eight hours a day was able to do all the butchering for the hotel. This particular hotel fabricated its own beef strips, top butts, filets, and chucks, ground its own hamburger, cut all of its lamb chops and ham steaks, made all of its veal cutlets, prepared all of its pork roasts, cut all of its calves liver, cut all of its fish for fillets, and in some cases, even bought its own fish dressed and finished its own portion cutting.

In larger institutions it has been standard practice for many years to have a single vegetable and salad preparation area, sometimes in the storeroom and sometimes in an isolated place in the kitchen, but use of the storeroom has only recently been adopted widely by hotels. Today, as a matter of fact, hotels doing as much as $6 million to $8 million worth of food business a year are preparing all bulk salads needed for the operation, including cole slaw, potato salad, vegetable salads, fruit salads, and greens, as well as cleaning and cutting all of the fresh vegetables needed for the operation.

Ingredient Rooms. Where it is possible to use standard recipes and sales forecasts, ingredients in the exact amount required by any one department for an entire day's production can be set out in the storeroom and issued as needed. Large institutions and food processors have for some time been rearranging their storerooms to allow for ingredient rooms. This trend, more prevalent in hospital and nursing home kitchens, now is gaining acceptance in large hotels. Not only is it an effective cost control measure, but it also helps in maintaining higher standards of quality.

Such a system has become feasible through the use of minicomputers, which makes ingredient and recipe control practical. The University of Massachusetts has been a leader in the development of this system.

Reserved Kitchen Storage Areas. It costs money to keep the main storeroom open, and it also costs money to have kitchen runners going to the storeroom to pick up a can of this and a box of that and a small bag of something else that another department has overlooked. Many large food operations have arranged to have a small, locked reserve storage area in each department where a par stock is maintained for daily use, and the keys are held by the head of the kitchen department. Such a reserve area eliminates costly trips to the storeroom.

Garbage and Trash Areas. Until a few years ago, the storage of garbage and trash and its disposal was one of the most unsanitary and least satisfactory phases of any food operation. Modern storage and disposal methods have greatly improved sanitary standards in the back areas of food operations.

In cities where sewage systems will permit, garbage is now ground by a very powerful garbage grinder and flushed down the drain. Only heavy bones are held out to be disposed of by other methods. Where the sewage system does not allow this, the old problem of collecting the garbage and transporting it to a refrigerated area or a dumpster container located at the back door still exists. Most city codes do, however, require that all garbage cans have liners and that the liner be closed and tied when the can is full. In this manner, fewer flies and vermin are attracted.

It is doubtful that many cities in the United States and Canada lack a trash removal system based on a portable compactor parked at the rear entrance of the operation. This system has even spread to the individual home and the apartment complex, and it is standard procedure for larger food operations.

Sanitary Requirements

Sanitary considerations are normally part of the responsibility of the architect and the kitchen contractor. All existing sanitary codes should be followed in laying out, designing, and constructing the storage and refrigerated areas. Details overlooked could result in problems for the operator after the establishment opens.

Floor and wall surfaces in storage and refrigerated areas should be constructed so that they are resistant to heavy trucks, easy to keep clean, and grease- and moistureproof. The best material for floors appears to be red quarry tile properly installed. In extremely wet areas Carborundum quarry tile is best suited to the purpose. There are substitutes, including poured mastic floors and treated cement floors, but they have not proved to be as satisfactory.

The best wall surface is glazed tile, but it is expensive. A special bonded cement or a glazed building block that can be easily cleaned is more often used in modern construction projects. Regardless of the wall surface used, it is best to have bumper guards to protect the walls; in time low and high trucks break through a building block wall or a metal surface refrigerator.

Local building codes normally specify

the height of the ceiling—generally a minimum of eight feet from floor to ceiling. If the cost of airconditioning the storage area is not allowed for in the budget, then there must be adequate forced-air ventilation. There must also be adequate lighting. Again, local building codes guide the architect in planning these details.

Operators should check the plans for the storeroom and refrigerated areas to make sure that there is drainage to facilitate cleaning refrigerators and scrubbing storeroom floors and walls.

Security and Control Measures

Securing against Entry. A well-planned food and beverage storeroom has one entrance through which everything enters and leaves. When the storeroom is locked, the key, which ought to be kept on a large ring, should be left at the front office in a large, sealed envelope, and there should be a record showing the name of the person who delivered it and the name of the person who received it.

The morning storeroom attendant should sign his name to the record when he receives the key, and, if the seal on the envelope has been broken, he should note that fact in the record. The controller should ascertain why it was necessary to use the key during the previous evening. Certainly emergencies do occur at night that require opening the storeroom. That is why the key is kept in the front office, under seal.

Another key to the storeroom should be kept in the vault in a sealed envelope and should be issued to the controller, the general manager, or the night manager, depending on the policy of management, but this should also be recorded and the general manager of the operation notified in writing.

The storeroom should be divided into three areas, each separately locked if possible. If the liquor storeroom is within the food storeroom area, then it is absolutely necessary that there be a separate key, with one person responsible for both the key and the liquor stock. When that person leaves, he should also lock the area, put the key in a sealed envelope, and leave it at the front office where it should be handled in the same way as the main storeroom keys. A liquor storeroom, whether it is inside the food storeroom or separate, should be as secure as a bank.

It is wise to have another small locked area in the dry storeroom to accommodate small valuable grocery items such as anchovy filets, boneless and skinless sardines, truffles, small jars of cocktail olives, smoked oysters, individual jars of jam for room service, and, in some parts of the country, certain bottled condiments.

A small locked area in one of the refrigerators is also advisable with the key in possession of the storeroom manager. Items most likely to be stolen, such as caviar, pâté de foie gras, small packages of smoked meats, and costly spices can be stored there. The keys to both small areas should be in the possession of the storeroom manager.

In large operations there should be a recording time lock on the door to the storeroom, and the tape from the time lock should go to the controller each day for review. Time locks can be useful. For example, a large New York hotel inexplicably lost about $1,500 a month from the storeroom. Everyone was blaming the figures except the control department. As a last resort, they installed a time lock on the storeroom door, and it was found, as a result, that the morning storeroom attendant was opening the storeroom forty-five minutes before the scheduled time. When questioned, he explained that he needed the extra time to prepare the storeroom for morning deliveries. The controller decided to give the morning storeroom person an afternoon shift so that he would not have to get up so early in the morning. The first day he was to work on the new schedule the storeroom attendant did not report for work, and it was subsequently learned that he had left the country. The storeroom shortages stopped immediately. Investigation revealed that the attendant had been removing valuable merchandise and concealing it around the hotel for friends to pick up during the day. For this "service" he received about half of the retail value of the merchandise.

The main entrance to the storeroom can be a Dutch door, with the lower half being closed at all times. All except storeroom personnel and deliverypeople, who should be observed when they are in the storeroom, can be excluded. Large issues on trucks can be delivered outside the door, and small issues can be handed over the shelf on it. The watchman's key punch station for the area should be near the entrance, and, if there is liquor stored in the food storeroom, the watchperson should punch in hourly at this point.

If possible, there should be no electrical panels and water control valves in the food storage area, and, if there are any ventilating shafts passing through the storeroom, they should be secured against entry into the storeroom. Any head space above drop ceilings should be thoroughly secured.

Perpetual Inventory Checks. The food and beverage manager should keep perpetual inventories on other "sensitive" items in the food storeroom such as bacon, tuna fish, anchovies, butter, expensive condiments, and cut meats and a complete perpetual inventory on all alcoholic beverages. Physical inventory checks on food stocks should be varied from month to month so that no one except the food and beverage controller knows what items are being spot-checked. A typical perpetual inventory card is shown in Exhibit 9-8.

Freezer stock should be controlled by a permanent perpetual inventory, including dating, to facilitate prompt use. Otherwise, freezer stock is an unknown quantity as it is difficult to get an actual count. Storeroom attendants are reluctant to spend much time in the freezer, even when provided with proper clothing. Security people should be instructed to check the freezer storage area occasionally since it is an out-of-the-way place for concealing merchandise stolen elsewhere.

Requisitions. The primary rule governing the control of all storeroom stock is that everything that goes into the storeroom be entered on a receiving sheet and everything that goes out leave upon receipt of a signed requisition. The simplest basic control is the monthly storeroom difference, which is determined by adding total storeroom purchases during the month to the opening storeroom inventory and subtracting merchandise issued from the storeroom for the month. The resultant theoretical inventory stock is then compared with the actual closing inventory.

If the difference between the theoretical inventory and the actual inventory is more than half of a percent of the closing inventory value, the food and beverage controller and the controller of the operation should investigate why this difference is greater than the minimum allowed.

A storeroom shortage can be the result of many different things that occur in the daily operation of the storeroom, or it can be the result of spontaneous or organized thievery. Some shortages occur because storeroom personnel are lax in getting a requisition for every item, because a requisition is unclear as to the size of the container, because there are inaccuracies in the number of cans or items issued, because items issued by weight may be carelessly weighed or repackaged

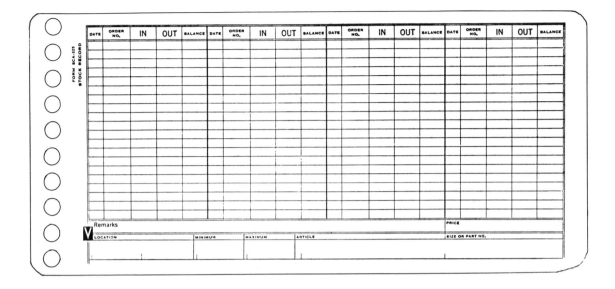

Exhibit 9-8. Perpetual inventory stock record

or requisitions may be mispriced. Occasionally the merchandise was never placed in the storeroom, and that fact was not noted for one reason or another.

Every requisition (see Exhibit 9-9) should bear the signature of a person designated by management as having the authority to sign it. A sample list of qualified signers, such as the one that appears below, with copies of the signatures, should be posted at the storeroom entrance behind sealed glass so that storeroom personnel can compare signatures on requisitions with the approved originals. Nothing should be issued without an approved signature, and the person signing the requisition should draw a line from the last item listed on a requisition to his signature so that no one can add items to the approved requisition.

Storeroom personnel should initial requisitions when they fill them. At the end of the day all requisitions should be totaled, clipped together with an adding machine tape, and sent to the food and beverage control office.

Office of the General Manager

Date _____

To all department heads:

The following named department heads are authorized to sign requisitions for food supplies from the storeroom. Storeroom personnel will not issue any stock unless one of the following signatures is on the requisition:

_____

John C. Smith—Food and Beverage Manager

_____

Anthony B. Brown—Chef

_____

Porter F. O'Brien—Sous Chef

_____

Gene A. Stryker—Night Chef

_____

Herman G. Shultz—Relief Chef

_____

Bertha A. Cotten—Pantry Supervisor

_____

Michael Lyzinski—Steward

_____

General Manager

Form 489

FOOD REQUISITION

S. L. 100 PADS 4/7)

N⁰ 6254

Date _____

ARTICLE	QUAN.	PRICE		AMOUNT	

_____   _____
Department Head

Exhibit 9-9. Typical storeroom requisition form

Most instructions on food and beverage controls say that requisition numbers should be closely regulated. The controller's department should account for all requisitions every day. This works well for liquor requisitions, but, under normal circumstances, accounting for all food requisition numbers is too costly. It is better to have a series of requisition books, in which each department is represented by its own distinct color, and to keep a continuous record from month to month. The food and beverage controller can run a series of spot checks on one color per week. In this way, adequate control is exercised over the numbers with a minimum of effort and expense.

Every piece of merchandise in the storeroom should bear a price on the package or on a meat tag (which is only needed in a large operation) attached to the merchandise. This enables storeroom personnel to price the requisition as the merchandise is issued, thereby providing more accurate daily food costs and eliminating storeroom differences at the end of the month. A broad, felt-tip pen is best for this purpose, although some storerooms use what are called supermarket pricing stamps. The two hours that the storeroom is closed in the afternoon is the best time to bring the pricing up to date, and slow evening periods can also be used to fill requisitions and price merchandise.

The month-end inventory can be priced according to the price of the merchandise that was received last. This saves averaging prices from different lots. From month to month, the total difference proves negligible.

Chapter 11 outlines new, computerized methods of storeroom control. New systems are being rapidly installed in the larger institutional and commercial food operations.

Rotation of Stock. Good storeroom management and operation insists on a true rotation of stock to avoid loss from spoilage, shrinking, and deterioration of quality. This is especially important for perishable foods and even more vital for such short-lived commodities as calves liver, melons, tomatoes, fresh strawberries,

raspberries, and blueberries, fish and seafood, milk, butter, cream, certain cheese items, and certain delicatessen items. A good storeroom manager, working with the chef and the food buyer, requests that these highly perishable items be purchased almost on a daily basis to avoid large losses.

During the past few years there have been a number of changes in storeroom operations because of changes in the packaging of food supplies. Many perishable items that originally came in large, bulk containers had to be sorted as soon as they were checked into the storeroom, with bruised and injured merchandise going directly to the kitchen for immediate use. Merchandise in good condition was generally repackaged in smaller units and held for issue when needed. Today practically everything is packaged in containers ready for storage. These containers protect the merchandise against damage and can be used for issuing merchandise to the using departments. This virtually eliminates "cooperage" accounts and many losses from inaccurate weighing and spoilage.

Since most merchandise now comes in containers that are more practical in size and shape, the amount of shelving, both in storerooms and in refrigerators, can be reduced to about half of that formerly needed. The merchandise in containers can be stacked on skids or pallets, and either the full container can be issued or the amount requisitioned can be removed from the top container. This method not only saves work; it also expedites daily taking of inventory to determine supplies needed and aids in taking the month-end inventory.

Good storeroom management also requires that all containers be stamped with the date or coded by color, with one color being reserved for each day of the week.

The date stamp is better for long-term storage, but color codes on perishable items have worked quite well, especially when storeroom personnel are unable to read or write.

Packaging can, however, be carried to extremes. It is costly, and many dry bulk items such as rice, beans, sugar, or specialty flours can be bought at a lower cost per pound in large units. The large containers can then be broken down into small packages, labeled, date stamped, and issued in smaller quantities in the storeroom. A net saving of as much as 30 percent is possible by repackaging bulk dry merchandise in the storeroom.

Even though items such as melons, tomatoes, apples, and other fruits are purchased "ready for use," it is always necessary, before issue, for storeroom personnel to unpack the containers, sort or trim the merchandise, or allow it to ripen, as required. This requires some shelving and tables for handling the merchandise. Some operations even have ultraviolet lamps with an off-and-on electrical control to ripen melons and certain fruits and berries.

Each storeroom shelf and storage area should be labeled with the name of the item to be stored and maximum and minimum stock levels. The minimum stock level is the point where storeroom personnel should request purchases to raise stock to the maximum level. Nothing ordered should be on hand more than ninety days except with the approval of management. At times when shortages are imminent and inflationary prices are expected, purchases of stock that exceed the ninety-day use period are desirable, almost necessary.

One category that always seems to be in excess supply is spices. Sometimes supplies of such things as mace, bay leaf, tarragon, and oregano adequate for three to four years of use are found. For some unknown reason there is sure to be too much poultry seasoning in almost every storeroom.

There are always those special items that some chef or banquet manager simply "has to have." As soon as a large quantity is on hand, however, the whole project is forgotten, and, unless the dead stock is recorded on a monthly basis and forced into the kitchen for use, it is eventually thrown out.

Inventory Taking. Month-end inventory taking can be an ordeal. Often it is so rushed that the results are inaccurate and unreliable. Frequently the work is assigned to someone who is poorly trained or uninterested, and errors result. Manipulating the figures to make them look accurate may well be the next step, and, as soon as this situation exists, someone is sure to see the possibilities in a systematic removal of stock.

The final responsibility for the taking of the month-end inventory lies with the controller and the accounting department. The controller, with the help of the head storeroom attendant and the food and beverage controller, must ensure a true and accurate accounting of all merchandise in the storeroom.

It is generally sufficient for the head storeroom attendant or storeroom manager working with the food and beverage controller to take the food and beverage inventory. From time to time, however, an independent representative from the accounting department should be present, and several times during the year the controller himself should participate in the taking of inventories.

The storeroom should be shut down during the taking of inventories, and it is helpful to have the storeroom crew count the merchandise and leave a ticket on each that shows the amount of merchandise on each stack of supplies. The inventory should be taken in a permanently bound inventory book with the items listed in the book in the order that the stock is arranged in the storeroom to facilitate a speedy and accurate count. The figures should be listed in the inventory book with a pen, and, once an entry is made, any change should be initialed by both the head storeroom attendant and the food and beverage controller.

Even though freezer stock should have a perpetual inventory, it is advisable to spot-check actual stock against the perpetual inventory on about a quarter of the items in the freezer. A different list of items should be spot-checked each month.

The liquor inventory, also perpetual, must be checked, item for item, against the actual inventory. This can be done at a later time by the food and beverage controller, who then determines overages or shortages by item.

One word of caution: the food and beverage inventory book should always be in the possession of the food and beverage controller. Once the book is priced, extended, and totaled, it should be kept under lock and key in the accounting office. Some large storeroom differences have been concealed by changing the storeroom inventory count when the book was available either in the storeroom or in the food and beverage control office. In one instance, the book was altered by a member of the accounting department who happened to have a taste for fine brandy.

Inspections. An inspection checklist should be prepared for management by the food and beverage manager in co-operation with the controller and the chief engineer. It should cover all requirements of the Occupational Safety and Health Act (see Chapter 3) and of local building codes. In addition to sanitary requirements in the storeroom operation, the checklist should cover all phases of the operation, including controls, hours of service, security measures, and any other pertinent information.

A copy of the major provisions of the local sanitary codes should be posted in the storeroom as a constant reminder to the staff. A regular cleaning schedule and a daily schedule of cleaning responsibilities should also be posted so that the storeroom would be ready for inspection by anyone at any time.

A good general manager of a hotel or large food operation will find time in his busy schedule to inspect the storeroom weekly. This does not have to be a formal matter; simply walking through the area helps to keep an operation alert.

Most food operations are required to conduct a formal monthly inspection and file a written report in the manager's office. The best inspections are often made by a team composed of two or three other department heads and the storeroom manager. Their checklist can be filed and used by outside inspectors.

Another practice has worked well for some large facilities. The general manager invites the local or state health inspector to visit the premises to help train the self-inspection team so that an effective monthly inspection can be made. This gives the health inspectors confidence in the attitude of management, and, if problems arise later, the operation is able to request the help of the health inspector who participated in the training process.

Other large operators have hired outside sanitation consultants on a regular basis to make a complete and thorough sanitary inspection of the premises and provide a written report with recommendations on compliance with local, state, and national health codes. Not only do these consultants help keep the premises in good shape; they can also help if there are any problems. The fact that management is interested enough to secure outside help often discourages lawsuits and keeps legal judgments at a low level.

In addition to regularly scheduled storeroom and sanitary inspections, there should be an understanding that certain department heads are expected to visit the storeroom, look over the operations, and offer any helpful comments or suggestions that they might have. These surprise inspections can be made by the food and beverage manager, the kitchen manager, the food buyer, the chef, the controller, the head bartender, the catering manager, or anyone else designated by the general manager of the operation.

Any reports from such inspections should be made to the general manager of the operation, as well as to the storeroom staff.

10 Controls and Checklists

Purpose: To examine how the control department and the internal control system of a good food service operation function in relation to the professional buyer's job.

INTRODUCTION

Control—like procurement, production, and sales—is one of the essential functions of a business organization. A food service operation, depending on its size and organizational complexity, may or may not have one controller responsible for all functions, but even if it does, there are some control activities that are the province of the food and beverage purchasing agent. This agent must be aware of how the control department functions in relation to the purchasing department and how the internal control system works.

THE CONTROLLER'S DEPARTMENT

As noted above, the four essential functions of a food service operation are control, procurement, production, and sales. This chapter is concerned primarily with the control function and how it relates to the professional food buyer.

A controller "responsible for the control and the security of all of the assets of the company" has broad authority indeed, and must be involved in the daily activities of all the departments in any food service operation. In addition, the controller is responsible for the accounting office and all members of the accounting staff.

The control department keeps a set of books and accounts as prescribed by law and recommended by the trade industry. It collects all income, accounts for bank deposits, pays bills, and keeps payroll records. The controller is responsible for establishing an internal control system and seeing that it works, auditing all incoming bills for accuracy, seeing that all payments are properly approved by management before payments are made, issuing daily operational reports, making special analyses for management, issuing regular monthly reports and annual tax reports, exerting necessary payroll controls, and assisting management in dealing with the unions. As if these duties were not sufficient, the controller is expected to act as an operations analyst and to advise management on decisions affecting the success or failure of the business. The controller or the control department basically observes, records, and reports every transaction of the entire operation. From these reports the controller is most competent to act as confidential advisor to management on financial matters.

This chapter is by no means an attempt to outline the operation of a control department. Instead, it represents an attempt to make the professional food buyer aware of how the controller and the control department function in relation to the food buyer's own job. The chapter also deals with the internal control system of a food service operation and how it operates on a day-to-day basis in departments that are under the direction of the food buyer, and points out why some of the steps in the internal control system are necessary.

INTERNAL CONTROL

The first control function related to food buying is the request from the various departments to the food buyer stating items and quantities needed. A suitable form is provided for making such requests. Then there are forms for recording price quotations, requests for bids, and purchase orders. There are additional forms for receiving incoming merchandise, including receiving sheets, receiving tickets, credit memorandums, and forms used for merchandise received without invoice. These were explained in Chapter 8. All of these forms make up the internal record-keeping documentation, which is necessary for verifying all purchases, items received, and returns.

Further control measures are the checking of incoming bills, the checking of merchandise against specification sheets, the control of the requisitions for the issue of merchandise, the keeping of necessary perpetual inventories and month-end inventories, as well as the proper pricing of requisitions and inventories, the issuing of dead stock reports, the storeroom

reports on overages and shortages, and the securing of the storeroom.

Specifications

The food and beverage controller and the receiving clerk are under the direct supervision of the controller. Through these persons the controller is kept aware of the proper use of specifications. If he or she receives word that there are deviations, the controller takes up the matter with the food buyer, and if necessary, with management.

Price Quotations

The food buyer's quotations, competitive and negotiated, support every price that is paid. The controller reviews such records and also sees that necessary purchase orders are issued and that orderly numerical files are kept of purchase orders and contracts.

Receiving Sheets

The internal control system in the food service industry generally requires the use of receiving sheets or tickets that give in detail the name of the purveyor and a listing of merchandise by item, quantity, price, and extensions. This information is supported by properly approved invoices. See Chapter 8 for full details concerning receiving.

Storeroom Controls

Storerooms include, in addition to food and beverages, such supplies as china, glassware, silverware, linen, utensils, paper, and cleaning supplies. In large operations, the value of the inventories can reach several hundred thousand dollars. A complete and detailed internal control system is designed to keep storeroom shortages to a minimum. The system begins with the receiving sheet where the quantity and price of all items that come into the operation are recorded. Effective storeroom operation dictates that as soon as merchandise is in the storeroom, it is date stamped and priced at cost so that requisitions can be priced properly by the storeroom staff as issues are made.

The next step is concerned with a properly made out and signed requisition bearing the signature of a department head authorized to make withdrawals from the storeroom. Nothing should be issued without such a requisition.

Then there are the minimum and maximum amounts of stock to be carried in the storeroom. The mini-maxi stock list is used as a basis for reordering as well as for keeping the stock value within the storeroom budget. The food and beverage controller, if there is one, the bookkeeper, or someone else from the controller's office should maintain a perpetual inventory on certain storeroom items such as liquor, freezer contents, and china, glassware, and silverware.

At the end of each month, a complete storeroom physical inventory of food and beverages must be taken by a member of the controller's office. (This duty can be delegated to the food and beverage control office.) The month-end inventory is used for determining accurate costs for the month, and, in addition, it is the basis for preparing an overage and shortage report on items kept on perpetual inventory. Exhibit 10-1 shows pages from typical storeroom inventory books.

Inventories of china, glassware, silverware, and linen are generally taken on a quarterly basis, and any necessary adjustments of the month-to-month cost of such items can be made at that time.

Production inventories are taken throughout the various departments of the operation, usually by the department head, assisted, on a spot-check basis, by someone from the controller's office. The taking of a production inventory can be a very sensitive matter, as there is always some question about what is of value once it is in production.

There must be a storeroom reconciliation made by the controller's department on both food and beverages. Such a report lists storeroom adjustments (sales made from the storeroom at cost, food spoilage, transfers at cost to other departments, employees' meals, public relations, and gratis foods). Any difference between the calculated month-end inventory and the actual physical month-end inventory has to be reconciled.

Another step in the internal control system is the dead stock report. It should be made out on a monthly basis for management's and the operating department's information. The dead stock report lists items that have been on hand in the storeroom for ninety days or more and that, for one reason or another, are not being used in production. Usually this stock has to be forced into the production line to ensure use before spoilage.

One of the more important facets of the internal control system in the storeroom is the logbook, kept where storeroom keys are turned in every night for security reasons. This logbook records the signatures of anyone who withdraws the keys, and the controller's office must investigate any withdrawal of the storeroom keys except to open the storeroom in the morning.

In large food service operations, management often authorizes the controller's department to bring in outside consultants for surprise inventories and for surprise receiving checks. Receiving checks must be done by people trained in the use of purchase specifications.

Other Activities Related to the Control System

Internal control in a food service operation also includes production controls in the kitchen, portion counts, recipe and portion-size control, daily food costs either in relation to sales, or, in the institutional

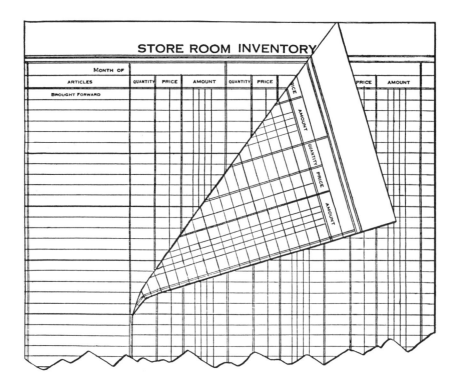

Exhibit 10-1. Pages from typical storeroom inventory books

field, cost per meal served, and the establishment of potential costs. Maintaining food and beverage control and production work sheets, checking and cashiering of all cash revenue, and control of restaurant checks, taking register readings, reconciling cash and charges, and accounting for all funds also require internal control.

Controls in Small- and Medium-Size Operations

The cost of an elaborate control system is unwarranted in a small operation. Management, generally the owner, can use visual control in place of a more detailed plan. Actually, an alert owner, with the help of family members or a partner, can exert a tight system just by staying constantly alert. If the operation is large enough to afford a full-time bookkeeper, that person can take care of some controls such as the control of cash, checking of invoices, and taking of inventories.

In a medium-size operation that is large enough to warrant a small controller's department, a fairly complete internal control system can be maintained by the controller through the spot-check method. If the controller's department varies the spot checks, the element of surprise can be almost as effective as an actual continuous control system.

A Word of Warning

The most elaborate internal control system possible means absolutely nothing unless it is correctly and fully used, with the controller ensuring such use. Management must take a very active part in policing the internal control system. A dishonest person in the controller's office can be a problem. The best guard against losses through such dishonesty is to have outside auditors and consultants come in occasionally on a spot-check

basis. Operators have learned that having outside spot checks conducted on an unannounced basis is an invaluable method of keeping employees honest.

The Controller's Role in Inspection Teams

Some parts of a food service operation do not require that the controller or a representative from the controller's department be on the self-inspection team, but any part of the operation involving the food buyer should have the controller or a representative of that department as a member of any inspection team.

Checklists concerned with the activities of the purchasing department should give attention to purchase requests by the various using departments, price quotations, butcher and cooking tests, specifications, receiving practices, requisitions for mechandise, pricing, and inventories. These are all part of the internal control system, and the controller is basically responsible for the manner in which that system is carried out.

CHECKLISTS

In a seminar on food and beverage purchasing during a summer school session at Cornell University, a well-known and higly regarded food buyer for a large industrial feeding operation was discussing the value and use of checklists. He attached great importance to their use, stressing that they help to make a person's job easier as well as more efficient. At one point the speaker stated that the use of checklists could save one's life. In the face of a rather skeptical reaction from his audience, the speaker went on to tell how the use of a checklist had done that. During World War II he was a passenger in a single-engine aircraft when the plane became lost in a heavy overcast so charged with electricity that neither radio nor direction finder could be used. As the pilot circled, in the hope that weather conditions would change and permit radio contact, the single engine quit. Pilot and passenger prepared to parachute from the plane, but not before the pilot, who had been trained in the use of an emergency checklist, proceeded to follow it. Within a few seconds the engine caught again, and twenty minutes later the pilot made radio contact and landed safely at an airport only two hundred miles from the intended destination. It was later discovered that the gas in the main tank had been exhausted, even though the gas gauge showed an ample supply. One of the procedures to be followed on the emergency checklist was to throw the emergency pump onto the reserve gas tank.

A food buyer may not owe his life to a checklist, but it is well known that one's best efforts are devoted to those phases of a job that are checked by others. A good checklist, properly used by both the departments and management, proves to be a helpful guide to both the operator and management.

One problem can arise in the use of checklists. If the person using the checklist considers himself to be perfect, he can cause difficulties for the operator. It would be better not to have a checklist than to use it in this manner.

The best system for the preparation and use of a checklist is for the department head, with the help of the staff, to compile one for the department and submit it to management. Once the checklist has been approved, department head and staff should be willing to use it because they designed it.

It is best to have teams from within the department make inspections, rather than a single individual. A team made up of one or two representatives from the operating department plus representatives from other departments helps to lessen the demoralizing effect. The self-inspection teams should fill out the checklist and review it with the department head before filing it in the department. Management can, on occassion, refer to this checklist when comparing its own inspection report with those of the self-inspection teams.

Sample Checklists

Food service personnel may be charged with preparing an operational checklist or lists covering a food and beverage purchasing operation. Exhibits 10-2 through 10-6 are examples of checklists now being used. These checklists, as they are set up, actually constitute a brief, condensed operating manual based on all the proven and successful methods of operation for a typical food service facility. If any food service operator could answer affirmatively all the items on these checklists covering purchasing, control, and sanitation, he would have an almost perfect operation, at least in terms of the areas checked.

The checklists for the food and beverage cost control system start with a list of "manager's spot checks," followed by a rather comprehensive list of questions that a manager should insist be answered in the affirmative so that he can be assured that back-of-the-house operations, especially the purchasing, receiving, storing, and issuing functions, are under control and that the food buyer is carrying out his responsibilities.

Sanitation Checklists

Sanitation requirements outlined in the Occupational Safety and Health Act will probably become much more strict as food service operations increase and consumers become more knowledgeable about how food poisoning can be transmitted.

Date: _____ Institution: _____

FOOD AND BEVERAGE PURCHASING CHECKLIST

Satis-factory	Unsatis-factory	N/A	Item description	Comments
			What specifications were used for purchasing?	
			Do all vendors have copies of the specifications for items they handle?	
			Are competitive bids being received from a minimum of two vendors on all items purchased competitively?	
			Are price quotations recorded on a market quotation list?	
			Are these lists kept on file for a period of one year?	
			Are the quantities to be purchased determined by forecasts?	
			Does the chef approve the quantities to be purchased before orders are placed?	
			Is a grocery price book maintained showing competitive prices?	
			Is the grocery price book up to date?	
			Is there a file supporting the decision to purchase certain products from single purveyors?	
			Are orders for fresh fish phoned to the vendor's office no later than 11:00 A.M. for delivery the next day?	
			Are orders for meats, provisions, poultry, fresh fruits and vegetables, frozen foods, and dairy items phoned to the vendor's office no later than 1:00 P.M. for the next day's delivery?	
			Are orders for canned goods and dry stores on a twice a month schedule?	
			Are orders for canned goods and dry stores phoned to the vendor's office at least forty-eight hours before desired delivery date?	
			Does the institution provide the vendor with a weekly forecast of requirements for ribs, strips, and top sirloin butts every Monday?	
			Are requirements given one week in advance for ribs and two weeks in advance for strips and top butts to allow the proper aging?	
			Are requirements for melons given to the vendor one week in advance to allow dealers time to purchase, select, and ripen melons?	
			Has the vendor furnished the institution with an approved vendor list?	
			Is there any deviation from this list?	
			Which major food items are not bought through the vendor? _____	
			Are certain perishable items that are used in small quantities bought by the pound or at retail instead of by the case lot?	
			Is no more than a three-month supply of spices bought to assure freshness and eliminate waste?	

Exhibit 10-2. Checklist for purchasing food and beverages (Courtesy: Sheraton Corporation of America, Boston, Massachusetts)

Date: _____ Institution: _____

FOOD AND BEVERAGE PURCHASING CHECKLIST

Satis-factory	Unsatis-factory	N/A	Item description	Comments
			How many days has the oldest supply of the following items been in the storeroom? Strawberries _____ Lemons _____ Chicken _____ Tomatoes _____ Oranges _____ Eggs _____ Grapes _____ Grapefruit _____ Butter _____ Romaine _____ Avocados _____ Coffee _____ Does the food purchaser verify invoices for agreement of amounts, prices, and items with orders placed? Has the quantity purchasing program to gain price advantage been implemented? Are the following items being purchased in accordance with Mr. Jones's memorandum of August 1973? Texas brown shrimp, 21-15 count? Sliced bacon, 21-14 count? Breakfast sausages, 14-16 size? Grade "A," large eggs? Vitality frozen orange juice? Instant hot cereal? Maple syrup, 15% blend? Are beverage purchase orders approved by the general manager before being placed? Are quantities ordered determined by par stock and banquet orders? Are all private and exclusive label beverages being purchased?	

Exhibit 10-2 (continued)

Date: _____ Institution: _____

FOOD RECEIVING INSPECTION CHECKLIST

Satis-factory	Unsatis-factory	N/A	Item description	Comments
			Is the receiving clerk responsible to the controller?	
			Is there a list of the items to be received showing vendor, items, quantities, and prices?	
			Are all items received (including those without invoices) written on the receiving sheet showing item, quantity, price, and total?	
			Are returns written on the receiving sheet?	
			List three items returned during the past week.	
			a) _____	
			b) _____	
			c) _____	
			What were the percentages of returns to total food purchases for the past two months? _____ % _____%	
			Are receiving sheets completed and added up daily?	
			Who prepares the receiving sheet?	
			Name: _____ _____	
			Are food receiving specifications posted in the receiving areas?	
			Are they readable from the scale?	
			Are the persons receiving food items familiar with the receiving specifications?	
			Does the general manager or food and beverage manager check the food receiving weekly?	
			Are the scales checked periodically by an inspector? Date: _____	
			Is a ruler attached to the receiving scale to measure the trim of the meat?	
			Is there an adequate scale for weighing merchandise received?	
			Are all items weighed in total and individual weights checked?	
			Are all meats, poultry, and fish items stripped of their wrappings before being weighed?	
			Are fruits and other items bought by size and count spot-checked to make sure that the size of the fruit is according to USDA grading marked on the box?	
			When receiving fruits, is the net weight as well as the count checked?	
			Are melons and pineapples taken out of their containers and checked for decay and ripeness?	
			Are unripened melons returned?	

Exhibit 10-3. Checklist for inspecting food and beverages received (Courtesy: Sheraton Corporation of America, Boston, Massachusetts)

Date: _____ Institution: _____

FOOD RECEIVING INSPECTION CHECKLIST

Satis-factory	Unsatis-factory	N/A	Item description	Comments
			Are berries checked as to net weight per pint?	
			Are cartons of oranges, grapefruit, and lemons turned over to see that the quality is consistent throughout?	
			When receiving lettuce, is at least one head of lettuce cut to check quality and see that it is free from decay?	
			Are fresh beans taken out of their containers and the net content weighed?	
			Are all perishable items date stamped?	
			Is ice cream weighed to check the overrun?	
			Is butterfat content checked on milk, cream, butter, and ice cream? Date of last check:_____	
			Are butter and coffee spot-checked for weight?	
			Are eggs weighed?	
			What merchandise was received before the food receiver came on duty?	
			Dealer Item Quantity Price Total	
			What merchandise was received after the food receiver usually goes off duty?	
			Dealer Item Quantity Price Total	
			Were the early morning and late afternoon deliveries emergency orders?	
			Is a "goods received without invoice" prepared when merchandise is received without invoice?	
			Is there a "notice of error and correction" prepared when merchandise is returned or an invoice is corrected?	
			Does the receiving clerk stamp and sign invoices?	
			Is incoming beverage merchandise checked against the purchase order?	
			Are cases of liquor weighed on a spot-check basis to find missing or broken bottles?	

Exhibit 10-3 (*continued*)

Date: _____ Institution: _____

FOOD AND BEVERAGE STORAGE AND ISSUING CHECKLIST

Satis-factory	Unsatis-factory	N/A	Item description	Comments
			Are designated opening and closing hours of the food and liquor storeroom maintained?	
			Is there a logbook maintained at the front desk recording the "in and out" of storeroom keys during the time the storeroom is closed?	
			Are all containers priced to facilitate inventory taking and costing of requisitions?	
			Are inventory items rotated, i.e., issued on a "first-in, first-out" basis?	
			Are sugar, spices, nuts, etc., prepackaged and priced in the quantities usually requisitioned?	
			Are items on shelves placed in order according to the inventory books?	
			Do the food and beverage storerooms operate out of single opened containers as far as possible?	
			Is a written requisition signed by an authorized person required for all items?	
			Is there a list of authorized signatures posted in the food storeroom?	
			Are requisitions signed by the person issuing the merchandise?	
			Are food requisitions priced by the storeroom clerk on a daily basis?	
			Are the keys to the liquor storeroom under the control of one person?	
			Is there an emergency key to the liquor storeroom in a sealed envelope at the front desk, and is it controlled by a signed in and out log?	
			Is the beverage perpetual inventory handled by a person other than the one who has the liquor storeroom keys?	
			Are bar requisitions handled as outlined in the food and beverage control manual?	
			a) Are the requisitions made out and signed by the bartender, are original and duplicate copies of the order sent to the wineroom, and is the third copy retained at the bar?	
			b) After filling the order, are the original and duplicate copies of the requisition signed by the wineroom storekeeper?	
			c) Does the bar boy sign the original and duplicate of the requisition before delivering the order?	
			d) Does the original requisition accompany the order to the bar and is the duplicate kept in the beverage storeroom?	
			e) Is the original rechecked and signed by the bartender on duty?	

Exhibit 10-4. Checklist for issuing food and beverages stored (Courtesy: Sheraton Corporation of America, Boston, Massachusetts)

Date: _____ Institution: _____

FOOD AND BEVERAGE STORAGE AND ISSUING CHECKLIST

Satis-factory	Unsatis-factory	N/A	Item description	Comments
			f) Is the signed original requisition forwarded to the food and beverage control office in a sealed envelope?	
			Is there a separate banquet bar used for the return and reissue of banquet stock to the regular bars?	
			Is there any open beverage stock in the wineroom?	
			Have storeroom operating hours been reduced to a minimum?	
			Are food, liquor, and general storeroom functions combined?	
			Has such a combination been examined for practicality?	

Exhibit 10-4 (*continued*)

Date: _____ Institution: _____

FOOD AND BEVERAGE SECURITY CHECKLIST

Satis-factory	Unsatis-factory	N/A	Item description	Comments
			Is there only one set of keys to the storeroom in circulation?	
			Does the morning storeroom person take the storeroom keys home to open the next morning?	
			Are the storeroom keys kept locked at the front desk when the storeroom is closed?	
			Are the storeroom keys kept in an unlocked drawer of the assistant manager's desk in the lobby?	
			Is there only one set of keys to the kitchen spaces in circulation?	
			Do the kitchen keys hang on a nail in the main kitchen all day and night till closing?	
			Are the kitchen keys kept locked at the front desk when the kitchen is closed?	
			Does the breakfast cook have a personal set of kitchen keys for speedy opening in the morning?	
			Is a logbook kept at the front desk to record the signing in and signing out of keys?	
			Are two signatures required for each entry: the person signing the keys in or out and the desk clerk?	
			Has anyone checked the entries in the front office key logbook during the past month?	
			When the storeroom must be opened after hours in an emergency situation, does the assistant manager accompany the person requesting merchandise to the storeroom?	
			Is a busperson or food runner sent alone to the kitchen for emergency withdrawals of food after the storeroom is closed?	
			Are designated opening and closing hours of the food storeroom maintained?	
			Do salespeople inventory the food purchases and tell the purchaser the institution's requirements?	
			Is a written requisition signed by an authorized person required for all items?	
			Does the storeroom man add forgotten items to food requisitions which are phoned in by a cook?	
			Is there a list of authorized signatures in the food storeroom?	
			Are food requisitions complete as to date, department, item, quantity, and size?	
			Are requisitions signed by the persons issuing the merchandise?	
			Is one responsible person entrusted with signing out kitchen keys?	

Exhibit 10-5. Checklist for securing food and beverages stored (Courtesy: Sheraton Corporation of America, Boston, Massachusetts)

Date: _____ Institution: _____

FOOD AND BEVERAGE SECURITY CHECKLIST

Satis-factory	Unsatis-factory	N/A	Item description	Comments
			Is a responsible person assigned the responsibility of locking all kitchen spaces at closing?	
			Are kitchen refrigerators left unlocked overnight?	
			Is there an established routine for putting all production food in locked areas overnight?	
			Are more employees' meals eaten in the main kitchen than the employees' cafeteria?	
			Are employees required to enter and leave through an employee entrance?	
			Are all bundles inspected before being taken from the premises?	
			Is there an organized method of salvaging usable butter, cream, and relishes from banquets?	
			Are restaurant and room service condiments stored in locked areas during hours when there is no service?	
			Are usable items salvaged from room service and restaurants during and at the close of operations?	

Exhibit 10-5 (continued)

Date: _____ Institution: _____

FOOD AND BEVERAGE COST CONTROL SYSTEM CHECKLIST

Satis-factory	Unsatis-factory	N/A	Item description	Comments

Manager's spot checks

Is the food and beverage control in this institution being carried out according to standard food and beverage control standards of the institution?

Do the general manager, food and beverage manager, chef, and banquet manager receive a daily flash food cost report?

Do the general manager, food and beverage manager, and controller receive a monthly summary of beverage sales, potentials, and costs (bar potential report)?

Is a monthly report of overages and shortages from the beverage perpetual inventory sent to the general manager and controller?

Are the monthly food and beverage inventories taken by the food and beverage cost controller and a representative designated by the controller?

Are menu prices adjusted on a quarterly basis to reflect fluctuating costs?

Is there a complete list of portion sizes posted at all points of service in the kitchen?

Are weekly cover forecasts prepared and distributed to the concerned department heads on a regular weekly basis?

Does the general manager receive the previous day's food and beverage invoices after they are properly approved by the purchasing agent, receiving clerk, and food and beverage controller?

Is the general manager getting current banquet information regarding: a) Food and beverage costs
  b) Guarantees
  c) Special prices

Is there a regularly scheduled weekly meeting of the general manager and food and beverage controller to review current food and beverage costs and trends?

Is there a weekly food and beverage meeting that the general manager attends?

Food and beverage cost control procedures

What standard system of food and beverage control is in use?

For large operation _____
For small operation _____
One-sheet control _____

Is the appropriate food and beverage control manual available to all concerned?

Is the manual understood by the persons responsible for controls?

Exhibit 10-6. Checklist used in establishing cost controls for food and beverages (Courtesy: Sheraton Corporation of America, Boston, Massachusetts)

Date: _____ Institution: _____

FOOD AND BEVERAGE COST CONTROL SYSTEM CHECKLIST

Satis-factory	Unsatis-factory	N/A	Item description	Comments
			Does the food and beverage cost controller report to the general manager?	
			Is the food and beverage cost controller responsible to the controller for carrying out accounting control procedures as prescribed in policy and procedures?	
			Are invoices written up completely on the receiving sheets showing the date, purveyor, item, quantity, price, and total?	
			Are receiving sheets completed and totaled daily?	
			Is the minimum practical number of items on direct charge?	
			Are the receiving sheets verified by the food and beverage controller before being sent to the auditing office?	
			Are controller's food and beverage purchase figures balanced monthly with the total purchases shown on the receiving sheets?	
			Are requisitions required for all food items issued from the storeroom?	
			Are meats issued by requisitions?	
			Are food requisitions complete as to date, department, item, quantity, size, and authorized signature?	
			Are requisitions signed by the person issuing the merchandise?	
			Are food requisitions priced by the storeroom clerk on a daily basis?	
			Is the standard (three copies) bar requisition used as prescribed in the food and beverage control manual?	
			Is the banquet beverage requisition in use?	
			Are monthly food and beverage inventories taken by the food and beverage cost controller and a representative of the controller?	
			Are the monthly food and beverage inventories recorded in pen in bound books which are secured in the auditing office when not in use?	
			Are all corrections of changes in the inventory books initialed by a representative of the controller?	
			Is the food production inventory taken according to policy and procedure?	
			Is the beverage perpetual inventory kept by the food and beverage cost controller?	
			Is a monthly beverage report of overages and shortages from the perpetual inventory prepared by the food and beverage cost controller and sent to the controller and general manager?	
			Do the general manager, food and beverage manager, banquet manager, and chef receive a daily flash food cost report?	

Exhibit 10-6 (*continued*)

Date: _____ Institution: _____

FOOD AND BEVERAGE COST CONTROL SYSTEM CHECKLIST

Satis-factory	Unsatis-factory	N/A	Item description	Comments
			Is the monthly summary of beverage sales, potentials, and costs prepared by the food and beverage cost controller and sent to the food and beverage office and to the general manager and controller?	
			Are the food and beverage reconciliations prepared by the food and beverage cost controller and sent to the food and beverage department and to the general manager and controller?	
			Is the monthly report of private label usage prepared by the food and beverage cost controller and sent to the food and beverage department and to the general manager and controller?	
			Are employees' meals accounted for and costed as explained in the policies and procedures?	
			Food and beverage cost control procedures — operations	
			Is there a file of competitive menus in the food and beverage control office?	
			Is there a regular monthly program of butcher tests and recipe costing?	
			Is there a list of portion sizes for all restaurant and banquet menu items?	
			Is a portion control maintained for steaks and other high-cost items?	
			Are menu prices adjusted on a quarterly basis to reflect fluctuations in purchase prices?	
			Are food covers forecast monthly by outlet and by meal period?	
			Are food covers forecast weekly by outlet and meal period?	
			Does the food and beverage controller furnish food costs by outlet as his contribution to the preparation of the quarterly profit and loss by outlet?	
			Are marked menus furnished to the chef of the institution on a continuing daily basis?	
			Are marked menus used in planning food production?	
			Is the chef's daily order and production record for the butcher shop used?	
			Is the chef's daily order and production record for the pastry shop used?	
			Is the nonproductive items control in effect?	
			Is the alcohol content of liquor spot-checked on a monthly basis with a hydrometer?	
			Are banquets costed daily?	

Exhibit 10-6 (*continued*)

Date: _____ Institution: _____   _____

FOOD AND BEVERAGE COST CONTROL SYSTEM CHECKLIST

Satis-factory	Unsatis-factory	N/A	Item description	Comments
			Are banquet checks compared with production records and the number charged verified for accuracy?	
			Internal accounting control	
			Are restaurant and bar checks signed for by waiters, waitresses, and captains when issued to them?	
			Are amounts posted by a cash register on bar checks by the bartender after each round of drinks is prepared and served to bar customers, and are the checks placed face down on the bar in front of the customers?	
			Are properly posted bar checks presented after each round of drinks to table guests by the waitress (waiter) by placing the check face down on the table after the service of drinks?	
			Are bar checks rung back through the cash register when checks are paid?	
			Are used bar checks put in a locked box?	
			Is there a daily missing check report prepared by the auditing office?	
			Are cash registers locked and readings taken only by representatives of the auditing office?	
			Is a cash register used in the coffee shop?	
			Control procedures—purchasing	
			Are revised purchase specifications used for purchasing?	
			Do all vendors have copies of specifications used for the items they handle?	
			Are competitive bids being received from a minimum of two vendors on all items purchased competitively?	
			Are these quotations recorded on a market quotation list?	
			Does the chef approve the quantities to be purchased before orders are placed?	
			Is a grocery price book maintained showing competitive prices?	
			Is the grocery price book up to date?	
			Is there a file supporting the decision to purchase certain products from single purveyors?	
			Does the purchasing agent verify invoices for agreement of amounts, prices, and items with orders placed?	
			Is the beverage purchase order approved by the general manager before being placed?	

Exhibit 10-6 (*continued*)

Date: _____ Institution: _____

FOOD AND BEVERAGE COST CONTROL SYSTEM CHECKLIST

Satis-factory	Unsatis-factory	N/A	Item description	Comments
			Are butterfat and bacteria tests taken on milk, cream, and ice cream on a quarterly basis?	
			Control procedures—receiving	
			Is the receiving clerk responsible to the controller?	
			Are receiving procedures being carried out as directed by the controller?	
			Are receiving specifications posted?	
			Has the receiving clerk been instructed in the use of the specifications?	
			Does the receiving clerk receive a list from the purchasing agent of items, amounts, and prices of orders placed to compare with the invoices for merchandise received?	
			Is there an adequate scale for weighing merchandise received?	
			Is the scale checked periodically by an inspector and a verifying seal attached to the scale?	
			Is a ruler attached to the receiving scale to measure the trim of meat?	
			What standard food and beverage receiving sheets are used?	
			Is the food receiving sheet filled out showing dealer, item, quantity, price, and extensions and totaled daily?	
			Is a "goods received without invoice" prepared when merchandise is received without invoice?	
			Are items received without an accompanying invoice recorded on the receiving sheet?	
			Is there a "notice of error and correction" prepared when merchandise is returned or an invoice is corrected?	
			Are corrections and returns noted on the receiving sheet?	
			Does the receiving clerk stamp and sign invoices?	
			Are all cartons and containers date stamped when received?	
			Are weights of certain items, e.g., eggs, written on the carton along with the date received?	
			Is incoming beverage merchandise checked against the purchase order?	
			Are cases of liquor weighed on a spot-check basis to find missing or broken bottles?	
			Are receiving procedures checked by the food and beverage controller?	

Exhibit 10-6 (*continued*)

Date: _____ Institution: _____

FOOD AND BEVERAGE COST CONTROL SYSTEM CHECKLIST

Satis-factory	Unsatis-factory	N/A	Item description	Comments
			Control procedures—storing and issuing	
			Are designated opening and closing hours of the food and liquor storerooms maintained?	
			Is there a logbook maintained at the front desk recording the "in and out" of storeroom keys during the time the storeroom is closed?	
			Are all containers priced to facilitate inventory taking and costing of requisitions?	
			Are inventory items rotated, i.e., issued on a "first-in, first-out" basis?	
			Are sugar, spices, nuts, etc., prepackaged and priced in the quantities usually requisitioned?	
			Are items on shelves placed in order according to the inventory book?	
			Do the food and beverage storerooms operate out of single opened containers as far as possible?	
			Is a written requisition signed by an authorized person required for all items?	
			Is there a list of authorized signatures posted in the food store-room?	
			Are requisitions signed by the person issuing the merchandise?	
			Are food requisitions priced by the storeroom clerk on a daily basis?	
			Are the keys to the liquor storeroom under the control of one person?	
			Is there an emergency key to the liquor storeroom in a sealed envelope at the front desk and is it controlled by a signed in and out log?	
			Is the beverage perpetual inventory handled by a person other than the one who has the liquor storeroom keys?	
			Are bar requisitions handled as outlined in the food and beverage control manual?	
			a) Are the requisitions made out and signed by the bartender original and duplicate copies of the order sent to the wine-room, and is the third copy retained at the bar?	
			b) After filling the order, are the original and duplicate copies of the requisition signed by the wineroom storekeeper?	
			c) Does the bar boy sign the original and duplicate of the requisition before delivering the order?	
			d) Does the original requisition accompany the order to the bar and is the duplicate kept in the beverage storeroom?	

Exhibit 10-6 (*continued*)

Date: _____ Institution: _____

FOOD AND BEVERAGE COST CONTROL SYSTEM CHECKLIST

Satis-factory	Unsatis-factory	N/A	Item description	Comments
			e) Is the original rechecked and signed by the bartender on duty? f) Is the signed original requisition forwarded to the food and beverage control office in a sealed envelope? Is there a separate banquet bar used for the return and reissue of banquet stock to the regular bars? Is there any open beverage stock in the wineroom?	

Exhibit 10-6 (*continued*)

The wise food operator will insist that his establishment be clean and sanitary at all times, and the best way to ensure this is to have a regular inspection checklist that covers all angles of the sanitation problem.

The food service operator not only needs a good reference manual on food service sanitation; he should also provide one for his staff, to serve as a guide for their daily activities and also as a guide for inspection. Such a manual has been prepared as an aid to the food service industry by the American Mutual Insurance Company's engineering department. The food service sanitation checklist (Exhibit 10-7), which is part of this publication, has been adopted by over forty states as a uniform and acceptable sanitation guide. It has also been accepted by the federal government and is used in many government-operated food services.

SURVEY REPORT
FOOD SERVICE ESTABLISHMENTS

CITY, COUNTY OR DISTRICT	NAME OF ESTABLISHMENT	ADDRESS	OWNER OR OPERATOR

SECTION B. FOOD

1. FOOD SUPPLIES

Reference Guide columns: 8G, 7F, 7E, 7C, 7D, 6B1-3
Specify: Bakery products, Poultry and poultry products, Meat and meat products, Frozen desserts, Shellfish, Milk and milk products

Item		Reference Guide	Demerit Points
1	Approved source		6
2	Wholesome - not adulterated		6
3	Not misbranded		2
4	Original container; properly identified		
5	Approved dispenser		2
6	Fluid milk and fluid milk products pasteurized	6B2	6
7	Low-acid and non-acid foods commercially canned	8H1	6

2. FOOD PROTECTION

(columns: Preparation, Storage, Display, Service, Transportation)

Item		Reference Guide	Demerit Points
8	Protected from contamination	8A1	4
9	Adequate facilities for maintaining food at hot or cold temperatures	8A2	2
10	Suitable thermometers properly located	8A2	2
11	Perishable food at proper temperature	8B1	2
12	Potentially hazardous food at 45° F. or below, or 140° F. or above as required	8B2,3	6
13	Frozen food kept frozen; properly thawed	9B5	6
14	Handling of food minimized by use of suitable utensils	9C1	4
15	Hollandaise sauce of fresh ingredients; discarded after three hours	9B4	6
16	Food cooked to proper temperature	9C3-6	6
17	Fruits and vegetables washed thoroughly	9C2	6
18	Containers of food stored off floor on clean surfaces	10D1,2	2
19	No wet storage of packaged food	10D3	2
20	Display cases, counter protector devices or cabinets of approved type	10E1	2
21	Frozen dessert dippers properly stored	11E3	2
22	Sugar in closed dispensers or individual packages	11E4	2
23	Unwrapped and potentially hazardous food not re-served	11E5	4
24	Poisonous and toxic materials properly identified, colored, stored and used; poisonous polishes not present	11G 1-7	6
25	Bactericides, cleaning and other compounds properly stored and non-toxic in use dilutions	12G4	

SECTION C. PERSONNEL

1. HEALTH AND DISEASE CONTROL

Item		Reference Guide	Demerit Points
26	Persons with boils, infected wounds, respiratory infections or other communicable disease properly restricted	12B	6
27	Known or suspected communicable disease cases reported to health authority	12B	6

2. CLEANLINESS

Item		Reference Guide	Demerit Points
28	Hands washed and clean	12C1-3	6
29	Clean outer garments; proper hair restraints used	13D1,2	2
30	Good hygienic practices	13E	4

SECTION D. FOOD EQUIPMENT AND UTENSILS

1. SANITARY DESIGNS CONSTRUCTION AND INSTALLATION OF EQIUPMENT AND UTENSILS

Reference Guide columns: 13A2, 13A2, 13A2, 13A3, 13A3, 13A1, 3, 14A, 4, 5, 9-11, 14A6-8
(Good repair, no cracks; No chips, pits or open seams; Cleanable, smooth; Approved material; No corrosion; Proper construction; Accessible for cleaning and inspection)

Item		Reference Guide	Demerit Points
31	Food-contact surfaces of equipment		2
32	Utensils		2
33	Non-food-contact surfaces of equipment		2
34	Single-service articles of non-toxic materials	15A12	2
35	Equipment properly installed	15B1-3	2
36	Existing equipment capable of being cleaned, non-toxic, properly installed, and in good repair	16C	2

2. CLEANLINESS OF EQUIPMENT AND UTENSILS

Item		Reference Guide	Demerit Points
37	Tableware clean to sight and touch	16D1	
38	Kitchenware and food-contact surfaces of equipment clean to sight and touch	16D2	4
39	Grills and similar cooking devices cleaned daily	16D2	
40	Non-food-contact surfaces of equipment kept clean	16D3	2
41	Detergents and abrasives rinsed off food-contact surfaces	16D4	2
42	Clean wiping cloths used; use properly restricted	16D5	2
43	Utensils and equipment pre-flushed, scraped or soaked	17F1	2
44	Tableware sanitized	16E1	
45	Kitchenware and food-contact surfaces of equipment used for potentially hazardous food sanitized	16E2	4
46	Facilities for washing and sanitizing equipment and utensils approved, adequate, properly constructed, maintained and operated	17-19 F	4
47	Wash and sanitizing water clean	17F3	
48	Wash water at proper temperature	17F3	2
49	Dish tables and drain boards provided, properly located and constructed	18F7	
50	Adequate and suitable detergents used	17F2	
51	Approved thermometers provided and used	18F6	
52	Suitable dish baskets provided	18F5	2
53	Proper gauge cocks provided	18F10B	
54	Cleaned and cleaned and sanitized utensils and equipment properly stored and handled; utensils air-dried	19G1,2	2
55	Suitable facilities and areas provided for storing utensils and equipment	20G2	2
56	Single-service articles properly stored, dispensed and handled	20H1,2	2
57	Single-service articles used only once	20H3	
58	Single-service articles used when approved washing and sanitizing facilities are not provided	20H4	6

SECTION E. SANITARY FACILITIES AND CONTROLS

1. WATER SUPPLY

Item		Reference Guide	Demerit Points
59	From approved source; adequate; safe quality	20A1	6
60	Hot and cold running water provided	20A2	4
61	Transported water handled, stored; dispensed in a sanitary manner	21B1,2	6
62	Ice from approved source; made from potable water	21C1	6
63	Ice machines and facilities properly located, installed and maintained	21C1	2
64	Ice and ice handling utensils properly handled and stored; block ice rinsed	21C2	2
65	Ice-contact surfaces approved; proper material and construction	21C4	

3364 1-66

Exhibit 10-7. Example of a report on food service santitation (Courtesy: AIG/New Hampshire Insurance Company, 70 Pine St., New York, NY 10270)

PAGE 2

Item	2. SEWAGE DISPOSAL	REFER. GUIDE	Demerit Points
66	Into public sewer, or approved private facilities	21A1	6
	3. PLUMBING		
67	Properly sized, installed and maintained	22A1	2
68	Non-potable water piping identified	22A2	1
69	No cross connections	22A1-3	6
70	No back siphonage possible	22A3	
71	Equipment properly drained	22B1-3	2
	4. TOILET FACILITIES		
72	Adequate, conveniently located, and accessible; properly designed and installed	23A 1-3	6
73	Toilet rooms completely enclosed, and equipped with self-closing, tight-fitting doors; doors kept closed	23A3	2
74	Toilet rooms, fixtures and vestibules kept clean, in good repair, and free from odors	23B1	2
75	Toilet tissue and proper waste receptacles provided; waste receptacles emptied as necessary	23B2	2
	5. HAND-WASHING FACILITIES		
76	Lavatories provided, adequate, properly located and installed	23A1-3	6
77	Provided with hot and cold or tempered running water through proper fixtures	24A4	4
78	Suitable hand cleanser and sanitary towels or approved hand-drying devices provided	24B1	2
79	Waste receptacles provided for disposable towels	24B1	2
80	Lavatory facilities clean and in good repair	24B2	2
	6. GARBAGE AND RUBBISH DISPOSAL		
81	Stored in approved containers; adequate in number	24A1,4	2
82	Containers cleaned when empty; brushes provided	24A3	2
83	When not in continuous use, covered with tight fitting lids, or in protective storage inaccessible to vermin	24A2	2
84	Storage areas adequate; clean; no nuisances; proper facilities provided	25B1-3	2
85	Disposed of in an approved manner, at an approved frequency	25D1	2
86	Garbage rooms or enclosures properly constructed; outside storage at proper height above ground or on concrete slab	25B4	2
87	Food waste grinders and incinerators properly installed, constructed and operated; incinerators areas clean	25C,D2	2
	7. VERMIN CONTROL		
88	Presence of rodents, flies, roaches and vermin minimized	26A1,2	4
89	Outer openings protected against flying insects as required; rodent-proofed	26B1-3,C	2
90	Harborage and feeding of vermin prevented	26A2	2

Item	SECTION F. OTHER FACILITIES 1. FLOORS, WALLS AND CEILINGS	REFER. GUIDE	Demerit Points
91	Floors kept clean; no sawdust used	26A1	2
92	Floors easily cleanable construction, in good repair, smooth, non-absorbent; carpeting in good repair	26A2,4	1
93	Floor graded and floor drains, as required	27A3	2
94	Exterior walking and driving surfaces clean; drained	27A5	2
95	Exterior walking and driving surfaces properly surfaced	27A5	1
96	Mats and duck boards cleanable, removable and clean	27A6	2
97	Floors and wall junctures properly constructed	27A7	2
98	Walls, ceilings and attached equipment clean	27B1	2
99	Walls and ceilings properly constructed and in good repair; coverings properly attached	27B3-5	1
100	Walls of light color; washable to level of splash	27B2	2
	2. LIGHTING		
101	20 foot-candles of light on working surfaces	28A1	
102	10 foot-candles of light on food equipment, utensil-washing, hand-washing areas and toilet rooms	28A1	2
103	5 foot-candles of light 30" from floor in all other areas	28A1	
104	Artificial light sources as required	28A1	2
	3. VENTILATION		
105	Rooms reasonably free from steam, condensation, smoke, etc.	28A1	2
106	Rooms and equipment vented to outside as required	28A2	2
107	Hoods properly designed; filters removable	28A3	2
108	Intake air ducts properly designed and maintained	28A4	1
109	Systems comply with fire prevention requirements; no nuisance created	28A5	2
	4. DRESSING ROOMS AND LOCKERS		
110	Dressing rooms or areas as required; properly located	29A1	1
111	Adequate lockers or other suitable facilities	29A2	1
112	Dressing rooms, areas and lockers kept clean	29A3	2
	5. HOUSEKEEPING		
113	Establishment and property clean, and free of litter	29A1	2
114	No operations in living or sleeping quarters	29A2	2
115	Floors and walls cleaned after closing or between meals by dustless methods	29B1	2
116	Laundered clothes and napkins stored in clean place	29C1	2
117	Soiled linen and clothing stored in proper containers	29C2	1
118	No live birds or animals other than guide dogs	30D1	2

REMARKS——

Note: This checklist indicates what areas are examined in a sanitation survey of food service establishments. The American Mutual Insurance Companies' engineering department has prepared a manual (**Food Service Sanitation: Valuable Information for Persons Concerned with the Food Service Industry**) that accompanies the checklist, and the numbers that appear as "Reference Guides" refer to page number and section where related information appears in the manual (e.g., 6B 1-3 refers to page 6, section B, subsections 1-3 on "Milk and Milk Products"):

1. All milk and milk products, including fluid milk, other fluid dairy products and manufactured milk products, shall meet the standards of quality established for such products by applicable State and local laws and regulations.

2. Only pasteurized fluid milk and fluid-milk products shall be used or served. Dry milk and milk products may be reconstituted in the establishment if used for cooking purposes only.

3. All milk and fluid-milk products for drinking purposes shall be purchased and served in the original individual container in which they were packaged at the milk plant, or shall be served from an approved bulk milk dispenser: **Provided,** That cream, whipped cream or half and half, which is to be consumed on the premises, may be served from the original container of not more than one-half gallon capacity or from a dispenser approved by the health authority for such service, and for mixed drinks requiring less than one-half pint of milk, milk may be poured from one-quart or one-half gallon containers packaged at a milk plant.

Exhibit 10-7 (continued)[1]

11 Technology in Food Service Purchasing

Purpose: To familiarize students with the advantages and challenges of technology use in food purchasing.

INTRODUCTION

The use of computers in purchasing and procurement in food service operations not only has made these functions more effective and efficient but also has opened doors to an unprecedented global market. Buyers may use the Internet to connect to vendors all over the world for products, equipment, and services. Internet technology enables the buyer to purchase the most advanced and highly desired products and services produced. The increasing use of the Internet and the growing amount of available products and services not only has led to more satisfied customers but has also presented a number of challenges.

CHALLENGES OF TODAY'S TECHNOLOGY

Vendors face one of the most perplexing challenges presented by today's technology. To stay abreast of the availability of the latest technology offered in the production of foods, beverages, supplies, and

new products, vendors must constantly monitor the industry. Vendors must engage in this time-consuming task if they are to meet the expectations of savvy customers and to remain competitive in the global market. The first vendor to deliver innovative production, delivery, and selection techniques to the customer is often the vendor or supplier viewed by the purchasers as the preferred service provider.

Another challenge is that increasing numbers of food service operations are using purchasing software and the Internet for the purchasing function. Unfortunately, vendors and supply companies cannot meet the growing demand for these products. The use of home computers for both business and personal uses has resulted in a dependence on the computer as a global window to information. For example, computers are used for education, for purchasing home products, business equipment, and supplies, and for planning trips via air, ship, and road. Customers expect to view products on their computer screen, to research and compare products by visiting competitors' web sites, and to make purchasing decisions by comparing price, quality, and ease of access. This expectation holds true not only for home computer users but also for purchasers in the commercial food service industry who must meet bottom-line income demands. Purchasers are searching for the best buys, product availability, and ease of getting products to their facility in the most effective and efficient manner. Therefore, food buyers will continue to use the Internet as the tool of choice for getting this information.

A third challenge of technology is that customized products and services continue to diversify, and the expectations for instant service are growing rapidly. Individually oriented or custom-designed services for groups are becoming a popular offering by vendors. With the global market open to customers and customers' increased ability to puchase, they want items in a variety of forms and quality. Price is not as important as depth and width of product lines, delivery time and avenues, and packaging. Marketing strategies for companies offering fast food, beverages, and groceries include commercials that rely on the feeling experienced, images generated, and popular celebrity association. Seldom do the spots concentrate on or mention price or value, which was the common marketing focus during the decades leading up to the 1980's, when the economy was in a recession.

For the above-mentioned reasons, the commercial food service industry is growing and aggressively seeking ways to attract new customers and satisfy existing ones. During this exciting and ever-challenging era, purchasers can look forward to a widening global market of products and services that will be available at their fingertips and delivered to their doorstep. Understanding how to use

the technology available will be the responsibility of the buyer; therefore, gaining knowledge in computer usage and related software is important to all future and current buyers.

SOFTWARE PROGRAMS

Some of the most popular software programs used by the commercial food service industry include those that are custom-designed by the vendor and those that are somewhat generic and designed by software companies to be used by a wide variety of vendors. Price is not often the deciding factor in which programs or software will be used, as was the case two decades ago. Currently, other concerns weigh heavily in a company's decision to either produce the purchasing software in house or use an already existing program. These concerns often include availability of equipment, upgrade requirements, maintenance of both software demands and equipment capability, in-house expertise, and features offered by both soft- and hardware.

Today, company size—a large factor some years ago—is also not always an indicator of the use of computer software and hardware. In the mid 1970's, when computer technology was beginning to be used in the commercial food service industry, hardware was large, bulky, and expensive. Software development was done mostly in house and not offered to customers. This software, compared to that used today, was simplistic and sluggish. However, those programs were effective and considered essential for internal communications and data collection on products.

The processes involved in tracking inventory and procurement were the first activities to be computerized, and thus were features of some of the first software programs offered in the industry on a retail basis. Similar to Microsoft Excel and Lotus, these spreadsheet-type programs were forerunners to others offering word processing, graphics, and many other features used by the industry today.

Professionally Designed Purchasing Software and Hardware

Medallion. Medallion is used with Microsoft products, permitting the use of spreadsheets (Excel), graphics (PowerPoint), e-mail, fax software, and word processing (Microsoft Word). This interfacing gives universal power for users to integrate a variety of files read by Microsoft products and also reduces training time to learn the program. The Microsoft products are used in the home, school, and businesses, making the software company one of the largest in the world and, therefore, one of the most familiar. Designing software to interface with Microsoft products in the Windows format eliminates the need for users to learn the buttons, navigation, and other features offered. On-line help is also a familiar feature as well as spelling, grammar, and formatting options.

Micros. This program is one of the most well-known and versatile systems used in the restaurant industry. Micros offers management of guest purchases, selections, pricing, inventory management, price comparisons, food cost percentage calculations, forecasting, profit projections, and menu management. This system includes specialized hardware with touch-screen terminals to read and produce guest tickets, production tickets, and financial information. Handheld terminals, which can be used tableside, are similar to the counter-based models, and permit order taking, calculation, selection of special diet requests, order changes, communication from the back of the house, and pricing. Considered an advanced point-of-sale (POS) system, Micros offers touch-screen usage, employee scheduling,

employee sales tracking, and built-in remote support and communications capabilities. Exhibit 11.1 shows some of the products offered by Micros.

Miracle. Catering and event management is one of the fastest growing arms of business in the food service industry. This demand for food at events has required the use of programs that would offer folio management, calendar postings, room set-up graphics, equipment location, food and beverage services, and client financial credit-debit options. Miracle is used by Marriott and Ritz-Carlton to track sales and schedule catered events, room assignments, customer food and beverage requests, room setup and special features, flower and other special-request orders, and client payment. This program interfaces with Encore, a popular property management system used by many hotel companies. Encore is used for guest check in, check out, rooms assignments, and housekeeping.

Sysco (eSysco.com) This program is an example of an interactive purchasing system designed to communicate prices, product information, company contact, and purchasing through the company's Internet site. This program is accessed through a URL address followed by pass codes, permitting the user to gain use of the site. Browse buttons and a window where the user enters key words to help find specific products quickly are options available to make searching easy and user friendly. Once a search is initiated, a list of available products can be perused by category, brand name, or product base name. For example, if a user wanted to search for Sysco Classic canned green beans in a specific can size, key words to this search would prompt the program to search the database and find the product. Also appearing would be other brands matching the same criteria. Prices, pack size, number of units in the pack, and market form are also listed so that the buyer

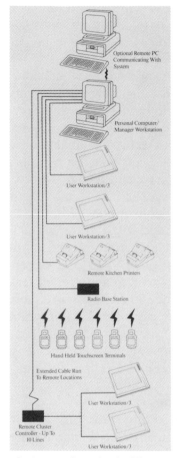

System configuration for Micros
8700 Hotel Management System

Micros point-of-sale hardware, including user workstation, remote
kitchen printer, and manager's PC workstation.

Exhibit 11-1. Examples of Micros products

can conduct price comparisons and make strategic decisions as to whether the pack would be convenient for the storage available. If a user would like to know more about a product, clicking a button and using the scrolling function to read the data can easily access information about items. Shipping information, company policies, history of the organization, and payment arrangements can be researched, and buyers can find their regional contact sales person.

Only those buyers who have contracts with Sysco can access Sysco's program. Hospitality students can gain access to Sysco only if their school purchases Sysco's products for the faculty club, school cafeteria, or other school food service outlets. For students, this access to company information is helpful when studying purchasing practices or developing purchase orders for laboratory experiments. At Florida State University, students are assigned recipes to manipulate in their food service courses and then required to research the Sysco site for pricing and product information. The recipes are then analyzed for correctness, and purchase orders are sent to the main purchasing division of the University Center Club, operated by Club Corporation of America, Inc. The purchase orders are used to place orders to the company and items delivered in time for the class laboratories. Students are responsible for receiving, storing, issuing, and managing inventory of the items purchased. They must also produce menu items for the public each week, so the purchasing cycle is a continuous one for both the student and Sysco, which supplies both edible and nonedible products.

More Internet sites are described in the last section of this chapter.

AUTOMATED INVENTORY MANAGEMENT—SCANNING BAR CODES

For decades, the commercial retail industry has used the bar code scanning system to manage inventory. It was not until the late 1980's that the food service industry used the same technology to receive and issue goods from both edible and nonedible goods storage with great success. Marriott was one company that used the early scanning system, adopted it for use in the large operations after testing it in several markets, and still uses the technology today. According to Marriott's Vice President of Procurement, Ron Winters, the technology not only has reduced costs due to over buying a product, but also has reduced theft, improved record keeping and accuracy of purchase orders, and increased effectiveness and efficiency of the procurement function at all sites.

How Scanners and Bar Codes Are Used

The use of scanners for control of purchasing and recording keeping is often accomplished by means of the vendors and the purchasers in a food service facility using a team approach. Vendors either supply products with bar codes on the containers of edibles and nonedibles or attach labels that are easily read by the purchaser's scanning device and software programs. Basically, a software package designed to read the ink bars on a sticky label interprets the bars as information that may include the package plant, date packaged, weight, details with regard to contents, and inspection codes associated with a particular item. Bar codes can be customized to include pricing information as well as storage recommendations or any other data that may be important to both the vendor and the purchaser, depending on what information they have agreed should be supplied.

Usually supplied by the packager or in some cases the purchaser once the product has arrived on the receiving dock, bar code labels are "read" by swiping them with a special wand, which serves as the encoding device. Often appearing as a red light shining from the end of the wand, the reading procedure takes only a fraction of a second and the bar code is copied into the software for interpretation. The software serves as both a decoding mechanism and a data base storage mechanism, so purchasers can quickly receive products and have the information recorded for inventory management. When items are issued from storage, the wand can also be used to swipe the bar code and the keyed item into the database as taken from current supplies. The result is a very defined record of the time items were taken from storage, the cost of the item, the date of issue, and the final product intended for its use.

For instance, if cherry pie were on the menu for Thursday lunch service, the inventory database would be programmed for cherry filling to be available for issue (based on planned menus) and the amount required for recipe precosted. Once the #10 can of filling is requested and the bar code on the can swiped during the issuing process, the item is automatically deducted from inventory, the cost deducted from financial records, and the leftover amount recorded for future use. At the end of the day, the food service manager or chef can request a report of all items used. He or she will receive a full report on all items used for the day, the time issued, the amount that should have been used and the amount that should remain available for future use. When the leftover cherry filling has been completely issued, an order will automatically be posted for purchase so that inventory levels can remain constant for the menu items offered.

WEB SITES FOR THE FOOD SERVICE MANAGER

The Internet offers many web sites of interest to food service managers. Web sites include, for example, software purchasing information, food buyer details including usage and trends, financial management for food service buyers, food service courses, and food buying texts. Following is an annotated list of some of the most useful sites.

The National Association of Purchasing Management (NAPM) Site (http://www.napm.org/MainBody/cfm). The NAPM supports purchasers of all goods and supplies in the United States in disseminating economic information such as usage, trends, forecasted buying behaviors, and advancements in industry. Seminars, conventions, trade show announcements, as well as expert advice through chat sessions and referrals to experts are also included in the services. The NAMP journal, *Purchasing Today*, presents information on purchasing and supply management strategies, advertisements on cutting-edge products and services and much more.

Vendor Inventory Purchasing (VIP) Hospitality Software Site (http://www.vipsoftware.com/maininfo/htm). This site explains the details of their inventory purchasing program and the ability of this program to integrate with other management systems. Users can download a version of VIP to investigate the program first-hand or view a video of the system in operation.

Hospitality Services Group—Cooperative Purchasing of Food and Supplies for Restaurants Site (http://www.hsgpurchasing.com). This is a consulting group specializing in training, research, and finance for the food service purchaser. Information on the company, career opportunities, price indexes, and training opportunities may be accessed on this site.

Mesa Food Service Program (http://www.inteergate.sdmesa.sdccd.cc.ca.us/food_service/food_service 140.htm). Mesa offers a course in operations, promotion, sales cost, and inventory controls for food and beverages. The courses will give professional continuing educational units, and credit may be transferred to major universities.

Quantity Food Purchasing Texts (http://www.vonl.com/chips/quanpurc.htm). This is the website of the Culinary and Hospitality Industry Publication Services, which offers texts on all hospitality topics. Books may be ordered on the Internet.

Food Service System (Foodpro) (http://www.services.software-directory.com/cdprod1/007/295.shtml). This site calls its software "a full service software application addressing all functional areas of the institutional food service business including forecasting and precosting, menu planning, food purchasing, production and inventory control, point-of-sale, post-cost reporting, and financial analysis." The site lists the equipment needed to run the software.

Menulink (http://www.menulinkinc.com). This restaurant software program is an active management system designed to help the restaurateur to track costs, purchasing, inventory, recipes, sales, and profit and loss statements. A version of the program is available for downloading and the site boasts that it takes only four hours for managers to become fully trained. Menulink offers users support, events to update training, and other product information for restaurant purchasing management.

Sysco (http://sysco.com). For edible and nonedible purchasing distributors, Sysco is an example of one company with a website that offers purchasing on-line. Once a buyer has contracted with the company to conduct business, a password is given to access the products and pricing on-line and submit an order. Buyers may obtain product information, ordering guidelines, comparable products, pack size, number of units in a pack, and unit and bulk pricing.

12 Common Market Practices: Ethical Considerations

Purpose: To provide an awareness of some of the dishonest practices that can result in large losses of revenue for the food service industry, how and why they occur, and how they may be reduced or eliminated.

INTRODUCTION

Losses resulting from a variety of illegal, dishonest, or fraudulent activities are a fact of life in all businesses, but in the food service industry there are more "loopholes and opportunities" than in most businesses. Knowing how to reduce losses to a minimum is an important responsibility of management.

A CONTROVERSIAL SUBJECT

This controversial subject is treated superficially, or it is not discussed at all, in many texts on purchasing. Perhaps in some businesses loss from "nonviolent crime" is of little concern. In the food business, however, losses from carelessness, indifference, bad habits, poor market practices, and deliberate thievery can determine whether a business continues to operate. Often the amount of money involved reflects the greater share of the profit. Knowing how to reduce losses to a minimum and keep them under control is an important responsibility of management today, especially in the food business.

Many thoughts on this subject have appeared in books and articles concerned with the great white-collar rip-off; the security service business has mushroomed; cameras and surveillance equipment are used; business psychologists attempt to provide "moral stabilization"; millions of dollars have been spent on seminars. Still, the "old payola" goes on.

Call it what you will: graft, payoff, payola, point system, cooperation, grease, nonviolent crime, rip-off, *comme-ca*, 2 percenters, 5 percenters, on the take, in the business, one of the boys, handouts, pig, easy mark, side money, black hat, or white hat. Whatever the name, it comes out of the boss's pocket, and he passes it along to the customer.

It is not the intent of this discussion to suggest that all dealers are dishonest, that every executive and employee spends working hours devising systems to "take" the boss, and that every customer is a potential thief. Large losses do, indeed, occur as a result of dishonesty and carelessness in the food business, but, on the whole, that business differs little from any other "buy and sell" business.

The real purpose of this chapter is to make management and employees alike aware of how large such losses can be, why they occur, and some methods of control. With awareness comes the potential for preserving not only one's job, but, on occasion, entire businesses.

THE HIGH COST OF DISHONESTY

No one really knows exactly how much white-collar crime costs the customer and business today. There have, however, been some in-depth studies of this problem, and the figures based on these conservative studies are staggering:

1. Nonviolent crimes cost the American businessman and customer approximately $40 a billion a year. Such crimes include employee theft, shoplifting, kickbacks, "promotional expense," and common practices that constitute cheating wherever they occur in the entire market system.
2. It has been reported that 90 percent of the body shops in the United States cooperate with their customers to steal from automobile insurance companies.
3. Losses from arson, largely covered by insurance, may reach between $4 billion and $5 billion a year. In only about half of the instances, however, is arson proved and the culprit punished.
4. Of the approximately 75 million shoplifting violations committed each year, which total about $2 billion in value, many go unprosecuted.
5. The advent of federally subsidized health benefits for older people has opened up one of the most lucrative sources of nonviolent crime the country has ever known, but doctors and lawyers who abuse such programs are seldom barred from practice when the abuses are discovered.

Similar abuses, whether the business involved is television, the theater, trucking, or food, are not difficult to find. About 18,000 businesses go broke each year from a combination of employee and management thievery. About a quarter of the instances involve some facet of the food industry. This helps to explain why four out of five restaurants fail in the first five years of operation.

The security business has enjoyed a greater rate of growth in recent years than any other business. Technological advances include use of the computer to allow exchange of information among agencies, use of lie-detecting equipment, and use of television cameras for surveillance. Candidates for employment are screened, and their records with previous employers are checked before they are hired. Federal and local laws have been passed that make bribery a felony, and undercover agents are used to detect problems.

WHO STEALS?

Stealing is not limited to any age group, sex, color, creed, educational level, or social status in a community or an organization. Even security personnel, hired to protect property, are not above practicing a little dishonesty on their own. The percentage of people caught stealing in the security business is somewhat lower than the general average, but there is also an effort to conceal such figures. Perhaps the best preventive measure is to remove temptation wherever it exists and to set up the kind of control within an organization that will, at reasonable cost, make it difficult to steal at any level in the organization. Many employees have defended their actions by claiming that the boss made it too easy and that the temptation was too great to resist. Unions have supported this defense, and many cases have been decided by the courts in favor of the defendant on the basis of lax management and lack of control.

WHY DO PEOPLE STEAL?

Security officers have produced a varied list of reasons why people steal and the reasons people give for stealing. The most important of these are reviewed below.

Mountain climbers, when asked why they risk climbing a mountain, have long responded, "Because it's there." This reasoning seems to prevail in the food business as well. A cashier, when asked why she systematically took ten dollars out of the till every night for a short period before she was caught, replied, "Because it was there." When psychologists researched this answer in the context of stealing, they found that some people simply cannot resist temptation, just as others cannot resist challenges.

Often employees begin stealing from the boss by "borrowing" a wrench, a dollar, a few bricks and pieces of lumber from the storage area, or a bottle of whiskey for a party. They originally intend to return the item, but somehow they never get around to it. It often does not stop at this point. Employees who have been caught have said that the first dime was the hardest to steal. After that, it became easier. Resentment toward management or the company that has a real or imagined basis is another reason employees often give for stealing. Some feel the company is not concerned about their welfare, that they are not being paid a fair wage, or that the boss is stealing. If unfair practices are tolerated at higher levels, these practices will be used to justify questionable activities at other levels.

There is the desire to be accepted that starts early in life, a desire that society reinforces by stressing group participation beginning at the kindergarten level. As children grow older, they often get into trouble because of the need to be "one of the gang." Even students who manage to avoid trouble before entering the business world are still conditioned to the need for belonging and being accepted. Sometimes this need makes them vulnerable to temptation or pressure from co-workers.

The most frequent reason employees used to give for stealing was that they needed the money. Fringe programs—unemployment benefits, group insurance, medical benefits, extended time payments, and more lenient terms for obtaining loans—are now available to fill some of the legitimate needs, but many employees still feel a real or an imagined need for money, and this leads them to steal.

People get trapped into living beyond their means, as do those who support another person with expensive tastes, those who attempt to supply their children with all of the "advantages," those who must pay off large debts, or those who have costly habits. When they see an opportunity to obtain the money that they need, they cannot resist temptation.

When the economy suffers reverses or business is in decline and unemployment levels are high, many people are tempted to steal in order to gain security. Benefits available to the unemployed and to senior citizens have helped to reduce instances of stealing for these reasons, but it is still one of the most important motives.

QUESTIONABLE PRACTICES IN THE FOOD MARKET

Some practices in this market are questionable, while others are patently dishonest. In dealing with questionable practices, the food buyer should heed the ancient warning: *caveat emptor* (let the buyer beware). Some practices have been used by dealers, their salespeople, and their delivery persons for so long that they have become standard operating procedure and dealers have developed arguments to support their position. Some of the shortcuts or profit builders most commonly used today are listed below, but the buyer should be aware that new ones may show up at any time.

Upgrading Quality

Upgrading quality is not only the most commonly used shortcut, but it is the hardest to prove. This practice is most common in the produce business and the portion-cut meat business. It seems, however, that each category of foods is vulnerable to some form of upgrading.

Produce

Because produce has the shortest storage life, it is not unusual to get spoiled commodities along with the good if one is not careful. The "sharp" dealer attempts to pawn off one- or two-day-old merchandise to the unsuspecting customer at top prices.

Ice Cream and Sherbet

A little extra profit can be made by the dealer who delivers ice cream with a lower butterfat content than was specified and billed. True fruit-flavored water ices and sherbets cost more to manufacture than articially flavored products, and the sharp dealer takes advantage by substituting artificial flavorings for the true fruit ones.

The best protection against substitution in this product category is to have an outside testing laboratory take a sample of the product being used and compare it with the specifications. This should be done every few months.

Milk and Cream

As with ice cream, a questionable practice is to deliver milk with a lower butterfat content than specified by the buyer. Half and half might be substituted for coffee cream. A little stabilizer added to medium cream makes it whip fairly well and brings the whipping cream price. These practices are illegal, but some dealers are willing to take the risk. Again, the best protection is to have the product tested periodically by an outside testing laboratory every few months.

Butter and Eggs

It is simple to substitute a lower-score butter for the higher one quoted and billed. When butter was being stored by the U. S. government in the Kansas salt caves, it was common practice to substitute frozen storage butter for fresh sweet cream butter. Also, a fifteen-ounce "pound" of butter is still quite in vogue. Butter in patties deteriorates rapidly, and another favorite practice is to deliver "old" butter as patties.

Upgrading eggs is another favorite way of getting a little extra profit from unsuspecting customers. The "sharp" dealer substitutes large eggs for extra-large ones, and one-size substitution down the scale. He also substitutes Grade A eggs for double A, and makes a similar one-grade substitution on through the grades.

Federally inspected and graded eggs are supposed to be delivered to the buyer in carefully and clearly makred cartons. This is a great protection. Occasionally, however, federally inspected eggs are repacked before delivery, and the cartons contain only Grade B and Grade C eggs in a sealed carton marked U.S. Grade A.

In the egg business a process known as oiling helps to maintain freshness in eggs. A dealer should not, however, substitute an oiled egg that may be a cold storage one if the specification calls for a fresh, nonoiled egg.

Poultry

A questionable practice of the "sharp" dealer is to "slack out" frozen poultry, repack it in ice, and sell it as being fresh. This can be done with turkeys, ducks, guinea fowl, and Cornish hens as well. It is around holidays, when there is a great demand for fresh-killed poultry, that the "sharp" dealer really makes a profit.

Fish and Seafood

Because fish and seafood are highly perishable and because there are many similar varieties, getting what one pays for is somewhat problematic. A clear understanding between the food buyer and the dealer, a good set of specifications, and a well-trained receiving clerk are the best guarantee of a good buy in the fish and seafood business. The two most common practices are the substitution of frozen for fresh fish and the substitution of similar, cheaper varieties for better eating, more expensive ones.

The practice of "slacking out" frozen fish, repacking in ice, and selling it as fresh can easily be spotted in whole fish because of the sunken appearance of the eyes and the grayness of the gills if the head is left on. If the head is off, the buyer should, without question, refuse delivery. It is somewhat more difficult to tell fresh fillets from previously frozen ones, especially after they have been treated with a salt water bath. A good receiving clerk can tell whether a fillet has been frozen or not from its feel.

The substitution of frozen green shrimp for fresh green shrimp is rather common in cities like New York, Boston, and Philadelphia, where there is a heavy demand for fresh shrimp. Because of the substantial profit involved, such a substitution may well indicate a substantial payoff to someone in the customer's organization.

Other common upgrading practices involve substitution of varieties: brown and pink Gulf shrimp for Mexican whites, smaller-size shrimp for larger ones by remarking boxes, Caribbean and African lobster tails for Australian, grouper for red snapper, mango snapper for red snapper or grouper, Gulf and Pacific snapper for Florida red snapper, haddock for cod and vice versa, pollock for haddock and cod, cusk for haddock or cod, flounder and fluke for gray and lemon sole, fluke for eastern sole, gray sole for lemon sole, lox for smoked salmon, and salmon from the Pacific Northwest, Canada, and Alaska for so-called Atlantic salmon.

Another favorite substitution is to cut up sea scallops and sell them as bay scallops or Long Island scallops. Alaskan scallops have recently been introduced; they are cut up and sold as sea scallops.

Coffee

Blending coffee is a highly specialized business. Large national distribution companies will not compromise their blends. Their coffees are blended according to certain basic standards and tastes, and there is no deviation.

"Sharp" local blenders can take advantage of the situation by submitting coffees for testing that contain a high ratio of Colombian and some very aromatic African coffees at a price per pound at or below their cost. If they get the business, they gradually reduce the ratio of Colombian coffee in the blend until the price is quite profitable. It is not difficult to decrease the dealer's cost by as much as 20 cents a pound without making a change in taste and aroma that is too noticeable.

Some dealers have found it easy to hold out an ounce of coffee from each bag. It is advisable for receiving clerks to weigh coffee frequently.

Meats

Following are some of the factors that allow unscrupulous meat dealers to cheat their customers:

1. New ink used in grading stamps disappears in a short time, leaving only a faint tint of color on the fat. An attractive piece of choice meat can be sold as prime if a customer accepts it.

2. There are three levels of quality in the choice grade of beef. It is a rare dealer who will volunteer to ship any customer all of his top choice, even though the customer is paying for it.

3. Substituting a packer grade for a U.S. Choice quality grade is not unusual, even though the packers' grades do not necessarily mean anything when it comes to quality.

4. Pork meat from grain-fed animals tastes and eats better than meat from animals fed refuse, but it is difficult to detect the latter without special training.

5. The possibility of upgrading in prefab portion-controlled meats is as likely as it is in the case of produce. It is not difficult to use U.S. Choice strips and cut "prime" sirloin steaks. Upgrading in portion-cut meats is the biggest drawback to buying these products.

6. Other upgrading practices found in the portion-control business are the substitution of New Zealand lamb for American lamb.

7. There is a legitimate place for meat additives, but the buyer should specify when these are suitable. A purveyor should not add meat extenders without the buyer's knowledge.

8. Directly behind the upgrading of quality comes another frequent abuse: short weights and counts. Many dealers do not weigh boxes of poultry and meats. They merely take the weight shown on the box and put it on the invoice sent along to the customer. If someone cheats them, they get their money back by charging it to the customer.

9. Invoices can show weights that include ice or wrappings in the weight of the products.

10. Excessive trim can mean excess fat covering, length of fat trim, or even the method of breaking the carcass down into wholesale cuts of meat. Unless specifications are clear and the receiving clerk is diligent, a dealer can pick up 10 percent additional profit on the excess fat left on prime ribs, strips, fillets, lamb racks, top butts, rounds, and pork loins.

Other Dishonest Practices

Buyers should watch out for these additional dishonest practices:

1. Unless the receiving clerk and the buyer are alert, a dealer can quote one price and then send the invoice through at another price.

2. Substituting brands of bacon, sausage, canned goods, oils, salad dressings, frozen goods, or any other item is a favorite way for the dealer to get a price advantage.

3. Every packer or purveyor repacks merchandise with the best side forward or the best products on top; it is up to the buyer and the receiving clerk to look beneath the first layer.

4. The practice of upgrading sizes is

quite easy, especially where lemons, oranges, limes, grapefruit, and melons are involved. Substituting 10-size Cranshaw or honeydew melons for 8's and 8's for 6's or 5's is almost standard operating procedure. A good packer can make a 36-size crate of cantaloupes look full by using 45's.

Chapter 8, "Receiving: A Hidden Hard Spot," lists eleven good rules for any receiving clerk to follow that are directed against the questionable practices discussed here.

DISHONEST PRACTICES IN THE FOOD MARKET

Whenever a questionable practice continues for any length of time, it is likely that at least one person in an organization is working with a purveyor or purveyors in some sort of dishonest scheme. Sometimes it takes two, often three, people in an organization to arrange a payoff scheme. Invariably someone is caught, but seldom prosecuted. It is usually the boss who both pays and loses.

Purveyors

Purveyors in the food industry are either scrupulously honest, inherently dishonest, or simply do what is expected of them in order to make a sale. It is unfortunate that so many dealers fall into the third category.

Most dealers conduct themselves and their business in such a manner that they are favored by food buyers and companies that insist on strict honesty. There are enough honest dealers to give an honest food buyer competitive prices. Then there are always the few dealers that, for one reason or another, simply do not know how to or will not do business in an honest manner even when offered the opportunity to do so. These companies are generally high-pressure or-

ganizations with overenthusiastic salesmen. Because the business was built on this type of policy, there is little reason to change at the risk of losing clients.

Though it is likely that most dealers would prefer to do business in a straightforward and honest manner, they are in the business to make a profit. If they have to make some sort of arrangement with the food buyer, the owner, or someone else in order to make a sale, most will do so. There does, however, seem to be an unwritten but almost universal law among this group of dealers that, if the dealer gives his word to an owner or food buyer that he will conduct his business in an honest manner, he either keeps his word or drops the account.

Food Buyers

There are only two categories of food buyers: honest and dishonest. This is discussed in detail in Chapter 5, "The Food Service Purchasing Agent."

The Bait

After the dealer has made an effort to become a regular supplier and has not succeeded, the next step is usually to suggest how the dealer can be of service to the buyer. This service can take many forms: use of a credit card, a friendly foursome for golf, dinner and nightclub entertainment, and the like. If the relationship with the buyer progresses, there is always the trip to Florida when the weather is especially bad in the North. For the interested golfer, the purveyor picks up initiation fees, club dues, and often a large share of the cost of the game.

Some dealers take the direct approach. They find out exactly how much the buyer wants. The bidding generally begins around 2 percent of the gross business from the dealer. The amount can increase to 5 percent, and in some cases go even higher.

If an aggressive dealer still does not

succeed in getting on the approved purveyor list, other methods can be tried. The food buyer's boss may be approached and offered services to influence the buyer. If the dealer is able to pick up club dues for the general manager or to compromise management in some other way, then the food buyer either compromises his principles or resigns.

In smaller operations a purveyor often arranges a business loan for an owner who might be having temporary financial problems. Naturally, the owner pays back part of the loan by giving business to the purveyor, so the purveyor makes an extra profit beyond his contribution.

Finally, there are dealers who are not above writing an anonymous letter to a food buyer's boss accusing the buyer of dishonesty or incompetence. The letter further indicates that the organization could get better prices if it used another set of dealers. The name of the dealer who wrote the letter is always included in the list of the better dealers.

Payoffs

It has been said that payoffs in the food business go all the way from peanuts to penthouses. It is, however, difficult to prove anything, and as long as bonding companies and kind-hearted bosses fail to prosecute, there will be more fiction than fact concerning payoffs. Only cases that have stood up under investigation can be termed fact.

PROTECTION AGAINST DISHONESTY

Whether top management feels that it has a problem or not, it is folly not to have a security program in operation. Professional security people agree on certain basic requirements for a good program, and the requirements are, surprisingly, relatively simple.

1. *Management must set an example.* If those who enjoy executive privileges are dishonest or behave in an avaricious or undignified manner, employees use this to justify their own similar actions.

2. *Management should let everyone know that honesty is the only policy.* If management has its own house in order, then the next step is to let everyone know, and to keep on letting them know, that there is no room for any kind of skimming process. Instant dismissal should result if such practices are discovered, even if only small amounts are involved.

3. *Management should be vigilant.* Management should be neither paranoid nor complacent. There is a lesson to be learned from the saying "Only thee and me are honest, and, at times, I doubt thee." Management has learned that no one is immune from being approached. The company should maintain job discipline and morale while using all security measures needed and making certain that all employees know that such measures are in effect.

4. *Management should maintain good employee relations.* Maintaining good employee relations has become one of the top jobs of management, for wages and benefits are not the only concerns. Other matters—employee meals and dining rooms, employee locker rooms and toilet facilities (as well as their care and maintenance), and social activities such as children's parties, sports, and other activities—are also of prime importance.

5. *Management should be available to employees.* Management that isolates itself from department heads,

especially those in sensitive positions, is asking for trouble. The door cannot be open at all times to all department heads or employees, but it is possible to talk to people on the job or to insist that department heads do this so that employees have a chance to express themselves regarding management policy and other matters.

6. *Management should seek the support of unions.* Occasionally a union will support a dishonest employee, but this support usually comes only when poor management has contributed toward the employee's dishonesty. When the facts indicate a case of dishonesty, it is a rare union that does not support dismissal and prosecution.

7. *Management should make the final decision regarding dealers.* Management should visit its purveyors, get to know them, and make clear to them that they do business with the operation because it is a management decision and not the decision of anyone else in the organization.

8. *All department heads should be thoroughly investigated.* An employer can check on his past employment, his credit rating, his bank account, his hobbies, and how he lives. If management prefers, there are public firms that specialize in character reference investigations.

9. *Department heads should be paid well enough to enable them to resist temptation.* Paying over-scale or above-custom wages does not ensure honesty, but a well-paid, happy, and satisfied employee is less likely to make deals or accept bribes.

10. *Specifications should be clear and complete.* This was dealt with in Chapter 7.

11. *There should be a good operations manual and checklist.* The purpose of such a manual and checklist is obvious, but it should be recognized that both tools are a waste of time if they are not used and supported by management.

12. *There should be regular inspections.* This is where the operations manual and a security checklist are needed. Self-inspection is helpful, but group inspection or inspection by another department head is more effective.

13. *The internal control system should be adequate and effective.* This was discussed in Chapter 10.

14. *An outside inspection service should be used.* Periodic use of an outside inspection service is well worth the expense. All management personnel and employees and the union representative should be aware that such services are being used.

15. *Offenders should be prosecuted.* One of the most disturbing things about the whole matter of dishonesty is that so few persons are caught, and even those who are caught are often permitted to resign. They are seldom prosecuted. There is, however, a growing realization that efforts made to punish offenders, even if such efforts are time consuming and expensive, serve to discourage further crime.

Part III
FOOD COMMODITIES

13 Meat

Purpose: To define various standards and other factors important in meat purchasing and to provide guidelines for writing purchase specifications.

INTRODUCTION

United States grade standards for quality, United States inspection for wholesomeness, legal definitions and standards of identity for product name and composition, and standard institutional meat purchase specifications for cut are discussed in this chapter. Sources, summaries, and samples of standards are provided for basic information and guidance in writing specifications and selecting meat. Factors to include in specifications are listed, and sample specifications are provided.

Hamburger, steaks, roasts, sausage, ham, wieners, and other meat items have been popular basic meal components for a long time. Whole businesses have been built on their sale. For example, McDonald's is the sales leader in the food service industry, based on the sale and hamburgers, and Outback Steakhouse is the nineteenth largest food service business, based on the sale of steak (Anonymous, 1999). Also, to satisfy customers, food service operators have generally emphasized the quality of meat entrees in a meal and paid less attention to the quality of accompaniments. Meat is not only an important factor in consumer satisfaction, it is also a critical component of food cost to both food service operators and customers.

To obtain maximum quality at least cost for preparing various meat items, a food buyer must know about animal structure, butchering techniques, the cuts appropriate for particular menu items, and meat quality grades. The meat buyer must also be aware that meat production and marketing have not remained static. Meat quality has changed due to breeding, variation in animal feeding practices, and interest in reducing the amount of fat in meat. Grade standards have been revised to reflect these changes in characteristics, with standards for inclusion in a quality grade revised to allow for reduced amounts of fat. Recently (1996), the meat inspection system has been totally revamped due to serious outbreaks of food poisoning, particularly from hamburger, and the perceived need for better control of sanitary quality.

Meat purchasing is challenging because of its involvement with the American agricultural economy and a dynamic meat production and marketing industry responding to changing societal demands. The goal is to acquire meat items that will yield high-quality menu items at controlled cost. Principal factors in purchase are quality grade, cut, weight of cut, cost, and, of most importance, the assurance of wholesomeness.

GRADE STANDARDS

Differences in *quality* and *yield* of meat are indicated by United States Department of Agriculture (USDA) grade standards. Use of USDA standards is voluntary, but if a U.S. grade has been assigned, then the standards for that grade must be met. A buyer should use grade standards in purchasing because they provide some quality assurance, a basis for legal recourse if a product does not meet expectations, and an excellent tool for communicating product requirements.

Grade standards for meat are established under the authority of the Agriculture Marketing Act of 1946, as amended. Complete descriptions of U.S. grades for meat are in the *Code of Federal Regulations, Title 7, Parts 53 to 209.*[1] Current standards indicate quality as related to palatability and yield. For beef and lamb, grades for quality and yield are separate; and for pork and veal, yield factors are incorporated in quality grades.

Class

Prior to grading, all animals are segregated by "class," and particular grades are applicable to each class. Definitions of class are included in U.S. grade standards to differentiate animals in terms of physical characteristics related to age, maturity, sex, and sex condition. Classes

---

[1]*Code of Federal Regulations, Agriculture, Title 7, Parts 53 to 209* (Washington, D.C.: U.S. Government Printing Office, 1993), p. 9.

of animals and distinguishing characteristics are shown in Exhibit 13-1. Essentially, the classes representing the youngest animals—males castrated when young and females that have not borne young—are considered for the highest quality grades. These include steers and heifers for beef, barrows and gilts for pork, and lamb for sheep. Older, more sexually mature animals tend to yield tougher, less finely grained, and less firmly muscled cuts of meat than do younger, less mature animals. Class is important to buyers because sometimes purchasing is done with the class name. Further, knowing class characteristics, particularly ranges in age, helps a buyer understand borderline quality and obtain proper meat at an appropriate price. Because U.S. grades are based on class, buyers can generally use quality grades and disregard class in buying.

Grading is in general based on factors contributing to palatability of lean, including conformation, muscling, and finish. Conformation refers to the shape of animal in relation to the proportion of meat to bone. Animals with good conformation are relatively short in height and length in relation to weight. Muscling essentially refers to muscle development, which represents usable meat. Finish is the amount and distribution of fat. Well-finished animals have a smooth coating of fat around cuts and fine-grained fat, called marbling or feathering, interspersed with lean. Marbling contributes to flavor and tenderness. Quality grades for animals of various species and classes are shown in Exhibit 13-2 and are based on specific factors applicable to each species and class.

Beef

Both yield and quality grades may be applied to beef. Factors in beef quality grades are the amount of and distribu-

Animal	Class	Characteristics
Cattle—bovine species		
	Steer	Male castrated when young with no development of the secondary physical characteristics of a bull
	Heifer	Immature female without physical characteristics associated with reproduction and age
	Bullock	Young male under 24 months of age (approximately), uncastrated or castrated, which has developed or begun to develop the physical characteristics of an uncastrated male
	Bull	Mature male 24 months of age or older (approximately), uncastrated or castrated, which has developed or begun to develop the physical characteristics of an uncastrated male
	Cow	Mature female with relatively large hips and mid section developed through reproduction or age
Vealer—Calves (bovine species that are young or very young)	Steer	Male, castrated
	Heifer	Female
	Bull	Male, uncastrated
Sheep—ovine species		
	Lamb	Immature animal usually under 14 months of age that has not cut its first pair of incisor teeth
	Yearling	Animal between 1 and 2 years of age that has cut its first but not second pair of incisor teeth
	Sheep	Animal over 24 months of age that has cut the second pair of incisor teeth
	Ewe	Female
	Wether	Male castrated when young
	Ram	Uncastrated male
Swine	Barrow	Male castrated when young
	Gilt	Young female that has not produced young or reached an advanced stage of pregnancy
	Stag	Male castrated after beginning development of secondary characteristics of an uncastrated male
	Boar	Uncastrated male
	Sow	Mature female that has reproduced or reached an advanced stage of pregnancy

Exhibit 13–1. Classes of animal species and principal distinguishing characteristics

Beef		Veal	Lamb and Yearling	Sheep	Pork	
Steer and Heifer	Bullock				Barrow and Gilt	Sow
U.S. Prime	U.S. Prime	U.S. Prime	U.S. Prime	U.S. Choice	U.S. No. 1	U.S. No. 1
U.S. Choice	U.S. Choice	U.S. Choice	U.S. Choice	U.S. Good	U.S. No. 2	U.S. No. 2
U.S. Select	U.S. Select	U.S. Good	U.S. Good	U.S. Utility	U.S. No. 3	U.S. No. 3
U.S. Standard	U.S. Standard	U.S. Standard	U.S. Utility	U.S. Cull	U.S. No. 4	U.S. Medium
U.S. Commercial	U.S. Utility	U.S. Utility			U.S. Utility	U.S. Cull
U.S. Utility						
U.S. Cutter						
U.S. Canner						

Note: Grades are given in descending order of quality.

Exhibit 13-2. U.S. government (USDA) grades for beef, veal, lamb, sheep, and pork

tion of finish, firmness of muscling, and physical characteristics associated with maturity. All grades of beef are applicable to steers and heifers. Cows cannot legally be graded Prime, but all other grades are applicable to that class. Separate grades are used for bullocks, which are relatively young castrated or uncastrated males under approximately 24 months of age. Bulls are not eligible for U.S. quality grades, and bull meat should be excluded from food service operations because the meat is very dark and strong in flavor. Animals from 9 to 30 months of age are considered essential to top quality meat. After 30 months, quality tends to decline in terms of color, texture, tenderness, the amount and distribution of finish, and firmness of muscling. Yield grades are based on confrontation, muscling, and amount of fat. In highest to lowest order, yield grades are 1, 2, 3, 4, and 5. In general, yield grades are inversely related to quality grades, with higher fat content being associated with higher quality and lower yield.

Veal

The meat known as veal is derived from young bovine animals (cattle), called "vealers," that are usually less than three months of age and fed largely on milk or "milk replacer," a formula substituted for mother's milk. The animals have trim figures (no middle paunch) because they have not been fed roughage. The predominate characteristic of veal is very light color of lean meat due to milk feeding. Buyers should know that animals can be fed milk formula well beyond three months of age to retain light color in lean and be classified as veal. While the market price may be somewhat lower than for younger animals, the quality is likely to be poorer. Quality will be reflected in the U.S. grade, but buyers should take care in purchasing.

Quality grades for veal are based on conformation; quality of flesh, based on the amount and distribution of fat; and the intensity of the color of flesh, based on maturity and feed. More intense color is associated with lower quality, and higher fat content with higher quality. No yield grades are available because yield factors are related to conformation and incorporated in the quality grades. Veal carcasses are classified as steer, heifer, and bull, but class is not considered in grading because all of the animals are young. Since class is not part of grading, and bulls approaching the age to be classed as beef cattle are likely to have poorer quality than animals in other veal classes, buyers may wish to consider class in purchasing.

Animals three to eight months of age that have been fed roughage, have developed a paunch, and have relatively intense color in flesh are termed *calves*. Quality characteristics are not so fine as for veal, and the meat is less expensive.

Pork

U.S. quality grades for pork barrow and gilt classes are based on the interrelationship of (1) backfat thickness over the last rib measured in inches and (2) scores for muscling. A mathematical equation based on these factors is used to assign grades. The highest grade is associated with a high amount of muscling and a medium amount of fat, and the lowest grade with an extremely large amount of fat and poor muscling. In between, meat with a small amount of fat and high muscling tends to fall into a higher grade, and meat with high fat and low muscling to a lower grade. Muscling is essentially the most important factor. An animal with "thin" muscling cannot be U.S. No. 1. Animals with superior muscling but excess fat for a grade can fall into the higher grade, but with inferior muscling and acceptable fat will fall into a lower grade. Note that pork grades are designated as No. 1, No. 2, No. 3, and No. 4, which is different than for other species, and grades for sows are different from other classes of pork. U.S. No. 1 grade sows are essentially the minimum grade for palatability. However, sows of any grade should not be selected for food service; in fact, specifications should exclude these animals from purchase.

Lamb

Buyers may specify quality grade, yield grade, and class in purchase of lamb (ovine species). Class is extremely important here because the older the animal, the stronger the flavor—from lamb (under 14 months of age), to yearling (1 to 2 years of age), to sheep (over 24 months of age). The characteristics of young lamb are generally those most highly prized, with the most desirable meat coming from animals well under 14 months of age. The strong flavor of sheep may be extremely objectionable to some consumers and should be purchased only when game meat is to be featured.

Quality grades are based on conformation and quality, with separate grades applied to each class of ovine animal. Conformation refers to general body proportions and the likely ratio of meat to bone based on the thickness of muscling. Graders must make evaluations of conformation by deft hand movements through an animal's fleece because differences in density and thickness of fleece can confuse evaluation of muscle made solely with visual methods. Quality is evaluated in terms of the quantity, distribution, and type of fat or finish. A firm, smooth, relatively thin layer of fat evenly distributed over an animal's body is characteristic of the Prime grade.

Yield grade is established in an evaluation separate from inspection for quality grade, though the factors evaluated are similar. Specifically, yield grade evaluation is based on measuring thickness of fat over the ribeye muscle cut. In highest to lowest order of lean meat and low amount of fat, yield grades are 1, 2, 3, 4, and 5. For Yield Grade 1, the average fat thickness is 0.00 to 0.15 inch; and for Yield Grade 5, 0.46 inch and greater.

Yield grades are inversely related to quality grades to an extent, but not directly. Top quality (Prime) grade meat requires some fat, but fat in the amount of Yield Grade 5 would generally not be graded Prime. For food service buyers, specification of yield grade is generally not so important as specification of quality grade, and specification of both yield and quality grades can be confounding because the grades are based on separate evaluations of interrelated factors.

INSPECTION

Based on the Federal Meat Inspection Act of 1906 as amended by the Wholesome Meat Act of 1967, the wholesomeness of meat, as assured by the mandatory federal meat inspection system, was taken for granted. However, the occurrence of deaths and severe illnesses attributable to bacterial contamination caused the system to be questioned. This included a nationally reported outbreak of *E. coli 0157:H7* food poisoning caused by hamburgers eaten in a major chain restaurant, and estimates by the U.S. Food Safety and Inspection Service that meat and poultry products with *Salmonella, E. coli 0157:H7, Camplybacter*, and *Listeria Monocytogenes* resulted in as many as 4,000 deaths and 5,000,000 illnesses annually.[2] These data precipitated a review of the meat industry and the meat inspection system that resulted in a totally new system for inspecting or insuring the wholesomeness of meat.

[2]Federal Register of Thursday, July 25, 1996, Part II, Department of Agriculture Foods Safety and Inspection Service (61 FR: 38807).

The new regulation (CFR 9, Parts 304 et al.) is called *Pathogen Reduction, Hazard Analysis and Critical Control Point (HACCP) Systems*. It involves industry self-inspection with detailed planning, controls at critical points, evaluations, plans for corrective action, records, and monitoring by the USDA Food Safety and Inspection Service. Requirements are that (1) all establishments develop and implement written sanitation operating procedures (SOP's); (2) slaughter establishments do regular microbial testing to verify the adequacy of process controls that prevent and remove fecal contamination and the bacteria associated; (3) all establishments producing ground meat products meet U.S. Department of Agriculture pathogen reduction performance standards for *Salmonella*, and (4) all establishments develop and implement a detailed system of preventive controls known as HACCP (Hazard Analysis Critical Control Points), with assessment or approval done by the Food Safety and Inspection Service (USDA). A more complete description of this regulatory rule (Federal Register, Thursday, July 25, 1996; 9 CFR, Parts 304, 308, 310, 320, 327, 381, 416, 417) is provided in Chapter 3, Exhibit 3.5. The rule is based on addition to or revision of the Federal Meat Inspection Act as amended by the Wholesome Meat Act.

Although the federal government has taken positive steps to assure the safety of meat and poultry products, food buyers with responsibility for the health and welfare of large numbers of consumers must not take chances. Buyers should inspect meat packing plants that are sources of supply, review HACCP records prepared for government review, work with government inspectors, and demand as a condition of purchase the highest sanitary quality in meat. Though enforcing rigid standards may increase the cost of the product and inspection time, that cost is low compared to the price paid for lawsuits, loss of life, and loss of business.

DEFINITIONS AND STANDARDS OF IDENTITY

Definitions and standards of identity or composition for various meat products have been established as a part of the Wholesome Meat Act Amendment to the Meat Inspection Act. These standards generally relate to the minimum or maximum amounts of a principal component and say what a product is in terms of federal law and a specific legal name that appears on the label. They form the basis for anyone's expectations for products in the marketplace and the basis for selection among products. For example, products labeled chopped beef, ground beef, hamburger, or fabricated steak may not contain more than 30 percent fat, and no water, binders, or extenders. A product labeled beef patties has no limitation for fat and may contain added water, binders, or extenders.

Special attention should be paid to definitions for cured and uncured smoked meats, particularly hams, to understand the characteristics of these items. Hams termed "cured" are prepared by injecting salt solution into muscle or immersing meat in salt solution to produce the characteristic color and flavors. In the process, hams frequently have excess water injected to increase weight. This reduces yield to the consumer and affects flavor. Previous standards required that hams with more than 10 percent added water be labeled "water added." This allowed for 10 percent added water without labeling. Current standards are stated in terms of "PFF," which is the minimum percentage of fat-free protein that must be present. Essentially this is a way to indicate the extent to which the protein naturally present in the meat is diluted with water or other substances. To obtain meat without added substances, buyers should specify "ham, common and usual" or just "ham." Designations in order of increasing amount of added substances are "with natural juices," "water added," and "ham and water product," with the percentage by weight of added substances indicated.

Hams termed "country ham," "country style ham," or "dry cured ham" are prepared with dry salt and dry sugar, potassium or sodium nitrate, and potassium or sodium nitrite as optional ingredients. They may be smoked or unsmoked. After preparation, the finished weight must be at least 18 percent less than the fresh. Dry cured hams, particularly smoked, have particular flavor characteristics that many people find highly desirable. Currently, dry cured hams and hams without water added are infrequently available in retail markets, and food service buyers will need to make a special effort to obtain ham of this quality.

Consumers generally do not know much about standards of identity and have limited ability to discriminate among products, but a professional buyer cannot afford this lack of knowledge. A partial list of defined items and important requirements are shown in Exhibit 13-3. A complete listing and details are found in the *Code of Federal Regulations, Title 9, Part 310*.[3]

Although standards of identity are important in obtaining good quality food and for discriminating among items, a buyer may wish something different in a product than is incorporated in the standard of identity, and this may be specified unless it is contrary to federal law. Perhaps 20 or 25 percent fat is preferred to 30 percent fat in ground beef, or ground beef from a particular cut is desired. Needless to say, not all canned beef stew,

ham, wieners, and other products on the market are the same, and most of these differences are not based on standards of identity. For convenience items with meat, choices may be made on the basis of product comparison and specification of brand name. If volume is large enough, production of the product may be contracted to a processor and produced according to a standardized formula provided.

INSTITUTIONAL MEAT PURCHASE SPECIFICATIONS

Identifying and writing specifications for particular cuts of meat desired requires considerable knowledge of animal skeletal structure and butchering techniques. Primal (wholesale) cuts of meat from beef, veal, lamb, and pork are shown in Exhibits 13-4, 13-6, 13-8, and 13-10. Meat may be further subdivided from these basic cuts. Sets of standardized specifications developed cooperatively by the USDA and the National Association of Meat Purveyors (NAMP) have made it easier to specify and supply the exact cuts of meat desired. Commonly used food service cuts of meat with institutional meat purchase specification numbers are shown in Exhibits 13-5, 13-7, 13-9, and 13-11 for beef, pork, veal, and lamb, respectively.

Institutional meat purchase specifications (IMPS) are available, as individual pamphlets, for fresh beef; fresh lamb and mutton; fresh veal and calf; fresh pork; cured, cured and smoked, and fully cooked pork products; cured, dried, and smoked beef products; sausage products; variety meats and by-products (such as liver, tongue, and heart); general requirements; and as quality assurance provisions. These purchase specifications are available (with the same titles as the items in the preceding list) from the U.S. Government Superintendent of Documents, Washing-

[3]*Code of Federal Regulations, Animals and Animal Products, Title 9, Part 200 to End* (Washington, D.C.: U.S. Government Printing Office, Jan. 1, 1993), p. 274.

Product Legal Name	Basic Requirements
Chopped beef for ground beef or hamburger or fabricated steak	Contains no more than 30 percent fat and no added water, binders, or extenders
Beef patties	May contain binders or extenders and added water; no limitation on fat
Barbecued meats	Must be cooked by direct action of dry heat such as burning hardwood to produce a brown crust. Finished weight must not exceed 70 percent of raw weight
Roast beef parboiled and steam roasted	Finished weight must not exceed 70 percent of raw weight
Corned beef, canned	Weight of finished product must not exceed 70 percent of raw
Corned beef, brisket	Finished weight must not be more than 20 percent above raw weight
Corned beef round or cured beef tongue	Finished weight must not be more than 10 percent above fresh weight
Cured pork products (ham)	Must meet minimum Protein Fat Free (PFF) percentage requirements specific to particular cuts and forms of preparation as for ham or loin, cooked, without added substances, 20.5 percent; with natural juices, 18.5 percent; with water, 17.0 percent; and with water and other ingredients, less than 17.0 percent
Country ham or dry cured ham, smoked or unsmoked	Uncooked, cured, dried, smoked, or unsmoked products made from a single piece of meat and prepared by dry application of salt and one or more approved optional ingredients according to prescribed methods. They must not be injected with or placed in curing solutions, and the finished weight must be at least 18 percent less than the original
Fresh pork sausage	Fat content must not exceed 50 percent; water content must not exceed 3 percent. Condiments may be added
Fresh beef sausage	Finished product must not contain more than 30 percent fat and 3 percent water. Condiments and other substances may be added in prescribed amounts
Breafast sausage	Must not contain more than 50 percent fat, 3 percent water, and 3.5 percent binders or extenders. Condiments may be added
Whole hog sausage	Must contain cuts of meat (edible portion) in natural proportion to the whole animal; may contain up to 50 percent fat and 3 percent water
Italian sausage	Is uncured, unsmoked, and must contain salt, pepper, and either fennel or anise. May contain a variety of other seasonings, up to 35 percent fat and 3 percent water
Ham patties, chopped ham, pressed ham, and similar products	Must meet minimum Protein Fat Free percentage requirements as: 19.5 percent, without additives; 17.5 percent with natural juices; 16.0 percent with water added; and less than 16.0 percent with water and other ingredients
Chopped ham	Prepared and formed from ham, curing agents, seasonings, and a variety of optional ingredients
Unsmoked smoked sausage	Smoked with hardwood or similar material and prepared from meat containing no more than 50 percent fat. Water must not exceed 3 percent
Frankfurter, wiener, bologna, knockwurst, and similar products	Finished products may contain no more than 30 percent fat and 10 percent water, and may contain various binders to the extent of 3.5 percent of the finished product. May be smoked or unsmoked and prepared from a variety of meats including beef, pork, chicken, and turkey
Liver sausage or braunschweiger	Must contain 30 percent liver and may contain up to 3.5 percent binders or extenders
Chili con carne	Contain not less than 40 percent meat
Hash and corned beef hash	Contain not less than 35 percent meat or corned beef, according to kind, on the basis of cooked trimmed meat
Meat stews	Contain not less than 25 percent meat of the type named on the label
Spaghetti with meat balls and sauce; spaghetti with meat and sauce	Contains not less than 12 percent meat
Spaghetti sauce with meat	Contains not less than 6 percent meat

Source: Abstracted from *Code of Federal Regulations, Animals and Animal Products, Title 9, Part 200 to End* (Washington, D.C.: U.S. Government Printing Office, Jan. 1, 1993).

Exhibit 13-3. Legally defined products and basic requirements.

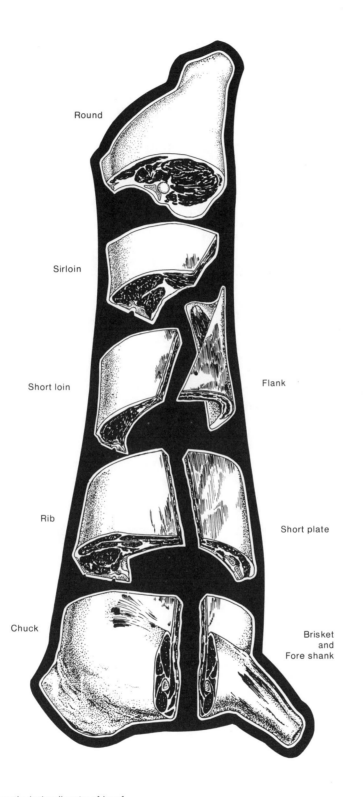

Exhibit 13-4. Wholesale (primal) cuts of beef
(Courtesy of the National Association of Meat Purveyors. This exhibit is copyrighted by the National Association of Meat Purveyors (NAMP) and may be reproduced only with the express permission of the NAMP.)

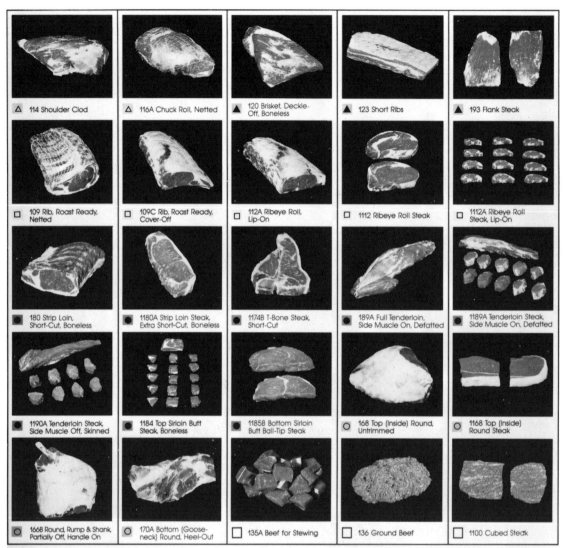

△ 114 Shoulder Clod

△ 116A Chuck Roll, Netted

▲ 120 Brisket, Deckle-Off, Boneless

▲ 123 Short Ribs

▲ 193 Flank Steak

□ 109 Rib, Roast Ready, Netted

□ 109C Rib, Roast Ready, Cover-Off

□ 112A Ribeye Roll, Lip-On

□ 1112 Ribeye Roll Steak

□ 1112A Ribeye Roll Steak, Lip-On

◑ 180 Strip Loin, Short-Cut, Boneless

◑ 1180A Strip Loin Steak, Extra Short-Cut, Boneless

◑ 1174B T-Bone Steak, Short-Cut

◑ 189A Full Tenderloin, Side Muscle On, Defatted

◑ 1189A Tenderloin Steak, Side Muscle On, Defatted

◑ 1190A Tenderloin Steak, Side Muscle Off, Skinned

◑ 1184 Top Sirloin Butt Steak, Boneless

◑ 1185B Bottom Sirloin Butt Ball-Tip Steak

○ 168 Top (Inside) Round, Untrimmed

○ 1168 Top (Inside) Round Steak

◉ 166B Round, Rump & Shank, Partially Off, Handle On

○ 170A Bottom (Goose-neck) Round, Heel-Out

□ 135A Beef for Stewing

□ 136 Ground Beef

□ 1100 Cubed Steak

The above cuts are a partial representation of NAMP/IMPS items. For further representation and explanation of all cuts see *The Meat Buyers Guide* by National Association of Meat Purveyors.

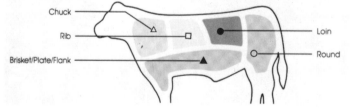

Chuck

Rib

Brisket/Plate/Flank

Loin

Round

Exhibit 13-5. Foodservice cuts of beef with Institutional Meat Purchase Specification numbers (IMPS/NAMP) (Courtesy of the National Association of Meat Purveyors. This exhibit is copyrighted by the National Association of Meat Purveyors (NAMP) and may be reproduced only with the express permission of the NAMP.)

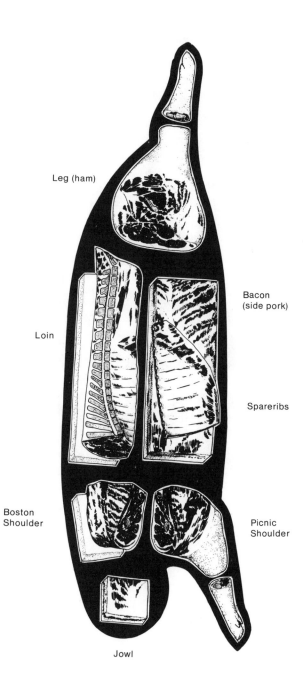

Leg (ham)

Bacon
(side pork)

Loin

Spareribs

Boston
Shoulder

Picnic
Shoulder

Jowl

Exhibit 13-6. Wholesale (primal) cuts of pork

(Courtesy of the National Association of Meat Purveyors. This exhibit is copyrighted by the National Association of Meat Purveyors (NAMP) and may be reproduced only with the express permission of the NAMP.)

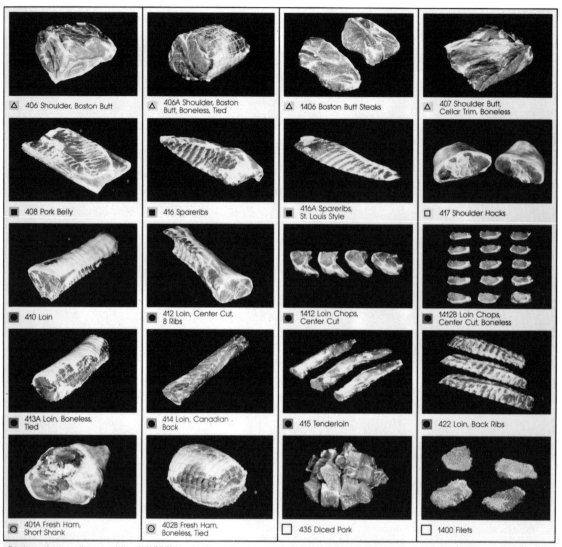

The above cuts are a partial representation of NAMP/IMPS items. For further representation and explanation of all cuts see *The Meat Buyers Guide* by National Association of Meat Purveyors.

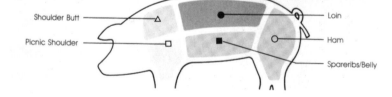

Exhibit 13-7. Foodservice cuts of pork with Institutional Meat Purchase Specification numbers (IMPS/NAMP) (Courtesy of the National Association of Meat Purveyors. This exhibit is copyrighted by the National Association of Meat Purveyors (NAMP) and may be reproduced only with the express permission of the NAMP.)

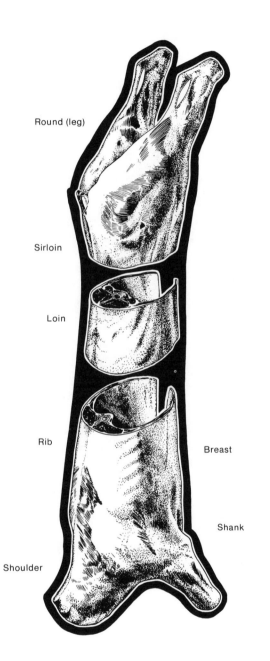

Round (leg)

Sirloin

Loin

Rib

Breast

Shank

Shoulder

Exhibit 13-8. Wholesale (primal) cuts of veal (Courtesy of the National Live Stock and Meat Board, Chicago.)

(Courtesy of the National Association of Meat Purveyors. This exhibit is copyrighted by the National Association of Meat Purveyors (NAMP) and may be reproduced only with the express permission of the NAMP.)

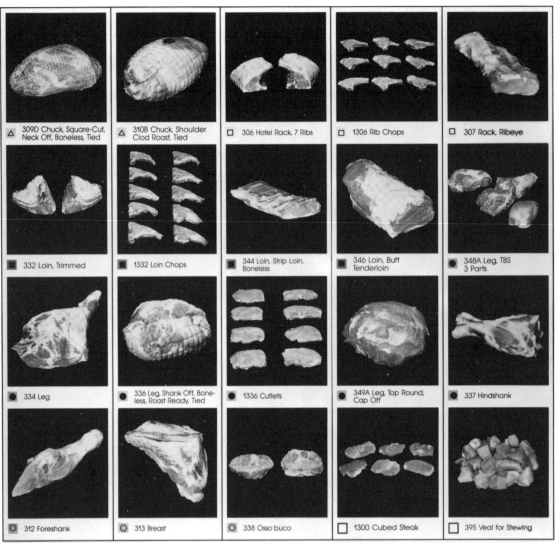

The above cuts are a partial representation of NAMP/IMPS items. For further representation and explanation of all cuts see *The Meat Buyers Guide* by National Association of Meat Purveyors.

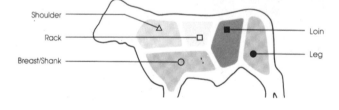

Exhibit 13-9. Foodservice cuts of veal with Institutional Meat Purchase Specification numbers (IMPS/NAMP) (Courtesy of the National Association of Meat Purveyors. This exhibit is copyrighted by the National Association of Meat Purveyors (NAMP) and may be reproduced only with the express permission of the NAMP.)

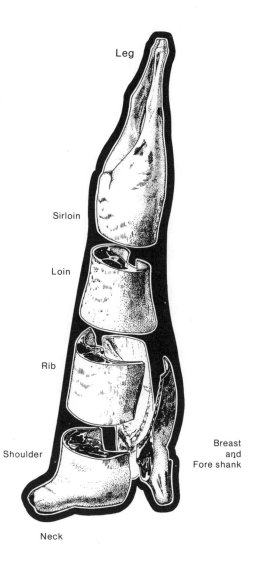

Leg

Sirloin

Loin

Rib

Shoulder

Breast
and
Fore shank

Neck

Exhibit 13-10. Wholesale (primal) cuts of lamb

(Courtesy of the National Association of Meat Purveyors. This exhibit is copyrighted by the National Association of Meat Purveyors (NAMP) and may be reproduced only with the express permission of the NAMP.)

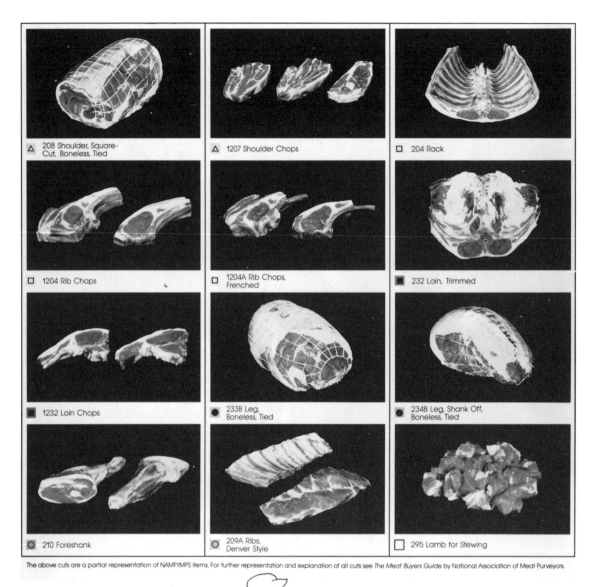

△ 208 Shoulder, Square-Cut, Boneless, Tied

△ 1207 Shoulder Chops

□ 204 Rack

□ 1204 Rib Chops

□ 1204A Rib Chops, Frenched

■ 232 Loin, Trimmed

■ 1232 Loin Chops

● 233B Leg, Boneless, Tied

● 234B Leg, Shank Off, Boneless, Tied

○ 210 Foreshank

○ 209A Ribs, Denver Style

□ 295 Lamb for Stewing

The above cuts are a partial representation of NAMP/IMPS items. For further representation and explanation of all cuts see *The Meat Buyers Guide* by National Association of Meat Purveyors.

Shoulder △

Rack □   ■ Loin

Shank/Breast ○   ● Leg

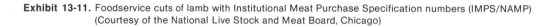

Exhibit 13-11. Foodservice cuts of lamb with Institutional Meat Purchase Specification numbers (IMPS/NAMP) (Courtesy of the National Live Stock and Meat Board, Chicago)

ton, D.C.[4] The same information is available from the National Association of Meat Purveyors in the form of a book, with color photographs, entitled *The Meat Buyers Guide*.[5] Indexes of fresh beef; portion-cut beef; fresh pork; cured pork; fresh veal and calf; and fresh lamb and mutton are items for which specifications have been written, and are provided in Exhibits 13-12, 13-13, 13-14, 13-15, 13-16, and 13-17. Items are listed by number, product, and weight ranges that reflect variations in animal carcasses. Descriptive specifications are provided (IMPS pamphlets) for all items listed in the indexes. Samples of IMPS descriptive material for various cuts of beef rib follow.[6]

- *Items No. 103—Beef Rib, Primal.* The primal rib is that portion of the forequarter remaining after removal of the cross-cut chuck and short plate and shall contain seven ribs (sixth to twelfth inclusive), the posterior tip of the blade bone (scapula), and the thoracic vertebra attached to the ribs. The loin end shall follow the natural curvature of the twelfth rib. The chuck is removed by a straight cut between the fifth and sixth ribs. The short plate shall be removed by a straight cut that is ventral to, but not more than 6.0 inches (15.0 cm) from, the longissimus dorsi at the loin end to a point on the chuck end ventral to, but not more than 10.0 inches (25.4 cm) from, the longissimus dorsi. The diaphragm and fat on the ventral surface of the vertebrae shall be removed.
- *Item No. 103A—Beef Rib, Regular.*

This item is prepared as described in Item No. 103 except that the short plate shall be removed by a straight cut that is ventral to, but not more than 3.0 inches (7.5 cm) from, the longissimus dorsi at the loin end to a point on the chuck end ventral to, but not more than 4.0 (10.2 cm) from, the longissimus dorsi. The protruding edge of the chine bone shall be removed.

- *Item No. 107—Beef Rib, Oven-Prepared.* This item is prepared as described in Item No. 103 except that the short plate shall be removed by a straight cut that is ventral to, but not more than 3.0 inches (7.5 cm) from the longissimus dorsi at the loin end to a point on the chuck end ventral to, but not more than 4.0 inches (10.0 cm) from, the longissimus dorsi. The chine bone shall be removed such that the lean is exposed between the ribs and the feather bone/vertebrae junctures, leaving the feather bones attached. The blade bone and related cartilage shall be removed.
- *Item No. 108—Beef Rib, Oven-Prepared, Boneless.* This boneless is prepared from Item No. 103. The loin end shall be exposed by a cut that follows the natural curvature of the twelfth rib mark and that exposes the spinalis dorsi not extending more than half the length of the longissimus dorsi. On the chuck end, the longissimus dorsi shall be at least twice as large as the complexus. Seven rib marks shall be present. The short plate shall be removed by a straight cut that is ventral to, but not more than 3.0 inches (7.5 cm) from, the longissimus dorsi at the loin end to a point on the chuck end ventral to, but not more than 4.0 inches (10.0 cm) from, the longissimus dorsi. All bones, cartilages, related intercostal

[4]Information may be obtained more directly from USDA, Agricultural Marketing Service Livestock and Meat Standardization Branch, Room 2603-S, P.O. Box 96456, Washington, D.C. 20090–6456.

[5]National Association of Meat Purveyors, 8365-B Greensboro Drive, McLean, Virginia 22102.

[6]From USDA, *Institutional Meat Purchase Specifications for Fresh Beef* (Washington, D.C., U.S. Government Printing Office, 1975), pp. 1, 2.

Item No.	Product Name	Range A	Range B	Range C	Range D
			Weight Ranges (Pounds)		
100	Carcass	500–600	600–700	700–800	800–up
100A	Carcass, Trimmed	475–575	575–675	675–775	775–up
100B	Carcass, Streamlined	335–400	400–470	470–600	600–up
101	Side	250–300	300–350	350–400	400–up
102	Forequarter	131–157	157–183	183–210	210–up
102A	Forequarter, Boneless	104–125	125–146	146–168	168–up
102B	Forequarter, Streamlined	91–110	110–128	128–147	147–up
103	Rib, Primal	24–28	28–33	33–38	38–up
103A	Rib, Regular	18–20	20–24	24–27	27–up
104	Rib, Oven-Prepared, Regular	19–22	22–26	26–30	30–up
107	Rib, Oven-Prepared	17–19	19–23	23–26	26–up
107A	Rib, Oven-Prepared, Blade Bone in	17–19	19–23	23–26	26–up
108	Rib, Oven-Prepared, Boneless	13–16	16–19	19–22	22–up
109	Rib, Roast-Ready	14–16	16–19	19–22	22–up
109A	Rib, Roast-Ready, Special	14–16	16–19	19–22	22–up
109B	Rib, Blade Meat	3–up			
109C	Rib, Roast-Ready, Cover Off	13–15	15–18	18–21	21–up
109D	Rib, Roast-Ready, Cover Off, Short-Cut	12–14	14–17	17–20	20–up
109E	Rib, Ribeye Roll, Lip On, Bone In	11–13	13–16	16–19	20–up
110	Rib, Roast-Ready, Boneless	11–13	13–16	16–19	19–up
111	Rib, Spencer Roll	10–12	12–15	15–18	18–up
112	Rib, Ribeye Roll	5–6	6–8	8–10	10–up
112A	Rib, Ribeye Roll, Lip On	6–7	7–9	9–11	11–up
113	Chuck, Square-Cut	66–79	79–93	93–106	106–up
113A	Chuck, Square-Cut, Divided	66–79	79–93	93–106	106–up
113B	Chuck, Square-Cut, Neck Off, Divided	35–40	40–47	47–55	55–up
113C	Chuck, Square-Cut, Neck Off, 2 Piece, Semiboneless	33–40	40–46	46–50	50–up
114	Chuck, Shoulder Clod	13–15	15–18	18–21	21–up
114A	Chuck, Shoulder Clod Roast	under 15	15–18	18–21	21–up
114B	Chuck, Shoulder Clod Roast, Special	under 15	15–18	18–21	21–up
114C	Chuck, Shoulder Clod, Trimmed	under 12	12–14	14–18	18–up
114D	Chuck, Shouler Clod, Top Blade, Roast	under 2	2–3	4–5	5–up
114E	Chuck, Shoulder Clod, Arm Roast	under 8	8–10	0–12	12–up
115	Chuck, Square-Cut, Boneless	54–65	65–77	77–88	88–up
115A	Chuck, Blade Portion, Boneless	22–25	25–29	29–34	34–up
115B	Chuck, Arm Out, Boneless	35–40	40–47	47–55	55–up
115C	Chuck, Square-Cut, Neck Off, Boneless	48–59	59–70	70–81	81–up
116	Chuck, Square-Cut, Clod Out, Boneless	40–48	48–57	57–65	65–up
116A	Chuck, Chuck Roll	13–15	15–18	18–21	21–up
116B	Chuck, Chuck Tender	under 1	1–3	3–up	
116C	Chuck, Chuck Roll, Untrimmed	16–18	18–20	20–22	22–up
116D	Chuck, Chuck Eye Roll	under 8	8–10	10–14	14–up
116E	Chuck, Under Blade Roast	under 8	8–10	10–14	14–up
117	Foreshank	7–8	8–10	10–12	12–up
118	Brisket	12–14	14–17	17–20	20–up
119	Brisket, Deckle On, Boneless	9–10	10–12	12–14	14–up
120	Brisket, Deckle Off, Boneless	16–8	8–10	10–12	12–up
120A	Brisket, Flat-Cut, Boneless	4–6	6–8	8–10	10–up
120B	Brisket, Point-Cut, Boneless	under 3	3–4	4–6	6–up
120C	Brisket, 2 Piece, Boneless	6–8	8–10	10–12	12–up
121	Plate, Short Plate	20–27	27–31	31–35	35–up
121A	Plate, Short Plate, Boneless	12–14	14–16	16–18	18–up
121B	Plate, Short Plate, Boneless, Trimmed	8–12	12–14	14–16	16–up
121C	Plate, Outside Skirt (Diaphragm)	1–2	2–3	3–up	
121D	Plate, Inside Skirt (Transversus Abdominis)	1–3	3–4	4–up	
121E	Plate, Outside Skirt (Diaphragm), Skinned	1–2	2–3	3–up	
121F	Plate, Short Plate, Short Ribs Removed	18–25	25–28	28–33	33–up
121G	Plate, Short Plate, Short Ribs Removed, Boneless	10–12	12–14	14–16	16–up
122	Plate, Full	28–37	37–44	44–51	51–up
122A	Plate, Full, Boneless	21–27	27–29	29–32	32–up
123	Short Ribs	2–3	3–4	4–5	5–up
123A	Short Plate, Short Ribs, Trimmed		Amount as Specified		
123B	Rib, Short Ribs, Trimmed		Amount as Specified		
123C	Rib, Short Ribs		Amount as Specified		
123D	Short Ribs, Boneless	1–2	2–3	3–4	4–up

Exhibit 13–12. Index of institutional meat purchase specifications for fresh beef products (From USDA, *Institutional Meat Purchase Specifications for Fresh Beef Products—Series 100* [Washington D.C.: U.S. Government Printing Office, effective October 1995], pp. 6, 7, 8, 9, 10)

Item No.	Product Name	Range A	Range B	Range C	Range D
			Weight Ranges (Pounds)		
124	Rib, Back Ribs		Amount as Specified		
125	Chuck, Armbone	77–88	88–103	103–118	118–up
126	Chuck, Armbone, Boneless	59–70	70–82	82–90	90–up
126A	Chuck, Armbone, Clod Out, Boneless	46–57	57–69	69–77	77–up
127	Chuck, Cross-Cut	86–103	103–120	120–138	138–up
128	Chuck, Cross-Cut, Boneless	68–81	81–95	95–109	109–up
130	Chuck, Short Ribs	2–3	3–4	4–5	5–up
130A	Chuck, Short Ribs, Boneless	0.5–1.5	1.5–2.5	2.5–3.5	3.5–up
132	Triangle	107–129	129–150	150–172	172–up
133	Triangle, Boneless	83–101	101–117	117–134	134–up
134	Beef Bones		Amount as Specified		
135	Diced Beef		Amount as Specified		
135A	Beef for Stewing		Amount as Specified		
135B	Beef for Kabobs		Amount as Specified		
136	Ground Beef		Amount as Specified		
136A	Ground Beef and Vegetable Protein Product		Amount as Specified		
136B	Beef Patty Mix		Amount as Specified		
136C	Beef Patty Mix, Lean		Amount as Specified		
137	Ground Beef, Special		Amount as Specified		
137A	Ground Beef and Vegetable Protein Product, Special		Amount as Specified		
138	Beef Trimmings		Amount as Specified		
139	Special Trim, Boneless		Amount as Specified		
155	Hindquarter	119–143	143–167	167–190	190–up
155A	Hindquarter, Boneless	90–108	108–126	126–143	143–up
155B	Hindquarter, Streamlined	96–115	115–134	134–152	152–up
155C	Hindquarter, Trimmed	110–132	132–155	155–178	178–up
157	Hindshank	7–8	8–10	10–12	12–up
158	Round, Primal	59–71	71–83	83–95	95–up
158A	Round, Diamond-Cut	63–76	76–89	89–102	102–up
159	Round, Primal, Boneless	44–53	53–62	62–71	71–up
160	Round, Shank Off, Partially Boneless	47–57	57–67	67–76	76–up
160A	Round, Diamond-Cut, Shank Off, Partially Boneless	50–60	60–70	70–80	80–up
160B	Round, Heel and Shank Out, Semiboneless	38–46	46–54	54–60	60–up
161	Round, Shank Off, Boneless	42–51	51–62	62–71	71–up
161A	Round, Diamond-Cut, Shank Off, Boneless	44–53	53–62	62–71	71–up
161B	Round, Heel and Shank Off, Without Knuckle, Boneless	30–37	37–44	44–51	51–up
163	Round, Shank Off, 3-Way, Boneless	41–50	50–58	58–66	66–up
163A	Round, Shank Off, 3-Way, Untrimmed, Boneless	42–50	50–58	58–66	66–up
164	Round, Rump and Shank Off	40–48	48–56	56–64	64–up
165	Round, Rump and Shank Off, Boneless	35–43	43–50	50–57	57–up
165A	Round, Rump and Shank Off, Boneless, Special	38–46	46–54	54–60	60–up
165B	Round, Rump and Shank Off, Boneless, Special	38–46	46–54	54–60	60–up
166	Round, Rump and Shank Off, Boneless	35–43	43–50	50–57	57–up
166A	Round, Rump Partially Removed, Shank Off	44–52	52–61	61–70	70–up
166B	Round, Rump and Shank Partially Off, Handle On	44–52	52–61	61–70	70–up
167	Round, Knuckle	8–9	9–11	11–13	13–up
167A	Round, Knuckle, Peeled	7–8	8–10	10–12	12–up
167B	Round, Knuckle, Full	10–12	12–14	14–16	16–up
167C	Round, Knuckle, Full, Peeled	9–11	11–13	13–15	15–up
167D	Round, Knuckle, Peeled, 2-Piece	5–7	7–9	9–12	12–up
168	Round, Top (Inside), Untrimmed	14–17	17–20	20–23	23–up
169	Round, Top (Inside)	14–17	17–20	20–23	23–up
169A	Round, Top (Inside), Cap Off	12–15	15–18	18–20	20–up
169B	Round, Top (Inside), Cap	1–2	2–3	3–up	
170	Round, Bottom (Gooseneck)	18–23	23–27	27–31	31–up
170A	Round, Bottom (Gooseneck), Heel Out	17–20	20–24	24–28	28–up
171	Round, Bottom (Gooseneck), Untrimmed	18–21	21–25	25–29	29–up
171A	Round, Bottom (Gooseneck), Untrimmed, Heel Out	17–20	20–24	24–28	28–up
171B	Round, Outside Round	8–10	10–13	13–16	16–up
171C	Round, Eye of Round	Under 3	3–5	5–up	
172	Loin, Full Loin, Trimmed	30–37	37–45	45–52	52–up
172A	Loin, Full Loin, Diamond-Cut	35–42	42–50	50–57	57–up

Exhibit 13-12 (continued)

Item No.	Product Name	Weight Ranges (Pounds)			
		Range A	Range B	Range C	Range D
173	Loin, Short Loin	17–24	24–30	30–35	35–up
174	Loin, Short Loin, Short-Cut	14–20	20–25	25–30	30–up
175	Loin, Strip Loin	11–14	14–18	18–22	22–up
180	Loin, Strip Loin, Boneless	8–10	10–12	12–14	14–up
181	Loin, Sirloin	16–19	19–24	24–28	28–up
181A	Loin, Top Sirloin	11–14	14–17	17–20	20–up
182	Loin, Sirloin Butt, Boneless	11–14	14–16	16–19	19–up
183	Loin, Sirloin Butt, Boneless, Trimmed	9–10	10–13	13–15	15–up
184	Loin, Top Sirloin Butt, Boneless	8–10	10–12	12–14	14–up
184A	Loin, Top Sirloin Butt, Semi Center-Cut, Boneless	7–9	9–11	11–13	13–up
184B	Loin, Top Sirloin Butt, Center-Cut, Boneless	5–7	7–9	9–11	11–up
184C	Loin, Top Sirloin Butt, Untrimmed, Boneless	8–10	10–12	12–14	14–up
184D	Loin, Top Sirloin Cap	1–2	2–3	3–4	4–up
184E	Beef Loin, Top Sirloin, 2-Pc	8–9	9–11	11–13	13–up
185	Loin, Bottom Sirloin Butt, Boneless	5–6	6–7	7–8	8–up
185A	Loin, Bottom Sirloin Butt, Flap, Boneless	1–3	3–up		
185B	Loin, Bottom Sirloin Butt, Ball Tip, Boneless	1.5–3	3–up		
185C	Loin, Bottom Sirloin Butt, Tri-Tip, Boneless	1.5–3	3–up		
185D	Loin, Bottom Sirloin Butt, Tri-Tip, Boneless, Defatted	1.5–3	3–up		
186	Loin, Bottom Sirloin Butt, Boneless, Trimmed	2–3	3–4	4–5	5–up
189	Loin, Tenderloin, Full	4–5	5–6	6–7	7–up
189A	Loin, Tenderloin, Full, Side Muscle On, Defatted	3–4	4–5	5–6	6–up
189B	Loin, Tenderloin, Full, Side Muscle On, Partially Defatted	3–4	4–5	5–6	6–up
190	Loin, Tenderloin, Full, Side Muscle Off, Defatted	2–3	3–4	4–up	
190A	Loin, Tenderloin, Full, Side Muscle Off, Skinned	2–3	3–4	4–up	
191	Loin, Tenderloin, Butt	1–2	2–3	3–4	4–up
191A	Loin, Tenderloin, Butt, Defatted	1–2	2–3	3–4	4–up
191B	Loin, Tenderloin, Butt, Skinned	Under 2	2–3	3–up	
192	Loin, Tenderloin, Short	2–3	3–4	4–up	
192A	Loin, Tenderloin Tails	Amount as Specified			
193	Flank, Flank Steak	Under 1	1–2	2–up	

Exhibit 13-12 (continued)

meat, and backstrap shall be removed. The rib shall be netted or tied when specified.

- *Item No. 109—Beef Rib, Roast-Ready.* This item is prepared as described in Item 103 except that the short plate shall be removed by a straight cut that is ventral to, but not more than 3.0 inches (7.5 cm) from, the longissimus dorsi at the loin end to a point on the chuck end ventral to, but not more than 4.0 inches (10.0 cm) from, the longissimus dorsi. The chine bone shall be removed such that the lean is exposed between the ribs and the feather bone/vertebrae junctures, leaving the feather bones attached. The blade bone and related cartilage, backstrap, latissimus dorsi, infraspinatus, subscapularis, rhom-boideus, and trapezius shall be removed. The exterior fat covering (that covered the latissimus dorsi and trapezius) shall not exceed 1.0 inch (25 mm) in depth at any point. The fat cover may be separated to accommodate removal of the backstrap and returned to its original position. The fat cover shall be trimmed even with the short plate side and shall not have holes larger than 2.0 square inches (12.9 sq cm). The rib shall be netted or tied when specified.

- *No. 109A—Beef Rib, Roast-Ready, Special, Tied.* This item is prepared as described in Item No. 103 except that feather bones are removed. The exterior fat covering (that covered the latissimus dorsi, trapezius,

Item No.	Product Name	Suggested Portion Weight Range (Ounces)
1100	Cubed Steak	3 – 8
1101	Cubed Steak, Special	3 – 8
1102	Braising Steak, Swiss	4 – 8
1103	Rib, Rib Steak	8 – 18
1103A	Rib, Rib Steak, Boneless	4 – 12
1112	Rib, Ribeye Roll Steak	4 – 12
1112A	Rib, Ribeye Steak, Lip On	4 – 12
1112B	Rib, Ribeye Steak, Lip On, Short-Cut	4 – 12
1114D	*Chuck, Shoulder Clod, Top Blade Steak*	*4 – 12*
1116D	*Chuck, Chuck Eye Roll Steak*	*4 – 12*
1121D	Plate, Inside Skirt Steak	*4 – 8*
1121E	Plate, Outside Skirt Steak, Skinned	*4 – 8*
1123	*Short Ribs, Flaked Style*	*3 – 10*
1136	Ground Beef Patties	Desired Ounces or Number per Pound
1136A	Ground Beef and Vegetable Protein Product Patties	Desired Ounces or Number per Pound
1136B	Beef Patties	Desired Ounces or Number per Pound
1137	Ground Beef Patties, Special	Desired Ounces or Number per Pound
1137A	Ground Beef and Vegetable Protein Product Patties, Special	Desired Ounces or Number per Pound
1138	Beef Steaks, Flaked and Formed, Frozen	Desired Ounces or Number per Pound
1138A	Beef Sandwich Steaks, Flaked, Chopped, Formed, and Wafer Sliced, Frozen	Desired Ounces
1138B	Beef Steaks, Sliced and Formed, Frozen	Desired Ounces
1150	*Top Side Steak, Boneless*	*4 – 16*
1167	Round, Knuckle Steak	3 – 10
1167A	Round, Knuckle Steak, Peeled	3 – 10
1167D	*Round, Knuckle Steak, Peeled, Special*	*4 – 8*
1169	Round, Top (Inside) Round Steak	*3 – 12*
1170A	Round, Bottom (Gooseneck) Round Steak	*3 – 24*
1173	*Loin, Porterhouse Steak*	*10 – 12*
1174	*Loin, T-Bone Steak*	*8 – 24*
1179	*Loin, Strip Loin Steak*	*8 – 24*
1179A	*Loin, Strip Loin Steak, Center-Cut*	*8 – 24*
1180	*Loin, Strip Loin Steak, Boneless*	*6 – 20*
1180A	*Loin, Strip Loin Steak, Boneless, Center-Cut*	*6 – 20*
1184	Loin, Top Sirloin Butt Steak, Boneless	4 – 24
1184A	Loin, Top Sirloin Butt Steak, Semi Center-Cut, Boneless	4 – 16
1184B	Loin, Top Sirloin Butt Steak, Center-Cut, Boneless	4 – 16
1184D	*Loin, Top Sirloin Cap Steak, Boneless*	*4 – 8*
1185A	Loin, Bottom Sirloin Butt, Flap Steak	3 – 8
1185B	Loin, Bottom Sirloin Butt, Ball Tip Steak	3 – 10
1185C	Loin, Bottom Sirloin Butt, Tri-Tip Steak	3 – 8
1185D	Loin, Bottom Sirloin Butt, Tri-Tip Steak, Defatted	3 – 8
1189	Loin, Tenderloin Steak	4 – 14
1189A	Loin, Tenderloin Steak, Side Muscle On, Defatted	3 – 14
1189B	Loin, Tenderloin Steak, Side Muscle On, Partially Defatted	3 – 14
1190	Loin, Tenderloin Steak, Side Muscle Off, Defatted	3 – 14
1190A	Loin, Tenderloin Steak, Side Muscle Off, Skinned	3 – 14
1190B	*Loin, Tenderloin Steak, Center-Cut*	*3 – 14*
1190C	Loin, Tenderloin Tips	Amount as Specified

Exhibit 13-13. Index of institutional meat purchase specifications for portion-cut meat products (From USDA, *Institutional Meat Purchase Specifications for Portion-Cut Meat Products—in Series 1000* [Washington D.C.: U.S. Government Printing Office, effective October, 1995])

longissimus dorsi, and spinalis dorsi) shall be separated to facilitate trimming of the underlying fat. The underlying fat covering the longissimus dorsi and spinalis dorsi shall be trimmed to a uniform thickness for the entire seamed surface. The exterior fat covering shall be returned and positioned so that it extends from the edge of the rib bones where the feather bones were, toward the edges of the rib bones at the short plate side. Fat cover extending beyond the short plate edges of the ribs shall be removed. The fat cover shall not exceed 1.0 inch (25 mm) in thickness at any point and have holes larger than 2.0 square inches (12.9 sq cm).

Item No.	Product Name	Range A	Range B	Range C	Range D
			Weight Ranges (Pounds)		
400	Carcass	120–150	150–180	180–210	210–up
400A	*Whole Roasting Pig*	*12–24*	*24–40*	*40–60*	*100–up*
401	Leg (Fresh Ham)	14–17	17–20	20–26	26–up
401A	Leg (Fresh Ham), Short Shank	14–17	17–20	20–26	26–up
401B	*Leg (Fresh Ham), Sirloin On*	*16–18*	*18–22*	*22–28*	*28–up*
401C	*Leg (Fresh Ham), Semiboneless*	*14–16*	*16–18*	*18–20*	*20–up*
402	Leg (Fresh Ham), Skinned	14–17	17–20	20–26	26–up
402A	Leg (Fresh Ham), Skinned, Short Shank	14–17	17–20	20–26	26–up
402B	Leg (Fresh Ham), Boneless	6–88–10	10–12	12-up	
402C	Leg (Fresh Ham), Boneless, Short Shank, Trimmed	6–8	8–10	10–12	12–up
402D	Leg (Fresh Ham), Outside	2–4	4–5	5–6	6–up
402E	Leg (Fresh Ham), Outside, Trimmed	2–3	3–5	5–up	
402F	Leg (Fresh Ham), Inside	under 3	3–4	4–5	5–up
402G	*Leg (Fresh Ham), TBS, 3-Way, Boneless*	*12–14*	*14–16*	*16–18*	*18–up*
403	Shoulder	8–12	12–16	16–20	20–up
403A	*Shoulder, Long Cut*	*10–14*	*14–18*	*18–22*	*22–up*
403B	*Outside Shoulder*	*8–12*	*12–16*	*16–20*	*20–up*
403C	*Inside Shoulder, Boneless*	*12–4*	*4–8*	*8-up*	
404	Shoulder, Skinned	8–12	12–16	16–20	20–up
405	Shoulder, Picnic	4–6	6–8	8–12	12–up
405A	Shoulder, Picnic, Boneless	2–4	4–6	6–8	8–up
405B	Shoulder, Picnic, Cushion		Amount as Specified		
406	Shoulder, Boston Butt	2–4	4–8	8–up	
406A	Shoulder, Boston Butt, Boneless	2–4	4–8	8–up	
406B	Shoulder, Boston Butt, Boneless, Special	2–4	4–6	6–8	8–up
407	Shoulder Butt, Cellar Trimmed, Boneless	1.5–3	3–4	4–7	7–up
408	Belly	10–12	12–14	14–18	18–up
409	Belly, Skinless	7–9	9–11	11–13	13–up
409A	*Belly, Single Ribbed, Skinless*	*10–12*	*12–14*	*14–18*	*18–up*
409B	*Belly, Center-Cut, Skinless*	*7–9*	*9–11*	*11–13*	*13–up*
410	Loin	10–14	14–18	18–22	22–up
410A	*Sirloin*	*2–4*	*4–8*	*8–10*	*10–up*
411	Loin, Bladeless	10–14	14–18	18–22	22–up
412	Loin, Center-Cut, 8 Ribs	4–6	6–8	8–10	10–up
412A	Loin, Center-Cut, 8 Ribs, Chine Bone Off	4–5	5–7	7–9	9–up
412B	Loin, Center-Cut, 8 Ribs, Boneless	2–4	4–5	4–6	6–up
412C	Loin, Center-Cut, 11 Ribs	5–7	7–9	9–11	11–up
412D Chine	Loin, Center-Cut, 11 Ribs, Bone Off	4–6	6–8	8–10	10–up
412E	Loin, Center-Cut, 11 Ribs, Boneless	3–5	5–6	6–7	7–up
412F	Loin, Center-Cut, Rib End, Boneless	1–1.5	1.5–2	2–up	
413	Loin, Boneless	6–8	8–10	10–12	12–up
413A	Loin, Roast, Boneless	6–8	8–10	10–12	12–up
413B	Loin, Boneless, Special	6–8	8–10	10–12	12–up
414	Loin, Canadian Back	3–4	4–5	5–6	6–up
414A	*Sirloin, Boneless*	*1–3*	*3–5*	*5–9*	
415	Tenderloin	0.5–1	1–1.5	1.5–up	
415A	Tenderloin, Side Muscle Off	0.5–1	1–1.5	1.5–up	
416	Spareribs	under 2.5	2.5–3.5	3.5–5.5	5.5–up
416A	Spareribs, St. Louis Style	1.5–2	2–3	3–up	
416B	Spareribs, Brisket Bones	0.25–0.33	0.33–0.5	0.5–0.75	0.75–up
416C	Spareribs, Breast Off	under 2.5	2.5–3.5	3.5–5.5	5.5–up
416D	*Breast Bones*	*under 1*	*over 1*		
417	Shoulder Hocks	0.25–0.75	0.75–1.5	1.5–up	
417A	Leg (Fresh Ham) Hocks		Not Applicable		
418	Trimmings		Not Applicable		
420	Pig's Feet, Front		Not Applicable		
420A	Pig's Feet, Hind		Not Applicable		
421	Neck Bones		As Specified		
422	Loin, Back Ribs	under 1.5	1.5–1.75	1.75–2.25	2.25–up
423	Loin, Country-Style Ribs	2–3	3–up		
435	Diced Pork		As Specified		
435A	*Pork for Stewing*		*As Specified*		
435B	*Pork for Kabobs*		*As Specified*		
496	Ground Pork		As Specified		
496A	Ground Pork and Vegetable Protein Product		As Specified		
496B	Pork Patty Mix		As Specified		

Exhibit 13-14. Index of institutional meat purchase specifications for fresh pork (From USDA, *Institutional Meat Purchase Specifications for fresh Pork—Series 400* [Washington D.C.: U.S. Government Printing Office, effective October 1995], pp. 5, 6, 7)

Item No.	Product Name	Suggested Portion Weight Range (Ounces)
1400	Steak Cubed	3–8
1401	Steaks Cubed, Special	3–8
1402	Cutlets	3–8
1402G	Leg Cutlets	3–8
1406	Boston Butt Steaks	4–8
1407	Shoulder Butt Steaks, Boneless	3–8
1410	Loin Chops	3–8
1410A	Loin, Rib Chops	3–8
1410B	Loin, End Chops	4–8
1411	Loin Chops, Bladeless	3–8
1412	Loin Chops, Center-Cut	3–8
1412A	Loin Chops, Center-Cut, Chine Bone Off	3–8
1412B	Loin Chops, Center-Cut, Boneless	3–8
1412E	Loin Chops, Center-Cut, One Muscle, Boneless	6–8
1413	Loin Chops, Boneless	3–8
1413B	Loins, End Chops, Boneless	3–6
1438	Steaks, Flaked and Formed, Frozen	Amount as Specified
1438A	Sandwich, Steaks, Flaked, Chopped, Formed and Wafer Sliced, Frozen	Amount as Specified
1438B	Steaks, Sliced and Formed, Frozen	Amount as Specified
1495	Coarse Chopped Pork	Amount as Specified
1496	Ground Pork Patties	Amount as Specified
1496A	Ground Pork and Vegetable Protein Product Parties	Amount as Specified
1496B	Pork Patties	Amount as Specified

Exhibit 13-14 (continued)

Size and Weight of Cut

The weight of meat cut specified by the buyer depends on the following: practicality of cutting based on size of animal parts; portion size desired for service; ideal weight for efficiency in cooking and serving; ideal weight in terms of quality; and ideal weight in terms of yield. Reasonable weights are indicated in the IMPS *Index of Specifications*. When selecting weights with indexes, weight range B or C is generally best. These include unportioned items such as roasts and portioned items such as steaks. Size ranges provided in indexes indicate reasonable weights of cuts as related to size of animal parts. However, since animals are not all built the same, the weight of a cut may not be in direct proportion to the carcass weight of the animal. For example, the weight of a rib may not be proportionately heavier as animal weight increases. Some animals have a relatively higher portion of bone or other inedible material. Thus, carcass weight should be specified only when the whole carcass is purchased and not along with cut weight.

Portion size of steaks may be specified in terms of weight or thickness but not both. In the same context, it is impossible for a purveyor to provide a 5-pound primal rib or a 10-pound primal round. These parts of beef cattle are not that small. However, a buyer may request that a particular item (cut) be cut in half (to make smaller roasts) or into cubes of a particular size or steaks of a particular weight, or be ground.

For all cuts of meat, a reasonable allowance for variation in weight must be written into specifications, since cutting meat to exact portion weight is not feasible. Recommendations for reasonable tolerance in IMPS are as follows: less than 6 ounces, ± ¼ ounce; 6 ounces to 12 ounces, ± ½ ounce; 12 ounces to 24 ounces, ± ¾ ounce; and 24.01 ounces or more, ± 1 ounce. Weight tolerance in roasts is generally specified within a range of 2 pounds, such as 8–10, 28–30, or 18–20 pound roasts, with no tolerance outside of the specified range. Tolerance for thickness in steaks is ± 3/16 inch for steaks 1 inch thick or less and ± ¼ inch in steaks more than 1 inch thick. Except when yield

Item No.	Product Name	Weight Ranges (Pounds)		
		Range A	Range B	Range C
500	Ham, Short Shank (Cured)	10–14	14–17	17–20
501	Ham, Short Shank (Cured and Smoked)	10–14	14–17	17–20
502	Ham, Short Shank, Skinned (Cured)	10–14	14–17	17–20
503	Ham, Short Shank, Skinned (Cured and Smoked), Fullly Cooked	10–14	14–17	17–20
504	Ham, Skinless, Partially Boned (Cured and Smoked)	8–10	10–12	12–14
505	Ham, Boneless (Cured and Smoked), Fully Cooked	8–10	10–12	12–14
505A	Ham, Boneless, Tied (Cured and Smoked), Fully Cooked	8–10	10–12	12–14
508	Ham, Boiled, Boneless (Cured), Fully Cooked	8–10	10–12	12–14
509	Ham, Boneless (Cured and Smoked), Fully Cooked, Special	5–11	11–16	
510	Ham, Honey Cured (Smoked), Partially Boned, Spiral Cut	8–10	10–12	12–14
511	Ham, Chunked and Formed (Cured), Fully Cooked	8–10	10–12	12–14
511A	Ham, Chunked and Formed (Cured and Smoked), Fully Cooked	8–10	10–12	12–14
512	Ham, Diced (Cured)	As Specified by Purchaser		
512A	Ham, Diced (Cured and Smoked)	As Specified by Purchaser		
514	Pork, Diced (Cured)	As Specified by Purchaser		
515	Pork Shoulder (Cured)	8–12	12–16	16–20
516	Pork Shoulder (Cured and Smoked)	8–12	12–16	16–20
517	Pork Shoulder, Skinned (Cured)	8–12	12–16	16–20
518	Pork Shoulder, Skinned (Cured and Smoked)	8–12	12–16	16–20
525	Pork Shoulder Picnic (Cured)	4–6	6–8	8–12
526	Pork Shoulder Picnic (Cured and Smoked)	4–6	6–8	8–12
527	Pork Shoulder Picnic (Cured and Smoked), Boneless, Tied	6–8	8–10	10–12
530	Pork Shoulder Butt, Cellar Trimmed, Boneless (Cured and Smoked)	1.5–3	3–5	5–8
531	Pork Boston Butt, Boneless (Cured and Smoked), Special	2–4	4–6	6–8
535*	Belly, Skin On (Cured)	10–12	12–14	14–16
536*	Bacon, Slab (Cured and Smoked), Skin On, Formed	10–12	12–14	14–16
537*	Belly, Slab (Cured and Smoked), Skinless, Formed	10–12	12–14	14–16
538*	Bacon, Slab, Center-Cut (Cured and Smoked), Skinless, Formed	8–10	10–12	12–14
538A*	Bacon, Sliced, Center-Cut (Cured and Smoked)	Number of Slices per pound 12–14; 14–18,18–22; 22–26; 26–30; 28–32: or as Specified		
539*	Bacon, Sliced (Cured and Smoked), Skinless	Same as Above		
541*	Bacon, Sliced (Cured and Smoked), Ends and Pieces	5- and 10-pound Containers or as Specified		
545	Pork Loin (Cured and Smoked)	10–14	14–17	17–20
546	Pork Loin, Bladeless (Cured and Smoked)	10–14	14–17	17–20
547	Pork Center Loin, 11 Ribs (Cured and Smoked)	5–7	7–10	10–12
547A	Pork Center Loin, Boneless (Cured and Smoked)	3–5	5–7	7–10
548	Pork Center-Cut Loin, 8 Ribs (Cured and Smoked)	4–6	6–8	8–11
548A	Pork Loin, Center-Cut, Boneless (Cured and Smoked)	2–4	4–6	6–10
550	Canadian Style Bacon (Cured and Smoked), Unsliced	3–4	4–6	5–6
550A	Canadian Style Bacon (Cured and Smoked), Sliced	5- and 10-pound Containers as Specified		
555*	Jowl Butts, Cellar Trim (Cured)	1–2.5	2.5–4	
556*	Jowl Squares (Cured and Smoked)	0.8–2	2–3	
558*	Spareribs, Fully Cooked	1.5–3	3–5	5–up
559*	Spareribs (Cured and Smoked)	1.5–3	3–5	5–up
559A*	Pork Spareribs, Fully Cooked, St. Louis Style	1.5–2	2–3	3–up
559B*	Pork Spareribs (Cured and Smoked), St. Louis style	1.5–2	2–3	3–up
560*	Hocks, Ham (Cured and Smoked)	0.5–1	1–1.5	1.5–2.5
561*	Hocks, Shoulder (Cured and Smoked)	0.5–1	1–1.5	1.5–2.5
562*	Clear Fatback (Cured)	6–8	8–10	10–12
563*	Feet, Front (Cured)	0.8–1.5		

Precooked Portion Items

Item No.	Product Name	Range A	Range B
1513	Ham Patties (Cured), Fully Cooked	3–5 ounces	As Specified by Purchaser
1531	Ham Steaks (Cured and Smoked), Boneless	5–12 ounces	As Specified by Purchaser
1545	Pork Loin Chops (Cured and Smoked)	3–8 ounces	As Specified by Purchaser
1548	Pork Loin Chops, Boneless, Center-Cut (Cured and Smoked)	3–8 ounces	As Specified by Purchaser
1596*	Pork Patty, Precooked	3–8 ounces	As Specified by Purchaser

*Style option not applicable to this item.

Exhibit 13-15. Index of institutional meat purchase specifications for cured, cured and smoked, and fully cooked pork products (From USDA, *Institutional Meat Purchase Specifications for Cured, Cured and Smoked, and Fully-Cooked Pork Products—Series 500* [Washington D.C.: U.S. Government Printing Office, effective January 1, 1992], pp. vi, vii, viii)

Item No.	Product Name	Weight Ranges (Pounds)			
		Range A	Range B	Range C	Range D
300	Carcass	60–90	90–140	140–175	175–245
303	Side	30–45	45–70	70–88	88–123
303A	Hindquarter, 2 Ribs	16–23	23–36	36–46	46–64
304	Foresaddle, 11 Ribs	29–43	43–67	67–84	84–118
306	Hotel Rack, 7 Ribs	5–9	9–12	12–14	14–18
307	Rack Ribeye	3–5	5–up		
308	Chucks, 4 Ribs	22–40	40–56	56–70	70–90
309	Chucks, Square-Cut	11–20	20–28	28–36	36–47
309A	Chucks, Square-Cut, 5 Ribs	12–21	21–29	29–37	37–48
309B	Chuck, Square-Cut, Boneless	10–19	19–26	26–33	33–40
309C	Chuck, Square-Cut, 5 Ribs, Boneless	11–19	12–27	27–35	33–43
309D	Chuck, Square-Cut, Neck Off, Boneless, Tied	9–18	18–25	25–32	32–42
309E	Chuck, Square-Cut, 5 Ribs, Neck Off, Boneless, Tied	10–19	19–27	27–35	35–45
309F	Chuck, Square-Cut, Neck Off, Arm Out, Boneless, Roast, Tied	6–12	12–19	19–26	26–38
310	Chuck Shoulder Clod	2–4	4–5	5–7	7–9
310A	Chuck Shoulder Clod, Special	2–4	4–5	5–7	7–9
310B	Chuck, Shoulder Clod Roast	2–4	4–5	5–7	7–9
310C	Chuck Scotch Tender	1/2–1	1–2		
311	Chuck Square-Cut, Clod Out, Boneless, Tied	9–18	18–25	25–32	32–42
312	Foreshank	1–2	2–3	3–4	4–5
313	Breast	3–6	6–8	8–10	10–12
314	Breast with Pocket	3–6	6–8	8–10	10–12
330	Hindsaddle, 2 Ribs	30–50	50–70	70–88	88–114
331	Loin	6–10	10–14	14–18	18–23
332	Loin, Trimmed	9–8	8–11	11–14	14–17
334	Leg	24–40	40–56	56–70	70–90
335	Leg, Boneless, Roast-Ready, Tied	9–15	15–21	21–26	26–33
336	Leg, Shank Off, Boneless, Roast-Ready, Tied	7–11	11–15	15–19	19–30
337	Hind, Shank	1–2	2–3	3–4	4–6
338	Shank, Osso Buco	1–3			
341	Back, 9 Ribs, Trimmed	9–15	15–20	20–25	25–32
344	Loin, Strip Loin, Boneless	3–4	4–6	6–up	
344A	Loin, Strip Loin, Boneless Special	2–3	3–5	5–up	
346	Loin, Butt Tenderloin	1–1 1/2	1 1/2–up		
346A	Loin, Butt Tenderloin, Skinned	1/2–1	1–up		
347	Loin, Short Tenderloin	1–up			
348	Leg, TBS, 4 Parts	24–32	32–40		
348A	Leg, TBS, 3 Parts	16–24	24–32		
349	Leg, Top Round,	8–12	12–16		
349A	Leg, Top Round, Cap Off	6–8	8–10		
395	Veal for Stewing			Amount as Specified	
396	Ground Veal			Amount as Specified	
396A	Ground Veal and Vegetable Protein Product			Amount as Specified	
397	Ground Veal, Special			Amount as Specified	
397A	Ground Veal, and Vegetable Protein Product, Special			Amount as Specified	

Note: When single hotel racks, square-cut chucks, loins, legs, etc., are specified, their respective weight shall be one-half of that prescribed for double cuts in the table.

Note: The weight ranges of cuts as shown in the above table do not necessarily reflect any relation to the carcass weight ranges. Studies have shown that not all carcasses within a given weight range will produce cuts that are uniform in weight. Therefore, in ordering cuts, purchasing officials should specify the weight range(s) desired without regard to the carcass weight shown in the various ranges.

Exhibit 13-16. Index of meat purchase specifications for veal and calf (From USDA, *Institutional Meat Purchase Specifications for Fresh Veal and Calf—Series 300* [Washington D.C.: U.S. Government Printing Office, pending approval January 1994], pp. 3, 4, 5)

Item No.	Product Name	Suggested Portion Weight Range (Ounces)
1300	Cubed Steak	3–8
1301	Cubed Steak, Special	3–8
1306	Rack, Rib Chops	4–8
1306A	Rack, Rib Chops, Frenched	4–8
1309	Chuck, Shoulder Arm Chops	4–8
1309A	Chuck, Shoulder Blade Chops	4–8
1332	Loin, Loin Chops	4–8
1336	Cutlets	3–8
1338	Steaks, Flaked and Formed, Frozen	3–8
1338A	Steaks, Flaked and Formed, Breaded, Frozen	3–8
1396	Ground Veal (or Calf)	2–8
1396A	Ground Veal (or Calf) and Vegetable Protein Product Patties	2–8
1397	Ground Veal (or Calf), Special Patties	2–8
1397A	Ground Veal (or Calf), Special, and Vegetable Protein Product Patties	2–8

Note: Because it is impractical to list all portion weights that purchasers may desire, the listed portion weights are suggested only. Other portion weights may be specified if desired.

Exhibit 13-16 (continued)

Index of Products and Weight ranges (Pounds)

Item No.	Product Name	Range A		Range B		Range C		Range D	
		Lamb	Mutton	Lamb	Mutton	Lamb	Mutton	Lamb	Mutton
200	Carcass	30–41	55–75	41–53	75–95	53–65	95–115	65–75	115–130
202	Foresaddle	15–21	28–38	21–27	38–48	27–33	48–58	33–38	58–65
203	Bracelet (Double)	5–6	8–11	6–8	11–14	8–10	14–17	10–12	17–19
204	Rib Rack (Double)	3–5	6–8	5–6	8–10	6–7	10–13	7–8	13–14
205	Chucks and Plates (Double)	12–16	22–30	16–21	30–38	21–26	38–46	26–30	46–52
206	Chucks (Double)	11–14	19–26	14–19	26–33	19–23	33–40	23–27	40–46
207	Square-Cut Shoulders (Double)	8–10	14–19	10–13	19–24	13–16	24–29	16–19	29–33
208	Square-Cut Shoulder, Boneless	3–4	6–8	4–6	8–10	6–7	10–12	7–8	12–16
209	Breast, Flank On	4–6	8–11	6–7	11–13	7–9	13–16	9–11	16–18
209A	Breast, Flank Off	3–5	7–10	5–6	10–12	6–8	12–16	8–10	16–18
210	Foreshank	1–1.5	2–3	1.5–2	3–4	22–2.5	4–5	2.5–3	5–6
230	Hindsaddle	15–21	28–38	21–27	38–48	27–33	48–58	33–38	58–65
231	Loin (Double)	5–6	8–11	6–8	11–14	8–10	14–17	10–12	17–20
232	Loin, Trimmed (Double)	3–4	6–8	4–5	8–10	5–7	10–12	7–8	12–15
233	Leg (Double)	11–14	19–26	14–19	26–33	19–23	33–40	23–27	40–46
233A	Leg, Lower Shank Off (Single)	5–7	9–12	7–9	12–15	9–12	15–19	12–up	19–up
233B	Leg, Lower Shank Off, Boneless	4–6	8–11	6–8	11–13	8–11	13–17	11–up	17–up
233C	Leg, Shank Off (Single)	5–7	8–10	7–9	10–12	9–12	12–15	12–up	15–up
233D	Leg, Shank Off, Boneless	4–6	7–9	6–8	9–11	8–11	11–14	11–up	14–up
233E	Hindshank, Heel Attached	Under 1	1–1.5	1–2	1.5–3	2–up	3–up		
234	Leg, Oven-Prepared	4–6	8–10	6–8	10–13	8–9	13–16	9–11	16–18
234A	Leg, Oven-Prepared, Boneless, Tied								
235	Back	9–12	17–23	12–16	23–29	16–20	29–35	20–23	35–39
236	Back, Trimmed	6–8	11–15	8–11	15–19	11–13	19–23	13–15	23–26
237	Hindsaddle, Long-Cut	20–27	36–49	27–34	49–62	34–42	62–75	42–49	75–85
238	Hindsaddle, Long-Cut, Trimmed	17–23	33–41	23–29	41–52	29–36	52–63	36–41	63–72

Note: When single chucks, backs, etc., are specified, their respective weights must be one-half of that prescribed for double cuts in the table. The weight ranges of cuts shown in the above table do not necessarily reflect any relation to the carcass weight ranges. Studies have shown that not all carcasses within a given weight range will produce cuts that are uniform in weight. Therefore, in ordering cuts, purchasing officials should specify the weight ranges(s) desired without regard to the carcass weights shown in the various ranges.

Exhibit 13-17. Index of meat purchase specifications for lamb and mutton (From USDA, *Institutional Meat Purchase Specifications for Lamb and Mutton—Series 200* [Washington D.C.: U.S. Government Printing Office, effective January, 1975], pp. v, vi)

Portion-Cut Products

Item No.	Product Name	Portion Size (Ounces)							
		3	4	5	6	7	8	9	10
1204	Rib Chops	X	X	X	X	X	X	X	X
1204A	Rib Chops, Frenched	X	X	X	X	X	X		
1207	Shoulder Chops		X	X	X	X	X		
1232	Loin Chops		X	X	X	X	X	X	X
1295	Lamb for Stewing*	Amount as Specified							
1296	Ground Lamb*	Amount as Specified							
1296A	Ground Lamb Patties	Size as Specified							

Note: Because it is impractical to list all portion weights that purchasers may desire, those identified by the letter "X" are suggested only. Other portion weights may be specified if desired.
*May also be prepared from yearling mutton or mutton as specified, in which case the appropriate name—Ground yearling mutton, etc.—shall apply.

Exhibit 13-17 (continued)

grade is specified or thickness of fat is specified in conjunction with an IMPS specification for a particular cut, fat tolerance should be specified for either steaks or roasts. IMPS-suggested options for fat thicknesses in roasts are ¾, ¼ or ⅛ inch or "practically free" as maximum *average* thickness with respective *maximum* thicknesses at any one point of 1, ½, ¼ and ⅛ inch. For steaks, options for maximum surface fat thickness at any one point are for ¼ or ⅛ inch. Other options for steaks and roasts are for "peeled denuded" with or without the surface membrane. The maximum fat thickness at any one point for peeled denuded roasts or steaks is ⅛ inch. For peeled denuded options with the surface membrane removed, the resulting cut surface must expose 90 percent lean.

In determining sizes of cuts and quantities of meat to purchase, the buyer needs to be aware of the difference between as purchased (A.P.) and edible portion (E.P.) quantities. A.P. means food as you buy it, including inedible parts such as bone. E.P. means the edible part of food as purchased (A.P.), which remains after food is cooked. This involves consideration of cooking loss through evaporation or rendering of fat or through trimming undesirable or inedible material such as bone, fat, or gristle.

In purchasing, the buyer needs to know if the meat is going to be portioned before or after cooking and the E.P. yield of the meat. Indication of E.P. yield of meat is listed in Exhibit 13-18. Further information on yield related to various cuts is presented in Appendix I, Table 1. Chops, steaks, and patties are generally purchased portioned and are listed with menu items by their A.P. weights. The 12-ounce steak or 4-ounce hamburger generally weighs less when it is served, due to loss in cooking. Calculation of cost and pricing is easy when food is portioned A.P. because the consumer takes the loss in terms of food she or he cannot eat. In these instances, meat needs to be purchased trimmed at least to the extent of being appealing when it is served. When meat is portioned after cooking or preparation, the buyer must determine losses that will occur in cooking and the extent of trimming to be done in the preparation process. The critical factor is cost per pound of edible portion.

Cuts for Particular Menu Items

A buyer selects cuts of meat according to the quality characteristics desired in the prepared menu item; and this is determined by the amount of fat and connective tissue interspersed with lean and the tenderness of muscle. Primal cuts

BEEF		VEAL		PORK	
Steaks		*Chops, Steaks,*		*Chops and Steaks*	
Chuck (arm or blade)	2	*Cutlets*		Blade chops or steaks	3
Cubed	4	Loin chops	3	Boneless chops	4
Flank	3	Rib chops	3	Loin chops	4
Porterhouse	2	Round steak	4	Rib chops	4
Rib	2	Shoulder steaks	2½	Smoked (rib or loin) chops	4
Rib eye (Delmonico)	3	Cutlets (boneless)	5	Smoked ham (center slice)	5
Round	3				
Sirloin	2½	*Roasts*		*Roasts*	
T-bone	2	Leg	3	Leg (fresh ham), bone-in	3
Tenderloin		Shoulder, boneless	3	Leg (fresh ham), boneless	3½
(filet mignon)	3			Smoked ham, bone-in	3½
Top loin	3	*Other Cuts*		Smoked ham, boneless	5
		Breast (riblets)	2	Smoked ham, canned	5
		Cubes	4	Blade shoulder (rolled) (fresh	
Roasts				or smoked) boneless	3
Rib	2			Blade Loin	2
Rib eye (Delmonico)	3			Top loin (rolled) boneless	
Rump boneless	3	LAMB		(smoked or fresh)	3½
Tip	3	*Chops and Steaks*		Center loin	2½
		Leg center slice	4	Smoked loin	3
		Loin chops	3	Arm picnic shoulder (fresh	
Pot Roasts		Rib chops	3	or smoked) bone-in	2
Chuck (arm)	2	Shoulder chops	3	Sirloin	2
Chuck blade	2	Sirloin chops	3	Smoked shoulder roll	3
Chuck boneless	2½				
Cross rib	2½	*Roasts*		*Other Cuts*	
		Leg, bone-in	3	Back ribs	1½
		Leg, boneless	4	Bacon (regular), sliced	6
Other Cuts		Shoulder, bone-in	2½	Canadian-style bacon	5
Beef for stew	4	Shoulder, boneless	3	Country-style back ribs	1½
Brisket	3			Cubes	4
Ground Beef	4	*Other Cuts*		Hocks (fresh or smoked)	1½
Short Ribs	2	Breast	2	Pork sausage	4
		Riblets	2	Spareribs	1½
		Cubes	4	Tenderloin (whole)	4
Variety Meats		Shanks	2	Tenderloin (fillets)	4
Brains	5				
Heart	5				
Kidney	4	*Variety Meats*		*Variety Meats*	
Liver	4	Heart	5	Brains, heart, kidney	5
Sweetbreads	5	Kidney	5	Liver	4
Tongue	5				

The servings per pound listed in this table are based on an average serving of 2½ to 3½ ounces per portion. However, it should be noted that the yield of cooked lean meat is affected by the method of cooking, the degree of doneness, the size of the bone in bone-in cuts, and the amount of fat that remains after trimming.

Exhibit 13-18. Servings per pound to expect from a specific cut of meat (From Barbara Bloch with the National Livestock and Meat Board, *The Meat Book.* [New York: McGraw-Hill Book Company, 1977]. Reprinted by permission of The Benjamin Company, Inc.)

of meat typically used in various food products are shown in Exhibits 13-19, 13-20, and 13-21. Selection of a section of a primal cut is a further refinement in selection. In addition, certain cuts may be more or less useful in preparation because of the quality grade. Prime or Choice grade round of beef may be very acceptable cooked by dry heat methods, while Good or Standard grades cooked the same way are likely to be tough. The primal cuts that are generally less tender and require moist heat or braising meth-

ods in cooking are round, chuck, brisket, foreshank, short plate, and flank. Some cuts of round, chuck, or flank of Prime or Choice quality grades may be successfully cooked, in terms of tenderness, by dry heat methods. The tender primal cuts are the rib, short loin, and sirloin; these cuts are also the most expensive.

Rib roast of beef may be the first choice for roasting, providing the cost is consistent with operational cost and pricing objectives. Sirloin, top round, or the

CUT	USES
Round	Roasts 　Top round 　Bottom round
	Steaks 　Cubed 　Swiss style
	Cubes (stew)
	Ground
Sirloin	Roast Steak Ground Cubed
Short loin	Steak 　Sirloin strip
Rib	Roast Steak
Chuck	Cubes (stew) Ground
Brisket	Corned beef (cured) Braised Boiled (soup)
Foreshank	Soup
Flank	Braised London broil
Short plate	Boiled (soup) Braised

Exhibit 13-19. Wholesale (primal) cuts of beef and desirable uses in food products

whole round (well trimmed from a small animal) are excellent cuts for roasting or pot roasting and may be cooked by either moist- or dry-heat methods. One reason that round and sirloin are good cuts of meat for roasting is that the muscle has relatively small amounts of fat and connective tissue, which means the product is appealing when mechanically sliced. Round or sirloin may be the first choice of cut for swiss steak, stew, or items to be cooked by braising methods where low amounts of visible fat and connective tissue are desirable. Round or sirloin cuts are highly desirable and generally expensive relative to chuck or other less tender cuts. Ground beef prepared from round is lean and desirable for lowfat diets, but

generally people prefer the taste of ground beef with higher fat content.

Chuck is very palatable but has considerable visible fat interspersed with lean and thus may not be so acceptable as round for some purposes. Chuck may be braised and merchandised as pot roast, but the connective tissue and fat make it less desirable than round for institutional or commercial use. Excellent stew or similar items may be made from chuck, but more trimming of the primal cut will be required, and the product will be relatively high in fat. Chuck may be the premium cut for grinding in terms of palatability. The meat is tasty, and the naturally higher fat content as compared to round is very acceptable. However, without taste testing, the average person is likely to think he or she prefers very lean meat.

Beef flank may be used for specialty items such as London broil or for ground beef or braised steak, but the item is in somewhat short supply, due to the size of a single flank in relation to the total animal. Short plate, flank, and brisket may be used for ground meat, cubed meat for stew, or braising steaks; these cuts are economical but tend to be tough except when ground.

The amount of trim made in a cut of meat, whether done by the processor or in a food service operation before or after cooking, affects the quality and the cost of the meat served. A rib of beef cut directly below the muscle makes a premium serving of beef of high-quality grade. At the other extreme, short ribs of beef served without any removal of fat or bone interspersed between lean may be repulsive to a consumer even if the serving of lean is sufficient. Size, shape, and trim of cubes or strips of meat can also determine the appearance and quality of a menu item. For high quality prepared menu items, cutting should be done

VEAL		LAMB	
Cut	*Use*	*Cut*	*Use*
Round (leg)	Roast	Leg	Roast
Sirloin	Cutlet	Sirloin	
	Cubed		
		Rib	Roast
Loin	Chops		Crown roast
	Roast		Chops
Ribs	Crown roast	Shoulder	Cubed (stew)
	Chops		Ground
Shoulder	Cubed	Breast	Ground
Breast	Ground	Foreshank	Soup (Scotch broth)
Shank	Soup		

Exhibit 13-20. Wholesale (primal) cuts of veal and lamb and desirable uses in food products

carefully either by the meat purveyor or within the operation. A buyer can choose to simply order beef cubes by IMPS number or to be more particular in quality requirements and specify a cut of meat to be cut into cubes or slices of selected dimensions.

Cost

Aside from general conditions of supply and demand in the market, the cost of meat is related to cut, quality grade, and the extent to which the primal cut is trimmed and deboned. As would be assumed, the tenderest cuts, the highest

CUT	USES
Leg (ham)	Roast (fresh)
	Bake (cured)
	Steak (ham)
	Cutlet (fresh)
	Ground fresh (sausage)
	Cubes (fresh)
Loin	Roast
	Chops
Boston shoulder	Ground, fresh (sausage)
Picnic shoulder	Ground, cured (ham patties. loaf)
	Cubed (fresh or cured)
Spareribs	Barbecue
	Roast
Bacon	Broil
	Pan fry

Exhibit 13-21. Wholesale (primal) cuts of pork and desirable uses in food products

quality grades, and the most closely trimmed and boned items are usually the most expensive. Cost of trimming and deboning depends on the weight of the material removed and the amount of labor used for this process. An institutional buyer must decide whether to bear the cost in labor of trimming or cutting down a primal cut or to pay a meat processor. Also, the buyer must determine the amount of fat, bone, gristle, or relatively undesirable part of muscle that will be served. Ease of service is a related factor. Bone must be removed if meat is sliced on a mechanical meat slicer; if hand carved, the bone is a factor in ease of carving. Purchasing decisions are made on the basis of desired quality, cost and pricing objectives, and the availability of skilled labor for cutting meat.

Packaging

Meat packaging should be consistent with good sanitation practices, standard market practices, and the particular needs of the individual operation. Packaging units should be selected based on the number of individual items needed or the recipe quantity of the meat ingredient; otherwise, food may be wasted or stored so long it deteriorates in quality. The way a product is used may also be a factor in package selection. For example, if chili is generally made in batch sizes requiring 20 pounds of ground meat, opening one 20-pound package is easier and more efficient than opening four 5-pound packages. Also, purchasing in 20-pound cases is more reasonable in terms of use of product than purchasing 30-pound cases. The USDA has developed requirements for packaging that may be useful to a buyer in writing specifications for particular packaging options, or the buyer may simply state that all meat must be packaged according to the USDA Institutional Meat Purchase Specifications General Requirements for packaging. In general, requirements are for meat to be placed in a plastic bag and a fiberboard carton. Examples follow:[6]

Packaging and Packing

1. Carcasses, sides, quarters, and primal cuts, *delivered frozen*, must be bagged in crinkled paper or wrapped in plastic held with a stockinette or completely wrapped in plastic and boxed. Buyers must specify packaging for this meat when *delivered chilled*.

2. Various cuts of meat such as roasts and steaks, made from primal or subprimal cuts and meat patties must be placed in fiberboard cartons lined with a plastic bag. Layers of portion-cut items or meat patties must be separated with waxed paper or plastic wrap, or items may be individually wrapped. Frozen meat items must be separated to prevent freezing in large blocks. Individually Quick Frozen (IQF) items such as meat patties may be packaged together in a plastic bag in a fiberboard carton.

[6]From USDA *Institutional Meat Purchase Specifications—General Requirements* (Washington, D.C.: U.S. Government Printing Office, 1992), p. 4.

3. Ground and diced meat items must be packaged in plastic bags or casings with air pockets forced out and the open end securely closed with a metal or plastic clip or tight fold.

4. *Unless otherwise specified in the purchase order*, products such as frankfurters, sliced bacon, sliced dried beef, linked or bulk pork or breakfast sausage, etc., must be suitably packaged and placed in immediate containers of the kind conventionally used for such products as illustrated in the following:

   a. *Frankfurters and linked sausage*—One- or two-pound retail-type individual vacuum packages or bulk-packed in 5- to 10-pound plastic-lined containers or *if specified by the purchaser* layer-packed with layers one link deep separated by waxed paper or plastic material.

   b. *Sliced bacon*—One- or two-pound retail-type individual packages or layout packed with sheets of waxed paper or plastic separating layers. *If specified by the purchaser* paper separating layers can be heat resistant to permit cooking without removing paper.

   c. *Bulk pork or breakfast sausage*—One-pound retail-type individual packages such as cello rolls or plastic bags, packed not more than 10 pounds net weight per container or in waxed or plastic-lined container with net weight not exceeding 10 pounds.

5. Shipping containers must be new and packed to full capacity without slack-filling or overfilling and meet bursting strength requirements with net weight not in excess of 90 pounds. Weather resistant containers may be specified.

Refrigeration State

Buyers must specify if meat is to be delivered chilled or frozen and the type of freezing desired. Guidelines for specifications or requirements are provided in the Institutional Meat Purchase Specifications pamphlet *General Requirements*.

If chilled, meat must be delivered at a temperature of not less than 28° F or higher than 40° F and must not have a temperature higher than 50° F at the time of initial inspection. Options for frozen meat are (1) bringing the temperature to at least 0° F in 72 hours; (2) individually "quick" freezing (IQF) individual portions, with internal temperature not to exceed 0° F in 24 hours; and (3) "deep" freezing with internal temperature of -10° F at the time of shipment and a temperature no higher than 0° F at the time of receipt.

Meat Acceptance Service

Buyers should be aware that the United States Department of Agriculture, through its Meat Grading Branch, makes available a meat acceptance service designed to certify that meat purchased meets the buyer's specifications for cut, grade, and other product characteristics. Factors considered and examination procedures are shown in the Institutional Meat Purchase Specifications pamphlets, entitled *General Requirements* and *Quality Assurance Provisions*.

Meat inspection and certification can be valuable since it can be based on Institutional Meat Purchase Specification Standards and any other factor (consistent with the law). This can be extremely important since IMPS specifications require higher quality and specify factors above the minimum legal standards. Large-volume users desiring this service should contact the Meat Grading and Certification Branch, Agricultural Marketing Services, Livestock Division, United States Department of Agriculture, 14th and Independence Avenues, S.W., Room 2628-S, Washington D.C. 20090–6456.

Specifications

Specifications for meat should include the following: name of cut; institutional meat purchase specification number; quality grade; weight of cut or portion weight or thickness; weight or thickness tolerance; fat limitation or tolerance; state of temperature (chilled or frozen); packaging requirements; and other factors related to particular needs or product characteristics. The following are sample meat purchase specifications:

- Beef rib, roast-ready, IMPS item no. 109, USDA Choice grade, weight of 16–18 pounds with no tolerance outside of this range; and maximum fat thickness of ½ inch at any one point. Chilled and packed according to IMPS general requirements for packaging.
- Steak, strip loin boneless special, IMPS item no. 1180B, USDA Choice grade; 14 ounces with weight tolerance of ¾ ounce and surface fat not exceeding ½ inch at any one point. Chilled, packed forty-eight pieces per container according to IMPS general requirements for packaging.

REFERENCES

Anonymous. 1999. The 400: Leading Concepts, *Restaurant and Institutions* 109 (19):60.

Bloch, Barbara. *The Meat Board Meat Book*, New York: McGraw-Hill Book Company, 1977.

Code of Federal Regulations, Agriculture, Title 7, Parts 53 to 209. Washington, D.C.: U.S. Government Printing Office, 1999.

Code of Federal Regulations, Animals and Animal Products, Title 9, Part 200 to End. Washington, D.C.: U.S. Government Printing Office, 1999.

Code of Federal Regulations, Animals and Animal Products, Title 9, Part 304, 308, 310, 320,

327, 381, 416, 419. Washington, D.C.: U.S. Government Printing Office, 1999.

Federal Register of Thursday, July 25, 1996 (61 FR 38806–38989). Washington, D.C.: U.S. Government Printing Office.

National Association of Meat Purveyors. *The Meat Buyers Guide*. McLean, Virginia: National Association of Meat Purveyors, August 1988.

USDA Institutional Meat Purchase Specifications. Washington, D.C.: U.S. Government Printing Office, 1995.

Institutional Meat Purchase Specifications—General Requirements.

Institutional Meat Purchase Specifications for Fresh Beef—Series 100.

Institutional Meat Purchase Specifications for Fresh Lamb and Mutton—Series 200.

Institutional Meat Purchase Specifications for Fresh Veal and Calf—Series 300.

Institutional Meat Purchase Specifications for Fresh Pork—Series 400.

Institutional Meat Purchase Specifications for Cured, Cured and Smoked, and Fully-Cooked Pork Products—Series 500.

Institutional Meat Purchase Specifications for Cured, Dried, Smoked, and Fully Cooked Beef Products—Series 600, Interim.

Institutional Meat Purchase Specifications for Variety Meats and Edible By-Products—Series 700, Interim.

Institutional Meat Purchase Specifications for Sausage Products—Series 800, Interim.

Institutional Meat Purchase Specifications for Portion-Cut Meat Products—Series 1000.

Institutional Meat Purchase Specifications—Quality Assurance Provisions.

14 Poultry and Eggs

Purpose: To discuss the law, standards, terminology, specifications, and other considerations in purchasing poultry and eggs.

INTRODUCTION

This chapter covers discussion of "class" as it relates to distinguishing characteristics of poultry, cuts, U.S. government grades for quality, U.S. government control of wholesomeness, legal standards of identity for name and composition, differences in canned items, size or weight of fresh poultry, and the current expansion in kinds of convenience products as bases for poultry selection and writing specifications.

U.S. government grades and sizes for fresh eggs, legal standards of identity for composition of processed eggs, inspection for wholesomeness, and considerations in selection of various processed egg products are discussed.

POULTRY

Poultry is a relatively inexpensive, nutritious, low-fat, and persistently popular food for use in entrees. Its popularity and profitability is indicated by KFC (Kentucky Fried Chicken) being the third largest food service operation in the United States (Anonymous, 1999) and McDonald's adding poultry items to their menus. The importance of poultry is further indicated

by U.S. government projections that poultry consumption will jump from 92.8 pounds (retail weight) per capita in 1998 to 114.5 pounds by 2008, and that poultry firms will continue to promote processed forms of products (National Restaurant Association, 1999). Considerations in the selection of poultry items are class; size or weight; grade; cut; form; packaging; standards of identity or composition for cuts, proportions of light and dark meat in relation to labeling terminology, canned poultry types, and various convenience items; sanitation of processing plants; and sensory evaluation as a basis for purchasing convenience forms of products.

Inspection

The Wholesome Poultry Products Act of 1968 mandated the inspection of all raw poultry products for wholesomeness, according to federal standards, whether they were sold in intrastate or interstate commerce. For many years, this seemed to ensure food product safety. However recent high-profile cases of *E.coli 0157:H* food poisoning, particularly in hamburger, and estimates by the U.S. Food Safety and Inspection Service (Federal Register, 1996) of 4,000 deaths and 5,000,000 illnesses annually associated with meat and poultry products contaminated with *Salmonella, E.coli 0157:H7, Camplybacter*, and *Listeria Monocytogenees* have led to new regulations (9 CFR, Parts 304 et al.) for the inspection of both poultry and meat. The regulation, called *Pathogen Reduction, Hazard Analysis and Critical Control Point Systems* is a sophisticated form of industry self-inspection involving detailed plans for sanitation and microbial control, measurements or evaluation, records of evaluations, plans for corrective actions, microbial testing for *E.coli*, and U.S. Food Safety and Inspection Service monitoring. This regulation has been reviewed in detail in Chapters 3 (Exhibit 3.5) and 13 of this text.

Although the federal government has taken steps to improve the microbial safety of poultry products, the most important part of buying may be to ensure safety, particularly when purchasing fresh or frozen forms. Buyers should visit processors' facilities and select those with the highest standards for sanitation. Further, buyers should consider the amounts purchased, package sizes, and forms of packaging in terms of use. If a product is to be thawed before cooking or use, the package size should be such that the food is held for only short periods of time (with refrigeration) during and after thawing. Also, fresh poultry should be purchased in small amounts so that the product is not held for more than two days (refrigerated). Buyers should also know that even with the best of sanitary controls, poultry meat (unless canned) is not sterile, and the microorganisms present will continue to live and grow. This is particularly true if the food is held outside a refrigerator or freezer or the food has been frozen and thawed. Ice crystals formed in freezing will cause some breakdown

of structure and produce greater surface area for microbial growth.

The extremely high volume of sale or use of poultry makes control of microbial quality difficult in all phases of product flow from the point of slaughter to final service to a consumer. Although the U.S. inspection system has been improved, the safety of these foods cannot be taken for granted and buyers should do everything possible to ensure the wholesomeness.

Class

Class means any subdivision of a product based on essential physical characteristics that distinguish among animals of the same kind and apply to chickens, turkeys, ducks, geese, guineas, and pigeons. Class indicates sex, species, quality, and age of poultry and is important in obtaining the characteristics desired in products. For example, if a buyer who wants to purchase chicken for roasting specifies "roaster," the poultry, by federal standards, should be young and tender. However, a buyer who purchases or specifies "hen," by definition will get poultry that has no limit on age and that, if old, is likely to be tough and may be *very* tough. Hens, however, may make excellent soup broth. Classes and the distinguishing characteristics of the various poultry items are indicated in Exhibits 14-1, 14-2, and 14-3.

Cut

Knowing the various definitions of cut will enable the buyer to order particular chicken parts. Defined cuts include breasts, breasts with ribs, wishbones, drumsticks, thighs, legs, wings, backs, stripped backs, necks, halves, quarters, breast quarter, breast quarter without wing, leg quarter, thigh, legs with pelvic bone, wing drumette, wing portion, cut-up poultry, and giblets. Complete descriptions of these cuts may be found in the volume of the Code of Federal

Class	Distinguishing Characteristics
Rock Cornish game hen or Cornish game hen	Young, immature, and usually five to six weeks of age; weighs not more than 2 pounds ready to cook and is prepared from a Cornish chicken or the progeny of a Cornish chicken crossed with another breed of chicken.
Rock Cornish fryer, roaster, or hen	Progeny of a cross between a purebred Cornish and a purebred Rock chicken with age and other characteristics as described for other breeds of fryer, roaster, or hen.
Broiler or fryer	Young and usually under thirteen weeks of age; is of either sex; tender-meated, and has soft, pliable, smooth-textured skin, and a flexible breastbone cartilage.
Roaster or roasting chicken	Young and usually three to five months of age; is of either sex; has tender meat, a soft, pliable, smooth-textured skin, and breastbone cartilage that may be somewhat less flexible than that of a broiler or fryer.
Capon	Surgically unsexed male chicken usually under eight months of age that is tender meated and has a soft, pliable, smooth-textured skin.
Hen, fowl, or baking or stewing chicken	Mature female chicken that is usually more than ten months of age with meat less tender than for a roaster or broiler and a nonflexible breastbone.
Cock or rooster	Mature male chicken with coarse skin, toughened and darkened meat, and a hardened breastbone.

Exhibit 14-1. U.S. classes for chickens and distinguishing characteristics

Class	Distinguishing Characteristics
Fryer-roaster	Young and usually under sixteen weeks of age; is of either sex; has tender meat, soft, pliable, smooth-textured skin, and flexible breastbone cartilage.
Young turkey	Young and usually under eight months of age with tender meat, and soft, pliable, smooth-textured skin. Sex designation is optional.
Yearling turkey	Usually under fifteen months of age and fully mature with reasonably tender meat and smooth-textured skin. Sex designation is optional.
Mature turkey or old turkey (hen or tom)	Old turkey of either sex which is usually over fifteen months of age and has coarse skin and toughened flesh.

Exhibit 14-2. U.S. classes for turkeys and distinguishing characteristics

Regulations entitled *Animal and Animal Products, Title 9, Part 200 to End.* Terms are generally self-explanatory, but the following points may be noted. For breasts or breasts with ribs, the breasts may be cut along the breastbone to make two equal halves, or the wishbone portion may be removed before cutting the remainder along the breastbone to make three parts. Turkey breasts may include some neck skin. Cut-up poultry is any cut-up, disjointed portion of poultry or any edible part thereof as defined. The buyer must beware if he merely specifies "cut-up" poultry. A buyer may wish to specify modifications in the defined product such as whole chicken breast without the rib section and not separated into parts or turkey breast without neck skin or chicken parts to include legs, wings, thighs, and breast quarters.

United States Government Grades

United States Department of Agriculture quality grade standards are available for

Ducks
  Broiler duckling or fryer duckling
    Young and usually under eight weeks of age; is of
    either sex, tender meated, and has a soft bill and
    windpipe.

  Roaster duckling
    Young and usually under sixteen weeks of age; is of
    either sex, has tender meat, a bill that is not
    completely hardened, and a windpipe that is easily
    dented.

  Mature duck or old duck
    Usually over six months of age; is of either sex, has
    toughened flesh and a hardened bill and windpipe.

Geese
  Young goose
    Young; tender meated; windpipe easily dented.

  Mature goose or old goose
    Is of either sex and has toughened flesh and a
    hardened windpipe.

Guineas
  Young guinea
    May be of either sex, has tender meat, and a flexible
    breastbone cartilage.

  Mature guinea or old guinea
    May be of either sex, has toughened flesh, and a
    hardened breastbone.

Pigeons
  Squab
    Young, immature pigeon of either sex with extra
    tender meat.

  Pigeon
    Mature pigeon of either sex with coarse skin and
    tough flesh.

Exhibit 14-3. Classes and distinguishing characteristics of ducks, geese, guineas, and pigeons

whole carcasses and parts of ready-to-cook poultry. Grade standards are also available for raw poultry roasts, rolls, and similar products. However, any poultry food product found to be unsound, unwholesome, or otherwise unfit for human consumption may not legally bear a U.S. grade.

Bases for Grading Poultry. Factors upon which the USDA grades are based are conformation, fleshing, fat covering, defeathering, exposed flesh, discoloration of the skin and flesh, and freezing defects. Conformation refers to deformities that detract from appearance and affect the normal distribution of flesh.

USDA Grades. USDA quality grade designations are A, B, and C. USDA Grade A poultry is free of deformities that affect normal distribution of flesh; has a well-developed covering of flesh and layer of fat well distributed in the skin; is free of pinfeathers, has no exposed flesh resulting from cuts or tears on parts and a carcass free of cuts or tears on the breast and legs; has a carcass free of broken bones; the carcass or part is practically free of discolorations of the skin and flesh resulting from bruising or blood clots; and the poultry is practically free from defects that result from handling or occur during freezing or storage.

For Grade A quality poultry roast, the deboned poultry meat used in the preparation is from A quality poultry with respect to fleshing and fat covering. In addition all material such as tendons, cartilage, blood clots, pinfeathers, and hair are removed; and 75 percent or more of the outer surface is covered with skin, but the combined weight of the skin and fat cover does not exceed 15 percent of the total net weight. Seasonings or flavor enhancers, if used, must be uniformly distributed; the product should be fabricated to retain its shape after defrosting and cooking; and no piece should separate into more than three parts after slicing.

A buyer may wish to purchase lots rather than individual heads of poultry. These are designated as United States Consumer grades and are the same as basic grade designations (A, B, and C). For a lot of the product to be Consumer U.S. Grade A, B, or C, each individual head must meet or exceed the quality standard for that grade. United States Procurement grades are also available, but standards for these are not so high as for Consumer or basic grades. For U.S. Procurement Grade 1, only 90 percent of the carcasses in a lot must meet the requirements of Grade A.

Poultry inspection mark (left) and grade mark (right).

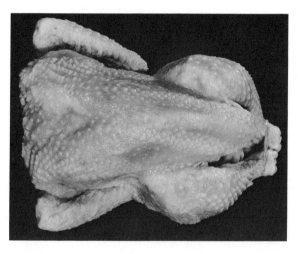

U.S. Grade A: full fleshed and meaty, well finished, attractive appearance.

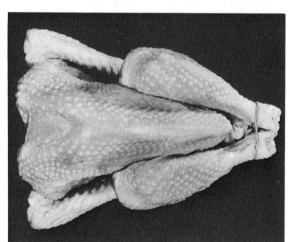

U.S. Grade B: slightly lacking in fleshing, meatiness, and finish, or some dressing defects.

Exhibit 14-4. The official poultry inspection marks of the U S Department of Agriculture are put on containers or affixed to the birds. The differences between a grade A and a grade B chicken may be noted in the pictures. (Courtesy of the United States Department of Agriculture, Washington, D.C.)

In view of the characteristics on which poultry is graded and the generally low cost of poultry as related to other high-protein entrees, a buyer will almost always purchase U.S. Grade A quality products. Yield from U.S. Grade A poultry may in itself compensate for the difference in cost between U.S. Grade A and U.S. Grade B or C. Furthermore, based on torn flesh, blood clots, and the various other characteristics that may be found in Grades B or C, these grades may not be acceptable to the consumer.

Convenience Forms—Standards of Identity

For many years, poultry products have been purchased in boneless, cooked, or uncooked forms to reduce the labor involved in carving or otherwise removing the flesh from the bone and the time required for cooking. These products have made great changes in restaurant menu offerings. For example, boneless chicken breasts are used in many kinds of chicken sandwiches and entrees, such as chicken picatta, chicken marsala, and chicken parmigiana, that are best-selling items.

Over the last several years, the varieties of convenience items has been greatly expanded and now foods made from these products are almost innumerable. Examples are deli-type roast, smoked, honey-smoked, pan-roasted, and oil-browned breast of turkey; chicken pot pie kits that include crusts and fillings that are ready to be put together and baked; breaded chicken products that are individually frozen; chicken nuggets and patties ready for deep-fat frying; ready-to-cook chicken chunks and strips with various types of seasoning and ready-for-preparing items such as fajitas and stir-fries; hand-wrapped burritos with shredded chicken, ready for deep-fat frying; hand-trimmed stuffed chicken breasts, with bleu cheese as chicken cordon bleu, with spinach as chicken Florentine, or with corn bread or apples; marinated chicken breast fillets that are vacuum tumbled for thorough penetration of sauce; and wings that are marinated, fully cooked, or breaded and ready for char-broiling or deep-fat frying. Further options for poultry products are for skin on, skin off, cooked or ready to cook, bone in or boneless, and fat free.

At one time, the quality of these items, particularly those such as chicken pot pie and veal cordon bleu, were not of acceptable quality for the average food service operation or equal in quality to the usual kitchen preparation. Now these products are served in elite hotels and high-volume chains, and some are of better quality than those formerly kitchen prepared.

Under the Wholesome Poultry Products Act of 1968 (*CFR 9:200-End.* 1999), legal standards of identity have been established for many types of processed poultry products. For most products, these are not particularly helpful, because they include only requirements for the minimal amount of the principal poultry component that must be present. However, buyers should be aware of their existence and consider their use.

Standards of identity are available for convenience-type poultry dishes or specialty items for all of the various classes of poultry, including the following: ravioli, soup, chop suey, chow mein, tamales, noodles, or dumplings with various kinds of poultry; stew; fricassee of wings; poultry with vegetables; gravy with sliced poultry; tetrazzini; poultry chili with beans; creamed poultry; cacciatore; fricassee; à la king; croquettes; sliced poultry with gravy and dressing; salad; chili; hash; and minced barbecue.

Standards of identity have also been established for poultry rolls, frozen poultry dinners and pies, burgers, patties, à la Kiev, canned boned poultry, steak, fillet, and poultry that is barbecued, barbecued with moist heat, or breaded. Burgers should consist of 100 percent poultry with skin and fat not in excess of natural proportions, but patties may contain fillers or binders. Chicken à la Kiev consists of poultry meat stuffed with butter, which may be seasoned, wrapped in sufficient skin to cover the meat, dipped in batter, fried, and frozen. Steaks or fillets are boneless slices or strips of poultry meat. Baked or roasted poultry is cooked by dry heat; barbecue has been cooked in dry heat and basted with sauce, and barbecued poultry prepared with moist heat has been cooked by the action and moist heat in a barbecue sauce.

In breaded products, the breading may not exceed 30 percent of the weight of the finished breaded product. Poultry rolls may have 2 percent binders or fillers in raw products, 3 percent in cooked, or more if labeled "binders added" or the particular binder added is named.

In purchasing convenience types of poultry products, general considerations are the same as for purchasing unprocessed forms of products. In fact, with so many boneless, cut up raw products available, convenience forms may include (depending on definition) a large portion of the poultry on the market.

When purchasing processed poultry, the buyer should conduct a survey to identify the purveyors and products available. Then, items should be initially screened to determine the extent to which they meet operational requirements for U.S. quality grade; "class" of poultry; pack; portion size or weight; form of product such as diced, cubed, or natural pieces; amount of light or dark meat in a pack; and preparation method such as "barbecued," "roast," or "baked," as defined in legal standards of identity. After screening, products should be extensively taste tested to determine the extent to which quality standards are met. Further, before any purchasing decisions are made, purveyors' processing plants should be inspected and evaluated in conjunction with U.S. HACCP requirements to determine the sanitary quality of products. Buyers should remember that convenience products have considerable handling outside the food service operation, and heating or cooking at the point of service may not be so great as for items that are totally kitchen prepared. Microorganisms that are present in food at the time of purchase may grow during product thawing or holding, and heating (particularly in microwave ovens) may not destroy the microorganisms that are present. Further, chicken may be purchased cooked and in bite-sized pieces for use in items such as chicken salad and should undergo no heat treatment that would destroy any microorganisms that might be present.

Canned Cooked Poultry. Canned boned poultry is prepared from cooked boned poultry meat and may contain skin and fat in natural proportion to the whole carcass (unless it is a solid pack product), 0.5 percent gelatin, stabilizers, or similar substances. Poultry is available as boned solid pack with a minimum of 95 percent meat and the remainder broth; boned with a minimum of 90 percent meat; boned with broth and 80 percent meat; or boned with a specified amount of broth not exceeding 50 percent.

Labeling Terms

A buyer should be familiar with the following terms when purchasing poultry products:

natural proportion—50–65 percent light, 50–35 percent dark

light or white meat—100 percent light, 0 percent dark

dark meat—0 percent light, 100 percent dark

light and dark meat—51–65 percent light, 49–35 percent dark

dark and light meat—35–49 percent light, 65–51 percent dark

mostly white meat—66 percent or more light, 34 percent or less dark

mostly dark, 34 percent or less light, 66 percent or more dark.

Deboned cut-up poultry meat, either cooked or uncooked in various forms such as cubed, diced, chunks, or chicken breasts, is widely used in food service operations. Standards specific to these items are generally unavailable, but the buyer may specify that items be prepared from poultry of a particular U.S. grade.

Size or Weight of Cut and Pack

To determine the weight of a cut of poultry or of a pack, the buyer needs to consider the typical weight of a bird of a particular class, the edible portion in relation to carcass weight, portion size or quantity needed for the particular recipe, the total quantity needed for a particular service period, and typical packs for commodities. If these factors are kept in mind, reasonable determinations for pack and weight of cut can be made. Typical weights or pack sizes for various poultry products are indicated in Exhibit 14-4. Other options include shrink plastic wraps and individual quick freezing (IQF) for various items.

Specifications

Factors that should be considered for inclusion in purchase specifications for poultry are species, class, cut, weight and weight tolerance, grade, form (fresh chilled, frozen, raw, or cooked), style (ready-to-cook), pack, and any other particular factors. The buyer should generally specify "ready-to-cook" to differentiate from "dressed" poultry, which may merely have the head cut off, and "live" birds. Sample specifications are as follows:

Chicken, broiler, halves, USDA Grade A, fresh chilled, ready-to-cook. Weight of 1 pound with tolerance of 4 ounces over or under. Packed forty-eight pieces per case according to standard market practice for protecting the product.

Chicken, boneless, white, raw, individually quick frozen chunks approximately 1 inch in diameter. Prepared from USDA Grade A poultry and packed 10 pounds per case according to standard market practice for protecting the product.

Weight for broiler or fryer	1½–3 lb.
Weight for half a broiler or fryer	¾–1½ lb.
Weight for a quarter broiler or fryer	6–12 oz.
Inedible portion and cooking loss (items with bone)	50 percent
Turkey (carcass with generally best yield in cooking)	28–30 lb.
Whole turkey	1, 2, 4, or 6 per box
Whole chicken	12–24 per box (generally in multiples of 6)
Frozen chicken whole legs	48 pieces per case
Frozen chicken breast halves (boneless)	50 per case
Frozen chicken fryer quarters	32 lb. per case
Frozen chicken chunks, cubes, or pieces	10 or 20 lb. per case or 6 5-lb. or 6-lb. packages per case
Frozen turkey breasts	6 per case

Exhibit 14-5. Typical weights and pack sizes for various poultry products

EGGS AND THEIR USES

Eggs are a very high-quality, low-cost protein food. They are a standard item on most breakfast menus and may be incorporated into luncheon and dinner menus to provide low-cost entree items.

Eggs may be purchased in either the fresh or processed form. The form selected will depend upon the intended use and the need for efficiency in operation. Frozen eggs produce excellent quality in baked goods and quite acceptable quality in scrambled eggs or omelets. They may be used for scrambled eggs in hospitals, dormitories, or commercial food service where several hundred to a thousand people must be served within an hour, and the time required to crack eggs would be too long. If eggs are to be served poached or fried, the fresh form of the product must, of course, be used.

Wholesomeness

The Egg Products Inspection Act of 1972 (Chapter 3) provides for mandatory inspection of egg-processing plants and considerable insurance of the safety of processed egg products. U.S. government grades for *fresh* eggs also provide some assurance of safety and quality of eggs. However, buyers must remember that fresh eggs are porous, that quality deteriorates rather quickly, and that the grade and wholesomeness at the time of delivery may not be the same as at the time of packing. Further, buyers should know that high-quality menu items, such as fried eggs, cannot be prepared from inferior-quality fresh eggs (the yolks will break). Also, the time and temperature for preparing high-quality fried eggs is probably not sufficient to destroy microorganisms, such as *Salmonella*, that may be present. To assure quality, buyers should inspect sources of supply to confirm sanitary

handling and cold storage sufficient to control microorganisms. They should also demand delivery of strictly fresh products.

Grades for Fresh Shell Eggs

The following U.S. government grades have been established for fresh eggs. U.S. AA, A, B, C, Dirty, and Checks. Eggs are graded on an individual basis, and then a grade is assigned to a case or lot based on the percentages of individual eggs of a particular grade that are in the unit. Specific standards are applied for U.S. Consumer, U.S. Wholesale, and U.S. Procurement grades and for quality at point of origin and quality at destination. U.S. Consumer grades in general have higher percentages of higher grades of individual eggs than U.S. Wholesale. For example, a case of U.S. AA Consumer grade eggs must be 85 percent AA at the place of origin, but up to 15 percent may be A or B grade, and not over 5 percent may be C or Check grade. At point of destination, 80 percent must be AA grade, 20 percent may be A or B grade, and not over 5 percent may be grade C or Check. Wholesale grade designations are U.S. Specials, Extras, Trades, Standards, Dirties, and Checks. For Wholesale grades, cases must be marked with the percentage of AA grade eggs in a case of Specials, the percentage of A quality eggs in a case of Extras, and the percentage of C quality eggs in a case of Trades. For U.S. Specials, the minimum percentage of AA eggs in the case must be 20 percent or more, and the remainder must be A quality or better. For U.S. Extras, 20 percent must be A quality or better, and the remainder, B quality; and for U.S. Trades, 83.3 percent or more must be U.S. C quality. Procurement grades are applied to lots which include several cases.

Quality standards are based on the following:

U.S. CONSUMER GRADES
Interior quality; condition and appearance of shell

top views

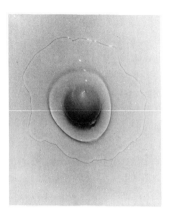 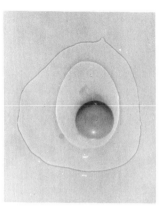 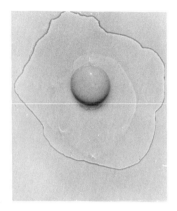

side views

 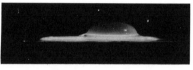 

Grade AA (or Fresh Fancy): egg covers a small area; white is thick, stands high; yolk is firm and high

Grade A: egg covers a moderate area; white is reasonably thick, stands fairly high; yolk is firm and high

Grade B: egg covers a wide area; has a small amount of thick white; yolk is somewhat flattened and enlarged

U.S. WEIGHT CLASSES
Minimum weight per dozen

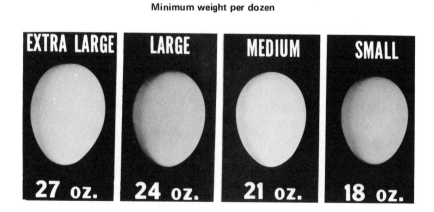

Minimum weight per thirty-dozen case: extra large, 50 lbs.; large, 44½ lbs.; medium, 39 lbs ; small, 33½ lbs.

Exhibit 14-6. Grade and size classification for eggs. (Courtesy of the United States Department of Agriculture, Washington, D.C)

Shell—cleanliness; breakage; shape; smoothness; uniformity in thickness

Air cell—depth

White—clarity; freedom from discoloration; thickness; viscosity

Yolk—shape indicative of firm membranes and tissue and yolk which will stand high; lacking indication of germ development

An AA grade egg is clean, unbroken, normal in shape, and has an air cell that does not exceed ⅛ inch. The white is clear and firm, and the yolk is practically free from defects. Dirty eggs have unbroken shells but adhering dirt and foreign matter. A Check has a broken shell or cracked shell, but the shell membranes are intact and the contents do not leak. An A grade egg is similar to AA, but the air cell may be larger and the white less firm. Grades B and C eggs have unbroken shells, but the shells may be stained, the yolk weakened, the air cell enlarged, and the yolk may show spots on the surface indicating some germ development.

Size

Size of eggs is not related to grade, but standard size designations have been established. Selection of size is based on intended use. Sizes are extra large, large, medium, and small. Large-size eggs are the most acceptable for general use. They are big enough to be attractive if served fried or poached, and, if used for other purposes, fewer will need to be cracked to obtain a particular volume. U.S. government standards have been established for minimum and average weights (lot basis) of eggs. The minimum net weight for an individual 30-dozen case of eggs is 50 pounds for extra large, 44.5 pounds for large, 39 pounds for medium, and 33.5 pounds for small. These values help the buyer determine whether the correct quantity of eggs has been delivered.

Processed Eggs

Standards of identity have been established for dried eggs, frozen eggs, liquid eggs, egg whites, dried egg whites, frozen egg whites, egg yolks, dried egg yolks, and frozen egg yolks. Legal standards pertain primarily to procedures for processing and preservation. This includes requirements for pasteurization and rendering products free from *Salmonella*. A dietitian, for example, would need to consider using processed eggs in liquid diets when eggs are not cooked.

When deciding which processed egg products to use, the buyer may wish to do some product testing. Products are quite specialized for particular purposes and may vary with the processor. Dried egg whites may be prepared with a whipping aid especially for use in meringue or angel food cake. Cake mixes may incorporate special forms of dehydrated eggs. Frozen egg whites, yolks, or whole eggs are available with additives that make them useful for particular purposes. A buyer may also purchase eggs cooked and frozen in various forms such as diced or chopped. These are quite useful and save considerable time in cooking and removing shells. No U.S. grade standards are available for processed eggs; thus, the best procedure is to assess the product by testing it for a particular use.

REFERENCES

Anonymous. 1999. The 400: Leading Concepts. *Restaurant and Institutions* 109 (19):60.

Code of Federal Regulations, Agriculture, Title 7, Parts 53 to 209. Washington, D.C.: U.S. Government Printing Office, 1999.

Code of Federal Regulations, Animals and Animal Products, Title 9, Parts 200 to End. Washington, D.C.: U.S. Government Printing Office, 1999.

Code of Federal Regulations, Animals and Animal Products, Title 9, Parts 304, 308, 310, 320, 327, 381, 416, 417. Washington, D.C.: U.S. Government Printing Office, 1999.

Code of Federal Regulations, Food and Drugs, Title 21, Parts 100 to 169. Washington, D.C.: U.S. Government Printing Office, 1999.

Federal Register of Thursday, July 25, 1996, Part II, 61FR 38806–38989). *Department of Agriculture, Food Safety and Inspection Service, Pathogen Reduction; Hazard Analysis and Critical Control Point (HACCP) Systems; Final Rule*. Washington, D.C.: U.S. Government Printing Office.

National Restaurant Association. 1999. Foodservice trends. *Restaurants USA* 19(4): 42.

15 Seafood—Fresh and Processed

Purpose: To give the purchasing agent the basic information required to make proper selections of fresh and processed seafood.

INTRODUCTION

Seafood can be a very difficult product to purchase, particularly in its fresh form. The problems with commitment to a fresh-fish purchasing program are that reliable sources are scarce. Even with a satisfactory purveyor, products in top condition are not always available. Since fish deteriorate very rapidly, even when handled properly, it is far easier to plan and implement a frozen-seafood program than a fresh-fish one. Purveyors are easier to locate; the products lend themselves to specifications better; and the handling problems are minimal.

FOOD VALUES OF SEAFOOD

It has been generally accepted that the best all around food available to mankind is fresh fluid milk, but fresh fish is nearly as nutritious. Since much of the world's population by necessity must use fish as one of the main sources of food, it is just as well that fish is an excellent source of protein. Fish and fish products also contain many valuable minerals and have a high vitamin content, largely in the B-complex series,

with generous amounts of Vitamin B_{12}, riboflavin, and thiamin. An average portion of fish will provide from 10 to 50 percent of the daily recommended allowance of these vitamins.

Fish is especially low in calories, contains almost no saturated fats, and is remarkably free of tough connective tissue, which makes seafood easily digestible even for persons with digestive disorders. Even though most fish is very low in fats, some fish, known as "fat fish," have flesh that contains as much as 25–30 percent fat. It is interesting to note that the most expensive types of fish are "fat fish." Lobster, crabmeat, salmon, pike, halibut, swordfish, shrimp, and oysters are high in fat content and also very flavorful. Bluefish and mackerel, however, are also high in fat content, but they are not particularly high on the gourmet scale.

The mineral content of fish is very important for certain persons who are in need of iodine in their diet. Fresh fish is also particularly high in calcium and phosphorus, plus other trace minerals. It might be interesting to note that most fish are high in iron content, and that fresh oysters are the highest in vitamin content of all seafoods.

A word of caution might be offered regarding the calorie content of various types of seafoods. A 5-ounce piece of lean haddock, broiled with lemon and a few herbs and paprika for color, would contain about 225 calories. If browned in lots of butter with a generous coating of breading material and adhesive, the calorie content jumps up to around 400 calories per portion. If you add a rich white wine sauce to the product, the calorie content of a single portion will rise to about 600 calories.

Fast food operators have been forced to rely primarily on fish sticks and heavily breaded fish items because of the dwindling supply of fresh fish and the continuous increase in price. These products are high in calories and fat, primarily because of the method of preparation and the materials used. This type of seafood may be a necessary part of the fast food operation, but it should be evaluated as a different product from fresh fish.

MARKET FORMS OF FISH AND SHELLFISH

Shellfish and fin fish are marketed in different ways. Food buyers should understand the various market forms of fish so that they can choose which is appropriate for their particular operation.

Fin Fish

Fin fish are initially sold whole or in the "round." Before the fish can be cooked, it must be scaled, and the entrails, head, tail, and fins have to be removed. The fish then can be used whole for baking, or it can be filleted, cut into steaks, sliced, or cut into chunks. If the fish can be broiled, then it should be cooked in this manner because it is the best way to preserve the fresh fish taste and because it can be broiled to order, thereby reducing overpreparation. Fish can also be deep fried, sauteed, baked, or poached and served with a sauce.

Drawn Whole Fish

In some market areas, local ordinances require that whole fish be at least eviscerated and cleaned thoroughly before marketing. Such "drawn" fish can then be cut up in the same manner as a whole fish or a fish "in the round."

Dressed or Pan-Dressed Fish

A dressed or pan-dressed whole fish is sold ready for cooking; it should be scaled, with the head and entrails removed and the tail and all fins cut off. Some fish, such as shad and trout, have to be boned or semiboned before they can be considered pan-dressed.

Fillets of Fish

Fillets of fish are produced by cutting the fish along the backbone from the head to the tail and then removing any bones that are left with the fillet. Fillets can be purchased without skin on one side, or they can be purchased completely cleaned of skin. These fillets, when washed, can be cooked in any manner desired by the kitchen manager. In the commercial market, fish are most commonly available in this form.

Steaks

Fish steaks are cut by slicing through a whole dressed fish and are generally about ¾ inch thick. These fish steaks are ready for cooking when received and are generally cut from salmon, halibut, swordfish, sturgeon, tuna, cod, and haddock.

Some fish are marketed as butterfly fillets and fish sticks. Smelts are generally marketed as whole fish, with the entrails removed, and some smaller fish, such as white bait, are marketed just as they come out of the water and are cooked whole.

Market Forms of Shellfish

Certain kinds of shellfish are marketed live, which requires considerable care and expense in their handling. The most com-

Whole or round fish

Steaks

Drawn fish

Single fillet

Dressed or pan-dressed

Butterfly fillet

Sticks

Exhibit 15-1. The major forms in which fin fish are marketed. (Courtesy of the United States Department of the Interior, Washington, D.C.)

mon forms of shellfish marketed live include oysters, clams, mussels, northern lobsters, soft-shell crabs, and in some instances, rock crabs and dungeness crabs. The most popular kinds of live shellfish on the market are Maine lobsters, oysters, and clams.

Shrimp are generally sold with the heads removed and frozen in blocks with the shell on, or cooked and shelled and deveined. Lobster tails, which are generally sold frozen, come from the spiny lobster or a large type of crayfish. Cooked, clear lobster meat is also available frozen, but it is very expensive and difficult to find.

Some forms of shellfish are marketed either cooked and canned or pasteurized. Uncanned crabmeat is marketed after being cooked, picked clean of shell, and packed in sterilized containers. This type of crabmeat is expensive and highly perishable. Oysters and clams that are sold fresh after being shucked from their shells are also highly perishable.

SOME DISTURBING FACTS ABOUT OUR SEAFOOD SUPPLY

The bells are tolling for what once seemed an inexhaustible supply of food, available even to the poor in the United States and throughout the world. In this country, seafood is becoming a luxury item; already lobster, shrimp, red snapper, crabmeat, striped bass, salmon, oysters, and swordfish are selling on the commercial market for higher prices than sirloin steak. These and other seafood items are getting more difficult to obtain every day.

The northern or "Maine" lobster will soon be gone from the market unless a successful method of lobster farming is developed. Some experimental lobster farming is underway, but since it takes ten to twelve years to grow a 1–1½-pound lobster, such methods are unlikely to be largely successful.

Our commercial supply of freshwater fish is now almost all farm fish. Reasonable supplies of freshwater fish are available, with trout, catfish, and shrimp being the most plentiful. Some progress is being made in the farming of striped bass, whitefish, lake trout, and pike. There are still some types of freshwater fish caught in the Great Lakes and marketed mostly through Chicago. These limited supplies of fish include buffalo fish, carp, catfish, chub, lake herring, lake trout, sheepshead, smelt, whitefish, yellow perch, and yellow pike.

An entire year's catch of freshwater fish is smaller than one month's catch of ocean perch, but even the great supply of ocean fish is declining. As people realize the excellent food value of seafood and the dangers of possible extinction, pressures are building to protect our existing supplies and increase our current fish-farming quotas. This movement is being led by conservation organizations.

What Brought on the Shortages

Seafood shortages did not happen overnight. Economists and scientists have for years been warning all of us, including the emerging countries' populations, that there was a day of reckoning ahead. One can readily understand why the poor continued trying to eke out a living and to supplement their diet by unrestricted harvesting of fish. Several other factors have contributed to the decline in fish and shellfish populations: a combination of rapidly increasing populations, people living longer due to better health care and diet, the overharvesting of some seafood supplies, changes in taste (some formerly acceptable fish are now regarded as "scrap fish"), pollution, and development by the commercial fishing industry of larger and more effective fishing boats and equipment.

Political efforts to set limits on fishing quotas have met with little success. However, there have been promising developments in other areas that concern our sea-food population. Here in the United States and in Canada, experimental programs in fish farming have proved successful, particularly with catfish, trout, and shrimp. Also, worldwide efforts to control contamination of our rivers, lakes, and oceans have produced some visible results: salmon can now be caught in the Thames River in England, Kennebec salmon are appearing again in our northeastern streams, and supplies of oysters and other shellfish are increasing in Long Island Sound. With many of the countries that previously relied on fish and shellfish as primary sources of protein now developing other food supplies, there is hope that the current decimation of this important food source will be stopped.

PROCESSED FISH

Processed fish are sold in much greater quantity than fresh fish. Some of the more important forms of processing and marketing seafood products are outlined in the following paragraphs.

Frozen Basic Market Forms of Fish

The seven basic forms of fresh fish are also available frozen. Because of the difficulties of marketing fresh fish, frozen versions of fish products far outsell fresh fish for commercial use and home consumption.

Smoked Fish

Smoking fish to make it easier to preserve and ship long distances was the common method of preservation until the late 1920's, when freezing became possible. Products still available in the smoked form are smoked salmon, smoked sturgeon, finnan haddie, smoked trout, bloaters, oysters, and clams. In some countries there is a considerable consumption of smoked eel and certain forms of reptiles.

Dried Fish

Dried salt cod is the most common dried fish in the United States, although other species of fish are dried in other parts of the world.

Canned Fish

In the food service industry, use of canned seafood is limited primarily to tuna, sardines, oysters, shrimp, and clams. In terms of general consumption, however, the United States uses more canned seafoods than all other seafoods combined. Some of the commonly used canned seafood products are salmon, mackerel, sardines, carp, lobster meat, crabmeat, herring, shad-roe, pike, squid, mussels, turtle meat, shrimp, and seafood soups.

Convenience Seafood Items

During the past ten years, the consumption of convenience seafood items, both cooked and raw, has increased at the rate of about 20 percent per year. The growth of fast food seafood restaurants and the increased consumption of heat-and-serve seafood items have been the basic sources of these increases. We are all well acquainted with fish sticks and fish portions and fish hors d'oeuvres, fish entrees, sauced fish entrees, but not too many of us are aware of the large quantities of fish used in the making of hot dogs and fish burgers.

SHOULD YOU OR SHOULD YOU NOT SERVE FRESH FISH?

There is no question that in the food service business the serving of fresh fish is very popular and nutritionally sound. But the use of fresh seafood may not be appropriate for federal or state institutions, high school or college cafeterias, the armed services, or large commercial food services such as Greyhound, Canteen, or Saga Corporations. There are three types of food service operations, however, that should give serious consideration to the service of fresh seafood.

The first is hospitals, where the service of fresh fish can be both nutritional and tasty in certain types of diets or psychological situations. It is true that it is costly, but when one considers the daily charges for hospitalization, the additional cost seems insignificant. The second type of operation that should serve as much fresh seafood as possible is the restaurant in a first-class hotel. Not only do the customers of these operations expect fresh seafood, but the operation can charge higher prices to offset any increased cost. In fact, fresh seafood can be a very profitable item.

Another type of restaurant that cannot afford to serve anything but fresh seafood is the specialty seafood restaurant. Most of the really successful seafood restaurants in the country serve nothing but fresh fish year-round except rock lobster tails, shrimp, and some forms of crabmeat or crab leg. And, of course, any resort hotel located on the coastline of the United States should make every effort to serve a good variety of the best seafood caught in the local area.

Don't Sell Oysters in Omaha

Most successful restaurant operators are the ones who have served the food that is popular in their particular region. As one particularly successful restaurateur observed, one doesn't serve French food in Plainview, Texas, or oysters in Omaha. If fresh seafood is not a big seller in the area in which the operation is located, then it would be wise to use seafood only as an auxiliary offering.

The Seafood Market in Your Area

If a buyer is interested in obtaining fresh fish or shellfish, and there are no good seafood markets in the area, it will need to be determined if there is any reliable means of delivery for seafood available. If the operation is within a hundred miles of a metropolitan area, there may be a dealer who delivers on a daily or semidaily basis to anywhere within a hundred miles of the market. Today, with regularly scheduled trucking, it is possible to schedule overnight deliveries of fresh seafood by refrigerated truck up to distances of 300 to 400 miles. The only problems with this system are weather and, in some cases, strikes or physical breakdowns.

If a food operation is willing to pay the cost of air freight, and is in a good location for this type of service, then it won't matter how far the operation is from its source of supply. For example, Hawaii receives fresh seafood every morning from Boston, New York, and Chicago, as well as from the West Coast on a six-day delivery basis. If the order is telephoned into Boston by 2 P.M., the shipment is placed aboard a one-stop air freight carrier at about 5 P.M. that day. With a refueling stop on the West Coast, the shipment reaches Hawaii by midnight of the same day. This shipment is then delivered that morning so that it can be served for lunch and dinner the day of delivery. As a matter of fact, there is more fresh seafood served in Hawaii that is delivered out of Boston than out of any other market in the United States. Hawaii has to import from the "Mainland" almost all of its fresh seafood and a good part of its frozen seafood because the local supply is extremely limited. The only fish that is available in any quantity in that state is mahi mahi, and it is very expensive. The poor fishing around Hawaii is the result of the extremely deep waters around the shores of the various islands, where there is little food available for fish.

QUALITY FACTORS FOR FRESH SEAFOOD

There is a saying along the Boston Harbor: "First you catch the fish and then you trust the dealer." It is a good adage to keep in mind when buying seafood because there is no other food that deteriorates faster after it is harvested. When selecting the primary dealer for the supply of fresh seafood, a food buyer should consider two things: first, whether the dealer has a good reputation for supplying fresh seafood for the particular area in which he or she operates; and second, how long the dealer has been in business selling fresh seafood. If the dealer has been in business for 20 to 25 years or longer, it is certain that he is selling quality food and giving service at a reasonable price, or he would have been out of business long ago.

No dealer, however, no matter how trustworthy, can take over the responsibilities of the food buyer. The food buyer has to let the dealer know enough in advance what the needs are going to be. A buyer cannot expect a dealer to come up with out-of-season fish on short notice; and when there are storms, the buyer must understand that the dealer may not be able to supply desired items.

Following are some quality factors to be considered regarding fresh seafood.

Fin Fish

A fish starts to decay at its head—so first look at the head of a fish. The eyes on a fresh fish look almost alive. They are bright, protruding, full, and they are not covered with a gray tint nor are they sunken into the head. Next, open the gills of the fish and look at their color. They should be bright pink or red, and if they have turned gray or almost black, the fish should be rejected. If the odor from the gills and the head is very strong and fishy, then either the fish is old or has been stored improperly. The flesh of the fish should be firm and elastic and when pressed should not leave an indentation.

The scales of a fresh fish are normally coated with a thin gelatinous matter that gives the impression of a smooth skin with a natural fresh sparkle. The fins and the tail of the fish should be whole and intact. If they are not, it may indicate that the fish has been badly handled or has been chilled or frozen and then "slacked out" and offered as a fresh fish. If the fish has been dressed, open up the cavity and look at the color of the flesh. If it is bright pink or red and is free of odor, then the fish is probably fresh. If the color is gray and looks washed out or dark in color, the fish should be discarded.

Fresh Northern Lobsters

The only fresh lobsters available in the United States are the northern or Maine lobsters, which can be shipped fresh and will remain fresh for several days if properly handled. When received, the lobster should still have considerable motility of claws and tail. If the movement is not there, the lobster is probably dead or near-dead. A fresh lobster has very little odor, and if the lobster is completely limp and has a pronounced odor, it should be discarded. Fresh lobster shipped any considerable distance should be packed in seaweed and fresh ice in a container that lets in some air.

Soft-Shell Crab

Fresh blue crabs can, in the soft-shell stage, be shipped fresh for some distance if they are packed in seaweed or seagrass and in a wooden container to prevent them from being crushed or from moving about. Again, watch for leg movement, and if there is no leg movement and the crab is completely limp, it should be discarded.

Clams and Oysters in the Shell

The shells of fresh, live clams and oysters are closed when the fish is alive. If any of the shells are open, these should be sorted out and discarded as unsafe. Shucked oysters should be plump and free of strong odor, and they should have a natural creamy color in a clear liquid. Shucked clams are generally frozen in a block or

When selecting fresh fish, a food buyer should keep in mind the following:

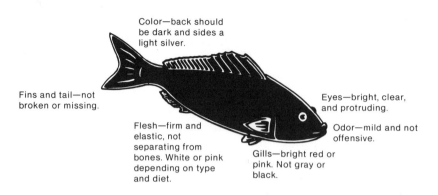

Color—back should
be dark and sides a
light silver.

Fins and tail—not
broken or missing.

Flesh—firm and
elastic, not
separating from
bones. White or pink
depending on type
and diet.

Gills—bright red or
pink. Not gray or
black.

Eyes—bright, clear,
and protruding.

Odor—mild and not
offensive.

Exhibit 15-2. How to tell a fresh fish (Courtesy of Sheraton Hotels Corporation)

canned. They deteriorate too fast after being shucked to be sold fresh, even if iced in small containers.

As has already been pointed out in the chapter on specifications, there are grade and quality standards available for almost every food item for sale in the United States. This holds true for fin fish and shellfish—both fresh and processed. The grade standards for fresh seafood are rather nebulous because fresh seafood can deteriorate minute by minute when it is not properly stored or transported. Processed seafood, however, can be closely graded, and the grade stamps will generally tell the customers the standard of the product they are buying within a reasonably short time after catch. This applies to frozen, canned, dried, smoked, breaded, and processed seafood.

GOVERNMENT STANDARDS

Government standards include standards for wholesomeness or required inspection, standards of identity, and grade standards. As for other commodities, standards for wholesomeness are meant to protect the public health and are mandatory for use. Standards of identity relate to composition such as species of

fish; amounts of breading (on shrimp) and packing medium such as water or oil in canned tuna fish; and size, such as count per gallon of oysters or count of shrimp per pound. U.S. grade standards indicate differences in quality. These standards are invaluable in ensuring wholesomeness and in obtaining the product characteristics desired. However, buyers should know that while approved inspection programs for wholesomeness (since 1995) and meeting standards of identity are required of fish processors, grading is not, and buyers must request and pay for this service. Grade standards, however, should definitely be used by food buyers.

Seafood Inspection

Prior to 1995, inspecting seafood for wholesomeness was not mandatory in the United States, although the Federal Food, Drug, and Cosmetic Act of 1938, Chapter VII, Section 702a (Code of Federal Regulations, Title 21, part 372a) made provision for this to be possible. The National Seafood Inspection Program was also available on a *voluntary basis* through the National Marine Fisheries Service of the National Oceanic and Atmospheric Administration of the U.S. Department of Commerce.

Due to consumer and regulatory interest in health and food safety, a new regulatory "rule" was enacted (1995) called *Procedures for the Safe and Sanitary Processing and Importing of Fish and Fishery Products* (21 CFR, Parts 123 and 1240) that requires all fish to be assured of wholesomeness using Hazard Analysis Critical Control Point procedures (HACCP). This regulation requires processors (both foreign and domestic) to develop comprehensive programs and plans for identifying and controlling any hazard to consumers for each species (fresh or frozen) that is marketed. A more thorough review of this law is found in Chapter 1 of this text. Because so much fish is consumed in the United States and fish was previously marketed with very limited regulatory control, this legislation meets a real need for assuring the safety of fish and is of great benefit to buyers and consumers.

Standards of Identity

Standards of identity are available for oysters, extra large oysters, large oysters, medium oysters, small oysters, very small oysters, Olympian oysters, large Pacific oysters, medium Pacific oysters, small Pacific oysters, extra small Pacific oysters, canned oysters, canned Pacific salmon, canned wet-packed shrimp in transparent containers, frozen raw breaded shrimp, frozen raw lightly breaded shrimp, and canned tuna (Code of Federal Regulations, Title 21, Parts 100 to 169).

For oysters, standards of identity are important in obtaining the size of oysters desired. Size is related to species, which is related to the area from which the oysters are harvested. Size designations are based on count per gallon or quart. For example, extra large oysters, which may also be called *counts* (generally from the Atlantic Ocean) are of such size that a gallon contains not more than 160 oysters, and oysters designated as "large Pacific" are of a size that a gallon contains not more than 64 oysters by count.

For canned salmon, a buyer needs the standard of identity to identify the species, form of product desired, and sizes of cans in which the product is generally packed. Species options, according to common names for similar species, given in groups, are chinook, king, spring; red, sockeye; coho, medium red, silver; pink; chum; and masou or cherry.

The standard of identity for canned tuna fish provides the buyer with the standards and language to select the product desired in terms of color (based on species), form, packing medium, and optional ingredients. Color options are white (which may also be identified as albacore based on species), light, dark, or blended. Canned tuna may be packed in any edible vegetable oil or mixture of oils (not including olive oil), olive oil, or water. Optional seasoning ingredients are salt, monosodium glutamate, hydrolyzed protein, spices or spice oils, vegetable broth, garlic, and lemon flavoring that has been prepared from lemon oil and citric acid. Specified optional forms of the product are solid, chunks, flakes, and grated. Any of the forms of the product may be smoked.

Standards of identity for frozen raw breaded shrimp and frozen raw lightly breaded shrimp include limits for amounts of breading material on shrimp and describe various forms of the products. The maximum permissible amount of breading for frozen raw breaded shrimp is 50 percent; and for frozen raw lightly breaded shrimp, 35 percent. Buyers should be aware that they may specify an amount of breading that is less than the maximum given in the standard. Names for various forms of the product are fantail or butterfly; butterfly, tail off; round; round, tail off; pieces; and composite units.

Grade Standards

U.S. grade standards have been established for basic classes of fresh and frozen fish under the authority of the Agricultural Marketing Act of 1946 (Code of Federal Regulations, Title 50, parts 200 to 599). These standards are administered through the National Marine Fisheries Service in the U.S. Department of Commerce. Included are standards for whole or dressed fish (fresh or frozen of any species), fish steaks, fish fillets, frozen fish blocks and products made from them, crustacean shellfish products (shrimp), and molluscan shellfish (scallops). Within these classes, standards for some specific species and products are available. These standards include salmon steaks, halibut steaks, and fillets of cod, haddock, perch, sole, and flounder.

Fresh seafood is sold only in A and B grades, but there are four grades for processed seafood. They are grades A, B, C, and substandard. It is only natural that the public demands a Grade A stamp on any processed food that is purchased in the market. The institutional trade uses most of the Grade B quality, and most of the Grade C and substandard is exported.

Grade A indicates the best quality and top grade. These Grade A products are uniform in size and color, free from most blemishes and defects, and of good typical flavor.

Grade B represents a good quality product, but the product may not be quite so uniform in size, can have a few blemishes, and may not present as appealing an appearance as the Grade A products. This grade indicates that the seafood is of good quality and is quite acceptable for most purposes.

Grade C and substandard grades are wholesome and safe to eat but have variations in size and appearance, and are generally used for export or for soup or processed fish dishes.

Collectively, grade standards cover most of the fish or fish products on the market.

Although using grade standards is not mandatory in terms of federal law, the provisions are highly advantageous to a buyer.

Grade standards for fish are unique in relation to other commodities in that flavor and odor are specific factors in grades. Other considerations include defects such as abnormal condition; appearance and consistency of flesh, eyes, and gills; excessive blood or drip; discoloration; dehydration; and miscut pieces.

Also included in grade standards are options and definitions of forms and styles of fish. Forms include fresh; frozen solid pack; and glazed or unglazed. Styles are whole; dressed (eviscerated); head on or headless; with or without fins; skin on, scaled, or unscaled; semiskinned; and skinless.

For salmon and halibut steaks, styles of pack may be random weight, uniform weight, or random-weight combination. "Random weight" means that fish are packed after cutting from head to tail. "Random-weight combination pack" means packing to include only cuts from selected parts of whole, dressed salmon; and "uniform weight" means that all cuts are generally of the same weight.

The grade standards for fish fillets include size as a factor in grading. This is protection against marketing very small fish. Also, "butterfly," "individually quick frozen (IQF)," and "single" are defined as forms of the product.

The product called "frozen fish blocks" is defined in the federal grade standard for that item. These are prepared from masses of fish of a single species that have been cleaned and frozen together in a large rectangular block. The fish may be skinless or have the skin on. Products termed "raw fish portions" are cut from frozen fish blocks, and options are provided for cutting the blocks into various shapes.

Frozen raw breaded fish portions are also cut from frozen fish blocks. According to the definition incorporated in the grade standard, portions of this product weigh more than 1.5 ounces and are at least ⅜ inch thick, and at least 75 percent of the total weight is fish rather than breading material.

Frozen fried fish sticks are similar to raw breaded fish portions except that only 60 percent of the total product weight must be made up of fish. The reduction in percentage of fish required makes provision for the weight of fat generally absorbed in frying.

Grade standards for shrimp cover essentially all forms including fresh, cooked, frozen, peeled, deveined, headless or with head on, split, and with or without the tail fin.

A special standard has been written for frozen raw breaded shrimp that provides designations of styles and types that are frequently used in specifications. Names and descriptions are Style I, regular breaded shrimp, which contains a minimum of 50 percent shrimp; and Style II, lightly breaded shrimp, which contains a minimum of 65 percent shrimp material. Type I breaded shrimp are fantail, and Type II are round. Within each type are subtypes A, B, and C, which indicate (A) with tail fin and shell, (B) with tail fin but no shell, and (C) without tail fin and shell. Uniformity in shrimp size and condition or breaks in breading are special factors in determining grades.

Provisions for grades of scallops (molluscan shellfish) are similar to those for other kinds of fish. They may be solid pack or individually quick frozen, and glazed or unglazed. Scallops that are breaded, whether raw or fried, must contain a minimum of 50 percent scallop meat and may be in Style I, random pack, in which the weight of individual scallops is not specified; or Style II, uniform pack, in which the pieces are of a specified weight.

Buyers should note that the terminology incorporated in federal grade standards is not uniform in terms of all classes and species. Therefore, depending on the particular fish, the grade standards in the Code of Federal Regulations (Title 50, Parts 200 to 599) or the standards of identity (Code of Federal Regulations, Title 21, Parts 100 to 169) should be reviewed to write proper specifications. However, after exact determinations are made, using the language in the grade standards and standards of identity can greatly facilitate fish purchasing.

SOME MARKETING FACTS ABOUT COMMONLY USED FISH AND SHELLFISH

In a recent listing, by the United States Department of Interior, of the various kinds of seafood available on the market today, there were sixty-eight kinds of fin fish from saltwater, fifteen types of freshwater fish from our lakes and rivers, and twenty-five varieties of shellfish. To this list we can now add five varieties of sharks that within the last two years have become popular. It is not within the scope of this book to examine all these varieties of fish, but the buyer needs to know a little about the more commonly used seafood.

Shrimp

The world's supply of shrimp is rapidly being depleted because of the popularity and high demand for this seafood. Even higher prices have not greatly affected the consumption of this very popular product. Not many years ago, fresh shrimp was selling in the New Orleans market for $.06, $.08, and $.10 per pound for brown gulf shrimp just off the shrimp boat. Today the price for the same shrimp varies from $3.00 to $4.00 per pound, and there is less than one-third the supply there was ten to fifteen years ago.

The United States imports twice as much shrimp as our own shrimp boats are able to bring in. Most imported shrimp come from the Mediterranean and the Indonesian

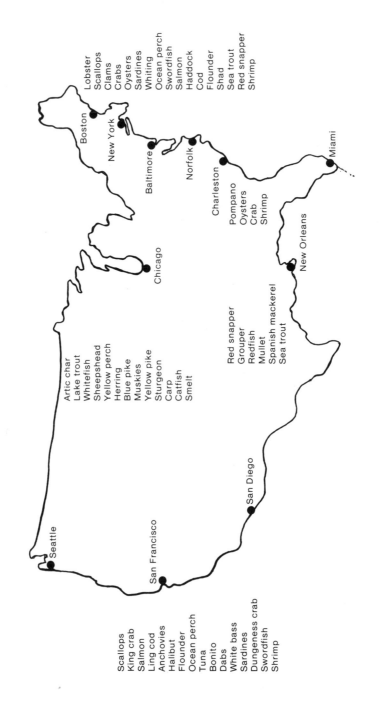

Exhibit 15-3. Primary fish markets of the United States and the main fish received.

Boston
Lobster
Scallops
Clams
Crabs
Oysters
Sardines
Whiting
Ocean perch
Swordfish
Salmon
Haddock
Cod
Flounder
Shad
Sea trout
Red snapper
Shrimp

New York

Baltimore

Norfolk

Charleston
Pompano
Oysters
Crab
Shrimp

Miami

New Orleans
Red snapper
Grouper
Redfish
Mullet
Spanish mackerel
Sea trout

Chicago
Artic char
Lake trout
Whitefish
Sheepshead
Yellow perch
Herring
Blue pike
Muskies
Yellow pike
Sturgeon
Carp
Catfish
Smelt

San Diego

San Francisco

Seattle
Scallops
King crab
Salmon
Ling cod
Anchovies
Halibut
Flounder
Ocean perch
Tuna
Bonito
Dabs
White bass
Sardines
Dungeness crab
Swordfish
Shrimp

ocean waters, with some coming from as far as Australia. The shrimp industry from the Indonesian area was purchased by the Japanese about twenty years ago, and the prices they set influence shrimp prices throughout the world.

Quality Factors of Shrimp. According to price schedules, the buying public seems to feel that white and pink shrimp are better than the brown or the deep-water red shrimp. The larger shrimp, called "prawns," which come from the Mediterranean, are reddish in color and are very much in demand for a seafood dish that is mistakenly called "shrimp scampi." Scampi merely means shrimp, but the name has come to mean shrimp cooked in butter, white wine, and spices. Actually, the quality and taste do not depend so much on the variety of shrimp but on where the shrimp are caught. Some of the brown shrimp caught in the New Orleans area and along the Gulf shores are apt to have an iodine taste, but brown shrimp harvested in the deep part of the Gulf are among the best-tasting shrimp marketed.

The author was involved in a series of tests concerning the taste and quality of various types of shrimp. One of the most interesting facts that came out of these tests was that the brown shrimp taken from the deep waters of the Gulf shrank less when cooked than either the white or pink varieties. These tests showed that 21- to 25-size brown shrimp, cooked and weighed, appeared the same as 16- to 20-size shrimp of the pink and white variety. This experience certainly should be checked out by today's food buyer and any users of large quantities of shrimp.

A few shrimp are sold live to places such as the exotic floating Chinese restaurants in the Hong Kong harbor, where they are kept in fish tanks. Most shrimp are marketed frozen, with the head removed. Shrimp are also marketed peeled, deveined, and quick frozen (in which case they are marked PDQ). Fantail, butterfly, round fantail, or solid shrimp is peeled, deveined, and cooked, and shrimp that is shredded and formed into shrimp shapes and deep-fried or sold raw for low cost is used for shrimp appetizers.

Shrimp is marketed under different names for the various sizes depending on the part of the country in which one is operating. However, most green headless shrimp are marketed in the following sizes: under 10s, which means there are from eight to ten of these extremely large shrimp per pound; 10 to 15s; 16 to 20s; and 21 to 25s. The next size category is for medium shrimp, which are 26 to 30s; 31 to 35s; 36 to 42s, and 43 to 50s. The count for small shrimp are generally 51 to 60 and 61 and over.

Scallops

Scallops are mollusks that live in either bays or the sea. Scallop meat is only the adductor or "eye" muscle that opens and closes the shell. It contains from 12 to 15 percent of the total meat of the mollusk. A gallon of bay scallops contains about 480 to 850 pieces and weighs around 8 pounds. Genuine Cape Cod scallops are considered the best of bay scallops; they are about the same size as other bay scallops but are very creamy white, tender, and full of flavor.

Sea scallops that come from the deeper waters of the bays are considerably larger and run from 100 to 185 scallops per gallon. Sea scallops vary considerably by size and some can be rather tough if the scallop is not young. Alaskan sea scallops are now coming to the market but have had a limited reception. The Alaskan scallop is rather large, dark in color, and often tough. The New York seafood market lists bay scallops in three different sizes: large, medium, and small. The large bay scallops are ¾ inch in diameter; the medium scallops are ½ to ¾ inch in diameter; and small scallops are ½ inch or less in diameter.

Reputable dealers will not substitute other products for quality scallops, but there are always a few dealers who are out to "make a buck," so the buyer must know what to look for. Today, shark meat is being cut into scallop-sized pieces and sold as scallops or mixed in with the regular scallops to sell to the inexperienced buyer. Some dealers will cut halibut into scallop-sized pieces, and some dealers will cut sea scallops into bay scallop sizes, but since sea scallops have started costing almost as much as bay scallops, this practice has fallen off.

Oysters

Fresh oysters, eaten from the half-shell, provide a taste thrill that cannot be duplicated by any other form of seafood. Of course, this applies only to those who like raw oysters. For those who do not, there is always oyster stew, scalloped oysters, fried oysters, and oysters in a seafood chowder. Any oysters sold in the United States through regular food supply channels come from shellfish beds that have been approved for sanitation by the U.S. Public Health Service. Products harvested from these areas are given labels containing the certification number of the area.

Oysters from the eastern shore of the United States are harvested all the way from the Canadian Maritimes to the Gulf of Mexico. The Chesapeake Bay bluepoint is the premium white oyster, with the Long Island oyster rated almost as good as the bluepoint. The Cape Cod oyster, especially from the area around Chatham, is in constant demand, as well as the small Chincoteague oyster found in the waters off the New England shore. The Gulf of Mexico produces a large, very dark oyster that is very strong in iodine but is highly prized in Creole cooking. The Pacific Ocean produces the Olympia and the Japanese Pacific oyster. The Japanese Pacific oyster is generally cooked, and the Olympia oyster, also known as the Western oyster, is used in cocktails.

Many varieties of oysters are sold on the half-shell, but the majority are shucked and sold by the pint, quart, or gallon to the retail and commercial trade. A gallon of shucked oysters, regardless of their size, should weigh approximately 8 pounds. Shucked oysters are sold fresh and must be properly iced as they deteriorate very rapidly.

Oysters in the shell are generally sold by count or by the bushel; in some areas, they are sold in 80-pound bags. The Chesapeake Bay bluepoints and the Long Island half-shells run about 250 to 300 oysters per bushel. The Cape Cod oysters average 200 to 250 per bushel, and the Chincoteagues average 300 to 350 per bushel. A bushel weighs 65 to 70 pounds gross weight with the net weight being 3 to 5 pounds less.

The Olympia oyster is a small oyster, being about one-third the size of a small Eastern or bluepoint oyster. On the other hand, the Japanese oyster taken in the Pacific is a very large oyster and averages 150 to 175 per bushel. On the West Coast, the Japanese oyster is generally marketed in 80-pound sacks, and the size averages about 200 per 80-pound sack.

Federal standards for shucked oysters list the following sizes per gallon (8 pounds):

Eastern oysters—extra large, 160 or fewer per gallon; large, 160 to 210; medium, 210 to 300; small, 300 to 500; very small, 500 and over.

Pacific oysters—large, 64 or fewer per gallon; medium, 65 to 96; small, 97 to 144; extra small, 144 and over.

Mussels

There is some demand for mussels in the United States, with the majority coming from the North Atlantic. Mussels are generally sold by the count or by the bushel. A bushel of mussels weighs 45 to 55 pounds and will contain from 350 to 400 medium-sized mussels. As the price of oysters continues to increase and they continue to become scarcer, the demand for mussels will grow. Mussels are beginning to be harvested from some freshwater areas where it has been determined they are safe for consumption.

Clams

There are two types of clams harvested from the shores of the United States that are of commercial importance: hard-shell and soft-shell clams. Of these types, four kinds are found on the Eastern shore of the United States: the New England soft-shell clam, the littleneck hard-shell clam, the cherry stone hard-shell clam, and the quahaug clam.

The New England soft-shell clam, which is harvested off the coast of New England from Cape Cod to the Canadian Maritimes, is the clam generally eaten at clambakes and shore dinners. New Englanders refer to this clam as a true clam, steamer clam, or long neck clam. The soft-shell clam is generally purchased by the bushel, which should weigh 75 to 78 pounds gross and contains from 700 to 800 steamer clams.

Littleneck clams, when purchased by the bushel, will average 675 to 700 clams per bushel. Cherry stones average 325 to 350 clams per bushel, and quahaugs have from 175 to 200 clams per bushel. The littlenecks, cherry stones, and soft-shell steamer clams can be eaten raw, but the larger quahaugs are too tough and are generally cut up and fried or used for chowders and similar dishes.

The Pacific clams are much like their Atlantic relatives. The Pacific soft-shell clam, which is called the razor clam, is 3 to 4 inches in length and is usually served deep-fried. The butter and littleneck clams that come from the Northern Pacific are hard-shelled clams that are normally eaten raw. The size of these clams is about the same as the littlenecks and cherry stones from the East Coast. The famous Pismo clam is a large clam like the quahaug from New England, and because it is tough, it is generally chopped and used to make clam chowders and other seafood dishes.

Shucked clams can be purchased in any of the larger metropolitan areas and can be purchased by the gallon, fresh or frozen. Fresh shucked clams should be kept packed in ice from the time they are shucked, and frozen shucked clams should be processed into the freezer within an hour of being shucked.

Crabs and Crabmeat

Crabs are harvested from both the Atlantic and the Pacific shores of the United States. Some are marketed live when in season, but most are frozen as crabmeat, crab legs, or cooked hard-shelled crabs to be eaten out of the shell. On the East Coast there is the blue crab, which is caught mainly off the middle-Atlantic shores, the New England rock crab that comes from the Cape Cod area, and the Florida stone crab, which is considered a delicacy by many crab devotees. The blue crab, which, before it has molded its hard shell, is known as a soft-shell crab, is very much in demand from early spring to mid-summer. After the hard shell is formed on the blue crab, it is harvested for crabmeat.

Eastern shore crabmeat, which is marketed both fresh and pasteurized, is graded for size as follows:

Jumbo lump or backfin lump—this is most desirable and is all large lump and white in color.

Lump—lump crabmeat consists of small chunks from the body and is white and fine tasting.

Mixed crabmeat or "special"—this must be more than 50 percent lump crabmeat with the remainder being flake.

Flake crabmeat—all white meat from the body of the crab that sometimes is full of bone.

Clawmeat—meat picked from the claws, brownish in color and containing considerable bone.

Rock crabmeat—very fine, on the watery side, rather bony; used commercially for prepared convenience food items such as crab imperial and inexpensive crab cakes.

The West Coast crabs of commercial interest are the dungeness, king, rock, tanner, and snow. Of this group, the dungeness and king crab are the most desirable and the most expensive. The dungeness crab is found all along the Pacific coast from Mexico to Alaska. The crabmeat is usually marketed cooked and is generally sold frozen. The dungeness crab is good sized and normally weighs from 2 to 3.5 pounds. Dungeness crabmeat is tender and sweet, but the lumps of the meat are small and rather moist, and the flavor does not compare favorably with the lump crabmeat of the eastern shore blue crab.

King crabs are caught only in Alaskan waters. Since World War II the king crab industry has jumped from almost nothing to the largest and most expensive source of crabmeat in the country. King crabs are normally marketed as cooked crab legs and cooked shucked king crabmeat. Both of these items are very expensive and already there are warnings that the king crab will go the way of the New England rock lobster.

Tanner crabs are mostly marketed locally, primarily for their claws. Snow crabs, found primarily in Alaskan waters, are also sold primarily for their claws. Almost all snow crabmeat is marketed cooked and frozen.

Lobsters and Lobster Tails

In certain areas of the Middle East, the fish market offers "rich man's fish" and "poor man's fish." Heading the list of rich man's fish are lobsters and lobster tails, closely followed by red mullet. In this country, too, lobster is a food that few people can afford. The true lobster and the spiny lobster are close to being endangered species, and they are already priced higher than any other items on a menu, including prime fillet of beef. The true or New England lobster is a two-claw lobster that is found primarily from Cape Cod north to the Maritime Provinces of Canada. Two-claw lobsters are also found off the shores of Denmark and Scandinavia, and an appreciable amount are taken from the Sea of Marmara near Turkey, where the clawless spiny lobster is also found.

The New York seafood market classifies lobsters as jumbo if they are 3 pounds and up, large if they are 1.5 to 2.5 pounds, quarters if 1 to 1.5 pounds, and chicken if ¾ to 1 pound. Usually a 1- to 1.25-pound lobster is considered a portion. However, a real lobster lover goes for the large lobster, which weighs from 1.5 to 2 pounds. Unfortunately, lobsters sometimes lose one claw, and then they have to be sold as culls and are generally used for cooked lobster meat. Cooked and picked lobster meat is available in 14-ounce cans, but is extremely costly and scarce because of labor costs.

Lobsters are normally available year-round; however, the harvest during February, March, and early April is usually curtailed by the weather. By law, lobsters cannot be harvested during their molting season, and as this happens during the inclement weather of the spring, this naturally cuts down the supply of lobsters tremendously as well.

The rock, or spiny, lobster can be found almost anywhere in coastal waters. The sources of rock lobster tails from the United States are the coast of Florida, the Gulf of Mexico, and the lower coast of California. But the majority of lobster tails are imported from other countries. The main sources of supply are Africa, New Zealand, and Australia. Before we got into a diplomatic crisis with Cuba, Cuban rock lobster tails were particularly sought after.

Rock lobster tails generally average about 8 ounces each, with some averaging considerably over 1 pound. The New York seafood market grades as jumbo those lobster tails that weigh 16 ounces and over. Tails that weigh 12 to 16 ounces are graded as large, 7 to 12 ounces as medium, and 6 to 9 ounces as small.

If you are a tourist in either Maine or Massachusetts, don't bother to order Danish or rock lobster tails. These two states prohibit the marketing of what is called a "mutilated lobster," which rules out the rock lobster and crayfish or the small Danish lobster tail.

SOME FACTS ABOUT FIN FISH

Some interesting facts about the more commonly used fin fish in the United States, which may be helpful to even the experienced food buyer, are outlined in the following paragraphs.

Bass

There are normally three varieties of saltwater bass available on the commercial market. The Atlantic varieties include striped bass or rockfish, sea bass or black bass, and white or common bass. Some freshwater white bass and small-mouthed bass are harvested in areas like the Great Lakes, but most of these fish are taken in sport fishing, and few are sold commercially. Although bass vary greatly in size and shape, the texture and flavor of the meat is pretty much the same. The flavor is generally pleasant and rich, and not so strong as some of the most oily fish, although the fat content is high. The fish flakes are in definite sections and, when cooked, turn white to gray white.

The West Coast varieties of bass are rockfish, striped bass, and white or common bass. The taste and quality of the West Coast bass are just as good as the East Coast bass. Supplies of both East Coast and West Coast bass are available year-round, but the best market harvest is in the spring, summer, and early fall. Bass vary greatly in size, ranging from ¾ to 1 pound for sea bass on the East Coast and up to 500 pounds for white bass found off the Pacific coast. The best sized striped bass to buy for fillets is from 4 to 10 pounds, with a 4-pound sea bass making four good portions of fillet of bass. For the hotel and restaurant trade, sizes of bass 10 pounds and under are generally more desirable than the larger sizes.

Bluefish

Bluefish normally caught along the middle-Atlantic shores are one of our best and most plentiful fish for commercial use. They are available year-round but are most plentiful from March through July. Bluefish vary from the small snapper blue that weighs around 1 pound to the large blue that weighs 7 to 8 pounds. Most chefs prefer a whole bluefish weighing 4 to 4.5 pounds or fillets cut from that size fish. The bluefish is a rather oily fish but is mild in taste and a good shipper. It also freezes well and, when properly wrapped, can be held up to six months.

Varieties of Codfish

The codfish, with its numerous varieties, is the most commonly used fish in the food service industry in this country. The catching and marketing of codfish is the backbone of the fishing industry in New England. The currents off the New England coast provide excellent feeding for these fish, and the supply seems to keep pace with heavy fishing.

Codfish harvested off the eastern shores of the United States are the common cod, cusk, both red and white hake, and some tom cod. The cod caught off the Pacific coast are mainly ling cod, tom cod, some common cod, and Pacific hake. Even though the Pacific cod differs from East shore cod to some extent, both types are white flaky fish that are low in fat and can serve many purposes. Cod is used in fish chowders and fish stews, or it can be broiled or baked. It is offered as "scrod" in many areas of the country. Codfish sold as "broiled scrod" is a far better seller than if it is listed on the menu as broiled cod.

Codfish are available in sizes from approximately 1 pound up to the whale cod, which sometimes grows to over 100 pounds. The best sizes for normal restaurant and food service use are from 1.5 to 10 pounds. Codfish is generally filleted for serving; however, some of the medium-sized fish are also cut into steaks. Buyers should keep in mind, however, that cod seldom dresses out to more than about 30 percent of the weight in the round.

Flounder and Sole

Most reference materials group flounder and sole under one heading because the fish are basically the same in shape, size, and eating qualities. The normal supply of Atlantic flounder are the blackbacks, which are caught in the winter; fluke, which is caught in the summer; sea dabs; gray sole; lemon sole; southern flounder; and the yellow tail, which is called both a flounder and a sole. On the West Coast, the most commonly used flounder are the wreck sole, the sand dab, and the Dover, or English sole, all of which are harvested year-round.

Most of the flounder family weigh from ¾ to 2 pounds; however, the summer fluke and the southern flounder often reach the size of 10 to 12 pounds. Most of the West Coast flounder weigh from ½ to 2 pounds.

Even though the main Pacific sole is called Dover, or English sole, the true Dover sole comes only from the English Channel. It takes a real connoisseur of seafood to tell the difference between "English sole" from the Pacific Coast or English sole from the English Channel. True English sole is marketed in the United States only in the frozen state, and it is very expensive compared to the Pacific sole.

Haddock

Haddock resembles cod in appearance and eating quality, but it is normally marketed as a separate variety of fish. Haddock averages from 3 to 7 pounds in the round and occasionally reaches a weight of 10 pounds. Haddock is harvested from the New England waters up into the Canadian Maritimes. The Newfoundland Banks, which are an extension of the George's Banks off New England, are the best haddock fishing grounds known.

About the turn of the century, there was so much baby haddock being harvested along with the other fish off the New England coast that it was considered a scrap fish and generally was made into fertilizer or else was just thrown out. There was a priest along the waterfront in Boston who was interested in helping the fishing industry, and he came up with the idea that it would be healthful, economical, and desirable from a religious standpoint to make Friday a fast day, in order to help consume the large oversupply of fish in the Boston area. The idea caught on, and for decades Friday was a Catholic fish day or fast day from meat in the United States, but nowhere else in the world. This custom has been dropped officially by the Church; however, the custom of eating fish on Friday still persists, much to the benefit of the New England fishing industry.

To improve the consumption of baby haddock, this same priest thought of serving this item as broiled scrod. This idea, too, caught on and worked so well that the supply of baby haddock became exhausted, and the public had to change to the various types of codfish to substitute for scrod.

Today, "broiled scrod" is one of our most popular fish dishes since almost any white flaky fish broiled to a crisp brown and served with lemon butter will serve the purpose.

Baby haddock, called scrod, are marketed in both Boston and New York at weights of 1.5 to 2.5 pounds. Haddock weighing less than 1.5 pounds are called small scrod in New York, and in Boston they are called snapper scrod. Haddock, like cod, is available the year round; however, the supply varies with the weather off the New England coast.

Halibut

Halibut is a flat fish that actually belongs to the flounder and sole family but is much larger than these two. Halibut is caught in both the Atlantic and Pacific oceans and even off the coast of Alaska. The United States also imports some halibut from the Scandinavian countries. There are few restrictions on the taking of halibut except off the Pacific coast where there is an agreement between the Japanese and Americans to restrict somewhat the taking of this fish.

Halibut varies considerably in size and can run from 5 pounds to well over 125 pounds for each fish. The classification of sizes for dressed halibut vary from the West Coast to the East Coast, but as a rule the size ratings of Boston and New York are accepted throughout the fishing industry. The New York classifications for halibut are: snapper, under 5 pounds; chicken, 5 to 10 pounds; medium, 10 to 50 pounds; large, 50 to 80 pounds; and whale halibut, over 80 pounds. From a buyer's viewpoint, the 8- to 10-pound size seems to cut out best for restaurant and other food services.

Halibut is a very highly rated fish with a medium to strong taste; the meat is fine, white, and considered to be some of the best on the market. It is exceptionally good served as steaks, which can be poached or broiled. A 4-ounce frozen halibut steak is a highly rated convenience food item in the food service industry. Halibut is considered a lean fish, but it does freeze and store well if flash frozen after being glazed with water and if the glaze is not broken or cracked in transit.

Halibut is also used in some ways that are frowned upon by the seafood industry. For example, in Chicago, halibut is sliced thin, breaded and deep fried, and sold as fried fillet of Eastern sole. Some restaurants and hotels in Chicago and the Midwest have tried true fillet of sole, but the customers seem to prefer the halibut even though it is a substitution. Halibut is also cut into bite-sized pieces and sold as scallops, and here again the customers have made it plain that they prefer the halibut scallops to the real thing.

Mackerel

Mackerel is harvested both in the Pacific and Atlantic oceans as well as in the Gulf of Mexico from Texas east. The eastern mackerel that are most plentiful on the market are the tinker mackerel, which weighs under 1 pound, and the Atlantic mackerel, which weighs from 1 to 3 pounds. The Spanish mackerel, caught in the Gulf of Mexico and around the Southern Atlantic, can reach weights of 6 to 8 pounds. The Pacific mackerel and the jack mackerel are found on the West Coast. The small Pacific mackerel are usually canned as large, inexpensive sardines, and the jack mackerel are canned in #1 tall cans and sold as an inexpensive substitute for salmon and tuna fish.

The English like their bloaters and golden eyes for breakfast, and in New England, the tradition of serving a small boiled salt mackerel with parsleyed potatoes is still a popular custom.

Red Snapper

Red snapper is one of the most desirable and expensive fish available in the restaurant and food service trade. It is caught in the Gulf of Mexico and Florida coastal waters, and off the shores of some of the Caribbean islands and Venezuela. The red snapper ranges in size from 1 to 20 pounds, but it dresses out to only 25 to 30 percent of its caught weight.

There is a mangrove snapper and a grouper that are caught along with the red snapper, and they are often marketed as red snapper at somewhat reduced prices. These two fish are excellent and can stand on their own, but they should not be confused with the true red snapper.

Salmon—The Finest of Them All

Salmon are the most desirable and high-priced fin fish in the restaurant and hospitality trade. They are caught in the coastal waters of the United States and in several other areas, including the coasts of Scandinavia, Russia, and Japan. This country harvests salmon from both the Atlantic and Pacific oceans. The eastern salmon caught in the estuaries of New England and Canada are called Kennebec and are prized for their texture and flavor. The supply of these salmon is very small. Most of it is sold as fresh salmon in the spring and summer months or made into smoked Kennebec salmon, which is extremely popular in Boston, New York, Washington, and Florida. Kennebec salmon are normally on the small side, weighing from 4 to 12 pounds each. However, some do reach sizes of up to 40 pounds.

There is some landlocked salmon (salmon which has adapted to being cut off from the sea) available in the country, but the supply is very limited and mostly consumed locally. In Canada there is a fish known as the Arctic char that is a cross between a landlocked salmon and a freshwater trout. These fish are small, seldom reaching more than 3 to 4 pounds, and are very expensive even in the round. The price for Arctic char is normally 2.5 to 4 times

the price of either Kennebec or the red sockeye salmon from the West Coast.

During the salmon harvest season, which is from early spring to late summer, large quantities of fresh salmon are air-lifted to just about every metropolitan area of the United States. There are five kinds of Pacific salmon marketed during the year, mainly during these summer months. The first and most important is the red salmon or sockeye salmon, followed by the Chinook or king salmon, the pink or humpback salmon, the silver or coho salmon, and the chum salmon (also called the white salmon). This fish is known to the Eskimos as the dog or keta salmon.

The red salmon is the one that is most desirable for canning, since it retains its red color after processing. Red salmon runs for only about a two-week period just before the Fourth of July of each year. It is not particularly large and generally weighs under 10 pounds.

Chinook salmon, which is often marketed as red salmon, is the largest normally caught and runs between 15 to 25 pounds on the average, though it can grow to a weight of 75 pounds. Chinook salmon appears on the market early in the season and can be taken as early as May in the shores off California.

Pink or humpback salmon is the smallest of the Pacific salmon, generally running between 3 to 5 pounds. Pink salmon has a very good taste and can be baked, fried, broiled, poached, or used in chowder. It stores well when properly glazed and frozen.

The silver or coho salmon is bright orange in color and is slightly larger than some of the other salmon, running between 10 to 12 pounds. The cohos run later in the summer, generally starting in late July and continuing into late September.

The chum or white salmon has the lightest flesh of the salmon family after it is cooked. Because of the whitish pink color of this salmon, it usually costs less, even though it has a good flavor. The chum migrates along with the red sockeye salmon, but the harvest season on the chum can go as late as the latter part of November.

About thirty-five to forty years ago, it looked as if the salmon were heading for extinction, with their spawning grounds being invaded by industry that not only polluted the waters but (by the introduction of dams for power) prevented the fish from reaching their spawning grounds. Fortunately, conservationists pressed the government to help clean up the waters and provide fish ladders for the dams. The government also persuaded the Japanese to be more conservative in their fishing methods. At the present, it appears that the salmon are staging a comeback. When one realizes it takes as much as eight years for a fingerling salmon to make its way to the ocean and return for spawning, it is easy to see how this fish could become an endangered species.

Smelts

Smelts are a small freshwater fish caught in the inlets of both the Atlantic and Pacific oceans and in the Gulf of Mexico. They are found as far north as the Arctic Ocean, where they are quite plentiful. For the commercial trade, they are caught primarily in the Great Lakes. These fish, which generally weigh from 1.5 to 3 ounces, are marketed—both fresh and frozen—in the round, dressed, or as boned fillets. They can be breaded and deep fried or sautéed. The flavor is rich and the texture of the meat is fine, but the flesh is rather oily.

Swordfish

Swordfish is one of our better market fish because of its fine-textured meat with a pleasant flavor and few bones. This fish, which can weigh as much as 300 pounds, is caught mainly in both the Atlantic and Pacific oceans and off the coast of Japan.

Some are caught off the coast of South America, and a few are caught off the shores of Canada. The Canadian swordfish is highly prized for its fine texture and taste.

Swordfish is usually marketed both fresh and frozen as steaks or center cut chunks, but some of the small ones are filleted or sold whole. The supply of swordfish is dwindling rapidly; consequently, the price is quite high. About thirty years ago, there was a scare about swordfish absorbing mercury that might endanger human health. A test was devised for detecting mercury in swordfish, but even though all swordfish marketed today are free of mercury, many people refuse to eat this great-tasting fish. All during the mercury scare, the Pier 4 restaurant in Boston specialized in swordfish steak. They advertised and promoted the product, and it became one of the leading menu items for the restaurant. Today it still is one of the best-selling items on the menu.

Shark

For years, no one would market shark meat under any circumstances. However, during the past five years, the demand for shark has grown to the point that it is now a highly profitable seafood item. Every kind of shark is being caught and sold, varying from the small sand shark to the large mako that can weigh 600 to 800 pounds.

Some shark meat is very dark in color, tough, stringy, with a rather unpleasant taste, but the mako shark is close in texture and taste to swordfish. In many instances, shark is being substituted for swordfish in the food service industry. Some shark meat is also being cut up into bite-sized pieces and sold as both bay and sea scallops, and although the practice is frowned upon in the industry, there is a considerable amount of shark meat consumed in this manner. Shark meat freezes well and is sold, like swordfish, as steaks and chunks.

Sea Trout

Along the Atlantic coast, and down through the Gulf, when all other fresh fish fail, there is always sea trout. This fish, also called weak fish, is available year-round when the weather is calm enough for fishermen to get offshore, and during the early spring and summer months it can be taken by surf-casting. Market sizes for this fish are from 1 to 6 pounds. The taste is not outstanding, but it is acceptable, especially when served fresh. It is not a particularly expensive fish and has found its biggest outlet in the supermarket, where price is an important factor.

Along the Atlantic coast, there is a gray sea trout as well as a spotted sea trout. In the Gulf of Mexico, there is a white sea trout which is not much different from the gray trout taken along the Atlantic coast. A small ¾-pound sea trout, boned, stuffed, and baked, is a very appetizing dish and considerably cheaper than the boned freshwater trout.

Freshwater Trout

Until recently, about the only freshwater trout that was available commercially was the Danish trout, which were marketed both fresh and frozen. A few farm-raised trout from Idaho were sold, but these were very expensive and difficult to obtain. But right after World War II, trout farms started to grow in leaps and bounds, and today there are actually more freshwater trout available commercially than sea trout.

The rainbow trout seems to be the best type of trout for the fish-farming business. Because of the volume available, prices have stabilized at fair levels, and the food service industry is utilizing this product to a great extent. The supermarkets, not to be left out, have specialized in freshwater trout, and fresh trout is now available year round, even in small towns. These trout are generally single-portion size (from ¾ to 1 pound). However, for special purposes, larger trout, ranging from 3 to 4 pounds and even up to 6 pounds, are available.

There are some lake trout available on the Chicago market taken from the Great Lakes, but because of the limited supply, this fish is consumed mostly close to the source.

Tuna Fish

Tuna fishing and canning is a large industry in itself. Tuna is taken in the Atlantic Ocean off the shores of South America, up through the Pacific, to the Alaskan shores, and down through the Japanese waters. Tuna, when caught, may be as small as 10 pounds, or they can reach 1,000 pounds. Fresh and frozen tuna are used throughout the United States in the food service trade. However, at least 95 percent of the tuna caught is canned, packed in either oil or water.

The United States imports a large volume of tuna from Japan, although some operators feel that the American processed tuna is of superior quality. Tuna fish is packed generally either in a 7-ounce can or in a large 66-ounce can. Some packers market a small individual 3-ounce can of albacore white-meat tuna that is in demand for cold plates in the Miami, Washington, and New York markets.

The best tuna fish is the albacore white chunk tuna packed in oil or water, followed by the southern and northern bluefin types of tuna down through the oriental, skip jack, and the big eye tuna. Canned bonito resembles tuna and for some purposes can be a less expensive substitute.

Tuna fish varies in price according to the quality and taste of the canned product. The darker and flakier the meat, the lower the cost; whiter meat in a more solid pack brings a higher price. For institutional trade, the darker flaked meat is perfectly satisfactory for tuna fish sandwiches and tuna fish salad.

REFERENCES

Code of Federal Regulations, Food and Drugs, Title 21, Parts 100 to 169. Washington, D.C.: U.S. Government Printing Office, 1986.

Code of Federal Regulations, Food and Drugs, Title 21, Parts 170 to 199. Washington, D.C.: U.S. Government Printing Office, 1986.

Code of Federal Regulations, Wildlife and Fisheries, Title 50, Parts 200 to 599. Washington, D.C.: U.S. Government Printing Office, 1987.

Compilation of Selected Acts Within the Jurisdiction of the Committee on Energy and Commerce, Volume II, Food, Drug, and Related Law. Washington, D.C.: U.S. Government Printing Office, 1987.

16 Dairy Products

Purpose: To provide the information necessary for the buyer to make rational decisions in the purchase of milk, cream, butter, ice cream, and cheese.

INTRODUCTION

Dairy products present unique problems in that they generally constitute only a small portion of the purchase dollar. Some dairy products may vary little in quality or price among different suppliers, but other products may vary considerably, so the buyer must choose suppliers carefully. There are also many products that can be successfully substituted for dairy foods.

THE DAIRY MARKET: AN OVERVIEW

Whole milk is considered to be the most nutritionally complete food available. The United States leads the world in the production of high-quality fresh milk and milk products.

Cows produce probably 95 percent of the milk and milk products, both fresh and processed, used throughout the world. But other animals are used for milk production, and in certain countries they provide a substantial amount of milk for human consumption. Goat's milk ranks second in volume, followed by ewe's milk, camel's milk, buffalo milk, milk from llamas and

yaks, and even mare's milk. Unfortunately, in some areas of the world the production of milk and other dairy products is handled in a very primitive and unsanitary way. Wherever funds are not available and training has not been given to improve the sanitary conditions, there are many sicknesses and deaths connected with the handling and consumption of milk and milk products.

In the United States the dairy industry is the most inspected and regulated industry in the country. The dairy industry has been used and abused by politicians, but fortunately government regulatory agencies have remained quite free of any irregularities in these matters. Along with federal regulations, we also have state and local regulations concerning dairy products, which in many areas are more strict than the federal laws. Most of the state and local codes are based on the federal ordinances and regulations of the U.S. Public Health Service, so there is an effective uniformity of control throughout the country.

The food buyer who purchases dairy products will need to become familiar with the system of federal and local controls popularly known as "price fixing." This price controlling stems from the fact that the government has set certain base prices that the dairy operators have to pay farmers for their raw milk product. Once this base price is established, it seems to carry through to the end product purchased by the food buyer. Whenever a purchasing agent tries to negotiate a price on milk or most dairy products, the dairies generally state that they are not permitted to sell anything for less than a basic fixed price established by the state or the federal government. Actually the federal government does not fix any selling prices except what is paid the farmers for the fluid milk in the original state. Most other price fixing is done by states or area control boards, and in many cases the prices are not mandatory. But in some states, such as California, the prices of fresh milk and cream and most dairy products are "fixed" by the state, and severe penalties are imposed on anyone deviating from this price schedule.

In an industry with so much control and regulation, and with such a product demand, it is not surprising that the competition sometimes leads to conditions that are not entirely ethical or legal. Some dairy companies offer inducements such as free equipment (where it is legal) and liberal expense accounts to both salespeople and clients. In a few cases, rather substantial cash payments for business are offered. The dairy industry is also proficient in bringing business pressure to bear when necessary, and the industry often has substantial connections to local politicians and government bureaus.

The conditions outlined in the above paragraph fortunately occur only in a very small number of cases. In view of the restrictions on the industry, the fact that there are so few irregularities speaks well for the self-policing that the dairy industry has done.

The entire text of this chapter could be taken up with material concerning the dairy industry, but we will restrict the material offered to the basic information a purchasing agent needs to know in buying and handling the dairy products normally used in the food service industry. This material will be offered under the following headings:

Fresh whole milk
Processed milk
Cream
Ice cream and frozen desserts
Butter
Margarine
Cheese
Yogurt

Some Thoughts for the Purchasing Agent

The operation of a dairy company involves a tremendous amount of financing; consequently there are not many marginal dairy companies in business. In many areas, especially in urban and resort areas, these products have to be delivered from considerable distances, and the buyer has to take this into account when selecting a dealer. The buyer must also be ready to pay an additional charge for long delivery distances.

Wherever there is a supermarket, the food buyer can normally find a dairy that operates in the area and can furnish the outlying motel and hotel. It is only in the larger metropolitan areas that the purchasing agent has any choice in selecting a dealer. Buying dairy products is the perfect example of a one-price buying system; the buyer has to look to other factors than price or switching business from one company to another to keep the dairy under control.

The purchasing agent and the dairy company with whom he or she is doing business should have a clear understanding of just what the specifications are for the products that are being purchased. Naturally, any federal, state, or local grade standards should be clearly specified, and periodic checks made to see that the product being delivered meets the standards. Taste tests by a purchasing committee (to which a representative of the dairy company should be invited) also help to prevent disagreements and trouble. Milk and cream tests for butterfat content and coli and bacteria count should be made occasionally by using an outside bonded laboratory specializing in such tests.

Receiving and inspecting dairy products is much simpler today than it was just a few years ago since every milk product is now sanitarily packaged and normally does not exceed the one-gallon size. A lot of time need not be spent checking everything into the premises every day, but a complete count on a random basis once or twice a week by the receiving department helps to insure full delivery of any product.

Fresh milk, cream, and butter will take on odors and tastes from other products very quickly. The worst offenders are blueberries and cantaloupes, quickly followed by fish, cheese, and smoked meats. In planning a hotel, restaurant, or institutional kitchen, the architect should always provide a separate refrigerator for fresh milk products. This refrigerator should have a temperature range from 30° to 40°F. Rotating stock in the dairy refrigerator also helps keep the products fresh. A list of the minimum and maximum stock requirement of each item carried in the dairy box should be posted in a conspicuous place and used in the ordering of dairy products.

A summary of the minimum legal standards for composition (standards of identity) for various dairy products is shown in Exhibit 16-1 to aid in purchasing. Complete details can be found in the *Code of Federal Regulations, Title 21, Parts 100 to 169.*[1]

---

[1] *Code of Federal Regulations, Food and Drugs, Title 21, Parts 100 to 169* (Washington, D.C.: U.S. Government Printing Office, April 1, 1995), pp. 266-295, 347-356.

FRESH MILK

Raw Whole Fresh Milk

Fresh milk just taken from the cows is listed as "raw whole fresh milk" and is seldom found in the public market because of the potential for bacteria, spoilage, and other contamination inherent in the product. Raw whole milk is generally consumed by country families that have a cow or two expressly for the purpose of having this rich product. Raw milk is also sold in certain countries where it is delivered door to door in milk cans strapped to the backs of large dogs or donkeys and is dipped out of the cans by a hand-dipper. Such delivery, of course, is illegal in the United States and should be elsewhere.

Pasteurized and Homogenized Fresh Whole Milk

Most of the fresh fluid milk sold in the United States is pasteurized for sanitary reasons and homogenized so that the milk and its cream do not separate. Fortified milk with additional vitamins is generally classified as vitamin D and/or fortified milk. Each state has its own standards and regulations for whole fluid milk that must meet with the standards set by the U.S. Public Health Service. Usually, states require that milk contain not less than 3.25 percent milk fat and not less than 8.25 percent milk solids. These standards vary from state to state; there are a few states that still require 4 percent butterfat and 10 percent milk solids.

In most modern dairy farms today, the cows on the milking wheel are washed and milked by automatic milkers. The milk is then transported to pasteurization equipment by tubing, where it undergoes one of two pasteurization methods before it is put into bulk containers and sent off to the intended dairy in refrigerated trucks for final processing and packaging. One

Food	Minimum Requirements
Milk	
Fresh whole	3.25 percent milk fat; 8.25 percent milk solids; pasteurization at 145°F–212°F
Ultrapasteurized	Heated to 280°F for at least 2 seconds to extend shelf life
Concentrated	7.5 percent milk fat; 25.5 percent milk solids; prepared by removing about half of the water from whole milk
Evaporated	7.5 percent milk fat; 25 percent milk solids; vitamin D added; homogenized
Sweetened condensed	8.0 percent milk fat; 28.0 percent milk solids; prepared by sweetening and then removing about half of the water from whole milk
Skim	0.5 percent or less milk fat; 8.25 percent milk solids; pasteurized; 2,000 International Units vitamin A
Evaporated, skimmed	0.5 percent or less milk fat; 20 percent milk solids; vitamins A and D added
Sweetened, condensed skim	0.5 percent or less milk fat; 24 percent milk solids; prepared by sweetening and then removing about half of the water from skim milk
Lowfat	0.5 percent, 1.0 percent, 1.5 percent *or* 2 percent fat; 8.25 percent milk solids; pasteurized or ultrapasteurized; 2,000 International Units vitamin A
Nonfat dry	1.5 percent or less milk fat; 5.0 percent or less moisture
Dry, whole	26 percent to less than 40 percent milk fat; 5.0 percent or less moisture; milk solids equal to whole milk
Lowfat dry	5.0 percent to less than 20.0 percent fat; 5.0 percent or less moisture; vitamin A added
Cream	
Heavy or heavy whipping	36 percent milk fat, minimum
Light whipping	30 percent but less than 36.0 percent milk fat
Light	18.0 percent but less than 30.0 percent milk fat
Half and half	10.5 percent but less than 18.0 percent milk fat
Sour	18.0 percent milk fat; 14.4 percent milk fat if sugar or flavoring substance added
Sour half and half	10.5 percent but less than 18.0 percent milk fat
Dry	40.0 percent but less than 75 percent milk fat; 5.0 percent or less moisture
Yogurt	Prepared by adding a bacterial culture to dairy ingredients; flavoring ingredients optional
Lowfat yogurt	0.5 percent but less than 2.0 percent milk fat; 8.25 percent milk solids; prepared by adding a bacterial culture to dairy ingredients; flavoring ingredients optional
Nonfat yogurt	Less than 0.5 milk fat; 8.25 percent milk solids; prepared by adding a bacterial culture to dairy ingredients; flavoring ingredients optional
Eggnog	Prepared from cream, milk, skimmed milk, or a combination of dairy ingredients; egg yolk containing ingredients, and a nutritive sweetener
Frozen desserts	
Ice cream and frozen custard	1.6 pounds total solids per gallon; weight of 4.5 pounds per gallon; 10.0 percent milk fat; 10.0 percent nonfat milk solids; less than 1.4 percent egg yolk solids for ice cream; 1.4 percent egg yolk solids for frozen custard; prepared from a pasteurized mixture of optional dairy ingredients, caseinates, sweetener, and flavorings
Ice milk	2.0 percent but not more than 7.0 percent milk fat; 11.0 percent milk solids; other ingredients similar to ice cream
Sherbet	1.0 percent but not more than 2.0 percent milk fat; 2.0 percent but not more than 5.0 percent nonfat milk solids; weight of 6.0 pounds per gallon; prepared from dairy ingredients, sweeter, and optional fruit ingredients
Water ice	Made with no milk or milk derived ingredients and no ingredient containing egg yolks; may contain egg whites
Mellorine	1.6 pounds total solids per gallon; weight of 4.5 pounds per gallon; 6.0 percent fat; 2.7 percent protein; *may contain animal or vegetable fat*
Goat's milk ice cream or ice milk	Prepared from goat's milk, but other standards similar to those for ice cream and ice milk

Source: *Code of Federal Regulations, Food and Drugs, Title 21, Parts 100 to 169* (Washington, D.C.: U.S. Government Printing Office, April 1, 1995), pp. 266-295, 347-356.

Exhibit 16-1. Distinguishing characteristics of dairy products in terms of legal requirements

accepted method of pasteurization is to raise the temperature of the raw fluid milk to 160°F and to hold it there for 15 seconds, then rapidly chill it down to 45°F. The more commonly used method is to raise the temperature of the raw fluid milk to 145°F, hold it at this temperature a minimum of 30 minutes, then chill it down to 45°F. Both processes kill pathogenic and nonpathogenic organisms and bacteria, making the milk safe for human consumption and aiding in the keeping quality of the milk.

Today, most pasteurized milk is also homogenized. This process breaks up the fat of the milk into tiny globules by forcing it under low heat through a series of very fine openings in a pressure tank. At this point in the processing, most fluid milks today have vitamin D added, as recommended by the Council on Food and Nutrition of the American Medical Association. Milk may also be fortified with vitamins A and B, or minerals, lactose, and, in some instances, nonfat dry milk.

Low-Sodium Milk

With the keen public interest in low-sodium diets, there has been a considerable increase in the sale of low-sodium milk. This is basically whole fresh milk that, through an ionization process, has had the sodium removed and replaced with potassium. The milk is then pasteurized and homogenized.

This low-sodium milk, used in diets that restrict the consumption of salt or other sodium compounds, permits the dieter to have the benefits of milk without danger to health. In addition to being sold fresh, it is also available dried or canned.

Fat Free Milk

Fat free milk is fresh fluid milk that has been almost entirely defatted. Vitamin A, which is removed in the defatting process, and vitamin D are frequently added for fat free milk. The remainder of the nutrients, such as protein, lactose, minerals, and other vitamins, remain in the fat free milk, making it a very healthful food.

2 Percent Milk

For those who want a milk with some butterfat left in it to enhance the taste, a product known as 2 percent milk is on the market that contains 2 percent butterfat with 8 to 10 percent of the milk solids. It is marketed both pasteurized and homogenized and is readily available in the dairy industry.

Buttermilk

Buttermilk used to be the by-product of the churning of cream to produce butter. What was left was sold as buttermilk, and it was a rather sour, grainy product. Today buttermilk is a cultured product and is made from fresh skim milk or from fresh whole milk.

Chocolate Milk

Chocolate milk is generally made with whole pasteurized, homogenized milk containing up to 1½ to 2 percent liquid chocolate plus sugar and stabilizers. It also contains all of the natural elements of whole fresh milk.

Chocolate Dairy Drink

The chocolate dairy drink now on the market is made from skim milk flavored with a chocolate syrup containing about 2½ percent butterfat and the other essential vitamins of skim milk. This product should not be confused with nondairy chocolate drink. This product, while meeting sanitary and other standards, does not have the taste or acceptance that chocolate milk has.

Other Fresh Milk Products

Over a period of time, certain areas of the country have developed localized fresh milk products. A food buyer should be aware that they are available, as in many cases certain diets require the use of these products. Included in this list are soft-curd milk, certified milk, multiple-fortified milk, concentrated fresh milk, concentrated frozen milk, concentrated canned milk, acidophilus or other cultured milks, and yogurt.

Container Sizes for Fresh Fluid Milk

Fresh fluid milk is normally packaged in half-pint, ¾ pint, full pint, quart, half-gallon, and sealed gallon containers. It is also available in 5-gallon plastic containers for use with milk monitors for the larger operation. Skim milk, low-fat milk, buttermilk, and flavored milks are normally available in half-pint, pint, quart, and in some areas, half-gallon containers.

PROCESSED MILK

About 40 percent of the fresh milk supply in the Western world is consumed as fresh milk, and the remainder is processed in various ways, producing a variety of products that are an important part of our food supply. Some of the more important milk products are canned milk, dried milk, butter, ice cream, frozen desserts, and cheese.

Evaporated Milk

Evaporated milk is made from fresh fluid milk that is pasteurized, and the water content is reduced to about 50 percent of the fresh product. The milk is homogenized, and in most cases vitamin D and other vitamins are added before the milk is sterilized and canned. Evaporated milk has a safe shelf life in the can of about one year. However, after opening, evaporated milk should be refrigerated and used within five days.

Sweetened Condensed Milk

Sweetened condensed milk is made much like evaporated milk; however, sugar is reduced. The product has a longer shelf life than evaporated milk, but when opened, it should be refrigerated and used within a week. Because of the high sugar content of this product, its use is more limited than that of evaporated milk. Commercially it is used more for making desserts; in some cases it is mixed with milk and cream and other products to make frozen desserts and whipped toppings.

Dried Whole Milk

Dried whole milk is a milk product from which only the water has been removed, leaving the milk and cream content intact. When reconstituted by the addition of water, the product must contain the same count of butterfat and milk solids as fresh fluid milk. Because this product includes an appreciable amount of cream or butterfat, if it is stored too long or stored under too high a temperature, it may become rancid and unsuitable even for prepared desserts.

Nonfat Dried Milk

This product is consumed in large quantities throughout the Western world. It is basically skim milk that has been pasteurized and homogenized and the water content removed through heat and evaporation. Nonfat dry milk can be used in the making of sauces, pastries, puddings, and other products that might use fresh milk products. This product is also produced in an instant form that is used primarily in the manufacturing of instant chocolate drinks, instant puddings, and other reconstituted desserts.

Malted Milk

Malted milk is a highly concentrated food product that has less than 3.5 percent moisture and a butterfat content of 7.5 to 10 percent. The remaining parts of the product are about 40 percent dried whole milk and 50 percent malt extract. Malted milk is used mostly in health food and soda fountain products and for dietary purposes.

CREAM

Some time back, when Umberto Gatti, the chef of the New York Plaza, was asked why the hotel had a reputation for fine food over the past fifty years, Mr. Gatti, who had been a cook, sous chef, and chef at the hotel for thirty years, promptly replied, "the cooks at the Plaza know when to lay on the butter, eggs, and cream." In the same program, GiGi Molinari, who was the maître d'hôtel at the Plaza and one of the best the hotel industry has ever seen, was asked why he thought the food at the Plaza was the best in New York City at that time. He promptly replied that the Plaza used more butter, eggs, and cream in the kitchen than any other hotel or restaurant in New York City. He also mentioned that the Plaza bought only heavy fresh cream for kitchen and dining room use.

For years, the Waldorf Astoria in New York has had the reputation of serving the best coffee in the city. Their secret was to buy one of the best coffees available, using only two gallons of water to one pound of coffee, and then offer heavy cream for a lightener. This standard was maintained through the entire house including at banquets and in the coffee shop. The kitchen crew had the same coffee and cream that the guests did in the dining room, but management felt that the extra cost was warranted because the cooks were aware of the high quality standards of the hotel. The author knows that this was true because he worked there for some time in the kitchen and can still remember the fine-tasting coffee.

Kinds of Cream and Their Use

The D. LaValle Company developed a cream separator about seventy-five years ago. Today the same system for separating cream from whole milk is used but in a more sophisticated and speedy manner. In this process, the cream or milk fat is separated from the whole fresh milk by centrifugal force and is then put up in sterile containers for distribution or for processing into dehydrated or frozen cream. The cream is derived from pasteurized but not homogenized fresh milk. Cream in itself does not separate unless diluted heavily with other products.

Coffee cream is generally packaged in small individual containers that measure from ½ to 2 ounces, and the cream in this container generally is half-and-half. These products are pure dairy products and should not be confused with the nondairy cream substitutes sold in the same type of package. Half-and-half, as the name implies, is half light cream and half milk with a butterfat content of 10 percent or slightly higher. Table cream (or coffee or light cream) must contain 16 to 18 percent butterfat, and medium cream is usually 24 to 26 percent butterfat but can go somewhat higher. Whipping cream normally contains 32 to 36 percent butterfat, and heavy whipping cream should contain 36 to 40 percent butterfat. Sour cream normally has a butterfat content of 16 to 20 percent and contains a lactic acid of up to two-tenths of a percent by liquid measure.

The various cream products are marketed in half-pint, pint, quart, half-gallon, and gallon containers, but the larger containers are distributed only to the larger commercial operations. Half-and-half cream and light cream can be obtained in 5-gallon plastic containers that fit a refrigerated milk and cream dispenser known as a milk monitor. This equipment ensures sanitary milk and cream dispensing and saves on packaging and delivery. In some instances the cost of the product is 30 to 40 percent less than when delivered in the smaller packages.

ICE CREAM AND FROZEN DESSERTS

Not too long ago, America was known for baseball, apple pie with ice cream, and

Chevrolets. Times have changed, and now America is known for football, light beer with pretzels, and Toyotas. But the great all-American dessert is still apple pie and ice cream. Until recent regulations were passed, however, "ice cream" could also mean ice milk, frozen custard, frozen soybean oil dessert, storage-butter ice cream, frozen palm-oil dessert, and of course, melorine-type frozen dessert. (To most customers, this means margarine.)

Truth-in-advertising laws have prompted the establishment of federal and state standards for ice cream and other frozen products, which is making it more difficult for some of the substitute products to be merchandised as ice cream. All of these products, however, are perfectly healthful and are apparently meeting the public's demand for a frozen dessert at a reasonable price. (In this case, the public is mostly composed of children and teenagers.) However, extensive tests have been made in which frozen custard and ice cream were both offered in drive-ins. Surprisingly, ice cream proved to be the more popular seller. In sit-down restaurants, even though frozen desserts other than ice cream have been tried, it is difficult to find any first-class restaurant or food service that offers anything other than ice cream today.

Current sales records show that ice cream is by far the most popular dessert in the United States food service industry. Vanilla is the most popular flavor, followed by chocolate, strawberry, and the three-flavor brick of chocolate, vanilla, and strawberry. Following these three most popular flavors, there is coffee, butter pecan, chocolate chip, burnt almond, peppermint stick, and a host of other specialties.

Milk sherbets and pure fruit ices are regular stand-bys and are offered on most first-class menus for those who wish to watch calories or avoid dairy products. Ice milk is gaining in popularity because of its low calories and comparatively low price.

In the past, ice milk had to contain at least 10 percent milk fat, but recently some states have permitted the manufacture of ice milk with a milk fat content of as low as 8 percent. French ice cream is the same as regular ice cream plus it must contain at least 1.4 percent egg solids by weight. When diluted by flavors, the egg solids have to be at least 1.125 percent.

Because of cost, premium ice creams are not always easy to find, but they are still available in the better class of food services. A premium ice cream used to contain 18 percent butterfat, 40 percent milk solids, and had an overrun of 60 to 80 percent. (Overrun means that a gallon of ice cream mix, when frozen, produces 1.6 to 1.8 gallons of ice cream because of the air mixed in during the freezing process.) One well-known company tried for quite a while to manufacture and sell a 22 percent butterfat vanilla ice cream. However, more often than not the ice cream turned into butter, and this plan had to be abandoned. Today any ice cream with a butterfat content of 14 percent or more is considered a premium ice cream, but there are still a number of premium ice creams that have a butterfat content of 16 to 18 percent with as high as 35 percent milk solids and a 60 to 80 percent overrun.

It is possible to have an 18-percent-butterfat ice cream and still come up with a very poor product because of the flavoring used. The majority of premium and good ice creams used the natural vanilla bean for flavoring before the country of Madagascar raised the price of pure vanilla beans some 5000 percent recently. Afterwards, the ice cream industry got busy and produced an artificial vanilla extract that produces a very satisfactory flavor. Some manufacturers try to keep prices down by substituting poor flavorings, some natural and some artificial, which has detracted from the whole concept of premium ice cream.

A Warning

Most ice creams and frozen desserts manufactured in the United States can be eaten by the public without anxiety about sanitation because of our high standards of manufacturing and inspection. But bacteria and coli can grow at amazing rates in ice cream and frozen desserts even though they are frozen solid. American standards for ice cream and frozen desserts state that the product cannot contain more than a 50,000-bacteria count per milliliter and not more than a 10-coliform count per milliliter. A smart food buyer or food operator should have milk, cream, butter, and frozen desserts checked by a licensed sanitary consulting firm since there is always the possibility of slipshod work regardless of the good intentions of the manufacturer and the standards of sanitation set by state and federal government.

In the tables in the appendices we have summarized some of the standards for dairy products in the United States. These standards will vary in some states, but on the whole they are current and acceptable for reference.

BUTTER

Until recently, most food service personnel thought that butter was an essential ingredient for cooking and for dining room service. But because of anxiety about cholesterol content and the price of butter, other products are now considered as substitutes. Butter is still generally the product of choice for most commercial food services, but margarine and other butter substitutes are being used more often by institutional services.

Products other than margarine that are being used in food preparation are products made from all-vegetable oils and fats, lard, combinations of animal and vegetable fats and oils, peanut oil, cottonseed oil, palm oil, and safflower oil. Recently a cooking product has come on the market that is part margarine and part butter. But in spite of costs, most first-class food operations and hotel and restaurant kitchens continue to use all butter in their food preparation. Some use butter substitutes for sauces and sautéed dishes, but when it comes to flavoring vegetables, cooking fish, and making pastries, there is no other product suitable for high-class food service.

What Is Butter?

Federal standards require that butter contain not less than 80 percent milk fat with 15 percent moisture and the remaining 5 percent milk solids, salt, coloring, and a small amount of stabilizer. The milk used in the butter-making process must be pasteurized at temperatures of not less than 165 to 185°F for as long as 30 minutes at 165°F or as little as 15 seconds at the higher temperatures. After pasteurization, the milk is treated with a milk acid to curdle it, and then the churning process produces the butterfat. The buttermilk that is left is then drained off and sold. The butter product is worked, colored, flavored if necessary, then graded, packaged, and marketed.

Grades of Butter

The best and highest-priced butter is sweet cream butter that is made exclusively from fresh pasteurized cream. It is generally scored double A or 93 score. This product contains no salt and because of this, the product has a short shelf life and is best used within five days after receipt from the distributor. This butter is often served in gourmet restaurants and in any food service establishment that follows kosher dietary laws.

Normally butter is scored AA (93 score), grade A (92 score), grade B (90 score), and grade C (89 score). Butter that does not score at least 89 or grade C still moves in the commercial market but is generally used in manufactured products. Butter is scored on the basis of flavor, body, salt, color, and packaging. Aroma is considered a part of flavor, and flavor is the basic determinant of the quality of butter.

The federal or state grader, who has to be trained and skilled in the grading of butter, assigns a grade to each "run" of butter, which is then packaged bearing the grade. Of course, the grade of butter is determined only at the time of grading. However, if butter is kept for any length of time, even in the most ideal refrigerated conditions, the actual grade will drop until the product can become unfit for consumption unless reworked and clarified.

The millions of pounds of butter stored by the government as the result of the milk support program are not normally part of the regular commercial chain of distribution of butter and butter products in the United States. However, these products are sold or given to certain countries, and recently the government has been giving huge quantities of storage butter to Americans on welfare.

Packaging of Butter

Butter is marketed in a wide variety of packages. Butter can be bought for table and dining room service in 5-pound packages with the butter pats cut into 60, 72, and 90 pats per pound. In some areas, the butter pats can be purchased foil wrapped for sanitary reasons, and this product is especially useful for hotel or motel room service. This product can be obtained in 48- to 90-count pats per pound.

Butter is also marketed in quarter-pound prints, pound prints, 30-pound cubes, and 64-pound cubes. Butter used in some commercial and manufacturing processes is shipped by the barrel or 100-pound cubes.

MARGARINE

Margarine is a fatty food made by blending fats and oils with other ingredients such as milk solids, salt, flavorings, vitamins, and coloring products. The government describes margarine as a "food, plastic in form, which consists of one or more of the various approved vegetable or animal fats mixed with cream." Good margarine contains at least 80 percent approved fats and not more than 15 percent moisture and 4 percent salt.

Margarine is not low in fat content; in fact, early margarines were almost as high in saturated fats as butter. However, now the majority of premium margarine products contain high levels of polyunsaturated fats with high iodine content. These special margarines contain up to 40 percent less unsaturated fats, as compared to regular margarines, and the iodine value in the special margarines can be as much as 30 percent higher than in regular margarine products.

Margarine is packaged and sold in the same way as butter, but it is not graded as strictly. Federal inspection of margarine is generally limited to an inspection for quality and suitability for consumption. Margarine sold to the public must be packaged so that the contents are clearly identifiable. Federal grading is not common for margarine products; however, some states provide a grading service and actually require the product to be identified by grade as well as quality.

CHEESE

Cheese has been around since early humans put thoughts down on papyrus, but which civilization started making cheese first has been impossible to determine. Some historians say that cheese was first made by the Phoenicians or the Greeks. We do know that cheese was mentioned in a Greek cookbook written by Apacus about 400 B.C. It is likely that the earliest cheese making resulted from the desire to use up excess milk and to ease the problem of storage and transportation of milk.

Today, cheese is a universal food, and every country has its own local cheese and also has access to many of the better-known cheeses on the market. The number of cheeses in the world today is actually unknown, but the *Larousse Gastronomique* states that there are more than one thousand registered brands and names of cheeses, plus all the local cheeses that never leave their own community. France alone has over seven hundred registered names. Although cheese is most commonly made from cow's milk, it is also made from the milk of goats, ewes, mares, camels, buffalo, and reindeer.

Most cheese is a good source of protein but is also high in fat and cholesterol. The average processed cheese is 30 to 40 percent milk fat, soft cheeses are 40 to 60 percent fat, and hard cheeses are from 30 to 42 percent fat. Cottage cheese made in the United States is normally about 80 percent moisture, 4 percent milk fat, and the balance milk solids. Cottage cheese made with only 2 percent milk fat is available for those on low-calorie diets. Cream cheese, which is extremely popular in the United States, has 30 to 35 percent milk fat, but cream cheese in other parts of the world may have up to 60 percent milk fat.

The average portion of cheese served as a separate course is from 1½ to 2 ounces, which means the portion has from 150 to 200 calories. When you add this to the 450 to 500 calories in a piece of homemade apple pie, one can see that cheese is not on the normal reducing diet. In fact, people with high blood pressure and vascular problems are advised to stay away from eating cheese completely. Lowfat cottage cheese, of course, is the general exception to this rule.

Cheese used to be a low-cost protein and meat substitute, but the price of cheese has risen to the point that it is now almost considered a luxury (the more exotic cheeses are definitely a luxury). The average price of cheese today varies between $2.00 and $8.00 per pound, and, if one wants to look for the exotic, the price can get as high as $18 to $20 per pound. Cottage cheese, sometimes known as farmer's cheese, is still a good buy at $1 to $1.50 per pound.

Cheese for Cooking

The cheeses used in cooking cover a large range of types. The most commonly used cooking cheese in the United States is the American cheddar, which varies from mild to sharp. Also used are brick cheese, both yellow and white, colby, Monterey jack, ricotta, Swiss, Parmesan and Romano, provolone, American processed, processed cheese food, and cottage cheese. American bleu cheese—and in some cases Gorgonzola and Roquefort cheeses—are used in salad dressings. (If "Roquefort cheese" dressing is listed on a menu, it must be made with true Roquefort cheese, or the eating place could be subject to lawsuit by the Roquefort cheese cartel in France.) Probably the most popular cooking cheese in the United States is Velveeta, which is a processed American cheddar-type cheese.

The consumption of cheese in the United States is about 45 percent cheddar and cheddar-type cheese, 38 to 40 percent cottage cheese, and 15 to 17 percent other types of cheeses. About 20 percent of the cheese sold in the United States is imported. Most of the imported cheese is from France. However, a great deal of cheese is imported from Italy, especially cooking cheese. Cheese imported from Italy is mostly of the hard-cooked and dried type, such as Parmesan, Romano, provolone, mozzarella, ricotta, scamorze, and sargo. Provolone and sargo are made from ewe's milk, and scamorze is made from buffalo milk.

Serving Cheese in the Dining Room

A few short years ago, it was almost impossible to give cheese away in the dining room, let alone sell it. However, operators looking for ways to spruce up their food service, started to use cheese in various forms, and today cheese is a major part of the menu in most first-class dining rooms and restaurants. The operators found that using cheese as an accompaniment to other foods and as part of buffet and salad bar service worked better than trying to sell cheese as a separate course at high prices.

Some of the ways cheese is being used today are briefly outlined as follows.

Nibbling cheese—these cheeses are used for snacking at home and in bars and dining rooms in restaurants. American cheddar and domestic Swiss cut into cubes and cold pack or club cheeses served in earthenware crocks are the most popular of these cheeses.

Snacks and hors d'oeuvres—cheese makers have found a bonanza in mixing cheese to acquire a cosmetic look, and they are now offering snack and hors d'oeuvre cheese mixed with dried fruits, nuts, and various smoked sausages and cured meats.

Cheese with the salad course—this service is a standard with formal banquet dinners. The after-the-main-course green salad is generally accompanied by a soft cheese such as Camembert accompanied by some hot, crusty, freshly toasted french bread. Of course, bleu cheese dressing on salads is well known and very popular.

Salad bar and buffet service—cheese has become a very popular part of salad bar and buffet service. A cheese board can be offered with these services with eight to ten cheeses, and it will often be selected as a substitute for dessert.

Table service of cheese—serving a variety of cheeses from a tableside wagon is gaining in popularity. Some service includes a glass of port or madeira wine plus fresh fruit and a variety of imported biscuits.

Almost everyone is familiar with a good piece of cheddar cheese served with fresh apple or other fresh-fruit pie or cobblers. In some parts of the country, these cheeses are known as "rat cheese," and no one apologizes for the name. One of the best all around American cheeses for home and public dining room service is the black diamond cheddar cheese made in Vermont. It is a light yellow cheese aged almost one year and comes in wheels as small as 1 pound to as large as 50 pounds. It is not an inexpensive cheese, but it is becoming very popular for wine and cheese bars and for gift giving.

Cheese is being used increasingly by the better resort hotels as an accompaniment for after-dinner coffee and cordials in the lobby during the proverbial after-dinner concert. This service is very popular in the northeastern part of the country, both in summer and ski resorts. Dry white wines, such as chablis, Leibfraumilch or Bernkastler, go well with practically any cheese. Some people prefer a burgundy or a dry red wine with the stronger cheeses such as Stilton or an aged English cheddar.

THE MAKING OF CHEESE

The basic method of making most cheeses is the same; the variations are produced by the use of different starters, acids, natural fermentation, and bacteria. A summary of how American cheddar cheese is made will give an idea of the basic steps in cheese making.

1. Fresh whole cow's milk is pasteurized to 145°F for about 30 minutes and then cooled to 85 to 88°F. Lactic acid is added during the cooling process.
2. A coloring material is added to the cheese curd to meet certain color standards.
   Rennet is added to curdle the milk further, and in about 30 minutes the entire mass becomes a large curd.

4. The temperature is raised to 100°F, and this is called "cooking." Temperatures can be raised to as high as 150°F to produce the harder cheeses.

5. As soon as the proper "cooking" temperature is reached, the mass is drained, leaving a large flexible bulk of cheese curd. This curd is cut in strips 8 to 10 inches square and about three feet long to make it easier to handle.

6. The curds are milled, salted, and placed in special molds. At this point, special bacterias can be added to produce specialty cheeses.

7. These molds are refrigerated for about two weeks to dry, and then they are paraffined and put in curing rooms to age.

Club or cold pack cheeses generally found in crocks are mostly ground cheddar cheeses with about 10 percent butter added. Some are flavored with wines, and others are mixed with other cheeses, nuts, and cured meats. These products are then pasteurized and sold in crocks. However, the user must keep in mind that these cheeses need constant refrigeration.

Processed cheese foods are a blend of various cheeses mixed with cream and other stabilizers; generally they are not aged. These products are very useful for cooking. They dissolve easily, resist curdling, and cost about half as much as regular cheddar cheese.

Classification of Cheeses

Cheeses are classified as hard, semihard, and soft. Hard cheese can be aged from 3 to 12 months, depending on the type; some cheeses are aged as long as sixteen months.

A complete listing of federal definitions and standards of identity can be found in the U.S. *Code of Federal Regulations, Title 21, Parts 100 to 169.*[2]

[2] *Code of Federal Regulations, Food and Drugs, Title 21, Parts 100 to 169,* (Washington D.C.: U.S. Government Printing Office, April 1, 1995), pp. 295-347.

Examples of hard cheeses are the Parmesan and Romano that are grated and used on lasagna, spaghetti, pizza, or hot bread. These cheeses are also sprinkled on soups and salads and used in making au gratin dishes. Some aged English cheddar cheeses are also classified as hard cheeses.

Semihard cheeses are ripened from 2 to 8 months and are used both for cooking and dining room table service. Some examples of semihard cheeses are the American cheddar, colby, Monterey jack, Swiss, provolone, Cheshire, Edam, and the French cantal.

Soft and semisoft cheeses are aged from 1 to 5 months, and certain soft cheeses, such as cottage, cream cheese, ricotta, and Neufchâtel, are not aged at all. Some of the better known semisoft cheeses are Brie, Camembert, Roquefort, bleu cheese, American, brick, and mozzarella.

Cheeses are also classified according to the following groupings. American cheddar is classified as *current,* which means that the cheese has been aged less than thirty days. *Medium* cheddar has been aged 30 to 180 days, and *cured* or *aged* cheddar is cheese that is aged over 180 days. Swiss cheese is *current* if it has been aged under ninety days, *medium* if aged from ninety days to six months, and *cured* or *aged* if aged over six months.

The shelf life of most cheeses, when kept under refrigeration, varies from a week to ten days for certain soft cheeses to over a year for Parmesan and Romano. Parmesan cheese can actually be kept at room temperature for about a year.

It is wise for the food buyer to plan his stock so that no cheese should be kept in the storeroom, even refrigerated, for over one month. Semisoft cheeses such as Camembert, Muenster, and Edam can be safely stored for 2 to 3 weeks under refrigeration. However, the softest cheeses, such as cream, cottage, farmer's, and pot cheese, should not be kept in the storeroom refrigerator for more than ten days.

Grading Cheese

Federal standards for grading certain American-made cheeses are summarized in the following list.

Cheddar—AA, A, B, C.
Colby and longhorn (cheddar type)—AA, A, B.
Monterey jack—AA, A, B.
American Swiss—A, B, C, D.

American-made cheeses are basically graded on factors of flavor, body, texture, and color. Flavors range from very mild for the fresh cheese to a well-developed, slightly acid taste for the cured or aged cheese. The body of the cheese should be smooth, firm, and slightly waxy and should not be crumbly or weak in texture. The color of the cheese should be typical for the type of cheese and should meet certain color chart specifications used by the federal grader.

Variety	Characteristics	Usage
Cheddar	White to orange interior. Semihard. Mild to sharp flavor. Many varied colors and coatings on exterior.	Great favorite on appetizer trays. With crackers, on pie, in sandwiches, in salads, in cooked dishes.
Colby	Light cream to yellow interior. Mild to mellow flavor. Firm, soft texture.	Flavorful mild sandwich cheeses. As appetizers and in cooked foods and salads.
Monterey Jack	White to light cream interior. Mild to mellow flavor. Firm, soft texture.	
Bleu	Gourmet cheeses for average budget. Tangy piquant flavor. Blue veined with crumbly semisoft texture.	In salads and salad dressings, in dips, on tray assortments, and with fruit for dessert.
Gorgonzola		
Brick	Creamy-yellow interior. Mild to sharp flavor. Semisoft.	"The nibbling cheeses." Great in a sandwich (especially on dark bread), on appetizer trays, with crackers, for dessert.
Muenster	Light yellow interior. Mild. Usually orange exterior. Semisoft.	
Edam	Red-wax coated. Mild nutlike flavor. Semisoft creamy yellow interiors.	Favorites for all ages. Colorful basis for cheese trays, in salads, in cooked dishes, in sandwiches.
Gouda		
Limburger	Pungent full flavor. Aromatic. Soft-textured creamy white interior, brownish exterior.	Wonderful on rye and pumpernickel, with snack items.
Port du Salut	Full rich flavor. Creamy texture. Brownish exterior, creamy yellow interior. Robust flavor.	Epicurean's delight. Serve with raw fruit, as dessert, on crackers, on cheese tray.
Ricotta	White, soft, moist, and grainy in texture. Bland but semisweet flavor.	In salads and dips. In cooking—especially Italian dishes such as lasagna, manicotti, ravioli. In desserts—cheese cake, cannoli.
Swiss	The "large eye" cheese. Light yellow color. Mild nutlike flavor. Firm.	A "must" sliced thin with cold meats. In salads, fondue, cooked dishes, sandwiches.
Parmesan	Creamy white interior. Very hard. Granular texture. Mild, nutty flavor. Grated for use.	Serve grated in lasagna, spaghetti, pizza, in or on breads. Sprinkle on soups and salads.
Romano	Yellowish white interior. Sharp, full flavor. Very hard. Granular texture. Grated for use.	

Exhibit 16-2. A food buyer's guide to domestic cheese

Variety	Characteristics	Usage
Provolone	Mellow to sharp, with smoky tang. Light creamy interior. Firm; smooth and somewhat plastic.	Favorite snack cheese. An appetizer, in cooked dishes, for dessert.
Scamorze / Mozzarella	Delicate, creamy white interior. Mild, slightly firm, but elastic texture. When heated, becomes stringy or stretchy.	In pizza and lasagna, in grilled sandwiches and cheeseburgers, in cooked dishes (meat loaf, casseroles).
Process	A pasteurized blend of natural cheeses uniform in flavor. Melts easily and quickly. Many varieties produced.	Versatile favorite. In sandwiches—grilled or not. In casseroles, on trays (try with cold cuts), in salads.
Club or Cold Pack	A blend of natural cheeses—may be flavored. Not pasteurized. Spreads and melts easily. Comes in various containers.	Always ready for the appetizer tray. With celery, on crackers.

Exhibit 16-2 *(continued)*

Name	Description	Uses	Wines
Bel Paese (I)	Soft, sweet, mild cheese made near Milan. A type of Bel Paese is made in the United States.	With bread or crackers. Appetizer, dessert, buffet, good for cooking.	Dry red, white
Brie (F)	Soft cheese with distinctive flavor. Similar cheeses are made elsewhere, including the United States.	With bread or crackers. Appetizer, buffet, dessert.	Dry red
Camembert (F)	Soft cheese with distinctive flavor. Similar cheeses are made elsewhere, including the United States.	With bread, crackers, fruit. Appetizer, dessert, cooking, buffet.	Dry red
Cantal (F)	Hard yellow cheese with piquant flavor and firm, close body.	With bread or crackers. Appetizer, buffet, dessert.	Dry red
Cheddar (E, U.S.)	English cheddar not generally available in the United States. American cheddar ranges from mild to sharp.	With bread or crackers. Appetizer, buffet, dessert, cooking, sandwiches.	Dry red
Cheshire (E)	Firm, cylindrical, salty, moist cheese not successfully imitated. Comes in red or white.	With bread or crackers. Appetizer, salads, cooking, dessert, buffet.	Dry red
Edam (N)	Ball-shaped with red rind. Semisoft to hard, with mild flavor and crumbly body.	With bread or crackers. Buffet, dessert.	Dry red, white
Emmenthal (S)	The original "Swiss cheese"; sweet, nutty flavor, made in the Emme Valley.	With bread or crackers. Buffet, sandwiches, cooking.	Dry red, white
Fontina (I)	Semisoft to hard cheese with nutty flavor and light brown crust. Made in Valley of Aosta.	With bread or crackers. Buffet, cooking (especially good in fondue), dessert.	Dry red, white
Gorgonzola (I)	Soft, blue-green veined cheese with strong flavor, made in Lombardy and Piedmont.	With crackers or bread. Appetizer, salad, dessert, buffet.	Red
Gouda (N)	Semisoft to hard sweet cheese. Wheel shaped with yellow casing.	With bread or crackers. Buffet, dessert.	Dry red, white

Country of Origin
(B) Belgium
(E) England
(F) France
(G) Germany
(I) Italy
(N) Netherlands
(S) Switzerland
(U.S.) United States

Exhibit 16-3 . A food buyer's guide for imported cheese

(Courtesy of Disabled American Veterans)

Name	Description	Uses	Wines
Gruyère (F,S)	Mild, nutty cheese similar to Emmenthal, with sharper flavor and brown, wrinkled skin.	With bread or crackers. Buffet, sandwiches, cooking (especially fondue).	Dry red, white
Liederkranz (U.S.)	Soft, very strong cheese similar to Limburger in body, flavor, and aroma.	Dark bread, onions. Sandwiches.	White
Limburger (B,G)	Semisoft cheese with strong flavor and aroma. Also made elsewhere, including the United States.	Dark bread, onions. Sandwiches.	White
Muenster (F,U.S.)	European variety is fairly strong, semisoft. American munster is milder and melts well.	With bread or crackers. Buffet, sandwiches, cooking.	Dry red
Neufchâtel (F)	Soft mild cheese, used either fresh or cured. American variety is moister and spreads well.	With bread or crackers. Appetizer, dessert, sandwiches.	White
Parmesan (I)	Hard, grainy cheese. Two major varieties: Parmigiano-Reggiano (true Parmesan), Grana Padano. Keeps for years at a time.	With bread or crackers. Dessert, grated, cooking.	White
Pont l'Eveque (F)	Distinguished semisoft cheese made in Normandy, not successfully imitated elsewhere.	With bread or crackers. Appetizer, buffet, dessert.	Red
Port Salut (F)	Creamy, yellow cheese that varies from mild to strong flavor with age.	With bread or crackers. Appetizer, buffet, dessert.	Dry red
Ricotta (I)	White, mild, creamy cheese similar to creamed cottage cheese.	Appetizer, salad, cooking (especially for stuffing pasta), desserts.	White
Roquefort (F)	Blue-veined semihard cheese. Sharp, pungent flavor. American bleu cheese is somewhat similar.	With bread or crackers. Appetizer, salad, dessert, buffet, cooking.	Red
Stilton (E)	Blue-green veined cheese of pebbly consistency. Rich, mellow, milder than Roquefort.	With bread or crackers. Buffet, dessert.	Red
Valencay (F)	Soft goat's milk cheese, pyramid shaped with strong flavor.	With bread or crackers. Appetizer, buffet, dessert, sandwiches.	Red

Exhibit 16-3 (*continued*)

YOGURT

Yogurt is cultured milk. Cultures are living organisms. The U.S. Food and Drug Administration (FDA) has set standards that require the use of two live active bacterial cultures—*Lactobacillus bulgaricus* (*L. bulgaricus*) and *Streptococcus thermophilus* (*S. thermophilus*)—to produce a product labeled "yogurt." When added to milk, these bacterial cultures convert the milk sugar (lactose) into lactic acid. This action changes the liquid milk into a custardlike substance—yogurt—that has a refreshingly tart taste.

Dannon adds a third culture to all of its refrigerated yogurts—*Lactobacillus acidophilus* (*L. acidophilus*). *L. acidophilus* is naturally present inside the human gastrointestinal tract. Of the three most commonly used cultures in yogurt, acidophilus has the strongest ability to survive the acid environment in the stomach to reach the intestines and replenish the body's own natural supply of *L. acidophilus*.

How Yogurt Is Made

Even though yogurt has only two basic ingredients—milk and bacterial cultures (some varieties include fruit), making yogurt is a complex process. Following is a step-by-step process of how Dannon makes yogurt:

1. Milk is skimmed to reduce the fat

content. After skimming, it becomes 98 to 99 percent fat free.

2. Nonfat milk solids are added to the skimmed milk to increase the protein content.

3. The milk mixture is then homogenized and pasteurized (flash-heated) in sterilized steel tanks. Pasteurization takes place before the yogurt cultures are added, since heat-treating deactivates the cultures and reduces the healthful properties of yogurt.

4. Live active yogurt cultures—*L. bulgaricus* and *S. thermophilus*—are added to the milk. In addition, Dannon Fruit on the Bottom, Plain, Classic Flavors and Blended varieties also contain a third culture, *L. acidophilus*. These cultures are carefully developed in the laboratories by yogurt technologists.

5. For set yogurts (Plain, Fruit on the Bottom, and Classic Flavors), the cultured milk is immediately piped into the cups with the appropriate fruits or flavors. The filled cups are then placed in cardboard boxes and stored in incubators for several hours. During this time, the yogurt cultures produce lactic acid, which causes the protein in the milk to coagulate and thicken. This action changes the liquid milk into a solid custardlike yogurt.

6. For blended yogurts, the cultured milk is incubated in a large vat. Once the yogurt has reached its custardlike stage, it is blended with fruit or flavor and then piped into individual containers.

7. The yogurt is then cooled overnight in refrigeration rooms at precisely controlled temperatures to preserve quality and to protect the highly perishable yogurt cultures. After cooling, the yogurt is ready for consumption.

REFERENCE

Code of Federal Regulations, Title 21, Parts 100 to 169. Washington, D.C.: U.S. Government Printing Office, 1995.

17 Convenience Foods

Purpose: To summarize the current situation regarding the supply and use of convenience foods so that management can determine the degree to which these foods should be used and the best ways to use them.

INTRODUCTION

Most foods purchased have some degree of "convenience" to them. Purchased ice cream is certainly a convenience food since the alternative is to make it yourself. Canned vegetables and fruits are also "convenience foods." But the term *convenience* is more often used for prepared dishes, particularly entrees and desserts that are purchased frozen. The advantage of these products is that they allow a greater degree of predictability, for the cost "in the back door" is basically the cost "on the plate." This has been the basic impetus behind the rapid growth of this category in recent years. It is expected that this growth will continue, and food and beverage operators will need to have a thorough understanding of the nature of convenience products and how to evaluate their cost and operating impact.

When a discussion of convenience foods comes up among a group of culinarians, it is difficult to get them to agree on a definition of convenience foods. Sooner or later, the group will be divided by three opinions:

1. The fast food operators do not have much trouble defining convenience food. It is raw-ready to ready food that requires minimum preparation and service.

2. Hotel operators and tablecloth restaurant owners will argue that convenience foods are entrees that are either partially or fully prepared and require only some reconstitution or heating to be ready to serve.

3. Food service managers for hospitals, schools, and institutional food services seem to have a better understanding of the use of convenience foods. They understand that canned goods and many frozen items are convenience foods but have been used so much they are accepted as standard foods. Consequently, they discount them in their discussions. To this group, convenience food primarily means convenience entrees and such items as vegetables prepared with a sauce or in a scalloped dish, precut and stuffed chicken breasts, fillets of fish, potato dishes, and a variety of breads and pastries. Many are fully prepared and others need final processing.

The fact is that large percentages of

283

convenience foods are being used throughout the entire food service industry, ranging from almost 100 percent in fast food operations to 50 percent in the institutional trade down to 15 to 20 percent in the hotel and tablecloth restaurant food service industry.

Convenience foods, depending upon the definition of the term, have been available for many years. Through much of that time they have prompted controversy within the industry, and there is as yet no firm consensus as to their acceptability in use. There is not even a universally accepted, exact definition of the term *convenience food.* However, for the purpose of this discussion, the following definition is offered: *a convenience food item is one in which all or part of the labor otherwise necessary for preparation is "built into" the product prior to purchase.* If this definition is accepted, a convenience food item is one that requires *less* on-site labor to prepare or otherwise make ready for service than would its nonconvenience counterpart.

TYPES OF CONVENIENCE FOODS

According to Bruno Maizel, there are three major types of convenience foods:

Minimally processed—food items that have some processing labor built in but that require additional on-site labor. They are generally designed to eliminate some semiskilled labor. Examples: peeled, whole potatoes; shredded, cleaned cabbage; various vegetable salad ingredients.

Partially processed—food items processed more extensively where profitable use is often related to such nonlabor factors as waste, by-products of processing, personnel scheduling. Examples: preportioned meats and entrees; breaded fish products.

Completely processed—the undisputed "convenience" foods that require little, if any, further preparation after purchase.

Examples: salad dressings; frozen, fresh-baked pies.

Minimally processed items can often be evaluated according to standards used to evaluate fresh products. Partially processed items should be evaluated relative to their suitability for the operation. There are, however, different criteria for completely processed products, and they are examined later in this chapter.

Many terms are used when referring to convenience foods, including fast foods, efficiency foods, ready-to-serve foods, ready service foods, frozen foods, prepared foods. Some of these terms are inaccurate when applied to the broader concept of convenience foods. For instance, not all convenience foods are frozen. Nor are all convenience foods ready to serve since some preparation may be necessary prior to service. It is this inability to arrive at an accepted definition which, in part, contributes to the continuing controversy over convenience foods.

For example, a purchaser may well encounter complaints about the poor quality of a preprepared, frozen beef stew because the establishment lacks the equipment to reheat it satisfactorily. If so, he should be aware of other market forms or intermediate types of products. In the case of a beef stew, there are canned products available, or it might be better to purchase intermediate components such as precut beef cubes, a prepared base for the gravy, canned vegetables, dehydrated chopped onion pieces and to incorporate these items into the beef stew recipe. The point is that there are many options, and, if any one or a combination of these products proves acceptable, the purchaser may well be less resistant to the general idea of using convenience foods. A negative bias toward one form (frozen) might be offset by the availability and suitability of other types of nonfrozen, convenience food products.

Perhaps it would be more helpful to consider convenience foods in terms of a raw-to-ready scale devised by B. Smith. The concept is based on the amount of on-site labor required before a food item is ready to serve. The linear (straight-line) scale or continuum begins with 1 and ends with 10, as shown below:

Raw   *Ready*

1   2   3   4   5   6   7   8   9   10

The higher on the scale a food item appears, the less on-site labor is required to prepare it for service. Conversely, an item that is placed at or close to the beginning of the scale requires more on-site labor before it can be served. Judgments as to where specific items appear on a raw-to-ready scale are frequently arbitrary. Exhibit 17-1 gives examples placed on points 1, 5, and 10 of the scale. The exhibit serves to indicate that there is a broad spectrum of convenience products available for purchase and that there are alternative forms of many individual items.

Many food items commonly considered convenience foods lie somewhere between point 5 (perhaps the point at which a food item that is somewhat complicated to prepare is made considerably less difficult to prepare) and point 10 (ready to serve). For example, canned and frozen vegetables, as well as other items, must generally be opened or unpackaged, placed into a pan or vessel for heating, and portioned prior

to serving, and the vessel must also be washed. Preparing these items for service is somewhat more complicated or at least more time consuming than it is for items close to or at point 10 on the scale.

Perhaps, with some exceptions in individual operations, items at point 10, which represents the epitome of convenience, are perishable in nature and tend to be purchased for immediate use rather than for inventory or storage purposes. Other items—fresh fruits, nuts, and other natural foods—might also be placed at point 10 on the scale, but even they require some preparation (washing, shelling, sorting) before service. They have been excluded from the raw-to-ready scale in order to satisfy the definition of convenience foods that does not consider items for which no alternative market forms are generally available.

When individual food items are considered higher on the raw-to-ready scale, this indicates that less on-site labor is necessary. For example, one might choose to purchase primal meat cuts that require in-house processing or bulk ground beef or portioned meat patties or even precooked, portioned meat patties. Each choice affects the amount of on-site labor required.

Where on the continuum a food product falls must be determined for each food service operation, and the purchaser must

Raw		Ready
1	5	10
Primal meat cuts	Preportioned, uncooked, ground meat patties	Baked pies, cookies, and other desserts
Flour, shortening, yeast, etc., used in preparation of bread and roll items	Frozen bread dough and related products	Baked, sliced bread
Fresh fruits and vegetables to be used in salads	Canned tomato and other sauces used as a base for on-site preparation of house sauces	Canned, ready-to-serve pie fillings and puddings
Oils, seasonings, etc., to be used in house salad dressings	"Instant" rice, macaroni, and similar products	Sweet rolls and doughnuts
Fresh whole (round) fish to be butchered on-site	Gravy bases and similar products that are built up to yield finished gravy and sauce products	Ice cream and prepared toppings
		Bottled salad dressings
		Milk and similar products

Exhibit 17-1. The location of sample food items on a raw-to-ready scale

have a clear understanding of the operation's exact needs. For example, frozen baked pies, which require thawing and, perhaps, warming, cannot be purchased if the operation needs a product that is at or at least very close to point 10 on the scale. In that case, fresh pies that require no warming before service might be purchased since they will require less equipment and labor time to make them ready for service (although the need to cut and dish each piece of pie and, perhaps, to wash the serving dish and utensils must be considered).

TRENDS IN THE USE OF CONVENIENCE FOODS

It can be said that the real father of convenience foods was Dr. Birdseye, who was operating out of the Geneva Experimental Station in upstate New York in the early 1930's. He was the first person to develop and commercialize quick freezing. He applied this technique originally to vegetables, the first two successful items being peas and cut string beans. At this time, small packages were frozen between two freezing plates, and many products could not be produced because the processors did not have the freezing capacity.

Blast freezing came into being around 1940, and at this time the processing and freezing of pie fruits, meats, and large containers of vegetables was developed. With blast freezing, raw-ready pastries were also introduced. These products met with instant success and are still very popular convenience foods. Today, practically all freezing is done in a nitrogen tunnel at approximately minus 390°F.

A few years later, the first convenience entrees appeared in the commercial field. Because of the difficulty of reconstituting sauces, most of these entrees were raw-ready items that required either deep-fat frying, roasting, or reconstituting in a water bath. It took several years of experiment-ing before the processors discovered that sauces using waxy rice flour rather than conventional recipes made it possible to develop sauce dishes such as fricassees, Newburgs, and the cheese, tomato, and brown sauces that are available today.

In 1950, the processors came out with soup bases, dehydrated soup bases, and dehydrated stock bases. These products found a ready market, and today they are a large segment of the convenience food business. These dehydrated soup and sauce bases are very convenient and can produce a good product. However, the quality of the product varies in direct proportion to the ingredients used. Some bases are almost all salt, monosodium glutamate, and other ersatz foods, and although they produce edible foods, they really are not worth considering for anything other than the lowest-priced food service.

Products known as deluxe food and soup bases, which are put out by a limited number of quality manufacturers, are excellent and are only slightly higher in price. These bases can be used in the best food service operations. Today it is a rare hotel or restaurant kitchen that has an old-fashioned stock pot being used to prepare its own supply of brown stock, white stock, or chicken stock. It is easier and more energy efficient to take a couple of tablespoons of deluxe chicken base rather than to cook a batch of chickens. When a butcher was in the kitchen and there was plenty of beef bones, it was a simple matter to make a good brown stock. Today, with beef bones costing 30 to 40 cents per pound, it is more economical to buy deluxe soup and stock bases.

Since the ingredients used must be listed by decreasing percentage, it is easy to tell a deluxe base from an economy base. A deluxe chicken base will have chicken as the first ingredient. An economy base will have salt as the primary ingredient and chicken may not even be listed at all! It is possible today to purchase deluxe food bases made from shrimp, lobster, clams, pork, ham, mushrooms, onion, and garlic.

Rapid Growth of the Use of Convenience Foods

Since 1950 the use of convenience foods by institutional food services has increased enormously. Hotel and restaurant businesses have also increased their use of convenience foods, but at a much lower rate. Some studies estimated that by 1975, over 55 percent of all foods served, other than in the home and fast food establishments, were convenience foods. Only about 15 to 20 percent of the food served in the hotel and restaurant trade were convenience items, but in some institutional fields, convenience foods comprised up to 85 percent of the food served.

Trends Since 1977

By the end of 1977, it was obvious that the large increase in the use of convenience foods was not continuing. The increase in 1977 was only 3 percent over the previous year. This same low rate of increase has continued to the present time. By 1980, food service industry investigations suggested various factors causing this slowing of demand. Some food service operators pointed to the rather excessive increase in the purchase prices of convenience foods, such as sauced vegetables and the items accompanying the convenience entrees. At the same time, unions were becoming concerned about the number of jobs available for their members and started making it very difficult to reduce staff. Many operators felt that since they had the personnel, they should use them for food preparation.

Also about this time, some of the large fast food operators started to augment their limited menus with salad bars and soups and vegetable dishes. These menus found great public acceptance, so food operators continued to offer these items. Hospitals and schools, noticing the customers' preferences and the trends toward increased fresh fruit and vegetable consumption, looked into the use of these items and found that their clientele were also interested in the broader and lighter menus.

Some food service operators became convinced that the dining-out public were becoming more sophisticated in their tastes and were starting to demand more for their money. Many of the smarter operators came to the conclusion that the convenience food fad was over and they had better find alternatives to augment their menu and produce a more interesting package for the public.

In the early part of 1982, *Institutions Magazine* made an in-depth study of the trends in the use of convenience foods and other types of foods, especially fresh fruits, vegetables, and meats. This study separated food services into the categories of full-service restaurants, hotels and motels, schools, hospitals, employee food services, and colleges and universities. The results were basically the same in all six categories. However, the greatest increase in the use of fresh and nonconvenience items was in full-service restaurants, hotels, and motels.

The following four charts show the course of the convenience food business from 1977 to 1981 in four of the above six groupings. It must be remembered, however, that the overall use of convenience food has increased during this five-year period by an average of 3 to 5 percent per year. Over 55 percent of all food consumed outside the home (not including fast food establishments) is convenience foods, including entrees and pastries. With these facts in mind, it does not appear that the convenience food industry is in danger of bankruptcy. With the producers concentrating on better quality and better packaging, there is no question that the convenience food industry is going to continue to grow as a major part of food service but in a more limited way than during the recent past.

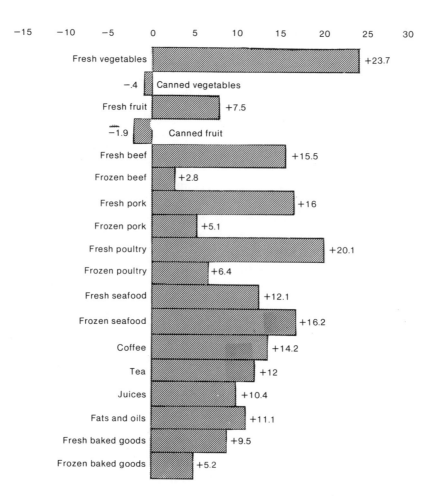

Full-service restaurants

In this most consumer-responsive of markets, the decade-long trends towards "freshness" and scratch cooking show little sign of abating. Besides this segment's obvious interest in fresh fruits and vegetables, restaurateurs also proportionately purchase the least kitchen-ready meat (28.4 percent) and poultry (30 percent). In order to play by the fresh-scratch rules and still maintain the benefits of convenience foods, more than half of the operations in this segment (55.4 percent) are now preparing and freezing their own food.

Still, manufactured convenience foods continue to retain their appeal where the virtues of short prep time, labor conservation and quality result can all be found in the same product. Frozen seafood may have successfully joined the select company of such items as frozen potatoes and frozen baked goods, as another category in which product is often "consumer approved" in its frozen form.

Exhibit 17-2. Usage trends: full-service restaurants*

Source: Institutions Magazine (September 15, 1980). Courtesy of Cahners Publishing Company.

All figures represent the mathematical difference between the percentage of operations in the given market segment that have reported an increase in the usage of the given item and those that have reported a decrease in its usage.

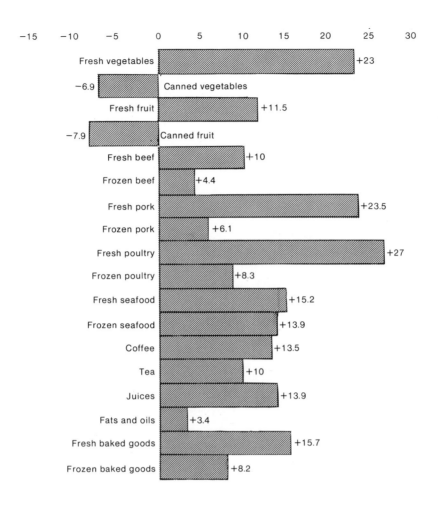

−15	−10	−5	0	5	10	15	20	25	30

Fresh vegetables +23
−6.9 Canned vegetables
Fresh fruit +11.5
−7.9 Canned fruit
Fresh beef +10
Frozen beef +4.4
Fresh pork +23.5
Frozen pork +6.1
Fresh poultry +27
Frozen poultry +8.3
Fresh seafood +15.2
Frozen seafood +13.9
Coffee +13.5
Tea +10
Juices +13.9
Fats and oils +3.4
Fresh baked goods +15.7
Frozen baked goods +8.2

Hotels/motels

For the most part, this industry segment remains defined by its high level of culinary talent (62 percent of the units have a trained chef) and the high quality expectations of its clientele. Although interest in truth-in-menu has at least temporarily plateaued in the industry as a whole, fully 33 percent of hotel/motel operators report that they have already changed menu *language* due to truth-in-menu pressures. A greater percentage of this segment (13.9 percent) than any other anticipates a decrease in the use of frozen entrees next year.

Interestingly, what holds true in the kitchen doesn't gel in the bakeshop. More than a fourth of this segment (26 percent) anticipates an increase in the use of frozen baked goods next year.

Watch for more hotel chains to capitalize on their bigness. Private-label products and automated, centrally located purchasing/inventory controls are already realities for some.

Exhibit 17-3. Usage trends: hotels/motels*

Source: Institutions Magazine (September 15, 1980). Courtesy of Cahners Publishing Company.

All figures represent the mathematical difference between the percentage of operations in the given market segment that have reported an increase in the usage of the given item and those that have reported a decrease in its usage.

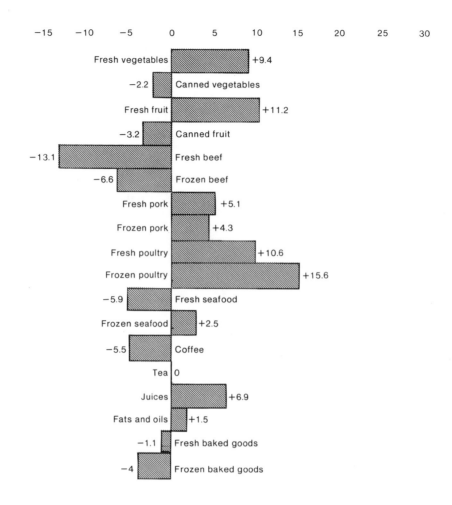

	−15	−10	−5	0	5	10	15	20	25	30

Fresh vegetables +9.4

−2.2 Canned vegetables

Fresh fruit +11.2

−3.2 Canned fruit

−13.1 Fresh beef

−6.6 Frozen beef

Fresh pork +5.1

Frozen pork +4.3

Fresh poultry +10.6

Frozen poultry +15.6

−5.9 Fresh seafood

Frozen seafood +2.5

−5.5 Coffee

Tea 0

Juices +6.9

Fats and oils +1.5

−1.1 Fresh baked goods

−4 Frozen baked goods

Schools

School feeding has already confronted some of the issues and problems facing nursing-home food service. It's partially a matter of similar bland diets and small portions; but the greatest correspondence is in their shared public poverty. Only these two market segments specify "food cost" as a more significant factor than "quality" in explaining their limited usage of frozen foods.

Schools, though, have managed to adopt a general menu policy that most people seem to agree is in the best public interest. Obviously, the key factors in this policy are *nutrition* and *commodities.* What results is a heavy dependence on protein extenders (52 percent of this segment uses them) and the industry's greatest usage of baked goods.

Public warehousing, volume economics, and unskilled labor have all contributed to the heavy reliance on satellite kitchen feeding (34.2 percent). School systems will do more regional and cross-agency purchasing.

Exhibit 17-4. Usage trends: schools *

Source: Institutions Magazine (September 15, 1980). Courtesy of Cahners Publishing Company.

All figures represent the mathematical difference between the percentage of operations in the given market segment that have reported an increase in the usage of the given item and those that have reported a decrease in its usage.

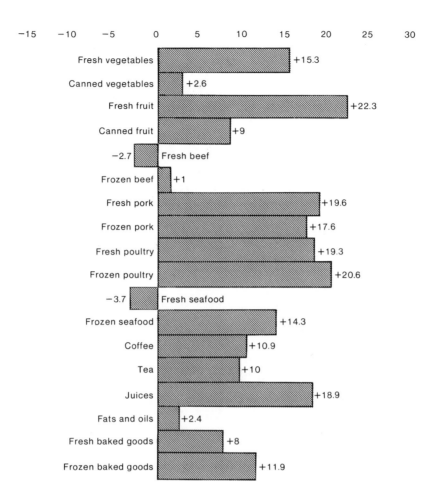

	−15	−10	−5	0	5	10	15	20	25	30

Fresh vegetables +15.3
Canned vegetables +2.6
Fresh fruit +22.3
Canned fruit +9
−2.7 Fresh beef
Frozen beef +1
Fresh pork +19.6
Frozen pork +17.6
Fresh poultry +19.3
Frozen poultry +20.6
−3.7 Fresh seafood
Frozen seafood +14.3
Coffee +10.9
Tea +10
Juices +18.9
Fats and oils +2.4
Fresh baked goods +8
Frozen baked goods +11.9

Hospitals

Due to the lack of trained kitchen manpower, the urgent complexity of nutritional requirements, and the considerable variety demanded by an especially captive clientele, hospitals have become the most enthusiastic customers of the convenience-food industry. More hospitals use frozen entrees (80.4 percent) and last year increased the use of frozen entrees (27.9 percent) and tried new canned entrees (52.8 percent) than did the units of any other market segment. Hospitals also led in usage of frozen baked goods (86.7 percent).

This expensive purchasing policy, which entails a very high rate of menu inflation, is a perennial sore point with hospital administrators. Expect more combined purchasing by government institutions, and more consolidation of suppliers and competitive pricing by independents. Hospital management corporations, with their bigger purchasing power and centralized controls, should thrive.

Exhibit 17-5. Usage trends: hospitals *

Source: Institutions Magazine (September 15, 1980). Courtesy of Cahners Publishing Company.

All figures represent the mathematical difference between the percentage of operations in the given market segment that have reported an increase in the usage of the given item and those that have reported a decrease in its usage.

VARIETIES OF CONVENIENCE FOODS

Today there are more than six thousand nationally distributed convenience food items available. This list continues to grow, and the food purchaser must stay abreast of the wide variety of items available in every conceivable category and within a large price range. Marvin Thorner, a leading food technician, has divided the seemingly endless number of convenience food items into product categories and provided examples of items within each category. A sample of foods within each category follows:

Appetizers, snacks, and hors d'oeuvres: juices, fruit cocktail, pâtés, egg rolls, stuffed cabbage, cheese puffs.

Soups: chowders, bisques, purees, minestrone, vegetable, chicken, cream of potato, green pea with ham, won ton.

Entrees: seafood, beef, poultry products, lamb, pork, pasta, casseroles, meat pies.

Specialty entrees: nationality foods such as beef Stroganoff, ravioli, cacciatore, lasagna, tortillas, tamales, chow mein, chicken Kiev, chicken Polynesian, sauerbraten, beef Burgundy.

Vegetables: potato dishes, onions, rice dishes, spinach souffle, varieties of vegetables.

Salads: fish, meat, tossed, fruit.

Bread and rolls: French toast, muffins, breads, rolls.

Desserts: puddings, fritters, cakes, pies.

Nonalcoholic beverages: iced tea (dispenser), soft drinks and juices (postmix dispensers), coffee (freeze-dried).

This list can only suggest the wide variety of convenience food items currently available.

One aspect of food service operations has always separated that industry from other businesses. The manufacture and sale of food service products have been confined to one site while most other businesses manufacture their product in one location and sell it in another (for example, clothing may be made by a garment manufacturer on the East Coast or the West Coast or even in another country and sold elsewhere). As the use of convenience foods becomes more widespread, the food service industry will also find itself purchasing food items made elsewhere. This permits the food service establishment to concentrate on serving and selling, rather than on manufacturing, food products.

FACTORS AFFECTING "MAKE OR BUY" DECISIONS

There are two types of make or buy decisions. If a food service system is to make total use of convenience foods, this affects the design of a new facility or leads to the remodeling of an existing one. On the other hand, convenience foods can be adopted on an item-by-item basis. There are some elements common to both approaches.

Price and Quality

Value is, according to Lendal Kotschevar and others, a function of price and quality. Value analysis suggests that value increases as price, relative to quality, decreases; value decreases as price, relative to quality, increases. These two factors—quality and price—are of the utmost importance in make or buy decisions. Quality in this sense is a subjective judgment by the food service manager as to how well the taste, appearance, consistency, or other aspects of a product meets the standards set for that product by the operation (the standard may be how well the operation itself can prepare the item).

Quality also reflects the food service manager's perception of the extent to which the customer will accept a product. If quality is not judged acceptable, a product *will not* be purchased regardless of price. If quality is acceptable, the product *may* be purchased if the price can be justified, or the product *will* be purchased if it cannot be prepared on-site. Quality and price cannot be separated when the decision to purchase convenience foods is made.

The price-quality difference between convenience foods and items prepared on-site was the basis for considerable early debate. There were allegations (perhaps accurate in many instances) of poor quality at a high price when convenience foods were being considered. Lack of precedent, defense of the status quo, fear for job or professional status, lack of proper equipment and other factors also affected the make or buy decision during the 1960's and early 1970's. A number of these same factors may remain important considerations today.

It is unfortunate that many food service operators do not make a careful, objective analysis of either quality or price when considering whether to make or buy. It is true that such an analysis can be complicated and time consuming. And, especially in large operations, this may constitute a further justification for establishing a separate purchasing department wherein a purchasing specialist might conduct a thorough analysis important in making the wisest decision. It is also true that, even in small operations, some objective study is critical to the decision-making process.

Quality analysis can require the use of taste panels. Specifications that suit the operation must be developed. Eligible suppliers must be selected. Proper receiving, storing, and issuing practices must be followed. The best preparation and service techniques must be determined. These responsibilities are of equal importance whether the food purchased is in convenience or more traditional form.

Price analysis, presuming equal quality, constitutes an attempt to identify and assess all costs relating to the use of on-site, prepared items and to compare that cost to the cost of using convenience food items. (This topic is discussed in a later section of this chapter.)

In addition to the obvious factors of price and quality, there are other factors involved in the make or buy decision. Each food service operation, being unique, will have specific concerns integral to its operation. Management experience is probably the best key to understanding these unique features, and the relationship between management and the purchasing department, if they are not the same, is an important one.

Acceptability

Some restaurant operators fear (and their fears are sometimes borne out) that customers will disapprove when they discover that entrees and other menu items were prepared off the premises. This disapproval stems, in part, from attitudes developed in the early days of convenience foods when quality was often low or inconsistent. There is also anxiety on the part of many operators that customers will discover that convenience foods are being used.

Actually a dichotomy appears to exist. What is widely acceptable in fast food or low-check average family, table service operations is frowned upon by customers in higher-check average gourmet table service restaurants. Operators must know their market and understand when convenience foods will be judged acceptable. Food service personnel are not generally anxious to educate their customers as to the quality available in convenience products. They must, therefore, utilize such products when it is assumed that they will be acceptable to the customer.

This problem is aggravated by requirements of the Federal Trade Commission and state and local governmental agencies relating to advertising. The spirit and intent of these regulations are that the customer should know exactly what he is buying so that he can make an informed choice between alternatives. Closely aligned to this need is recent legislation in some areas of the country where there is concern for "truth in menu writing." If a menu indicates that toasted cheese sandwiches, for example, are available, then processed cheese food products cannot be used; nor can ice cream be ice milk. These are just two of many possible examples. Some areas have even considered legislation requiring that menus indicate where items offered for sale have been prepared. This need to inform the public is another important consideration when one is deciding whether to make a food item or buy a convenience food alternate.

Other Considerations

Certainly the above concerns are common in any establishment. Other considerations peculiar to each establishment include: equipment, the number and availability of qualified personnel, time available for preparation, size and type of available packaging of convenience food products, consistent availability and quality of product, versatility in use, and the reputation of the supplier. The following questions should be asked by those who purchase food in order that they might be more discerning in their selection of convenience products:

Is specialized equipment needed to prepare or serve on-site, or must equipment be purchased?

If equipment is to be purchased, is there space for it?

Is skilled labor available for on-site preparation?

Is food service management aware of all operational changes required if convenience food items are to be incorporated into the menu?

Which type of packaging is best suited to the needs of the establishment? (For example, beef stew can be purchased in a "boil-in-the-bag" form. It can be canned or frozen in containers that vary in size.)

Is a food item easy to serve?

Do changes in preparation or service (such as batch cooking or cooking to order) create problems in inadequately designed production-serving areas?

Are the food items, in amounts needed by the operation, consistently available?

Is the product consistent in quality, or does quality vary in each shipment?

Are the suppliers who handle the product reputable?

Can the product be varied, given available personnel skills, to make it distinctive from the same product used by a competitor?

All factors involved in the make or buy decision are important. The task is difficult when menu items are considered separately. The task is monumental when decisions involve the initial design and construction of an establishment that is or is not to be "total convenience."

ADVANTAGES AND DISADVANTAGES IN USING CONVENIENCE FOODS

The trend toward increased use of convenience foods within the food service industry must be an indication that food service operators are finding convenience foods more acceptable, but a complete discussion of this topic is difficult because food service operations vary. No listing of advantages or disadvantages can apply to all operations. In addition, there have been continuous improvements in product, distribution, and processing procedures that serve to reduce perceived disadvantages. The following represents an attempt, in spite of the difficulty, to list some possible advantages and disadvantages. Many of these have been enumerated by Thorner.

Advantages

It is appropriate to begin with the advantages that might accrue to management from the use of convenience foods. For one thing, more attention can be devoted to the merchandising and serving of menu items rather than to preparation of the products. Also, equipment malfunction and supply problems are less likely to occur or, if they do occur, they are often easier to resolve.

In terms of purchasing, the computation of food costs and the keeping of records are simpler since there is not the same need for high levels of raw material purchase, alertness in receiving, extensive inventory and complicated preparation. Reliable suppliers—often fewer are needed—and manufacturers' representatives may assist with problems stemming from the initiation or daily operation of a convenience product or system. Purchasing can be done in quantities and assortments that meet the needs of an operation, and packaging requests can be meshed into the general operation. Waste as a result of shrinkage, spoilage, pilferage, careless handling, or theft can be more carefully controlled. And, if nutritional information is needed, it is available on the label.

Less production space is needed when an efficient work system design is incorporated into the facility. This is especially true for a new facility that is planned around the use of convenience foods. Production needs during the peaks and valleys of meal service can be scheduled more accurately, and menus can be varied without a corresponding increase in planning and production effort. The ability to prepare food in batches can reduce or eliminate overproduction, and there is more control over portion sizes.

The time lag between production and service of a food item also decreases, and this improves the quality of the item being served. Proper processing, distribution, storage, and reconstitution of a convenience food item may be less detrimental than on-site preparation followed by hours of holding at a high temperature level. The quality of a convenience product is more likely to remain consistent from day to day and from cook to cook, and some larger operations can develop their own standards of quality for convenience products.

Production personnel need not have high skill levels (purchased by management at a high wage or salary level) if convenience products are used and the gross number of labor hours needed for production decreases. Working conditions on-site improve, with fewer odors, lower humidity, and cooler temperatures emanating from production equipment.

The food service operator is always concerned about sanitation in food production and service. The number of sanitation and cleaning tasks in the care of facilities and of large and small equipment is reduced. With the production process (or much of it) eliminated, there could be less danger of food-borne illness. Food service personnel must still be concerned about and follow all proper food-handling procedures when convenience foods are used, but there is some assurance that convenience food products entering the facility will be wholesome and not contaminated. It has been pointed out by Karla Longree that, with proper handling and care of precooked, frozen food items, the quality component involving high sanitation levels can be met.

Disadvantages

Careful analysis and adequate planning are critical before introducing a convenience food item. This takes time, and frequently the assistance available to management is limited. Certainly the purchase of new equipment or the remodeling of facilities may require increased capital. That equipment is often complicated and requires highly skilled personnel to repair malfunctioning units, and, even then, the machinery often does not work smoothly at first. For these and other reasons implementation of a new convenience food item or system does not always produce an immediate increase in business or profits. One additional threat is strikes by employees of manufacturers and shippers. Obviously the convenience system cannot be as closely controlled as is possible within a single establishment.

There are also some disadvantages in the purchasing area. There is no effective standardization of product quality or size and type of packaging between products offered by competing manufacturers. Comparing the merits of, for example, a beef stew or a poultry casserole item being offered by two different manufacturers is difficult. The availability of so many convenience items can also be confusing and result in inadequate or incorrect merchandising and sales programs. Certainly there is reliance on specific manufacturers and suppliers for quality, and consistent, reliable product distribution may be limited in some instances to metropolitan areas. As a general rule, the overstocking of convenience foods because of "special buys" is not economically justifiable.

Disadvantages in the production area relate, first, to customer dissatisfaction. Quality must be maintained or the reputation of the establishment suffers. Improper handling or processing of a convenience product, on or off the premises, can affect quality, and instructions accompanying a product may be inadequate or not carefully followed. Although the people preparing the product may not need to be as highly skilled, they must be creative in

their approach so that the convenience product becomes more acceptable to the customer.

Convenience systems, are often implemented with improperly or inadequately trained management, production, and serving personnel. This situation is not improved when employees see convenience foods as a threat to job security, as limiting creative ability, or as "cheating" the customer. In order to reassure them, union contracts or other personnel agreements may prohibit the termination of employees or any reduction in employee hours worked because of the increased use of convenience foods. Such documents may be specifically worded to prohibit the closing of any preparation department or prohibit the use of any convenience foods unless the facility operates as a "totally convenience" operation.

The Final Judge—The Consumer

In the 1960's and 1970's, some food service operators adopted convenience foods too enthusiastically, and the resulting problems and misconceptions are still with us today. Many operators are trying to make a final decision on the use of convenience foods based on cost, claims and counterclaims, storage space, labor costs, and training programs. They have depended upon committees to come up with decisions, but in many cases they overlooked the "final judge": the consumer. Those in the hospitality field will remember what happened to Howard Johnson when that organization used only frozen foods and may also recall what happened at the University of Maryland. It's hard to forget all the protests about grade-school food service and "enforced" institutional feeding.

Today, food service operators are endeavoring to research the customer's reaction before committing their operations to the use of convenience foods. Because of this caution, the demand for better quality frozen entrees has grown until many of the entrees available today can be served even in hotels and the better restaurants without fear of embarrassment. This care for quality is good for the overall continued growth of convenience foods.

IMPLICATIONS OF THE USE OF CONVENIENCE FOODS

Careful analysis of all factors involved in the potential use of convenience foods is important as make or buy purchasing decisions are made. Many of these factors, as well as possible advantages and disadvantages to the use of convenience foods have been noted, but there are several additional matters that should be considered if convenience programs are to be implemented in existing food operations.

Employee training in the proper procedures for handling convenience items is critical to the success of any implementation program, and training should begin with a defense and justification of operational changes in order to counter any existing prejudice against their use. Apprehension about job security must also be relieved. Training must be thoroughly planned and involve everyone from top management through storeroom personnel. It might be wise to experiment with different handling techniques before procedures are standardized. As was noted earlier, some existing equipment may need to be replaced by items specifically designed for heating and reconstituting convenience foods. It is often tempting to try to make do with available equipment, but it should be recognized that this could compromise the quality of the finished product. Existing operational procedures may need to be changed as convenience foods are used. These changes affect far more than work flow and employee scheduling in the production area. Pur-

chasing systems, receiving methods, storage facilities and practices, record-keeping, and other activities are affected, and change in these areas must also be accommodated. It must by now be obvious that there is a great need for commitment to convenience foods as expressed by an allocation of sufficient time and monies to the implementation or conversion task.

One additional point to be considered is the time saved by using convenience foods. Exhibit 17-6 indicates the general impact on prime costs (food and direct labor) of traditional and convenience food systems. The exhibit suggests that, if convenience foods are used, a food service operator can generally expect a higher food cost than if nonconvenience food items are prepared on-site. This seems reasonable since processing and other costs incurred by the manufacturer are passed on to the buyer. These charges are not usually present when raw products are purchased.

On the other hand, the food service operator can generally expect lower labor costs when convenience foods are used than when nonconvenience food items are utilized. This also appears logical since at least some processing was done prior to purchase and does not need to be repeated on-site. It is this labor cost reduction that, in many instances, encourages the purchaser to choose the convenience product.

Even a cursory review of Exhibit 17-6 should suggest that any analysis of prime costs must be carefully undertaken in order to determine whether total prime costs (food and labor) are higher or lower when a convenience alternate (either an item or an entire system) is proposed. This discussion of prime cost analysis presumes equal quality in the convenience and nonconvenience food item being considered. This discussion likewise excludes the very necessary analysis of financial and other

Cost category	When convenience foods are used	When convenience foods are not used
Food cost Labor cost	Will be higher Will be lower	Will be lower Will be higher

Exhibit 17-6. Fiscal implications of convenience foods use on prime costs

factors unrelated to prime cost discussed earlier in this chapter.

But, in the opinion of Michael Coffman, many food service operators in different establishments find themselves comparing food, labor, and other expenditures without considering operational differences that contribute to variable costs. Thus, to find that a neighboring establishment is working on a higher or lower food cost percentage is not usable information in itself. There may be easily explainable reasons for differences. Certainly an establishment utilizing convenience foods can expect to operate on a higher food cost percentage than one making less use of convenience foods. One must then look further, determining costs for other categories in order to assess the true fiscal status of an operation. For example, the operation with a higher food cost percentage may well have a much lower labor cost percentage than the neighboring establishments, which has the net effect of lowering the total prime cost.

"Paper" savings in labor costs when convenience foods are used are meaningless unless the actual number of dollars spent for labor decreases. If the amount spent for labor does not decrease and if food costs increase, the food service operation will find itself in an unsatisfactory financial position. The question then becomes: What do we do with the labor hours saved through the use of convenience foods? (This same question applies when labor-saving equipment is being considered for purchase.) Ideally, hours can be reduced through employee attrition,

but, if this is not feasible, then other alternatives must be carefully reviewed and decisions made prior to the implementation of a convenience foods program.

Potential problems in employee scheduling must also be considered and resolved during the make or buy decision-making process. For example, if a convenience food item is used on some days but not on others, can employee schedules reflect this vacillation in need for man-hours? Perhaps cleaning, training, or other activities can be scheduled for days when it is necessary to utilize man-hours saved. There are other ways to redirect and reschedule employee hours in order to accommodate the changes that come as a result of using convenience foods, but these must be planned for by management if available labor is to be used most efficiently.

The implications that the use of convenience foods have for the entire fiscal and operational structure of the food service operation are great. Time must, therefore, be spent in planning, employee training, supervision, and operational monitoring if there is to be a successful transition to the use of convenience foods.

COST ANALYSIS IN A MAKE OR BUY DECISION

Assuming that the quality of food items prepared on-site and those purchased in convenience form is equal or at least acceptable, cost differences must be considered. The typical food service operator probably does not have the time, the ability, or access to complicated measuring equipment required to conduct sophisticated tests of time, energy, and other factors to be considered when the usefulness of convenience products is analyzed. It is possible, however, to conduct a reasonable study and analysis of major cost differences between alternate purchase forms of menu items. It is also possible to consider, even if only subjectively, many other factors before substituting a convenience food item for one prepared on-site. The following examples show how this analysis can be done.

Example 1

A small restaurant prepares twelve pecan pies daily. It has sufficient equipment (ovens and mixer) to produce the pies since the equipment needed is multipurpose and is used for many other production tasks. The assistant cook who prepares this item is scheduled to retire, and the decision has already been made to purchase several other bakeshop items needed. It is necessary to decide whether to continue on-site preparation of the pies. What are the prime cost implications of preparing and buying pecan pies (assuming that an item of equivalent quality is available)?

First, calculate the standard food cost from the standardized recipe that is (or at least should be) used in preparing the pecan pies. Labor time can be determined from personal observation, interviews with production personnel, time-motion study, or, perhaps, a combination of these procedures. The results of such an analysis appear in Exhibit 17-7.

The time necessary to portion slices, plate, perhaps heat, serve, wash plates, or other activity is the same regardless of whether the pie is purchased or prepared on-site. There are other costs that have not been considered. Utility charges apply for on-site preparation, and the cost of disposing of pie tins must be considered for the prepared product. The large cost differential, however, indicates that there may be an economic advantage to the continued on-site production of the pecan pies. Other noneconomic factors to consider in this make or buy decision were examined earlier in this chapter.

Example 2

The same food service operator was informed by a friend at a restaurant convention that money could be saved by purchasing a canned spaghetti sauce and

---

Labor time required to produce twelve pecan pies	
Prepare dough	20 min.
Roll out 12 shells	32 "
Prepare filling	18 "
Portion pies	7 "
In/out oven	3 "
Check-in process	2 "
Clean equipment and work station	6 "
Wash pie pans	5 "
Total labor time	93 min.

Bakery employees at $10.00 per hour
Fringe benefits (10%)@ 1.00 per hour
93/60 = 1.55 hours x $11.00 = $17.05 to produce 12 pies
$17.05/12 = $1.42 labor per pie
Material cost @ $2.87 per pie + $1.42 labor = $4.29 per pie
Cost for purchase frozen pie = $4.70

Exhibit 17-7. Example of a cost analysis to determine whether to make or buy pecan pies

modifying it on-site with additional spices and seasonings. Since there always seemed to be production bottlenecks on days when spaghetti sauce was being prepared, the alternative certainly seemed worth considering. The analysis that appears in Exhibit 17-8 would be appropriate in this instance.

The cleaning time for the work area and the equipment for either alternative would be similar. Utility costs may be higher for the on-site item since the range oven or steam kettle will be used for a longer period of time. Time for preparing spaghetti and portioning costs would be the same. Since the cost of the convenience item is less and the quality is acceptable and since use would, with operational changes, help to eliminate production bottlenecks, it might be wise, after evaluating all other factors, to buy the convenience item. However, unless scheduling results in an actual reduction in employee time spent in production, these are "paper" savings, as noted earlier, which do not, in themselves, reduce labor cost. In this case, the expense involved in utilizing the convenience item may be acceptable even without a subsequent reduction in employee time be-cause of the elimination of the bottleneck in work procedures.

THE SUPPLIER'S PERSPECTIVE

The advantages and disadvantages of using convenience foods have thus far been seen from the viewpoint of the food purchaser. The suppliers who sell the products also have interesting viewpoints. Suppliers who offer full-line service (different market forms of many different products) have noted a trend toward significant increases in convenience food sales. Growth rates of 300 percent or more in convenience food sales within a period of several years are not uncommon. Many suppliers suggest that more convenience products are used in institutional food service operations than in their commercial counterparts.

Suppliers often hear the following four reasons why an operator decides to adopt a convenience item:

1. Convenience foods are frequently used as the basis for preparing meals for employees of the food service operation.
2. Convenience foods are more con-

Cost	Make sauce		Buy sauce	
	Time (minutes)	Money (dollars)	Time (minutes)	Money (dollars)
Standard food cost (36 cups or approximately 3 # 10 cans)		$12.50		$15.60
Additional seasoning		0.00		0.32
Estimated total		$12.50		$15.92
Production Clean, weigh, chop, sauté vegetables)	40			
Add canned tomato sauce, other ingredients, stir, season to taste	15			
Measure or weigh and add seasoning, stir			10	
Total	55		10	
Labor*		6.05		1.10
TOTAL		$18.55		$17.02

*The assistant cook is paid $6.00 per hour with an additional 10 percent in fringe benefits ($6.00 + .60 = $6.60). Thus, with on-site preparation labor, the cost is 55/60 x $6.60, or approximately $6.05. Labor for the convenience food product raises the cost 10/60 X $6.60 = $1.10. The preparation labor when the convenience food item is used is, then, $1.10.

Exhibit 17-8. Cost analysis to determine whether to make spaghetti sauce or to buy and modify a prepared product

sistent in quality than the corresponding product prepared on-site.

3. There is less waste than with on-site preparation.

4. Convenience foods can be used to reduce labor costs.

The primary disadvantage of convenience foods, from the viewpoint of the supplier, is that many food purchasers complain about quality. During the early years of fast growth, many convenience foods were of inferior quality. As these items entered the marketplace, food purchasers experimented, found the products inferior, and returned to the use of nonconvenience foods. Attitudes formed then still remain with purchasers today, even though there have been many improvements. Larger, nationally known, reputable companies that started slowly in terms of convenience foods now, in many instances, dominate the field. Products produced by these companies are of higher quality, and, as use increases, suppliers believe that there will be fewer complaints.

Although suppliers readily agree that the quality of the convenience product has not always been satisfactory, they also point out that longtime users of convenience products are generally pleased, with few subsequent problems reported to the supplier. This suggests that there is frequently an awkward period between the time a convenience food is tried for the first time and the time it is accepted for use. Such periods are trying for both the operator and the supplier. Suppliers share the feeling that growth in the use of convenience foods will continue, primarily because product quality will improve through advances in technology. As for handling convenience products, suppliers find it easier. Perishability and sanitation concerns are lessened, and shelf life is increased. Most suppliers work hard to overcome the suspicions of food purchasers and encourage the use of high-quality convenience products.

THE BUYER'S PERSPECTIVE

The Product

Considering convenience foods from the perspective of the food purchaser has prompted most of the comments in this chapter so far. The purchaser must recognize that acceptability varies according to the type of operation. Also, because quality levels may be different, the purchaser must make comparisons and choose reliable suppliers if he is to obtain a high-quality product that can overcome any subsequent customer resistance. Even if there is little chance or desire to convert an entire operation to the use of a convenience system, it is possible to defend the purchase and use of many individual convenience items in terms of consistent quality, lower labor costs, lower capital costs, and ease of operation.

Equipment

One benefit that comes from the use of convenience foods is that such products require less equipment for reheating or reconstituting than would be required for more traditional processing. This seems logical since some (or all) of the food preparation task is performed off-site, but it is also true that convenience foods often require more specialized equipment for highest quality presentation of the item to the customer. Many properties must, however, use older, more traditional equipment to prepare convenience foods, at least until the use of these items increases enough to justify purchase of new equipment.

There are three major concerns when purchasing specialized equipment:

1. Some equipment may need to be purchased (if not already available) as a convenience foods program is implemented.

2. Equipment models constantly change or improve. Newer items have many

options or features not available on older models.

3. The wide variety of equipment available makes selection difficult.

The criteria used to select equipment used in the processing of convenience foods does not differ greatly from criteria used in the purchase of most other food service equipment. These criteria have been identified by Kotschevar and Margaret Terrell as:

Need (Will the addition of an equipment item help to improve the quality, increase the quantity, or reduce time for or cost of the operation being performed?)

Cost (Can the equipment be cost justified not only in terms of initial purchase expense, but also in terms of subsequent installation, repair and maintenance, operating, and other charges?)

Performance (Does the equipment perform adequately, from the purchaser's perspective, the job it is supposed to do?)

Satisfaction of need (Does the equipment have the proper capacity and operational ability to fill present and future needs?)

Safety and sanitation (Is the equipment safe to use and easy to clean? Does it have the approval of recognized agencies such as Underwriter's Laboratories [electrical] and the National Sanitation Foundation [cleanliness]?)

Appearance and design (Does the equipment fit into the operation, and does its design provide for simple operation, maximum space utilization, and other needs?)

General utility value (Are mobility, size, quietness of operation, or some other factor matters of concern?)

With these criteria in mind, one can consider equipment items as they relate to convenience foods systems.

Refrigeration. Preparation facilities planned years ago generally provide for considerably more refrigerated storage (32° to 40°F) than for frozen (−10° to 0°F) storage. With the dramatic increase in the use of convenience foods (especially frozen food items) this relationship has changed. Newly designed operations frequently contain more frozen than refrigerated storage space. Walk-in refrigerated and frozen units have proved more useful for bulk or central storage. Upright, under the counter, reach-in, and pass- or roll-through units can often be justified in work and serving centers in terms of increased employee productivity and efficiency.

Several types of "thawing" units are also available for fast, sanitary thawing of frozen foods. These units are designed for automatic thawing of frozen foods and subsequent holding at a proper, preset temperature. There are units that can also be programmed to cook, bake, or otherwise heat for service the items being held. It is known that proper storage and thawing of frozen foods are important to protect the quality of the frozen product. Odd tastes, poor texture, shrinkage, discoloration, and spoilage can frequently be traced to improper storage and thawing. It is important to follow closely instructions provided by the supplier for the storage and processing of convenience items, and this might require specialized storage, heating, or serving equipment.

Heating. Many convenience items must also be heated prior to service. Often traditional bake or roast deck ovens, rotary ovens, or range ovens already on the premises must be used as convenience food programs are being implemented. It should be recognized, however, that several new and improved types of equipment are available:

Convection ovens. These units utilize one or more fans inside the oven cavity to circulate heated air through the oven chamber. It is the convection current created that gives rise to the name. This oven enables the operator to prepare items at a lower temperature and in a shorter period of time than is possible with a conventional oven. These features, along with compact size, enable more efficient utilization of space. (A stacked convection oven [two units] can hold approximately twenty-two 18-inch x 26-inch pans of hamburger patties, cookies, or some other item, using less floor space than a single-tier conventional oven holding just two such pans would require.) Convection ovens lend themselves to fast reheating of rather large quantities of convenience food products, and the sale of these ovens is increasing. In fact, traditional ovens are not being placed in many facilities being constructed or remodeled today.

Microwave ovens. These ovens make use of short radio waves (hence, the name microwave) produced by magnetron tube(s) in the oven unit. Molecules in foods placed in the oven absorb this energy, and it is the friction generated by the fast-moving molecules within the food that produces heat. The molecular movement occurs deep within the food item at the same time that the surface is being heated. This greatly shortens the required cooking time. These ovens can heat on an order-by-order basis or in somewhat greater bulk items for subsequent service. The advantages have been listed by Julie Wilkinson as:

1. ability to heat small amounts of food quickly,
2. capacity to complement existing equipment,
3. fast thawing of frozen items,
4. fast cooking, and
5. reduction in labor costs because there is less food handling.

There are disadvantages to the use of microwave units. For example, bulk preparation of large amounts of food is not generally possible; some items, such as breaded products, do not lend themselves to microwave cookery; position, size, shape, consistency of thaw, and weight of items to be cooked must be considered to ensure consistent quality in the product being cooked (heated); browning is impossible without a special attachment.

The advantages, however, frequently outweigh the disadvantages. It has been estimated by Thorner that, by the end of the 1980's, 85 percent of all food service operations will be making some use of microwave heating units. With personnel trained to utilize equipment correctly, entire systems can eventually be designed around microwave ovens. With the increased use of convenience foods, it seems likely that there will be a corresponding increase in the use of microwave ovens for the heating of those foods.

Infrared (quartz) ovens. These ovens were originally designed to reconstitute bulk-pack frozen foods, but they are also used to heat, roast, and brown. They are much faster than convection ovens, but do not heat as quickly as microwave ones. They have the advantages of both types since they brown and can satisfy quantity needs. A quartz plate at the top of the oven diffuses infrared rays around the ambient area. This provides uniform heat transfer. The ovens are useful for broiling and are particularly good for finishing dishes that may have been heated in a microwave oven and are then browned and crisped in the quartz oven (in much the same fashion as occurred with the more traditional "salamander" or back-shelf broiler units). This piece of equipment comes close to being perfect for cooking to order in a large-volume operation.

Re-Con ovens. These ovens can be used to reconstitute frozen, prepared entrees, or they can be used as high-speed, conventional ovens that, because of the temperature range, can broil or roast as needed. Because of their flexibility and because they are offered in various sizes (from a small unit that produces forty portions to one that can yield six hundred breasts of chicken at one time), this piece of equipment has been well received and is gaining wide use by institutions, airlines, catering operations, and hotels and restaurants.

Steam equipment. Self-contained steam equipment units are in frequent use today since efficient, centrally located sources of live, clean steam are not always available. Self-contained units are usually cleaner, less expensive to operate, energy saving, and faster than direct hookup counterparts. Local ordinances may require that a licensed engineer be on the premises whenever high-pressure steamers are used, but these ordinances can usually be bypassed if self-contained units are employed.

High steam pressure means more efficient and faster cooking, with less nutrient loss. Several different types of steam cooking equipment are available that make it possible to do both basic cooking and reheating of convenience foods. There are stationary or tilting models that range in size from several quarts to many gallons. Traditional compartment steamers are of a low-pressure type (approximately five pounds of pressure per square inch). They range in size from one to four compartments (each of which can be separately controlled and will hold several steam table pans) and can be used for the heating of canned and frozen vegetables and many other convenience items. A faster-operating model (called a high-pressure steamer since it operates at approximately fifteen pounds of pressure per square inch) is also available. It is frequently smaller than low-pressure units and cooks much faster, thereby lending itself to small batch or "to order" cooking requirements. Small counter top units, which generate steam in a spray and can be used for single-order purposes, are also available. These units can frequently be moved between work stations and are utilized in many fast food operations for such purposes as melting cheese

on hamburgers and warming buns. A recent innovation in terms of steam heating equipment is the convection steamer, which circulates steam around food products placed within the cooking compartment. It does not operate under pressure, and it is useful for cooking and heating many types of convenience food products.

Specialty Equipment. There are many specialty equipment items available for use in the processing of convenience foods. Examples include: spaghetti-handling equipment that cooks, washes, stores, and reheats spaghetti products; water-heating units developed to heat "boil in the pouch" items; hot dog and hamburger cookers; "computerized" deep fryers that automatically adjust to quantities and types of food items being fried (some have automatic lowering and lifting devices for fryer baskets).

Other Items. Depending upon the market form and the amount of preparation built into the convenience foods being purchased, many items of traditional equipment (steam kettles, tilting fry pans and grills, ovens) can and are used in the on-site processing of convenience food items. As volume of production-service increases, there are equipment items (even if of a single-purpose, specialty nature) available for use in the more efficient processing of convenience products.

SOME SIGNIFICANT DEVELOPMENTS OF THE LAST TEN YEARS IN CONVENIENCE FOODS

Ever since Clarence Birdseye froze the first package of peas at an experimental station in upstate New York, there has been a debate among food service operators: would the industry be taken over by preserved frozen foods, or would convenience foods be just a fad and disappear?

Many millions of dollars were spent in

developing convenience foods. It was quite a while before the public would accept them. Literally thousands of items were introduced by the food service industry and great claims of payroll savings and reduction in costs were promoted. In the long run, the public has made the decisions on how far this new industry could progress.

For about fifty years, the great debate went on. During the last ten years, the public has made some very important decisions, and set trends for the future, in accepting convenience foods. The highlights of these developments can be summarized as follows.

Convenience foods (entrees and at least 50 percent prepared dishes of all nature that can be completed by microwave or some other fast heating equipment) are here to stay. Nutritionists have found nothing wrong with the food value or taste, and customers have accepted the quality and taste of these foods for home use and for use in institutional food service. Customers have said loud and clear that they don't want convenience foods served in hotels and restaurants and some other food services. The average customer has said he or she will not pay high prices and eat the same quality and variety as at home.

The customer and the economics of the business have clearly stated that convenience foods are the way to go in almost all institutional food services, fast food service, family meals for two-income families, schools, social and correctional institutions, and hospital and convalescent homes. The jury is still out on just what type of food is going to be taken into the space age by our astronauts.

As a result, we now have two definite branches of the food service industry. First, the hospitality industry covers hotels, restaurants, retirement homes, convalescent centers, and the home entertainment business, which has grown to significant size and importance. These industries cater to the more affluent, who can patronize a place that they choose themselves and who are not there because of some regimenting social or economic force. In this industry, from 50 to 60 percent of food purchased for this group is composed of half-prepared to fully prepared convenience foods.

The other industry is known as the institutional food service. This industry covers almost all food service other than the free-choice hospitality industry. Most chain-operated fast food services, although they use convenience foods, cannot be classified as institutional food service operations because freedom of choice, heavy competition, and wide variety is offered to the public.

The institutional food service industry uses about 85 to 90 percent clearly defined convenience foods. All the classic claims for convenience foods hold true here. The most important reason is that not enough help is available to allow the use of ordinary methods of food preparation and service to take care of the immense number of people being fed in institutions.

These factors, coupled with the high cost of modern prep kitchens, storage facilities, losses from spoilage, the increased number of people needed in the kitchen operations, and hassles with trade unions and with government regulatory departments and services, have produced this distinct division within the food service industry.

THE FUTURE OF CONVENIENCE FOODS

After many years, during which the use of convenience foods by the food service industry has increased, there is still some debate about the acceptability of convenience items. This makes it even more difficult to look into the future and make predictions about the use of convenience foods. We do know that the American public is spending more money and eating more meals away from home. It has been estimated that, by the end of the 1980's, 40 percent or more of all meals consumed by Americans will be eaten outside the home.

We also know that there is, and probably will continue to be, a proliferation in fast food, family-style, table service restaurants. That is the area where company owned and franchised operations are most active. Since it is these types of operations that make the fullest use of convenience foods, and since, in terms of numbers of meals and dollars of sales, these operations are growing, this indicates a continued, even dramatic, increase in the use of convenience items.

Other operations (fast food hamburger, chicken, and similar counter-service types) are designed around the complete, or almost complete, use of convenience foods. This type of operation, which enables owners to invest less capital in equipment and space and to make use of unskilled workers, is actually growing quickly *because of* the availability and utilization of convenience foods.

The future may also see still greater variety in the types of convenience foods available. The most striking increase in variety may be seen in the area of more elaborate cuisine items. High-quality items such as beef Wellington, elegant canapes, and beef Stroganoff are already available. There will be more such items as procedures used in the processing of simple items are adapted to the more difficult ones.

The quality of convenience foods will improve still further in the future. New methods of reheating (probably accompanied by still newer equipment or, at least, further modifications in existing equipment) or for other processing tasks on-site will also be developed.

Some observers envision (perhaps still very far off in the future) credit cards being used to activate a keyboard from which one selects a complete meal, reserves a table, and is billed. Two or three employees (really technicians) would be needed to operate a computerized kitchen that automatically prepares food items for service. After dinner the table is automatically cleaned, sanitized, and reset.

Other observers, probably thinking of the more immediate future, do not see "kitchenless" facilities. They see food service operations in which facilities are modified, using new and different types of equipment, and management tasks are redesigned to allow for new methods of purchasing, receiving, storing, issuing, and obviously, production-service.

Perhaps kitchens will be viewed as "assembly points," rather than the more traditional "processing units," again with the result that management emphasis can be placed on merchandising, selling, and service, rather than, as at present, needing to be split between these same duties and actual production.

The restaurateur who operated a facility twenty years ago but who has not been in a commercial kitchen since would probably be amazed at the equipment now being used and the many alternate market forms of food items available for purchase. It appears that the restaurateur of today who "leaves the scene" for twenty years would, should he return about the year 2010, be equally amazed. It is likely that there will still be gourmet, high-check, average operations still preparing a large percentage of their food items on-site. There will not, however, be the growth in this segment of the food service industry to compare with that in fast food, lower-check, average properties making maximum (perhaps, in the near future, even total) use of convenience foods. This being the case, then, the percentage of food service dollars used to purchase convenience foods will increase dramatically, to the end that the vast majority of all dollars spent will be used to purchase convenience items. Convenience foods, then, it would appear, will be important in the future of the food service industry.

18 Fresh Fruits and Vegetables

Purpose: To identify particular characteristics of the fresh fruit and vegetable market and provide information that will enable a buyer to write specifications and purchase these commodities.

INTRODUCTION

Fluctuation in the fresh fruit and vegetable market based on product perishability, methods for purchasing, major production areas, and seasons for various commodities are discussed in this chapter in relation to product availability and price. Commodity varietal differences, packs, and U.S. government grades are considered as bases for selection. Special consideration is given to commodities that are frequently purchased. Guidelines for writing specifications and a sample specification are provided.

MARKET

Consumer interest in fresh foods and merchandising fresh fruits and vegetables seem to be increasing in food service operations. This is evidenced in the salad bars appearing in almost all commercial restaurants, including fast food ones, and the fresh fruit and vegetable items appearing on menus. Interest in fresh fruits and vegetables may relate to an increased concern in American society for physical fitness and a healthy diet. Fresh fruits and vegetables are increasingly important meal components and as such are important for quality and cost control in purchasing. Purchasing fruits and vegetables involves market considerations, including principal producing areas; methods of purchasing; U.S. grade standards; size and pack; and variety, type, or maturity of particular commodities.

Fresh fruits and vegetables are one of the most difficult and perhaps most interesting commodities to purchase because of the fluctuation that continually occurs in the market. Perishability of products and inconstancy of supply are the two principal causes of fluctuation, both in quality and price. Supply and quality are based on weather and general environmental conditions, climate, and season in the various growing areas of the United States or the world. If the supply is large, the price will generally be low because the food is perishable and will rot if it is not sold for direct use or preserved by canning or freezing. A buyer can therefore engage in a certain amount of bargaining that may affect price on a fairly short-term basis. Several relatively large-scale buyers refusing to buy a particular perishable commodity because the price is too high may quickly bring down the price if the seller has a large supply on hand. Also impinging on supply are labor and economic problems. An organized group of laborers may decide to strike rather than pick a crop, or growers may decide to let a crop rot in order for the commodity to gain a higher market price, or a commodity may be unavailable because of turmoil in a particular part of the world.

Purchase Method

Traditionally, fresh fruits and vegetables have been purchased on a fairly informal basis or on what has been termed the open market. Because of the high perishability and variability in quality of fresh fruits and vegetables, a buyer may wish to go to the wholesale market to inspect and compare quality of products in addition to using U.S. grades. A buyer may purchase informally by calling various produce dealers, sometimes called commission merchants, to check commodity availability in terms of specifications, quality, and price. After produce availability is determined and prices compared, an order is placed. Produce should always be inspected when received, particularly if the buyer has not gone to the market to make the purchase. Produce that has deteriorated is generally expensive, regardless of the price, in terms of waste and time required to trim away bruises, rot, or unusable material.

Currently, some commodities are purchased on a contract or formal basis. This is true for commodities such as potatoes to be used for french fries by fast food chain operations. Buyers may go to growing areas and contract for specific characteristics in the commodity. For potatoes, this may include requirements for variety, starch, sugar, and specific gravity.

At one time fruit and vegetable commodities were brought, principally by rail, to large wholesale markets in large cities, where they were sold by auction to large buyers and then resold or redistributed. Prior to the beginning of the auctions, the commodities were available for inspection. This method of initial sale has largely been displaced. Commodities may be sold at the point of production, and a variety of modes of transportation are available, including air and trucks. Today, areas of production are more diverse, and better facilities, including controlled atmosphere, are available for storing fresh commodities.

GRADES AND FACTORS IN GRADES

U.S. government grade standards are available for most commodities under authority of the Agricultural Marketing Act of 1946 but are not mandatory for use. However, if grades are applied, the commodity must meet the specifications or requirements for that grade. Considerable quality assurance is provided through the use of grade standards, but a buyer should remember that fresh fruit and vegetable commodities are perishable and should be inspected carefully as well as purchased by grade. Also, a buyer should specify that the condition of the product at the time of delivery should equal the grade specified. Fresh fruits and vegetables, unlike many other commodities, have no legal standards of identity. Standards of identity are definitions of products in terms of composition or ingredients and are thus not particularly relevant to fresh food.

The bases on which fresh fruits and vegetables are graded are particular to individual commodities. Factors may include variety, shape, color, cleanliness, disease or decay, damage or defects, freezing damage, size, pack, maturity or firmness, or trim. The primary consideration in variety is that all units in a container or lot are the same. This is important to a user because variety affects chemical and physical characteristics and the possible use of an item. For example, Russet Burbank variety potatoes are particularly good for baking and have different chemical and physical characteristics from the Irish Cobbler variety. Characteristics, such as starch, sugar, and solids content, are highly important relative to quality of food items. In addition, cooking time for different varieties may vary, and cooking large quantities of different varieties at the same time would cause considerable difficulty.

The form or shape of a commodity is important to a buyer in terms of the appearance, the amount of usable material, and the ease or time required in preparation. A pointed or elongated grapefruit would not make attractive halves. Carrots with long stem ends of small diameter are wasteful and expensive in terms of the weight of trim and the labor involved in trimming.

Cleanliness is an important factor because of the cost in labor of washing items (such as potatoes for baking) and the cost of the weight of soil, rock, stems, or other inedible material included when an item is purchased by the pound. Disease, decay, damage, or freezing are similar in effect in terms of purchasing fresh commodities. All of these conditions produce inedible portions, whether in the form of rot, scab, bruises, deep cracks or cuts, or black interiors resulting from disease or freezing. Inedible portions are costly in terms of material thrown away and the cost of labor for trimming.

PRODUCTION AREAS

In working with the fresh fruit and vegetable market, a buyer can gain considerable knowledge of major production areas and season of principal production. Detailed production data are available from the U.S. Department of Agriculture, but keeping in mind a few basic geographical facts about commodities may be of more value to a buyer than statistics. In general, fruit and vegetable commodities require warmth, sunlight, and water to grow well, but they will be burned up by intense heat. Southern states, such as Texas, Arizona, and Florida, are major producers in late autumn and winter but are too warm in the summer. The central states (such as Ohio and Michigan) and eastern states (such as New York) are suited to production in the summer but are too cold in the winter. Southern states, such as Georgia, Virginia, and North Carolina, may not produce all winter but produce earlier in the spring than states farther north. California is a major producer of numerous commodities both winter and summer, but for some commodities, the season tends to be summer. Tropical types of fruit, such as citrus, tend to be in season in California during the summer and in Florida during the winter. Well-known producers of particular commodities are Washington—apples, berries, and other fruits; Idaho and Maine—potatoes; Michigan—red sour cherries; Georgia, North Carolina, and South Carolina—peaches; Florida—citrus and other fruit and vegetables such as lettuce and tomatoes. California is an extremely important producer of almost all commodities.

COMMODITY TYPE, VARIETY, SIZE, AND PACK

Variety or type, pack, and size are primary considerations in purchasing fresh fruits and vegetables because these are basic determinants of product characteristics and cost. Some of these factors are incorporated into U.S. grades; others are not. Packs of items commonly purchased are indicated in Exhibit 18-1. Following are some basic facts about items frequently purchased.

Commodity	Pack
Apples	Box of 80, 88, 100, or 113 count
Bananas	Box of 40 pounds or per pound as required
Cantaloupe	Crate of 27, 36, or 45 count
Grapefruit	Carton of 4/5 bushel with counts of 27, 32, 36, or 40; from Texas, 7/10 bushel carton with similar counts
Grapes	Lug or carton of 23 pounds, but weights vary
Lemons	Carton of 38 pounds with count of 140 or 150
Oranges	Carton of 4/5 bushel with counts of 80 or 100; from Texas, 7/10 bushel carton with counts of 64, 80, or 100
Broccoli	Carton of 14 bunches
Cabbage	Carton or bag of 50 pounds
Carrots	Crate or mesh bag of 50 pounds; cartons of 2 dozen bunches; or carton with 48 film bags
Celery	Crate of 2½ dozen stalks and weight of 55–60 pounds
Lettuce, iceberg	Carton with 2 or 2½ dozen heads and minimum net weight of 42 pounds
Onions, dry	Mesh bag of 50 pounds
Potatoes	Bag of 50 or 100 pounds or carton with 50 pounds net weight and counts of 100, 110, or 120
Tomatoes	Lug or carton of 20, 28, or 30 pounds.

Exhibit 18-1. Standard or commonly used packs for fresh fruit and vegetable commodities

Lettuce

Several types of lettuce are available; these include iceberg, butterhead, bibb, romaine, and leaf. All have particular characteristics of form, color, and flavor. Variation and mixtures in type can add interest and variety in salad preparation, and some types of lettuce are particularly suited to certain salads. Tossed salad prepared from a mixture of greens may be more attractive and tasty than when prepared using only iceberg lettuce. A jello salad will not tip so readily, can be more quickly assembled, and may be better displayed on a leaf of lettuce or garnished with a few pieces of endive than in the bottom of an iceberg lettuce cup. However, iceberg lettuce cups may be needed to display large salads such as chicken, shrimp, or fruit used as entrees. Thus, consideration should be given to salad design in terms of basic material and variety of lettuce.

Iceberg lettuce is the most commonly used lettuce, and for a fresh product the commodity is highly standardized. Grades for lettuce are U.S. Fancy, U.S. No. 1, and U.S. No. 2. Standard pack recommendations are specified in conjunction with grades. Lettuce packed in a standard lettuce container should have a net weight of not less than 42 nor more than 50 pounds. The standard pack of lettuce is 2 or 2½ dozen heads per case. The case with 2 dozen heads is most generally used. Minimum weight requirements should generally be specified at 42 pounds for the case of 2 dozen heads and at 50 pounds for 2½ dozen heads.

Potatoes

Type or variety of potato affects cooking quality, appearance, and use. Skin color may be important if red-skin potatoes are to be merchandised, and shape may be important in terms of length of a cut for french fries. Potatoes with relatively high specific gravity have a high proportion of starch compared to sugar. Generally, a high (minimum 1.08) specific gravity is considered important in potatoes for baking and french frying but not as important in those to be boiled or pan fried. However, potatoes with low specific gravity and high sugar content may produce gummy mashed potatoes. Types of potatoes include long russet, long white, round white, and round red. Type may be more important than variety since varieties within types may be difficult to distinguish. Long russet potatoes are long and cylindrical with a netted skin. Potatoes of this type have typically been grown in the northwestern part of the United States (very frequently in Idaho), but they are also grown in other parts of the country. These potatoes are very high in specific gravity and are considered a premium quality potato, particularly for baking. Long white, round red, and round white types have variable amounts of sugar, starch, and solid matter, but these types generally have lower specific gravity and starch content than the long russet. Probably the most important variety of long russet potato is the Russet Burbank, and the most important long white is the White Rose. Important round white varieties are Katahdin, Kennebec, and Irish Cobbler. Red Pontiac is an important variety of round red type potato.

U.S. grade standards are available for potatoes and include specifications for minimum size as well as quality. Grades are U.S. Extra No. 1, U.S. No. 1, U.S. Commercial, and U.S. No. 2. U.S. Extra No. 1 potatoes are at least 2¼ inches in diameter or 5 ounces in weight and do not vary more than 1¼ inches in diameter or 6 ounces in weight. Thus, potatoes of this grade have some uniformity in size and are not inordinately small. U.S. No. 1 grade potatoes have a minimum diameter of 1⅞ inches, and U.S. No. 2, a minimum diameter of 1½ inches unless the buyer specifies something different in conjunction with grade.

U.S. Commercial meets the size requirement of U.S. No. 1. In addition to minimum requirements for size that are a part of U.S. grades, terminology for other size specifications is provided in conjunction with grades. Size may be specified in terms of diameter or count per 50-pound box. Size based on count per 50-pound box is related to weight of individual potatoes, and, in general, the weight of individual potatoes is equal to 50 pounds divided by count. For example, size 50 potatoes weigh about 1 pound each; size 100, 8 ounces.

When specified in terms of diameter, sizes are A at 1⅞ inches with 40 percent of the potatoes 2½ inches or larger; B at 1½ to 2¼ inches; small at 1¾ to 2½ inches; medium at 2¼ to 3¼ inches; and large at 3 to 4½ inches. In terms of counts per 50-pound box, weight ranges for the various size designations are as follows: Under 50, 15 ounces; 50, 12 to 19 ounces; 60, 10 to 16 ounces; 70, 9 to 15 ounces; 80, 8 to 13 ounces; 90, 7 to 12 ounces; 100, 6 to 10 ounces; 110, 5 to 9 ounces; 120, 130, 140, and over 140, 4 to 8 ounces. Since considerable range in weight is incorporated in size designations, buyers may wish to specify more precise size requirements in purchasing. For example, a buyer may specify size 120 potatoes at 6 ounces with 1 ounce tolerance over or under. This may be particularly pertinent to portion control in potatoes to be used for baking. Also, a hospital patient on a controlled diet would certainly prefer a whole baked potato purchased at a fairly precise weight to a potato that has been cut, after baking, to the size required for the dietary purpose. Size is also important in terms of baking time, fitting covers over plates, and in control of cost.

Tomatoes

Tomatoes are available around the year and are used extensively as a salad or a salad garnish. In order for standards to appropriately reflect the characteristics of the commodity, several sets of U.S. standards are available; these include U.S.

standards for "fresh tomatoes" and U.S. "consumer standards for fresh tomatoes." Consumer standards for fresh tomatoes are applicable only to field-grown products and not to tomatoes grown in greenhouses. Grades for fresh tomatoes are U.S. No. 1, U.S. Combination, U.S. No. 2, and U.S. No. 3. U.S. Consumer grades are U.S. Grade A and U.S. Grade B. Color and size characteristics, as well as typical factors in quality, are incorporated in grades. In standards for greenhouse tomatoes, size designations are in terms of minimum and maximum diameter in inches and 1/32 of inches. Sizes and minimum diameters in inches are extra small—1 28/32 inches; small—2 4/32 inches; medium, 2 9/32 inches; large—2 17/32 inches; extra large—2 28/32 inches; maximum large—3 15/32 inches. Differences between minimum and maximum diameters are only fractions in 1/32 inches, which means that the difference in size among tomatoes with a particular size designation is extremely small. Consequently, specifications would not need to be more precise than the size designation.

Terms for color classification are green—completely green in color; breakers—color other than green on not more than 10 percent of the surface; turning—10 to 30 percent of the surface pink or red; pink—30 to 60 percent of surface pink or red; red—more than 90 percent red; mixed color—product that does not meet standards for any of the preceding. For U.S. consumer standards, size classification is in terms of weight. Tomatoes under 3 ounces are small; 3 to 6 ounces, medium; 6 to 10, large; and over 10 ounces, very large.

U.S. Consumer grade designations for color or maturity are: turning—some part less than half is pink; pink—½ to ¾ of surface is pink or red; hard ripe—¾ or more of surface pink or red; and firm ripe—¾ or more of surface red.

Apples

Apples are grown commercially in many states, including Washington, New York, Michigan, Virginia, California, West Virginia, Ohio, Massachusetts, New Jersey, Illinois, North Carolina, and Oregon. Apple varieties should be selected according to intended use. Some varieties are best if eaten raw, others are better cooked, and some are considered good for all purposes. Principal commercial varieties of apples are Red Delicious, Golden Delicious, McIntosh, Roman Beauty, York Imperial, Winesap, Jonathan, Cortland, Rhode Island Greening, and Northern Spy. Red Delicious apples are the principal variety for eating raw but do not cook well. Winesap, Roman Beauty, Northern Spy, McIntosh, Jonathan, and Grimes Golden are good all-purpose apples; Roman Beauty is particularly good for baking because the skin is not prone to shrivelling and the fruit is mealy. Rhode Island Greening is excellent for sauce and pie but is not particularly good served raw.

U.S. grades for apples are well defined and include U.S. Extra Fancy, U.S. Fancy, U.S. No. 1, and U.S. Utility. Packing and marking requirements are important factors in grades. Packing requirements are meant to prevent bruising of the fruit and involve packing in cartons with or without cells or trays for individual fruit or in wooden boxes or baskets in such a manner as to prevent the apples from moving. Apples on the face of any container must be reasonably representative in size, color, and quality of the contents. The numerical count or the minimum diameter of the apples packed in a closed container must be indicated on the container. Thus, apples are one of the most standardized and easily purchased fresh commodities.

Count of apples in a standard container indicates size and should be specified by a buyer. Counts of 48, 56, 64, and 72 indicate extra large fruit; counts of 80, 88, and 100, large; 113, 125 and 138, medium; and 150, 163, and 175, small. Apples of 180 count correspond to 2¼ inches in diameter; 160, 2½ inches; 140, 2⅝ inches; 120, 2¾ inches; 96, 3 inches; and 80, 3½ inches. Sizes 80, 88 or 100 are generally selected for serving a whole apple and are also suitable for cooking or salad preparation since fewer fruits of this size need to be peeled to yield a specific amount of product. Small-size fruits may be used for serving a whole apple to small children in elementary or nursery schools where a larger apple is likely to be partly wasted. Extra fancy quality extra large fruit is beautiful but expensive and should be purchased only for special occasions or merchandising efforts.

Bananas

Bananas are almost totally imported into the United States. They are an unusual commodity because they are used extensively, but no U.S. grade standards have been established. Brand name can be an important indicator of quality, and purchase may be made in terms of brand.

Size of fruit and degree of ripeness may be important to a buyer. Selection of size is based on intended use and portion size. If a whole banana is to be served, size will affect cost per serving since the fruit is commonly priced by the pound. Size is typically indicated as small, medium, and large. Generally about three medium-size bananas will weigh 1 pound. Ripeness in bananas selected for purchase is based on time of intended use. Common trade designations for ripeness are full ripe—bright yellow color flecked with brown and no green; hard ripe—bright yellow with no brown; turning ripe—pale yellow with a green tip. Bananas are cut in bunches of 40 pounds, sometimes called hands, and shipped in 40-pound cartons, but they may

also be purchased by the pound in the quantity desired.

Grapefruit

Grapefruit has different characteristics depending on its growing area. Several U.S. grade standards have been established that reflect these differences. Separate standards have been established for grapefruit from Texas and states other than Florida, California, and Arizona; Florida; and California and Arizona. Differences in product characteristics and packs can be confusing, but the following considerations need to be kept in mind by a buyer. Florida grapefruit are generally bigger than Texas grapefruit, even though they are designated the same size, because size is related to number of fruits per box. The standard box for Florida fruit is 4/5 bushel; the standard box from Texas is 7/10 bushel. California and Arizona fruit are generally brighter colored but thicker skinned and less juicy than Florida fruit. Packs of fruit from Florida, California, and Arizona are generally similar, but a 4/5 bushel of Florida grapefruit will generally weigh considerably more than 4/5 bushel of California or Arizona fruit. Difference in weight generally reflects difference in the juice content of the fruit. Florida and Texas fruit are generally in greatest supply from October through May, and the California and Arizona fruit from May through September. The most important varieties are Marsh or Pink Marsh, which are seedless, and Duncan or Florida Common grapefruit, which has seeds. U.S. grades for Florida grapefruit are U.S. Fancy, U.S. No. 1 Bright, U.S. No. 1 Golden, U.S. No. 1 Bronze, U.S. No. 1 Russet, U.S. No. 2, U.S. No. 2 Bright, U.S. No. 2 Russet, and U.S. No. 3. Sizes and counts of Florida grapefruit are indicated in U.S. grade standards. In terms of a 4/5 bushel box, these are 14, 18, 23, 27, 32, 36, 40, 48, 56, and

64. Sizes 27 through 40 are generally acceptable for half-grapefruit servings, although a size 40 tends to be somewhat small in terms of attractiveness.

Processed Fresh Commodities

Fresh commodities have been considered highly expensive in terms of the labor required for preparation. Presently, most produce houses sell almost any form of fresh commodity in prepared or convenience form. These are usually packed 5, 10, 25, or 30 pounds to a plastic bag. Examples of the forms of various commodities available include the following: cabbage heads—whole, halved, quartered, shredded coarse, shredded medium, or shredded fine; carrots—whole, cut in 2-inch lengths, cut in sticks, shredded medium, shredded fine; celery—whole, sticks, or diced; lettuce—heads, chopped, or shredded fine; onions—whole, diced, or sliced; peeled potatoes—whole, quartered, sliced, diced, or French cut; and tossed salad. When purchasing prepared forms of fresh commodities a buyer may specify the grade, variety, type, and size of a raw commodity as well as the form of the processed product.

SPECIFICATIONS

Factors to consider in writing a specification for fresh fruits or vegetables include the following: specific commodity name, form of commodity (fresh—not frozen, canned, or dried), variety or type, grade, geographic area of production if relevant, size or count, pack including weight tolerance if relevant, processing required, color if relevant, condition upon delivery, and any other factors necessary to obtain a product with the desired characteristics. Any of these factors that are relevant to the particular commodity to be purchased and characteristics desired in the product should be included in the specification, but not all may be necessary.

Sample Fresh Fruit and Vegetable Specifications

Potatoes, fresh, Russet Burbank variety, U.S. Extra No. 1 grade; size 100, 7 ounces with weight tolerance of no more than ½ ounce per potato; Idaho grown; packed in fiberboard box with minimum net weight of 50 pounds; condition upon delivery equal to grade indicated.

Apples, fresh, Red Delicious; U.S. Fancy grade; count and size of 88 per Western box; Washington grown; condition upon delivery equal to grade indicated.

Lettuce, Iceberg; U.S. No. 1 grade; packed 24 heads per fiberboard carton with minimum net weight of 42 pounds; California grown; condition at delivery equal to grade indicated.

In the preceding sample specifications a growing area has been indicated. While growing area is important in relation to commodity quality characteristics, precise specification of growing area is limiting in terms of product acquisition; it may make little sense in terms of quality and availability from other growing areas, may make the commodity unnecessarily costly, and generally should not be strictly adhered to.

REFERENCES

Code of Federal Regulations, Agriculture, Title 7, Parts 2800–2851. Washington, D.C.: U.S. Government Printing Office, 1981.

National Restaurant Association. *Buying, Handling, and Using Fresh Fruits.* Chicago, Illinois: National Restaurant Association, n.d.

National Restaurant Association. *Buying, Handling, and Using Fresh Vegetables.* Chicago, Illinois: National Restaurant Association, n.d.

United Fresh Fruit and Vegetable Association. *Container Net Weights.* United Fresh Fruit and Vegetable Association, 1976.

19 Processed Fruits and Vegetables

Purpose: To describe legal standards and other factors important in purchasing processed fruits and vegetables and to provide guidelines for writing purchase specifications.

INTRODUCTION

Standards of identity, which legally define products in terms of ingredients, and standards of quality, which indicate legally permissible defects such as bruises, pits, or skin remaining after peeling, are covered in this chapter as are legal standards for fill of container and U.S. grade standards,which are used to differentiate product quality. Standard container sizes are indicated, and standards useful in purchasing frozen fruits and vegetables are discussed. Guidelines for writing specifications and a sample specification are provided.

The purchase of processed fruits and vegetables is simplified by their relatively consistent and predictable quality because of product stability and highly developed U.S. government standards. A buyer who understands government standards and services can readily communicate requirements for ingredients, form, and quality in products purchased. Further, a dietitian can have some knowledge of food composition because permissible or required ingredients in many commodities are defined by law. Important government standards are standards of identity, standards of quality, standards of fill of container, and grade standards.

STANDARDS OF IDENTITY

Standards of identity are available for many processed fruit and vegetable products, including fruit and vegetable juices. A standard of identity, under authority of the Federal Food, Drug, and Cosmetic Act administered by the Food and Drug Administration, defines a product in terms of its ingredients and composition. Identity standards include required and optional ingredients, minimum quantities of required ingredients, packing medium, options in variety, and options in color type.

The term "Brix" may be noted in conjunction with packing medium. Canners traditionally have used an instrument called a Brix hydrometer with gradients calibrated to read degrees in terms of the percentage of sucrose in solution. The percentage in a packing medium may be specified either in degrees Brix as a specific value or by terms such as "light syrup," "heavy syrup," or "extra heavy syrup," which denote specific percentage concentrations of sugar. An example of a standard of identity follows.

Canned Apricots, Standard of Identity

Ingredients. Canned apricots is the food prepared from mature apricots of one of the optional styles specified in paragraph (a)(2) of this section, which may be packed as solid pack or in one of the optional packing media specified in paragraph (a)(3) of this section. Such food may also contain one, or any combination of two or more of the following safe and suitable optional ingredients:

(i) Natural and artificial flavors.

(ii) Spice.

(iii) Vinegar, lemon juice, or organic acids.

(iv) Apricot pits, except in the cases of unpeeled whole apricots and peeled whole apricots, in a quantity not more than one apricot pit to each 227 grams (8 ounces) of finished canned apricots.

(v) Apricot kernels, except in the cases of unpeeled whole apricots and peeled whole apricots, and except when optional ingredient under paragraph (a)(4) of this section is used.

(vi) Ascorbic acid in an amount no greater than necessary to preserve color. Such food is sealed in a container and before or after sealing is so processed by heat as to prevent spoilage.

(2) Optional styles of the apricot ingredient. The optional styles of the apricot ingredient referred to in paragraph (a) of this section are peeled or unpeeled:

(i) Whole.

(ii) Halves.

(iii) Quarters.

(iv) Slices.

(v) Pieces or irregular pieces.

Each such ingredient, except in the cases of unpeeled whole apricots and peeled whole apricots, is pitted.

(3) Packing media (i) The optional packing media referred to in paragraph (a)(1) of this section, as defined in 145.3, are:

(a) Water.

(b) Fruit juice(s) and water.

(c) Fruit juice(s).

Such packing media may be used as such or any one or any combination of two or more safe and suitable nutritive carbohydrate sweetener(s) may be added. Sweeteners defined in 145.3 shall be as defined therein, except that a nutritive carbohydrate sweetener for which a standard of identity has been established in Part 168 of this chapter shall comply with such standard in lieu of any definition that may appear in 145.3.

(ii) When a sweetener is added as a part of any such liquid packing medium, the density range of the resulting packing medium expressed as percent by weight of sucrose (degrees Brix) as determined by the procedure prescribed in 145.3(m) shall be designated by the appropriate name for the respective density ranges, namely:

(a) When the density of the solution is 10 percent or more but less than 16 percent, the medium shall be designated as "slightly sweetened water"; or "extra light sirup"; "slightly sweetened fruit juice(s) and water"; or "slightly sweetened fruit juice(s)," as the case may be.

(b) When the density of the solution is 16 percent or more but less than 21 percent, the medium shall be designated as "light sirup"; "lightly sweetened fruit juice(s) and water"; or "lightly sweetened fruit juice(s)," as the case may be.

(c) When the density of the solution is 21 percent or more but less than 25 percent, the medium shall be designated as "heavy sirup"; "heavily sweetened fruit juice(s) and water"; or "heavily sweetened fruit juice(s)," as the case may be.

(d) When the density of the solution is 25 percent or more but not more than 40 percent, the medium shall be designated as "extra heavy sirup"; "extra heavily sweetened fruit juice(s) and water"; or "extra heavily sweetened fruit juice(s)," as the case may be.[1]

In spite of the apparent complexity of standards of identity, the definitions are commonly accepted in the marketplace, and understanding them is necessary for intelligent purchasing by a food buyer. Further, these standards are an excellent means to facilitate purchasing. For example, a buyer may specify canned apricots packed in water. With these few words, the buyer can expect to receive everything that has been described in the standard of identity for these characteristics in the product. Although the average homemaker and some uninformed volume food service buyers may not have heard of standards of identity, people generally have definite expectations as to the appearance of canned tomatoes, peaches, or green beans because the products are highly standardized and defined by federal law.

STANDARDS OF QUALITY

Legal standards of quality for canned goods define products in terms of texture and the defects that may be present. This includes firmness or toughness; peel or stems that may remain; size; and gouges or off-center cuts that may produce nonuniform shape. As standards of identity assure food composition, so legal standards of quality mean that a buyer may expect definite quality characteristics in canned food.

Canned Apricots, Standard of Quality

The standard of quality for canned apricots is as follows:

(i) All units tested in accordance with the method prescribed in paragraph

(b)(2) of this section are pierced by a weight of not more than 300 grams.

(ii) In the cases of whole apricots, halves, and quarters, the weight of the largest unit in the container is not more than twice the weight of the smallest unit therein.

(iii) Not more than 20 percent of the units in the container are blemished with scab, hail injury, discoloration, or other abnormalities.

(iv) In the cases of whole apricots, halves, and quarters, all units are untrimmed, or are so trimmed as to preserve normal shape.

(v) Except in the case of mixed pieces of irregular sizes and shapes, not more than 5 percent of the units in a container of 20 or more units, and not more than 1 unit in a container of less than 20 units, are crushed or broken. (A unit which has lost its normal shape because of ripeness and which bears no mark of crushing shall not be considered to be crushed or broken.)[2]

STANDARDS OF FILL OF CONTAINER

Legal standards of fill of container exist for numerous commodities. However, these standards are probably the least helpful of all standards available for canned food. The standard for fill of container for canned apricots is: "the maximum quantity of the optional apricot ingredient that can be sealed in the container and processed by heat to prevent spoilage, without crushing or breaking such ingredient."[3] Obviously, this standard is inadequate in terms of a

---

[1]*Code of Federal Regulations, Food and Drugs, Title 21, Parts 100–169* (Washington, D.C.: U.S. Government Printing Office, April 1, 1982), p. 271.

[2]*Code of Federal Regulations, Food and Drugs, Title 21, Parts 100–169* (Washington, D.C.: U.S. Government Printing Office, April 1, 1982), p. 272.

[2]*Code of Federal Regulations, Food and Drugs, Title 21, Parts 100–169* (Washington, D.C.: U.S. Government Printing Office, April 1, 1982), p. 273.

buyer knowing what quantity of food is in a can. Although not mandatory for use, recommendations for "fill weight" or "drained weight" may be found in conjunction with U.S. grade standards.

GRADE STANDARDS

United States Department of Agriculture (USDA) grade standards are not mandatory for use by a food processor and are infrequently found on the labels of canned fruits and vegetables in the retail market. These standards are, however, very well developed for almost all canned or frozen fruits and vegetables and should be used by the food buyer as a means to specify the quality characteristics desired.

USDA grade standards are essentially quality standards based on standards of quality defined in the Federal Food, Drug, and Cosmetic Act. The lowest grade of a commodity is basically the same as the minimum standard of quality. Factors involved in determining a quality grade differ among commodities, but in general they are color; uniformity of size and symmetry; defects; character or texture; and, for commodities such as applesauce, consistency. Defects are peel, bruises, pits, or imprecise cutting. Character or texture refers to firmness, based on degree of ripeness or extent of processing, or toughness, based on fibrous material in the raw commodity.

Grades for commodities are determined by scoring various product characteristics. Points may be assigned to each characteristic with a minimum score for each grade or be based on the numbers of minor, major, severe, critical, and total defects related to each characteristic. Grade designations are not consistent among commodities but in general are "A," "B," "C," and "Substandard." "A" may also be termed "Fancy"; "B," "Choice"; and "C," "Standard." In some instances,

"Grade B" is termed "Extra Standard," and some commodities may have only two grades. The importance of reading the grade standard and the standard of identity before buying food or writing a specification for a commodity cannot be overemphasized. Without this knowledge, a buyer does not know product characteristics in terms of grade or ingredients or the proper terms for use in purchasing.

The U.S. standard for grades for canned apricots is provided as an example.

Grades for Canned Apricots

(a) "U.S. Grade A" or "U.S. Fancy" is the quality of halves, slices, and whole canned apricots that:

(1) Have similar varietal characteristics;

(2) Have normal flavor and odor;

(3) Have at least a reasonably good color that scores not less than 17 points;

(4) Are at least reasonably uniform in size and symmetry for the applicable styles except for limits of off-suture cuts in the style of halves;

(5) Are practically free from defects;

(6) Have at least a reasonably good character; and

(7) For those factors which are scored in accordance with the scoring system outlined in this subpart the total score is not less than 90 points.

(b) "U.S. Grade B" or "U.S. Choice" is the quality of canned apricots of any style that:

(1) Have similar varietal characteristics;

(2) Have a normal flavor and odor;

(3) Have at least a reasonably good color;

(4) Are at least fairly uniform in size and symmetry for the applicable styles except for the limits of off-suture cuts in the style of halves;

(5) Are at least reasonably free from defects;

(6) Have at least a reasonably good character; and

(7) For those factors which are scored in accordance with the scoring system outlined in this subpart the total score is not less than 80 points.

(c) "U.S. Grade C" or "U.S. Standard" is the quality of canned apricots of any style that:

(1) Have similar varietal characteristics;

(2) Have a normal flavor and odor;

(3) Have at least a fairly good color;

(4) Are at least fairly uniform in size and symmetry for the applicable style;

(5) Are at least fairly free from defects;

(6) Have at least a fairly good character; and

(7) For those factors which are scored in accordance with the scoring system outlined in this subpart the total score is not less than 70 points

(d) "Substandard" is the quality of canned apricots that fail to meet the requirements of U.S. Grade C.[4]

Information that is not a part of a quality grade may be presented in conjunction with grade standards. Included is information on style, packing medium, and recommendations for drained or fill weight. This kind of information is highly valuable and should be used in writing product specifications but must be stated in addition to the requirements for grade.

PACK AND FILL OF CONTAINER

Contents of containers may be stated as drained weight, fill weight, or net weight. Traditionally, cans have been labeled for net weight, which means the weight of the total can content including solid content and liquid packing medium. From net

[4]Code of Federal Regulations, Agriculture, Title 7, Part 2852 (Washington, D.C.: U.S. Government Printing Office, July 1, 1981), p. 557.

weight labeling, a buyer can have no knowledge of the part of total weight that is solid content, such as peach halves, and the part that is liquid. Drained weight is the weight of the solid material in a can after the liquid has been drained away. Recommended values for "drained weight" and procedures for determining weight have been established by the USDA for some but not all commodities and are stated in conjunction with U.S. grades.

Recently (1973), government standards have been established for determining "fill weight," which is the weight of the commodity filled into a can. The USDA has established recommended fill weights in conjunction with U.S. grades for canned Freestone peaches, Kadota figs, Clingstone peaches, pears, red tart pitted cherries, sweet cherries, apricots, grapes, plums, and asparagus. Values for fill or drained weight are important and should be a part of specifications written by a buyer. When fill weight information is unavailable, a buyer should open sample cans to make drained-weight determinations and comparison of products. Symbols used to denote fill of a can and definitions are as follows:

$\overline{X}_d$—Minimum average drainage weight of all the units in a sample.

LL—Lower limit for drained weight of an individual sample unit.

$\overline{X}_{min}$—Minimum lot average fill weight.

LRL—Lower reject limit for individual fill weight measurements.

PACKAGING

Commodities are packed in numerous sizes, types, and shapes of cans. Complete information on available cans may be found in The Almanac of the Canning, Freezing, Preserving Industries, which is published annually. The size of cans in the United States is described by two three-digit numbers. The first three-digit number (reading

Common Name	Size	Capacity (water weight)		Number Per Case
		Avoir. Oz.	Pounds	
No. 10	603 x 700	109.45	6.8	6
No. 3 cyl. (46 oz.)	404 x 700	51.70	3.2	12
No. 303	303 x 406	16.85	1.05	24
No. 2	307 x 409	20.50	1.28	24
No. 2½	401 x 411	29.75	1.86	24
No. 5	502 x 510	59.10	3.69	12
No. 5 squat	603 x 408	68.15	4.26	6

Source: The Almanac of the Canning, Freezing, Preserving Industries (Westminster, Maryland: Edward E. Judge & Sons, 1989).

Exhibit 19-1. Names, sizes, capacity, and pack of common cans

from left to right) indicates the diameter of the can, and the second indicates height. For each of the three-digit numbers, the first digit denotes inches, and the second two denote fractions of an inch in units of 1/16. Thus, a size 603 x 700 can is 6 3/16 inches in diameter and 7 inches high. Data on commonly used can sizes, capacity, and pack are presented in Exhibit 19-1. Buyers need information of this kind to communicate in the market and for specifying quantities of food to be purchased.

Frozen Fruits and Vegetables

U.S. grade standards but not standards of identity, quality, or fill of container are available for many frozen fruits and vegetables. In general, grade standards for frozen fruits and vegetables are simpler than for canned foods but are still very useful in writing product specifications. Fruit may be packed without sugar or with sugar in varying proportions such as four or five parts of fruit to one part of sugar by weight. Fruits or vegetables may be individually quick frozen (IQF) or frozen in solid blocks. Food may be bulk packed in a case or can or divided into a number of smaller units and packed in a case. Common packaging units are in Exhibit 19-2.

Vegetables are generally packed in a plastic bag or bags in a fiberboard case or in plastic-coated boxes in a fiberboard case. Fruit may be in cans, plastic-coated boxes, or plastic bags packed in a fiberboard carton.

Grade and Other Certification

The Food Safety and Inspection Service of the USDA, for a fee or contract, will certify grade and other factors such as condition, style, size, syrup density, and weight. A buyer may and probably should require that a seller provide a USDA "Inspection Certificate" as a condition for purchase. A processor (seller) may provide the "Inspection Certificate" on the basis of one of the following: lot inspection; continuous inspection; pack certification under a designated lot contract; or pack certification under a quality assurance contract.

Lot inspection means inspection and grading of a group of containers of the same

Fruit	Vegetables
Bulk Pack	Bulk Pack
30-lb. can	20-lb. bulk-pack case
20-lb. case	
10-lb. case	Unit Pack
	12/2-lb. packages per case
Unit Pack	12/2.5-lb. packages per case
6/6-lb. per case	12/3-lb. packages per case
6/5-lb. per case	
6/6.5-lb. per case	
6/8.5-lb. per case	
12/4.5-lb. per case	
12/12-oz. per case	
12/20-oz. per case	
12/4.5-oz. per case	

Exhibit 19-2. Frozen fruit and vegetable packaging

size and type which contain a processed product of the same type and style located in one place and available for inspection at the same time. The location of the commodity may be a company or commercial warehouse, truck, rail car, or other storage facility or conveyance consistent with industry practice. Usually the inspector has no knowledge of the conditions under which the product was produced, and evaluation is based on inspection of the finished product.

Continuous inspection is performed in an approved plant where at least one inspector is present at all times the plant is in operation. Grading and inspection are based on checks made during preparation, processing, packing, and warehousing of all products under contract. Pack certification is based on inspection and grading in an approved plant where one or more inspectors make checks during preparation and processing of products but are not in the plant at all times. Pack certification may be made under a designated lot or quality assurance contract. For designated lot contracts, inspectors will grade and certify only those lots specified by the applicant. In a quality assurance contract, lots will be certified on the basis of information provided by the processor's quality control records and by grading lots at random to verify that the records are correct.

SPECIFICATIONS

Based on the information in this chapter, a buyer who knows product requirements for a particular operation should be able to write specifications for processed fruit and vegetables. The following factors should be considered for inclusion:

1. Specific legal or common name
2. Style
3. Type or variety
4. Grade; possibly minimum score
5. Packing medium
6. Size
7. Pack
8. Fill, net, or drained weight or count
9. Particular factors relevant to a specific operation

An example of a specification for canned apricots is provided.

Specification for Canned Apricots

Apricots, canned unpeeled halves. U.S. Grade A. Packed in light syrup in No. 10 Cans with $\overline{X}_{min}$ fill weight of 69.5 ounces; 6 No. 10 Cans per Case.

REFERENCES

Code of Federal Regulations, Food and Drugs, Title 21, Parts 100–169. Washington, D.C.: U.S. Government Printing Office, 1982.

Code of Federal Regulations, Agriculture, Title 7, Part 2852. Washington, D.C.: U.S. Government Printing Office, 1981.

The Almanac of the Canning, Freezing, Preserving Industries. Westminster, Maryland: Edward E. Judge & Sons, 1982.

20 Groceries

Purpose: To identify characteristics of grocery products based on legal standards of identity for composition, processing technology, and basic chemical characteristics of the foods.

INTRODUCTION

Flour and cereal; sugars, jams, and jellies; fats and oils; pickles and olives; spices and flavorings; coffee, tea, and chocolate products are discussed in terms of the differences in product characteristics. Chemical properties of flour, sugars, and fats are described to indicate appropriate use for particular purposes. Standards of identity, grade standards, and other considerations are identified to provide a basis for product differentiation. Standard packs for various products are indicated.

Grocery items are staples in food service operations. They are quite varied in composition and in availability of standards for use in purchasing. These items are usually readily available, but diversity in what appear to be similar items makes knowledge of product characteristics essential since certain products will be suitable only for particular purposes. Some discussion of individual commodity items follows.

FLOUR AND CEREAL PRODUCTS

Flours are blended and marketed for particular purposes and should be selected for purchase in terms of their intended use. Flour is variable in chemical and physical composition based on wheat variety or type and milling. Basic types of wheat, which include numerous varieties, are hard red spring, grown primarily in the northern Great Plains states; hard red winter, produced largely in the southern Great Plains; soft red winter, from states east of the Mississippi River and below the Great Lakes; and white wheat, grown in small quantities in many areas of the country.

The terms hard and soft refer to the hardness of the grain and are indicative of the protein content and best use for the product. Soft wheats are generally relatively low in protein, high in starch, and are the ideal type for use in preparing bakery items such as cakes, cookies, biscuits, or other items not leavened by yeast. Cake flours have 7 to 8 percent protein, are high grade, and are bolted (sifted) through fine mesh. Pastry flour for biscuits and similar products is 7 to 9 percent protein, may be lower grade than cake flour, and is not so finely sifted. Hard wheats are higher in protein (14 percent or more) and are excellent for use in bread or preparation of pasta products.

Wheat may be selected by millers in terms of U.S. quality grades and types of wheat relative to the type of flour to be produced. The miller determines the ultimate chemical composition of the flour produced through selecting and mixing various varieties of wheat and through the milling process. Wheat must be selected and mixed to provide for uniformity in the flour over time. In milling, the bran and germ are separated from the endosperm or principal part of the wheat kernel and are ground into a fine powder or flour. This involves a repeated sequence of grinding, sifting to separate large from small particles, and regrinding.

Grades of flour are related to the separation process. The first grinding results in the most refined product. With successive grindings more bran and germ become part of the flour, the product becomes darker, and the ash (mineral) content increases. Grades are extra short or fancy patent flour, short or first patent, short patent, medium patent, long patent, and straight, which is flour from the major part of the grain with just the bran layer removed.

A buyer may purchase flour on the basis of specifications for protein, starch, ash, lipid, cellulose, and moisture. The better procedure may be to purchase products marketed as high-grade cake, bread, pastry, or all-purpose flour (depending on need), based on trade name and performance in product preparation. The buyer must always remember that the type of flour is of major importance in product preparation. Bread prepared from cake flour or cake made from bread flour is quite likely to be inedible; gravy or pie filling will probably never thicken if bread flour is used as a thickener.

Various types of flours and cereal products have been defined in terms of legal standards of identity. These may be found in the *Code of Federal Regulations. Title 21, Part 137.* Included are definitions of flour, bromated flour, enriched flour, instantized flours, phosphated flour, self-rising flour, cracked wheat, crushed wheat, whole wheat flour, and various products. A buyer or dietitian may be interested in these definitions in terms of knowing food composition or use for a particular purpose.

Various rice, pasta, corn, and wheat items have federal standards of identity related to the composition of products. These may be found in the *Code of Federal Regulations, Title 21, Parts 100–169.* Many forms of these items are available, and product definitions should be consulted to identify exact items desired. For example, one may buy white corn flour, yellow corn flour, corn grits, enriched corn grits, quick grits, yellow grits, white corn meal, bolted white corn meal, enriched corn meal, degerminated white corn meal, self-rising white corn meal, self-rising yellow corn meal, yellow corn meal, bolted yellow corn meal, or degerminated yellow corn meal according to federal definition. These should be selected in terms of use in particular menu items, and federal definitions should be consulted for information on the composition of these and similar types of wheat, rice, and pasta products.

SUGARS, JAMS, AND JELLIES

Chemically, sugars occur in many different forms. These include sucrose, glucose, dextrose, fructose, and lactose. Although all are sugars, they do not have the same properties and cannot be substituted for one another with the same result. A buyer must be certain to receive the correct form since substitutions are sometimes made in the market. Sucrose, the sugar most commonly used in food service, is available in several frequently purchased forms. These include granulated sugar, brown sugar, and powdered sugar. Granulated sugar is refined; brown sugar is less refined than white granulated; and powdered sugar is ground granulated sugar.

What we generally call sugar (sucrose) is obtained from sugar cane by crushing and shredding the stalks, concentrating extracted juice by boiling, and then centrifuging to separate liquid from crystals. The initial substance produced is raw sugar, which is further refined to produce typical white crystals. Granulated sugar is available in varying sizes of grains for use in particular products. Coarse (large) grained sugar, called sanding sugar, is used for coating or sprinkling on confectionery products to add sparkle; very fine grains are used for making fondant where a smooth creamy end-product is desired. Sugar with medium granules may be selected for general use, but finer sugar, called extra fine granulated or bar sugar may be used for beverages (bar) or baking so that granules will dissolve quickly. Powdered sugars are ground to various degrees indicated by X's for increasing degrees of fineness, including XXXX, XXXXXX , and 10X.

Brown sugars are composed of tiny sugar crystals covered with a fine film of cane syrup, and they result either from incomplete refining of granulated sugar or adding cane molasses to fully refined sugar. Brown sugar is available in various gradients of color or refining. Commonly available on the market are light brown, dark brown, and medium. Color selected is based on strength of molasses flavor desired.

Standards of identity are also available for other sugar products, such as anhydrous dextrose, dextrose monohydrate, glucose syrup, dried glucose syrup, lactose, cane syrup, maple syrup, sorghum syrup, and table syrup (*Code of Federal Regulations, Title 21, Part 168*). These may be useful in purchasing or for knowledge of sugar concentration when making dietary calculations. Grade standards are available for sugar-cane syrup, sugar-cane molasses, refiners' syrup, and maple syrup.

Grades of maple syrup may be of particular interest; they are U.S. Grade AA, Fancy; U.S. Grade A, U.S. Grade B, and Unclassified. Maple syrup must be made from the sap of a maple tree, contain not more than 35 percent water, and weigh not less than 11 pounds per gallon.

Jams, jellies, and related products have legal standards of identity (composition) and, in terms of these standards (*Code of Federal Regulations, Title 21, Part 150*), minimum requirements for fruit or juice in the product. However, differences in flavor and stiffness or consistency occur among products prepared by various manufacturers. Grade standards are available to indicate these differences. U.S. grades have been established for fruit jelly, fruit preserves or jams, orange marmalade, and apple butter. Grades for jelly, based on consistency, color, and flavor, are U.S. Grade A, Fancy; U.S. Grade B, Choice; and U.S. Grade D, Substandard. For jams or preserves the grades are U.S. Grade A, Fancy; U.S. Grade B, Choice; and Substandard, based on consistency, color, absence of defects, and flavor. Grades for apple butter are U.S. Grade A, Fancy; U.S. Grade C, Standard; and Substandard based on color, consistency, finish (size and texture of apple particles), defects, and flavor.

Orange marmalade is available in various kinds, styles, and types which are defined by grade standards. Orange marmalade may be sweet if prepared from Valencia or navel oranges; bitter if prepared from Seville or other sour types; or sweet and bitter if prepared from both types. Styles are sliced or chopped depending on whether the peel is in thin strips or small irregular pieces; and type is clear or natural depending on whether the gel is translucent or cloudy. Grades are the same as for other jams and preserves based on similar factors.

Related products that do not have standards of identity but are graded are honey and comb honey. Honey has various official color designations, but color is not a factor in grade for extracted honey. However, flavor may be directly related to color, and flavor is a principal (50 percent) factor in grade. While grades are useful in the purchase of various jams, jellies, and related products, a buyer should make sensory evaluations and compare price in terms of the clientele to be served.

FATS AND OILS

Fats and oils are useful for particular purposes depending on naturally occurring physical and chemical properties, chemical additives, and processing. Fats and oils used as food are principally triglycerides and are obtained from either plant or animal sources. They are composed of long- or short-chain fatty acids and are either saturated or unsaturated. Saturation refers to whether double bonds are present that can be broken to add additional substances such as hydrogen to the molecule. Fats from animal sources in general are composed of short-chain fatty acids, are saturated, and are solid in their natural form. Fats from vegetable sources are composed primarily of long-chain fatty acids, are unsaturated, and are liquid. Complete saturation would indicate that no double bonds were present and would generally mean a solid fat. Fats with long-chain fatty acids generally decompose less readily when heated than those with short chains. Basic animal fats are lard and butter; vegetable fats are cottonseed, peanut, corn, and soybean oils.

Fats may be used in relatively natural form or may be highly processed for particular purposes. Processes that may be applied to basic fatty substances include bleaching to remove undesirable color pigments, deodorization to improve aroma, winterization to remove solid crystals and prevent the fat from solidifying at refrigerator temperatures (useful for salad oil),

tempering to eliminate brittleness and improve consistency, plasticizing to produce creaminess, hydrogenation to eliminate double bonds and thus stabilize and solidify the product, and other processes that produce chemical and physical alteration of the product.

Chemical substances that may be incorporated as additives include mono- and diglycerides, glycerol monostearate, propylene glycol monostearate, or lecithin to provide stability from separation and allow the user to incorporate greater amounts of substances such as sugar in cake formulations; butylated hydroxyanisole (BHA) or butylated hydroxytoluene (BHT) to hinder decomposition or oxidation; citric acid or other substance to serve as metal scavengers to prevent the metal ion that may be present from accelerating decomposition of the fat; silicone dioxide to prevent foam formation, lecithin to promote foam formation for shortening to be used in cake making; and sodium benzoate, benzoic acid, or potassium sorbate as antimicrobial agents.

Salad oil, frying fat, shortening, fat for specialty bakery products, butter, and margarine are basic types of fat that may be purchased for restaurants or institutional use. Salad oils include winterized cottonseed or soybean oils. Frying fats may be simple corn or peanut oil, or simple fats that are highly processed and designed for particular purposes. Shortenings are used to produce tenderness and are generally hydrogenated oils. Lard is an excellent shortening for pie crust and is available in processed and unprocessed forms. Unprocessed lard has a distinctive flavor that some people like, and others do not. Fat for preparation of Danish or puff pastry may be specially prepared for plasticity and flavor. Shortenings are available that have substantial amounts of emulsifiers added. These are termed "high ratio" because the emulsifiers make it possible to use a high ratio of sugar in cake formulas.

A buyer may choose to purchase fats that are highly specialized and chemically designed or fats that have not been highly processed. In general the less processing, the less expensive the product. However, the buyer must purchase in terms of the particular needs of the operation. If baking is an important aspect, special fats may need to be purchased. Product testing may be necessary. Oils marketed and designed as frying fats may be considerably more expensive than peanut or corn oil, which has little processing. However, the chemically designed fat may turn out to be less expensive based on longer use before decomposition of the product.

Fats that are designed for particular purposes should be purchased with the particular purpose in mind since many types cannot be used interchangeably. A shortening with large amounts of emulsifiers may be essential to prevent a cake with a high proportion of sugar from falling but totally unacceptable for frying where the emulsifiers, combined with direct heat, are likely to accelerate the fat decomposition. Conversely, a frying fat with antifoaming additives would be disastrous if used for cake baking.

SPECIALTY PRODUCTS

Catsup, chili sauce, peanut butter, French dressing, mayonnaise, and salad dressing are commonly termed specialty products. They have legal standards of identity for basic composition (*Code of Federal Regulations, Title 21, Parts 100–169*), and some grade standards have been established. Standards distinguish between similar products and protect against dilution of basic ingredients in these items. Products defined as mayonnaise and salad dressing are similar in appearance, but salad dressing has a starch base, whereas mayonnaise is primarily oil and eggs. Numerous products of these kinds are available on the market, and each may have a particular flavor characteristic. Decisions on purchase may be based on eating quality, menu or recipe requirements, and cost.

PICKLES AND OLIVES

U.S. grade standards are available for various pickle products with types, styles, and sizes indicated in conjunction with grades. These may be found in the *Code of Federal Regulations, Title 7, Part 2852*, and are necessary for terminology in writing proper specifications. Styles of pickles include whole, sliced crosswise, sliced lengthwise, cut, and relish. The two basic types of pickles are cured and fresh pack. Cured pickles are fermented in a salt brine, whereas fresh-pack pickles are not cured or fermented but merely packed in a vinegar solution with other ingredients. The two types are very different in flavor.

Types of cured pickles include the following: natural or genuine dill pickles cured in salt with dill herb; processed dill pickels packed in vinegar solution with dill flavoring; sour pickles packed in vinegar; sweet pickles and mild sweet pickles packed with vinegar and sweetener; sweet mixed pickles packed with cauliflower, onions, vinegar, and sugar; sour mustard pickles or sour chow-chow packed in prepared mustard sauce; sweet mustard pickles or sweet chow-chow packed in sweetened prepared mustard sauce; sour pickle relish, finely cut pickles packed in vinegar solution; and sweet pickle relish, finely cut pickles packed with vinegar and sugar.

Types of fresh-pack pickles are dill pickles with vinegar and dill flavoring; sweetened dill pickles with vinegar and sugar; sweetened dill relish, finely cut with vinegar, dill, and sugar; sweet pickles, with vinegar and nutritive sweetener; sweet relish, finely chopped cucumbers with vinegar and sugar; and dietetic pickles, with or without sugar or salt.

Sizes of pickles are based on diameter and count packed per gallon. From smallest to largest, the sizes include midget, small gherkin, large gherkin, small, medium, large, and extra large. Grades applied to the various types are U.S. Grade A, Fancy; U.S. Grade B; Extra Standard; and Substandard. Factors on which grades are based are color, uniformity of size, defects, and texture.

Ripe and green olives may be purchased according to U.S. grades, which incorporate information on style or type and size. Green olives are completely fermented, cured, and packed in brine. Styles are whole or plain (unpitted); pitted; stuffed (pitted and stuffed with pimento, onion, almond, celery, or other ingredients); halved (cut lengthwise); sliced (cut parallel); chopped or minced; and broken pitted or salad pack, which are whole olives that have been accidentally broken. Grades of olives are U.S. Grade A, Fancy; U.S. Grade B, Choice; U.S. Grade C, Standard; and Substandard. Factors on which grades are based are color, uniformity of size, absence of defects, and character. Size designations for green olives are in terms of counts per pound calculated from drained weight of sample units. From smallest to largest, sizes are subpetite; petite or midget; small, select, or standard; medium; large; extra large; mammoth; giant; jumbo; colossal; and super colossal.

Ripe olives are generally prepared from a different variety and maturity of olives than green olives and they are processed differently. Two types of ripe olives are available, which are designated as ripe type and green type in U.S. grade standards. Ripe type are oxidized in processing to produce a uniformly dark color. Green type have not been oxidized in processing and are yellow with green or green with yellow. Grades for ripe olives are U.S. A, B, and C based on scores for color, absence of defects, and character. Styles are whole, pitted, halved, segmented (cut lengthwise

into three or more parts), sliced, chopped, and broken pitted (olives broken during pitting but not sliced or cut). Sizes of olives, which are related to count per pound calculated from drained weight, are small, medium, large, extra large, and colossal.

SPICES AND FLAVORINGS

Spices, according to the Federal Food, Drug, and Cosmetic Act (Title 21, Part 101.22) are aromatic vegetable substances that are whole, broken, or ground and are used primarily for seasoning rather than nutritional value and from which no volatile oil or principal flavor ingredient has been removed. Numerous plant substances have been identified as being "generally recognized as safe" (*Code of Federal Regulations, Title 21, Part 182.10*) for use as food ingredients. Included are anise, basil, bay leaves, caraway seed, cinnamon, cloves, mustard flour, nutmeg, oregano, and pepper. Not included are items like celery, onions, and garlic, which contribute considerable food substance as well as imparting flavor. Spices are generally imported into the United States and are regulated for wholesomeness under the Federal Food, Drug, and Cosmetic Act. Spices are variable in both price and fullness of flavor. Selection is based largely on brand name, price, and established source of supply for grocery items. Grades for use in purchasing by institutional or commercial food services are not available.

Flavoring may be either natural or artificial (*Code of Federal Regulations, Title 21, Part 101.22*). Artificial flavoring is any substance used to impart flavor that is not derived from a spice, fruit or fruit juice, vegetable or vegetable juice, yeast, meat, fish, poultry, dairy product, eggs, or fermentation of these products. Conversely, natural flavor is the essential oil, oleoresin, essence or extractive, protein hydrolysate, distillate, or product of roasting, heating, or enzymolysis extracted from these substances. Natural flavoring is generally more expensive to purchase than artificial, but some artificial flavoring such as lemon and vanilla is highly acceptable and frequently purchased. Selection of flavoring may be quite a fine point in sensory quality of food. Choice may be based on specific organizational considerations related to cost and required quality.

COFFEE

Factors to consider in purchase of coffee are blend, grind, roast, packaging, and service. Standards for quality of coffee sold on the wholesale market for restaurants and institutions are basically unavailable. Differences in quality are indicated in names of company blends and in price. Selection is based on tasting various products, organizational decisions on whether the top or a lesser quality is to be served, price, and considerations relative to service provided by various companies. While top blends are richest and most flavorful, middle-of-the-line products are quite acceptable when well prepared. Numerous processors produce high-quality coffee, and differences among companies are not generally great for top-, middle-, or bottom-of-the-line products.

Basic quality characteristics of coffee are determined by the processors. The flavor and other characteristics of a particular blend or brand of coffee are determined by coffee tasters selecting and mixing coffee beans of various grades from various parts of the world. Most coffee is not prepared from beans of a single type. Coffee may come from South America, Central America, Mexico, Hawaii, the West Indies, Africa, or Asia. Quality varies from area to area and within areas according to the weather and growing conditions. Beans must be selected to produce blends with particular color, flavor, body, and aroma at a particular price. A coffee

taster must have great skill because of the variability in availability, quality, and price of raw material and the expectation or demand that a particular brand of coffee always taste the same and be sold at a fairly constant price.

Selected green coffee beans must be roasted to produce the particular flavor characteristics desired in a beverage. The longer the roasting, the darker the beverage. Roasts are generally termed light, medium, or dark; medium is the most commonly used. The dark roast is used in particular for espresso or French-type beverages. Roast selected for purchase is based on the characteristics desired in the beverage.

An important factor both in processing and selection of coffee is grind. Standards for grinds of coffee have been established by the Bureau of Standards, U.S. Department of Commerce. Grinds are fine or vacuum, drip or urn, and regular. Grind selected is directly related to the equipment to be used for coffee making. Both grind and precision of grind have important influence on coffee flavor and clarity. When a coffee bean is cracked in a grinder, not all particles are the same size. Very fine particles may go through a coffee filter to produce a muddy or flocculent beverage; in large particles, flavor will be difficult to extract because less surface area is exposed. Large coffee processors generally have very fine grinders that cut with great precision. While coffee ground on the premises of a commercial restaurant has a pleasant aroma which in effect contributes to perception of flavor in a brew, such grinding may not be so effective as when done by a processor.

TEA

Standards for purity and quality of tea are established under the Federal Food, Drug, and Cosmetic Act and the Tea Importation Act and may be found in the

Code of Federal Regulations, Title 21, Parts 800–1299. Standards are based on tasting and inspection of samples of the actual product. The Board of Tea Experts is appointed by the Secretary of Health and Human Services and submits actual samples representing standards for various types of tea that are in effect from May 1 until April 30 of each year. The Tea Board is appointed by the Secretary of Health and Human Services by February 15 of each year.

Standard teas are Formosa oolong, black tea for all black teas except those from China and Formosa, black tea for tea from China and Formosa, green tea, Canton oolong for Canton types from Formosa and China, scented black tea, and spiced tea. Black teas are fermented; oolong, semifermented; and green teas, unfermented. The extent of fermentation produces distinctly different flavor characteristics.

From the various teas imported into the country, blends are prepared for marketing under particular brand names. Quality characteristics in tea are related to the part of the plant from which leaves are picked and the elevation at which the plant is grown. For black tea, leaves from the tip of the plant are known as orange pekoe, from the middle, pekoe, and from the base, souchong. For green teas, the end leaves are called gunpowder, the middle-sized leaves, young hyson, and the largest, imperial. Leaves from the tip of the plant are most delicate in flavor and leaves become larger and the flavor, stronger from the middle to the bottom of the plant. Leaves picked at higher elevations are generally of better quality than those from lower altitudes, and large leaves from higher altitudes may be better quality than small leaves from lower altitudes. Thus, various interrelated factors must be considered in developing blends of tea.

In buying tea for restaurant or institutional use, a buyer should not be so concerned about basic quality as selecting among the numerous brands available which produce a good quality beverage. Black tea is the generally accepted basic beverage served in food service operations. Important considerations for a buyer may be the packaging of tea, the manner of service, and the number of cups that can generally be made from one bag. Three 6-ounce cups of tea can generally be made from 0.07 ounce of good tea, and this quantity is often contained in one tea bag. A user may wish to consider whether to serve water with tea sufficient for more than one cup or use a tea bag with lesser quantity of tea and provide one tea bag per cup of water. This can make some difference in ease and cost of service. Many flavors of tea are currently on the market; basis for selecting these products is related to personal preference and choices relative to serving these products.

COCOA AND CHOCOLATE

Numerous cocoa beverage mixes are available on the market. These may or may not contain rather large amounts of sugar, nonnutritive sweetener, different forms of cocoa, and dried milk. Buyers will need to taste-test the product and to consider the ingredients, convenience of use, and cost. If the largest portion of a mix is sugar, this might be less expensive purchased separately; however, perhaps the convenience and flavor of the mix is worth the cost. For knowledge of beverage and basic cocoa or chocolate products, the federal standards of identity should be consulted (*Code of Federal Regulations, Title 21, Part 163*). Definitions are available for cacao nibs, chocolate liquor, breakfast cocoa, cocoa, low-fat cocoa, sweet chocolate, milk chocolate, buttermilk chocolate, skim milk chocolate; sweet cocoa and vegetable fat coating; and milk chocolate and vegetable fat coating.

PACKAGING

Common packs for grocery items are indicated in Exhibit 20-1. These may be useful in specifying quantities of products to be purchased.

REFERENCES

Code of Federal Regulations, Agriculture, Title 7, Part 2852. Washington, D.C.: U.S. Government Printing Office, 1981.
Code of Federal Regulations, Food and Drugs, Title 21, Parts 100–169. Washington, D.C.: U.S. Government Printing Office, 1983.
Code of Federal Regulations, Food and Drugs, Title 21, Parts 170–199. Washington, D.C.: U.S. Government Printing Office, 1983.
Code of Federal Regulations, Food and Drugs, Title 21, Parts 800–1299. Washington, D.C.: U.S. Government Printing Office, 1983.
Junk, W. R., and Pancoast, H. H. *Handbook of Sugars for Processors, Chemists, and Technologists.* Westport, Connecticut: Avi Publishing, 1973.
Matz, S. A. *Bakery Technology and Engineering.* Westport, Connecticut: Avi Publishing, 1972.
Pan-American Coffee Bureau publications No. 117; No. 4. New York: Pan-American Coffee Bureau.
Pomeranz, Yeshajahu, and Shellenberger, J. A. *Bread Science and Technology.* Westport, Connecticut: Avi Publishing, 1971.
Weiss, T. J. *Food Oils and Their Uses,* 2d ed. Westport, Connecticut: Avi Publishing, 1983.

Product	Pack	Container
Flour	100-pound	bag
Macaroni	20-pound	box
Noodles, egg	10-pound	box
Spaghetti	20-pound	box
Cereal, Cream of Wheat	12/28-ounce boxes	case
Cereal, rolled oats	8/42-ounce boxes	case
Cereal, dry	70 boxes (individual)	case
Baking powder	10-pound	can
Baking soda	24/1-pound boxes	case
Cornstarch	25-pound	bag
	or 24/1-pound boxes	case
Rice	100-pound	bag
Coconut	5-pound	box
Molasses	6/½-gallon cans	case
Sugar, granulated	50- or 100-pound	bag
Sugar, granulated, individual packets	2,000 individual paper packets	case
Sugar, powdered	50- or 100-pounds	bag
Salad dressing	4/1-gallon jars	case
Mayonnaise	4/1-gallon jars	case
Salad dressing, individual	100 packets	case
Oil, salad	6/1-gallon cans	case
Oil, frying	5- or 10-gallon	can
Shortening, hydrogenated	50-pound	box
Catsup	6/number 10 cans	case
Catsup, individual	200 individual packages	case
Mustard, yellow	4/1-gallon jars	case
Mustard, yellow, individual	200 packages	case
Pickles	4/1-gallon jars	case
Tobasco sauce	24/2-ounce bottles	case
Worcestershire sauce	12/10-ounce bottles	case
Flavoring	Pint, quart, or gallon	bottle
Vinegar	4/1-gallon bottles	case
Spices	1 pound	can
Pepper, individual packets	5/boxes of 1,000	case
Salt	50- or 100- pound	bag
	or 24/26-ounce boxes	case
Salt, individual	5/boxes of 1,000 individual packets	case
Gelatin	12/24-ounce boxes	case
Jelly	6/number 10 cans	case
Jelly, individual	200/½-ounce packages	case
Cocoa	50-pound	drum
Hot chocolate mix, individual	6 boxes of 50 packages	case
Tea bags	10 boxes of 100 bags	case
Coffee	96/2-ounce packages	case
	or 24/1-pound packages	case

Exhibit 20-1. Commonly used packs for grocery products

21 Special Dietetic Foods

Purpose: The purposes of this chapter are to identify the foods purchased for special dietary needs and to describe provisions in the legal standards of identity and the Nutrition Labeling and Education Act of 1990 to provide an understanding of the bases for purchasing these kinds of foods.

INTRODUCTION

Various foods purchased for special diets are identified in this chapter. Standards of identity, which are legal definitions of product composition for normal food, are discussed as an important basis of purchasing for special diets. Provisions of the Nutrition Labeling and Education Act of 1990 and the Dietary Supplement Health and Education Act are outlined, and important implications for purchasing foods for special dietary purposes are discussed.

FOODS

Types of foods that are typically purchased for dietary use in hospitals are those that eliminate added sugar; salt, particularly sodium chloride; spices, particularly pepper; fat, including total fat, saturated fat, and cholesterol; and caffeine.

Particular food items that are typically purchased without salt are butter or margarine, bread, and canned vegetables. For very restricted diets, milk, which is naturally high in sodium, may be purchased with the sodium removed. The items usually purchased without sugar are canned fruits, gelatin, jellies, and ice cream. These may be prepared with saccharin or another nonnutritive sweetener. Fat may be reduced or altered in low-calorie salad dressings and in margarines high in polyunsaturated fatty acids, low in cholesterol, or with reduced fat. The fat may be reduced because large amounts of water or air are incorporated into the product.

Diet packs that contain particular combinations of spices or condiments for particular diets are also frequently purchased. Packs may eliminate salt, pepper, or sugar and include salt substitute or nonnutritive sweetener as required by a particular diet. Purchase of commercially prepackaged seasoning helps to eliminate employee error in selection of the appropriate combination of spices and saves the time in tray assembly that would be required to pick up several items.

STANDARDS OF IDENTITY

Knowledge of legal standards of identity can provide an important base for purchasing food for special dietary pur-

333

poses. Standards of identity are legal definitions of food composition in terms of ingredients and quantities of ingredients that must or can be present. Through reading standards of identity, a dietitian or buyer can select, by name and options, items to meet special requirements. Water is an optional packing medium for most fruits and vegetables and can be specified. Fruit ice rather than sherbet can be purchased to eliminate egg yolk and fat. Purchasing skim milk will eliminate milk fat.

Types of commodities for which standards of identity are available include cacao products and confectionery; milk and cream; cheeses and related cheese products; frozen desserts; bakery products; cereal flours and related products; macaroni and noodle products; canned fruits; canned fruit juices; fruit butters, jellies, preserves, and related products; canned vegetables; vegetable juices; frozen vegetables; eggs and egg products; fish and shellfish; nonalcoholic beverages; margarines; sweeteners and table syrups; food dressings and flavorings; and processed meat and poultry products. Some of these are more relevant to purchasing for special dietary purposes than others. All are of some importance to persons interested in food composition.

Definitions that may be of particular interest in relation to purchasing the correct or a proper commodity are frozen desserts including ice cream, frozen custard, ice milk, mellorine, sherbet, and water ice; milk and milk products including acidified milk, cultured milk, concentrated milk, sweetened condensed milk, sweetened condensed skim milk, lowfat dry milk, nonfat dry milk, nonfat dry milk fortified with vitamins A and D, evaporated milk, evaporated skimmed milk, lowfat milk, acidified lowfat milk, cultured lowfat milk, acidified skim milk, cultured skim milk, heavy cream, light cream, sour cream, acidified sour half and half, yogurt, lowfat yogurt, and nonfat yogurt; numerous cheese products, particularly dry curd cottage cheese, lowfat cottage cheese, and part-skim mozzarella cheese; canned fruits, including artificially sweetened canned apricots, cherries, fruit cocktail, peaches, pears, and pineapple; artificially sweetened fruit jelly; and canned fruit juices, including cranberry juice cocktail, lemonade, and canned fruit nectars. These definitions are important in terms of specifying and buying food to eliminate or reduce milk, egg, sugar, fat, or any other particular substance from a person's diet.

Standards of identity are provided and discussed in this text in relation to basic kinds of food. A complete listing for items other than meat and poultry may be found in the *Code of Federal Regulations, Title 21, Parts 100 to 169.* Definitions for meat and poultry are in the *Code of Federal Regulations, Title 9, Parts 200 to End.*

NUTRITION LABELING AND EDUCATION ACT

The Nutrition Labeling and Education Act of 1990, which became effective May 8, 1994, has completely changed food labeling and the perspective of purchasing food for special dietary needs. The Act amended the Federal Food, Drug and Cosmetic Act to provide legal authority for the Food and Drug Administration to require nutrition labeling of food and . . . "establish those circumstances whereby claims can be made about nutrients in foods." The objectives were "(1) to make available nutrition information that can assist consumers in selecting foods that can lead to healthier diets, (2) to eliminate consumer confusion by establishing definitions for nutrient content claims that are consistent with the terms defined by the Secretary,[1] and (3) to encourage product innovation through the development and marketing of nutritionally improved foods."[2]

The Act was developed to promote public health through encouraging a particular way of eating as expressed in federal nutrition policy stated in the "Dietary Guidelines for Americans."[3] Recommendations were to "eat a variety of foods; maintain desirable weight; avoid 'too much' fat, saturated fat, and cholesterol; eat foods with adequate starch and fiber; avoid 'too much' sugar; avoid 'too much' sodium; and drink alcoholic beverages only in moderation if at all.

Provisions resulting from the Nutrition Labeling and Education Act are as follows:

1. Mandatory nutrition labeling of all processed foods (including meat and poultry) and most other foods
2. Voluntary nutrition guidelines for labeling each of the twenty kinds of fruits, vegetables, and fish most frequently consumed in a year
3. New nutrient standards, called Reference Daily Intakes (RDI), Daily Reference Values (DRV), and Daily Values to replace the U.S. Recommended Dietary Allowances (U.S. RDA)
4. Required labeling of all food ingredients, including those with legal standards of identity
5. New labeling format requirements
6. Definitions for descriptors such as "light," "reduced," and "high," which are used in labeling foods for special dietary applications
7. Legal authority for the Secretary of Health and Human Services to modify the legal standards of identity to permit food modification and innovative product development of benefit to consumer health
8. Procedures for allowing the Secretary of Health and Human Services to determine the situations in which claims can be made for a product's usefulness in alleviating or preventing disease
9. Bases for states to enforce federal regulations and for states to petition for exemption from federal regulations

Labeling

The bases for new labeling requirements are a specified serving size, Daily Reference Values (DRVs), Reference Daily Intakes (RDIs), and Daily Values (DVs). RDIs apply to essential vitamins and minerals, and are similar to the standards formerly called U.S. RDAs. DRVs are applied to fat, saturated fatty acids, cholesterol, total carbohydrate, fiber, sodium, potassium, and protein based on a 2,000-calorie diet for adults. The Daily Value is an overall term that encompasses DRV and DRI standards and is used to simplify labeling.

The required and voluntary components of nutrition fact labeling for a serving, in the required order of listing, are shown in Exhibit 21-1. The required format is shown in Exhibit 21-2.

Health claims that have been approved for labeling include the relationships of low fat and high fiber from fruits, vegetables, and grains to reduced risk of cancer and coronary heart disease; calcium and reduced risk of osteoporosis;

[1] "Secretary" refers to the Secretary of Health and Human Services in the President's Cabinet.

[2] *Federal Register* of Wednesday, January 6, 1993, Book 2 of 2, 58 FR 2301, column 3. Washington, D.C.: U.S. Government Printing Office.

[3] U.S. Department of Agriculture and U.S. Department of Health and Human Services, "Nutrition and Your Health, Dietary Guidelines for Americans," *Home and Garden Bulletin* No. 232, 2d edition. Washington, D.C.: U.S. Government Printing Office, 1985.

Required	Voluntary
Serving size	
Servings per container	
Total calories	
Calories from fat	Calories from saturated fat
Total fat	
Saturated fat	Polyunsaturated fat
	Monounsaturated fat
Cholesterol	
Sodium	Potassium
Total carbohydrate	
Dietary fiber	Soluble fiber
	Insoluble fiber
Sugars	Sugar alcohol
	Other carbohydrates
Protein	
Vitamin A	
Vitamin C	
Calcium	
Iron	Other vitamins and minerals
	(essential)
Vitamins and minerals	
added as supplements	
Percent daily values based on a 2,000 calorie diet	

Exhibit 21-1. Required and voluntary components of nutrition fact labeling in prescribed order

saturated fat and cholesterol to coronary heart disease; fat to cancer; sodium to high blood pressure; and folic acid to neural tube defects. Claims disallowed are for antioxidant vitamins and cancer; zinc and enhanced immune function in the elderly; omega-3 fatty acids and heart disease; and general statements relating dietary fiber to cancer and heart disease.

Exempted from nutrition labeling or subjected to special labeling requirements are the following: processed food sales of $500,000 or less or direct consumer sales of $50,000 or less; restaurants or other types of food service operations, provided no nutrition claims are made; food products sold to food service operators; foods, including plain coffees and teas, condiment-type dehydrated vegetables, flavor extracts, and food colors that contain "insignificant" amounts of all constituents for which nutrition labeling is required; infant formulas; baby foods other than infant formulas; dietary supplements of vitamins and minerals; medical foods that are generally liquid formulas designed for tube feeding or meeting particular medicinal needs; and food products used in food manufacturing.

Descriptor Definitions

Approved descriptors for products designed to cater to persons with particular dietary needs are shown in Exhibit 21-3. These terms are fundamentally important for buyers to obtain foods with desired characteristics.

Summary of Provisions

Major provisions of the Nutrition Labeling Act that influence food buying are:

Foods that were formerly designed for special dietary purposes in a clinical sense have been made applicable to the total population as a prescribed way of eating.

Alteration in regulations has been made to allow modification of ingredients in foods with legal standards of identity to permit developing and marketing foods with lower amounts of basic materials such as fat, sugar, and eggs.

Labeling all food ingredients, including those with legal standards of identity (formerly excluded), is required.

An official nomenclature has been developed (see Exhibit 21-3) for labeling foods designed for special dietary purposes.

Infant formulas, dietary supplements, medical foods, wholesale packs of foods for restaurants or institutional food service, and food served in restaurants and similar operations have been exempted.

The new food label will carry an up-to-date, easier-to-use nutrition information guide, to be required on almost all packaged foods (compared to about 60 percent of products up till now). The guide will serve as a key to help in planning a healthy diet.*

Nutrition Facts
Serving Size 1/2 cup (114g)
Servings Per Container 4

Amount Per Serving

Calories 90	Calories from Fat 30
	% Daily Value*
Total Fat 3g	5%
Saturated Fat 0g	0%
Cholesterol 0mg	0%
Sodium 300mg	13%
Total Carbohydrate 13g	4%
Dietary Fiber 3g	12%
Sugars 3g	
Protein 3g	

Vitamin A	80%	*	Vitamin C	60%
Calcium	4%	*	Iron	4%

* Percent Daily Values are based on a 2,000 calorie diet. Your daily values may be higher or lower depending on your calorie needs:

	Calories	2,000	2,500
Total fat	Less than	65g	80g
Sat Fat	Less than	20g	25g
Cholesterol	Less than	300mg	300mg
Sodium	Less than	2,400mg	2,400mg
Total Carbohydrate		300g	375g
Fiber		25g	30g

Calories per gram:
Fat 9   *   Carbohydrates 4   *   Protein 4

* This label is only a sample. Exact specifications are in the final rules.
Source: FDA Backgrounder 5-10-93; Food and Drug Administration 1992

Exhibit 21-2. Nutrition fact labeling format

Previous regulations related to nutrition and special dietary foods have essentially been abolished, except for the definition of foods for "special dietary use," the requirements for labeling hypoallergenic foods, and the particular regulations applicable to infant formulas and medical foods (including liquid formulas for parental or enteral feeding). Marketing foods, such as canned fruits and vegetables that are sugar or salt free, as "dietetic" packs, has become essentially illegal.

SPECIAL DIETARY FOODS

The definition of particular special dietary foods may be found in the *Code of Federal Regulations, Title 21, Part 105.* Foods for "special dietary use" are legally defined as those supplying particular dietary needs based on (a) particular physical, physiological, pathological or other conditions including diseases, convalescence, pregnancy, lactation, allergy to food, underweight, and overweight; (b) supplying special dietary needs that ex-

Descriptive Terms	Definition (per reference amount customarily eaten)
General	
High; rich in; excellent source of	Contains 20 percent or more of the RDI or DRV of a food.
Good source; contains; provides	Contains 10 percent to 19 percent of the RDI or DRV
More; fortified; enriched; added	Applies to the level of protein, vitamins, minerals, dietary fiber; means the food contains at least 10 percent more of the RDI or DRV
Light; lite	Fat reduced 50 percent if the food derives 50 percent or more of calories from fat; calories are reduced by 33 $1/3$ percent or fat reduced 50 percent for foods that naturally have 50 percent of calories derived from fat; quantitative information is shown for fat and calories relative to a standard product; food meets definition for low fat and low calorie; and sodium is reduced 50 percent.
Calories	
Calorie free; free of calories; no calories; without calories; trivial source of calories; negligible source of calories; dietarily insignificant source of calories	Contains fewer than 5.0 calories per reference serving
Low calorie; few calories; contains a small amount of calories; low source of calories; low in calories;	Contains fewer than 40 calories per reference amount
Reduced calorie; fewer calories	Contains at least 25 percent fewer calories
Sugar	
Sugar free; free of sugar; no sugar; zero sugar; without sugar; sugarless; trivial source of sugar; negligible source of sugar; dietarily insignificant source of sugar	Contains less than 0.5 gram sugar
No added sugar	No amount of sugar has been added
Reduced sugar; reduced in sugar; sugar reduced; lower in sugar	Contains at least 25 percent less sugar
Sodium	
Sodium free; free of sodium; no sodium; zero sodium; without sodium; trivial source of sodium; negligible source of sodium; dietarily insignificant source of sodium	Contains less than 5.0 milligrams sodium
Very low sodium; very low in sodium	Contains 35.0 milligrams or less sodium
Low sodium; low in sodium; little sodium; contains a small amount of sodium; low source of sodium	Contains 140.0 milligrams or less sodium
Reduced sodium; reduced in sodium; sodium reduced; less sodium; lower in sodium	Sodium reduced 25 percent
Salt free	Contains less than 5.0 milligrams sodium
Unsalted; without added salt; no salt added	Sodium chloride is not added in processing, while in similar food salt is usually added
Fat	
Fat free; free of fat; no fat; zero fat; without fat; nonfat; trivial source of fat; negligible source of fat; dietarily insignificant source of fat	Contains less than 0.5 gram fat
Low fat; low in fat; contains a small amount of fat; low source of fat; little fat	Contains 3.0 grams fat or less
Reduced fat; less fat; lower fat	Contains at least 25 percent less fat
____ percent fat free	Meets criteria for "low fat" or "fat free"
Saturated fat free; free of saturated fat; no saturated fat; zero saturated fat; without saturated fat; trivial source of saturated fat; negligible source of saturated fat; dietarily insignificant source of saturated fat	Contains less than 0.5 gram saturated fat and less than 0.5 gram *trans* fatty acids

Exhibit 21-3. Descriptors for foods designed to meet special dietary needs.

Descriptive Terms	Definition (per reference amount customarily eaten
Low in saturated fat; low saturated fat; contains a small amount of saturated fat; a little saturated fat	Contains 1.0 gram or less of saturated fatty acids
Reduced saturated fat; reduced in saturated fat; saturated fat reduced; less saturated fat; lower saturated fat; lower in saturated fat	Contains at least 25 percent less saturated fat
Cholesterol	
Cholesterol free; free of cholesterol; zero cholesterol; without cholesterol; no cholesterol; trivial source of cholesterol; negligible source of cholesterol; dietarily insignificant source of cholesterol	Contains less than 2.0 milligrams cholesterol and 2.0 grams or less saturated fatty acids
Low cholesterol; low in cholesterol; contains a small amount of cholesterol; low source of cholesterol; little cholesterol	Contains 20 milligrams or less cholesterol and 2.0 grams or fatty acids
Reduced cholesterol; less cholesterol; lower cholesterol	cholesterol reduced by 25 percent
Extra lean	contains less than 5.0 grams total fat, less than 2.0 grams saturated fat, and less than 95 milligrams cholesterol
Lean	Contains less than 10.0 grams total fat, 4.5 grams or less saturated fat, and less than 95.0 grams cholesterol

Exhibit 21-3 (continued)

ist by reason of age such as infancy; (c) supplementing or fortifying the usual diet with any vitamin, mineral, or other dietary substance; and (d) use of artificial sweeteners for regulation of calories, available carbohydrate, or diets for diabetics.

If a special dietary food is marketed as being hypoallergenic, the label must bear the common or usual name of the product; the quantity or proportion of each ingredient including spices, flavoring, and coloring; a qualification of the name of the product or of each ingredient to provide clearly the plant or animal source of each ingredient; and the nature and effect of any treatment or processing if that treatment or processing has changed the allergenic property of the food.

DIETARY SUPPLEMENT HEALTH AND EDUCATION ACT

The Dietary Supplement Health and Education Act of 1994 is a further development related to national interest in health and nutrition—particularly consumer interest in purchasing vitamins and other types of nutraceutical products typically available in health food stores. This act assured consumers' access to safe types of these products and integrated them into the regulatory system. In terms of this legislation, "dietary supplements" are regulated as a *special category of foods* rather than as drugs. They include vitamins; minerals; herbs or other botanicals; amino acids; dietary substances such as fish oil, blue-green algae, bee pollen, bone meal, and melatonin used to supplement total dietary intake; and concentrates, metabolites, or combinations of any of the substances named above. Although these substances are considered a *special category of food*, they must be labeled as "dietary supplements" and sold in the form of pills, capsules, tablets, gelcaps, liquids, powders, or other forms and not be represented for use as conventional foods.

The labeling of supplements is similar to that required by the Nutrition Labeling and Education Act (NLEA). As of March 1999, dietary supplement packages must have a "Supplement Facts" panel similar to the "Nutrition Facts" required for nutrition labeling. Also, health claims on dietary supplement labels must meet the same criteria as for labeling conventional foods (NLEA). However, health claims allowed for supplements are more limited and include only relationships between calcium and osteoporosis, folate and neural tube birth defects, soluble fiber and coronary heart disease, and sugar alcohols and dental caries.

IMPLICATIONS FOR BUYERS

National interest in nutrition, affirmed in the Nutrition Labeling and Education Act, has resulted in development of an extensive array of food products with reduced cholesterol, sugar, calories, and salt or with increased fiber. These include complete meals, vegetable entrees to substitute for meat, desserts, cereals, fats or oils, and dairy products including ice creams, cheeses, and various forms of yogurt. Fruits, vegetables, pastas, poultry, and fish, which are naturally low in fat, have also been extensively promoted. This has partially been made possible by the act's providing options for modifying legal standards of identity.

Modifying standards of identity will further facilitate product development, but can make a buyer's job somewhat more difficult. With definitely applied legal standards of identity, purchases can be made with a product name, and the exact composition and characteristics will be known. For example, "mayonnaise" contains not less than 65 percent vegetable oil, egg yolks, and an acid substance such as vinegar, and may contain salt, sweetener, spice, monosodium glutamate, sequestrants, and crystal inhibitors. With the legal option to alter the standards of identity, a "lowfat mayonnaise" might be developed and called "light mayonnaise." Buyers should know

that despite provisions to alter, standards of identity still exist and in many instances provide the best basis for food identification and buying either for usual or special dietary purposes. For example, using standards of identity, fat-free milk can be obtained merely by ordering "skim milk." And canned foods such as fruits and vegetables without added sugar or salt may be ordered by using the food name, such as canned peaches, and specifying "packed in water," which is a standard-of-identity option.

The provision of mandatory labeling of ingredients, including those with standards of identity, can be helpful to buyers. This means information on composition is available without needing to refer to a source book of federal standards. However, the source book may be important because food service buyers purchase many foods with written specifications rather than through selection at a supplier's facility, and labeling is not required for wholesale foods sold to institutional or commercial food service buyers.

Knowing the new nomenclature for labeling is essential knowledge for a buyer selecting foods in the general market, since it provides the language (in addition to that in the standards of identity) for writing specifications or selecting foods to meet particular needs. Terms are provided to indicate a reduced amount (light) or total elimination of an ingredient, such as fat (fat free). The buyer must first determine the extent of the reduction desired according to customer demand or patient need and then select the proper term to obtain the product desired.

It is important to know that specially modified foods are not good for all purposes. Ingredients with modified fat or other substances cannot be directly substituted in recipes and should not be purchased unless the recipe is thoroughly developed and tested with the modified ingredient. Further, if a recipe is tested and developed with a particular modified ingredient, other similar products should not be substituted. When ingredients are highly engineered, the resulting food quality in recipes is unpredictable and requires testing.

Exclusion of institutional packs of food from mandatory labeling means that if buyers want this information, they must ask the processors or manufacturers. The information should be requested if a health claim such as for a reduced calorie or light meal is to be made on a menu, nutrient data such as calories or fat is to be provided to customers, or nutrient data is needed by hospital dietitians. Exemption of infant formulas, dietary supplements, and medical foods is similar to previous law in treating these foods more like medicine than food. Generally, these substances are treated as pharmaceutical products and are purchased with pharmaceutical rather than dietary products. The feeding is generally provided on the order of a physician. However, the Dietary Supplement Health and Education Act has made commercially formulated, nutritionally complete, liquid diets such as "Ensure" readily available for public purchase in supermarkets, drugstores, and other types of retail establishments. Newborn infant formulas are generally handled outside the department of dietetics. Buyers should know that companies are highly competitive in marketing various nutritional products, and prices can vary considerably. Food purchasing agents in the future may buy these products, based on selection by dietitians or other health professionals.

The Dietary Supplement Health and Education Act has provided a further basis for product development. While food service buyers are not likely to purchase items such as blue algae, bee pollen, or vitamins to be added to food products, food processors wishing to capitalize on consumers' interests in healthful foods may add these types of substances to conventional food products such as cereal. In a legal sense, marketing these types of foods as supplements may be easier than marketing them as conventional food products with food additives and nutrition labeling.

For a food buyer, a wide choice of special foods is highly attractive, but greater choice and, in a sense, fewer standards make food selection more difficult. Further, diets are not limited to hospital food service, but have become a generally accepted way of eating in a large segment of society. Decisions on the kinds of these products to purchase and incorporate in special diets or for general food service use are very complicated and require overall dietary planning and total assessment of product composition, physiological effects, and sensory quality. For effective purchasing, buyers must read labels, taste test, compare price, consider marketability, and work cooperatively with dietitians or scientists, managers, and consumers to make selection of food. A new way of eating perhaps means a new way of buying with less ability to buy using established standards and greater need to explore and assess market offerings. Consumer interest and the legal provision for marketing healthful foods or nutraceuticals is present. Their future is yet to be determined.

REFERENCES

Code of Federal Regulations, Food and Drugs, Parts 100–169. Washington, D.C.: U.S. Government Printing Office, 1993.

Dietary Supplement Health and Education Act of 1994, Public Law 103–417, Oct. 25, 1994, 21 USC 301 *et seq.*

Federal Register of Thursday, July 19, 1990, part III (55 FR 29476–29533). Washington, D.C.: U.S. Government Printing Office.

Federal Register of Monday, December 18, 1995, Part II. 60 FR 65197–65202. *Department of Health and Human Services, Food and Drug Administration, Procedures for the Safe and Sanitary Processing and Importing of Fish and Fishery Products; Final Rule; Code of Federal Regulations Title 21*, Parts 123 and 1240. Washington, D.C.: U.S. Government Printing Office.

Federal Register of Wednesday, Jan. 6, 1993, Book 1 (58 FR 2066–2300). Washington, D.C.: U.S. Government Printing Office.

Federal Register of Wednesday, Jan. 6, 1993, Book 2 (58 FR 2302–2964). Washington, D.C.: U.S. Government Printing Office.

Federal Register of Monday, December 18, 1995, Part II. 60 FR 65197–65202. *Department of Health and Human Services, Food and Drug Administration, Procedures for the Safe and Sanitary Processing and Importing of Fish and Fishery Products; Final Rule; Code of Federal Regulations Title 21*, Parts 123 and 1240. Washington, D.C.: U.S. Government Printing Office.

Mermelstein, Neil H. "A New Era in Food Labeling," *Food Technology* 47 (February 1993): 81–96.

Public Law 101–535, Nov. 8, 1990. An act cited as the Nutrition Labeling and Education Act of 1990, 101st Congress.

The Almanac of the Canning, Freezing, Preserving Industries. Volume 1. Westminster, Maryland: Edward E. Judge & Sons, 1993.

The Almanac of the Canning, Freezing, Preserving Industries. Volume 2. Westminster, Maryland: Edward E. Judge & Sons, 1993.

The Almanac of the Canning, Freezing, Preserving Industries. Westminster, Maryland: Edward E. Judge & Sons, 1998.

U.S. Department of Agriculture and U.S. Department of Health and Human Services, "Nutrition and Your Health, Dietary Guidelines for Americans," Bulletin No. 232, 2nd ed. Washington, D.C.: U.S. Government Printing Office, 1985.

22 Alcoholic Beverages

Purpose: To present and discuss the basic information that a purchasing agent and management should have in order to buy and control the use of alcoholic beverages in the food service industry. Of equal importance, to review for the reader some ethical and legal aspects concerning the use of alcoholic beverages.

INTRODUCTION

Only in the last eight to ten years has the subject of selling alcoholic beverages even been discussed in "good company." Today, with over 11 percent of the total sales and 20 percent of the profit in the industry coming from the sale of alcoholic beverages, operations are seeking to increase profits from this source and at the same time to control the negative effects of drinking.

The Bad and the Good

First, the bad—any beneficial food, drug, medicine, exercise, and health regimen, if abused, can turn dangerous and destructive. This is especially true of alcohol. The medical profession warns us that alcohol is an addictive drug that can cause tragedy in human life.

Properly controlled and used, however, alcoholic beverages can be profitable business builders, providing some social amenities. And some research suggests that one drink a day is correlated with better health, enjoyment of living, and longer life. But the highway casualty lists, broken bones and marriages, job losses, millions of homeless people, human derelicts, stunted careers, interrupted educational careers, declining health, and human tragedies and death are all well known.

RED FLAGS AND POTHOLES TO BE AVOIDED BY BOTH MANAGEMENT AND PURCHASING AGENTS

Experience has told us many times over that it is the little things that cause the biggest problems, not the most publicized problems. This is certainly true when it comes to beverage operations.

The following is a list of thirty axioms and warnings that the author has formulated from experience since the repeal of Prohibition in 1934. These potholes have caused many operators to complain loudly. "Why didn't someone tell me?" Read carefully; these traps can be very costly.

1. A purchasing agent should buy any samples required. This will give both him and his company good status in the trade and reduce criticism of the buyer from jealous colleagues.

2. Never play golf or cards with sales-people.

3. Always use the triplicate requisition system for issues from the liquor storeroom.

4. The purchasing agent should not have a set of keys to the liquor storeroom. Only the person in charge of the storeroom needs the keys.

5. The liquor storeroom manager should sign any liquor receiving sheet.

6. Management should insist that an accurate perpetual liquor storeroom inventory be kept by the accounting department.

7. Month-end liquor storeroom inventory should be taken by the controller's office and liquor storeroom manager.

8. Train the "security" department to check every public function with the legal occupancy limits.

9. It is illegal to have any open liquor, beer, or wine bottles in the liquor storerooms.

10. Destroy all empty liquor or wine bottles daily. A properly designed bottle breaker is a good investment.

11. Federal laws permit you twenty-four hours to use up any premixed cocktails if you have a specific order from a party that had a short-fall in attendance.

12. House stamp all liquor bottles to prevent any liquor from being carried in by bartenders for sale.

13. Be alert for any bartender who is especially popular with the maids or service crew.

14. Do not leave any emergency keys to liquor stores with the engineering department. These keys should be kept in the front office and signed out in emergencies.

15. *All* cash registers and checking machines should be factory-sealed so that only progressive readings can be taken. Failure to do so cost one hotel

$85,000 in revenue losses before the night auditor discovered this oversight.

16. Hydrometer tests for alcoholic contents should be made on a surprise basis on operating bars.

17. Never buy anything but quality brands of wines or liquors regardless of price. Your customers like to be known as quality oriented to their friends.

18. Do not use any automatic or mechanical dispensers on front bars. Customers hate them.

19. A purchase order, approved by management, should be issued for purchase of wines and liquors. No purchases should be made for any product not listed on an approved list of brand names.

20. Do not serve cheaper liquor for banquets than on the public bars. The same applies to the size of drinks and quality of glassware. Use better-quality liquor and wines and more attractive glassware than your competitors.

21. Fifty quality wines are usually enough for a good list. Don't tie up money on an excessive amount of wines and liquors in the storeroom.

22. Management should "walk" the bars and liquor storeroom at least once a day and once a week at closing time.

23. Have a regular "shopping service" on all public bars and let beverage staff know you have such a service.

24. Steward sales of any food and beverage product should not be permitted, even for the management staff.

25. Be extremely careful about underage drinking at "sweet sixteen" and high school parties.

26. Train your own bartenders. Good bartenders are not looking for jobs.

27. Management should sign a regular guest check for all liquor service.

28. The controller's office should be responsible for setting up and operating an adequate control system over the

beverage operation.

29. Don't forget—even the best computerized beverage control system can be rigged. It happened to the author, and it was very embarrassing.
30. Remember the old adage—"You can beat a system, but you can't beat an honest man."

THE PURCHASING AGENT AND THE LIQUOR-BUYING PROCESS

In Chapters 5 and 6, we reviewed the place the purchasing agent takes in the overall food and beverage purchasing process. Here we provide a more detailed discussion of the purchasing agent and department in the beverage-buying process.

Harold Grossman, an outstanding consultant and authority on beverage operations, used to say that he could tell you "how to buy liquor and wine in five minutes—but teaching you what to buy would take five years."

The rest of this chapter will be devoted to teaching you (1) how to buy, (2) where to buy, and (3) what to buy.

How to Buy

Any purchasing agent can look at the liquor storeroom shelves, make a list of what seems to be needed, and then pick up the phone and place some orders. Or he can wait until "salesman day" and place an order. The chance that he or the hotel will fill out and mail a purchase order is rather remote—unfortunately, that is the way most purchasing is done.

The following outline shows an adequate and properly controlled beverage-purchasing system that will fit most hotel, restaurant, or food service operations.

1. *Establish responsibility.* Management can best do this by issuing a functional organization chart for the food and beverage department.
2. *Use a management-approved inventory stock list.* Management should, after consulting staff, approve a list of

beverages to be used in the beverage operation.

3. *Establish inventory quantities.* Minimum and maximum amounts of each item to be carried in inventory should be established. These levels set average monthly inventory turnover. Each item should turn over at least once.
4. *Issue purchase orders.* Issue purchase orders approved by management for all beverage purchases.
5. *Manager should approve purchase.* Management and the purchasing agent should agree on an approved list of purveyors.
6. *Independent receiving.* Incoming merchandise should be received and recorded by the receiving clerk under the control of the accounting and controller's office.
7. *Establish one-person control of stockroom.* One person should have the only key to the stockroom and make all stock issues based on triplicate requisitions. A reserve key should be held in the safe, under management control. Perpetual inventory, either manual or computer programmed, should be kept on wine, liquor, and beer stocks.
8. *Internal control system.* The entire purchasing system should be under the internal control system established by the controller's office and approved by management and outside auditors. The system should cover taking of inventories, over and short reports, perpetual inventories, signature verifications, and dead stock report.

A Word About Glassware

About every two years, some enterprising bar manager comes up with a bright idea that introduces a trend in the bar business. Since the repeal of Prohibition, some of the better ideas have been (1) dry martini on the rocks; (2) the Knott Hotels increasing the drink size by 50 percent over standard; (3) Sheraton's fixed mark-on over cost on full-bottle wine sales; (4) the introduction of port and wine bars, (5) the effort to curb drinking and driving, and to have a designated sober driver for drinking guests; and (6) Restaurant Associates' introduction of unique, "wild," oversize, but quality bar glassware. One large hotel chain that introduced a "large attractive glass program" increased sales and profits from 12 to 30 percent because of good reception by the public. Today, one glassware manufacturer lists thirty-two pages of bar glassware in its catalogue, featuring machine-made, hand-blown, and pressed lead crystal glassware. So "better and different" is paying off well in the bar business.

Minimum Acceptable Sizes of Bar Glassware. Exhibit 22-1 shows the minimum sizes of bar glassware that seem to be acceptable in the trade, from a study of current supply catalogues.

Where to Buy

The "alcoholic beverage" business has more controls than any other business in the country. From the federal government down through the state, county, municipality, ward, police, health department, trade union, and the W.C.T.U. (Women's Christian Temperance Union), everybody and every politician takes a crack at it and a big bite out of it. And it still is the most profitable department of the hospitality business.

Where to buy? Each state will tell you. Currently our fifty states are divided into three groups on where to buy. Briefly, they are as follows:

Closed states—you must buy wine and spirits from state stores.

Open states—you must buy wine and spirits from state-licensed distributors.

Semiclosed states—you must buy spirits from state stores; may buy wine from state-licensed wine distributors.

Beer may be purchased for an "on premises" operation from state-licensed beer distributors.

Type	Standard	Metric
Shot	2 oz. with 1-oz. line	60 ml with 30-ml line
Double Shot	3 oz. with or without 2-oz. line	90 ml with 60-ml line
Old-Fashioned	7–9 oz.	210–270 ml
Highball	7–8 oz.	210–240 ml
Tom Collins	9–10 oz.	270–300 ml
Chimney	11–12 oz.	330–360 ml
Pilsner	11–12 oz.	330–360 ml
Cocktail	4½ oz. with 3-oz. line	135 ml with 90-ml line
Champagne (saucer)	5 oz.	150 ml
Champagne (tulip)	8 oz. (fizz glass)	240 ml
All-purpose wine	8 oz.	240 ml
Sherry	2½ oz.	75 ml
Liqueur	1 oz.	30 ml
Brandy	2 oz. with 1-oz. line	60 ml with 30-ml line
Cognac inhaler (balloon)	16 oz.	480 ml
Whiskey Sour	4½–5 oz.	135–150 ml
Specialty	Any size, depending on size of special	

Exhibit 22-1. Minimum sizes of bar glassware

Management and purchasing agents must be alert to the laws on enticement that are in effect in some states. For example, in several states you cannot give away free peanuts or pretzels in a bar. In other states, free food is prohibited, and so are so-called happy hours at reduced prices. Most states require that appropriate food be served in a bar during open hours.

A few states will not permit the words "bar" or "lounge" on the outside of a building housing a hotel or restaurant, and in others the food menu cannot list the names of cocktails or wines available. The customer must ask for the wine list.

What to Buy

The rather large but interesting subject of what to buy is discussed in three parts: (1) wines, (2) distilled spirits, and (3) beers and ale.

Let's take wines first, because most readers seem to think it is the most interesting area.

AN INVITATION TO ENJOY WINE

In this section, we discuss information regarding wines that we feel would be interesting and useful to both the average reader and the gourmet diner. You can augment this introduction from many sources. The California Wine Growers Institute has published an inexpensive, but an amazingly complete, story of wine and its uses. You can start with this booklet, and if you can absorb all the information contained in this booklet, you could almost be rated a wine expert. Many people get so interested in the subject that they read through an entire library on wines and its uses. I also suggest two books that anyone interested in wines should have at hand. One is *The Noble Grapes and the Great Wines of France,* by Andre L. Simone. The other is *Grossman's Guide to Wines, Spirits and Beers,* which has been in print for at least forty years and is being revised and reissued.

Selecting Wines

Even the use of a product as traditional and historical as wine does swing like a pendulum with time. However, it does not fluctuate as extremely as the use of other beverages and foods.

In 1934, when Prohibition was repealed in the United States, people talked a lot about the "proper" wine to drink with the foods being served or what wine to drink when one was just enjoying a glass. Some wine experts held that drinking a red wine that went well with beef was gastronomically "wrong" with a roast of lamb, or only a Grand Cru burgundy should be consumed with pheasant, quail, and charcoal-broiled steaks.

Very light-colored fish could be eaten with a French pouilly fumé. However, pink-colored fish had to be accompanied by a pouilly fuissé, a sauterne, or a dry Rhine wine. Ports and sherries were consumed only as meal starters and finishers, except when sherry was served with terrapin á la Maryland or Lobster Newberg.

Naturally, all this tradition was unnecessary. The next thing we knew, wine experts told us that any wine could be consumed with any food, if that was what the customer wanted. This theory was as poor as the previous one, and soon people who were interested in wines started a new pattern of wine consumption with food that was easy to understand and made for more enjoyable gourmet dining.

Wines are now classed as appetizer wines, red and white table wines, sparkling wines, and dessert wines. The only point of discussion is whether one should drink a red or white table wine with the meal. This has been solved quite simply by public acceptance that red meats require a red table wine or rosé; fish, fowl, and other light-colored meats go best with white table wines such as chablis, white burgundies, sauternes, or Rhine wines.

The Art of Tasting

No discussion of wine would be complete without the traditional discussion on the art of tasting and selecting. Most wine experts agree with traditional wine-tasting practices. They emphasize that experience—judiciously drinking various qualities and varieties of wine with food—is the only sound basis for tasting and selecting wine for their own use and consumption as well as for others'.

First You Look. Wine in an appropriate clear, clean glass looks good if it is a good wine. Knowing what looks good, of course, is the key to this first step in testing. Young wines are bright and clear and free of sediment; however, as they age some become dull, show some sediment, and actually change color. For example, a young claret or red bordeaux, as well as young red burgundies, is clear and bright red; as they age, their color turns brownish-red. The aged wines are slightly cloudy, but don't have excessive sediment. However, sediment will be stirred up if the wine is badly handled. This is one reason why good wines should be opened and allowed to rest for a while, to let the sediment settle to the bottom of the bottle.

Then You Smell. Most wines are sampled from an 8-ounce bordeaux-type wine glass, which gives the wine a chance to develop its aroma or bouquet if gently swirled around the glass. Again, experience is the key to recognizing quality in the aroma of the various wines. It doesn't take much experience to detect a wine that has "gone bad," because it smells like vinegar. Some wines, when they "go bad," reek of alcohol.

Some kinds of wines, basically varietal types and German wines, carry the distinct odor of the type of grape from which the wine is made. A good wine taster can immediately identify the grape. At this stage, a wine taster begins to feel as if he or she really knows something about wines.

At wine tastings, one can hear the experts talking about the "nuttiness" and flavor of some of the wines being tasted. In some wines, this nuttiness is a decided advantage. The flavor comes from the crushed seeds of the grape, plus the skins, which lend some astringency to the taste of the wine even when it is consumed. Wines made from muscat grapes, and sauvignon blanc grapes have a very definite taste and odor of the grapes, whereas some others, such as pinot blanc and pinot noir, are much more subtle in taste and aroma.

Most wine makers know that consumers seek a pleasant and outstanding bouquet in the wines that they drink. Good wine makers also realize that their standing in the profession and trade depends on how skillfully they can develop the bouquet of their wines.

Finally, You Taste. Remember that the odor of the grape and the color of the wine also have some effect on what you taste.

A dry wine is not sweet. Most red wines, and a few white wines, fall into the dry category. Some sparkling wines, as well as appetizer wines, also fit into the dry category. Wines that taste of natural grape sugars fall into the semisweet to supersweet categories. These sweet wines include most of the white wines and rosés, a few of the sparkling wines, such as sparkling burgundy, the sweeter champagnes, and cold duck.

Beginning wine drinkers generally like the lighter, sweeter wines and gradually move to the drier red wines, which contain a greater variety of flavors and aromas.

Grapes, being a fruit, have a natural proportion of fruit acids somewhat similar to pears and apples. Some grapes are tart, and unless some sugar (cane sugar) is added, the wine made from them would not be satisfactory for drinking. Consequently, we have what is known as the "fortified" wine. A good wine maker knows how to blend added sugar to the natural tartness of a wine to develop its distinctive taste.

Astringency in Wine. Certain wines have a "puckeriness" that carries over from the natural grape. This tannin, the same astringency found in tea leaves and certain green leaf vegetables, can be quite strong. Red wines seem to have more of this taste, especially in the younger wines. Food with which this wine is served must be strong in flavor. This is why most light-colored and light-tasting fish cannot compete with the tannin of red wines; white wines suit these goods better.

Alcohol Content

Most table wines throughout the world contain from 10 to 13 percent alcohol by volume, which can be interpreted as about 6 proof. Some appetizer wines can be as high as 20 percent alcohol by volume, and some sparkling wines are as low as 8–10 percent alcohol by volume.

From this rating of the alcoholic content of wines, you can easily see that anyone having more than two to three side glasses of wine has had the equivalent of at least two to three drinks of whiskey or spirits.

Learning How to Select Wines

In discussing selecting wines with wine experts, you will notice that they talk a lot about experience, and this experience can be summarized in two words: *look* and *listen.*

Look. What do you look for? Look at the sales records of the hotel or restaurant. If a certain wine is selling well, you can accept that the customer wants it. Look over your wine list. If it is full of slow-moving items, start tasting and looking for new wines. Look at your competition's wine list to see what wines are moving there. Look at the labels on the bottles. The label can tell you a great deal about vintage year, the name of the shipper, the name of the winery, whether it is a quality, boutique, or production-line winery. Look in the newspaper and trade journals for articles on wine. One should certainly read regularly publications put out by the California Wine Growers Institute, the French and Italian governments, and any other trade association sponsored by wine growers, regardless of the country involved.

Listen. Any purchasing agent wishing to become expert in wine purchasing should join a local wine and food society and enter into the fun and training with a positive attitude. Listening to the experts can provide valuable knowledge that can never be found in a book. Listen to what your customers say about your wine. Have the waitresses listen to them, as well as the captains, head waiters, and the bartenders. Keep a guest comment log book at the bar, at the various outlets, and in the banquet office. Get the cooperation of your associates in recording any comments that they hear from the guests or their own suggestions to help improve wine sales.

A Final Thought. A number of years back, I attended a seminar headed by Harold Grossman, who was then one of the world's outstanding authorities on wines. He was asked, "What is the best way to train one's palette for selecting quality wines?" Grossman advised the asker not to drink anything but a recognized, quality wine. Then, if you taste something out of the ordinary, you will know that it is not a good wine.

Over the years we have tasted some very fine wines, including Cabernet Sauvignon Special Reserve from Robert Mondavi Winery, a case of which costs $300. We remember the first time that we tasted a Château Lafite-Rothschild, as well as a 1929 chablis at Antoine's in New Orleans. It is hard to beat a Romanee-Conti or a La Tache Burgundy or Dom Perignon Extra Dry Champagne. We discovered our favorite wine while touring Germany, a moselle wine known as Bernkasteler Doktor-Doktor Thanisch. And don't sell American wines short. It is very easy to get hooked on a cabernet sauvignon blanc from the winery in Barboursville, Virginia—the site of one of the original wineries when Virginia was settled during the 1600's.

The Quality of Wines

The Egyptians are reputed to have started making wine about 4000 B.C. Some of their early records outline certain requirements for making good wine. The government took steps to ensure the making of "quality products" and naturally levied a tax to pay for the administration of the law. Some people rebelled at the idea of a tax but were "quickly whipped into submission."

Today, our universal authorities on wine making likewise agree on the basic requirements for the making of quality wines, summarized as follows:

1. Type and quality of the grape or fruit used in the wine-making process
2. Cultivation and harvesting of the grape
3. Kind of soil and locality of growth
4. Equipment and processing used
5. Aging
6. Blending
7. Bottling—method and sanitation
8. Care and skill of cellar master and staff

Types of Wines. Six different types of wines are recognized throughout the wine industry, which helps identify the characteristics of wines included in each grouping.

The use of these wines varies by the country in which they are consumed. In the United States and Canada, dry white still wines and sparkling wines are the most popular; the sweeter red wines, sparkling wines, and vermouths are less in demand.

Classifying Wines. Wines are classified by type pretty much the same the world over. Most authorities and texts use the following summary as a basis for the classification of wines by types. Other classifications of wines are quite varied, such as area of growth, vintage or nonvintage, demi-sec to brut in sweetness, fortified or natural, authoritative quality standards, and "fad" wines such as jug wines, blush wines, wine coolers, and slurpies. There are fruit wines and flavored wines, and there is actually a "Red Ripple."

A purchasing agent should be familiar with the following recognized classifications by type.

Appetizer or aperitif wines
Dry sherry
Vermouth
Dubonnet
Blonde Dubonnet
Byrhh
Pink champagne
Dry champagne
Sparkling rosé
Cold duck
Chablis
Sparkling Leibfraumilch
Tawny port

Type	Characteristics
Fortified	To which alcohol has been added to gain a desired content or "proof"
Sparkling and coolers	Contain CO_2, whether natural or added
Still	Contains no CO_2
Aromatized	Treated with special herbs—vermouth, cassis
Dry	Contains up to 1 percent natural sugar
Sweet	Can contain up to 6 percent sugar, either natural or added.

White table wines
Chablis
Rhine
Sauterne
Chardonnay
Chenin blanc
French colombard
Gewürztraminer
Riesling
Alsatian
Moselle
Semillon
Sylvaner
Sauvignon blanc
Pouilly fuissé
Soave
Anjou—white

Red table wines
Red bordeaux
Rhône
Red burgundy
Chianti
Cabernet sauvignon
Gamay beaujolais
Zinfandel
Lancer's
Mateus
Rioja
Pinot noir
Chianti reserve
Barbera
Claret
Bandolino

Sweet dessert wines
Port
Sweet sherry
Madeira
Tokay
Muscatel
Sweet sauternes
Sweet German wines

Sparkling wines
Champagne

Pink champagne
Cold duck
Asti Spumanti
Lancer's crackling
Sparkling Rhine wines

AMERICAN WINES

American wines are made from basically two varieties of grapes: the native muscadines, which are still a very popular vine in the country, and the hybrids developed from some of the native grapes such as the hybrid muscadine, the Delaware, the Catawba, Diana, Niagara, Ontario, the Concord family, and the Norton, to name a few of the most popular and universally grown in the United States for American wines.

Blended and Varietal Wines

Practically all American wines, as well as most imported wines, are either blended wines or varietal wines made from one specific variety of grape such as the cabernet sauvignon.

The following list shows the most popular blended wines used in the United States and Canada and in western Europe:
Port
Sherry
Chablis
Burgundy
Muscatel
Claret
Sauterne
Champagne
Rhine
Moselle
Alsatian
Rosé
Riesling

Some of the more popular varietal wines in the United States are:

Red
Cabernet sauvignon
Gamay beaujolais

Zinfandel
Pinot noir
Ruby cabernet

White
Sauvignon blanc
Chenin blanc
Pinot chardonnay
French colombard
Riesling
Zinfandel—white
Traminer

California Wine Districts

Before 1980, California wines took their geographical identities from the counties in which the grapes grew. However, since then they have taken on a sharper focus and identity. The federal government has formed more than a score of "approved viticultural areas" (AVAs) within the state and continues to name additions as needed. These AVAs have been grouped into five major wine-growing districts within the state for easier identity, but these districts do not necessarily cover all the wine-producing areas of the state.

Exhibit 22-2 shows the wine-growing districts of California, the counties in each district, the acreage in grape cultivation, and the main varietal wines produced in each district.

Outstanding Vineyards of California

Earlier in this chapter, we discussed the basics of selecting a wine. The reputation of the vineyard is vital to the success of its products, and tells the buyer and the public more about the quality of its wine than anything else. Fine restaurants with good wine sales seem to offer selections from only a few reputable wineries, for both domestic and imported wine. Wine drinkers are quick to air their views on quality wines, and all the buyer has to do is "listen."

Since the mid-1930's when the U.S. wine industry was revitalized, certain vineyards have grown in reputation because of the quality of their products over a stretch of time. Some, but not all, of the better vineyards of California are listed here. In addition, many small "boutique" vineyards in California intentionally remain anonymous—their product is so good that it sells out each season to "standing room only."

Korbel
Beaulieu Vineyards (B.V.)
Schramsburg
Inglenook
Wente Brothers
Robert Mondavi
Paul Masson
Beringer
Firestone
California Cellars
Almadén
Louis Martini
Christian Brothers
Gallo
Italian Swiss Colony
Souverain
Heitz
Stag's Leap
Simi Reserve
Stony Hill
Free Mark
Sterling
Dry Creek
Chauteau Montelarne
Frog's Leap
York Creek
Stone Creek
M. La Mont
Fappiano
Concannon
Sonoma

A novice can't go wrong with these labels. There are at least 300 other "good labels" from California, but I have not had the time to evaluate them all.

Other Wine-Producing Regions of the United States

Given the success of the wine industry in California, it could be easy to forget that many U.S. regions already have established

Area	Acres	Grape Variety (principal varietal wines)
Northwest District		
Lake County	3,000	Cabernet sauvignon
		Zinfandel
Mendocino	10,000	Colombard chardonnay
Napa	25,000	Sauvignon blanc
		Chenin blanc
Sonoma	28,000	White Riesling
		Pinot noir
Solano	1,000	Carignane
Central Coast		
Alameda County	1,700	Grey Riesling
		Zinfandel
Monterey	35,000	Cabernet sauvignon
		Chardonnay
San Benito	4,000	Pinot noir
		Petit sirah
San Luis Obispo	5,200	Chenin blanc
		Sauvignon blanc
Santa Clara	1,700	Gewürztraminer
Santa Barbara	10,000	
South Coast		
San Bernadino County	5,000	Mission
		Zinfandel
Riverside	3,000	Sauvignon blanc
		White Riesling
San Diego	400	Chardonnay
Central Valley		
Sacramento Valley	210,000	French colombard
San Joaquin	225,000	Thompson seedless*
(indlcudes Fresno, Kern, Madera,		Chenin blanc
Merced, San Joaquin, Tulare, Yolo,		Zinfandel
Clarksburg, and Merritt Island		Barbera
counties)		Grenache
		Ruby cabernet
Sierra Foothills		
El Dorado County	1,200	Zinfandel
Amador	800	Sauvignon blanc
Calavaras	300	Pinot noir

*Primarily used in blended dry white wines such as chablis

Exhibit 22-2. Wine-growing districts of California

wine industries. Some enthusiasts claim that by the turn of the century, every state will have a wine industry. Some of the abandoned oil fields of West Texas are being converted to huge vineyards and new varieties of hardy grapes are being developed, so this claim could become true. Some experimental vineyards already exist on the southern Pacific slopes of Alaska. Canada produces large quantities of wine with some similar climatic conditions.

Washington State and Oregon. The region of Washington and Oregon is really an extension of California. The soil is similar, the weather mild, and the grape varieties very similar to the original imports from Europe by way of South America.

Wines from this area are known for being light, fruity, and low in alcoholic content. Their rosé wines are particularly good and in demand. The list of wines produced is similar to California's, except for champagne, which is somewhat of a stranger here.

New York State. The Finger Lakes District of upstate New York has been known from colonial times for its fine table wines, sherries, and champagne. These wines are produced on native root stock that can resist the harsh winters and parasites. The slopes of the Hudson River and Sullivan

County are ideal for producing table wines. Many wine authorities feel that some New York State champagnes can compete with the best West Coast champagnes.

The Catawba and the Delaware varieties of grapes are the mainstays and backbones of the eastern wine industry, but the Niagara, Norton, Diana, and Ontario are gaining in use.

The Middle Atlantic States. Colonial wine production started in the middle Atlantic states mainly in what is known as Virginia today. The original Virginia Dare Winery existed up to the time of Prohibition but then moved to California and survived by producing cooking wines until repeal. The areas now involved are the Carolinas, Maryland, Pennsylvania, and the Virginias. The cabernet sauvignon wines of this area, both red and white, are particularly fine.

Ohio and Missouri. Earlier in this century, these areas—resembling the Rhine River valley—showed great promise in wine production. Some good champagne still comes from Missouri. The wines of Ohio are basically American versions of German wines. Some areas along Lake Erie have been fairly successful with table wines.

Other Wine-Producing Areas. Some wines are also produced in New Jersey, Michigan, Tennessee, and Florida, mostly white table wines.

Types of Eastern American Wines

Most eastern wineries produce both red and white table wines, but the great majority are white wines labeled as European types such as sauternes, riesling, chablis, French colombard, and chardonnay. The eastern ports and sherries are excellent and are well distributed.

Eastern champagne is considered by many to be the best in the United States, especially made from grapes from the Finger Lake area of New York, the shores of Lake Erie, and the slopes of the Missouri River.

American wineries have tried to develop the use of American-named wine types but so far have been unsuccessful. Somehow "New York State chablis" tastes better than "New York State Elvira white table wine."

FRENCH WINES

An introduction and a sincere compliment: when you think of France, you immediately think of fine food, fine wines, and a fine relaxed style of living. This reaction is the same the world over. Twenty-five years ago, a booklet published by Food and Wines from France, Inc., had an introduction that said it all:

Wine is one of the great and civilized pleasures of the world, a symbol of friendship, good living, joy and romance. It is a diversified pleasure that comes in seemingly endless variety, a versatile pleasure that is right any time, any place. Above all, wine is a simple pleasure, a product of the earth born out of devotion and hard work. It needs no special ceremonies. It follows no rigid rules. While a few serving suggestions may add immeasurably to your satisfaction, wine asks only to be drunk to be enjoyed.

France, more than any other wine-producing country, offers these pleasures in abundance. French wines are unequaled in quality and variety. They span every taste sensation and include some of the greatest wines the world has ever known. Great wines are never inexpensive. But because French wines are so varied, they cover a broad range of prices. And while a few are indeed costly, most French wines are very appealing wines at very reasonable prices. In short, anyone who enjoys wine can enjoy—and afford—a French wine.

Blessed with an ideal combination of soil, climate and a long tradition of dedicated wine making, France has over the centuries created wines that are the standards against which all other wines are judged.

About one million Frenchmen grow grapes. From these grapes comes wines of every nuance, each different from those of other regions. And the only way to understand these differences is to taste the wines.

French Wine Laws

The French feel that every wine is unique, the product of many different factors. The most important factors by far are (1) where the grape is grown and (2) how it is made into wine.

Fine wines, especially, carry the imprint of the place where the grapes were grown and the condition under which they became wine. Generally, the more limited the size of the winery and the better-controlled the conditions, the more distinctive the wine and the higher its rating. The French have always recognized the truth of this maxim, and if you check the French wine laws back to the Middle Ages, you will see that the French government and the wine-making industry have always observed definite requirements and limitations.

In 1935, France passed the first comprehensive wine legislation the world had ever seen. These laws were called the Appellation de Origine Contrôlée (AOC), or Controlled Place of Origin. These laws cover every aspect of wine making—from the soil and vine to bottling and labeling—because of the far-reaching control. They offer the strongest possible protection both to the consumer and to the reputation of France's fine wines. These wine laws have been so successful that they have become the model and pattern for almost all wine legislation that followed in Europe and other wine-producing countries of the world.

Not all French wines are AOC wines. On an average, about 16 percent of the total wine production of France can be labeled as AOC wine, meeting the strict requirements of the government. The second class of quality-rated wines in France are known as VDQS (vins délimités de qualité súperieure), which are good wines and are only slightly different from the AOC-quality wines. Although these wines are not quite as highly rated as AOC wines, they are carefully controlled, with growing areas and grape varieties clearly specified and the alcoholic content and other pertinent requirements clearly defined. Each bottle of these wines is labeled with a distinctive label specifying it as a VDQS wine.

French wine laws provide for a third class of wine that in quality is just slightly below the VDQS rating: "vins de pays." These wines, known as "country wines," are good and are consumed with great confidence by the average French consumer. These wines are not poor wines; their source of origin and quality are very closely monitored, and they must meet certain minimum standards to be given this label.

Points Covered. The French wines laws are applicable, in varying degrees, to all the different wine-making districts of France. They can become quite complicated, as illustrated by the fact that a Bordeaux claret has one set of rules for the Medoc area and a different set of rules for the Bordeaux area as a whole. As noted, the smaller the area, the stricter the rules and regulations, and the higher-quality wine is thus produced with higher profitable margins. The six main points covered by the laws are

1. Place of origin
2. Grape variety
3. Minimum alcohol content
4. Maximum yield per acre
5. Grape-growing practices
6. Wine-making procedures and customs

The most important regulations are those dealing with place of origin and hence the established wine-producing districts of France.

The French Wine Districts

Although wine is produced in every town and parish of France, the French government and the worldwide wine industry have designated certain areas of the country as recognized wine-making districts, with their own proprietary products and qualities. Exhibit 22-3 shows the various recognized wine-making districts.

The Loire Valley. The Loire Valley grape-growing district is one of the most beautiful valleys in northern France, and it is known for the "beautiful" white and rosé wines that are dear to the average French citizen's heart.

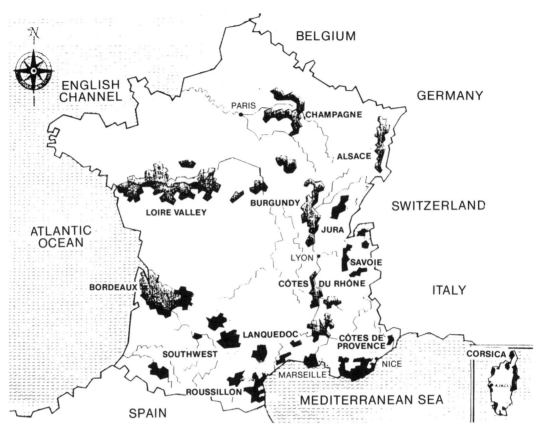

Exhibit 22-3. The wine districts of France

The best-rated wine from this district is the pouilly-fumé, which is a light white wine that goes especially well with delicate fish and summer salads. Pouilly fumé is not to be confused with pouilly-fuissé, which is a white burgundy, but they both serve the same purpose when it comes to fine dining, especially in banquets featuring a fish course as well as a meat course.

The Anjou district of the Loire Valley produces some white wines; however, the rosé wines from this district are better known and are quite excellent and are in demand even in the United States and England.

The most successful wine grapes are the sauvignon blanc and the chenin blanc. However, the darker red grapes do not seem to thrive well in this area. Although some red wine is made, it is seldom seen outside the immediate vicinity of the winery.

The area turns out a light wine known as *muscadet,* an excellent everyday white table wine. It is offering some competition to chablis, the white table wine so popular around the world today.

Bordeaux. Bordeaux is one of the most important wine-making areas in the world, producing about one-third of the wines of France. No other area produces better or finer wines. Great numbers of wines are produced in this area from the great variety of grapes grown. The variety of soil and weather is unique in this area, helping to produce outstanding wines—both red and white.

The Bordeaux area is located on the Atlantic Coast toward the southwest section of France. Records show that fine wines have been made in this area for over 2,000 years. When the Romans moved in about 50 B.C., they found the industry was well established and encouraged further growth.

In the year A.D. 1152, management of the Bordeaux wine area fell into the hands of the English. The Bordeaux wine area became the leading wine-producing area of the world. Bordeaux wines are by far the most popular wines in England and were so throughout the British Empire before it became a commonwealth.

Bordeaux is best known for its fine red wines, which are made from the cabernet sauvignon and the cabernet franc, which together with the merlot, give the red wines tannin, taste, and long life.

The white wines from this area, although not as great as the red wines, are, on the whole, outstanding. They are not as dry as some of the white wines from the other wine-producing areas of France, but are semisweet, high in taste and aroma, and can hold their own with almost any food product.

Almost all the Bordeaux wines, both red and white, are blended wines and not made from any particular variety of grape. There are so many varieties, with so many outstanding attributes, that the French have perfected the art of blending to produce the great wines that come from this region.

The Four Basic Categories. Bordeaux wines, both red and white, are marketed under four different categories. These are described briefly as follows:

1. The *chateau bottled wines* category tells the buyer that the wine grapes and the wine processing and bottling were done on the premises stated on the bottle label. A majority of the first growths of wine rated by the French government are found in this category.
2. The second category is for wines grown in certain chateaus where they are processed and then sold by the barrel to shippers who bottle and sell these wines both in France and abroad.
3. By far the largest category is the *regional appellation wines* which are sold in bulk to shippers who bottle them, label them under the labeling laws, and market them throughout the world.
4. The *monopole* wines are wines blended by merchant shippers and given a controlled brand name. To identify these wines, the brand name is often coupled with the region or the name *monopole*.

The Principal Red Wines. Because of the great variety of grapes and kinds of wine produced in Bordeaux, the wines produced in certain areas have been designated for a distinct type of a Bordeaux wine. Although these areas are rather limited in number, there seems to be no limitation on the number of chateaus or vineyards in each area. For example, in the Medoc area, over 500 chateaus or wineries are officially listed as producing a named brand of a red medoc wine. Some of the other areas claim only two or three hundred chateaus or wineries; well over 1,500 chateaus and wineries produce wines in the Bordeaux area alone.

Medoc. The wines of the Medoc appellation are all red and are true claret wines, which means they are light to medium in color. When young they contain a great deal of tannin, which with proper aging mellows and helps give the wine its distinctive flavor and the ability to age in the bottle for long lengths of time.

The Medoc area is further divided into Haut-Medoc, Saint-Estephe, Pauillac, St. Julien, Margaux, and St. Emilion.

Graves. The area of Graves produces distinctive flavored and garnet-colored wines that are as rich, full-bodied, and appealing as any of the Medoc wines.

The vineyards of Graves were classified in 1959, and the top chateaus were all rated equally as Crus Classes. The one exception is the Château Haut-Brion, which was given the classification "first growth," one of five such in France.

Saint-Emilion. The district of Saint-Emilion is one of the oldest wine-making areas known in France. The wines are full-bodied and deeply colored, but do mature somewhat more quickly than the other red wines of Bordeaux.

Saint-Emilion wines are all reds and are generally classified under the rating of "first" or "second growth" of French wines.

Pomerol. Pomerol wines are very sturdy and have the unique quality of being rather velvety in taste. The Pomerol area is rather small, and the vineyards have not been rated to date.

Other Red Wines of Bordeaux. There are many other distinctive red Bordeaux wines typical of the area, marketed under the label Côtes de Bordeaux.

The Principal White Wines. With all the publicity given to red wines of Bordeaux, it is surprising to find out that about half of the entire production of the Bordeaux wine district is of white wines. These wines are good everyday drinkable wines, reasonable in price, and vary from very dry to semisweet, are pale yellow to straw yellow, and range from a strong aroma to a pleasant light aroma.

Graves. About two-thirds of the wines produced in the Graves area are white. Some of the Graves wineries make both red and white. Recently the white Graves wines were raised to the rating equal to Crus Classes.

Entre-Deux Mers. One of the major Bordeaux areas for good drinkable white wine has a rather tricky name. The wines are light, pleasant, and said to be sound by the local inhabitants.

Sauternes and Barsac. This area is known for its luscious, golden, unique sweet wines, which are among the greatest dessert wines of the world. Château Yquem, which comes from this area, is acknowledged to be the finest dessert wine in the world.

The extra sweet wine is made by leaving the grapes on the vine past the normal picking time, which increases what is called the "noble rot." This risky procedure develops the sugar in the grapes very highly. However, if a frost sets in, the winery ends up with fields full of rotten grapes and must wait until next year.

Special Rating for Bordeaux Wines. A committee sponsored by the French government has rated the greater majority of wines produced in the Bordeaux district. These ratings are "first growth," "second growth," "third growth," "fourth growth," and "fifth growth." The rest of the wineries' products are unclassified.

There are only five recognized first growths of Bordeaux wines. Keep them in mind, as you may be asked to order a superior wine on some occasion.

Their wines are all red and are clarets:
Château Lafite-Rothschild
Château Margaux
Château Haut-Brion
Château Latour
Château Mouton-Rothschild

For years there were only four first growths of Bordeaux wines, but in 1955, due to public pressure, the committee rated Mouton-Rothschild a first growth. It was in greater demand than the other four, and was hurting their sales and volume drastically.

Any AOC-rated Bordeaux wine will be a good-to-excellent wine regardless of its name because of the strict control of the growing, production, and bottling processes. The consumer can absolutely depend on this control feature.

Many years back, a very large and prestigious bottler and exporter was tempted to tamper with the control laws and was immediately discovered, disgraced, and put out of the wine business.

Bordeaux wines can command extravagant prices. During one severe wine shortage, French wine prices soared to such heights that the industry gained a very bad reputation. So leaders in the industry promised to prevent this from happening again. This was topped off when a very wealthy person paid over $10,000 for a single bottle of red Bordeaux wine at an auction. He immediately opened it and served it to his guests at the table. Asked to comment on the price, he remarked "If you must consider the price, you couldn't afford it."

Champagne. Only the French can regally say, "Champagne, with its shimmering bubbles and fresh fruity taste, is the best and most famous wine in the world. It is the wine of celebration, elegance, and dreams; in its charm and vivaciousness, it is like the spirit of France; in its incomparable style and finesse, it is unique."

The Champagne wine-producing district is located about ninety miles east of Paris and is the northernmost wine-making area in France. Only certain grapes can grow satisfactorily this far north, because of occasional severe winter weather. Although champagne wine is made throughout the world, true champagne is made only in this area and is the only sparkling wine that has the right to carry the name *champagne*. Champagne was made in this area even before the Romans invaded from the south, and the Romans did everything they could to further develop the making and use of champagne. The old Roman wine cellars are still used today, augmenting modern production procedures.

True champagne is made from three grapes. The juice from the white chardonnay grape is blended with the juice from the pinot noir grape and the pinot meunier grape. Some champagnes are made only from the white chardonnay, and they are known as blanc de blanc. To keep the champagne white, the black skins are removed before fermentation begins.

The making of champagne involves two different fermentation processes. The first fermentation is done in bulk in the wine cellars of the winery. It is here that the skill of the wine maker really counts in the blending of the various juices and the handling of the young wine.

After this initial process, the wine is bottled with a small amount of sugar and stored in the wine cellars for the second fermentation process to begin.

Sizes of Bottles. Champagne is marketed—not only from France, but from other "champagne" areas—in various sizes of bottles. Some other sparkling wines are offered in the same-size bottles.

Bottle	Ounces	Metric
Split	6.5 oz.	18.75 centiliters
Half-bottle	13.0	37.5 centiliters
Bottle	26.0	75 centiliters
Magnum	52.0	1.5 liters
Jeroboam	104.0	3 liters

Bottles larger than a jeroboam are known as "curiosity" bottles and are individually filled at the winery:

Bottle	Ounces	Metric
Rehoboam	156.0	4.5 liters
Methuselah	208.0	6
Salmanasar	31.0	9
Balthasar	416.0	12
Nebuchadnezzar	520.0	15

Labeling. The label on a bottle of champagne is very informative and helps the buyer make the right decision. The most important pieces of information are

    The name of the winery
    Vintage year or nonvintage status
    Sweetness of the wine
    Name of shipper and importer
    Size of the bottle and contents
    Alcoholic contents by volume

For further information, refer to the section "How to Read a Wine Label" at the end of this discussion of French wines.

Degrees of Sweetness

Degree	Description	Amount of Sweetness
Brut or natural	Very, very dry	0.5 to 1.5% sugar
Extra dry	Fairly dry	1.5 to 3% sugar
Sec or dry	Medium sweet	3 to 5% sugar
Demisec	Quite sweet	5 to 7% sugar
Doux	Very sweet	Over 7% sugar

Brut and extra dry are the choice of the American wine consumer. The others are available but difficult to obtain.

Alsace. Near the central eastern border of France, where the Vosges Mountains look down on the Rhine River over to Germany, is the wine-making district of Alsace. This area is about 70 miles long and about 2–3 miles wide, and is located about halfway up the side of the mountain.

Not surprisingly, wines from Alsace are a great deal like the wines from the German side of the Rhine—basically, white wine with a fruity-nutty taste and a pleasing aroma. Because the wines are predominantly like the grape from which they are made, the wineries have adopted the practice of naming their wines after the grapes from which they are processed. Most Alsatian wines are further graded as Vin de Alsace or a slight variation, such as Vin Fine de Alsace.

Some finer Alsatian wines are further defined by law as Grands Vin or Grands Cru. Many shippers add to this designation the words *Grands Reserve* or *Exceptionale,* which calls to the buyer's attention the confidence the shipper has in the product. Almost all the Alsatian wines develop early, and are at their best when consumed when young and with lighter foods.

Some of the more important Alsatian wines are briefly described in the following paragraphs.

Riesling. This wine is generally accepted as the best wine of Alsace. Made from the Riesling grape, it is light, has an excellent bouquet, develops early, and is particularly good when consumed with cold meats and cold salads.

Gewürztraminer. The Gewürztraminer wine is the most distinctive and individual of Alsatian wines. In German, the word *gewürz* means "spicy." The spiciness is the most distinctive characteristic of the wine. It is a delicious, fruity wine, rarely overly dry, and might be called a semisweet wine. It is a big, rich wine that can be aged properly. With its high bouquet, it can be consumed with some rather highly spiced foods such as curries and some of the more spicy foods from Mexico and South America. Some Gewürztraminer wines are sweet enough to be served with dessert.

Sylvaner. Sylvaner wines are fresh, fruity, and dry. They develop within the first year and are best consumed with seafood. Sylvaner wines can also be used as aperitif wines.

Burgundy. The famous wine-producing district of Burgundy is located about seventy miles due east of Paris and extends about 225 miles down to the city of Lyon. It is not the largest wine-making district and produces only about one-tenth the amount of wine as Bordeaux. However, the wines it produces are considered some of the finest in France.

Located at the far north of the Burgundy wine district is Côte de Chablis, which produces only white wine, mainly chablis, the popular dry white wine.

As you travel south, the area is known as the Côte d'Or and just to make it more complicated, the Côte d'Or is divided into the Côte d'Nuits and the Côte d'Beaune. This area is the home of some of the greatest red wines of France, and to many wine connoisseurs the wines of this area are superior to even some of the best wines of Bordeaux. From this point south, the district borders the Rhône River and is known as the Golden Slope. The grape-growing areas located along this slope are not as famous as the areas further north and their wines are not as heavy and do not have as high a quality. However, they contribute a great deal to the reputation of the Burgundy area.

In the southern part of Burgundy is the Beaujolais district, where the very popular Beaujolais wine is produced. This light, semidry wine matures quickly and is usually consumed within one to two years after being produced. Some of it is consumed as soon as it is bottled, and London restaurants and hotels compete to put the first beaujolais on the table early in the fall.

Burgundy produces both red and white wines, but it is the red wines for which Burgundy is best known. The red wines of Burgundy age well but do not require the long aging to reach perfection that some of the red Bordeaux wines require.

The wines of Burgundy have been rated by the AOC as Grand Cru, Premier Cru, and "village." The Grand Cru wines of Burgundy compete very well with the "first growth" rating of the Bordeaux area.

The Red Wines. At the northern end of the Côte d'Or is located the Chambertin winemaking district. This district has about nine different areas, each producing its own variation of Chambertin Burgundy wines, both red and white. To identify these wines, each area has its own connotation, but all include the word chambertin. For example, there is the wine known as Chambertin itself and others such as Gevrey-Chambertin and Chambertin—Clos De Beze.

In this area is the village of Vougeot, the home of the Conferie des Chevaliers du Tastevin, a society organized in 1934 to propagate the qualities of Burgundy wines. In this area are produced some of the greatest wines of Burgundy, including the Romanee-Conti, the Vosne-Romanee, La Tache, and Richbourg, which are the great burgundies of France.

At the far south of the Burgundy area is the Beaujolais wine-making district. Beaujolais wines, noted for their light fruity aroma and enjoyable taste, are bottled under four different categories:

1. The first, or lowest category, or grade as approved by the French government, is Bas-Beaujolais.
2. Beaujolais Superieur is essentially the same grade as Beaujolais, but must have 1 percent more alcohol content.
3. Beaujolais—Villages comes from the nearby villages and is rated a step up in elegance and balance.
4. The most outstanding wine of the district is the Cru Beaujolais, which comes from any one of the nine villages of the area where the granite soil brings out the best of the gamay grapes. This grape variety adds to the soft elegance

of the wine and also makes it a longer-lived wine than wine from the other areas in Beaujolais.

The White Wines. Although the vineyards of Burgundy, on the whole, produce both red and white wines, the only white wine that has much significance is chablis, which basically comes from the far north of the area.

Four categories are authorized for the rating and bottling of chablis. The best is known as petit chablis. It is rated as a Grand Cru wine to be consumed while young.

Chablis Premier Cru is the second rated wine and is best consumed while on the young side, like petit chablis.

The most elegant chablis wines are known as the "great growths" of chablis. Some shippers label them as the Great Grand Cru Chablis. These wines have the most distinctive burgundy taste of all the white wines of Burgundy.

Other great white wines of Burgundy are the Grand Cru Corton, Meursault, and Puligny-Montrachet.

The best known of all the southern Burgundy wines from the Macon area is pouilly fuissé, a slightly green-tinted, pale golden, very dry white wine that competes with pouilly fumé from the Loire area for the menus of the outstanding banquets of the world.

Côtes du Rhône. The Côtes du Rhône wine-producing district is a small narrow strip of land that begins just south of the Burgundy wine-making area and extends down to the Mediterranean Sea. This area is consistently warm, and the strong grapevines produce full, highly colored, and perfumed wines. Both white and red wines are produced but less than 10 percent of the wine production is white, the balance being red and a small percentage being tavel rosés.

The district is divided into the northern and southern vineyards. Each area has its own distinct group of wines, each with its own particular outstanding qualities.

The red wines have a high sugar content and tend to have a higher alcohol content than some of the white wines. Both the red and white wines take some time to mature, but they do develop into smooth, highly bouqueted, and enjoyable wines.

The Northern Vineyards. The four main vineyards of the northern part of the Côtes du Rhône all produce strong red wines that have high bouquets and can stand considerable aging without spoilage. The vineyards of the area are the Côte Rotie, Heritage, Saint-Joseph, and Cornas.

The only white wine of significance produced by the northern vineyards is the hermitage blanc, which, if the weather is just right, can be an outstanding wine and in much demand by the local population.

The Southern Vineyards. The southern vineyards are responsible for about 80 percent of the wine production of the Côtes du Rhône. The most celebrated of the Rhône wines is the Chateauneuf-du-Pape, a big, pungent, strong and deep-colored product that can be made from as many as thirteen different authorized grape varieties of the area. This wine generally matures somewhat earlier than the Rhône wines from the northern district.

The ground where these grapes are grown is covered with large stones that draw the heat from the atmosphere in order to encourage fast and vigorous growth, resulting in the high flavor and aroma.

Other wines in the area are marketed under the label Côtes du Rhône, which is a catch-all label. These wines are considered very good average table wines and are used in blending other wines throughout France.

Other Wine-Producing Regions of France. Some wine-producing areas in France mainly produce the everyday drinking wines of the French nation and nearby countries. Some of these areas produce enormous quantities of good wines, and some of the areas produce small quantities of certain wines that have very distinctive

qualifications and help to contribute to France's reputation of having the greatest variety of wines in the world.

The best known of these areas are Jura, Savoie, Provence, Languedoc-Roussillon, Southwest, and Corsica, located in the Mediterranean.

These areas produce a great variety of mostly red wines; however, they do produce some very good rosé wines and some notable sparkling white wines.

WHAT IS A VINTAGE YEAR?

There seems to be some confusion to the exact meaning of the word *vintage* in reference to wine making—whether the wines are imported or produced in the United States, or other countries where the word *vintage* appears on the label. The word has several meanings:

1. A *vintage* is a gathering of the grapes and pressing them and making wine. This is part of the regular wine-making process, so there is a vintage every year.
2. The date on the bottle of wine shows the year in which the wine was produced—the vintage year.
3. Some vineyards bottle and date every year's production; others date only the better years.
4. Certain regions, notably Champagne, date only the wines of exceptional years. Because such conditions do not exist every year, the champagnes, when dated, are known as "vintage years."
5. Even though one region can have an outstanding year, this does not necessarily mean that all regions will be equally outstanding. For example, in one year the Burgundy region may produce some of the finest wines in its history, but that does not necessarily mean that in the same year the Bordeaux region will produce wines

outstanding for Bordeaux. The same applies to the United States, Italy, and other major wine-producing countries.

Vintage charts are published that list the various districts of a country and comment on the quality of the wines. These wine charts and comments are quite accurate because wine consumers have learned to depend on these charts when selecting wines. However, the various wine authorities in France, Italy, Germany, and the United States contend that you can best make your own choice by sampling and drinking wines from the various vintage years. When you find one that is very pleasing to your taste and within your price range, you should decide what is "the best vintage year."

HOW TO READ A WINE LABEL

As already pointed out, French wine laws go back to the middle ages, and the origin and authority for enforcement was sometimes vague. However, in 1935, the French government drew up a set of standards requiring that certain information be contained on the label for bottled wines produced in France.

1. The wine is a product of France.
2. The region in which the wine was produced—for example, Burgundy, Bordeaux, Champagne.
3. The appellation for which the wine qualifies accompanied by AOC (Appellation d'Origine Contrólée; or V.D.Q.S. (Vins Délimités de Qualité Supérieure), except in the case of Champagne, where the label need only read "Champagne."
4. The name and address of the shipper, except in the case of Champagne where, usually, the Champagne house (brand) is also the shipper.
5. The name and address of the importer.
6. The alcoholic percentage by volume.
7. The net contents of the bottle.
   The following is optional information that may appear on the label:
8. Vintage
9. Brand name or chateau name
10. "Estate bottled," "Chateau bottled," or similar phrase.

Exhibit 22-4. How to read a wine label (Courtesy: French Wines Correspondence Course, Food and Wines from France, Inc., New York, New York)

Acceptance by the public and industry was so good that the United States, Canada, Italy, Germany, and the majority of all wine-producing countries adopted the French wine-labeling codes.

The information required on the label is shown in Exhibit 22-4.

ITALIAN WINES

Italy produces more wines, both in variety and gallonage, than any other country in the world. Each year they produce an average of over 2 billion gallons of wine and export about 350 million gallons to other countries. The United States imports more wines from Italy than from all other countries, over half of these wines being bottled table wines.

Italian wines, because of the weather, soil, and grape varieties, are distinctive, with their own tastes, color, and aroma. Italians categorize wines as whites, reds, and rosés, dessert, and sparkling (see Exhibit 22-5). Over three hundred kinds and blends of wines have been registered by the government for production and sale, both locally and for export.

The production of Italian wines is not a "Mom and Pop" farm operation anymore. Production is now centered in the large single estate; the estate cooperatives have become corporate cooperatives with hundreds of members. The most modern equipment is used, and every step of the process is inspected and regulated. Some of the traditional farm wineries are still in operation

Type of Wine	Suggested Varieties	
WHITE WINES		
Mellow whites	Frascati abboccato	Prosecco
	Orvieto abboccato	Recioto di soave
Dry, light-bodied whites	Corvo bianco	Marino bianco
	Est! Est! Est!	Pinot bianco
	Frascati secco	Pinot grigio
	Lugano	
Dry, medium-bodied whites	Castel del Monte Bianso	Tocai
	Orvieto secco	Trebbiano di Romagna
	Soave	Verdicchio
RED WINES		
Semidry reds	Lambrusco	
Dry, light-bodied reds	Bardolino	Marino rosso
	Lago di caldaro	
Dry, medium-bodied reds	Castel del Monte Rosso	Inferno
	Cabernet	Montepulciano
	Chianti	d'Abruzzo
	Dolcetto	Merlot
	Freisa	Nebbiolo
	Grignolino	Sangiovese di
	Grumello	Romagna
		Sassella
		Valpolicella
Robust reds	Amarone	Chianti riserva
	Barbera d'Asti	Corvo rosso
	Barolo	Gattinara
	Barbaresco	Ghemme
	Brunello di Montalcino	Vino Nobile di
		Montepulciano
ROSÉ, DESSERT, and SPARKLING WINES		
Rosé wines	Castel del monte	Marino rosé
	Charietto	
Dessert wines	Marsala	Vin santo
Sparkling wines	Asti spumante	Prosecco spumante
	Nebbiolo spumante	Spumante brut

Exhibit 22-5. Types of Italian wines

mainly because the tourist bureau has insisted on maintaining them.

The Law and DOC (Denominazione di Origine Controllata)*

Italians may have been the first people to create laws to control the origins and protect the names of wines. The Romans named and defined production areas for dozens of wines and the Grand Duke of Tuscany in 1716 delimited the zones for Chianti, Pomino, Carmignano and Valdarno di Sopra.

But only in the last two decades has government control been applied nationwide to wine of "particular reputation and worth" under what is known as *denominazione di origine controllata* or, by the initials, as DOC.

There are now some 220 DOCs, all delimited geographically, though a zone may extend through an entire region or apply to only a few choice plots in a single community. Six of the

---

*From Burton Anderson, *Wines of Italy* (New York: Italian Trade Commission, 1986). Courtesy of the Italian Wine Center, Italian Trade Commission.

classified wines have been distinguished as DOCG (the G for *garantita* or guaranteed authenticity by government-appointed commissions). These are Barbaresco, Barolo, Brunello di Montalcino, Chianti, Vino Nobile di Montepulciano and Albana di Romagna.

In the 220 zones, more than 800 types of wine are defined—red, white or rosé; still, bubbly or sparkling; dry, semi-sweet or sweet; natural or fortified; young or aged; *classico; superiore;* and more.... Or they may be referred to by grape varieties, i.e. Trentino DOC with 18 varietals in its 20 subcategories.

Yet DOC and DOCG—which may also carry the European Common Market designation of VQPRD or, for sparkling wines, VSQPRD, account for only 10 to 12 percent of Italy's production. Non-DOC sparkling wines may be referred to as *spumante,* fizzy as *frizzante,* sweet as *amabile* or *dolce,* fortified as *liquoroso,* but other unclassified wine must be sold as *vino da tavola.*

Even this anonymous mass breaks down into two categories. One is table wines with geographical indications, which may be as sweeping as an entire section of the country

Exhibit 22-6. An Italian wine label (Courtesy: Italian Wine Center, Italian Trade Commission. From Burton Anderson, *Wines of Italy,* 1986)

(Pinot Grigio delle Venezie might have originated in any of three regions) or a region (Barbera del Piemonte) or a community (Moscato di Strevi). The other is simply labeled *vino da tavola* and cannot carry a vintage date.

Gradually, some table wines with geographical indications are due to be brought into an official classification known as *vini tipici*, roughly equivalent to the French *vins de pays*.

It is important to note, though, that while DOC and DOCG verify authenticity and denote quality, many good to excellent Italian wines are not classified. The reason might be that the grapes came from a non-DOC area or the wine was made under a special formula or that the producer chose to retain an individual identity. In the end, the most reliable guide to the quality of any wine from anywhere is the reputation of the individual producer or estate. Certain names are well worth getting to know.

All Italian wines imported into the United States must carry the INE seal of approval for export on a red neck label. Labels must state the bottle size in milliliters, alcohol by percentage of volume, a description such as "red table wine, product of Italy" and the importer's name and location.

GERMAN WINES

The wines of Germany are produced in the farthest northern grape-growing region of Europe. The soil is rocky (shale), and it is a tribute to the farmers of northern Germany that they can produce a wine crop of any magnitude at all. Even in good years, the volume of the crop is rather limited and the grapes grown are not particularly juicy. The wines produced in an ordinary year are quite good, and when the weather is right, the wines are some of the best in the world.

Back in the 1700's, the wines produced along the Rhine River near the Holland border were exported to England in large quantities under the Hochheimer label. This name was shortened to Hoch, and for years German wines were known in England as Hoch or Hochs. For some reason, this nickname was applied only to Rhine wines and not to the Moselle or Stein wines, which are also produced in the area of the Rhine and Moselle rivers.

The Rhine wine-producing area is divided into three districts: The Rheingau, the Rheinhess, and the Rhinepfalz. Both the Moselle and Stein wine areas are divided into small districts of Germany; however, most of these wines and wineries are grouped under Moselle and Stein wines.

German Wine Vintage

As with the French wines, the word *vintage* is used to cover the processing of a wine during any one year. The words "Vintage of 1980" means that the wine was produced in that year.

The Germans label their wines with certain descriptive wording that gives the prospective buyer a good guide as to what to expect. The following are brief descriptions of some of the terms used.

When the label on a bottle of wine carries the word "*naturrein*," the buyer knows that this is just a good all-around wine made in the natural method with no added sugar. The alcohol strength of such wines varies from 8 to 10 percent.

When *auslese* appears on the label, the wine is made from fully ripened but selected grapes. These wines are very good and are medium dry to medium sweet.

Spätlese means that the wine is made from grapes picked late in the season, when the sugar concentration is the highest. These wines are made only in good years and may be somewhat sweeter then the *auslese* wines.

Some of the finest wines produced anywhere in the world are the German *trocken beeren auslese*, which means that the wine is made from dried or shriveled grapes left on the vines until past late autumn. Often the grapes are wiped out from early frost, but if they survive, the wines are some of the world's best. In some years, as few as 20 to 25 cases of this wine are produced, due to unnaturally early frosts. These wines bring a price of about $1,000 per case at the vineyard—a good beginning bid at an auction.

German wine labels carry such information as whether the product is estate bottled, or is bottled by the shipper. The labels also show a district or township where the wine was produced and the trademark of the shipper. The label generally carries, or is required to carry, the vintage year of the wine, the district where produced, the alcohol content, and the name of the shipper. If the wine is sent to the United States, the name of the importer must also appear on the label.

Grape Varieties

Only a few varieties of grapes will survive the rocky soil and the northern climate of the Rhine Valley. The grapes that do survive produce very fine quality wines. The most important grapes for the production of German wine are the riesling, sylvaner, traminer, and the burgunder, which is the pinot noir of the Rhine Valley. Some red wines are produced from this grape, but less than 8 percent of the wines produced in Germany are red wines and are seldom exported. The excellent white wines dominate wine production in Germany.

Outstanding German Wines

Anyone who takes pride in knowing wines will say that there are three outstanding wines in Germany, and can recite the legends that have made these wines famous.

Bernkasteler Doktor, a moselle wine, was named after a wine that cured the Bishop of Bernkastel of a deadly fever in the fifteenth century. When the bishop recovered, he called the wine the Doktor of Bernkasteler. The vineyard was on the property of Dr. H. Thanisch, and today the vineyard is still in the hands of the Thanisch family. The wine is one of the best made in Germany.

Liebfraumilch Blue Nun is a Rhine wine from the Rheinhess, and it is the single largest-selling imported wine in the United States today. Originally, the wine came from a vineyard that the shadow from the "Church of our Beloved Lady" fell on each day, which limited the volume of wine production. Years ago the German wine authorities ruled that the name could be applied to any "Gott" wine from the township and so it remains today. The wine is soft, aromatic, lightly nutty in flavor, semisweet, pleasant to drink, and reasonably priced. The Americans "drink it up."

Schloss Johannisberg is a product of a vineyard going back to the Napoleonic wars. The vineyard was the scene of several battles and changes of ownership, but the quality of wine remained outstanding. The wines are rather heady and semisweet, and have a full bouquet and their own character and taste. They develop slowly but do not last more than about ten years.

Because of the German wine-labeling laws and the introduction of strict production standards, certain wines and vineyards have established reputations for outstanding quality. The following is a representative listing. (In a German wine listing, the township name generally precedes the winery name.)

Rhine Wines
Schloss Johannisberg
Rudesheimer Schlossberg
Schloss Vollrads
Steinberger Auslese
Hochheimer Domdechaney
Oppenheimer Schlossberg
Niersteiner Domthal
Oppenheimer Goldberg
Forster Jesuitengarten

Moselle Wines
Bernkasteler Doktor
Piersporter Goldtropfschen
Graachen Himmelreich
Zeltinger Schlossberg
Moselblümehen (district name)
Zeltinger Riesling

The *vintage* means the same in Germany as in other countries—each year has a vintage, but some years are better than others. Few German wines keep over six years, and even the best will "go" after ten years.

The vintage of 1921 is referred to in a hushed voice in German wine circles. It is the standard by which all vintages are judged.

SPANISH WINES

Sherry and Port

When Spain is mentioned, one immediately thinks of sherry and port. These two centuries-old wines were developed in these two countries and exported around the world.

Even before the time when Greece was at its pinnacle of power, Venetian sailors had visited the Iberian peninsula and found it almost totally barren. Together the Phoenician and Greek sailors established trading posts and started vineyards, and sherry wine was born.

The wine industry in Spain flourished several hundred years before the birth of Christ. When the ruins of Pompeii were excavated hundreds of years later, many wine casks from Spain were found, some still containing wine.

In the 1500's, an industrious Spanish wine merchant went to England with some samples of sherry and port and found that the English were unenthusiastic, but with a little merchandising the Spanish sherry and port eventually succeeded in England. The English spread the word about the therapeutic value of these two wines when England ruled the seas.

Sherry wines come in seven different types ranging from very, very dry to very, very rich and sweet. The two best-known sherry wines in the United States are Harvey's Bristol Cream, a very rich, brown sherry, and La Ina Pale Dry, which has gained considerable fame for being an excellent aperitif.

Other Wines of Spain

Spain is best known for its sherry wine, but it must not be forgotten that the total wine production of Spain is well over 500 million gallons per year. Only about 10 percent of this is sherry, part of which is exported. With the exception of one other wine, most of this production is consumed by the local population as table wine.

These wines are light, have a stronger alcohol content, but are often used with a mixture of fruit juices and sparkling waters. Because of these fruit mixtures and the fact the wine is consumed during the day as well as at meals, these wines have been dubbed "Spanish Lemonade."

Riojas Wines. The leading Spanish table wine in the world market is the riojas wine, which comes both in red and white. It is a light, semidry table wine, and because of its similarity to the French Bordeaux wines, it is often called the Spanish claret and sauterne.

PORTUGUESE WINES

The legendary wine from Portugal, not surprisingly, is port. Port was introduced to England about 1700 but was a failure—the wine was raw, dark, and had an unpleasant aroma. After several decades of experimentation, the vintners came up with a process whereby they put some brandy in the wine plus some sugar during the fermentation process. This proved successful. Port is now a traditional after-dinner drink about the civilized world. Of the four types of port produced, only ruby and tawny port are exported in any appreciable quantity.

Port wines mature very slowly in wooden casks, and most ports are aged as much as thirty years before bottling. Ruby ports have a bright red color and are made from a blend of the younger eight- to twelve-year-old ports, whereas the tawny ports are made from blends of twenty- to thirty-year-old ports.

The Portuguese prefer the lighter, low-alcohol wines known as Lisbon wines. In the

1950's, the Portuguese developed the lancer wines, which are still very popular. These wines, similar to a rosé, come both as a sparkling wine and a still table wine.

The Wines of Madeira

In the late 1400's the Portuguese started producing a wine on their colonized island of Madeira some 550 miles southwest of Lisbon, Portugal. Both the French and English ships plying the ocean lanes of commerce stopped at Madeira and picked up a supply of wine to take back to the home ports, where it was considered a very high-quality product.

From 1500 through the turn of the nineteenth century, Madeira wines were considered a mark of distinction in wealthy families. Every sideboard or buffet in the large English country homes had a decanter or cask of Madeira wine that was offered to the guests of the lord of the manor. During World War I, with shipping curtailed by submarine warfare, the distribution of Madeira wines shrank almost to zero. For some reason, it has never recovered.

Madeira wines are somewhat sweet and slightly heavy in body, which discourages people from drinking very much. They are not wines imbibed to get drunk, which may explain their decline in popularity in the last century.

Madeira wines are the longest-lived wines in the world. You will seldom see an exported Madeira wine that is less than 20–25 years old. Madeira wines continue to improve with age up to 90–100 years, if properly stored in sound wooden casks.

Bottled Madeira wines are a blend of various types of Madeira wines and usually include various ages of wine. The wine is marketed at about 20 percent by alcoholic volume, and if the wines, when blended, need some additional alcohol, they are fortified with sugar and permitted to age some additional years.

One peculiarity of Madeira wines is that the fermentation of the wine and the initial ageing is done by what is known as the "baking method." Instead of the fermentation being done at the usual room temperature, these wines are put in "hot houses" with temperatures up to 175°F for 3–4 months. The wines are permitted to ferment, and this processing gives them their outstanding taste, flavor, and aroma. Madeira is the only wine processed in this way in the world today, except for a few districts in the hills of China.

THE TWO VARIETIES OF VERMOUTH

French Vermouth

French vermouth the world over is known as the dry vermouth. Before Prohibition, it was used mostly as an aperitif. After Prohibition, it was used mostly as a cocktail mixer, especially in the United States. However, it is still used as a premeal aperitif in most other countries.

French vermouth is made from a good-quality blended white wine produced in central France, but has little commercial value other than locally. This wine is mixed with up to forty different flavorings such as plants, roots, seeds, nuts, and other botanicals. The wine is steeped with these flavorings for about a month and then drawn off, filtered, and allowed to age from two to three years in wooden casks. Most French vermouth is marketed at just under 20 percent alcohol by volume, but some of the so-called extra-dry vermouths are marketed at as little as 10–11 percent alcohol by volume.

Italian Vermouth

Until recently, Italian vermouth was known as the sweet vermouth and in many parts of the world it still is. Italian vermouth is made primarily the same as French vermouth; however, Italian vermouth contains some quinine. This addition was useful several hundred years ago because of the fact that quinine helps to cure malaria, which was very prevalent when vermouth was introduced.

Italian vermouth is marketed with two different versions. The first is an aperitif type, which is rather sweet and heavy. It is strong enough to stand on its own, and can be served on the rocks.

Italian vermouth is also produced as a cocktail vermouth that is lighter in body and flavor and blends well with other liquors to make a pleasing or straight up on-the-rocks drink. Italian vermouth is marketed with an 18–20 percent alcohol content by volume and is an important commercial export from Italy.

An interesting thing has happened with both the French and Italian vermouths over the last 25–30 years. Originally, French vermouth was known as the dry vermouth and was the accepted mixer for martini cocktails. The Italian vermouth was accepted as the sweet vermouth and was the mixer normally used for manhattan cocktails. When the Americans went berserk over the idea of a dry martini, the Italians developed an extra dry vermouth that made an ideal dry martini, and took the dry vermouth business away from the French. The French, not to be outdone, set out to take the sweet vermouth business away from the Italians, and were successful to some degree. However, the Americans stopped drinking manhattans, so in the long run the French lost to the Italians.

Some vermouths are made in other parts of the world such as the United States, South America, and Australia. However, most so-called local vermouths are of such low quality that they ruin the liquor with which they are mixed. No self-respecting bar manager would have any of them in a first-class bar operation.

OTHER WINE REGIONS OF THE WORLD

Switzerland, with its sunny mountain-sides and slopes, produces a very fine line of wines similar to those found in the Alsace region of France. These wines are the riesling, sylvaner, and traminer types, quite similar to the majority of the lighter German wines. They are a little on the sweeter side and have a fine, fruity aroma and taste and are considered some of the better beverage wines to accompany good food.

Austria

Before World War II, Austrian wines held a unique place in world trade. They were light, fruity, and seemed to remind people of the gay life of Vienna. Of course, the war destroyed most of their business; however, after the war, even though the country produces good wines, they have not seemed interested in exporting their wines. Austrian wines are still good, but producers lack aggressive advertising and the will to compete in the world market.

Until the last few years, Hungary had a good thing going with a wine nicknamed Rosebud. It was quite popular in the United States, a heavy, dark red wine with a rather high alcoholic content. The producers became involved in some adulteration, and the demand for the wine around the world evaporated. Whether or not it ever recovers remains to be seen.

Russia

Before the Russian revolution in 1918, Russia was an important competitor in the world wine trade. Records show that Russia exported as much as 40 million gallons of wine a year, mostly white wines and some heavy, sweetish champagne.

Russia still exports a small amount of wine, but it has not been well accepted worldwide. Most of the wines produced in Russia are consumed by the new middle class that is emerging.

Greece and Turkey

Greek wine culture began thousands of years ago; it was highly refined by the time of the Trojan War, and the Homeric epic poems describe many episodes of wine drinking. The wines were originally light and pleasant, but according to some historians, the Greeks wanted a stronger, most flavorful and distinctive wine. They accomplished this by storing their wines in large earthenware crocks lined with a pine resin, which gave them the distinctive resinous taste. The Greek wine *retsina* has this taste even today.

For modern Greece, however, the wine producers of the country have developed white wines that are free of the resinous taste. Some of these wines are exported to the United States and other countries to satisfy demand from Greeks who have emigrated to other countries.

In this century, Turkey started to produce a line of wines and distilled spirits that if not of the finest in the world, are some of the strongest. The biggest problem for the wine industry in Turkey is the lack of bottles and the hard currency to buy them from the other parts of the world that produce glass. In some cases, the deposit on the bottles costs more than the contents. This holds especially true for champagne.

Turkish wines are very strong and heavy, and their distilling methods are, at best, questionable. Their vodka is safe to drink; however, two drinks of their gin and the tourist will have a headache for the next two or three days.

North Africa

North Africa, meaning Tunisia, Morocco, and Algeria, have produced quite a bit of wine, which has been exported mostly to France, Spain, and Italy for blending with those countries' finer wines. These countries still export some wine for blending, but they lost their market primarily to the huge supply of good wines available in California. (Records show that one of the biggest customers of the California wine industry is the wine industry of France, which uses the wines for blending with popular wines and then ships the blended wine back to the United States.)

Australia

During the past fifty years, the Australians have become more involved in the wine-producing business. The weather and soil along the southern coast is very similar to California, Oregon, and Washington, and the wines produced are almost identical to the wines of California.

The grapes used in wine production here are the same variety used in the western United States and in South America. A list of the wines available for export reads much like an advertisement for the larger wineries of California.

The Australians, in naming their wines, are not reluctant to refer to their wines as *burgundy, champagne, claret,* or *sauterne.* They do not feel it necessary to add the word *type* or to qualify the name of the wines, as is done in California.

The Argentine

It may come as a surprise to many that Argentina is the fifth largest wine-producing country of the world. Until recently, this was a well-kept secret, and only in the past few years has an effort been made to promote the sale and export of Argentine wines to the rest of the world.

These wines are being exported as named after their counterparts in the European wine trade, such as claret, burgundy, sherry, and rosé.

The wines are good, sound, pleasant drinking wines. However, they are on the bland side and do not have distinct wine type flavors or tastes, which has held back the growth of the export business. We understand that the wine-producing associations of the area are developing better techniques and quality vines for wine production.

Chile

Over the past century, Chile has become host to a considerable number of emigrating Germans, Swiss, and mid-Europeans. Most of these colonists were knowledgeable about wines and have set up quite a wine-producing industry in Chile, which is known for producing consistently high-quality wines for export and local consumption.

Most wines produced in Chile are of the German type, being light, bright, fruity in taste, and quite similar to Rhine and Alsatian wines. For some reason, the wine growers have bottled their riesling wines, which is one of their best, in a typical stein wine bottle, which seems to be the trademark of the Chilean wine industry in the export trade.

The Chilean government for years has limited the cap on the price that the local hotels and restaurants can charge for wine. Consequently, the price of wine in Chile is very reasonable. The last time we were in Chile, about ten years ago, we were able to get a bottle of the finest and highest-priced Chilean wine in the best restaurant of Santiago for the equivalent of $7.50 per bottle.

DISTILLED SPIRITS

When the art of distillation was discovered or who first used it is a mystery. There are some records of distillation in ancient Egyptian history. Around 2000 B.C., the Chinese were making a drink or beverage from distilling wine from rice. About 350 B.C., Aristotle, the great Greek philosopher, announced and proved that sea water could be made potable through distillation. Captain Cook, on his trip around the world in the 1700's, found in the South Pacific that the natives of those distant islands had available some beverage that obviously had been made by distillation. By A.D. 1000, the words *alcohol* and *still* were both in use in Europe.

By the time European colonists came to the Western Hemisphere, most of the current different types of alcoholic beverages were known. Scotch whiskey, Irish whiskey, rum, and brandy figured as important trade items in the slave trade. At one time, a pint of whiskey served as a standard for trade.

In the early 1600's, an English trading company came to the Jamestown, Virginia, area with the expressed purpose of setting up a whiskey distillery, to establish trade as a source of income for the colonies and England. The Berkeley Plantation at the mouth of the James River claims the distinction of developing what is now known in the United States as bourbon whiskey.

Back in the 1500's these distilled spirits were called the "water of life" because the imbibers seemed to have been given the exuberance of health and vitality. But even then some doctors, noticing drunkenness and ill effects on health, started countermeasures to try and control the effects of the so-called water of life.

Classifying Distilled Spirits

In today's market, distilled spirits are classified as follows:

Whiskey
Gin
Vodka
Brandy
Rum
Liqueurs (or cordials)
Other spirits
Rectified spirits

Although familiar with most of the classified spirits, most readers may require more information on rectified spirits. Rectifying is considered to be any process that changes the character of a spirit on which tax has already been paid, and it must be performed in a taxed rectifying plant. Here are some examples:

Blending and bottling any distilled spirit
Blending two different whiskeys made either in the same plant or in different plants
Blending whiskeys with neutral spirits

Redistillation of spirits that have been stored in barrels

Adding coloring or anything else except water

Redistillation of neutral spirits for potable uses

Redistillation of neutral spirits with a flavoring agent

Compounding neutral spirits with flavoring oils for gin or liqueurs, or adding other flavoring substances

Bottle Sizes and Number of Drinks

Exhibit 22-7 shows, in both the standard and metric systems, the common bottle sizes, the number of bottles per case, and the number of drinks per case usually obtained for distilled spirits.

Alcoholic Content

Bottles of distilled spirits are labeled as being a certain proof, such as 86°, which is actually 43 percent alcohol by volume, just 50 percent of the rated proof. Exhibit 22-8 shows some of the more common "proofs" for distilled spirits.

How Spirits Are Metabolized

A few years back, the *New England Medical Journal* published an article stating that if you want to drink, at least you should know what you are drinking. The article went on to list the time that it took the average person to absorb and eliminate an ounce of alcohol from various types of spirits. The types of alcohol and length of time it takes for the average person to absorb and eliminate each spirit are listed here:

Gin and vodka (1 oz.): 1 hour

Liqueurs or cordials (less than 60 proof) (1 oz.): 5–6 hours

Scotch, Irish, and Canadian Whiskey (1 oz.): 6 hours

Beer or ale (12 oz.): 6–8 hours

Table wine or champagne (3 oz.): 6–8 hours

Bourbon and light rum (1 oz.): 8 hours

Dark rum (1 oz.): 10–12 hours

Brandy and cognac (1 oz.): 24 hours

WHISKEYS

Almost all the whiskey of the world is produced in four countries. The most famous is Scotland, followed by Ireland, the United States, and Canada. Some whiskeys are made in other countries, but they are of minor importance. The Japanese put out a product under the Suntori label, and some

Size of bottles	Number of bottles per case	Number of Servings in Standard-Size Containers			
		1-oz. servings per bottle	1.5-oz. servings per bottle	1-oz. servings per case	1.5-oz. servings per case
Half gallon	6	64	42.6	384	256
Quart	12	32	21.3	384	256
Fifth	12	25	17	307	204
Pint	24	16	10.7	384	256

Size of bottles	Number of bottles per case	Number of Servings in Various-Size Metric Containers			
		30-ml per bottle	45-ml per bottle	30-ml per case	45-ml per case
1.75 liters	6	59.2	38.8	355	232.8
1 liter	12	33.8	22.2	405	266.4
750 ml	12	25.4	16.6	304	199.2
375 ml	24	12.7	8.3	304	199.2

Note: These figures for drinks per case or individual bottle are not exact, but have been rounded off to the appropriate figure.
Source: Courtesy of Creative Bar Management, Inc.

Exhibit 22-7. Bottle sizes and number of drinks for distilled spirits

Spirits	Proof
Whiskies: Scotch, Irish	80, 86, 93
Bourbon: rye, corn, wheat	80, 86, 90, 94, 100, 110
Canadian	80, 86
Gin	80, 86, 90
Vodka	80, 90, 100
Rum	80, 86, 100
Brandy	80, 86, 100
Cordials	45, 50, 60
Tequila	80
Vermouth	16–20% by volume

Note: Whiskey bottled in bond is always marketed at 100°.

Exhibit 22-8. Common proofs for distilled spirits

American-type whiskeys are produced in Mexico, Chile, Argentina, and Brazil. These products carry the name of the U.S. company under which they are licensed and made.

Some European countries produce a whiskey-like product that is generally called *schnapps,* which is rather strong, high in alcoholic content, and raw in taste. The cherry schnapps from Germany is about the only product of this type that is imported into the United States.

Scotch Whisky

Both Scotland and Ireland argue about who began making whisky first in this area. When the process of distilling whisky was developed in either country is still in question. It is pretty well agreed, however, that both Scotch and Irish whisky were being made somewhere about A.D. 900. Both whiskies are made in almost the same way, with the exception of one step we discuss briefly later.

Scotch whisky is made and identified from four different areas of Scotland. These areas are the Highlands, the Lowlands, Campbell Town, and Islay. Each area produces its own particular type and taste of whisky. However, most scotch whiskey is a blend of at least two of these regional scotches, sometimes a blend of all four plus a grain whisky.

Scotch whisky is made with five main processes:

1. Malting or sprouting of the grain
2. Mashing
3. Fermenting
4. Distilling
5. Maturing and blending

Most scotch whisky is made from barley, which is plentiful, reasonably priced, and produces a good product.

First the barley is brought into the receiving area, where it is sieved to remove weeds, hay, and other foreign substances. It is then spread on the malting house floor, where it is wet down, for about three weeks until the grain starts to sprout.

After the grain has sprouted, it is transferred to a kiln where the sprouted grain is placed on screens over open peat fires. These peat fires are quite smokey and as they dry the green malt, the grain takes on some of the smoky taste. In the heat, the starches start to develop into sugars, which are necessary for fermentation.

After the dry grain is screened, it is moved over to the so-called mashing vats. In the mashing vats, the grain is thoroughly ground and mixed with warm water and then is blended with a mixture of wort (green, or starter beer) from a previous batch that contains alcohol and yeast. This alcohol and yeast then starts fermentation with the new wort—at this point it is called *beer.*

The beer is then passed on to pot stills, where it ferments until it reaches the proper alcohol content. Then it goes through "low distillation." What remains in the pot stills is a residue that used to be thrown out until it was discovered that it made great cattle food. Aberdeen angus are the best all-around beef cattle in the world.

The product from the first distillation is then redistilled to about 180 proof, at which time the distillation is put into oak casks for aging and blending. Today these oak casks and barrels are obtained primarily from the United States, but in earlier times, scotch whisky was put in old wine barrels, especially sherry wine barrels, if they were available.

These new scotch whiskies are left in the

casks, where they are aged in government-controlled warehouses, so that there will be no opportunity for substitution.

Scotch whisky is not blended and bottled until the scotch has matured in the oak casks for a minimum of three years. In certain cases, the whisky is permitted to mature up to twelve years and even twenty years.

Until about 1850 all scotch whisky was straight whisky of one run. However, the newfound American trade seemed to prefer a milder, less smoky taste. This brought about the artful blending that produced the fine-tasting scotch whiskies of today.

The matured whiskies are thoroughly mixed through air filtration and mechanical devices. With a few exceptions, all scotch whisky is blended, a mixture of the four basic scotch regional whiskies plus grain whisky, which is made with a mixture of other grains. However, they are grain whiskies, not alcohol or distilled water.

At this point these whiskies are bottled and stored for export or immediate consumption. However, many finer scotches are put back in oak barrels and cured for an additional period of time so as to cater to the more affluent gentry and the U.S. trade, which is constantly seeking a status symbol in aged scotch. Yet age in a whisky, especially scotch, does not necessarily mean a fine product. It just means that the product has been aged for a certain length of time. Remember that aging whisky costs considerable money, because of taxation, evaporation, and cost of investment. The successful distiller does not normally age poor whisky, except by accident. Scotch whisky experts continually point out that many of the finest scotch whiskies are marketed at four and five years of maturity and that it is quality rather than age that produces a fine reputation, demand, and high prices.

Irish whisky is made with the same processes as scotch whisky, with the exception that the kiln used in drying the sprouted Irish barley has a solid floor. The smoke from the peat, or heating element, is not exposed to the sprouted grain, thus making irish whisky less smoky and harsh but somewhat sweeter than the average scotch whisky. It is considered more of a "sipping whisky" than scotch.

Premium Scotches. About three thousand distilleries in Scotland make a premium scotch, in some cases called "liqueur" scotch. All these distilleries seek to market their prestige scotch in the United States, because the additional profit here is quite substantial. However, cracking this market is very difficult and costly.

Since the repeal of Prohibition, several attempts have been made to establish a new prestige scotch in the United States, but only one has really taken hold and that is Chivas Regal, which today is one of the best and most expensive prestige scotches available in the United States.

According to import records, the most popular prestige scotches over the past fifty years have been Johnny Walker Black Label, Haig & Haig Pinch, Chivas Regal, Catos 12, Dewar Ne Plus Ultra, Buchanan's Liqueur Oval, and Ambassador 12. All these scotches have been aged twelve years and some for twenty years. However, scotch does not improve very much after twelve years, and the extra cost involved doesn't help the sales.

All these scotches have an eight-year version that is the commonly accepted "good" scotch for the true scotch drinker. Some of the better "standard" scotch whiskies are used in the average bar and liquor store in this country. Some of them are Black & White, Dewar's White Label, White Horse, J&B Rare, Teacher's, 5 Star, Martin's VO, Peter Dawson, Old Smuggler, John Beg, White Heather, and Checkers. There are, of course, many more labels for good to excellent scotches. However, no class bar operation could go wrong by pouring any one of the above-named scotches as its bar scotch.

DCL Scotch. DCL (Distillers Combine Limited) is a marketing corporation with roots in Scotland, headquarters in England, and branches around the world. This marketing group controls about 75 percent of the better-selling scotches and other spirits exported from Scotland. Its activities establish some stability in the scotch market, and DCL scotches also tend to be slightly more expensive than some of the independent scotches. DCL also controls some marketing practices: you will never see a DCL scotch bottled domestically in the United States.

Domestic Bottled Scotch. After the repeal of Prohibition, some of the independent scotch producers, noticing the success of U.S. blended whiskey, decided that in view of increased bottling costs, taxes, transportation, and marketing costs, it might be wise to try to bottle some of their product in the United States under the U.S. rectifying laws. Several companies, all independent of DCL, experimented with this idea and it soon took root in the United States. Today it is a large factor in the marketing of scotch whisky. Under this program, a blend of all-malt whiskies at high proof are brought into this country in barrels and then reduced in proof, using American neutral spirits and bottling and distributing in the United States. This process is somewhat different from the blending of the malt whiskies in Scotland with their grain whiskies. However, the difference in taste is very slight, providing the scotch is of good quality and palatable in the pure malt state.

The success of this idea has allowed retail prices for domestic bottled that are about 60 percent those of imported bottled scotch. In the United States today, the biggest-selling scotch, according to beverage sales records, is Old Smuggler, which is a domestic bottled scotch used a great deal as a bar scotch across the country.

American Whiskeys

One New England historian commented that when the settlers came to the Virginia colonies, they brought along their stills and their thirst, whereas when colonists came to New England, they brought along their Bibles. It is true that whiskey was made in Virginia about the time the colonists landed at Plymouth Rock.

The Southern colonists started making whiskey because they had a readily available supply of rye grain. More importantly, there was abundant limestone-filtered water, which is necessary in making any good whiskey, regardless of type. This limestone water has the same chemical qualities as the red sandstone water used in making scotch and irish whiskey. If this red sandstone-filtered water had been available in England or France, we probably would be drinking English or French whiskey instead of scotch.

This limestone-filtered water is available from Maryland and parts of Virginia through southern Pennsylvania, to Indiana and through Tennessee and Kentucky and into Illinois. Early U.S. settlers went west along this route, distilling as they went, helped by the fact there was considerable agitation over the taxes on liquor and political opinion as to whether there should be prohibition and control of the making and selling of whiskey. Bourbon whiskey was developed with the addition of the maize cultivated by Indians. The name was taken from Bourbon County, Kentucky. At one time in early American history, as noted earlier, a pint of whiskey was used as a standard of exchange. The whiskey standard was more stable than the U.S. dollar. We had the first tax rebellion over taxes on whiskey during the first term of President Washington's administration. Fortunately, it was a bloodless revolution, and it established the right of the federal government to tax the making of whiskey for public sale. The settlement was a compromise whereby people could make their own whiskey for their own consumption without paying taxes, but if it was sold they had to pay taxes. The situation stands pretty much the same today.

How American Whiskey Is Made. American whiskey is made basically the same as scotch and irish whiskey but is made by an even simpler method. American distillers have cut out the green malting and kiln drying of the grain and start with the grinding of the grain mixture with water and yeast and the distillation of the so-called beer. American whiskey is distilled at about 100–102 proof, whereas the scotch is distilled out as high as 180 proof.

Because American whiskeys are distilled at lower proof, the initial product or green whiskey contains a chemical that if not removed through aging, would cause the problems that arose during Prohibition (blindness, excessive drunkenness, staggering, ulcers, and death). Any marketed American whiskey today is aged a minimum of four years in charred oak casks, preferably white oak, and the American whiskeys are reduced from the original distillation rate down to 80–86 proof. In comparison, 90–100 proof whiskey was popular until 15–20 years ago.

U.S. whiskeys continue to age successfully up to about eight years, when they reach their maximum in taste and aroma. Further aging does not seem to improve the product—all it does is result in higher costs. After Prohibition was repealed, quite a bit of seventeen- and eighteen-year-old bourbon was available in warehouses in Kentucky. It was marketed very successfully, featuring the fact that it was long-aged whiskey. It was marketed and totally consumed but at a premium price, but some was of very poor quality, being musty and with a dark brown color and a rather unpleasant odor.

Kinds of American Whiskeys. Five kinds of American whiskey are recognized by the federal government. They are listed as follows, with a brief description of their ingredients:

Straight whiskey is a whiskey distilled from a mixture of small grains with no one grain constituting over 50 percent of the mixture. This whiskey is made in Virginia, Pennsylvania, and Illinois and is generally known as a light whiskey.

Rye whiskey is made from a mixture of fine grains of which 51 percent or more is rye grain. Other grains can be corn, barley, millet, and wheat.

Bourbon whiskey is made from a mixture of fine grain of which 51 percent or more is corn, with other grains being rye, barley, wheat, and other fine grains.

Corn whiskey is made from a mixture of nothing but various kinds of corn grain.

Wheat whiskey is made from 100 percent wheat grain in the conventional method.

Sweet Versus Sour Mash. In making American bourbon and rye whiskeys, after the grain and water mixture has been cooked into what is known as a *beer,* the next step is to add a certain measured amount of yeasting material to cause the beer to ferment before it is put into the distilling process. Some distilleries use what is known as a "sour mash method" of adding yeast, which merely means that a certain amount of yeast and distillation from a previous run of the product is added to the new beer, plus some additional yeasting materials to cause the fermentation. Other distillers feel that it is better to use new, pure yeast from the laboratory to start the fermentation process. This "sweet mash method" is recommended, as it is easier to control and does not encourage stray bacteria in yeast, as can occur using the sour mash method.

Today, with our modern, closely controlled production processes in whiskey making, there is very little chance for any wild yeast to ruin a run of whiskey production. All whiskeys are the result of a carefully planned production process, which follows a very closely supervised routine. A good whiskey made according to the recipe, properly supervised, and made from quality grains with the right limestone-filtered water and the proper aging in charred oak casks, will be high quality whether it is made with the sour mash or sweet mash method. In short, Jack Daniels Black Label, Old

Fitzgerald's Cabin Still, and Baltimore Pure Rye would be the same whether they were made by either production method.

From a merchandising standpoint, there is considerable value in the idea of sour mash whiskey. Bourbon drinkers, as well as martini drinkers, have their own ideas about what is quality liquor. A bourbon drinker who is dedicated to a sour mash product will not like a sweet mash product even though others will think the sweet mash product is superior. The sales representatives for the various liquors have quite a number of claims that they use to prove that their product is better than the others, but we doubt that very many people will remember whether their favorite brand of bourbon or rye is made with a sour mash method or some other method. All they know is the brand name and that they like it, and they will be very loyal to that brand name.

Types of American Whiskeys. American whiskeys are classified by type in Exhibit 22-9.

Canadian Whiskey

Canadian whiskey is made the way American whiskeys are but under Canadian rules and regulations. A straight Canadian whiskey is made from a mixture of fine grains with a balanced amount of the grains used. A "straight" is also made from a single run of whiskey and distillation. If a straight Canadian whiskey is blended with other than a "straight," it must be designated and labeled as a blended Canadian whiskey.

OTHER DISTILLED SPIRITS

Gin

In the late seventeenth century, the poor people of England were drinking a distilled spirit that was made by distilling the leftover wort from the making of Scotch whiskey. This drink was rather distasteful and the people let the government and distillers know they were dissatisfied about the fact they did not have a cheap drink. After considerable trial and error and aggravation, by the 1800's the English came up with a London dry gin and an Old Tom gin about the time the Dutch came up with their Holland and Geneva gins. Today, all the gins made are of these two types.

European Gins. There are two types of London dry gin used throughout the world today. The first is a distilled gin and the second is a rectified gin or what was known during Prohibition as a "bathtub" gin. Regardless of the name and the labeling, gin is pure grain alcohol distilled and drawn off at high proofs so that it is a pure, safe drink with a kick but without the effects of some spirits that are not distilled at sufficiently high proof.

London dry gin is distilled from a beer made from a mixture of ground corn, wheat, and barley, and the first run is drawn off at about 180 proof. This first run of alcohol is blended with some essential flavoring oils and materials such as juniper berries. Then it is distilled a second time in pot stills and drawn off at around 120 proof. Finally it is

Type	Explanation
Straight rye	Made from a single run of rye whiskey
Straight bourbon	Made from a single run of bourbon whiskey
Blended rye	Made from a blend of 35 percent or more of straight rye whiskey and the balance from neutral spirits
Blended bourbon	Same as for blended rye except bourbon whiskey is used. In some parts of the east, this product is known as "rye" whiskey
A blend of straight rye or bourbon whiskeys	A mixture of a number of straight rye or bourbon whiskeys
Bottled in bond	A whiskey that meets the requirements for a bottled-in-bond whiskey: A straight whiskey 100 proof when bottled Aged four years in new white oak barrels Stored in a bonded warehouse under government supervision

Exhibit 22-9. Classification of American whiskeys by type

reduced to the 80–100 proof levels with distilled water.

The English have a gin known as Old Tom gin, which is just London dry gin with some sweetening. It makes a gin ideal for gin and tonic, but is not a good mixer for the ever-popular martini.

Holland gin is made quite differently from the English London dry gin. The water is different, as is the distilling process. The Holland gin is a mixture of flavoring products with a mash made with wheat, barley, and corn. After fermentation, it is distilled off at 100–110 proof, which results in a heavier-bodied product that is better taken straight and in smaller quantities than the English dry gin.

American Gins. American gins are made almost exactly like the English London dry gins. The difference in flavor comes from the different water used. The water used in England makes a better product than the American water. American gin is double-distilled, using various flavoring materials on the second run. It is drawn off at over 190 proof, which leaves a slight difference in taste but a very pure and palatable drink with very few afteraffects when consumed in moderation.

Fruit Gins. A great number of fruit gins are available, made primarily by rectifying or mixing fruit flavors with London dry gin. The result is a pleasant gin when mixed with ice and soda.

Aging of Gin. Because of its method of preparation, gin lacks most of the by-products that cause physical problems. However, some areas in the world make gin in ways more resembling the first stages of sour mash whiskey, with the result that the product is heavily tainted with esters, fusel oil, and animal hides that make the product dangerous to drink. Travelers and tourists in the Middle East should not drink any locally made gin. If no imported gin is available, drink vodka, preferably from Russia, if available.

Vodka

Vodka, the other member of the "white-goods family," is pure grain alcohol. It is distilled out over 190 proof, is double-distilled, and is used instead of gin.

Rum

Rum is the most versatile distilled spirit there is. It can be consumed straight or in long (tall) fruit juice coolers, makes great cocktails and mixed drinks, and is used extensively in cooking, especially in sauces and pastries.

There are records of rum being known in ancient China. About the fifteenth century, it became a noted product in the West Indies. Even today, the best source of good rum is the West Indies.

Rums are made by distilling the molasses obtained from ground-up sugar cane. It is distilled at 180–190 proof for the light rums and somewhat lower (160) for the dark, heavier rums.

Rums can be consumed after one year of aging in oak barrels. However, the better rums are aged four to six years before being bottled and sold. The older rums such as the Cuban and Yale are aged up to twenty years, but not all rums will stand up for this lengthy aging.

Back in the sixteenth century, the English navy ruled the waves. One reason for their dominance was that sailors could spend more time on the ocean without getting scurvy if they got a ration of rum each day. Today's modern diet of fresh fruits, juices, and vegetables replaces the rum ration.

There are three kinds of rum in the world today. First is the light rum sometimes known as Cuban rum. Second is the dark rum known as Jamaica rum. Third is Batavia rum, which is made in the East Indies and is a unique-tasting rum.

There are no "types" of rums. Each rum is a specific kind and is designated by the source of the sugar cane from which it is made.

Before Cuba challenged the United States for dominance of the Caribbean, Cuban rum was considered the best light rum. The best rum from Cuba was Bacardi, but with the advent of Castro, Bacardi moved to Puerto Rico and set up its rum processing there. Today, Bacardi Puerto Rican and Carioca Puerto Rican rums are the most widely used in the United States and are considered very good. Good light rums are also imported from the West Indies, Santo Domingo, and Haiti. Jamaica also imports a good light rum under the name of Appleton's, in addition to its well-known Jamaican rum.

Jamaica is known for its dark rum. Trinidad, Demerara, Barbados, and Martinique also export good dark rums, and New England producers still put out a good dark rum made from sugar cane and molasses imported from the West Indies.

Batavia rum or arrack is made in the East Indies, primarily on the Island of Java. The water from which it is made and the introduction of some fried rice cakes into the beer just before it is distilled give this rum a unique and pleasing taste.

Proof of Rum. Most rums, regardless of where they come from, are marketed at 80 and 86 proof. These proofs seem to fill the public's demand at the present time. However, an excellent rum called Demerera is marketed at 151 proof. This rum is used primarily for the making of rum sours and rum punch, and it is an excellent product.

One of the finest long drinks made in the world is the Mai Tai. This rum drink is featured by Trader Vic and the Kon-Tiki restaurants and about every other hotel in Hawaii and the nearby islands.

Cognac and Brandy

All cognac is brandy, but not all brandy is cognac.

By law, cognac is a brandy made from grapes grown, distilled, aged, and bottled in the Cognac district of France. The French government closely supervises all steps in the production of cognac to protect quality standards.

Brandy is made the same way as cognac. However, it can be made anywhere in the world except where grapes will not grow or a wine cannot be produced from some fruit grown in the area. Quality standards, as well as taste, vary from country to country, but basically it is the same product, made in the same way, and has the same aging requirements to be potable.

The process of making cognac, as well as brandy, is not particularly complicated. However, the small details involved in the making of cognac make the difference. That is why the French government sets such strict standards for making cognac, such as locking up all the public-owned stills as well as community-owned stills when the quota of wine to be made into cognac has been met.

After it is made, the cognac wine is held in oak barrels for about a year and then it is doubled-distilled in pot stills. Each distillation is a separate process, which adds to the cost, whereas in other parts of the world the process is continuous. After the double-distillation, it is put in new oak barrels to age.

The proper aging of cognac is quite debatable. However, because of certain impurities it is necessary to age the product for as long as necessary. This means from a period of six years to a century. Good cognacs are aged from twenty to forty years. Most brandies are aged from six to eight years.

After the cognac has aged, various products are blended together to obtain the final taste and then permitted to meld for several months before being filtered and bottled. Cognac, as with other wines, liquors, and whiskeys, does not age once it has been bottled and corked or sealed.

Labels on cognac bottles do carry certain indications of the quality of the product as well as the age. The number of stars on a bottled cognac is not very meaningful; the stars are just part of the name. Certain abbreviations do indicate some quality standards. For example, VSOP stands for "Very Superior Old Pale" cognac. Eight initials are used on the cognac labels to represent the following standards:

E Especial	S Superior
F Fine	P Pale
V Very	X Extra
O Old	C Cognac

Making cognac is not a complex, big manufacturing procedure. Almost all the cognac made in the area is produced on individually owned farms, hence the product must be blended to be the same from year to year. The brand name shippers such as Hennessey, Martell's, Lejon, and Courvoisier are like cooperatives. They buy up the product, blend it, establish their standards, and then bottle, market, and ship it.

Other Brandies from Around the World

Armagnac. Armagnac is practically the same as cognac but it is made in the Bordeaux area of France and is made from claret wine. It is double-distilled in a continuous distillation process, and it is aged in a different type of oak barrel, which gives armagnac its distinctive color.

Spanish Brandy. Spanish sherry, of course, is fortified with brandy. Consequently, Spanish brandy was developed to fill this need. Spanish brandy is made in a process resembling that which produces cognac and armagnac. However, the resulting brandy is somewhat sweeter and has become the third most popular brandy in the foreign trade. Probably the two most popular brands of Spanish brandy are Pedro Domec and Gonzales Buyas.

American Brandies. The State of California produces most American brandies, about 3 million gallons per year. Beverage brandies are aged in white oak casks for six to eight years and are sold for drinking as brandy. In addition to beverage brandy, California produces up to 15 million gallons of blending brandy used primarily in rectifying cordials and liqueurs, which is a very important aspect of wine production in California. California brandies are made the same as other brandies, including cognac in France.

The United States produces a substantial amount of apple brandy, which is basically the same product as the French produce under the name of Calvados. Most U.S. apple brandy is produced in New Jersey, and it is also marketed as bottled in bond, which meets the requirements of bottled-in-bond whiskey. So-called apple jack is aged in charred oak casks two to six years and is used in cooking as well as certain beverage drinks such as the Jack Rose cocktail.

Other Fruit Brandies. Some true distilled apricot, blackberry, and plum brandies are produced in the United States as well as the middle European countries. However, most fruit brandies are made by soaking California brandies with fruit juices and dried fruits for a period of time in earthenware containers and filtering out the residue, leaving a product known as a fruit brandy or a cordial. These products are not aged together in oak because the brandies or cordials would take on an oak taste and color, which is not desirable.

Pisco Brandy. The only brandy produced in South America of any importance is that produced in the port city of Pisco, Peru. This great brandy is sold as Pisco or Pisco Punch, depending on the distillery and shipper. It is a very "sneaky" product that doesn't seem to have any effect on the drinker until he or she has consumed too much—and then the reaction is rather violent and long-lived.

Greek Brandies. The best brandy produced commercially in Greece is mataxa, which is quite good and is valuable to the foreign exchange of Greece. The Greeks also produce another brandy, called *raki,* that is not aged very long and is harsh and often dangerous. Greece also produces an anise-flavored brandy called *ouzo,* which is the popular aperitif of Greece. This licorice-flavored drink is consumed straight as an aperitif or mixed with water as a beverage drink. It is very popular in Greece, but not in the United States.

Liqueurs (Cordials)

According to history, learned medieval monks and alchemists spent their efforts in trying to solve two problems: (1) how to convert base metal into gold; and (2) how to come up with the elixir of life, which was supposed to extend normal human life ten to twenty years. Obviously, they didn't solve the first problem, and there is considerable debate over whether they solved the second. They did, however, discover a health aid that can make the last few years of one's life better than expected. This elixir was known as liqueurs.

Liqueurs, made from natural products, are rich, sweet alcoholic beverages, made from fruits and/or roots of certain plants, to which natural sweeteners have been added. These drinks, because of their heavy sweetness, have been used primarily as an after-dinner drink, and the consumption of these drinks is heavier in Europe and Asia than in the United States. In the United States, many beverage authorities refer to liqueurs as cordials, and the two names are used interchangeably throughout the world.

Liqueurs (cordials) are divided into two classes: rectified fruit liqueurs, and plant liqueur made from seeds, plant roots, and other vegetation. The fruit liqueurs are made by macerating a good-quality brandy with fruit, which gives it color and taste. This soaking period continues for four days, after which the pulp is filtered out and the proof adjusted by adding simple syrup and/or distilled water.

The plant liqueurs are made somewhat differently, from a mixture of flavorings with brandy, which is fermented and distilled off as a clear liquid. This liquid is then flavored and colored by adding certain oils and flavorings. The resulting product is aged in held-over oak barrels, which are one of the producer's most valuable assets. One producer in the Champagne district of France said that his cooperage was guarded better than the gold bullion stored in Fort Knox, Kentucky. The formulas and techniques of processing of most of the famous liqueurs in the world are better-kept secrets than the formula for making Coca Cola Classic.

The Best-Known Liqueurs. The following are the best-known liqueurs or cordials that generally appear on good bar lists around the world:

Dom benedictine
Cherry heering
Crême de cacao
Drambuie
Gilka kümmel
Strega
Ouzo
Triple sec
Chartreuse
Curacao
Cointreau
Grand Marnier
Creme Yvette
Creme de menthe
Sloe gin

BEERS AND ALES

History of Beer

According to the *Anheuser-Busch Companies Fact Book*, the origins of beer are older than recorded history, extending into the mythology of ancient civilizations. Beer, the oldest alcoholic beverage, was discovered independently by most ancient cultures—the Babylonians, Assyrians, Egyptians, Hebrews, Africans, Chinese, Incas, Teutons, Saxons, and the various wandering tribes of Eurasia. These ancient peoples left records that indicate they not only enjoyed their beer, but considered brewing to be a serious and important job.

Babylonian clay tablets more than 6,000 years old depict the brewing of beer and give detailed recipes. An extract from an ancient Chinese manuscript states that beer, or "kiu" as it was called, was known to the Chinese as early as the twenty-third century B.C.

Beer was enjoyed by ancient peoples at all levels of society. Of course, some drank with more style than others. For example, the University of Pennsylvania Museum displays a golden straw used by Queen Shubad of Mesopotamia for sipping beer.

With the rise of commerce and the growth of cities during the Middle Ages, brewing became more than a household activity. Municipal brew houses were established, which eventually led to the formation of brewing guilds. Commercial brewing on a significantly larger scale began around the twelfth century in Germany.

Although native Americans had developed a form of beer, Europeans brought their own version with them to the New World. Beer enjoys the distinction of having come over on the Mayflower and, in fact, seems to have played a part in the Pilgrims' decision to land at Plymouth Rock instead of farther south, as intended. An entry dated 1620 in a journal kept by one of the passengers states that the Mayflower landed at Plymouth because "we could not now take time for further search or consideration, our victuals being much spent, especially our beere . . ."

The first commercial brewery in America was founded in New Amsterdam (New York) in 1623. Many patriots owned their own breweries, among them Samuel Adams and William Penn. Thomas Jefferson was also interested in brewing and made beer at Monticello. George Washington even had his own brew house on the grounds of Mount Vernon, and his handwritten recipe for beer is dated 1757 and preserved in his diary.

Some Definitions of Beer Products

Beer is a food product made from barley malt, hops, grain adjuncts, yeast, and water. The alcohol in beer results from the fermentation by yeast of an extract from barley malt and other cereal grains. In addition to alcohol, beer commonly contains carbohydrates, proteins, amino acids, vitamins (such as riboflavin and niacin) and minerals (such as calcium and potassium) derived from the original food materials. Ale is made much as beer is, but is heavier in consistency, more aromatic, contains more hops, is fermented at higher temperatures, and is produced with a different type of yeast.

Stout is a very dark ale made with a malt flavor, and is somewhat sweeter than ale.

Porter is a variation of ale, with a rich creamy foam. It is made with a very dark malt and is very hoppy and sweet. Porter is not as hoppy, sweet, or strong as Stout.

Bock beer is a special, heavy brewed beer that is prepared during the winter for spring distribution and sales. The German word *Bock* means male goat or buck, and has a connotation of giving the drinker vigor and energy (more imagination than fact).

Lager beer is a bright, clear, light-bodied, and effervescent beer, made more sparkling by plowing back into the beer some of the carbon dioxide that escapes during fermentation. Some call it the ginger ale of beer. Most American beers are of the lager type.

Alcohol Content

Through custom, the general public has come to refer to the alcohol content of American beers as either "3.2 percent" or "5 percent." The 3.2 percent designation refers to percent of alcohol by weight and the 5 percent designation refers to percent of alcohol by volume. To clarify the real difference in percentage designation, 3.2 percent (an alcohol by weight designation) is equivalent to 4 percent by volume, and 4 percent by weight is equivalent to 5 percent by volume. In comparing the "by volume" numbers, it is clear that there is really only about a 1 percent difference in alcohol by volume between so-called 3.2 percent and 5 percent beers.

Quality Factors for Beers and Ales

The key words in the beer industry are *consistent quality*. There are no secrets within the industry, just care and direction and the willingness to accept a little less profit than average.

Quality assurance begins with the testing of ingredients before brewing ever begins. Perfection can be achieved only through close scrutiny extending down to the smallest detail of the packaging operation, including bottle crowns and can lids. Pure water is also a key ingredient in brewing great beer. Water must be checked as rigidly as other ingredients. When necessary, the water must be treated to ensure conformity to exacting standards.

No scientific test, however, can replace tasting as the final judgment of quality. In a fine brewery, flavor panels meet daily to judge the aroma, appearance, and taste of packaged, filtered, and unfiltered beer.

Control of quality does not cease at the brewery. Wholesalers play a key role in seeing that the quality that begins with the ingredients and continues through the brewing and packaging processes is preserved until the beer reaches consumers. Such care by wholesalers requires controlled-environment warehouse systems that maintain beer freshness during storage.

Packaging

Beers are packaged for sale in kegs, bottles, and cans. Wooden kegs must be lined with a nontasting plastic, and if a metal keg is used, it too must be lined. Aluminum kegs can be used without a lining. A barrel of beer contains 31 gallons, or the equivalent of 13.8 cases of 12-ounce cans or bottles (24 cans or bottles in each case).

The 12-ounce brown bottle is the most popular for beer, and the 12-ounce green bottle is used primarily for ale. The colored glass filters out light, which affects the quality of beer and ale very rapidly. Some 7-ounce bottles are in use throughout the country, but they have not proven very popular.

Beers and ales, regardless of how packaged, should be stored in a clean, dry, dark storeroom with a temperature tightly controlled between 40° and 50°.

A purchasing agent will need to become informed and involved when beer is served, especially if draught beer is served. The technicalities of the length of the beer lines, the maintenance of temperature along the lines, the cleanliness of the lines, and the pressure maintained are all too complicated for the average bar operation to handle. At this point, the purchasing agent must bring in a skilled representative of the company from which the beer is bought. Most beer distributors furnish this inspection and service without cost to protect their product. However, if such a service is not available without cost, it is well worth paying for it if you want to stay in the draught beer business.

Experience shows that a bar operator can take care of all the basic necessities to draw a good glass of beer at the tap, but if the glasses into which the beer is drawn are not "beer clean," his or her business will disappear. The dishwashing machine and techniques of delivering beer-clean glasses to the bar are vital!

Nonalcohol Brew

Prior to the introduction of Sharp's nonalcohol brew by the Miller Brewing Company in 1989 and O'Doul's by

Anheuser-Busch shortly thereafter, the market for nonalcohol brew was dominated by imported nonalcohol brews. Moussy from Switzerland led the parade in the 1970's followed by brands like Kaliber from Ireland and Clausthaler from Germany. Since 1990, the local brands—particularly O'Doul's, Sharp's, OMNA (old Milwaukee Non-Alcoholic) by Stroh's, and Coors' Cutter—have dominated the market, with Heileman's Kingsbury running far behind in fifth place. Currently, five of the top twenty nonalcohol brews on the market are imported, but together they account for only 4 percent of total sales.

In 1993, the total nonalcohol brew volume in the United States was 2.8 million barrels. With a total brew volume of 196 million barrels, the volume of nonalcohols constitute only about 1.5 percent of the total volume.

Exhibit 22-10 shows supermarket sales of the leading American brands of nonalcohol brews.

A number of factors have contributed to the appeal and marketability of nonalcohol brews. For one, the continuing trend toward moderation and fitness has many people freely choosing to drink fewer alcoholic beverages or none at all. This is consistent with the demand for lower alcoholic content in whiskies, gin, vodka, and the light beer featured by most American breweries. Also helping the market for nonalcoholics are ongoing efforts to stiffen drunk-driving penalties. In 1993, five states lowered the required blood alcohol content (BAC) threshold at which a person is considered legally drunk. While still small, the nonalcohol brew category continues to gain momentum. O'Doul's, which commands the largest share of the market, is targeted to adults 28 years of age and older.

Concerning the manufacture of nonalcohol brew, O'Doul's brand manager, Anne Suppiger, says, "At Anheuser-Busch, we believe the best way to produce a nonalcohol brew is to start with a quality beer. We fully ferment, age, and finish a premium beer. Then, in an extra step, the alcohol is removed, leaving real beer taste and only 70 calories."

Brand	Brewer	Case Sales	Market Share
O'Doul's	Anheuser-Busch	3,410,663	32.6%
Sharp's	Miller Brewing	1,993,270	19.1
OMNA	Stroh Brewery	1,387,765	13.3
Coors' Cutter	Coors' Brewing	1,083,655	10.4
Kingsbury	G. Heileman	481,383	4.6
Total		8,356,736	79.9%
Other Brands		2,105,761	20.1
Total Nonalcohol Brews in Supermarkets		10,462,497	100.0%

Exhibit 22-10. Supermarket sales of the leading U.S. nonalcohol brews

Part IV
SUPPLIES AND SERVICES

23 The Big Four: China, Glassware, Silver, and Linen

Purpose: To describe these standard supply items and to discuss quality, cost, cost control, and buying plans.

INTRODUCTION

The items in the title of this chapter gained this sobriquet because they are the major "other expenses" (departmental expenses other than food cost and payroll) in a typical restaurant or hotel operation, including both the rooms department and the food and beverage operations.

The budgeted costs for these items are shown in the following brief schedule.

Rooms Department	Percentage of Room Sales
Linen and glassware	1.8%
Food and Beverage	
China and glass	1.5%
Silver*	.6%
Line	.7%
Total	2.8%

* Includes silver and stainless steel flatware and holloware.

The apparent need for control of these items is better illustrated if we look at the dollars involved. In the rooms department, 1.8 percent of sales represents $18,000 per $1,000,000 in sales. Likewise, in the food and beverage departments, the 2.8 percent amounts to $28,000 per $1,000,000 in sales. The hotel and restaurant industries buy over $125,000,000 of the "big four" items annually.

CONTROL OF BIG FOUR COSTS

Management's most valuable technique in controlling big four costs is to resist change merely for the sake of change. Inevitably, changes in personnel, refurbishing, or introduction of a decorator's ideas result in calls for a total new look. Management must avoid this costly trap.

Basic to keeping the cost of these items under control is for the accounting department to put all storeroom stock on a perpetual inventory card, or preferably, a computer. Management should review, on a regular basis, what department is getting these items, how the use of these items compares, period to period, and how the usage compares with industry averages. Each item thus becomes a controllable item rather than a percentage of overall cost.

When management has this information (and it should be expressed in terms of units used per hundred covers or hundred guest days), it should investigate how the supplies are used. Some of the questions that arise are, "Do we have the proper warewashing equipment?" "Is our night security of expensive items adequate?" "Is our linen being used for home use or is it being carted out (which it often is) in large quantities and resold?" In South America, it is almost impossible to keep any silver flatware or holloware safe in a hotel because of the locals' desire to accumulate silver. Consequently, stainless steel, aluminum, and plastic are often substituted even in the highest-class operations.

Overbuying of some items is a common cause of excess cost. This is usually the result of lack of good stock information and month-end inventories. The accounting department should issue an excess-stock report each month or each quarter so that the department heads can plan ways to use it. It may pay to donate excess china and glassware to charitable organizations to obtain the benefit of a tax write-off. Failure to anticipate replacement needs in time for delivery when needed may result in purchase of fill-ins so stocks become mismatched and obsolete.

Knowing How to Buy Big
Four Items

E. M. Statler is known as the great innovator of guest services, but he and his executive staff were also known for running the "tightest ship" in the business. They operated their hotels on the theory that it was necessary to know where every penny was spent and why. Some of the systems that they designed to control costs were very unusual and wouldn't apply today, but their innovative system of buying big four items introduced in the 1920's is still used by practically all purchasing agents who have expertise in this area.

Until recently, when hotels and restaurants obtained computers, all statistical information had to be kept on cards along with quarterly and annual inventories. Calculations and reports were all made by hand. When an inventory clerk earned $60.00 per week, this was feasible, but those days are gone forever. However, the Statler system of buying remains the best in the business.

Statler's Plan

Statler accumulated consumption figures over a five-year period and then calculated the figures for the average quarter so that he could plan to use up supplies on a quarterly basis as well as on an entire year's basis. His next step was to negotiate on a new basis with all the companies involved each year with the idea of making a deal with a price that would hold for the entire year. The supplies and materials would be withdrawn and paid for by the hotel each quarter and the balance of the stock would be carried by the manufacturer and held at the same price for the entire year.

One of the problems that arose was what to do about overages and shortages at the end of the year. Statler found that being honest and fair with the manufacturers was the best policy. He agreed that if the hotel had underbought at the last withdrawal by more than 5 percent, they would pay and withdraw up to 5 percent of the year's total. Mr. Statler also agreed to take the remaining 5 percent during the first three months of the next year regardless of whether they renewed the purchase agreement with the company holding the 5 percent or not.

On the other hand, Statler expected that if the hotels were using more than they expected through the third quarter, then the hotel should be granted permission to increase the last quarter withdrawal by an additional 5 percent and the dealers would be expected to fill the orders without any increase in cost. The big advantage of such a plan is that the hotel gets the advantage of large-quantity purchasing through yearly negotiated prices and also saves money by dealing directly with the manufacturer. This system also enables management to monitor the rate at which stock needs to be replaced at each facility and to make comparison between these rates for different facilities. The following incident illustrates the benefits of such a comparison.

After bringing the statistics up to date and starting to compare the breakage of cups hotel by hotel, it was found that the Statler Hotel in New York City was breaking about one-third the number of cups per hundred covers as the Statler in Washington, D.C. A single visit to the Statler in Washington revealed the cause of this excessive breakage. The steward at the hotel was being criticized for coffee and tea stains in the cups so he came up with the idea of soaking the cups after each use in a strong detergent solution. He had built two large stainless steel soaking tanks, one near the kitchen dishwasher and one in the banquet kitchen where banquet coffee cups were brought back. As the waiters cleared tables, they set the coffee cups aside and then unceremoniously dumped them into these tanks, which were filled with water and the soapy solution. Excessive breakage resulted. In fact, the steward had hung up two coal scuttles just above the tanks that were used to remove the broken cups into trash cans when the tanks were cleaned at the end of the day.

Further investigation showed that the hotel in New York had the same problem with stains; however, they worked with their detergent supplier and found a combination detergent that removed the coffee stains and, with the use of a rinse-dry, had solved the problem. The cleaning supply company used in Washington was a different company. Needless to say, the necessary changes were made.

Using the Statler Plan—Buy and Hold

The Statler buying plan may be summarized as follows:

1. Determine accurately the quarterly and yearly consumption of each type of big four item.
2. Determine that the items you are buying are appropriate for the use for which they are intended.
3. Thoroughly research the market to determine what items are available that will fill the need best for the least money.
4. Prepare a clear set of specifications covering the required items.
5. After you have determined the first four, prepare yearly requirements on a quarterly basis and obtain the best price on the specified goods on a buy-and-hold quarterly basis.

CHINA

We are concerned here with tableware or dinnerware, whatever its material. Ten different products are now available to the food service industry, and we list them not necessarily in the volume in which they are being used overall but rather by their use in the food service industry.

These items are:
1. Earthenware or stoneware
2. China
3. Fireproof china
4. Bone china
5. Alumilized china
6. Pyroceram—prolon products
7. Pyrex
8. Plastics—reusable
9. Single-service plastics—throwaways
10. Coated paper throwaways

The paper and plastic throwaways, better known as single-service ware, are used almost 100 percent in the fast food industry, airlines, railroads, and practically all institutional food services. Use of the other types of dinnerware for service is pretty much restricted to hotel or "tablecloth" restaurants.

Types of Tableware Generally Used by Hotel and Tablecloth Restaurants

Molded Plastic Dinnerware—Melamine. Some molded plastic dinnerware is still in use in the food service industry. Although it is almost impossible to break, it does have a tendency to scratch and become worn looking in a short time. Molded plastics are now being used for salad bowls and items that are substituted for cut glass serving pieces.

The main problem with molded plastics is that they are not hard enough to resist absorption. These molded plastics will take heat only up to about 600°F, and the majority start melting around 450°F, so it is impossible to put a hard glaze on them. The health departments around the country have taken a dim view of the use of molded plastic dinnerware; consequently, their use has been mostly restricted to containers for the service of food or buffet service in lower-priced operations.

Pyrex Dinnerware. For years we have had Pyrex cooking utensils, which are heat-resistant glass items. About twenty years ago, Corning Glass started making dishes and dinnerware out of Pyrex after they found out how to color the material and put designs on the glass before firing. For a while, these products found ready acceptance because they were low in price and resisted breakage. However they chipped badly around the edges, and it also seemed that the dining-out public did not want to be served on the same type of low-priced dinnerware they were using at home. Even though Pyrex is still used today in many operations, it is not used in better hotels and restaurants.

Alumilized China. For years the china companies have looked for a way to reinforce regular china with some substance that would make it less breakable. Just about every type of product was used, including fiberglass and even vegetable fibers, but none seemed to improve its fragility, or if it did, it made the product so heavy that it was not practical. One manufacturer has now developed what they call alumilized china, which is regular china with powdered aluminum dust mixed in to make it stronger. The company claims that it has reduced the breakage rate by 30 percent.

The problem with this product is that it is heavy, since it has to be made a little thicker than ordinary china, and it tends to leave a black ring on other china when stacked in the kitchen ready for use. This black ring is difficult to remove even with the strongest of detergents and the best warewashing equipment. Consequently, the popularity of this product has been limited.

Fireproof China. The Hall China Company developed a product known as "ovenproof china" over fifty years ago that has become the standard for all cook-and-serve china in the country. All food service operators unquestionably are familiar with the green and brown china with the white inside finish. Recently the company has developed a large range of color combinations, plus many interesting shapes that can be used for purposes other than oven cooking. They have developed salad bowls, serving platters, and coffee cups and have recently marketed what might be called contemporary-pattern china. This china has been developed for table service and offers unusual designs for standard serving pieces. It is very popular and is used extensively in the typical grill-room type of operation.

At one time, there was a three- to four-month waiting period for delivery of this china. Even today, the purchasing agent of a company using this type of china would do well to have at least a three-month backup of all pieces to avoid embarrassment in case of a shortage.

Bone China. This is the finest kind of china made and generally carries the name of Rosenthal, Royal Dalton, Spode, and other well-known trade names. Such china can be found only in the finest stores and in homes that can afford this very expensive but beautiful china. Its use in hotels and restaurants is usually limited to demitasse coffee service in certain luxury dining rooms.

Pyroceram. About twenty years ago when NASA was looking for a substance to protect the surfaces of the capsule carrying the astronauts when reentering the earth's atmosphere, they came up with a product made of glass that would withstand heat up to 5,000 to 6,000°F. This product was pyroceram, and it was basically the same product that is being used today to make the tiles that cover the space shuttle. This material is very strong, resists breakage, and is creamy white in color and very lightweight. It was inevitable that the company making this product would introduce tableware made of Pyroceram since they were already making Pyrex dinnerware.

When introduced, Pyroceram dinnerware was plain white and limited in shape and size but still attracted the attention of the food service operator. The coffee cups were easily adapted into many china patterns, and tests showed that the breakage rate of Pyroceram cups was one-fourth that of regular china cups. The manufacturer soon learned how to tint Pyroceram and how to put attractive decals and prints on the product. With expansion of the use, the cost came down to where it became a serious contender for the dinnerware business and even some of the better food service operations.

Earthenware—Stoneware. The best way to describe earthenware is that it is a low-grade china which, when handled properly, answers all the needs for dinnerware for a food service operation. It can be decorated like china, is fired like china, has a fairly hard glaze to resist contamination, and is fairly resistant to breakage. The

English make earthenware for sale in this country at prices considerably under those for regular china, and buyers should give serious consideration to the use of these products.

A great deal of the dinnerware used for outdoor dining and colorful dinnerware for home and specialty restaurant use is made from earthenware. It has a considerable market value because it is attractive and it is low priced.

Vitrified China. Vitrified china is still the standard by which all other dinnerware is judged. Although some lines are very costly, more than 80 percent of white-tablecloth restaurants and hotels are using this product for table service.

Of the many reasons for this popularity, the most important is that people expect china when they spend the money to eat in a first-class restaurant. They will not accept use of the same product that they probably use at home. They want something special, and if they don't get it, they will go elsewhere. Another reason is that china can be made in different shapes and sizes; it can be decorated very attractively, and food has enhanced appeal when displayed on china. China is sanitary since its surface is covered with a hard glass glaze that contamination cannot penetrate. China also washes easily and doesn't require special handling other than use of current detergents and warewashing equipment.

China is heat resistant and can be placed in the oven for a very short time or actually put under a broiler for a few seconds to give the dish a final heating before it is sent into the dining room for service.

In spite of the increase in price of china over the past years, it is still fairly inexpensive. With care in warewashing operations, breakage can be reduced by use of the proper diswashing racks and storage procedures. Incentive programs among warewashers to reduce breakage have also been very successful.

Decorating China. China lends itself to glazed decoration as well as hand-painting with exotic patterns. China can be bought in plain body colors such as white, off-white, and adobe. Any color can be purchased other than the standard three, but the buyer must remember that the paint or dye is sprayed on the china bisque before it is glazed and fired.

China is decorated in basically three ways. The china bisque can be sprayed with colors through templates to make certain decorative patterns, or it can be brushed with dyes and paints to obtain the desired effect. Finally, china can be decorated with decals which, when applied to the china bisque, result in the many attractive patterns that are available today.

It used to be that the prints and decals had to be applied to the china bisque by hand, which slowed up the process and kept the price of decorated china very high. About fifteen years ago, the Shenango China Company developed a fully automated system of decorating china that revolutionized the china business. It is this process that today enables china manufacturers to offer a satisfactory product to the public at affordable cost.

Overglazed China. China made with gold-leaf decoration is extremely attractive and food looks great on it. But unfortunately gold-leaf decoration under glaze is not possible. Gold decorations and hand-painted patterns have to be put on by hand over the glaze of the china. Although such china is very attractive, the decoration is short-lived in heavy commercial use. These products, therefore, are limited to very expensive dining room service or home use.

THE PLACE OF GLASSWARE IN THE FOOD SERVICE INDUSTRY

Not too long ago the only glassware used in the food service industry was the old barrel-shaped water tumbler that was machine pressed and built to resist breakage. Today, glassware is one of the most versatile products used in the food service industry. As one research scientist said, "If we run out of wood and building materials, we'll just dig up the earth, melt it, and turn it into glass." As we look around at the glass towers in our cities, glass houses in the country, fiberglass wires running under the ocean and across our plains, and our astronauts wearing fiberglass clothing, innovating with glass clearly doesn't have to wait until we run out of wood and building materials. The food service industry has its share of innovative glassware.

Main Types of Glassware

Two main types of glassware are used in the food service industry: (1) Lead crystal, a hand-blown, hand-shaped product; and (2) machine-made glassware, the backbone of the industry. A few fine hotel restaurants still use a certain amount of hand-blown crystal stemware, especially in serving wines and bar beverages. The use of the hand-shaped vases, fruit bowls, and other decorative pieces has declined almost to zero because of the high cost involved.

When you talk about Steuben glassware, Baccarat, Orrefors, Rosenthal, or Waterford, you are talking about museum pieces, kept in vaults to protect them from pilferage because of their value. So we have to rule out lead crystal and hand-shaped, hand-blown glassware from use in today's food service industry.

Machine-Made Glassware

The real boom in the use of glassware in the food service industry and, in fact, in everyday living, started about thirty years ago when a company in England developed machinery and techniques that allowed stemware to be made by machine. Costs dropped, shapes and sizes proliferated, and food service operators saw the possibility of food merchandising using the new shapes and sizes for serving specialty foods and bar drinks.

The Decorative Value of Glassware

Decorators are finding that glassware can be very useful in table settings and can be used to enhance the general decorative scheme of dining rooms and public spaces.

Accountants have developed techniques using certain sizes of glassware for cost control features. We all are familiar with glass cookware and ovenware, which is actually better than metal in certain instances, especially for pastry.

Glassware is noted for being sanitary, and we have already pointed out that china is made more sanitary by glazing (spraying on glass that is then baked on).

Glassware is reasonably inexpensive for the amount of use it gets, and because manufacturers have learned to temper glass, breakage is not as troublesome as it used to be.

Colored glassware can get rather expensive, especially the ruby-red kind, which gets its outstanding color from adding pure gold to the molten glass. Fortunately, the manufacturer averages the cost out, or you wouldn't see any ruby glassware on the market.

Types of Commercial Glassware

The great bulk of commercial glassware is machine-made, either drawn or pressed, and is made with fully tempered glass, partially tempered glass, or a mixture of lead crystal (generally about 24–25 percent of the total product). The better commercial glassware has been treated with a patented anealing process that gives the edge of the glassware some breakage resistance. The most popular of this type of product is the no-nick edge on the Libby Owens glassware.

Glassware can be decorated with hand cutting or machine cutting. It can be hand or machine painted. One process uses acid to etch the glass by use of decals and spraying.

A popular method of decorating glass is that of applying gold leaf over an etched decoration. As a merchandising idea for the sales department, this style goes fine with sterling silver flatware and gold-leaf-decorated bone china. Of course, the costs are tremendous. However, some people in the world will pay for such frills, and the purchasing agent should be able to explain this market to the sales department and to other staff who meet the public.

A few years back, there was a great rage to decorate glassware and then suddenly the practice fell off. Today, most glassware depends on its shape and size for its attractiveness. Some hotels and restaurants thought it was good advertising to put decals all over the glassware, but that is pretty much over. About the only glasses that are decorated are the water goblets in the higher-class dining rooms.

One of the most popular lines of glassware ever marketed is the "Georgian" line from Libby Owens Manufacturing Company. It is chip- and break-resistant and attractive in design. The cost is low because the plant is fully automated.

Exhibit 23-1 reprints a page from the Libbey Owens product catalogue, showing the many shapes and sizes available.

A Cheer for the Home Team

We hear much these days about how poorly made U.S. products are in comparison to Asian products and European products. But our glassware is not poorly made, nor are our china, textiles, and stainless steel products.

I have had the privilege of opening hotels all over the world. In some instances, because of monetary and exchange problems, it is not possible to buy American glassware in these countries. One must resort to other countries, where the barter system exists. In all the years we were in operation, never once did we find a glassware product from any country that

GEORGIAN STEMWARE

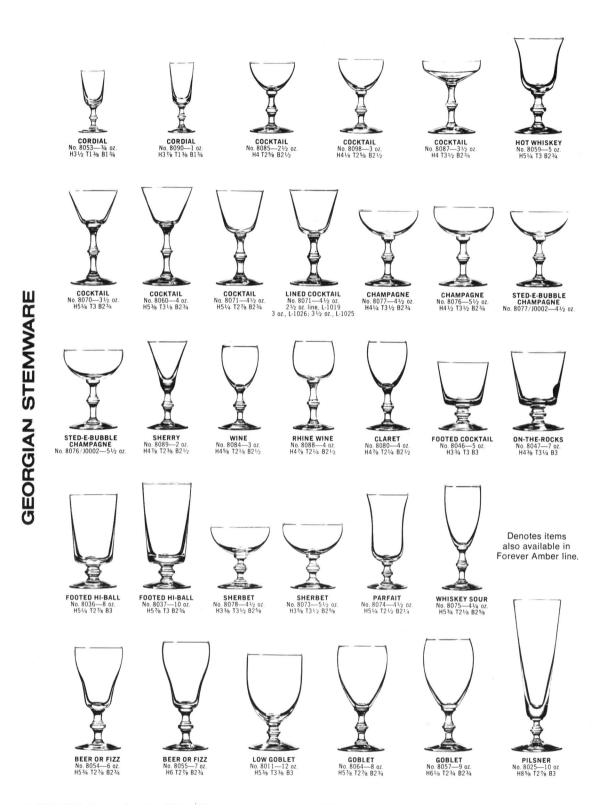

CORDIAL
No. 8053—¾ oz.
H3½ T1⅜ B1¾

CORDIAL
No. 8090—1 oz.
H3⅞ T1⅜ B1¾

COCKTAIL
No. 8085—2½ oz.
H4 T2⅝ B2½

COCKTAIL
No. 8098—3 oz.
H4⅛ T2⅝ B2½

COCKTAIL
No. 8087—3½ oz.
H4 T3½ B2¾

HOT WHISKEY
No. 8059—5 oz.
H5¼ T3 B2¾

COCKTAIL
No. 8070—3½ oz.
H5¼ T3 B2¾

COCKTAIL
No. 8060—4 oz.
H5⅜ T3⅛ B2¾

COCKTAIL
No. 8071—4½ oz.
H5¼ T2⅞ B2¾

LINED COCKTAIL
No. 8071—4½ oz.
2½ oz. line, L-1019
3 oz., L-1026; 3½ oz., L-1025

CHAMPAGNE
No. 8077—4½ oz.
H4¼ T3½ B2¾

CHAMPAGNE
No. 8076—5½ oz.
H4½ T3½ B2¾

STED-E-BUBBLE
CHAMPAGNE
No. 8077/J0002—4½ oz.

STED-E-BUBBLE
CHAMPAGNE
No. 8076/J0002—5½ oz.

SHERRY
No. 8089—2 oz.
H4⅞ T2⅜ B2½

WINE
No. 8084—3 oz.
H4⅝ T2⅛ B2½

RHINE WINE
No. 8088—4 oz.
H4⅞ T2¼ B2½

CLARET
No. 8080—4 oz.
H4⅞ T2¼ B2½

FOOTED COCKTAIL
No. 8046—5 oz.
H3¾ T3 B3

ON-THE-ROCKS
No. 8047—7 oz.
H4⅜ T3¼ B3

FOOTED HI-BALL
No. 8036—8 oz.
H5¼ T2⅞ B3

FOOTED HI-BALL
No. 8037—10 oz.
H5⅞ T3 B2¾

SHERBET
No. 8078—4½ oz.
H3⅜ T3½ B2⅝

SHERBET
No. 8073—5½ oz.
H3⅝ T3½ B2⅝

PARFAIT
No. 8074—4½ oz.
H5¼ T2½ B2¼

WHISKEY SOUR
No. 8075—4¼ oz.
H5¾ T2⅛ B2⅝

Denotes items
also available in
Forever Amber line.

BEER OR FIZZ
No. 8054—6 oz.
H5¾ T2⅞ B2¾

BEER OR FIZZ
No. 8055—7 oz.
H6 T2⅞ B2¾

LOW GOBLET
No. 8011—12 oz.
H5⅜ T3⅜ B3

GOBLET
No. 8064—8 oz.
H5⅞ T2⅞ B2¾

GOBLET
No. 8057—9 oz.
H6⅛ T2¾ B2¾

PILSNER
No. 8025—10 oz.
H8⅝ T2⅞ B3

Exhibit 23-1. A page from the Libbey Glass glassware catalogue (Courtesy: Libbey Glass, Toledo, Ohio)

could even approach the durability and attractiveness of American products. One time in the Middle East, where we were forced to use some European glassware, we bought an entire year's supply of glass because of the import restrictions. We had modern, American-built dishwashing machines with temperature and detergent controls. It was quite a shock when at the end of two weeks, we found ourselves running short of glassware because it literally fell apart in the dishwasher. (About the only products worse were the paper supplies available on the barter system, and two of the worst were tissue and toilet tissue.)

Glassware Against Plastic

Even though glassware has improved greatly in durability, it still breaks. Now that the appearance of plasticware has improved, some parts of the food service industry have adopted "glassware" made of plastics. These single-service products are in demand and are practical when food service is given away from an established base, in airline service, meeting room service for conventions, and in circumstances where sanitation is more important than appearance.

Some plasticware can be reused after machine washing, but plasticware does get scratched and cannot be used more than two or three times. Hotel supply houses comment that one of the most popular places where plastic beer mugs and glasses are used is around military bases, where some of the customers are inclined to drink a bit too much and may start throwing the plasticware around.

SILVERWARE—FLATWARE AND HOLLOWARE

This category in today's *Uniform System of Accounts* often lists the cost of many other items in addition to silverware, flatware, and holloware. Substitutes for these traditional eating utensils include stainless steel, plastics, pewter, cast aluminum, hammered aluminum, and even plastics used for banquet service.

Holloware

The holloware classification covers chafing dishes, platters, covers, candelabra, and all of the other service pieces that go with serving banquets plus tureens, platters, covers, coffee pots, and other pieces used in fine dining room service. When silver was selling for $.65 an ounce and artisans in the silver trade were being paid $10,000 to $12,000 a year, no self-respecting hotel or restaurant would have anything for banquet service pieces except silverplate, or in some cases, sterling. Now silver is selling for over $7.00 an ounce and few artisans have the skills for producing silver holloware. Consequently, costs are so high that few hotels and restaurants will spend the money necessary to equip their food service with silverplated holloware.

Twelve years ago, when the author set up the Sheraton Center Hotel in Toronto, the cost of silver, flatware, and holloware was budgeted at $485,000. It was a showplace, and the owners decided it was worthwhile to have silver service. Today, the same silverware would cost well over $3,000,000 and probably wouldn't be purchased.

Because of the extremely high cost of silver holloware (for example, $850 for a full-size, lightweight silverplated chafing dish), stainless steel has been substituted even in some of the best hotels and restaurants in the country. Other products used are aluminum, glass, and plastic. Aluminum, although widely used, has the drawback of becoming corroded in contact with a strong detergent; glass breaks too easily; and clear plastics, although at first quite attractive, quickly become cloudy and have to be replaced in a short time.

Flatware

Many of the better hotels and white-tablecloth restaurants use silverplated table flatware. With the recent decline in silver prices, the use of this product will probably increase, since it produces a very attractive service. Flatware today comes in three different weights: commercial, which is lightest and cheapest; heavyweight, which is considerably heavy, but still reasonably priced; and extra-heavyweight, which is the heaviest and most expensive. Certain pieces come in all three weights, and some pieces can be purchased with reinforced silver-plating on areas that tend to wear, such as the backs of spoons and forks. It doesn't make sense to buy anything but the lightest weight teaspoons and demitasse spoons, but it does pay to buy reinforced forks, serving spoons, soup spoons, and any other pieces that are subject to constant use.

The base metal used in making both flatware and holloware is a very important part of the quality of manufacture. The best base metal is known as nickel silver, which has replaced the once-standard German silver. When nickel silver became in short supply, silver manufacturers tried to silver-plate ordinary steel, but this turned out to be a disaster. The steel had to be copper-plated first, and copper was in shorter supply than silver. The silver manufacturers also tried stainless steel, but it took many years before the method of getting silver to adhere to stainless steel was discovered. By that time, stainless steel cost more than nickel silver, so the manufacturers went full circle and are now back to some of the original specifications.

Quality Considerations. The quality of silver flatware is based on the quality and weight of the blanks (forms before silverplating) and the amount of silver used in the electroplating process. The weight of the silverplate is measured by the ounces per gross of teaspoons, which varies from 2½ ounces per gross for lightweight com-mercial to 8 ounces for extra-heavyweight. Usually a gross of blanks for teaspoons will weigh 9 to 11 pounds.

Stainless Steel Flatware

A good pattern of American-made stainless steel is not an inexpensive item and is acceptable today for flatware in all but the higher-priced hotels and restaurants. The American product is heavy in weight, has good design, is polished and free of sharp edges, and can be detarnished with detergent to look almost new after washing.

Stainless steel holloware and flatware can be purchased with either an attractive polished surface or with a brushed finish that, over a long period of time, will probably stand up better than the bright finish. Stainless flatware and holloware is imported from all over the world, but the best comes from Germany, the United States, Switzerland, and Canada. Less desirable products come from the Far East and South America. Certain Japanese stainless steel is excellent, but the buyer must carefully check the reputation of the manufacturer and shipper. South American stainless steel, although inexpensive, has a slightly bluish color and has the reputation of pitting badly when used with certain detergents.

Quality Considerations. Inexpensive flatware is stamped out of lightweight sheets of stainless steel of gauges as thin as 22-gauge. Little polishing is done, and the edges sometimes will scratch surfaces and cut fingers and lips. Fork tines will bend, spoons will double, and the knives will not "cut butter." Quality stainless flatware is stamped from contoured sheets of stainless steel rolled to give extra weight at the stress points. Rough edges are ground and polished to present an attractive product. Good stainless is stamped from 10- and 12-gauge sheets of 18/8 or 17/7 chrome nickel alloys of stainless steel.

TEXTILES OR LINENS

At one time, the expensive category in the *Uniform System of Accounts* was rather clear—"linens" meant materials used in the rooms department and the food and beverage department made of cotton or linen. Today, with literally hundreds of materials being used for these purposes, it is best that we talk about textiles and their uses in the hospitality industry. New materials are being added every year. After a testing period, they are either accepted as an improvement and/or a savings in cost, or they are dropped and the search goes on for new and better materials.

Buy for the End Use

Textiles in the food service industry should be bought to serve a purpose—not because of history or habits, or the desires of the housekeeping department or the catering manager, and certainly not on salespeople's claims of superiority or unbeatable price.

There are four standards by which materials are purchased:
1. The materials have to be suitable for the use for which they are intended.
2. They have to be serviceable and durable.
3. Materials must be economical, giving due consideration to the suitability and long life.
4. The materials must be attractive when they are placed in use.

REVIEW OF CURRENT AVAILABLE TEXTILES FOR THE FOOD SERVICE INDUSTRY

Books have been written on textiles and their uses; however, there are probably only twenty-five to thirty materials and blends of materials that are in common use in the food service industry. Let's review these materials and look at some of their uses.

Categories of Materials

Today's textiles can be broken down into two categories: natural fibers, which consist of cotton, silk, linen, and wool; and synthetic or manufactured fibers, which run into the hundreds.

Cotton. Cotton materials are still very extensively used for room linen and for the food and beverage department table service. Cotton is blended with other materials and used for uniforms, toweling, and even some decorative materials. Cotton is inexpensive when blended with other materials such as polyester and rayon. It is comfortable in uniforms because it "breathes" and it absorbs moisture but keeps the uniform dry and cool. Cotton launders well, although unless it is blended with polyester, it has to be ironed if it is expected to produce a good appearance. Cotton has a tendency to be stronger when wet, which means that it holds up to much laundering. The main problem with cotton, other than ironing, is that it shrinks very badly.

Manufacturers of cotton materials have come up with a process called Sanforizing that will reduce the shrinkage in cotton to 1 percent or less. The processor will guarantee this shrinkage and the buyer should make sure that he buys only Sanforized products and that he receives a written guarantee.

"Preshrunk" cottons can be purchased and the manufacturer will state the percentage of shrinkage that the material is guaranteed against. For some uses, preshrunk materials with 2 to 3 percent shrinkage are considerably less in cost, and as long as the shrinkage is known, the buyer can plan on the amounts to purchase.

Silk Materials. At one time silk was used in the food service industry for exotic-appearing uniforms and some decorative materials. Silk was woven into heavy materials for certain uniforms, such as those of head waiters and captains, where a neat, classic uniform was required. But today silk is so expensive that it is rarely used in the industry.

Linen. Linen is made from the flax plant; although rather expensive, it still has many uses in the food service industry. Linen absorbs moisture well, is cool, makes very attractive waitress uniforms, is good for hand towels for rooms, is excellent for glass towels, and makes attractive tablecloths and napkins. It has the drawback of wrinkling very easily and must be ironed before it is used. When blended with other materials, however, linen is easier to iron and also less expensive.

Wool. Wool has some uses in the food service industry, such as for winter uniforms, door attendant's uniforms, uniforms for waiters in elegant restaurants, luxury suite carpets, and luxury hotel blankets. Wool is very expensive, shrinks badly, is ruined in hot water, and has the bad habit of "pilling" around areas that show wear. Wool materials, however, are very warm, comfortable, and resilient. In carpets and blankets, they are long wearing, easy to dye, and easy to process.

Manufactured Fibers—General Use in the Food Service Industry

A review of manufactured fibers in general use in the food service industry, with a listing of the good and bad points, should be valuable to the buyer.

Rayon. Rayon was the first synthetic material made and offered to the public. This material, in blends with cotton and wool, has been available for over fifty years. When introduced, rayon was considerably less expensive than any of the natural materials. It had good absorption and comfort qualities. However, it wrinkled very badly and had to be ironed. It was highly flammable and when it was first used in draperies, some very serious fires resulted, ending its use for this purpose. Today, however, rayon, blended with other materials and flameproofed, is used not only for draperies but also for chair coverings and low-priced carpeting.

Nylon. The next synthetic fiber to meet with acceptance was nylon. It is strong, soft, and in many ways resembles silk. It makes good carpets, especially when blended with wool. It is fairly inexpensive and lends itself very easily to manufacturing. Nylon will burn, however. It will smolder rather than flame. It has a high incidence of static buildup, and it has low moisture absorption. For these reasons, pure nylon materials do not make good uniforms or undergarments.

Acetates. The acetates resemble silk in many ways and are used for draperies after being fireproofed. The main problem with these materials is that they fade in ordinary atmospheric conditions. In most cases, they have been superceded by other synthetics.

Acrylic. Acrylic materials are very light in weight and are very warm. This material has been used as a substitute for wool for blankets and has practically eliminated the use of pure wool blankets in the hotel industry. Acrylic has one serious drawback: it is very flammable.

Mono-Crylic. Because of the fire hazard of acrylics, the synthetic manufacturers brought out mono-crylic, which has all of the good points of acrylic but is nonflammable and thus more acceptable for blankets.

Saran. Saran fibers are very stain- and moisture-resistant. This material is used in carpeting for problem areas and is also used in blends with other materials to resist staining from food spills. It is rather stiff, which limits its possible uses.

Olefin. This material is lightweight, warm, and flexible; it won't wrinkle or pile up at wear points; it has low static buildup;

and it is wear-resistant. It is used basically in indoor-outdoor carpeting and in many upholstery materials.

Antron. Antron is a synthetic that was recently developed primarily for carpeting. It is very strong, resists stains, is fire-resistant, and can be blended well with other materials for carpeting such as polyester, olefin, and wool. Refinements of this product have been marketed as Antron II, III, and IV, but the materials are basically the same.

Polyester. This synthetic material has been around for fifteen years and is probably used more than any other synthetic for blending with other materials. Polyester itself is not a particularly attractive material but blended with other materials, it has the property of making the blend wrinkle-resistant. This is why a great majority of table linens today are a blend of cotton and polyester; no-iron bed linens are either a 50-50 blend of polyester and cotton or a blend of 65 percent polyester and 35 percent cotton. Polyester can also be blended with antron to make inexpensive but very serviceable carpets.

One of the most widely used materials for tablecloths and napkins is a 50 percent blend of dacron polyester and 50 percent cotton treated with resins to resist stain absorption and greatly reduce ironing for regular dining room use. (However, napkins and tablecloths look better when touched up with the mangle or an iron.) These materials take dye well and do not fade when laundered, thus reducing the problem of different shades of tablecloths within a room.

Polyester-cotton blends lend themselves very well to the permapress process that eliminates the need for ironing, which is especially good for washable uniforms. Over 90 percent of uniforms and costumes offered in food service catalogues are made from polyester-cotton blends.

Basic Weaves

In purchasing materials, the buyer will need to be acquainted with certain terms that the textile industry uses. Two words commonly used are the *warp* and *weft* of the material. The warp are the threads that run the length of the material in the weaving process. The weft are the crossthreads that are used to complete the weave. The weft is also sometimes called the "filling."

Plain or Basket Weave. The most common weave in the textile industry is the plain or basket weave. It is an over-and-under weave with each thread of both the weft and warp perpendicular to each other. It is used for sheets, pillow cases, toweling, and table linens as well as a number of uniform materials.

True Bias Material. A true bias material is woven with the warp in its natural position and the filling woven in at a 45-degree angle. A bias material has very little yarn slippage; it has smaller shrinkage and is a longer-life material. Uniforms made from this weave fit well, look well, and are long wearing. Bias materials are generally woven with a selvage edge that prevents raveling when the material is cut.

Twill-Weave. A twill-weave is a bias material that is very attractive and very strong. It is frequently used in uniforms.

Satin Weave. A satin weave is a regular basket weave with a floating thread that gives a shiny attractive appearance to the material. This weave has the tendency to have bad thread slippage; it is a short-life material and is used primarily for a certain quality of sheets and uniforms.

Pile Weave. Pile weave materials are made with a regular basket weave plus extra threads that stick out perpendicular to the surface of the regular material. This produces a velvet material that is useful for carpeting, clothes, and terrycloth toweling.

Specifications for Purchasing

It has been noted many times in this text that there is a specification for almost every product for sale in the United States. This is certainly true for textiles. In setting up specifications on any particular material, the following points should be considered and included in the list.

1. The breaking strength of the material should be considered. There is a standard test for breaking strength and this measurement should be specified.

2. Resistance to yarn slippage should be listed in the specifications. Satin-weave materials are very prone to yarn slippage and wear.

3. Color fastness is another item that should be spelled out in the specifications. Some materials, because of their makeup, do not take or hold dyes well.

4. Maximum shrinkage should be spelled out; this information should be available from the manufacturer. Certainly no material, regardless of how unusual, should have more than 6 percent maximum shrinkage.

5. The manufacturer's grading on resistance to abrasion should be in the specifications.

6. The specifications should list whether the material is wash-and-wear, wash-and-iron, dry-clean only, or washable in hot water or cold water, and the type of detergent to use.

7. The specifications should state if the material is water repellent or if it soaks up moisture quickly, making it unsuitable for certain purposes.

8. The specifications should state whether a material has high resistance, medium resistance, or low resistance to soil staining.

9. The specifications should answer the following questions concerning flammability: Is the material flameproof? What degree of flameproofing has the material been subjected to? Does it have natural resistance to fire? How does it have to be treated when cleaned or laundered?

10. Specifications should call for thread counts, type of weaves, treatment of finish, material and blends of material, or any other information that is necessary to prevent any misunderstanding as to the properties of the material.

BASIC COMPLEMENTS FOR BIG FOUR ITEMS

It is not an easy job for a purchasing agent, or any other person in the food service business, to sit down and make out an order for big four items based on what is really needed, the losses from the year, and the par stocks necessary to meet normal operations of a hotel or restaurant.

In Appendix III of this text, there is a complete list of big four items needed, based on a five-year study in Statler, Hilton, and Sheraton hotels. This information has been found very helpful and accurate.

HOW TO USE THE BASIC COMPLEMENT RECORD

One question facing a purchasing agent who is opening a new hotel or restaurant is how much to buy of the big four products for the different food services that are being offered, including coffee shops, food operations, room service, banquet service, and bar service. In many instances, when the operation opens, very necessary items are missing, which puts a crimp in the entire operating style of the hotel.

And how much will be lost during the first year of operation? Often replacements must be anticipated and ordered with the opening order. Down the pike, alert management will look at the replacement figures and ask whether breakage and replacement figures are anywhere near normal. It doesn't take a wizard to determine that a loss of 10,000 dozen teaspoons in the first year of operation of a 500-room resort hotel is out of line—but just how low can the loss be kept? This same question is asked in every hotel and restaurant operation. It is good to have a reference that can be checked, to compare your figures with some known operating figures from a well-managed company.

These problems are specifically answered by the basic complement schedule for big four items. All you need to know is the size of the various restaurants, the number of rooms in a hotel, and the seating capacity of the function rooms, and the basic complement will show you what items you need, what sizes you need, the amount to buy for the opening of the property, and how much you can expect to lose through breakage and slippage during the first year of operation. The basic complement will also indicate the par stocks necessary for such items as linens for rooms and banquet service as well as dining room service for a normal operation.

We advise accountants, management, and a purchasing agent to learn how to use this basic complement information. To our knowledge, it's the only reference for this type of information that has been collected and put into one source.

24 Cleaning and Operating Supplies

Purpose: To identify the various cleaning and operating supplies used in food and beverage operations and to gain an understanding of the factors involved in the selection and procurement of these products.

The problem presented by this category is that it consists of many items, none of which constitutes a significant portion of the operating statement; but collectively, they account for a considerable expense. It is sometimes difficult for an operator to justify the time necessary to plan and implement an effective purchasing program based upon each individual item, but—considering the total expense—it is worth the effort.

Fifty Thousand to One He Can Supply Your Needs

The Edward Don Company of Chicago, Miami, and Philadelphia, at present one of the leading food service and hotel supply companies in the country, introduces his excellent catalogue with the statement that he sells over fifty thousand items for the hotel and food service operator. He believes that he has in stock almost any item needed; if not in stock, he knows where to obtain it. A national distributor for accounting forms and related paper items claims that it stocks twenty-five thousand items and has been able to fill 90 percent of all orders from stock over the past five years. The Sheraton Supply Company catalogue lists some thirty-five thousand supply items, and Innkeepers' Supply lists over thirty thousand items on their computer price lists.

When we look at numbers such as these, it is obvious that a textbook cannot deal with all of these items on an individual basis. From a practical viewpoint, we have divided these operating-expense items into two categories:

Cleaning Supplies and Equipment
Other Operating Supplies

CLEANING SUPPLIES AND EQUIPMENT

Because cleaning supplies involve a lower number of items and represent the largest single cost factor in the total operating supplies, we will look into this expense category in some detail. As the largest cost factor, cleaning supplies offer the best opportunity for economies but are often ignored while the more obvious costs of food, beverage, payroll, and energy receive all the attention.

What Should Your Cleaning Supply Cost Be?

Present-day accounting systems, whether operated by hand or computer, can readily tell you what your cleaning supply costs are and can give you the breakdown of pounds, gallons, and other measurements of supplies used. To date, no one has had the opportunity or the desire to determine exactly what cleaning costs *should be* for a specific volume of business or type of operation in the hospitality field.

Our *Uniform System of Accounts* and national accounting firms regularly publish what these costs are running on an annual basis for different sizes and location of operation. As operators, at present, the best we can do is compare costs with national averages.

Overall, cleaning supplies for the rooms department of a hotel should not exceed six-tenths of 1 percent of the room revenue if these costs are to be considered in line with industry averages. When we look at the food and beverage departments, we find that cleaning supply costs usually vary between 1.5 to 2 percent of the total food and beverage volume. The leading cleaning supply companies and manufacturers say this figure is higher than necessary and if costs run over 1 percent of total food and beverage sales, a review should be made of operating methods and use of detergents. The detergent supplier should be asked for help in determining how to bring costs into line.

Selecting a Supplier

The first and most important step in the control of cleaning supply costs is the selection of a supplier for these items and the service and training programs that necessarily accompany the products. The chief executive officer of the largest cleaning supply and service company in the country insists that there are no secrets as to the makeup of the various detergents available and that prices are reasonably competitive. It is the service and training programs that determine the final costs. The value of the different programs offered should be the deciding factor in selecting a cleaning supply dealer.

In selecting a supplier, the purchasing agent should investigate the various products recommended for dishwashing, floor cleaning, detarnishing silverware, toilet sanitation, scrubbing pots and pans, and other kitchen chores. Prices will depend a great deal on the volume of business and the service program offered by the company. The larger, better-known companies may have their own service staff and pay their salespeople on a commission-plus-salary basis. Some suppliers hire service companies to maintain the equipment. These varied methods of operation must be analyzed and compared by the purchasing agent or operator with the responsibility for selecting a supplier. If a service company is hired, close attention must be given to the activities of the outside supervision to insure economical operation of the equipment.

There are many reputable detergent companies of national scope throughout the United States. Each locality seems to have a local company that has a good reputation, renders good service, is active in the Chamber of Commerce, and contributes to the community. These factors must be considered by the purchasing agent and food service manager.

A Service Program to Benefit the Buyer. In negotiating a service program with the supplier, the buyer should first give the salesperson an opportunity to outline the service program and tell why it is the best available. The service programs offered by the various companies under consideration should be reviewed, and the one most suited to the conditions selected.

Such a program should start with at least a monthly checkup and then be adjusted as needed. During this monthly physical check of the operations, there are a number of services that the sales representative should perform for the operator. The salesperson should make sure that all of the dispensing equipment is working properly. If minor repairs are needed, these should be made by the supplier.

Most cleaning supply companies are quite proud of their training program for dish-room operators. The company generally posts instructions both in Spanish and English showing illustrations of how the equipment should be operated and how the dish area should be cleaned after each warewashing shift. Most companies offer to do minor repairs on the dishwashing equipment. However, the operator is expected to pay for any additional major parts. If major repairs are needed, the supplier is not expected to do more than to call this fact to the attention of the operator.

Service Reports. Each detergent supply company submits a service report after the monthly service check. It is a good idea for the food and beverage manager, or in some cases, top management, to sit down with the supply representative and review the service report. Necessary work can be outlined at this meeting, and management has an opportunity to check the consumption of various cleaning supplies and compare it to the organization's standards.

Each salesperson normally has a card on which he records the shipment of the various cleaning materials made each month to the operation. If the operation maintains a par stock of these supplies, it is easy to measure the consumption of the various cleaning materials. By checking the number of covers served with the amounts used, it is possible to locate areas in the operation that need attention.

Research and Development. It is wise to select a supplier with a good research and development program. Economics Laboratory is probably the leader in this field and spends approximately $15,000,000 on research and development each year. Other suppliers have similar programs.

Some of the new products that have been introduced in the past few years have been rinse-dry products and dispensers, a new solid-block detergent that, when put in the dispenser, can be ignored until it is gone, and various detergents that will meet almost any water condition. The most recent development is a low-temperature dishwashing machine. This development, a cooperative effort with the machine manufacturers, can result in energy savings of up to 35 percent in the day-to-day operation of dishwashing machines. A more detailed discussion of low-temperature dishwashing machines is given in a later part of this chapter.

A Supplier With a Complete Line of Products. A complete product line also includes the necessary cleaning materials for laundry, the rooms department, and the engineering department, as well as for the food and beverage department. One of the leading detergent companies offers in their supply catalogue twenty-one different types of warewashing detergents for machines, automatic dispensers, hand washing, and pot washing, or other specific uses. They also offer two tableware presoak detergents, five rinse-dry additives, five floor-care products, four germicidal detergents, seventeen laundry products, and twelve specialty products from those that will clear the lime out of dish machines to aerosol sprays that will clear the air of odors.

Complete Line of Dispensers. Normally, a detergent supplier will furnish, at cost, the necessary dispensing equipment to regulate use of the product prescribed for the operation. In some cases, with very large users, this equipment is furnished free. However, it remains the property of the detergent supplier. This equipment will include the usual soap dispenser for the dishwashing machines, the equipment necessary for rinse-dry mixture, grease filters for hoods, central dispensers of dishwashing detergents and laundry detergents, and portable equipment for sanitizing outside areas. The most successful portable equipment is the combination detergent-sanitizer dispenser used on back docks and dumpster equipment. These areas are always dirty, covered with flies and other vermin. The Mikro-spray put out by Economics Lab can, if used daily, keep the area sanitary and odor-free.

A good supplier will maintain this equipment, help train the staff in the use of it, and notify management if it is being improperly used.

An Adequate Training Program. Management, in deciding which supplier to select, should spend considerable time learning the details of the training program offered by the potential supplier. If the company under consideration does not have a training program, it should be eliminated from further consideration. Some suggestions for a training program are offered in the following paragraphs.

Suggested Training Program

1. Whatever training program is agreed upon between the buyer and the seller, it should be written out in sufficient detail so that there will be no misunderstanding on either side.

2. The training program should be run in connection with the monthly inspection service offered by the supplier. During these visits, the sales representative should time his visits to observe the warewashing operations in action and spot problems or shortcomings that can be called to the attention of the steward or the food and beverage manager. In most cases, instructions can be given at that point to correct obvious problems. If a more complete instruction class is needed, the details can be worked out by the sales representative and the food and beverage manager.

3. Illustrated-action instructions and bilingual explanations should be posted near the warewashing areas so that the staff can refresh their understanding of the instructions. A good training program should include sound-slide films outlining in simple terms and with simple instructions the warewashing procedures normally followed in good operations.

4. The larger companies have a series of well-orchestrated sound-color movies that they will be glad to show to a group of employees or supervisors. Usually these movies show four or five different phases of warewashing operations with attention given to cost analysis, storage, and purchasing reminders as well as active warewashing instructions.

5. Giveaways—manufacturers and supply companies are constantly putting together catalogues, brochures, reports on conventions, and articles by well-known operators pertaining to warewashing procedures, costs, and products. The supplier who is selected for the trial should be expected to produce some of these so-called "giveaways" from time to time so that the supervisors of the hotel or restaurant will be aware of new developments in the field.

6. Participation—some dedicated sales representatives have actually worked as warewashers for several hours with a crew. Under such circumstances, the crew learned more quickly and performed better.

Emergencies. In selecting a supplier, the buyer should have a clear understanding as to what services the supplier will furnish in case of emergencies. Invariably, warewashing emergencies seem to fall on a holiday or weekend or late during the dinner hour. The cause of the emergency can be generally attributed to the operator's neglect, but that doesn't get the dishwashing machine back in operation and the dishes washed and put away.

When a new hotel opens, it is a rare occasion when the dishwashing machine or other warewashing facility doesn't become clogged or break down, adding to the confusion during the opening banquet and reception. The better suppliers have emergency phone numbers and will furnish, either free or at a low cost, mechanics or personnel that will respond to the emergency and make whatever necessary repairs or adjustments are needed to get the operation back on line. If the operation is in the United States, service and repairs can be obtained on a reasonably short notice. But if it is located in Istanbul or Cairo, Buenos Aires, Tel Aviv, or Hong Kong, the hotel operator will be very thankful if the buyer has made the proper arrangements for service or standby service at these opening functions.

The Real Cost of Washing Dishes

A warewashing cost analysis completed during the first part of 1981 showed the cost of washing dishes can be broken down into five basic categories: (1) labor, (2) hot water and steam, (3) detergent and cleaning supplies, (4) breakage, and (5) miscellaneous operating costs. This cost analysis also showed that the overall cost of warewashing in a modern, well-managed operation averages approximately one cent per piece washed. In making this test, a single glass and dish was considered a "piece to be washed," whereas it took ten pieces of flatware to be considered "one piece."

In breaking this cost down further, it was found that of the one cent per dish washed, 48 percent was for labor, 19 percent for replacement cost, 19 percent for indirect operating costs, 8 percent for steam and hot water, and only 6 percent for detergents and cleaning supplies necessary for the

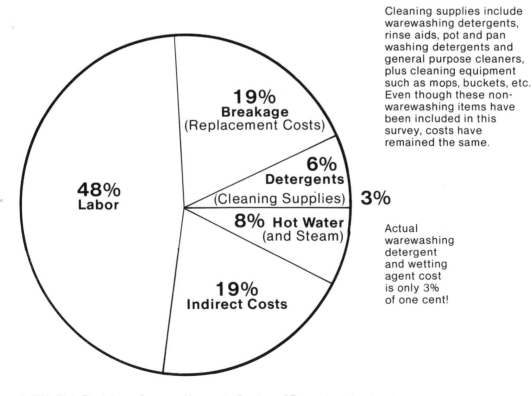

Cleaning supplies include warewashing detergents, rinse aids, pot and pan washing detergents and general purpose cleaners, plus cleaning equipment such as mops, buckets, etc. Even though these non-warewashing items have been included in this survey, costs have remained the same.

Actual warewashing detergent and wetting agent cost is only 3% of one cent!

Exhibit 24-1. Breakdown of warewashing costs (Courtesy of Economics Laboratory, Inc.)

warewashing operation. It was also found that about half of that total cost for detergents and cleaning supplies was for the detergents used in the warewashing process and the balance was for the cleaning of the kitchen floor, walls, and so on.

These breakdowns are shown in the previous chart (see Exhibit 24-1). This chart illustrates the fact that the cost of detergents is so small in the warewashing process that it would be "penny wise and pound foolish" to try to save a few cents on the price of detergents when a more sophisticated formula is needed to obtain the correct results. A professional food buyer will keep these thoughts in mind when researching the type of detergent to be used in warewashing equipment.

Are You Paying Full-Time Wages for Part-Time Help?

From the foregoing chart, it is obvious that labor is the largest single cost of warewashing. But the solution to controlling labor costs does not lie in fighting wage rates. The good food service operator controls labor costs through the full utilization of the employee while on duty and by reducing labor turnover. To control warewashing labor costs, you must schedule your staff to work only when needed. In some operations, an entire warewashing crew is brought in at 7 A.M. and changed at 3 P.M. There is little work for warewashers between 7 and 9 A.M. Between 9 and 10:30 A.M., the crew can be busy after which they take a break until 1 P.M. The situation is the same for the evening shift. This results in abnormally high labor costs for warewashing. A good operator will schedule a warewasher to come in early in the morning and stack the dishes. One or two assistants will arrive later who will clean up the breakfast dishes as well as the pots and pans. They will then help ready the dining room for lunch.

When work is distributed as described above, the warewasher is no longer "just" a warewasher but falls under a higher-rated category known as a utility person, which meets union requirements and labor board standards for a small additional increase in the hourly rate. A rate for a utility person can be established that then permits this employee to move around the kitchen in all the places where allied work is involved. Unions also encourage employees to prepare themselves to take over higher-rated jobs such as cook's helpers, pantry employees, assistant stewards, banquet waiters, and housepeople, jobs that are a step up the ladder to more professionalism and higher pay.

New Boy on the Street

In 1974, in response to the fuel shortage, a research program cosponsored by the Warewashing Equipment Manufacturers and the detergent manufacturers sought to produce warewashing equipment that could operate at low temperatures. Today there are low-temperature warewashing machines on the market that have proven to be satisfactory. Actual tests have shown they can pay for the cost of installation through energy savings in about a year's time. Savings in energy for hot water have amounted to 40 percent over high-temperature standard warewashing equipment.

It would appear that this type of equipment was the answer to all of our warewashing problems. However, we are currently in the midst of the trial period. There are a number of problems still to be solved involving hardness of water, foaming action, and the sanitizing agent used to kill bacteria at lower temperatures. It is possible to convert regular dishwashing machines to low-temperature machines, but there are drawbacks. Low-temperature machines use typical codine-based or chlorine-based sanitizing agents in the wash and power rinse cycles of operations, but use rather sophisticated and strong agents in the final rinse cycle. These final rinse agents can attack pumps and other internal parts of converted high-temperature machines. The cost of installing new pumps and other equipment must be considered when deciding to convert a high-temperature machine. Most warewashing machine manufacturers and detergent suppliers agree, however, that low-temperature machinery is the wave of the future.

A nationally known food service operator has recently completed replacing all thirty-eight of his high-temperature warewashing machines (including pot washers) with low-temperature equipment, and actual energy savings costs will enable the company to pay for all conversion costs in less than two years. In a small luncheon club serving about 125 covers per day on a five-day-a-week basis, the entire cost of installing a new "box-type" Hobart AM-9 low-temperature dishwasher was paid for in energy savings in just fifteen months.

Low-temperature machines work on the basis that regular hot water temperatures normally found in a hotel or restaurant are sufficiently high to safely wash dishes. This requires a detergent that is known as a highly refined polyphosphate. The first wash cycle of this equipment is done at a temperature of 140°F. However, the power rinse is also done at 140°F without additional energy to raise it to the 160°F of the high-temperature method. The real savings comes in the final rinse, done without the use of a power booster, with the equipment using just the water from the regular hot water line. A highly specialized low-temperature sanitizer is pumped into the final rinse line so as to eliminate any bacteria that still might be on the dishes as they pass through the final rinse.

At present, there is an ample oil supply on the market, and the switch to low-temperature machines has slowed down. However, if the price of oil increases again, there will be pressure put on manufacturers to perfect this equipment and convert old equipment to the low-temperature warewashing procedure. Any food service operator considering new warewashing equipment or any purchasing agent looking at the renovation of a kitchen and the modernization of the warewashing equipment should investigate the low-temperature warewashing equipment to see if it is adaptable to his situation without some of the adverse side effects that occur in various parts of the country because of local water conditions.

Some energy cost savings have been quoted amounting to over $1,000 per month for large equipment and high-volume operations. This may appear too good to be true, but when the figures come from one of the most respected and successful food service operators in the country, it behooves all food service operators and purchasing agents as well as management to check this equipment out thoroughly before making a final decision on any warewashing equipment purchase.

How Did the New Kid Make Out?

Back in the early 1980's there was a question of whether the trade would accept "low-temp" warewashing, so we decided to find out how the "New Kid" was doing in the 1990's.

We went to the management of one of the largest U.S. food operations (a class hotel chain), and when we asked the managers about their experience with low-temp washing, the reply was "we didn't know that any other type of machine was made."

Exhibit 24-2 shows one of the most successful warewashers of this type today.

Some Thoughts on Buying Detergents and Cleaning Supplies

Detergents and cleaning supplies are purchased for the cleaning and sanitation of all food service equipment. The buyer should realize that price means nothing if the product does not do the job intended.

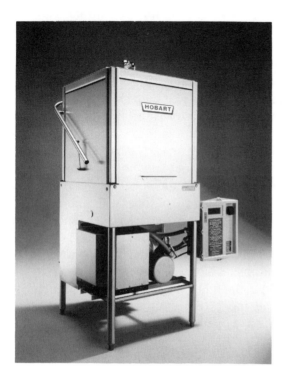 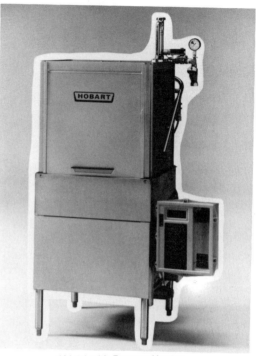

AM-14 with Booster Heater

OUTSTANDING STANDARD FEATURES

- Energy Efficient — High production and readily convertible to:
  Hot Water Santizing — 150°F Wash Temperature minimum, 180°F Final Rinse, 53 racks per hour.
  Chemical Sanitizing — Normal Duty — 120°F Minimum Wash and Final Rinse Temperature (140°F Recommended), Injection of Sodium Hypochlorite required, 62 racks per hour.
  Chemical Sanitizing — Light Duty — 130°F Minimum Wash and 120°F Minimum Final Rinse Temperature (140°F Recommended), Injection of Sodium Hypochlorite required, 80 racks per hour.
- Low water consumption (1.2 gallons/rack).
- Rinse system with exclusive Sani Dwell Cycle (Hot Water Sanitizing only).
- Microcomputer controls.
- LED Display of Cycles (Fill, Wash, Rinse) and Temperature.
- Built-in service aids for enhanced serviceability.
- Choice of Electric Heat, Gas or Steam Injectors.
- Microcomputer control of water temperature and positive protection against tank heat damage.
- All stainless steel revolving upper and lower interchangeable wash arms.
- All stainless steel revolving upper and lower rinse arms.
- Microcomputer protection.
- Door actuated drain closer.
- Exclusive all stainless steel interior.
- Self-flushing stainless steel strainer pans.
- Large, removable scrap basket.
- Snap-in stainless steel front panel (on AM-14).
- Field adjustable control box height 4⅝" to 12⅝".
- Inspection Door (on AM-14).
- Manual By-Pass Controls.

All of these standard features make this Hobart AM Dishwasher an outstanding value for exceptional dishwashing performance, with built-in Hobart reliability.

Exhibit 24-2. Low-temperature washers (Courtesy: Hobart Food Equipment, Troy, Ohio)

SPECIFICATIONS listed by Underwriters Laboratories Inc. and by National Sanitation Foundation. Meets Requirements of A.S.S.E. Standard No. 1004.

The microcomputer-based control system is built into the AM-14 Series Dishwashers. Model AM-14 is for straight-through operation with a third (front) door for inspection, and AM-14C for corner installations. Each is available in standard electrical specifications of 100-120/60/1, 200-230/60/1, 200-230/60/3, 400-460/60/3 and all are equipped with a reduced voltage pilot circuit transformer.

*CAUTION: CERTAIN MATERIALS, INCLUDING SILVER, ALUMINUM, AND PEWTER ARE ATTACKED BY SODIUM HYPOCHLORITE (LIQUID BLEACH) IN THE CHEMICAL SANITIZING DISHWASHER MODE OF OPERATION. WATER HARDNESS MUST BE CONTROLLED TO 2-6 GR. FOR BEST RESULTS.

CONSTRUCTION: Tank and wash chamber constructed of #16 gauge stainless steel, arc-welded. Unitized welded stainless steel tank, frame and stainless steel feet. Wash chamber and front of tank above motor compartment are polished, satin finish. New stainless steel snap-in front panel—no fasteners required.

DOOR LIFT: Doors coupled by chrome-plated door handle, spring counter-balanced (except the front inspection door). All doors guided for ease of operation and long life.

PUMP: With Ni-Resist impeller, integral with motor assures alignment and quiet operation. Pump shaft seal with stainless steel parts and a carbon ceramic sealing interface. Easily removable impeller housing permits ease of inspection. Capacity 160 GPM. Pump is completely self-draining.

MOTOR: Hobart-built, 1 HP, with solid state thermal protection, grease-packed ball bearings, splashproof design, ventilated. Single-phase is capacitor-start, induction-run type. Three-phase is squirrel-cage, induction type.

MICROCOMPUTER CONTROL SYSTEM: Hobart microcomputer controls, assembled within water-protected enclosure, provide built-in performance and reliability.

The microcomputer control, switches and contactors are housed in a single enclosure, mounted on right-hand side of dishwasher below table level. Control enclosure is field adjustable to an alternate lower position to clear standard 12" deep table trough or table sink installation. The line voltage electrical components are completely wired with 105°C, 600V thermoplastic insulated wire with stranded conductors and routed through electrical metallic tubing or liquid-tight flexible conduit. Low-voltage electrical components are wired with type ST cord. Line disconnect switch NOT furnished.

CYCLE OPERATION: The microcomputer timing program is started by closing the doors, which actuates the door cycle switch. The microcomputer energizes the wash pump motor contactor during the wash portion of the program. After the wash, a dwell permits the upper wash manifold to drain. At the end of the dwell, the final rinse solenoid valve is energized, after the final rinse valve closes, Sani-Dwell (Hot Water Mode only) permits sanitization to continue. The Rinse LED remains on during this period, completing the program. If the microcomputer is interrupted during a cycle by the door-cycle switch, the microcomputer is reset to the beginning of the program. **Hot Water Sanitizing — 62 seconds (53 Racks/hr.):** 40 Second Wash, 4 Second Dwell, 9 Second Rinse, 9 Second Sani-Dwell. **Chemical Sanitizing (Normal Duty) — 53 Seconds (62 Racks/hr.):** 40 Second Wash, 4 Second Dwell, 9 Second Rinse. **Chemical Sanitizing (Light Duty) — 40 Seconds (80 Racks/hr.):** 27 Second Wash, 4 Second Dwell, 9 Second Rinse (130°F Minimum). All of the above programs and many more can be pre-selected by your Hobart service technician.

WASH: Hobart revolving stainless steel wash arms with unrestricted openings above and below provide thorough distribution of water jets to all dishware surfaces. Arms are easily removable for cleaning and are interchangeable. Stainless steel tubing manifold connects upper and lower spray system.

RINSE: Eleven overhead rotating rinse spray nozzles with two nozzles mounted to spray and sanitize the interior of the chamber. The stainless steel upper and lower rinse arms are easily removable without tools and feature curved ends for greater uniformity of rinse coverage. Lower revolving rinse arm with nine nozzles lifts out for inspection. Diaphragm-type rinse control solenoid valve mounted outside machine. Machine is equipped with special hot water vacuum breaker on downstream side of rinse valve—mounted 6" above uppermost rinse opening. Easy open brass line strainer furnished.

FILL: Microcomputer controlled fill valve installed on upstream side of rinse vacuum breaker. Ratio fill method is used giving the correct fill at any flowing water pressure. (20 PSIG necessary for proper rinsing.)

DRAIN AND OVERFLOW: Large bell type automatic overflow and drain valve controlled from inside of machine. Drain automatically closed by lowering doors. Drain seal is large diameter, high temperature "O" ring. Cover for overflow is integral part of stainless steel strainer system.

STRAINER SYSTEM: Equipped with large, exclusive self-flushing, easily removable perforated stainless steel strainer and large capacity soil basket. Submerged soil basket minimizes frequent removal and cleaning.

HEATING EQUIPMENT: Standard tank heat is 5KW electric immersion heating element. Energy-saving burner with gas regulator and automatic solid state pilot igniter (no constant burning pilot light). Optional at extra cost. Gas Heated Dishwasher: For natural gas, gas pressure (customer connection) not to exceed 7" W.C. For liquefied petroleum, gas pressure to burner (customer connection) not to exceed 11" W.C. If gas pressure is higher than 7" W.C. or 11" W.C. a pressure regulating valve must be supplied (by others) in the gas line to the dishwasher. Regulated ¾" steam injector optional at extra cost. Water temperature regulation is controlled by a thermistor sensor in combination with microcomputer controls. The tank heat and positive low water protection microcomputer circuits are automatically activated when the main power switch is turned "ON". If tank is accidently drained, low water protection device automatically turns heater off. These features are standard with the Hobart microcomputer control system.

STANDARD EQUIPMENT: In addition to the standard features listed on the front are the following—latest design door cycle switch, ratio fill, stainless steel adjustable feet. Adjustable height control panel. Chamber, tank and all doors of 16 gauge stainless steel. Detergent injector and sensing connections provided as well as connection in fill line for rinse agent and sanitizer dispensing. Manual by-pass switch. Two Peg and two Combination 19¾" × 19¾" Hobart heavy duty all-plastic racks.

OPTIONAL EQUIPMENT AT EXTRA COST—ELECTRIC BOOSTER HEATER: Electric booster adequately sized to raise 120°F inlet water to 180°F. Pressure/temperature relief valve and pressure gauge for incoming water.

ACCESSORIES: Desirable functional accessories can be furnished at added cost. See listed options and accessories on this specification sheet. Write to the factory for special requirements not listed above.

As continued product improvements is a Hobart policy, specifications may be changed without notice.

HOBART
CORPORATION
EXECUTIVE OFFICES
TROY, OHIO 45374

Exhibit 24-2. *(continued)*

Because of the complications in the formulas needed to overcome all of the problems in warewashing, it is rare that a low-priced detergent is adequate for the job.

One of the leading detergent manufacturers and service companies lists fifty-eight different products that are intended for use in a food service operation. This does not include cleaning supplies for rooms and public spaces. One can quickly see the problem facing a purchasing agent responsible for obtaining the proper cleaning detergents.

Almost any detergent or cleaning supply purchased from a reputable supplier will do a fair job, especially on china or hard plastic tableware. Such a situation can continue for a while, but one day a health inspector will come along and give the operator ten days to correct his warewashing operation or face a shutdown. At this point, the operator or food and beverage manager quickly becomes an expert on sanitation through a crammed course on supplies and cleaning procedures.

The operator will learn quickly that he is looking for three things in a detergent. These are:

1. The ability to counteract minerals in the washing water.
2. Defoaming action where excess sudsing is a problem.
3. Chlorinating action where a chlorine-type detergent is used.

Counteracting Minerals. No one uses distilled water in the warewashing procedure. Consequently, the water used contains minerals and ranges from "soft" water to extremely "hard" water, causing problems in proportion to the degree of hardness. This is one of the reasons that the detergents offered vary in formulation so as to meet the hard water problems that we know as "bathtub ring."

If the water is really soft, as found in some resorts, a phosphate detergent known as "trisodium phosphate" would probably be adequate to do the job. As the hardness increases, the formulation must become more sophisticated. Most detergent manufacturers use trisodium phosphate as a basic ingredient for their detergents, but they add their own special formulation to meet the mineral problem. Pyrophosphates are adequate to handle some uncomplicated situations. However, more than half of the detergents sold in the country come under the heading of a highly refined polyphosphate. This enables the detergent to completely neutralize the mineralization of the water that otherwise would cause streaked tableware. Therefore, to be sure of the best results, a detergent containing highly refined polyphosphates should be selected.

Defoaming Action. A quick look in the dishwashing machine while it is in action will show whether there is excess sudsing. If there is more than ½ inch of foam, the operator should check the detergent's formula. The best way to determine whether any detergent has the proper defoaming action is to insist on a series of demonstrations from the supplier. If necessary, bring in other suppliers and give them a chance to demonstrate their low-sudsing detergent before making a selection.

Chlorinating Action. Food stains do appear on dishes, especially from coffee, tea, and certain vegetables. In the past such stains required soaking these dishes in a highly chlorinated bleach. However, today's detergents make it possible to dispense chlorine into the warewashing cycle without the soaking procedure. It is true that in some areas of the country, because of the soft water, this is not troublesome, but such a situation is rare.

A Word of Caution. One can have the most sophisticated and most expensive detergent available, but if the detergent dispensing equipment is not designed for the product and/or is not in good working condition, the results will be poor, and money will be wasted. Your detergent manufacturer should prescribe the type of dispenser needed. The manufacturer must also make sure the dispensers are working properly when making monthly service calls to the operation.

Rinse Additives. Not long ago, most kitchens were set up with a separate glass-washing and silver-washing machine because it was impossible to run these items through the regular machine without water spotting when drying; even the dishes showed water spots. In many cases it was standard procedure to have a crew wipe glasses, silverware, and dishes before putting them back into service.

Today, almost every dishwashing machine is equipped with a dispenser that pumps a softening agent into the final rinse so that the water does not adhere to the surface of dishes, silverware, or glassware. The water rolls off as the tableware is rinsed, so that it comes out of the machine free of any water spots and actually surface dry. As soon as the tableware has cooled down, it can be put back into service without toweling off.

The rinse-dry additive must be adjusted to the degree of the hardness of the water used in the final rinse. Again, the food service operator should obtain demonstrations from the supplier to prove that the product being used is the best available for this purpose.

Getting Rid of the Flies

It is common to have a serious fly problem around the back dock of a food service operation. The back dock is generally near a dumpster or trash bin with its usual unsanitary conditions. Hotels and resorts featuring outdoor dining are especially troubled with fly and insect problems. The solution to this problem is a twice-a-day hose-down in the areas in need of cleaning and sanitizing. Excellent equipment for this purpose is available under different brand names. The equipment for pest control from Economics Laboratory and Wyandotte has proven effective. It can be

mounted on the back dock and requires only a hot water tap; it does not require steam or high-pressure water. It is safe to use regularly on a twice-a-day basis, and it is very effective in hosing down dumpsters, trash bins, and garbage refrigerators at the back dock. Even though the cans have plastic liners, the cans themselves have to be cleaned and sanitized at least weekly. This equipment does the job with a minimum of time and work.

Examples of Detergent/Sanitizer Equipment

Many types and makes of this equipment are on the market and can be furnished by any reputable cleaning supply and service company. We show cuts of two pieces of equipment, one portable and one wall mounted, from a typical equipment catalogue (see Exhibit 24-3).

Specials

Other products useful in a food service operation are known as "specials" in the trade. Included in these specials are degreasers, descalers, hand soaps, bathroom cleaners, window cleaners, coffee urn cleaners, nonabrasive equipment cleaners, floor cleaners, laundry detergents, and air deodorizers. No one expects a purchasing agent to know all the details of these products or how they are best used. For this reason, we have recommended that the use of these products be part of the training program agreed upon with the detergent supplier for the hotel or other food service operation.

OTHER OPERATING SUPPLIES

Comparative operating statements published by hotel and restaurant accounting firms (when the statements are set up on the *Uniform System of Accounts*) show that the total cost of operating expenses amounts

DETERGENT/SANITIZER DISPENSERS
Environmental Sanitation
MIKRO-SPRAY•, MODEL J

The Mikro-Spray unit is used to inject a predetermined portion of liquid germicide and/or detergent into water being used to spray-clean any surface that may be cleaned with water. Proportioning is adjustable and precise. The unit operates on water line pressure, has no moving parts. Equipped with hose and spray nozzle instantly adjustable by lever action from full-off to a fine misty spray to full-on. Knob turn provides clear rinse water. Draws product direct from shipping container. Also available in wall-mounted Model C-3, with 48 oz. reservoir, and Model B-3 mobile unit.
U.S. Pat. No. 3,698,644.

PORTA-WASHER•

A unitized high pressure cleaning system. Delivers 3 gallons per minute at 700 psi maximum. Selector valve permits alternating detergent wash to fresh water rinse. Offers high pumping efficiency and unidirectional flow. Floating pistons and "viton" seals assure long pump life with low maintenance. High pressure 40' hose, wand, spray tip and suction hose filter screen are standard equipment.

A convenient foamer attachment converts the Porta-Washer for foam cleaning without external air connections. The attachment fits directly over the standard wand and allows either foaming or conventional high-pressure spray cleaning.

Exhibit 24-3. Detergent/sanitizer dispensers (Courtesy: Economics Laboratory, Inc.)

to about 8 percent of the total revenue of the operation. Of course, this figure will vary according to size, class, type, and location of operation. The big four—the trade name given to china, glass, silver, and linen—generally take up 3 percent of the total of other operating expenses. Cleaning supplies can take up to 2 percent of the total revenues, which leaves 3 percent of total sales generally applied to other operating supplies.

Major Expense Categories Included in Other Operating Supplies

It has already been pointed out that there are literally thousands of expense items normally used in a hotel and restaurant operation. If purchasing agents researched every one of these items, they would spend all of their time nitpicking on certain expense categories where the possible savings are practically nil and neglecting the important part of the job. There are certain expense categories, however, that are sufficiently large and important to mention. Included in this list would be uniforms (which are often listed separately in the accounting report), paper dining room napkins, paper cocktail napkins, placemats, facial tissues, toilet tissues, doilies, tray covers, disposable tablecloths, carryout containers, skirting for banquet tables, matches, gifts for the catering department, picks and stirrers for the cocktail lounge, Christmas and holiday decorations, doggy bags, children's games, and disposable tumblers, highball glasses, and tableware.

In the rooms department, the most important expense items are writing paper, envelopes, and pens for guests' use. Other expense items for consideration are the so-called "perks" for the rooms, such as shoeshine cloths, sewing kits, laundry and valet bags, disposable glassware, sanitary toilet seat covers, soap, and facial tissue.

In the luxury hotels, there are other costly expense items for the rooms: the daily newspaper, imported scented soap, electric shoe polishers, shower caps, bathrobes, extra-sized towels, disposable shower slippers, shoehorns, shaving kits, sewing kits, cologne, first-aid kits, mints, and in many cases, mineral water (Perrier, Vichy), spring water, and quinine water.

Sources of Supply

With literally hundreds of items available to the purchasing agent and dozens of purveyors and specialty houses anxious to sell, a good purchasing agent will generally pick two or three dealers who offer a complete line of products in these categories. After making spot checks of dealers' prices to find their so-called "loss leaders," the purchasing agent will, on a regular basis, place orders with these selected suppliers.

In the retail business, the salesperson representing the supply houses normally takes a periodic inventory, with the storeroom keeper, of the supplies of products on hand, and together they come up with a list of supplies needed. With this preliminary work accomplished, the salesperson can then go to the purchasing agent and in this way aid the buyer while promoting his account. There is certainly nothing wrong with this approach for the food service buyer, providing the buyer spot checks the prices being charged to him with competitive prices from outside sources or another dealer with whom he is doing business on a regular basis.

Buying for the End Use

In deciding which item to buy, the purchasing agent should consider the following questions: (1) Is it suitable for the use intended? (2) Is it a practical item and not a gadget or specialty item? (3) Is it durable? (4) Is the economy of the item acceptable for the product being obtained? (5) What is its effect on the public image?

In selecting items that may cause the guest to pass judgment on the general tone and quality of the operation, the purchasing agent has to give first consideration to this potential. In practice, items acceptable to the public are rarely the least expensive. But there are certain items that guests simply will not compromise on. It would be well if we listed some of these items under the heading of *Buyer Beware.*

Red Flag Items—Buyer Beware

Toilet tissues and facial tissues: The purchasing agent has to carry out management's policy on certain items, but management should set the standards for only the best. This is true for toilet tissue and facial tissue for the bedrooms and public restrooms. Any quality less than a two-ply sheet roll that contains 500 double sheets of facial tissue quality should not be considered. Some tissues of this quality come in different colors and in certain scents, which can add to the luxury of the product as well as to the cost. The name "Kleenex Facial Tissues" is a quality standard below which no item should be purchased. Other brand names that meet the same quality standards are acceptable.

Cocktail picks, stirrers, and mixers: If there is anything more irritating to a customer than to pay $2.50 for a small-to-medium-sized drink served in the cheapest type of highball glass with a chopped-off piece of straw for a mixer, the beverage service business has not come up with it. There is plenty of profit even in dollar drinks to permit the operator to use a suitable stirrer for highballs or cocktail pick for olives and cherries.

Food and beverage service napkins: These two items give the operator a chance to make a good impression on the customer by the quality of the product plus the decorative effect obtained through either color or design. Of course, individualized paper napkins are available, but it requires a sizeable order if you are to keep the cost down. However, almost every supply house has a wide variety of stock paper napkins, placemats, and cocktail napkins that enable the operator to vary the appearance of these items at will and to take advantage of the many seasonal and holiday items that are offered by the paper supply companies.

It would be unwise for the operator to buy anything of less quality than two-ply facial quality paper napkins or cocktail napkins. Of course, single-ply dispenser napkins are adequate for certain fast service restaurants and employees' cafeterias where economy is essential.

Placemats: Many food service operators today use a breakfast placemat on which the breakfast menu has been printed. In this manner, the service is speeded up. However, for lunch and dinner, a cleverly designed placemat made of good paper is generally used and is accepted by the public for coffee shop and semiformal dining room service. For specialty dining rooms, plastic placemats with special designs are suitable. For the so-called white-tablecloth restaurants, a colored tablecloth with matching or contrasting "linen" cloth and napkin are required.

Uniforms: For the past several years, many food service operators have attempted to save money by permitting their waiters and waitresses and bartenders to wear their own street clothes with the addition of an apron or vest. This is a very unsanitary practice. It is also an imposition on the employees, and unless you are running a cheap saloon, informality is entirely wasted on the customer. You seldom see this practice in a quality food service operation.

Uniform houses have expanded their designs to the point where it is not necessary for any operator to call in a special designer to come up with a suitable uniform for any food service. The operator who is running a unique operation, however, might wish to bring in a designer to produce the type of uniform that would go best with the style of the operation.

Carryout service: Many hotels and restaurants are profiting from developing a good carryout service in office lunches, box lunches for travelers, and take-home food for fast dinner preparation or for outside snacking. This gives the food operator a chance to publicize the name and to produce a quality product in a quality container that helps to sell the whole operation. Today molded plastic or paper containers designed to hold any food offered for carryout service are available. Hot and cold cups for carryout coffee and iced drinks come in both lined paper cups and molded plastic cups that act as insulators for hot and cold drinks and protect the customer against burned fingers.

Guest room stationery: Deluxe hotels offer not only regular writing paper but notepaper with appropriate envelopes. The design is exclusive, and the quality of the paper and the embossing reflect the quality of the hotel. Room items such as service directories, including room service and cocktail lists, and other writing materials are used for the same purpose. Even in the "econo-hotels," guests should be offered a suitable quality and design in guest room stationery since they are quick to notice poor quality in this item.

Banquet tables and chairs: These items are normally considered capital expenditure items, but it is important that purchasing agents and operators consider them in terms of their effect on the public as well as of their cost and durability.

25 Maintenance and Service Contracts

Purpose: To acquaint management, department heads, and the purchasing agent with the various types of maintenance and service contracts available.

INTRODUCTION

Management must make decisions regarding purchase of services as well as products. Services are not distributed in the same manner as products. As there are few national service organizations, the food and beverage operator must usually deal with smaller local firms. In purchasing services, the buyer needs first to be able to determine expertise and qualifications and then to establish standards of evaluation.

Chain and franchise operators in the hotel and food service field have the advantage of getting advice and help from their corporate headquarters, although, often because of location and distance, even these operators are left to their own devices. For the independent operator, help can be available when needed if a program is laid out in advance, with arrangements for outside contractors to provide services on short notice.

One problem facing the independent operator is that reliability of these outside contractors is often unknown until after the services begin. For this reason, an independent operator should spend adequate time investigating the reputation of the service contractors and talking with the contractors to get a clear understanding of what their services involve and what their standards of performance are. The operator should be sure to get everything in writing and to have the contracts reviewed by the legal services of the food service operation.

RESEARCHING THE CONTRACTORS

The general manager of the food service operation, together with the owner, is responsible for determining what outside services are required. The general manager must also see that the prospective contractors are thoroughly checked out for performance and that contracts are drawn up correctly and are reviewed and approved by the legal services of the hotel or food service operation.

At present, there are about fifty different types of maintenance and contract services available to the average-sized hotel and food service operation. It is also a well-known fact that when the majority of these food service contracts are signed, there is little opportunity on the part of the operator to maneuver if he is not satisfied with the services rendered. In the metropolitan areas, there are certain "gentlemen's agreements" in force that limit the operator's ability to make any changes after the original contract is signed. There are many instances on record where the contractor has taken advantage of this situation and literally robbed the operator before legal action could be taken.

Even though the general manager has the final responsibility for the service contracts, it is nearly impossible for one person to do all the necessary research on the contracts and contractors. It is best for the general manager to delegate these responsibilities and then give final approval after receiving satisfactory research reports. In a small motor inn or small food service operation, the general manager can call in the various department heads and ask them to review their outside service needs and to discuss their needs with the contractual services and then come to the general manager for approval of the contracts.

In the larger operations, it has been found advisable to use the purchasing department as the coordinator for research on contractors and for preparing the contracts. The purchasing agent would be wise to review the needs of the various departments with the department heads and, working with these department heads, to come up with recommendations as to what contractors and what services should be acquired by management. Some of these contracts are very lucrative; with two people working together representing management, the chances of "cooperation" with the contractors is greatly reduced. Also, with two people participating, there are fewer chances of misunderstandings.

Researching the contractors and drawing up contracts and getting them approved is only half of the job. Someone has to monitor the performance of the contractor, and this is best done through the cooperative efforts of the department head and the controller. The controller is responsible for overseeing all expenditures of the hotel, and, if he feels there is any laxness in the services being rendered, it is his responsibility to report it to management. Management should spot check the performance of the contractors, independently of the department head and controller, for reassurance that these two sources of supervision are functioning properly.

ORGANIZATION CHART FOR OUTSIDE CONTRACTUAL SERVICES

The following functional organization chart for outside and contractual services shows the various department heads and the services normally under contract for these departments. It is to be remembered that almost every operation, from medium-sized up, has certain situations that make it necessary to handle certain contracts and services in a specialized manner. In some cases, department heads are strong in certain phases of their operation but very weak in others, thereby requiring some additional help from management or some other department head who has the ability and time to offer assistance.

There are forty-four different contractual services listed in the foregoing organizational chart, which seems to cover any service a medium to large hotel or food service operation would require. However, there may well be additional services that could be utilized by management.

Red Flag Items to Be Watched

The majority of these contractual services are not too difficult to research, assuming that the department head and purchasing agent are proficient in their jobs and that management takes the necessary time to review their research. However,

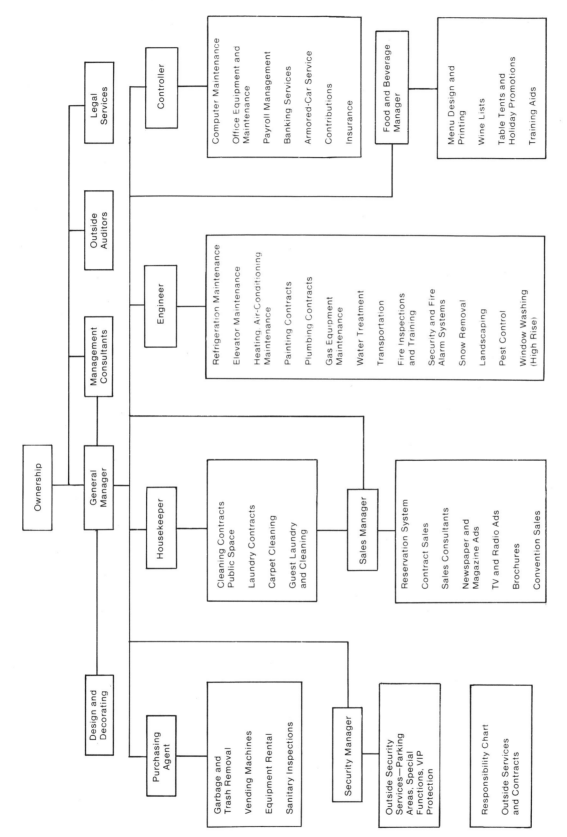

Exhibit 25-1. Chart for contractual services

there are certain "red flag" items and situations to watch out for.

Are These Services Necessary?

The first question management has to answer is if the contemplated outside services are really necessary, or can the work be done better by in-house staff? Experience has shown that when there is sufficient work to keep one person busy performing any function throughout the operation, it is usually less expensive to do the work in-house. Where there is alert departmental supervision, the quality of work can be as good as or better than that performed by an outside contractor.

There are some services required in a hotel or food service operation that cannot be done in-house, and it is necessary to go outside to get adequate service and performance. In many cases, this professional help is required by law or by insurance companies that realize certain professional services are best done by outside contractors.

Garbage and Trash Removal

If the city or community in which the hotel or food service is operating has adequate sewage capacity to permit garbage grinders, the problem of garbage and trash removal can be reduced by at least 50 percent. Today, any acceptable trash removal company is able to furnish dumpsters that can be located at the back dock of the operation. Most of this equipment is tightly closed and should not present much of a vermin or small-animal problem for the operation. Larger operations have these dumpsters removed daily and replaced with other dumpsters that have been washed and sanitized so that the problem of odor or unsightliness is minimal.

It is up to the operator to see that the entire dock area (including the dumpster) is washed down at least daily with a detergent and sanitizing agent. In some cases it is necessary to perform this chore two or three times a day. As a rule, the steward or food and beverage manager is held responsible for monitoring the manner in which this service is performed.

Vending Machines

Vending machine operations in metropolitan and nearby suburban areas are mostly controlled by an outside group representing the machine operators. These companies furnish the food and vending products, repair the machines, collect and distribute the revenue and commissions, and protect the vending machine areas from petty thievery and invasion by those who would "take over" a particular vending area. These "gentlemen's agreements" cover the kind of equipment furnished, leasing arrangements, commissions, and service responsibilities.

We have known certain operators to purchase and service their own vending machines. We have also seen what some of these machines look like after being assaulted by persons unknown. The general manager and owner should take a large part in any negotiating and granting of vending machine contracts as this is a substantial and lucrative business for outsiders who have not shown much inclination to relinquish it to in-house operators.

Equipment Rental

These services generally apply to the rental of tables and chairs and convention paraphernalia and are especially valuable for large exhibitions, where the contractor can bring in the necessary display equipment. It would be expensive and wasteful for the hotel to try to maintain adequate supplies of this convention material. The contractors come in and set it up and when the function or the exhibition is over, they clear up the equipment and leave the area ready for the next use.

There is other equipment available for

rent, especially for food service needs, and some operators take advantage of it. It is debatable whether it pays to rent this equipment or to own it. Some of the equipment now being rented includes coffee makers, warewashing machines, automatic fire extinguishing systems, and liquor dispensing systems. One of the largest cleaning supply dealers offers a service that furnishes not only detergents but also warewashing machines and tables, plus the actual workers and supervision to handle the complete warewashing function. This type of service is now growing and could possibly become an integral part of the food service business.

Sanitary Inspection and Consultants

This is a growing contractual service, primarily due to the many lawsuits against food service operators for actual or imagined food poisoning. From a protective viewpoint, these services can be very desirable; no operator, however, should have to admit that he needs outside help to keep the premises clean. If any operation has a detergent supplier that cannot, with the help of management, figure out how to keep the tableware and premises clean, then management should throw out the detergent supplier and find one that can do this job satisfactorily. If the in-house staff cannot keep the premises clean, then it may be necessary to find a new steward or food and beverage manager.

Laundry Alternatives

During the late 1950's and early 1960's, the management of in-house laundries was becoming more difficult because $1.00-per-hour labor was no longer available, and unions and OSHA were pushing for improved working conditions. The older heavy equipment was wearing out, and the cost of replacing it had skyrocketed. The end cost to the operators, both hotel and food service, was getting seriously out of line.

About 1965, many hotel or motel and large food service operators switched to renting their clean linens from commercial laundry services, which the institutional field and the small restaurant operator had been doing for years. (Of course, in-house guest laundries, as well as in-house dry-cleaning services, were also passed on to outside cleaning services, which were not only better but cost the customer less.) For a considerable length of time, this seemed to be the answer to all food service laundry problems. However, there were drawbacks: the quality of linens was low, the laundry operators were forced to increase rates due to union activities, new equipment costs were extremely high, and service became difficult due to gasoline shortages and lack of space for laundries near the metropolitan areas. While all this was going on, products were introduced that necessitated a whole new look at the laundry problem. These products were no-iron linens and a new breed of small, high-capacity washers, spin dryers, and related laundry equipment.

By the mid-1970's, conversions back to in-house laundry were so successful that a trend was started. Today many medium to large operations have gone back to in-house laundry. But the majority of food service operators have found it best to stay with laundry rentals, and only the largest food service operators have installed their own laundry equipment and staff.

Frank D. Borsenik, well-known professor and author, says that today the hotel and large food service operator has several options when it comes to handling laundry services. These alternatives include the following:

1. Purchasing linens and installing on-premise laundry facilities.
2. Renting clean linens from a commercial laundry.
3. Purchasing linens and using an off-premises laundry service.

4. Using disposable products (a growing practice, especially in low-cost motels and institutions).
5. A combination of the first four alternatives.

Even with five alternatives, no single alternative is satisfactory in itself insofar as both cost and service are concerned. Another factor involved in the selection of the proper alternative is the customers' reactions. If the product or service has a negative effect on customers, the operator should forget it and make every effort possible to give customers what they want.

Some Facts an Operator Should Know About Linen Rental. There are some strict rules that are adhered to by all the linen rental service companies, and customers are obliged to observe these rules if they want any service. A purchasing agent discussing a contract with any sizeable company in the metropolitan areas or nearby suburbs will soon find this to be true.

When a purchasing agent opens negotiations for a linen rental contract, the agent will find that he is free to discuss such a contract with only a limited number of companies because only they are willing to discuss a contract with the new operator. The new operator will also find very little variance in rates, services promised, or quality of product. Most importantly, the new operator will find out that once the negotiations are over and the contract is signed, the operator is permanently "married" to the linen rental company until "one or both goes bankrupt."

If an operator is dissatisfied with the service or the product or with increasing rates, there is only one alternative—to try to negotiate something better with the present linen rental service. If the operator tries to negotiate a new contract with a competitive company, it will soon be found that there is no competitive company interested in taking over the business.

How this situation originated and who enforces the practice is pretty well known in the industry. What is not well known, however, is what to do about it. At present the food service operator should investigate every possibility of the contract and spell out in the contract everything that is to be agreed upon by both the operator and the linen rental service. A good lawyer can be a valuable aide to the operator in achieving a clear contract that covers all the details.

The operator should make sure that the contract includes a clear description of how the linen will be checked into and out of the hotel or restaurant, who is responsible for checking the numbers of pieces, who is responsible for determining the cost of lost linen (which the operator is expected to pay for), and what tolerances will be allowed for torn and unusable clean linens delivered to the hotel or restaurant. If colored linens are used, there should also be a signed agreement stating how much variation due to fading will be allowed before the linen rental service has to redye or purchase new linens.

Outside laundry services usually follow the same practices as the linen rental services. The same operating practices should apply.

Commercial Laundry Service Alternative. If enough capital is available, many operators find it very satisfactory to purchase their own linen and then contract for the washing, drying, and folding with a commercial laundry. This practice requires an inventory of three to five times the normal daily requirements because of the necessary time lapse for processing laundry. There is also a need to maintain a reserve stock on hand to meet emergencies. And, in the northern areas, service delays due to weather conditions are always a possibility in the winter.

The food service and hotel operator has more freedom to change laundry service when he owns his own linen. However, in certain metropolitan areas, it is a known fact that a switch in this type of laundry service cannot be accomplished without at least one year's advance notice. And, if he reads the fine print, an operator may find there is a penalty clause in switching laundry services.

On-Premise Laundry Alternative. For the past fifteen years, the larger operator has reevaluated the advantages of on-premise laundries. Of course, the benefits of lower cost, lower inventory, and better service have to be weighed against the problems: union pressures, space considerations, adequate supervision and possible theft (which can turn out to be a very large consideration). In one large chain-operated hotel, the losses of good cotton damask napkins amounted to 10,000-dozen the first year of operation. When the hotel switched to a rather scratchy plain-colored momie-cloth napkin, the losses ended. The new napkins were also rectangular, a shape that did not lend itself well to being folded for diapers.

Disposable Linen Alternative. This alternative cannot be readily dismissed without being given full consideration. For the medium to small food service operator, this alternative is already accepted, especially with the improvement in the weight and appearance of disposable tablecloths. Throw-away banquet tablecloths are now available which are almost impossible to distinguish from the ordinary momie-cloth tablecovers. Three-ply heavy-duty paper napkins of tissue quality are being accepted in banquets and food service operations, except for the most exclusive ones. These products have the advantage of being sanitary. Until the feel of the product is improved to more closely resemble linens, however, the acceptance of disposables for hotel room bed linens will probably be delayed for some time. However, disposable linens are already taking over the institutional and hospital field. It would

appear that disposable linen alternatives are best when used with table linens.

Choosing the Right Alternative. In the end, food service operators will have to decide for themselves which of the above alternatives or combination of alternatives will suit the needs of their particular operation. The information provided above should furnish a guideline for developing an effective program.

Contract Cleaning

During World War II and immediately afterward, the hospitality industry turned to contract cleaning services because of help shortages and because the industry was flourishing and could afford contract help. Today, almost every large hotel or food service operation uses a number of contract cleaning services. These services provide daily cleaning of public spaces including lobbies, ballrooms, private dining rooms, and restrooms. Some contract cleaners have even offered attractive contracts for complete cleaning, including guest rooms. But even though this complete cleaning service is very popular and widely used in hospitals and nursing care and retirement homes, the costs have worked out to the disadvantage of the potential buyer in the hospitality business.

Experience has shown that contracts for specific types of cleaning services have worked out the best for the operator, if not for the provider. Over the past ten years, cost-conscious operators have analyzed their contract cleaning costs and have found in many cases that they can do the daily work at a considerable savings (often ⅔ the cost) compared to having it done by outside contractors. Still, a rather appreciable number of large hotel and restaurant operators have outside crews that come in at night and do the necessary cleaning. But the smaller operator finds that hiring contractors for periodic cleaning, such as shampooing and vacuuming of public space carpets, hallway carpets, drapes and ceiling areas, is generally the best plan.

One other cleaning service that is sometimes a problem, especially in high-rise buildings, is that of window washing. The supervision of this service is often given to the housekeeping department in low-rise buildings, but in a "glass tower" it is usually necessary to hire a professional window-cleaning crew and to place the supervision of the work under the chief engineer. We do know of certain compromise situations where the housekeeper and her personnel are expected to keep the windows of the lobby floor clean, and anything above that would be done by contract service on a periodic basis.

The decision to use outside cleaning contractors depends entirely on the attitude of the owner and management. A manager who is primarily interested in sales and promotion rightfully will probably push for an outside contract. If ownership is very devoted to cost management and is assisted by a cost-conscious controller, the situation can be altered to suit the needs of the operation.

CONTRACTS MONITORED NORMALLY BY SALES MANAGER

Really good sales managers who are capable of handling all of the programs necessary for a successful operation are hard to find, and they command high salaries. This type of person is normally found in the larger hotel and food service operation, while in the smaller operation this phase of the work is usually covered by the general manager assisted by some outside consultants and contract services. But for all food service operations, a good advertising program is essential for maximum profitability. For the medium to small operator, the local newspaper and radio are the best media for advertising. It is only the larger operation that can afford magazine or TV advertising.

In addition to outside advertising, there are many in-house promotional ideas that are used by operators who realize the value of selling to the customer who is already in the house. Brochures, flyers, menus, elevator advertising where permitted, and printed material distributed in lighted signs throughout the house are some of the more common methods of internal promotion. Another in-house promotional piece used extensively is the telephone directory with all the house services listed in it. Closed circuit television with screens throughout the property can also be used for periodic promotions of house services. Highway billboards are a necessity for the suburban motor inn and restaurant, but this service can be expensive and the value of such a service has to be carefully evaluated by management.

The best local advertising and business promotion is the feature story appearing in the local media or broadcast over the local radio station. Themes for feature stories include the arrival of VIP guests, conventions with national speakers, and employee activities such as softball and bowling teams. Even soccer teams are now receiving considerable attention.

All of the foregoing facts are usually well known to a sales manager or a sales-oriented general manager. It is simply a matter of finding time to work up a sales program of this nature and to decide what is to be contracted out and what is to be done in the house.

Reservation and Convention Sales

For the chain operator or franchise operator, the essential part of a promotional program is not much of a problem because these services are almost always furnished by the franchisor or corporate headquarters. However, there are many independent operators who have found it advisable to contract a telephone reservation service. Recently, contract services that book conventions, training institutes, and school functions have been very effective in bringing business to the independent operator.

OUTSIDE SERVICES FOR THE ENGINEERING DEPARTMENT

Heating Services

Until recently, if a building was set up with oil heat, management continued with this type of heat regardless of the cost. Some old coal-fired heating systems were still in existence, and regardless of the problems of ash disposal and air pollution, these systems continued to operate. Gas heat became very popular when the oil shortage developed, but with the removal of controls, the cost of gas heat has rapidly approached that of oil. Many cities operate their own gas company, and it was only natural that they would start selling steam as the supply channels became compatible in price.

In the mid-1970's, because of the steady climb in fuel costs, heating services began to be managed differently. Instead of building with traditional equipment and accepting rate increases, the manufacturers of heating equipment, working with building management, developed new compact, low-cost equipment that made it profitable for the operator to switch from one type of heating energy to another based on a five-year projection of energy costs. Many operators that were buying steam in metropolitan areas found it profitable to install gas-fired boilers to create their own steam and in some cases, use steam to operate electric generating equipment. In other areas, gas-fired equipment became expensive to operate, and after some study, many building managers switched back to oil with quite appreciable savings.

The cost of hot water in the hotel and food service industry can run as high as 25 to 30 percent of the total energy cost. Consequently, rapid strides are being made in the use of solar energy for hot water heating. At the present time, solar energy has not been widely accepted in large operations, but solar powered air-cooling has made appreciable inroads in air-conditioning management.

Recently, some heating equipment manufacturing companies have used a three-year cycle for projecting energy costs instead of the currently popular five-year cycle. The potential for saving costs by switching fuels and modification of equipment is real. However, management must be very careful about who does the analysis on which management's decision is to be based. This is where good outside independent engineering consultants are necessary. After studying the situation they may recommend a course of action that could result in appreciable savings in heating and air-conditioning costs.

Gas Equipment Maintenance

About 90 percent of the kitchen equipment in use in the United States today is gas-fired. Usually some small equipment is operated by electric power, and the rest is powered by steam (such as steam-jacketed kettles, coffee urns, and hot water boosters for dishwashing machines). The need for servicing this equipment varies according to the quality of equipment purchased in the first place and the care and use of the equipment. It is not economical even for some of the largest operations to have a person on the staff capable of repairing and maintaining this equipment. Consequently, most operators have a service contract on their gas equipment either with the gas company selling the energy to the operator or, in some cases, with an independent equipment service maintenance company that can offer maintenance service for all types of kitchen equipment as well as gas-fired equipment.

Elevator and Escalator Maintenance Contracts

It has been estimated that there are more people moved each day by elevator and escalator than by all other forms of transportation combined, including the automobile. Elevators and escalators are also rated as one of the safest modes of transportation. (Horizontal transportation such as moving walkways are not included in these statistics.) The low accident rate for elevator and escalator transport is the result of stringent rules for the safety and maintenance of equipment. Numerous inspections by city or state elevator inspectors (with the posting of the results in the elevator) assure the passengers that the equipment is safe.

When an elevator breaks down, it is a simple matter of shutting down the elevator until it can be repaired, while passengers use the other elevators. Freight elevators can be out of service for a short time without causing too many problems, but where there is only one passenger elevator available, the need for quick repair and maintenance is essential. Most engineering departments have at least one man on duty that is trained to investigate elevator stoppages and to take care of minor repair work. But it is usually required by the state that the operating company have a contract with a licensed elevator maintenance service. Normally, this service is contracted with the company that produced the equipment. However, in some instances, this service is furnished by an independent company specializing in elevator service and maintenance. These services generally consist of regular maintenance inspections, testing of safety features, replacement of worn parts, and a regular schedule of shutting down the individual elevators for a complete physical and maintenance check. Anyone who depends on elevator service must have this kind of inspection and maintenance service. It would be very foolish on the part of the operator to try to stint in any way in procuring an adequate service contract for this equipment.

Airport Limousine Service

Airport limousine service is an important factor in the operation of motor inns catering to the airplane traveler. This service is normally under the supervision of the engineering department. Depending on the area in which the operation occurs, some limousine services may be restricted to taking passengers from a motor inn or hotel to the airport but not be permitted to carry passengers from the airport to the motor inn. This is generally due to political pressure put on by the cab company or limousine service that has the contract with the airport for general transportation services.

As a rule, airport motor inns purchase a small limousine or two for this service, and when a call comes in from the airport, one of the bellmen will take the limousine over to the airport and pick up the passengers. Motor inns generally maintain a regular taxi schedule to aid guests in planning their departure times.

A few of the larger operators will lease their limousine with full maintenance included in the contract. Most of the smaller operators have an agreement with the local garage to take care of all the needs of the limousine, with payment made on a job basis. Naturally, whether the limousine is leased or owned, the operator is required to have a minimum of liability insurance adequate to cover any injuries to passengers or other motorists in case of accident.

Water Treatment

Normally, water for a hotel or food service operation comes from two basic sources: (1) the city water supply, or

(2) from wells on land controlled by the operator. Resort operations sometimes depend on their own reservoir or water pumped from a nearby lake or stream. In the latter case, the operator may need to acquire a license, and the water must be tested for safe consumption. The first consideration for a water supply is whether it is free of toxic chemicals. If the water is tested and found to be pure, the next concern is the degree of hardness of the water and its effect on the equipment in the hotel or food service operation. Water that has 0 to 5 grains of salt precipitates per million parts of water is considered soft water and will not damage machines or plumbing. Water with 5 to 10 grains of precipitates is considered medium-hard and will require some treatment to prevent lime deposits building up in the water pipes and in equipment such as dishwashing machines, laundry equipment, and some air-conditioning equipment. Water with over 10 grains of precipitates must be given a regular and continuous water-softening treatment if it is to be used as the main source of the operation's water supply. Without such treatment, pipes will become clogged, lime deposits will form on the inside of dishwashing equipment, dishes will be spotted and slimy, and laundry will be discolored and streaked.

At the time of the hotel's construction, any good architect will take samples of the water and, with the aid of a water treatment consultant, will specify an adequate treatment system designed to meet the needs of the operation. Factors affecting the water supply may increase water hardness at a later date, and then it is up to the operator to install a treatment system adequate for the needs of the hotel or food service operation. Sometimes these installations become very expensive, but in most instances, especially food service operations, there are compact systems, which can be installed and operated at a minimum cost, that do a

perfectly good job of softening the water. Detergent suppliers can be very helpful in locating the cause of water hardness and can be helpful in recommending equipment and softening materials.

Most municipal water supply companies treat their water to bring it within the medium-to-low hardness range. With this level of hardness, the problems for the operator will not be critical. However, pumping water from a well or taking water from a lake can prove to be a big problem, and may require that the operator call in a water treatment consultant.

Pest Control

This is one area where it would be a mistake for a hotel or food service manager to think that the service can be adequately provided in-house. Because of the toxic effect of so many of the chemicals used in pest control, there is considerable danger to food, employees, and guests from exposure to these chemicals. Pest control is a highly specialized service, and it is unlikely that the typical food service manager would have sufficient knowledge of the subject. A true story will illustrate the problem. A newly assigned manager of a restaurant that was only five months old noticed, in examining the service contracts, that there was none for pest control. The restaurant was new, well-constructed, and appeared quite clean, so the manager figured he could put off this expense for a time. From time to time, he would spot a roach, but he didn't begin to worry until the service crew complained of seeing roaches in the dining room. He called in a reputable local pest control service, whose representative told him that if he saw one roach there were undoubtedly thousands of them. The manager scoffed: It was not possible, the problem was a minor one, but he would like to get rid of the few roaches he had. The man from the pest control company invited the manager to come back that evening when, after closing, he would fog both the kitchen and dining room. The manager did, and to his amazement and horror, saw thousands of roaches pouring out, seemingly, from everywhere. The next morning the dead insects were vacuumed up in the dining room and swept up in the kitchen.

Needless to say, that operation immediately went on a regular pest control program. Not only is this story true, it is not unusual. Of course, the physical structure must be properly constructed, and the operation must be kept immaculately clean, but this is not enough to assure freedom from insects and vermin. It is absolutely essential to have a professional pest control service under contract.

If there is a national pest control company available, it would be best to deal with them, but they do not cover all areas. In such cases, management will have to determine which available service is best qualified. The best criterion for selecting a local dealer is their reputation for performance with other operations in the area.

Another criterion that a manager should check into is the training the pest control company gives its own employees. If they cannot produce evidence that they have a regular training program for their own personnel, management would be advised to look elsewhere and find a company with an ongoing training program.

An additional benefit of having a contract with a pest control service is that if a health inspector should find some evidence of pests, the food service operator can prove that he has made an effort to control them. Many health inspectors will overlook minor evidence of pests when shown the service contract. The inspector's report should then be reviewed with the pest control service.

In the northern part of the country, it would be wise to have an inspection and treatment at least twice a month, with provisions for emergency inspections and treatment. In the southern areas, it is almost always necessary to have a weekly inspection and treatment if waterbugs, roaches, and other types of pests are to be controlled. Throughout the Caribbean, there do not seem to be any standards for inspection and treatment by the local governments; in fact, some areas have no pest control services at all. Under the circumstances, the hotel or food service operator is required to train someone on staff to see that the reputation of the operation is not ruined by infestations of pests.

The author has had some experience in pest and fly control in the Caribbean area and was surprised to find that it was relatively easy to control this situation by the application of a few basic rules and regular use of nontoxic materials. The back dock of an operation is where most infestation starts, and these infestations are generally the result of unsanitary floor areas, trash storage areas, garbage disposal dumpsters, and soiled driveways. In the chapter on cleaning supplies, there is a discussion of types of equipment and detergents that can be effectively used for keeping all outside areas around a food service operation clean, odorless, and free of flies and vermin. By the use of certain equipment, the author was able to clean up a situation that had become so bad that the outside dining terrace had to be closed because of the fly situation. With two weeks' attention to cleaning up and spraying the area, including some of the nearby woods, it was possible to reopen the terrace—much to the pleasure of the guests, who were tired of eating in an air-conditioned room.

Landscaping and Snow Removal

Downtown hotels and restaurants, as a rule, are not bothered with these problems if they have their own inside garage facilities. If they do not have these facilities, they generally have a contract with the parking lot operator whose job is to see that the parking areas are clear of snow and valet parking service maintained where necessary. In suburban areas, landscaping and snow removal become an important phase of the overall operation. Unless shrubbery, trees, and other plants are cared for, the premises readily take on a seedy look and discourage customers from using the facilities. The parking areas must be kept clear of snow and other debris. The usual solution is to contract with a local company to provide landscaping and snow removal.

As with other service contracts, the operator must make sure that the service company being considered has a good reputation for performance, reliability, and responsibility. It is best if the operator has a contract written up by management or someone on the staff competent to do so. The contract should clearly specify type and frequency of services. Some of these organizations will have standard contracts, and the operator is advised to make whatever modifications are necessary. The best type of contract is one that identifies the basic services to be provided for a fixed fee and spells out in detail what the fees will be for certain additional services.

Some of the details that should be spelled out include whether the landscape service is responsible for watering shrubs and other plantings, what substitutions can be accepted for the replacement of dead plants, what fertilizers are to be used on lawns and shrubs, when the fertilizer is to be applied, and what measure of snowfall is necessary for the snow removal service. The responsibility for snow removal and landscaping can sometimes be delegated to the chief engineer and/or the housekeeper in some of the smaller suburban motor inn properties. In many instances, a housekeeper is best suited to supervise these services. The important point is that someone other than the property manager be responsible for monitoring these services.

Other Services

Outside plumbing and painting contracts are best done on a per-job basis. A good operator, however, will have an ongoing painting program in order to maintain the appearance of the unit. There should then be options for additional services at specified fees. This system would also apply to plumbing maintenance and emergency plumbing jobs.

Fire Inspections and Safety Training

These services are becoming more of an operating problem for the hospitality industry every year. Good operators make sure that the chief engineer is not only qualified but sincerely interested in safety and fire prevention. All the knowledge in the world is worthless unless that individual makes safety a high priority. Competent management makes certain that they themselves have an up-to-date training and inspection program to guard against the possibly tragic results of carelessness or lack of information. Most community fire departments offer fire inspection services and help in training staff to recognize fire hazards. If the local fire department does not provide these services, the operator should hire adequate inspection and training services.

Nearly every community in the country now has an underwriters' approved set of rules for the installation and maintenance of fire alarm systems in hotels and food service operations. Most local ordinances provide for periodic inspection and testing of all fire alarm systems by members of the fire department. If these tests are not routine, a responsible operator will request them. If the service is not provided, the operator should pressure the local community politicians to make the service available. The operator may also find that if it is necessary to hire an inspection service, the cost may be compensated by lower insurance rates.

CONTRACT SERVICES MONITORED BY THE CONTROLLER'S OFFICE

Certain types of contract services are normally handled by the controller's department, which works out the contract details for management and then monitors the service. Such services include computer maintenance, accounting office equipment service and maintenance, outside payroll services, banking services, armored-car service, insurance, and political fund management.

One of the most important services now required by the medium- to large-sized hospitality industry operator is that of computer maintenance. With the introduction of computers that can be purchased for less than $2,000, even the small operator may now be involved in computer maintenance. Most computer maintenance contracts are offered either by the sales company or the manufacturer, who have a vested interest in providing good service. When considering a computer maintenance program, the two most important criteria are twenty-four-hour, seven-day availability of competent service personnel and speed of response to emergency calls. The research on the maintenance service is generally done prior to a management decision as to which computer to purchase. The dependability of the equipment often has a value of several thousand dollars, so no compromise should be made between purchase cost and dependable, trouble-free equipment.

Payroll Preparation and Management

Only very small operators today take care of their own payroll records, for payroll "service bureaus" have improved their skills and reduced the cost of their services. In some instances they even furnish statistical information and management consultation on the control of payroll. In larger communities, there are usually three or four companies in this type of business, usually associated with other banking services.

Banking Services

Even though the controller's department and management might be asked to review and make a decision as to what bank should provide the necessary banking services, this decision must take into consideration the financial investors. It would be very unwise for a manager to ignore the institutions that control the actual ownership of the property. Normally, controlling financial institutions such as banks and insurance companies are interested in keeping an eye on the day-to-day financial operations and will offer lower fees to have the opportunity to monitor their funds in operation.

The more banking services an operation can put under one umbrella, the better the rates will be for the individual services. Not all banks charge the same fees for their services; they will negotiate on the fees to be charged depending on the variety and amount of service required. Banks are very interested in checking accounts, payroll accounts, short- and long-term loans, employee check cashing, and financial consulting. Today, we see banks offering their computer services to the individual operation for payment of bills and deposits of cash, and banks are even getting into the techniques of day-to-day purchasing of operating supplies.

The medium to small operator generally tries to put as many of these services as possible into the hands of one local bank. However, large corporate financial managers have shown that it is best to divide these services into three or four groups, thereby getting an additional competitive edge in the negotiations.

Armored-car service for the pickup and delivery of cash generally comes under the heading of banking services. This may not, however, always be the case, as the armored-car service may be independent of any

bank. Banks are particularly interested in the types and size of insurance policies carried by the operator. Banks do not offer insurance policies because of legal requirements, but to protect their own funds, they are interested in the type and size of the policies carried by the operator.

Insurance

In purchasing insurance, the first consideration has to be the organization's political nature. If the operation is owned by an insurance company, it would expect to insure its own property. Unfortunately, no single insurance company offers a comprehensive policy covering all the needs of the hotel and food service operator. According to insurance companies, this is due to the need for special services and a desire to spread out all the risks involved in such insurance.

When selecting insurance, the buyer wants to be fully protected while keeping the insurance rates as low as possible. But in an operation that is serving the public, adequate protection should take precedence over cost. Insurance policies should cover personal injury, false arrest, food poisoning, automobile insurance, and crime coverage for burglary and robbery.

Today it is a rare operator that does not carry worker's compensation and health insurance for employees. Some companies carry a form of life insurance as part of the employee relations program and may also provide benefits such as legal services, dental coverage, and insurance covering any injury to an employee while participating in any sporting event connected with the hotel or food service operation. If the operation has a contract with the unions, many of these health and welfare benefits are covered by the union contract. Of course, the operator pays insurance costs, but the problems of administration are reduced for the operator, and in many instances the union contract actually is less expensive for the operator than trying to

place the insurance on his own. A reputable insurance agent plus the assistance of a competent lawyer are basic requirements if an operator is to be adequately covered by insurance, but not to the point of paying excessive dollars for unneeded insurance that could perhaps best be covered by a self-insurance fund set aside for such a purpose.

Contributions

One of the best insurance policies an operator can have, which doesn't come under the heading of insurance expense and is not discussed very openly except in a tightly controlled office, is an adequate holiday contribution fund. This fund can include a few dollars to the police and firemen's benevolent association, a contribution to local political campaign funds, and remembrances to the various offices of city, county, and state services.

In certain metropolitan areas, these contributions can become substantial. On the other hand, experience has shown that these contributions are almost routine in acceptance and essential in case of certain problems. The value of such goodwill was brought home to the author on one occasion when a fire was started in a hotel due to carelessness on the part of an employee. After the fire was out and reporters and the insurance adjusters started the usual questions, the captain from the fire department stepped in and answered all the questions and protected the hotel by stating the cause of the fire was unknown and, as far as he could ascertain, accidental.

In another instance, when a regional strike of food service employees occurred, the union calling the strike set up a branch headquarters in a food service operation with which the author was involved. For six weeks, that restaurant operated without any problem at full capacity and profitability simply because the local business agent had been permitted to sign a few food checks amounting to $50.00 a month over the past six months of operation.

Printing Needs

If the food and beverage operation is of sufficient size to warrant having the position of a food and beverage manager, it should be able, with the help of management and a good menu printer, to take care of any menu design and printing necessary for the operation, plus adequate wine lists, table tents, and holiday promotions. When the local staff is involved in the preparation of menus, wine lists, and other internal promotion, experience has shown that the backing of any program is far better and the results more profitable than if outside consultants had been brought in to do the original design work.

OWNERSHIP AND MANAGEMENT RESPONSIBILITIES FOR OUTSIDE SERVICES

Owners, for their own protection, should insist on making the final decision as to the selection of any outside auditors or auditing service. Owners should also have the final say as to the selection of legal services for the firm and will often participate in the placement of insurance policies and the selection of banking services.

If a major rehabilitation program is to be undertaken for the property, owners, with the assistance of the general manager, should make the final decision in selection of the designer or decorator. If the owners are not satisfied with the operating results, they have the privilege and the responsibility of bringing in outside management consultants to assist the general manager in improving operating results. It is a smart general manager who will take the attitude of "I'm happy for the help," because if he doesn't, the owners will invariably make a change. It doesn't mean that the general manager has to agree with everything the consultants say, but he should keep an open mind and work as closely as possible with the consultants to do everything possible to improve the profitability of the operation.

SECURITY

There has always been a need for a security program and security personnel in large hotel operations and even in certain large food service operations. But during the past fifteen years, the need for security services has become necessary even for the small motor inn operator.

Most hotels with food service have an in-house security crew headed by the chief security officer, and they cover night patrols as well as daytime surveillance of employees and customers. Those operations that have extensive banquet facilities may have a contract with an outside security service. Some have a standby service whereby their employees, and off-duty police/firepeople, watch over the premises during conventions, when certain VIPs are on the property, and to augment the local or in-house security for the protection of parking areas and guests going from their cars to the entrance of the hotel or restaurant. The important considerations for the operator are (1) who will be checking on the honesty and performance of the outside security guards and (2) what is the reputation of the outside security forces? Unfortunately, problems have arisen due to expanding security services being offered to the public. Often the personnel hired by the outside security services have been anything but satisfactory. For their own protection, the operators have to make sure that they are dealing with a reputable company that is adequately covered with liability insurance for failure to perform satisfactorily or for dishonesty of its employees.

Appendix I Guides to Purchasing Food

Table 1. Portion of Yield Factors for Meats, Poultry, Fish, and Shellfish—Hotels and Good Restaurants

Wholesale Cut	IMPS Code Number	Entree	Yield Factor (percent)	Portion Factors		
				Size and State	Cost	Average Number of Servings
MEATS						
Beef						
Rib, primal (regular, 34 to 38 lb.)	103	Roast ribs of beef	26	15 oz., cooked	3.60	10
				11 oz., cooked	2.64	14
				9-½ oz., cooked	2.23	16
				8-½ oz., cooked	2.04	18
Oven ready (20 to 22 lb.)	109		44	15 oz., cooked	2.10	10
				11 oz., cooked	1.49	14
				9-½ oz., cooked	1.32	16
				8-½ oz., cooked	1.17	18
Top round (roast ready), 19 to 23 lb.)	168	Pot roast	55	8 oz., cooked	.91	23
				6 oz., cooked	.68	30
		Round steak	65	10 oz., raw	.96	21
				8 oz., raw	.77	27
		Roast round	57	8 oz., cooked	.88	23
				6 oz., cooked	.66	31
				4 oz., cooked	.44	47
Bottom round (25 to 28 lb.)	170	Pot roast	55	8 oz., cooked	.91	28
				6 oz., cooked	.68	37
		Hamburger	90	8 oz., raw	.55	47
				6 oz., raw	.42	63
				5 oz., raw	.35	76
Strip loin (bone in, 10-inch trim, 18 to 20 lb.)	175	Sirloin steak (2-inch tail, 1/8-inch fat)	50	16 oz., raw	2.00	10
				14 oz., raw	1.75	12
				12 oz., raw	1.50	14
				10 oz., raw	1.25	16
				8 oz., raw	1.00	20
Strip loin (boneless, 12 to 14 lb.)	180	Sirloin steak (2-inch tail, 1/8-inch fat)	70	16 oz., raw	1.42	10
				14 oz., raw	1.24	12
				12 oz., raw	1.06	14
				10 oz., raw	.89	16
				8 oz., raw	.71	20
Top sirloin butt (boneless, 12 to 14 lb.)	184	Top butt steak	62	10 oz., raw	1.01	12
				8 oz., raw	.81	16
				6 oz., raw	1.01	20
		Roast top sirloin	75	8 oz., cooked	.67	20
				6 oz., cooked	.50	26
				4 oz., cooked	.34	38

Table 1 *(continued)*

Wholesale Cut	IMPS Code Number	Entree	Yield Factor (percent)	Portion Factors		
				Size and State	Cost	Average Number of Servings
Tenderloin (full, 7 to 9 lb.)	189	Tenderloin steak	50	10 oz., raw	1.25	5 to 7
(short, 5 to 6 lb.)	192			8 oz., raw	1.00	7 to 9
				6 oz., raw	.75	9 to 12
		Roast tenderloin	40	8 oz., cooked	1.25	5 to 7
				6 oz., cooked	.94	7 to 9
				4 oz., cooked	.63	11 to 14
Corned brisket (kosher style,	120	Corned beef	45	8 oz., cooked	1.11	10 to 12
12 to 14 lb.)				6 oz., cooked	.83	14 to 16
				4 oz., cooked	.56	21 to 25
Fresh brisket	120	Same as corned brisket				
Chuck (square cut, boneless,	116	Pot roast	66	8 oz., cooked	.76	82 to 95
62 to 72 lb.)				6 oz., cooked	.57	109 to 126
				4 oz., cooked	.38	163 to 190
		Stew meat or hamburger	90	8 oz., raw	.56	111 to 129
				6 oz., raw	.42	148 to 172
				4 oz., raw	.28	220 to 380
Veal						
Veal leg (single, 25 to 28 lb.)	334	Roast leg	40	8 oz., cooked	1.25	20 to 22
				6 oz., cooked	.94	26 to 28
				4 oz., cooked	.63	40 to 42
		Veal cutlets	47	8 oz., raw	1.06	23 to 26
				6 oz., raw	.80	31 to 35
				4 oz., raw	.64	47 to 52
		Veal stew	68	12 oz., raw	1.10	22 to 25
				10 oz., raw	.92	27 to 30
Veal rack (double, trimmed,	306	Veal chops	60	10 oz., raw	1.08	9 to 11
10 to 12 lb.)				8 oz., raw	.86	12 to 14
		Roast loin	38	8 oz., cooked	1.32	7-½ to 9
				6 oz., cooked	.99	10 to 12
				4 oz., cooked	.66	15 to 18
Veal chuck (square cut, 8 to	309	Veal stew	68	12 oz., raw	1.10	7 to 10
12 lb.)				10 oz., raw	.92	8 to 13
				8 oz., raw	.74	10 to 16
		Roast shoulder	40	6 oz., cooked	.94	10 to 12
				4 oz., cooked	.63	14 to 16
Calves liver (3 to 5 lb.)	Fresh	Calves liver	85	6 oz., raw	.44	4 to 6
				4 oz., raw	.30	6 to 10
Sweetbreads (12 to 16 oz.	Frozen	Sweetbreads	50	6 oz., raw	1.00	1
a pair)				6 oz., raw	.75	1
Veal kidneys (4 to 5 oz.	Fresh	Veal kidneys	40	8 oz., raw	1.25	4 per serving
each)				6 oz., raw	.94	3 per serving
Lamb						
Lamb chuck (15 to 17 lb.)	206	Lamb stew	55	12 oz., raw	1.37	11 to 13
				10 oz., raw	1.14	13 to 15
				8 oz., raw	.91	16 to 18
Lamb rack (6 to 8 lb.)	204	Lamb chops	50	8 oz., raw	2.00	6 to 8
				6 oz., raw	.87	8 to 10
				4 oz., raw	.50	12 to 16
		Roast rack	45	8 oz., cooked	1.11	5 to 7
				6 oz., cooked	.83	7 to 9
				4 oz., cooked	.56	10 to 14
Lamb leg (16 to 18 lb.)	233	Roast leg	44	8 oz., cooked	1.14	14 to 16
				6 oz., cooked	.85	18 to 21
				4 oz., cooked	.57	28 to 31
Pork						
Ham (fresh, 12 to 14 lb.)	401	Baked ham	55	8 oz., cooked	.91	14
				6 oz., cooked	.68	19
		Ham steak	80	10 oz., raw	.78	16
				8 oz., raw	.62	21
Ham (pullman, 7 to 9 lb.)	Trade	Ham, ready to eat	85	8 oz., raw	.59	12 to 15
				6 oz., raw	.44	16 to 20
Prosciutto (bone in, 12 to	Trade	Hors d'oeuvres	50	4 oz., raw	.50	24 to 28
14 lb.)				2 oz., raw	.25	48 to 56

Table 1 (continued)

Wholesale Cut	IMPS Code Number	Entree	Yield Factor (percent)	Portion Factors		
				Size and State	Cost	Average Number of Servings
Shoulder (4 to 8 lb.)	404	Roast shoulder	40	8 oz., cooked	1.25	3 to 6
				6 oz., cooked	.94	4 to 8
				4 oz., cooked	.63	6 to 12
Pork loin (10 to 12 lb.)	411	Pork chops	82	8 oz., raw	.61	16 to 19
				6 oz., raw	.46	22 to 26
		Roast loin	50	8 oz., cooked	1.00	10 to 12
				6 oz., cooked	.75	13 to 16
				4 oz., cooked	.50	20 to 24
POULTRY						
Roasting chicken (3 to 4-½ lb.)	N.A.	Roast chicken	30	4 oz., cooked	.83	3 to 5
				3 oz., cooked	.75	4 to 7
				2-½ oz., cooked	.53	5 to 8
		Breast of chicken	—	11 oz., raw	1.43	—
				10 oz., raw	1.30	—
				9 oz., raw	1.17	—
		Chicken leg	—	11 oz., raw	.73	—
				10 oz., raw	.66	—
				9 oz., raw	.59	—
Fowl (5-½ to 6-½ lb.)	N.A.	Chicken pot pie	25	4 oz., cooked	1.00	5 to 6
				3 oz., cooked	.90	7 to 8
Turkey (22 to 26 lb.)	N.A.	Roast turkey or turkey salad	23	6 oz., cooked	1.63	13 to 16
				4 oz., cooked	1.08	20 to 24
				3 oz., cooked	.98	26 to 32
Duckling (4-½ to 5 lb.)	N.A.	Roast duckling	—	½ per serving	2.38	2
Broiling chicken	N.A.	Broiled or fried chicken	—	1 per serving	—	—
FISH						
Bass, sea (whole, 1 to 1-¼ lb.)	N.A.	Sea bass, fillet	48	8 oz., raw	1.04	1
				6 oz., raw	.78	1-½
Bass, striped (whole, 8 to 12 lb.)	N.A.	Striped bass, fillet	40	8 oz., raw	1.25	6 to 9
				6 oz., raw	.94	8 to 12
Bluefish (whole, 3 to 8 lb.)	N.A.	Bluefish, fillet	40	8 oz., raw	1.25	2-½ to 6
				6 oz., raw	.94	3 to 8-½
Codfish (whole, 5 to 8 lb.)	N.A.	Codfish, fillet	40	8 oz., raw	1.25	4-½ to 6
				6 oz., raw	.94	6 to 8-½
Flounder (whole, ¾ to 2 lb.)	N.A.	Flounder, fillet	33	8 oz., raw	1.52	½ to 1
				6 oz., raw	1.14	½ to 1-½
Haddock (whole, 3 to 8 lb.)	N.A.	Haddock, fillet	36	8 oz., raw	1.39	2 to 5-½
				6 oz., raw	1.04	3 to 7-½
Halibut (whole, 10 to 12 lb.)	N.A.	Halibut, fillet	55	8 oz., raw	.91	11 to 13
				6 oz., raw	.68	15 to 17
		Halibut, steak	81	8 oz., raw	.91	16 to 19
				6 oz., raw	.68	21 to 25
Mackerel (whole, 1 to 2 lb.)	N.A.	Mackerel, fillet	50	8 oz., raw	1.00	1 to 2
				6 oz., raw	.75	1 to 2-½
Pompano (whole, 1 to 1-¼ lb.)	N.A.	Pompano	40	8 oz., raw	1.25	1
				6 oz., raw	.94	1-¼
Red snapper (whole, 8 to 12 lb.)	N.A.	Red snapper, fillet	40	8 oz., raw	1.25	6 to 9
				6 oz., raw	.94	8 to 12
Salmon (head off, 8 to 12 lb.)	N.A.	Salmon, fillet	65	8 oz., raw	.77	10 to 15
				6 oz., raw	.58	14 to 20
		Salmon, steak	85	8 oz., raw	.59	13 to 20
				6 oz., raw	.44	18 to 27
Scrod (whole, 5 to 7 lb.)	N.A.	Scrod, fillet	40	8 oz., raw	1.25	4-½ to 5
				6 oz., raw	.94	6 to 6-½
Shad (fillet, ½ to 1 lb.)	N.A.	Shad, fillet	100	8 oz., raw	.50	1 to 2
				6 oz., raw	.37	1 to 2-½
Shad, roe (pair, 6 to 14 oz.)	N.A.	Shad roe	100	8 oz., raw	.50	1 to 1-½
				6 oz., raw	.37	1 to 2
Sole, English (whole, 1 to 2 lb.)	N.A.	Dover sole	100	1-½ lb., raw	1.50	1
				1 lb., raw	1.00	1
Swordfish (center cut)	N.A.	Swordfish, steak	90	8 oz., raw	.55	—
				6 oz., raw	.42	—
Whitefish (whole, 2 to 3 lb.)	N.A.	Whitefish, fillet	50	8 oz., raw	1.00	2 to 3
				6 oz., raw	.75	2½ to 4

Table 1 *(continued)*

Wholesale Cut	IMPS Code Number	Entree	Yield Factor (percent)	Portion Factors		
				Size and State	Cost	Average Number of Servings
SHELLFISH						
Clams, cherrystone (320 to 360 per bu.)	N.A.	Clams, fresh	95	6 per serving	.019	50 to 55
Clams, little neck (600 to 700 per bu.)	N.A.	Little neck clams	95	12 per serving	.019	48 to 55
				6 per serving	.009	95 to 110
Crab meat (1 lb. tin)	N.A.	Cocktail or entree	95	5 oz.	.33	3
				3 oz.	.24	5
Crab meat (frozen)	N.A.	Cocktail or entree	95	6 oz.	.39	2-½
				4 oz.	.26	4
Live lobster	N.A.	Whole lobster	100	2 lb., raw	2.00	—
				1-½ lb., raw	1.50	—
				1-¼ lb., raw	1.25	—
		Lobster cocktail or lobster meat	20	6 oz., cooked	1.87	—
				4 oz., cooked	1.25	—
				2 oz., cooked	.63	—
Lobster meat (fresh)	N.A.	Lobster cocktail or lobster meat	95	6 oz., cooked	.39	2-½
				4 oz., cooked	.26	4
				2 oz., cooked	.13	8
Lobster meat (frozen, 14 oz. can)	N.A.	Lobster meat	80	6 oz.	.47	2
				4 oz.	.31	3
Oysters, Chatham	N.A.	Oysters in half shell	95	12 per serving	.52	15 to 20
				6 per serving	.26	30 to 40
Scallops, Long Island (480 to 640 per gal.)	N.A.	Cape Cod scallops	100	24 per serving	.04	20 to 26
				18 per serving	.03	26 to 35
Scallops, sea (8 lb. per gal.)	N.A.	Sea scallops	95	6 oz., raw	.05	20
				5 oz., raw	.04	24
Shrimp (headless, frozen, 16 to 20 lb.)	N.A.	Shrimp cocktail or entree	—	10 per serving	.55	1-½ to 2
				7 per serving	.39	2 to 3
				5 per serving	.27	3 to 4

Note: N.A. indicates not applicable. Lines indicate that there is too much variation to be specific.

Table 2. Amounts of Foods for 50 Servings—For Institutional Food Service Operations

Food and Purchase Unit	Amount per Unit	Approximate Serving Size	Servings per Pound (AP)	Amount to Buy for 50 Servings	Comments
MEATS					
Beef					
Rib roast, rolled, boned, 7-rib	12 to 15 lbs.	2-½ to 3 oz. cooked (3-½ to 4-½ inch slice)	2-½ to 3	17 to 20 lbs.	May use sirloin butt, boned
Rib roast, standing, 7-rib	16 to 25 lbs.	3 to 3-½ oz. cooked	2 to 2-½	20 to 25 lbs.	
		4 to 5 oz. cooked	1-⅓ to 1-⅔	27 to 36 lbs.	
Chuck pot roast, bone-in, top	9 to 12 lbs.	3 to 3-½ oz. cooked	2 to 2-½	20 to 25 lbs.	
Chuck pot roast, bone-in, crossarm	6 to 9 lbs.	3 to 3-½ oz. cooked	2 to 2-½	20 to 25 lbs.	Top chuck is more tender
Round steak		4 to 4-½ oz. clear meat, un-cooked	2-½ to 3	17 to 20 lbs.	Bottom round requires longer cooking than top round
Stew, chuck and plate, clear meat		5 oz. stew	3 to 5	10 to 17 lbs.	Yield per lb. of raw meat depends on amount of vegetables added to stew
Lamb					
Leg roast	6 to 8 lbs.	2-½ to 3 oz. cooked (3-½ to 4-½ inch slice)	1-½ to 2-½	20 to 35 lbs.	Great variation is due to difficulty in carving
Shoulder roast, boneless	4 to 6 lbs.	2-½ to 3 oz. cooked (3-½ to 4-½ inch slice)	2-½ to 3	15 to 20 lbs.	
Stew, shoulder and brisket, clear meat		5 oz. stew	2-½ to 3	17 to 20 lbs.	Yield per lb. of raw meat depends on amount of vegetables added to stew
Pork					
Loin roast, trimmed	10 to 12 lbs.	2-½ to 3 oz. cooked (3-½ to 4-½ inch slice)	2 to 2-½	20 to 25 lbs.	
Ham					
Fresh, bone-in	12 to 15 lbs.	3 to 3-½ oz. cooked	2 to 2-½	20 to 25 lbs.	
Smoked, ten-derized, bone-in	12 to 15 lbs.	3 to 3-½ oz. cooked	2-½ to 3	17 to 20 lbs.	Smoked shoulder may be substituted for ground or cubed ham in recipes
Canned, boneless, ready-to-eat	2 to 9 lbs.	3 oz. cooked	4 to 5	10 to 12 lbs.	
Veal					
Leg roast	15 to 20 lbs.	3 to 3-½ oz. cooked	1-½ to 2-½	20 to 35 lbs.	Great variation is due to difficulty in carving
Shoulder roast, boneless	8 to 14 lbs.	3 to 3-½ oz. cooked	2-½ to 3	17 to 20 lbs.	
Cutlet		4 to 5 oz. uncooked	3 to 4	12 to 17 lbs.	May use frozen cutlets
Ground Meat					
Patties	1 lb. raw meat measures 2 C. packed	4 to 5 oz. uncooked (1 or 2 patties)	2-½ to 3	17 to 20 lbs.	May use one kind of meat only or combinations, such as 10 lbs. beef and 5 lbs. veal or pork, or 10 lbs. fresh pork and 5 lbs. smoked ham

Table 2 *(continued)*

Food and Purchase Unit	Amount per Unit	Approximate Serving Size	Servings per Pound (AP)	Amount to Buy for 50 Servings	Comments
Loaf or extended patties	1 lb. raw meat measures 2 C. packed	4 to 4-½ oz. cooked	3-½ to 4	12 to 15 lbs.	May use one kind of meat or a combination
Bacon					
Sliced	30 to 36 medium or 15 to 20 wide strips per lb.	3 strips	10 to 12	5 to 6 lbs.	1 lb. cooked and diced measures 1-½ C.
		2 strips	7 to 10	5 to 7 lbs.	
Canadian, sliced	12 to 16 slices per lb.	2 or 3 slices	5 to 8	7 to 10 lbs.	
Liver		4 oz. cooked	3 to 4	13 to 17 lbs.	
Sausage					
Links	8 to 9 large per lb.	3 links	3	17 to 20 lbs.	Yield varies with proportion of fat that fries out in cooking
Cakes		6 to 8 oz. raw (2 cakes)	2 to 2-½	20 to 25 lbs.	
Wieners	8 to 10 per lb.	2 wieners	4 to 5	10 to 11-½ lbs.	
POULTRY					
Chicken					
Fryers, dressed	2-½ to 3-½ lbs.	¼ fryer		35 to 40 lbs.	Dressed means bled and with feathers removed
Fryers, eviscerated	1-¾ to 2-½ lbs.	¼ fryer		25 to 30 lbs.	Eviscerated means ready to cook
Fowl					
For fricassee, dressed	3-½ to 6 lbs.	4 to 6 oz. bone-in	1 to 1-½	35 to 50 lbs.	
For fricassee, eviscerated	2-½ to 4-½ lbs.	4 to 6 oz. bone-in	1-¼ to 2	25 to 35 lbs.	
For dishes containing cut-up cooked meat, dressed		1 to 2 oz. clear meat	2-½ to 3	17 to 20 lbs.	4 lbs. raw yield about 1 lb. cooked boned meat
For dishes containing cut-up cooked meat, eviscerated		1 to 2 oz. clear meat	3 to 4	13 to 17 lbs.	3 lbs. raw yield about 1 lb. cooked boned meat
Turkey					
Young tom, dressed	12 to 23 lbs.	2 to 2-½ oz. clear meat	1 to 1-½	35 to 50 lbs.	1 lb. raw yields 4 to 5 oz. sliced clear meat or 5 to 6 oz. cooked boned meat
Young tom, eviscerated	10 to 18 lbs.	2 to 2-½ oz. clear meat	1-½ to 2	25 to 35 lbs.	Yields of all turkeys depend on type and size of bird: broad-breast and larger birds yield more than standard type and smaller birds
Old tom, dressed	20 to 30 lbs.	2 to 2-½ oz. clear meat	1 to 1-½	35 to 50 lbs.	
Old tom, eviscerated	16 to 25 lbs.	2 to 2-½ oz. clear meat	1-½ to 2	25 to 35 lbs.	

Table 2 *(continued)*

Food and Purchase Unit	Amount per Unit	Approximate Serving Size	Servings per Pound (AP)	Amount to Buy for 50 Servings	Comments
FISH					
Fresh or Frozen Fillets		4 to 5 oz.	3 to 4.	14 to 17 lbs.	
Oysters					
For frying	24 to 40 large per qt.	4 to 6 oysters		7 to 8 qts.	
For scalloping	60 to 100 small per qt.			4 to 5 qts.	
For stew	60 to 100 small per qt.	4 to 6 oysters		3 qts.	
VEGETABLES*					
Asparagus, by lb. or in bunches	2 to 2-½ lbs. per bunch; 32 to 40 stalks per bunch	3 oz. or 4 to 5 stalks	3 to 4	12 to 16 lbs.	Yield may be increased if tough part of stalk is peeled
Beans, green or wax, by lb.	1 lb. measures 1 qt. whole or 3 C. cut up	2-½ to 3 oz. or ½ C.	4 to 5	10 to 12 lbs.	
Beets					
by lb.	4 medium per lb. (1-½ to 2 C. cooked and diced)	2-½ to 3 oz. or ½ C.	4 to 4-½	12 to 14 lbs.	
by bunch	4 to 6 medium per bunch	2-½ to 3 oz. or ½ C.	4 to 4-½	12 to 14 lbs.	
Broccoli, by lb. or in bunches	1-½ to 2-½ lbs. per bunch	2-½ to 3 oz.	2-½ to 3	17 to 20 lbs.	Yield may be increased if tough part of stalk is peeled
Brussels sprouts, by qt. berry basket	1 to 1-¼ lbs. per basket	2-½ to 3 oz.	4 to 6	10 baskets or 12 lbs.	
Cabbage, by lb.					
Raw	4 to 6 C. shredded per lb.	1 to 2 oz.	8	8 to 10 lbs.	
Cooked	2 qts. raw shredded per lb.	2-½ to 3 oz. or ½ C.	4	12 to 15 lbs.	
Carrots, by lb.					
Cooked	6 medium per lb.	2-½ to 3 oz. or ½ C.	3 to 4	14 to 16 lbs.	1 lb. raw yields 2 C. cooked and diced; after cooking, 3-¼ C. diced weigh 1 lb.
Raw		strips, 2 to 3 inches long		2 to 2-½ lbs.	3-½ C. diced raw weigh 1 lb.
Cauliflower, by head, trimmed	1 to 3 lbs. per head	3 oz. or ½ C	2	28 to 32 lbs.	A 3-lb. head yields 3 qts. raw flowerets
Celery, pascal, by bunch					
Cooked	1 medium bunch weighs 2 lbs.	2-½ to 3 oz. or ½ C.	3 to 4	7 to 10 bunches	1 medium bunch yields 1-½ qts. raw diced
Raw	1 medium bunch weighs 2 lbs.		8 to 10	3 to 4 bunches	1 qt. raw diced weighs 1 lb.
Cucumbers, single	1 cucumber weighs 10 to 14 oz.	5 to 7 slices (¼C.)		8 to 9 cucumbers	1 medium yields 1-¾ to 2 C. of peeled slices

Table 2 *(continued)*

Food and Purchase Unit	Amount per Unit	Approximate Serving Size	Servings per Pound (AP)	Amount to Buy for 50 Servings	Comments
Eggplant, single or by dozen	1 small eggplant weighs 1 lb.	2-½ oz. (1-½ slices)	4	10 to 12	A 1-lb. eggplant yields 8 to 9 slices
Lettuce, by head	1 medium head weighs 1-½ to 2-½ lbs. before trimming	⅙ to ⅛ head		4 to 5 heads for garnish; 6 to 8 heads for salad	10 to 12 salad leaves per head; 1 head untrimmed yields 1-½ to 2 qts. shredded; 2 qts. shredded weigh 1 lb.
Mushrooms, by lb. or basket	1 basket weighs 3 lbs.				1 lb. raw sliced tops and stems measures 7 C.; 2-½ C. sautéed weigh 1 lb.
Onions, by lb.	4 to 6 medium per lb.	3 to 3-½ oz. or ½ C.	3 to 4	14 to 16 lbs.	1 lb. yields 2-½ to 3 C. chopped; 1 C. chopped weighs 5 oz.; 1 C. sliced weighs 4 oz.
Parsley, by bunch	1 bunch weighs 1 oz.				1 medium bunch yields ¼ C. finely chopped; 1 C. chopped weighs 3 oz.
Parsnips, by lb.	3 to 4 medium per lb.	2-½ to 3 oz.	3 to 4	15 lbs.	
Peppers, single or by lb.	5 to 7 per lb.				1 lb. yields 2 C. finely diced; 1 C. chopped weighs 5 oz.
Potatoes, sweet, by lb.	3 medium per lb.	3-½ to 4 oz.	2-½ to 3	17 to 20 lbs.	
Potatoes, white by lb.	3 medium per lb.	4 to 4-½ oz. or ½ C. mashed or creamed	2 to 3	15 to 20 lbs.	1 lb. yields 2-¼ C. diced
by bushel	1 bu. weighs 60 lbs.	4 to 4-½ oz. or ½ C.	2 to 3		
by bag	1 bag weighs 50 lbs.	4 to 4-½ oz. or ½ C.	2 to 3		
Rutabagas, by lb.	1 to 2 per lb.	3 to 3-½ oz. or ½ C.	2 to 2-½	20 to 25 lbs.	1 lb. yields 1-½ C. mashed or 2-½ C. diced
Spinach, by bag or bushel	10 or 20 oz. per bag	3 to 3-½ oz. or ½ C.	2-½ to 3	17 to 20 lbs. home-grown or 12 to 15 10-oz. bags cleaned	A 10 oz. bag yields 2 qts. raw, coarsely chopped for salad
Squash Summer, by lb.		2-½ to 3 oz. or ½ C.	3 to 4	13 to 16 lbs.	
Winter, by lb.		3 oz. or ½ C. mashed	2	25 to 30 lbs.	
Tomatoes, by lb., 8 lb. basket, or 10-lb. carton	3 to 4 medium per lb.	3 slices raw	5 (sliced)	10 lbs. for slicing	1 lb. yields 2 C. diced or cut in wedges
Turnips, white, by lb.		3 oz. or ½ C.	3 to 4	15 to 20 lbs.	

FRUITS*

Apples by lb.	2 to 3 medium per lb.	½ C. sauce		15 to 20 lbs. for sauce or pie	1 lb. before peeling yields 3 C. diced or sliced; 4-½ to 5 C. pared, diced, or sliced weigh 1 lb.
by pk.	1 pk. weighs 12 lbs.	½ C. sauce		15 to 20 lbs.	1 pk. (12 lbs.) makes 4 to 5 pies, 4 to 5 qts. of sauce, 7 to 8 qts. of raw cubes

Table 2 *(continued)*

Food and Purchase Unit	Amount per Unit	Approximate Serving Size	Servings per Pound (AP)	Amount to Buy for 50 Servings	Comments
Apples (continued)					
by bu.	1 bu. weighs 48 lbs.	½ C. sauce		15 to 20 lbs.	
by box	1 box contains 80 to 100 large or 113 to 138 medium	½ C. sauce		15 to 20 lbs.	
Bananas, by lb. or dozen	3 to 4 medium per lb.	1 small	3 to 4	15 lbs.	1 lb. yields 2 to 2-½ C. sliced thin or 1-¼ C. mashed; for 1 C. sliced or diced, use 1-⅓ medium; for 1 C. mashed, use 2-¼ medium
Cranberries, by lb.	1 lb. measures 1 to 1-¼ qts.	¼ C. sauce	12 to 14 for sauce	4 lbs. for sauce	1 lb. makes 3 to 3-½ C. sauce or 2-¾ C. jelly
Grapefruit, by dozen, box, or half-box	54 to 70 medium per box; 80 to 126 small per box				1 medium-small yields 10 to 12 sections or 1-¾ C. broken sections
Lemons, by dozen, box, or half-box	210 to 250 large per box; 300 to 360 medium per box; 392 to 432 small per box			25 to 30 lemons (1-¼ qts. juice) for 50 glasses of lemonade	1 medium yields ¼ C. juice and 1 t. grated rind; 4 to 5 medium yield 1 C. juice
Oranges, by dozen, box, or half-box	80 to 126 large per box; 150 to 200 medium per box; 216 to 288 small per box	½ C. sections		40 to 50 oranges	Use medium oranges for table and salad; 1 medium yields 12 sections and ½ to ⅔ C. diced
Peaches					
by lb.	3 to 5 per lb.	3 oz. or ½ C.	4	10 to 12 lbs. for slicing	1 lb. yields 2 C. peeled and diced
by pk.	1 pk. weighs 12-½ lbs.	3 oz. or ½ C.	4		
by ½ bu.	½ bu. weighs 25 lbs.	3 oz. or ½ C.	4		
Pineapple, single	1 medium weighs 2 lbs.	½ C. cubed		5 medium	1 medium yields 3 to 3-½ C. peeled and cubed
Rhubarb, fresh, by lb.		½ C. sauce	5	10 lbs.	10 lbs. yield 6 qts. sauce
Strawberries, by qt.	1 qt. yields 3 C. hulled	½ C.		10 to 13 qts.	1 qt. yields 4 to 5 servings of fruit
	1 qt. yields 1 pt. hulled and crushed	⅓ C. for shortcake		8 to 10 qts.	1 qt. yields 6 servings of sauce for shortcake
STAPLES*					
Cocoa	1 lb. measures 4 C.; 1 C. weighs 4 oz.			2 C. (½ lb.) for 50 C. beverage (2-½ gals.)	
Rice	1 lb. raw measures 2-⅛ C.	1 no. 16 or no. 12 scoop	15 to 20	2-½ to 3 lbs.	1 lb. cooked measures 1-¾ qts.
Sugar					
Cubes	50 to 60 large or 100 to 120 small cubes per lb.	1 large or 2 small	50 to 60	¾ to 1 lb.	
Granulated	1 lb. measures 2-⅛ C.; 1 C. weighs 7 oz.	1-½ t. to sweeten coffee	50 to 60	¾ to 1 lb.	

Table 2 *(continued)*

Food and Purchase Unit	Amount per Unit	Approximate Serving Size	Servings per Pound (AP)	Amount to Buy for 50 Servings	Comments
Bread, by loaf					
White and whole wheat	1-lb. loaf yields 18 slices	1-½ slices to accompany meal	12	4 loaves	
	2-lb. club loaf yields 24 slices	1-½ slices	8	3 loaves	
	2-lb. Pullman (sandwich) loaf yields 36 slices	1-½ slices	12	2 loaves	
Rye	1-lb. loaf yields 17 slices	1-½ slices	11	4-½ loaves	
	2-lb. short loaf yields 29 slices	1-½ slices	10	5 loaves	
	2-lb. long loaf yields 36 slices	1-½ slices	12	2 loaves	
Butter	1 lb. measures 2 C.; 1 oz. measures 2 T.		48 to 60	1 to 1-½ lbs.	Available in wholesale units cut into 48 to 90 pieces per lb.; 60 count gives average size cut
Cheese					
Brick	1 brick weighs 5 lbs.	1-oz. thin slices for sandwiches	16	3-¼ lbs. for sandwiches	
		4/5-oz. cubes for pie	20	2-½ lbs. for pie	
Cottage	1 lb. measures 2C.	no. 10 scoop (approximately ½ C.)	8 to 9	6 lbs.	1 lb. yields 12 to 13 of the no. 16 scoops and 25 of the no. 30 scoops
Coffee					
Ground	1 lb. drip grind measures 5 C.			1 lb.	Makes 50 C. when added to 2-½ gals. of water
Instant				2-½ C.	Add to 2-½ gals. of water
Cream					
Heavy (40 percent) to whip		1 rounded T.		1 pt. (yields 1 qt. whipped)	Doubles its volume in whipping
Light (20 percent) or top milk for coffee	1 qt. yields 64 T.	1-½ T.		1-¼ qts.	
Fruit or vegetable juice	1 46-oz. can measures approximately 1-½ qts.	4-oz. glass or ½ C.		4-⅓ 46-oz. cans (6-½ qts.)	
	1 no. 10 can measures 13 C. or 3-¼ qts.	4-oz. glass or ½ C.		2 no. 10 cans (6-½ qts.)	
Fruits, dried					
Prunes	1 lb. contains 40 to 50 medium	4 to 5 for stewed fruit		5 to 6 lbs.	
Honey	1 lb. measures 1-⅓ C.	2 T.		5 lbs.	
Ice cream					
Brick	1-qt. brick cuts 6 to 8 slices	1 slice		7 to 9 bricks	Available in slices individually wrapped
Bulk, by gals.		no. 10 scoop		2 gals.	1 gal. yields 25 to 30 servings
Lemonade		8-oz. glass (¾ C.)		2-½ gals. (25 to 30 lemons for 1-¼ qts. of juice)	
Peanut butter	1 lb. measures 1-¾ C.			4 lbs. for sandwiches	
Potato chips	1 lb. measures 5 qts.	¾ to 1 oz.		2 lbs.	

Table 2 (continued)

Food and Purchase Unit	Amount per Unit	Approximate Serving Size	Servings per Pound (AP)	Amount to Buy for 50 Servings	Comments
Salad dressings					
Mayonnaise, by qt.		1 T. for salad		1 to 1-½ qts. for mixed salads; 3 to 4 C. for garnish	
French				¾ to 1 qt.	
Sandwiches					
Bread	2 lb. (14-in.) loaf cut 30 to 35 medium or 35 to 40 very thin slices	2 slices	7 to 8 medium; 9 to 10 very thin	3 loaves	
Butter, by lb.		spread on 1 slice		¾ lb.	
		spread on 2 slices		1-½ lbs.	
Fillings		2 T. or no. 30 scoop		1-¾ to 2 qts.	
		3 T. or no. 24 scoop		2-½ to 3 qts.	
Tea, iced	1 lb. measures 6 C.			3 oz.	Makes 50 glasses when added to 2-½ gals. water and chipped ice
Vegetables, dried					
Beans, navy	1 lb. measures 2-½ C.			5 to 6 lbs.	

Source: Marion Wood Crosby and Katharine W. Harris, *Purchasing Food for 50 Servings,* rev. ed., Cornell Extension Bulletin no. 803 (Ithaca: New York State College of Home Economics. 1963). Reprinted by permission of the Cornell Cooperative Extension.

Note: Can be used for hotel and restaurant food service.

Table 3. Summary of Federal Standards for Grading Meats, Poultry, Fish and Shellfish, Eggs, Dairy Products, Fruits, and Vegetables

MEATS

Beef

USDA grade	Steers and heifers	Cows	Bullock (young bull under 18 months of age)	Bull or stag (old bulls graded only for yield)
Prime	X	—	X	—
Choice	X	X	X	X
Good	X	X	X	X
Standard	X	X	X	—
Commercial	X	X	—	X
Utility	X	X	X	X
Cutter	X	X	—	X
Canner	X	X	—	X

Grading considerations:	Quality grades				
	Prime	Choice	Good	Standard	Commercial
Quality factors					
Texture of meat	Very smooth	Fairly smooth	Slightly smooth	Slightly ropey	Ropey
Firmness of flesh	Very firm	Quite firm	Firm	Slightly firm	Soft
Marbling and fat	Abundant	Medium abundant	Moderate	Slight	Traces
Color of flesh	Bright cherry red	Medium cherry red	Red	Bluish red	Dark bluish red
Age (condition of bone, 1-½ to 3 years)	1	2	3	4	5
Buttons (feather bones)	Large, soft decreasing to hard, small.				

YIELD GRADES (ratio of usable meat to total carcas weight)

Quality grades	Yield grades				
	Most usable 1	2	3	4	Least usable 5
Prime	—	X	X	X	X
Choice	X	X	X	X	—
Good	X	X	X	—	—
Utility	X	X	—	—	—
Cull	X	X	—	—	—

Veal

USDA grade	Calf	Veal (under 3 months of age)
Prime	X	X
Choice	X	X
Good	X	X
Standard	X	X
Utility	X	X
Cull	X	X

No yield grades for veal.

Lamb

USDA grade	Lamb (under 1 year old)	Yearling 1 to 1-¼ year old	Mutton (over 1-¼ year old)
Prime	X	X	—
Choice	X	X	X
Good	X	X	X
Utility	X	X	X
Cull	X	X	X

Quality grade	Yield grades				
	Most usable 1	2	3	4	Least usable 5
Prime	—	X	X	X	X
Choice	—	X	X	X	X
Good	X	X	X	X	X
Utility	X	X	X	X	X

Table 3 (continued)

Pork

USDA grade	Barrow	Gilt	Stag	Boar
Fresh				
No. 1	X	X	—	—
No. 2	X	X	X	X
No. 3	X	X	X	X
No. 4	X	X	X	X
Utility	X	X	X	X
Smoked (hams, bacon, picnics, loins, Canadian-type bacon)				
No. 1	N.A.	N.A.	N.A.	N.A.
No. 2	N.A.	N.A.	N.A.	N.A.
No yield grades for pork.				

POULTRY
(includes chickens, turkeys, ducks, geese, guinea fowl, and squab pigeons)

USDA grades for ready to cook carcasses	USDA grades for wholesale market
A	Extra
B	Standard
C	Trade

Grading considerations:
  Physical condition (edible)
  Properly cleaned (inside and out)
  Fleshing (full)
  Conformation (no abnormalities)
  Fat (well covered)
  Pinfeathers (free)
  No defects (broken bones, skin tears, freezer burns)

FISH AND SHELLFISH

USDA grades for fresh fish
  A
  B
  Substandard (SS)

Standards for classification as to:

Source (all fish and shellfish marketed in the United States must come from waters approved by the U.S. Health Department)
  Salt water
  Fresh water
  Fresh and salt water
  Cultivated or farm fish

Condition
  Fresh
  Frozen
  Canned
  Dried
  Processed

Market form (fresh fish)
  Whole or round (as caught)
  Drawn (eviscerated and scaled)
  Dressed (eviscerated, head, tail, fins off)
  Steaks (cross sections of dressed fish)
  Fillets (flesh cut lengthwise off back bone)
  Chunks (pieces of drawn or dressed fish)
  Sticks (fillets cut into pieces)

EGGS

USDA grades for fresh shell eggs
  AA (fresh, fancy)
  A
  B (all eggs below this grade are sold to processors)

Table 3 *(continued)*

Fresh shell eggs

	Weight	
Size	Minimum net weight per dozen (ounces)	Gross weight per case (including 4-pound allowance for carton) (pound)
Jumbo	30	60
Extra large	27	54
Large	24	49
Medium	21	43
Small	18	38
Peewee	15	28

Classification of eggs:
  Fresh shell (under 29 days old)
  Storage shell (over 29 days old)
  Processed storage (shell oiled before storage)
  Frozen—mixed whole
          —whites only
          —yolks, plain
          —yolks, sugar added (9:1)
  Dried—freeze-dried
        —dehydrated

DAIRY PRODUCTS

Butter
USDA grades

  AA
  A
  C
  Cooking (CC)

Classification of butter:
  Sweet cream (made only from sweet cream)
  Sweet (contains no salt, but can be made from sour cream)
  Creamery (factory made from milk and cream from many sources)
  Salted (contains salt, also called lightly salted butter)
  Farm (generally made on a farm and often unpasteurized)
  Sour cream (made from naturally soured cream)

Milk (all milk products must conform to state and federal standards for pasteurization, addition of vitamins, and coliform and bacteria counts)
Classification of milk:
  Fresh, whole (contains a minimum of 3-¼ percent milk fat and 8-¼ percent nonfat milk solids)
  Homogenized
  Pasteurized
  Nonfat
  Buttermilk
  Acidophilus
  Dried
  Cream
    Light (contains 16 to 18 percent milk fat)
    Table (contains 20 to 30 percent milk fat)
    Whipping—light contains 30 to 34 percent milk fat
            —heavy contains 34 to 40 percent milk fat
    Half and half (mixture of milk and light cream, about 10 percent milk fat)

Table 3 (continued)

Ice Cream and Frozen Desserts

Government standards	Product				
	Vanilla ice cream	Flavored ice cream	Ice milk	Sherbet	Ices
Minimum percent milk fat	10	8	2	1	0
Minimum percent milk solids	20	16	11	2	0
Minimum weight per gallon (in pounds)	4.5	4.5	4.5	6	6
Percentage of overrun	80 to 100	80 to 100	80 to 100	35 to 40	25 to 30

FRUITS

Fresh	USDA grades at the wholesale level
Apples	Extra Fancy, Fancy, No. 1, No. 1 Cookers, No. 1 Early, Utility
Apricots	No. 1, No. 2
Avocados, Florida	No. 1, Combination
Cantaloupes	No. 1, Commercial
Cherries, sweet	No. 1, Commercial
Cranberries	Grade A (Consumer grade)
Dewberries and blackberries	No. 1, No. 2
Grapes, American bunch	
Grapes, European, sawdust pack	Fancy, Extra No. 1, No. 1
Grapes, table	Fancy No. 1
Grapefruit (California and Arizona)	Fancy No. 1, No. 2, Combination, No. 3
Grapefruit (Florida)	Fancy, No. 1, No. 1 Bright, No. 1 Golden, No. 1 Bronze, No. 1 Russet, No. 2, No. 2 Bright, No. 2 Russet, No. 3
Grapefruit (Texas)	Fancy, No. 1, No. 1 Bright, No. 1 Bronze, Combination No. 2, No. 2 Russet, No. 3
Honeydew and honeyball melon	No. 1, Commercial, No. 2
Lemons	No. 1, Combination, No. 2
Limes (Persian), Tahiti	No. 1, Combination, No. 2
Nectarines	Fancy, Extra No. 1, No. 1, No. 2
Oranges (California and Arizona)	Fancy, No. 1, Combination, No. 2
Oranges and tangelos (Florida)	Fancy, No. 1 Bright, No. 1, No. 1 Golden, No. 1 Bronze, No. 1 Russet, No. 2 Bright, No. 2, No. 2 Russet, No. 5
Oranges (Texas)	Fancy, No. 1, No. 1 Bright, No. 1 Bronze, Combination No. 2, No. 2 Russet, No. 3
Peaches	No. 1, No. 2
Pears, summer and fall	No. 1, Combination, No. 2
Pears, winter	Extra No. 1, No. 1, Combination, No. 2
Pineapples	Fancy, No. 1, No. 2
Plums and prunes	Fancy, No. 1, Combination, No. 2
Rhubarb	No. 1, No. 2
Strawberries and raspberries	No. 1, No. 2
Tangerines	Fancy, No. 1, No. 1 Bronze, No. 1 Russet, No. 2, No. 2 Russet, No. 3
Watermelon	No. 1, Commercial, No. 2

Processed	USDA grades	Trade grades
Canned and frozen	A or Fancy B or Choice C or Standard Below U.S. Standard (water packed)	
Dried	A or Fancy B or Choice C or Standard	Good Reasonably good Fairly good

Table 3 (continued)

VEGETABLES	
Fresh	USDA grades at the wholesale level
Artichokes, globe	No. 1, No. 2
Asparagus	No. 1, No. 2 (Washington No. 1, Washington No. 2 are more used in the markets)
Beans, lima	No. 1, Combination No. 2
Beans, snap	Fancy, No. 1, Combination, No. 2
Beets	No. 1, No. 2
Beet greens	No. 1
Broccoli, Italian sprouting	Fancy, No. 1, No. 2
Brussels sprouts	No. 1, No. 2
Cabbage	No. 1, Commercial
Carrots, bunched	No. 1, Commercial
Carrots, topped	Extra No. 1, No. 1, No. 2
Carrots, short-trimmed tops	No. 1, Commercial
Cauliflower	No. 1
Celery	Extra No. 1, No. 1, No. 2
Collard or broccoli greens	No. 1
Corn, green	Fancy, No. 1, No. 2
Cucumbers	No. 1, No. 1 large, No. 2
Cucumbers, greenhouse	Fancy, No. 1, No. 2
Dandelion greens	No. 1
Eggplant	Fancy, No. 1, No. 2
Endive, escarole, chicory	No. 1
Garlic	No. 1
Kale	No. 1, Commercial
Lettuce	No. 1, No. 2
Lettuce, greenhouse leaf	Fancy, No. 1
Mushrooms	No. 1
Mustard greens and Turnip greens	No. 1
Okra	No. 1
Onions, Bermuda, Granex	No. 1, No. 2, Commercial
Onions, Creole	No. 1, No. 2, Combination
Onions, northern grown	No. 1, No. 1 Boilers, No. 1 Picklers, Commercial No. 2
Onions, green	No. 1, No. 2
Parsley	No. 1
Parsnips	No. 1, No. 2
Peas, fresh	Fancy, No. 1
Peppers, sweet	No. 1, No. 2
Potatoes	Fancy, Extra No. 1, No. 1, No. 2, Commercial
Potatoes sweet	Extra No. 1, No. 1, Commercial, No. 2
Radishes	No. 1, Commercial
Romaine	No. 1
Rutabagas or turnips	No. 1, No. 2
Shallots, bunched	No. 1, No. 2
Spinach, fresh	Extra No. 1, No. 1, Commercial
Squash, fall and winter type	No. 1, No. 2
Squash, summer	No. 1, No. 2
Tomatoes, fresh	No. 1, Combination, No. 2
Tomatoes, greenhouse	Fancy, No. 1, No. 2

Processed	USDA grades	Trade grades
Canned and frozen	A or Fancy	
	B or Extra Standard	
	C or Standard	
	Below U.S. Standard (water packed)	
Dried	A or Fancy	Good
	B or Choice	Reasonably good
	C or Standard	Fairly good

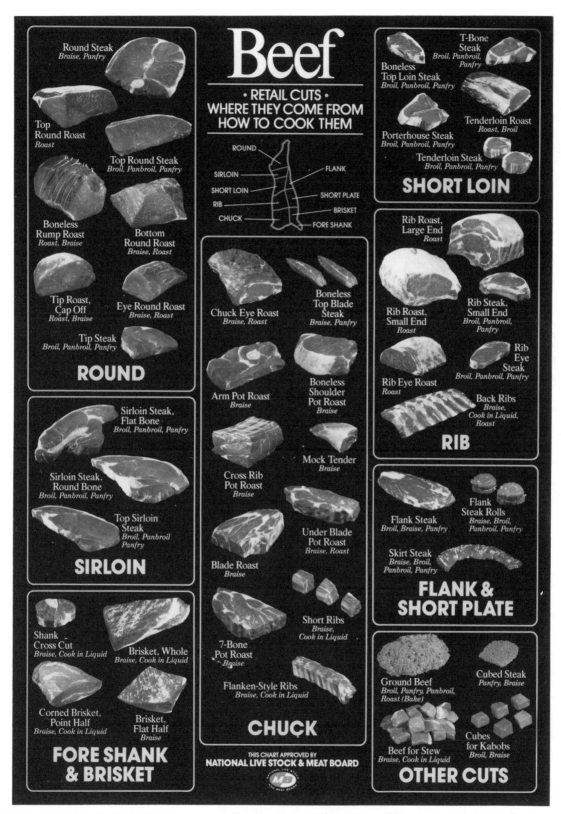

Figure 1. Chart of the Primal and Retail Cuts from Beef Animals, Indicating the Acceptable Preparation Methods. (Courtesy of the National Association of Meat Purveyors. This exhibit is copyrighted by the National Association of Meat Purveyors (NAMP) and may be reproduced only with the express permission of the NAMP.)

Figure 2. Chart of the Retail Cuts of Veal. Since the vealer is a young beef animal, the bone configuration and cuts are the same as those of beef, although flesh color, taste, fat covering, and use of the meat differ.

(Courtesy of the National Association of Meat Purveyors. This exhibit is copyrighted by the National Association of Meat Purveyors (NAMP) and may be reproduced only with the express permission of the NAMP.)

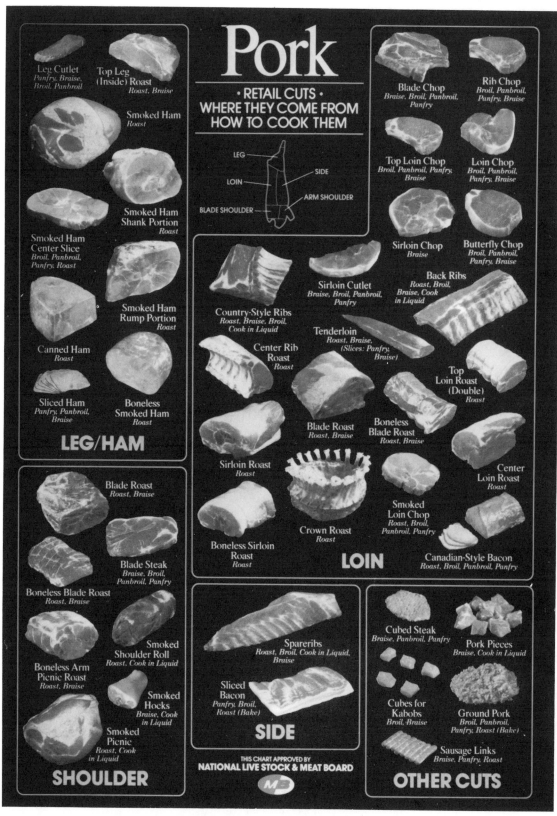

Pork
• RETAIL CUTS •
WHERE THEY COME FROM
HOW TO COOK THEM

LEG
SIDE
LOIN
ARM SHOULDER
BLADE SHOULDER

LEG/HAM

Leg Cutlet
Panfry, Braise, Broil, Panbroil

Top Leg (Inside) Roast
Roast, Braise

Smoked Ham
Roast

Smoked Ham Shank Portion
Roast

Smoked Ham Center Slice
Broil, Panbroil, Panfry, Roast

Smoked Ham Rump Portion
Roast

Canned Ham
Roast

Sliced Ham
Panfry, Panbroil, Braise

Boneless Smoked Ham
Roast

SHOULDER

Blade Roast
Roast, Braise

Blade Steak
Braise, Broil, Panbroil, Panfry

Boneless Blade Roast
Roast, Braise

Smoked Shoulder Roll
Roast, Cook in Liquid

Boneless Arm Picnic Roast
Roast, Braise

Smoked Hocks
Braise, Cook in Liquid

Smoked Picnic
Roast, Cook in Liquid

LOIN

Blade Chop
Braise, Broil, Panbroil, Panfry

Rib Chop
Broil, Panbroil, Panfry, Braise

Top Loin Chop
Broil, Panbroil, Panfry, Braise

Loin Chop
Broil, Panbroil, Panfry, Braise

Sirloin Chop
Braise

Butterfly Chop
Broil, Panbroil, Panfry, Braise

Sirloin Cutlet
Braise, Broil, Panbroil, Panfry

Back Ribs
Roast, Broil, Braise, Cook in Liquid

Country-Style Ribs
Roast, Braise, Broil, Cook in Liquid

Tenderloin
Roast, Braise, (Slices: Panfry, Braise)

Center Rib Roast
Roast

Top Loin Roast (Double)
Roast

Blade Roast
Roast, Braise

Boneless Blade Roast
Roast, Braise

Sirloin Roast
Roast

Crown Roast
Roast

Center Loin Roast
Roast

Smoked Loin Chop
Roast, Broil, Panbroil, Panfry

Boneless Sirloin Roast
Roast

Canadian-Style Bacon
Roast, Broil, Panbroil, Panfry

SIDE

Spareribs
Roast, Broil, Cook in Liquid, Braise

Sliced Bacon
Panfry, Broil, Roast (Bake)

OTHER CUTS

Cubed Steak
Braise, Panbroil, Panfry

Pork Pieces
Braise, Cook in Liquid

Cubes for Kabobs
Broil, Braise

Ground Pork
Broil, Panbroil, Panfry, Roast (Bake)

Sausage Links
Braise, Panfry, Roast

THIS CHART APPROVED BY
NATIONAL LIVE STOCK & MEAT BOARD

Figure 3. Chart of the Retail Cuts from Pork Animals and Their Preparation Methods.
(Courtesy of the National Association of Meat Purveyors. This exhibit is copyrighted by the National Association of Meat Purveyors (NAMP) and may be reproduced only with the express permission of the NAMP.)

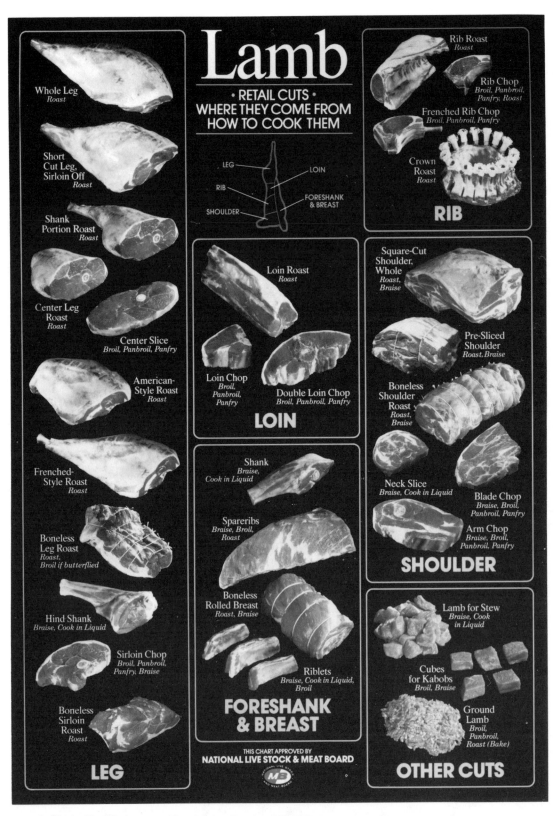

Figure 4. Chart of the Wholesale and Retail Cuts of Lamb and Their Preparation Methods.
(Courtesy of the National Association of Meat Purveyors. This exhibit is copyrighted by the National Association of Meat Purveyors (NAMP) and may be reproduced only with the express permission of the NAMP.)

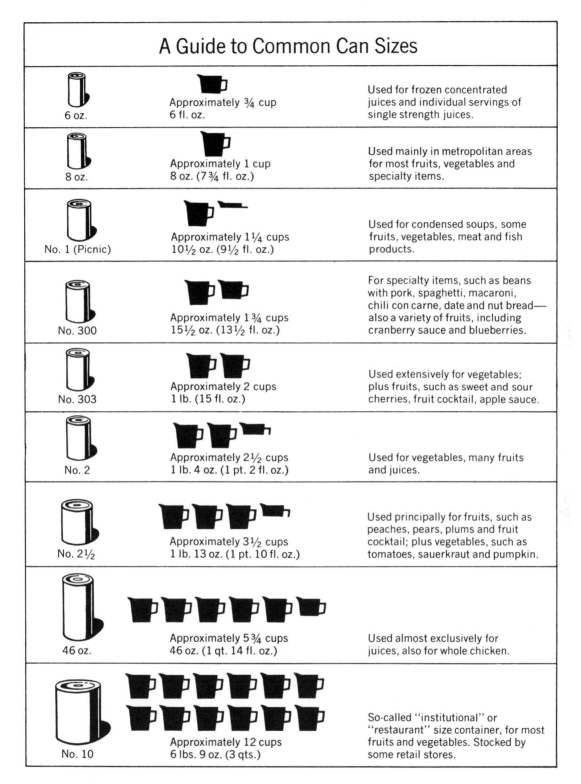

A Guide to Common Can Sizes

6 oz.	Approximately ¾ cup 6 fl. oz.	Used for frozen concentrated juices and individual servings of single strength juices.
8 oz.	Approximately 1 cup 8 oz. (7¾ fl. oz.)	Used mainly in metropolitan areas for most fruits, vegetables and specialty items.
No. 1 (Picnic)	Approximately 1¼ cups 10½ oz. (9½ fl. oz.)	Used for condensed soups, some fruits, vegetables, meat and fish products.
No. 300	Approximately 1¾ cups 15½ oz. (13½ fl. oz.)	For specialty items, such as beans with pork, spaghetti, macaroni, chili con carne, date and nut bread—also a variety of fruits, including cranberry sauce and blueberries.
No. 303	Approximately 2 cups 1 lb. (15 fl. oz.)	Used extensively for vegetables; plus fruits, such as sweet and sour cherries, fruit cocktail, apple sauce.
No. 2	Approximately 2½ cups 1 lb. 4 oz. (1 pt. 2 fl. oz.)	Used for vegetables, many fruits and juices.
No. 2½	Approximately 3½ cups 1 lb. 13 oz. (1 pt. 10 fl. oz.)	Used principally for fruits, such as peaches, pears, plums and fruit cocktail; plus vegetables, such as tomatoes, sauerkraut and pumpkin.
46 oz.	Approximately 5¾ cups 46 oz. (1 qt. 14 fl. oz.)	Used almost exclusively for juices, also for whole chicken.
No. 10	Approximately 12 cups 6 lbs. 9 oz. (3 qts.)	So-called "institutional" or "restaurant" size container, for most fruits and vegetables. Stocked by some retail stores.

Figure 5.   Average Container Sizes. One No. 10 Can Can Equals Two No. 5 Cans, Two 46-Ounce Cans. Four No. 2 1/2 Cans, or Five No. 2 Cans. (Courtesy of American Can Company, Greenwich, Connecticut.)

456 APPENDIX I

Table 4. Approximate Quantities Required for Some Common Fruits and Vegetables

Item	Shipping Container	Approximate Net Weight in Pounds, as Purchased per Container	Miscellaneous Shipping or Portioning Data	Portion Size as Served	Portions per Pound as Purchased	Approximate Amount to Purchase as Purchased for 100 Portions
FRUITS						
Apples, whole	Western box, 113's	44		1 each	2.3	44 lbs. (1 box)
Apples, baked	Western box, 88's	44		1 each	1.8	55 lbs. (1-¼ box)
Apples, for pies	Bu. basket	48	20 pies per bu.; 2-½ lbs. used per 9-in. pie	1 pie slice[a]	2.5	40 lbs.
Apples, rings	Western box, 113's	44	5 rings per apple	2 rings	6.7	15 lbs. (⅓ box)
Apple salad, Waldorf	Western box, 113's	44	15 slices per apple	½ C. diced	4.5	22 lbs. (½ box)
Apple slices, small	Western box, 113's	44	16 to 20 qts. per bu.	3 slices	14.0	7-½ lbs. (20 apples)
Applesauce	Bu. basket	48	8 to 12 per lb.	½ C.	2.8	36 lbs. (¾ bu.)
Apricots, whole	Till, 60's	5		2 each	5.0	20 lbs. (4 till)
Apricots, whole	Los Angeles lug	20	100 apricots per lug	2 each	2.5	40 lbs. (2 lugs)
Avocados, half	Flat, 18's	13	30 slices per avocado used in grapefruit salad	half	2.0	52 lbs. (4 flats)
Avocados, sliced	Flat, 24's	13		4 slices	25.0	4 lbs. (8 avocados)
Bananas, whole	Box	40	3 per lb.	1 each	3.0	33 lbs. (.8 box)
Bananas, sliced	Box	40	2 to 2-½ C. per lb. or 30 slices per banana	½ C.	4.0	25 lbs.
Blackberries	Crate, 24 qts.	30	(use 1 qt. per pie for pies)	½ C. with cream	6.0	17 lbs. (13 boxes)
Blueberries, for pies	Crate, 12 qts.	8	¾ qt. per 9-in. pie	1 pie slice[a]	7.0	15 lbs. (24 pts.)
Blueberries, pudding	Crate, 24 qts.	30		½ C.	12.1	8-¼ lbs. (6-½ qts.)
Cherries, sweet, whole	Lug	15		12 cherries	5.0	20 lbs. (1-⅓ lug)
Cherries, sour, pie	Bushel	54	1-¼ qt. per 9-in. pie	1 pie slice[a]	3.3	33 lbs. (⅔ bu.)
Cranberries, sauce	Box	25	Cooked sauce	¼ C.	3.5	7-½ lbs.
Cranberries, sauce	Box	25	Chopped raw	½ C.	6.0	17 lbs.
Figs	Flat, 48's	6		3 medium figs	2.8	36 lbs. (6 boxes)
Grapes, Concord, whole	Basket	6		¼ lb.	4.0	25 lbs. (4 baskets)
Grapes, European, whole	Box	28	70 grapes per lb.	½ C.	3.6	28 lbs. (1 box)
Grapefruit	⅘ bu. carton, 32's	40		Half	0.8	125 lbs. (3-⅛ boxes)
Grapefruit, sections	⅘ bu. carton, 32's	40	12 sections per grapefruit	6 sections (salad)	0.8	125 lbs. (3-⅛ boxes)
Grapefruit, juice	⅘ bu. carton, 40's	40	6-½ qts. juice per carton	4 oz.	1.3	80 lbs. (2 boxes)
Lemons, juice	⅘ bu. carton, 85's	38	For lemonade: 1 pt. juice per dozen; 8 qts. per carton	2 oz. juice	3.6	28 lbs. (12 doz.)
Lemons, slices	⅘ bu. carton, 85's	38	8 slices per lemon	1 slice	40.0	2-¼ lbs. (1 doz.)
Lemons, wedges	⅘ bu. carton, 85's	38	6 wedges per lemon	1 wedge	25.0	3-½ lbs. (1-½ doz.)
Limes, juice	Dozen		For limeade	1-¾ oz. (1 lime)		9 doz.
Limes, wedges	Dozen		4 to 5 wedges per lime	1 wedge		2 doz.
Melons						
Cantaloupe[b]	Crate, 45's	70 to 80		half	.8 to 1.0	90 lbs. (1.2 crates)
Cantaloupe, rings	Crate, 45's	70 to 80	8 rings per melon, each ring used to hold chopped fruit for salad	1 ring	4.0	22 lbs. (13 melons)
Cantaloupe, balls	Crate, 45's	70 to 80	30 balls per melon; used for melon ball cup	9 balls	1.8	51 lbs. (30 melons)

Item	Container	Servings	Notes	Serving		Weight
Cantaloupe, diced	Crate, 45's	70 to 80	10 oz. meat per melon	3 oz.	1.8	51 lbs. (30 melons)
Casaba, wedge^c	Crate, 8's	50		1/8 melon	1.3	82 lbs. (13 melons)
Watermelon, slice	Individual melon	35		1 lb.	1.0	100 lbs. (3 melons)
Nectarines, whole	Lug, 120's	20		2 whole	2.4	34 lbs. (1-2/3 lug)
Oranges, whole	Carton, 88's	38		1 whole	2.3	43 lbs. (8-1/3 doz.)
Oranges, juice	Carton, 88's	45	10-1/2 qts. per carton	4 oz.	2.2	55 lbs. (1-1/4 cartons)
Oranges, slice	Carton, 88's	45	6 slices per orange for salad	3 slices	4.0	26 lbs. (50 oranges)
Oranges, sections	Carton, 88's	38	9 sections per orange	6 sections	w	28 lbs. (5-1/2 doz.)
Peaches, sliced	Lug	20	4 per lb.; 6 C. sliced per lb.; 8-1/2 qts. sliced per lug	1/2 C.	3.6	60 lbs. (3 lugs)
Peaches, pie	Basket, 20's	5 to 6	3 pies per basket; 2 C. per pie	1 slice pie^a	1.7	30 lbs. (5 to 6 baskets or 2/3 bu.)
Peaches, pudding	Bushel	45		1/2 C.	3.4	18 lbs.
Pears, whole	Box, 120's	40	3 per lb.	1 whole	5.5	34 lbs.
Pears, diced	Bushel	48		1/2 C.	3.0	32 lbs. (3/4 bu.)
Persimmons, whole	Flat, 28's	14	(6 sections can be obtained per persimmon)	1 each halved	3.0	50 lbs. (8-1/3 doz.)
Pineapple, diced	Crate, 24's	70	20 oz. diced per pineapple	1/2 C.	2.0	60 lbs. (20 pineapples)
Pineapple, sliced	Crate, 24's	70	10 round slices per pineapple	1 slice	1.7	30 lbs. (10 pineapples)
Plums, whole	Basket, 5 x 5	5	18 to 24 medium per basket	3 medium	3.3	22-1/2 lbs. (4-1/2 baskets)
Plums, pie	Basket, 4 x 5	5	2-1/2 to 3 9-in. pies per basket	1 pie slice^a	4.4	30 lbs. (6 baskets)
Raspberries	Crate, 24 pts.	18		3 oz. (2/3 C.)	3.3	16 lbs. (20 pts.)
Raspberries, pie	Crate, 16 qts.	20	3/4 qt. per pie	1 pie slice^a	6.3	17 lbs. (13 qts.)
Raspberries, cobbler	Crate, 16 qts.	20		1/2 C.	6.0	10 lbs. (8 qts.)
Rhubarb, hothouse	Flat	5	Used for sauce	1/2 C.	10.0	20 lbs.
Rhubarb, pie	Crate	40	3 C. rhubarb sliced per pie	1 pie slice^a	4.0	15 lbs.
Strawberries	Crate, 24 qts.	30	6 servings to qt.	2/3 C.	6.6	20 lbs. (17 qts.)
Strawberries, pie	Crate, 24 qts.	30	1 qt. per pie	1 slice pie^a	5.0	20 lbs. (17 qts.)
Strawberries, sauce	Crate, 24 pts.	18		1/4 C.	5.0	10 lbs. (13 pts.)
Tangerines	Crate, 125's	40	10 sections per tangerine; used for salad	1 tangerine	10.0	35 lbs.
Tangerines, sections	Crate, 125's	40		5 sections	3.0	16 lbs. (4-1/4 doz.)

VEGETABLES

Item	Container	Servings	Notes	Serving		Weight
Artichoke, globe	Artichoke box, 72's	40		1 each	1.8	56 lbs. (8-1/3 doz.)
Asparagus	Crate	29	1 bunch is 2-1/2 lbs. and contains 24 stalks	3 oz. (3-4 stalks)	2.6	38 lbs.
Beans, lima, Fordhook	Bu. basket	30	Yields 8 qts. shelled	3 oz. (1/2 C.)	2.1	48 lbs.
Beans, lima, baby	Bu. basket	28	Yields 8 qts. shelled	3 oz. (1/2 C.)	2.2	45 lbs.
Beans, lima, fava	Bu. basket	28	Yields 8 qts. shelled	3 oz. (1/2 C.)	2.1	48 lbs.
Beans, lima, shelled	Basket	1/4		3 oz. (1/2 C.)	5.3	19 lbs.
Beans, snap	Bu. basket	30		3 oz. (1/2 C.)	4.5	22 lbs.
Beets, with tops	Crate, 36 bunches	45		3 oz. (1/2 C.)	2.1	46 lbs.
Beets, topped	Bu. basket	52		3 oz. (1/2 C.)	4.0	25 lbs.
Beet greens	Bu. basket	18	1 bunch is 2 to 2-1/2 lbs.	3 oz. (1/2 C.)	2.3	43 lbs.
Broccoli	Crate, 18 bunches	63		3 oz. (1/2 C.)	2.9	35 lbs.
Brussels sprouts	Drum	27		3 oz. (1/2 C.)	4.1	24 lbs.
Cabbage, shredded	Bag	50	Cooked 1 lb. shredded cabbage yields 2-1/2 C.	3 oz. (1/2 C.)	4.0	25 lbs.

Table 4 *(continued)*

Item	Shipping Container	Approximate Net Weight in Pounds, as Purchased per Container	Miscellaneous Shipping or Portioning Data	Portion Size as Served	Portions per Pound as Purchased	Approximate Amount to Purchase as Purchased for 100 Portions
Cabbage, shredded	Bu. basket	40	Raw 1 lb. shredded cabbage equals 3-½ C.	½ C. slaw	6.5	15 lbs.
Cabbage, Chinese	Bu. basket	40	Diced raw	2-½ oz. (½ C.)	4.0	25 lbs.
Carrots, with tops	Crate, 36's (bunches)	45		3 oz. (½ C.)	2.8	35 lbs.
Carrots, with tops	Crate, 36 bunches	45	Strips raw	2 oz. (4 strips)	4.3	23 lbs.
Carrots, topped	Bag	50	Strips raw	3 oz. (½ C.)	3.9	26 lbs.
Carrots, topped	Bag	50	Strips raw	2 oz. (4 strips)	5.8	17 lbs.
Cauliflower	Crate, 12's	24		3 oz. (½ C.)	2.0	50 lbs.
Chard	Bu. basket	18		3 oz. (½ C.)	3.7	27 lbs.
Celery	Crate, 30's	30	Stalk pieces raw (small)	3 oz. (2 stalks)	3.7	27 lbs.
Celery	Crate, 30's	30		2 oz. (2 stalks)	6.0	17 lbs.
Cucumbers, pared	Bu. basket	45	75 cucumbers; 1 9-in. cucumber yields 25 to 30 slices	2-½ oz. (5 slices)	5.8	18 lbs.
Cucumbers, unpared	Bu. basket	45		2-½ oz. (5 slices)	7.6	13 lbs.
Endive, Belgium, chopped	Basket	5	15 to 25 heads	2 oz. (½ or ⅓ head)	7.1	14 lbs.
Collards	Bu. basket	20	12 bunches	3 oz. (½ C.)	4.3	23 lbs.
Corn, on the cob	Wirebound crate	40	5 doz. ears each ear approximately 10 to 12 oz. as purchased	7 oz. (1 ear)	1.7	60-75 lbs. (8-⅓ doz.)
Corn, kernels from cob	Wirebound crate	40		3 oz. (½ C.)	1.5	66 lbs.
Eggplant	Bu. basket	40	24 to 30 eggplant; eggplant pared and steamed	3 oz. (½ C.)	4.0	25 lbs.
Eggplant, sliced	Bu. basket	40	Unpared, batter-fried	3-½ oz. (1 slice)	4.3	23 lbs.
Escarole, diced, raw	Bu. basket	25	2 doz. heads	2 oz.	5.8	17 lbs.
Chicory, curly leaf	Bu. basket	22	2 doz. heads	2 oz.	6.0	17 lbs.
Kale	Bu. basket	19		3 oz. (½ C.)	3.7	27 lbs.
Kohlrabi	Bu. basket	22	3 to 5 per lb.	3 oz. (½ C.)	2.9	35 lbs.
Leeks	Bu. basket	18	18 bunches, 3 to 5 per bunch	3 oz. (½ C.)	2.2	45 lbs.
Lettuce, iceberg	Carton, 24's	25	Chopped raw	2 oz. (½ C.)	5.9	17 lbs.
Lettuce, iceberg	Carton, 24's	25	Underliners for salad; 12 per head average		11.1	9 lbs.
Lettuce, leaf	Bu. basket	18	Raw	2 oz.	5.3	19 lbs.
Lettuce, Boston or Bibb	Bu. basket	24	Raw	2 oz.	5.1	20 lbs.
Mushrooms, chopped	Carton	1		1 oz. (2 T.)	11.1	9 lbs.
Mustard greens	Bu. basket	18		3 oz. (½ C.)	3.1	32 lbs.
Okra	Bu. hamper	38	Diced and cooked	3 oz. (½ C.)	5.1	20 lbs.
Onions, dry	Sack	50	French-fried	3 oz. (½ C.)	4.0	25 lbs.
Onions, dry	Sack	50	Raw diced or sliced	2-½ oz.	5.0	20 lbs.
Onions, dry	Sack	50		2 oz.	7.1	14 lbs.
Onions, green	California ⅔ crate	50	8 doz. bunches to the crate	1-½ oz. (2 onions)	3.9	25 lbs.
Parsnips	Bu. basket	45		3 oz. (½ C.)	4.2	24 lbs.
Peas, green	Bu. basket	28	8 qts. shelled	3 oz. (½ C.)	1.9	53 lbs.

Peppers, green	Sturdee crate, 1-¾ bu.	30	Chopped raw	1 oz.	13.1	8 lbs.
Peppers, green	Sturdee crate, 1-¼ bu.	30	Halves steamed	2 halves	4.0	25 lbs.
Potatoes, Irish	Sack	100	Whole, pared	1 (5 oz.)	2.6	39 lbs.
Potatoes, Irish	Sack	100	Baked	1 (7 oz.)	2.1	47 lbs.
Potatoes, Irish	Sack	100	Hash brown	4 oz.	2.3	44 lbs.
Potatoes, Irish	Sack	100	Mashed	4 oz.	3.3	30 lbs.
Potatoes, Irish	Sack	100	Raw-fried	4 oz.	1.7	59 lbs.
Potatoes, Irish	Sack	100	French-fried	3 oz.	2.7	37 lbs.
Potatoes, sweet	Bushel	50	140 potatoes; mashed	4 oz.	3.3	30 lbs.
Potatoes, sweet	Bushel	50	Candied	4 oz.	3.4	30 lbs.
Potatoes, sweet	Bushel	50	Baked	6 oz.	2.7	36 lbs.
Pumpkin	Bushel	40		3 oz. (½ C.)	3.4	30 lbs.
Radishes	Dozen bunches	10	Raw	1 oz.	10.0	10 lbs.
Rutabagas	Bushel	45		3 oz. (½ C.)	3.8	27 lbs.
Spinach	Bushel	18		3 oz. (½ C.)	3.2	31 lbs.
Spinach, trimmed and washed	Bushel	18		3 oz. (½ C.)	4.0	25 lbs.
Squash, summer	Bushel	40		3 oz. (½ C.)	4.2	24 lbs.
Squash, acorn	Bushel	50	50 squash	1 half	2.0	50 lbs.
Squash, Boston marrow	Pound		Mashed	3 oz. (½ C.)	4.1	24 lbs.
Squash, Boston marrow	Pound		Baked	4 oz.	2.9	35 lbs.
Squash, butternut	Pound		Mashed	3 oz. (½ C.)	2.4	41 lbs.
Squash, butternut	Pound		Baked	4 oz.	1.7	59 lbs.
Squash, Hubbard	Pound		Mashed	3 oz. (½ C.)	3.1	33 lbs.
Squash, Hubbard	Pound		Baked	4 oz.	2.2	46 lbs.
Tomatoes, unpeeled	Lug, 5 x 5	30	75 tomatoes; raw	3 oz.	4.9	20 lbs.
Tomatoes, peeled	Lug, 5 x 5	30	Raw	3 oz.	4.7	21 lbs.
Turnips, topped	Bushel	50		3 oz. (½ C.)	4.0	25 lbs.
Turnips, with tops	Crate, 18's	36		3 oz. (½ C.)	3.3	31 lbs.
Watercress	Basket, 14 bunches		Raw	2 oz.	5.9	17 lbs.

Note: All vegetables cooked unless otherwise noted.
a Each pie cut 6.
b Yield on honeyball melons is same as for cantaloupes if 45 per crate.
c Yield on honeydew and Persian melons is same as for casabas if 8 per crate.
Source: U.S. Department of Agriculture.

Table 5. Egg Equivalency Table

Fresh or frozen:
1 whole egg. . . . . = 3 T.
8 whole eggs. . . . . = 1½ C.

Fresh or frozen:
16 egg whites. . . . . = 1 pt.
24 egg yolks. . . . . = 1 pt.

Dried whole egg powder:
   Sifted. . . . . ½ oz. or 2½ T.
+ Water. . . . . 2½ T.

= Number of eggs. 1

Dried whole egg powder:
   Sifted. . . . . 4 oz. or 1⅓ C.
+ Water. . . . . 1⅓ C.

= Number of eggs. 8

Dried whole egg powder:
   Sifted. . . . . 6 oz. or 1 pt.
+ Water. . . . . 1 pt.

= Number of eggs. 12

Dried whole egg powder:
   Sifted. . . . . 12 oz. or 1 qt.
+ Water. . . . . 1 qt.

= Number of eggs. 24

Source: Reprinted by permission of Rykoff-Sexton,
Inc., from *Recipes and Menus for All Seasons*

Table 6. Milk Conversion Table

Nonfat dry milk	13 oz.
+ Water	7¾ pts.
= Liquid skim milk	1 gal.

Nonfat dry milk solids	1½ oz.
+ Water	14½ oz.
= Liquid skim milk	1 lb.

Nonfat dry milk	3¼ oz.
Butter	1⅔ oz.
+ Water	1 qt.
= Whole milk	1 qt.

Dry whole milk	1 lb.
+ Water	7¼ pts.
= Liquid whole milk	1 gal.

Dry whole milk	2 oz.
+ Water	14 oz.
= Liquid whole milk	1 lb.

Dry whole milk	4½ oz.
Sugar	6½ oz.
+ Water	5 oz.
= Sweetened condensed whole milk	1 lb.

Nonfat dry milk solids	4 oz.
Sugar	7 oz.
+ Water	5 oz.
= Sweetened condensed skim milk	1 lb.

Source: Reprinted by permission of Rykoff-Sexton, Inc., from *Recipes and Menus for All Seasons*

Table 7. Dipper Equivalency Measures

Dipper Size	Equivalent
No. 8	½ C. or 8 T.
No. 10	⅖ C. or 6 T.
No. 12	⅓ C. or 5⅔ T.
No. 16	¼ C. or 4 T.
No. 20	⅕ C. or 3⅓ T.
No. 24	⅙ C. or 2⅔ T.
No. 30	⅛ C. or 2 T.

Source: Reprinted by permission of Rykoff-Sexton, Inc., from *Recipes and Menus for All Seasons*

Table 8. Common Container Sizes

Industry Term	Approximate Amount Contained			Principal Content	Approximate Number of Servings
	Net Weight	Fluid Measure	Cups		
8 oz.	8 oz.		1	Fruits, vegetables, specialties[a] for small families	2
Picnic	10-½ to 12 oz.		1-¼	Mainly condensed soups. Some fruits, vegetables, meat, fish, specialties[a]	2 to 3
12 oz (vacuum)	12 oz.		1-½	Principally for vacuum-pack corn	3 to 4
No. 300	14 to 16 oz. (14 oz. to 1 lb.)		1-¾	Pork and beans, baked beans, meat products, cranberry sauce, blueberries, specialties[a]	3 to 4
No. 303	16 to 17 oz. (1 lb. to lb. 1 oz.)		2	Principal size for fruits and vegetables. Some meat products, ready-to-serve soups, specialties[a]	4
No. 2	20 oz. (1 lb. 4 oz.)	18 fl. oz. (1 pt. 2 fl. oz.)	2-½	Juices,[b] ready-to-serve soups, some specialties[a], pineapple, apple slices. No longer in popular use for most fruits and vegetables	5
No. 2-½	27 to 29 oz. (1 lb. 11 oz. to 1 lb. 13 oz.)		3-½	Fruits, some vegetables (pumpkin, sauerkraut, spinach and other greens, tomatoes)	5 to 7
No. 3	33 oz. (2 lbs. 1 oz.)		4	Some juices	
No. 3 cylinder or 46 fl. oz.	51 oz. (3 lbs. 3 oz.)	46 fl. oz. (1 qt. 14 fl. oz.)	5-¾	Fruit and vegetable juices[b] pork and beans. Institutional size for condensed soups, some vegetables	10 to 12
No. 5	56 oz. (3 lbs. 8 oz.)		7		
No. 10	6-½ lbs. to 7 lbs. 5 oz.		12 to 13	Institutional size for fruits, vegetables, and some other foods	25

Notes: Strained and homogenized foods for infants, and chopped junior foods, come in small jars and cans suitable for the smaller servings used. The weight is given on the label. Meats, poultry, and fish and seafood are almost entirely advertised and sold under weight terminology. The labels of cans or jars of identical size may show a net weight for one product that differs slightly from the net weight on the label of another product, due to the difference in the density of the food. An example would be pork and beans (1 lb.), blueberries (14 oz.), in the same size can.

[a]A specialty is usually a food combination such as macaroni, spaghetti, Spanish-style rice, Mexican-type foods, Chinese foods, tomato aspic, etc.

[b]Juices are now being packed in a number of can sizes.

Sources: National Canners Association; Reprinted by permission of Rykoff-Sexton, Inc., from *Recipes and Menus for All Seasons*

Table 9. Food Serving Chart—Canned, Frozen, Preserved

CANNED VEGETABLES

Cans per Case and Container Size	Food	Style	Type	Approximate Net Weight	Range in Contents per Container	Suggested Portion per Serving	Approximate Portions per Container	Approximate Drained Weight	Miscellaneous Information
6/5 squat	Asparagus	Colossal all-green spears	California	4 lbs. 1 oz.	50 to 60	2 spears	25 to 30	2 lbs. 14 ozs.	
6/5 squat	Asparagus	Mammoth large all-green spears	California	4 lbs. 1 oz.	85 to 95	3 to 4 spears	21 to 34	2 lbs. 14 ozs.	
6/5 squat	Asparagus	Blended mammoth large all-green spears	California	4 lbs. 1 oz.	80 to 85	3 to 4 spears	20 to 26	2 lbs. 8 ozs.	About 25 percent tips
6/10	Asparagus	Cut, all-green	Michigan	6 lbs. 5 ozs.	300 to 375	½ C.	24	3 lbs. 15 ozs.	
6/5 squat	Asparagus	Colossal whole green-tipped and white	California	4 lbs. 1 oz.	50 to 60	3 to 4 spears	12 to 15	2 lbs. 10 ozs.	
6/5 squat	Asparagus	Mammoth whole green-tipped and white	California	4 lbs. 1 oz.	60 to 70	4 to 5 spears	12 to 14	2 lbs. 14 ozs.	
6/10	Beans, green	Tiny whole	Northwest Blue Lake	6 lbs. 5 ozs.		½ C.	29	3 lbs. 13 ozs.	No. 1 sieve
6/10	Beans, green	Small whole	Northwest Blue Lake	6 lbs. 5 ozs.		½ C.	30	3 lbs. 13 ozs.	No. 2 sieve
6/10	Beans, green	Salad whole	Northwest Blue Lake	6 lbs. 5 ozs.	420	12 to 14 pieces	30 to 35	3 lbs. 13 ozs.	No. 3 sieve
6/5 squat	Beans, green	Whole vertical pack		4 lbs.	200	10 to 12 pieces	18 to 20	2 lbs. 8 ozs.	No. 4 sieve
6/10	Beans, green	French-style	Northwest Blue Lake	6 lbs. 5 ozs.		½ C.	30	3 lbs. 13 ozs.	
6/10	Beans, green	Cut	Northwest Blue Lake	6 lbs. 5 ozs.		½ C.	26	3 lbs. 15 ozs.	1½-inch cuts, No. 3 sieve
6/10	Beans, green	Cut	Northwest Blue Lake	6 lbs. 5 ozs.		½ C.	26	3 lbs. 15 ozs.	No. 4 sieve
6/10	Beans, kidney	Dark red		6 lbs. 12 ozs.		½ C.	24	4 lbs. 12 ozs.	
6/10	Beans, lima	Garden run Fordhook	Eastern Fordhook	6 lbs. 9 ozs.		½ C.	24	4 lbs. 8 ozs.	Fresh
6/10	Beans, lima	Small green	Eastern Henderson Bush	6 lbs. 9 ozs.		½ C.	24	4 lbs. 8 ozs.	Fresh
6/10	Beans, lima	Medium green	Eastern Henderson Bush	6 lbs. 9 ozs.		½ C.	24	4 lbs. 8 ozs.	Fresh
6/10	Beans, oven-baked		New England	6 lbs. 14 ozs.		½ C.	25	6 lbs. 14 ozs.	New England pack with salt pork
6/10	Beans, red		Idaho Red	6 lbs. 12 ozs.		½ C.	24	5 lbs. 2 ozs.	
6/10	Beans, wax	Cut	King Horn Variety	6 lbs. 5 ozs.		½ C.	26	3 lbs. 15 ozs.	No. 3 sieve
6/10	Beets	Cubed	Eastern Detroit Red	6 lbs. 8 ozs.	400 to 450	½ C., 15 cubes	26 to 30	4 lbs. 7 ozs.	¾-inch cubes
6/10	Beets	Diced	Eastern Detroit Red	6 lbs. 8 ozs.		½ C.	27	4 lbs. 7 ozs.	
6/10	Beets	Julienne	Eastern Detroit Red	6 lbs. 8 ozs.		½ C.	30	4 lbs. 8 ozs.	
6/10	Beets	Sliced	Northwest Detroit Red	6 lbs. 8 ozs.	200 to 250	½ C., 10 slices	20 to 25	4 lbs. 8 ozs.	
6/10	Beets, rosebud	Whole	Oregon Detroit Red	6 lbs. 8 ozs.	Over 250	6 to 8 pieces	30 to 40	4 lbs. 5 ozs.	
6/10	Cabbage, red		New York	6 lbs. 3 ozs.		½ C.	30	5 lbs.	
6/10	Carrots	Diced	Northwest Chantenay	6 lbs. 9 ozs.		½ C.	28	4 lbs. 8 ozs.	
6/10	Carrots	Julienne	Northwest Chantenay	6 lbs. 9 ozs.		½ C.	29	4 lbs. 6 ozs.	
6/10	Carrots	Quartered	Northwest Chantenay	6 lbs. 9 ozs.	86	3 pieces	28	4 lbs. 8 ozs.	
6/10	Carrots	Small sliced	Northwest Chantenay	6 lbs. 9 ozs.	325 to 375	6 to 8 slices	43 to 54	4 lbs. 3 ozs.	
6/10	Carrots	Tiny whole	Northwest Chantenay	6 lbs. 9 ozs.	Over 200	6 to 8 pieces	30 to 35	4 lbs. 6 ozs.	1½ inch diameter
6/10	Carrots	Small whole	Northwest Chantenay	6 lbs. 9 ozs.	Over 100	6 to 8 pieces	24 to 30	4 lbs. 6 ozs.	
6/10	Celery	Cut	California	6 lbs. 2 oz.		½ C.	23	4 lbs. 2 ozs.	Packed in brine
6/10	Corn, cream-style	Little kernel Country Gentleman	Midwest White	6 lbs. 10 ozs.		½ C.	25	6 lbs. 10 ozs.	
6/10	Corn, cream-style	Golden sweet	Midwest	6 lbs. 10 ozs.		½ C.	25	6 lbs. 10 ozs.	
6/10	Corn, whole grain	Golden sweet	Midwest	6 lbs. 10 ozs.		½ C.	26	6 lbs. 10 ozs.	
6/10	Hominy	Golden	Southern	6 lbs. 2 ozs.		½ C.	22	4 lbs. 1 oz.	
6/10	Kale	Chopped	Wisconsin	6 lbs. 8 ozs.		½ C.	23	3 lbs. 12 ozs.	
6/10	Mixed vegetables					½ C.	25	4 lbs. 1 oz.	Carrots, potatoes, celery, green beans, peas, corn, lima beans
6/10	Mustard greens	Chopped	Southern	6 lbs. 2 ozs.		½ C.	20	3 lbs. 12 ozs.	
6/10	Okra	Cut	Southern	6 lbs. 2 ozs.		½ C.	25	4 lbs. 1 oz.	
6/10	Onions	Tiny whole	Eastern	6 lbs. 5 ozs.	Over 200	10 pieces	20	4 lbs.	
6/10	Onions	Small whole	Eastern	6 lbs. 5 ozs.	Over 100	5 pieces	20	4 lbs.	
6/10	Peas, early June	Extra sifted	Wisconsin Alaska	6 lbs. 9 ozs.		½ C.	24		No. 2 sieve
6/10	Peas, early June	Sifted	Wisconsin Alaska	6 lbs. 9 ozs.		½ C.	24		No. 3 sieve

Table 9 *(continued)*

Cans per Case and Container Size	Food	Style	Type	Approximate Net Weight	Range in Contents per Container	Suggested Portion per Serving	Approximate Portions per Container	Approximate Drained Weight	Miscellaneous Information
			CANNED VEGETABLES *(continued)*						
6/10	Peas, alsweet	Sifted	Wisconsin Alsweet	6 lbs. 9 ozs.		½ C.	24		No. 3 sieve
6/10	Peas, telephone	Sweet	Wisconsin Sweet	6 lbs. 9 ozs.		½ C.	25		No. 5 sieve
6/10	Potatoes, white	Tiny whole	Midwest	6 lbs. 6 ozs.	Over 150	6 pieces	25	4 lbs. 6 ozs.	
6/10	Potatoes, white	Small whole	Midwest	6 lbs. 6 ozs.	Over 100	4 pieces	25	4 lbs. 6 ozs.	
12/3 cyl.	Potatoes, sweet	Small whole	Louisiana yams	3 lbs. 3 ozs.	20 to 25	2	10 to 12	2 lbs. 3 ozs.	In heavy syrup
6/10	Sauerkraut		Midwest	6 lbs. 3 ozs.		½ C.	37	5 lbs.	
6/10	Spinach	Leaf	California	6 lbs. 2 ozs.		½ C.	18	3 lbs. 12 ozs.	
6/10	Spinach	Sliced	California	6 lbs. 2 ozs.		½ C.	15	3 lbs. 12 ozs.	
6/10	Tomatoes	Italian-style	California	6 lbs. 6 ozs.	28	1 whole	28	4 lbs. 4 ozs.	Trace of calcium chloride added
6/10	Tomatoes	Whole	Midwest	6 lbs. 6 ozs.	20	1 whole	20	4 lbs. 8 ozs.	Trace of calcium chloride added
6/10	Tomato paste	Sweet	California blended, round and plum tomatoes	6 lbs. 15 ozs.			12 cups	6 lbs. 15 ozs.	30 percent solids
6/10	Tomato puree	Extra heavy	California	6 lbs. 9 ozs.			12 cups	6 lbs. 9 ozs.	1.07 specific gravity
6/10	Tomato puree	Superb	California	6 lbs. 9 ozs.			12 cups	6 lbs. 9 ozs.	1.06 specific gravity
6/10	Turnip greens	Chopped	Southern	6 lbs. 2 ozs.		½ C.	20	3 lbs. 12 ozs.	
			DEHYDRATED VEGETABLES						
6/1¾ #	Onions, white	Slices		1 lb. 12 ozs.					Yields 2½ gallons when reconstituted
6/10	Potatoes	Flakes		1 lb. 12 ozs.		½ C.	90		
6/10	Potatoes	Instant	Powdered	6 lbs.		½ C.	112		
			CANNED FRUITS						
6/10	Apple sauce		New York State	6 lbs. 12 ozs.		½ C.	26	6 lbs. 12 ozs.	Heavy coarse finish
6/10	Apricots	Unpeeled halves	Blenheim	6 lbs. 14 ozs.	75 to 85	3 halves	25 to 28	4 lbs. 2 ozs.	In syrup
6/10	Apricots	Whole peeled	Blenheim	6 lbs. 14 ozs.	40 to 50	2 pieces	20 to 25	4 lbs. 4 ozs.	In syrup
6/10	Apricots	Sliced, peeled	Blenheim	6 lbs. 14 ozs.		⅓ to ½ C.	20 to 25	4 lbs. 2 ozs.	In syrup
6/10	Boysenberries		California Genuine Variety	6 lbs. 12 ozs.		12 berries	26	3 lbs. 7 ozs.	In syrup
6/10	Cherries, bing	Unpitted	Pacific Northwest	6 lbs. 12 ozs.	220	11 cherries	20	4 lbs. 5 ozs.	In syrup
6/10	Cherries, bing	Pitted	Pacific Northwest	6 lbs. 14 ozs.	300 to 350	11 cherries	27 to 32	4 lbs. 2 ozs.	In syrup
6/10	Cherries, red	Pitted	Michigan Montmorency	6 lbs. 14 ozs.		½ C.	23	4 lbs. 12 ozs.	In syrup
6/10	Cherries, Royal Ann	Light sweet unpitted	Pacific Coast	6 lbs. 12 ozs.	250 to 300	11 cherries	23 to 27	4 lbs. 2 ozs.	In syrup
6/10	Cranberry sauce	Home-style	Cape Cod or Wisconsin	7 lbs.		¼ C.	50		2 ozs. or No. 48 souffle
6/10	Cranberry sauce	Strained	Cape Cod or Wisconsin	7 lbs.		¼ C.	50		2 ozs. or No. 48 souffle
6/10	Figs	Whole	California Kadota	7 lbs.	70 to 90	3 pieces	23 to 30	4 lbs. 4 ozs.	Slice of orange added in syrup
6/10	Fruit cocktail		California Fancy	6 lbs. 14 ozs.		⅓ C.	27	4 lbs. 8 ozs.	In syrup
6/10	Fruit for salad		California Fancy	6 lbs. 14 ozs.		½ C.	20	4 lbs. 6 ozs.	Peach slices, pear slices, grapes, apricot halves, pineapple tidbits, maraschino cherries in syrup
12/3 cyl.	Grapefruit	Segments	Florida	3 lbs. 2 ozs.	50 to 60	4 segments	12 to 15	2 lbs. 1 oz.	In syrup
12/3 cyl.	Grapefruit and orange	Segments	Florida	3 lbs. 2 ozs.	65 to 75	5 segments	13 to 15	2 lbs.	In syrup
6/10	Grapes	Seedless	California Thompson	6 lbs. 14 ozs.		½ C.	22	4 lbs. 3 ozs.	In syrup
12/3 cyl.	Orange	Segments	Florida Valencia	3 lbs. 2 ozs.	65 to 75	6 segments	11 to 13	2 lbs. 1 oz.	In orange juice syrup
6/10	Orange, mandarin	Segments	Japanese	6 lbs. 6 oz	425 to 450	½ C.	20	4 lbs. 3 oz.	In syrup
6/10	Peaches, ambrosia	Halves	Ambrosia yellow cling California	6 lbs. 14 ozs.	25 to 30	1 half	25 to 30	4 lbs. 10 ozs.	In syrup
6/10	Peaches, ambrosia	Sliced	Ambrosia yellow cling California	6 lbs. 12 ozs.		6 slices	16	4 lbs. 10 ozs.	In syrup
6/10	Peaches, yellow cling	Diced	Midsummer yellow cling California	6 lbs. 12 ozs.		½ C.	21	4 lbs. 5 ozs.	In syrup

6/10	Peaches, yellow cling	Halves	Midsummer yellow cling California	6 lbs. 14 ozs.	30 to 35	1 half	30 to 35	4 lbs. 2 ozs.	In syrup
6/10	Peaches, yellow free	Halves	Yellow free Elberta California	6 lbs. 14 ozs.	25 to 30	1 half	25 to 30		In syrup
6/10	Peaches, yellow free	Sliced	Yellow free Elberta California	6 lbs. 14 ozs.	150	6 slices	25		In syrup
6/10	Pears, Bartlett	Halves, peeled	Pacific Northwest Bartlett	6 lbs. 10 ozs.	30 to 35	1 half	30 to 35	4 lbs. 2 ozs.	In syrup
6/10	Pears, Bartlett	Halves, peeled	Pacific Northwest Bartlett	6 lbs. 10 ozs.	35 to 40	1 half	35 to 40	4 lbs. 3 ozs.	In syrup
6/10	Pears, Bartlett	Halves, unpeeled	Pacific Northwest Bartlett	6 lbs. 10 ozs.	25 to 35	1 half	25 to 35	3 lbs. 10 ozs.	In syrup
6/10	Pears, Bartlett	Diced	Pacific Coast Bartlett	6 lbs. 10 ozs.		½ C.	21	4 lbs. 9 ozs.	In syrup
6/10	Pears, Kieffer	Halves	Michigan Kieffer	6 lbs. 10 ozs.	40 to 50	2 halves	20 to 25	3 lbs. 15 ozs.	In syrup
6/10	Pineapple	Crushed	Hawaiian Cayenne	6 lbs. 12 ozs.		½ C.	20	5 lbs. 5 ozs.	In syrup
6/10	Pineapple	Crushed	Hawaiian Cayenne	6 lbs. 11 ozs.		½ C.	18	4 lbs. 10 ozs.	In juice
6/10	Pineapple	Dessert cut	Hawaiian Cayenne	6 lbs. 12 ozs.	250 to 300	8 pieces	31 to 37	4 lbs. 5 ozs.	In syrup
6/10	Pineapple	Sliced	Hawaiian Cayenne	6 lbs. 13 ozs.	52	1 slice	52	4 lbs. 8 ozs.	In syrup
6/10	Pineapple	Sliced	Hawaiian Cayenne	6 lbs. 13 ozs.	66	1 slice	66	4 lbs. 3 ozs.	In syrup
6/10	Pineapple	Tidbits	Hawaiian Cayenne	6 lbs. 12 ozs.	850 to 900	½ C.	23	4 lbs. 12 ozs.	In syrup
6/10	Plums, Green Gage	Whole unpeeled	California	6 lbs. 14 ozs.	27 to 35	2 pieces	13 to 17	3 lbs. 12 ozs.	In syrup
6/10	Plums, Green Gage	Whole peeled	California	6 lbs. 14 ozs.	27 to 35	2 pieces	13 to 17	3 lbs. 12 ozs.	In syrup
6/10	Plums, prune	Whole unpeeled	Northwest Italian	6 lbs. 14 ozs.	60 to 70	3 pieces	20 to 23	4 lbs.	In syrup
6/10	Prunes	Prepared	Santa Clara	6 lbs. 14 ozs.	150 to 160	5 pieces	30 to 32	4 lbs. 7 ozs.	40 to 50 cut out prunes per pound
6/10	Prunes	Ready-to-serve	San Jose	7 lbs.	110 to 115	4 to 5 pieces	30 to 35	5 lbs. 2 ozs.	Water and sugar added
6/10	Rhubarb		Michigan	6 lbs. 9 ozs.		½ C.	18	4 lbs. 1 oz.	U.S. certified food coloring added in syrup

VACUUM-PACKED SHELLED NUTS

6/3#	Almonds	Sliced	Blanched	3 lbs.	3 qts.				
12/1#	Almonds	Slivered	Blanched	1 lb.	1 qt.				
6/4#	Nut topping			4 lbs.	4 qts.				Peanuts, cashews, almonds, pecans
6/3#	Pecans	Halves		3 lbs.	3 qts.				
6/3#	Pecans	Pieces		3 lbs.	3 qts.				
6/2¾#	Walnuts	Halves and pieces	Light California	2 lbs. 12 ozs.	2¾ qts.				
12/1#	Walnuts	Halves and pieces	Light California	1 lb.	1 qt.				
12/1#	Walnuts, black	Kernels	Eastern	1 lb.	1 qt.				

DRIED FRUITS

6/2#	Apple	Pie slices	Low moisture fruit	2 lbs.	1½ gal.		5—9-in. Pies		Used 1 quart for each pie
6/2½#	Apple	Sauce nuggets	Low moisture fruit	2 lbs. 8 ozs.	3¼ gals.	½ C.	104		
30# Carton	Apricots	Dried	Blenheim	30 lbs.	2550	6 to 7 pieces	364 to 425		
6/10	Apricots	Slices	Low moisture fruit	3 lbs. 8 ozs.	2¼ gals.	½ C.	72		
30# Carton	Figs	Dried	Calimyrna jumbo	30 lbs.	702	3 pieces	234		
5# Bag	Figs	Dried	Calimyrna jumbo	5 lbs.	117	3 pieces	39		
6/10	Fruit cocktail mix		Low moisture fruit	2 lbs. 12 ozs.	2¼ gals.	½ C.	72		Maraschino cherries, apricots, peaches, apples, grapes
30# Carton	Fruit	Dried	Mixed	30 lbs.	690 prunes 432 apricots 114 peaches 84 pears	5 pieces	264		Blenheim apricots, Lake County pears, Muir peaches, Santa Clara prunes
30# Carton	Peaches	Dried	Muir	30 lbs.	1134	3 pieces	378		
30# Carton	Prunes	Dried	Santa Clara	30 lbs.	540 to 720	2 pieces	270 to 360		Size 18/24
5# Can	Prunes	Dried	Santa Clara	5 lbs.	90 to 120	2 pieces	45 to 60		Size 18/24
30# Carton	Prunes	Dried	Santa Clara	30 lbs.	600 to 900	3 pieces	200 to 300		Size 20/30
5# Can	Prunes	Dried	Santa Clara	5 lbs.	100 to 150	3 pieces	33 to 50		Size 20/30
30# Carton	Prunes	Dried	Santa Clara	30 lbs.	900 to 1200	4 pieces	225 to 300		Size 30/40
5# Can	Prunes	Dried	Santa Clara	5 lbs.	150 to 200	4 pieces	37 to 50		Size 30/40
30# Carton	Prunes	Dried	Santa Clara	30 lbs.	1200 to 1500	5 pieces	240 to 300		Size 40/50
5# Can	Prunes	Dried	Santa Clara	5 lbs.	200 to 250	5 pieces	40 to 50		Size 40/50

Table 9 (continued)

Cans per Case and Container Size	Food	Type	Style	Approximate Net Weight	Range in Contents per Container	Suggested Portion per Serving	Approximate Portions per Container	Approximate Drained Weight	Miscellaneous Information
PREPARED PIE FILLINGS									
6/10	Apples	Greenings		7 lbs 4 ozs			3—9-in Pies		Apple slices, sugar, lemon juice and water. Used 1 quart for each pie
6/10	Blueberry	Maine		7 lbs 4 ozs			3—9-in Pies		Contains blueberries, sugar, lemon juice, starch, salt and water. Used 1 quart for each pie.
6/10	Cherry	Michigan		7 lbs 8 ozs			3—9-in Pies		Contains cherries, cornstarch, sugar, lemon juice, food coloring and water. Used 1 quart for each pie
6/10	Lemon			7 lbs 14 ozs			3—9-in Pies		Sugar, corn syrup, eggs, cereal, lemon juice, stabilizers, vegetable shortening, salt, fruit acid, lemon flavoring. Used 1 quart for each pie
6/10	Peaches	Yellow cling	Sliced	7 lbs 4 ozs			3—9-in Pies		Freestone peaches, sugar, starch, lemon juice and water. Used 1 quart for each pie.
PIE FILLINGS									
6/10	Apples	York Imperial	Sliced	6 lbs 12 ozs			16½ C	6 lbs 12 ozs	No syrup
6/10	Apricots	Blenheim, Royal or Tilton	Unpeeled halves	6 lbs 10 ozs			11¾ C	6 lbs 10 ozs	Preheated solid pack pie apricots, no syrup
6/10	Blackberries	Washington State Evergreen		6 lbs 7 ozs			12½ C	4 lbs 15 ozs	Packed in water
6/10	Black raspberries	Michigan		6 lbs 6 oz			8 C	3 lbs 3 ozs	Packed in water
6/10	Blueberries	Maine or Canada Genuine Variety		6 lbs 6 ozs			9¾ C	3 lbs 12 ozs	Packed in water
6/10	Boysenberries	California or Oregon		6 lbs 7 ozs			6¾ C.	3 lbs 6 ozs	Packed in water
6/10	Cherries, red sour	Michigan or Wisconsin Montmorency	Pitted	6 lbs 7 ozs			11¾ C.	4 lbs 7 ozs	Packed in water
6/10	Gooseberries	Northwest or Michigan		6 lbs 5 ozs			11¾ C.	3 lbs 13 ozs	Packed in water
6/10	Mincemeat	Olde English		7 lbs 12 ozs			13½ C.	7 lbs 12 ozs	Contains raisins, evaporated apples, sugar, boiled cider, candied fruits, beef suet, cider vinegar, spices
6/10	Peaches, yellow cling	Midsummer or Phillips yellow cling California	Halves or slices	6 lbs 8 ozs			14 C	6 lbs 3 ozs	Preheated solid pack pie peaches, no syrup
6/10	Pumpkin	California		6 lbs 10 ozs			14 C	6 lbs 10 ozs	Dry pack
SPICED FRUITS									
6/10	Apples, spiced	Jonathan	Rings	6 lbs 10 ozs	70 to 80	1 ring	70 to 80	3 lbs 13 ozs	Colored, unpeeled, cored in heavy syrup
6/10	Apricots, spiced	California Blenheim	Whole peeled	6 lbs 14 ozs	35 to 40	1	35 to 40	4 lbs 4 ozs	Pit loosened in extra heavy syrup
6/10	Cantaloupe, preserved		Cubed	8 lbs	214	2	107	5 lbs 11 ozs	In heavy syrup
6/10	Crab Apples, spiced	Michigan Hyslop	Whole	6 lbs 10 ozs	50 to 60	1	50 to 60	4 lbs 1 oz.	Colored red, cored in extra heavy syrup
12/5	Honeydew melon, preserved		Cubed	8 lbs.	226	2	113	5 lbs 13 ozs	In heavy syrup
6/10	Kumquats, preserved	Florida	Whole	3 lbs 8 ozs	70 to 75		70 to 75	2 lbs 8 ozs	In syrup
6/10	Peaches, yellow cling, spiced	California	Whole	6 lbs 14 ozs	25 to 30	1	25 to 30	4 lbs 10 ozs	Pit loosened in extra heavy syrup
6/10	Pears, Bartlett cinnamon-flavored	California	Halves	6 lbs 12 ozs	25 to 30	1	25 to 30	3 lbs 10 ozs	Colored red in extra heavy syrup

6/10	Pears, Bartlett peppermint-flavored	Halves	California	6 lbs. 12 ozs.	25 to 30	1	25 to 30	3 lbs. 10 ozs.	Colored green in extra heavy syrup
6/10	Pears, Kieffer, spiced	Whole	Michigan	6 lbs. 10 ozs.	40 to 50	1	40 to 50	3 lbs. 15 ozs.	Colored red in heavy syrup
6/10	Pears, Seckel, spiced	Whole	New York Seckel	6 lbs. 12 ozs.	70 to 80	1	70 to 80	4 lbs. 9 ozs.	In extra heavy syrup
6/5	Prunes, spiced	Whole	D'Agen	3 lbs. 4 ozs.	62	1	62	2 lbs. 10 ozs.	Sometimes available in No. 10 cans
6/10	Watermelon, preserved	Cubed		8 lbs.	194	2	97	5 lbs. 9 ozs.	
			FRUIT JUICES, NECTARS, AND BEVERAGE BASES						
4/1 gal.	Apple	Cider		1 gal.		4 oz.	32		
12/46 oz.	Apple	Juice	Unsweetened	46 oz.		4 oz.	11½		
12/46 oz.	Cherry	Juice	Red	46 oz.		4 oz.	11½		Sugar added
4/1 gal.	Cranberry	Juice	Cocktail	1 gal.		4 oz.	32		Sugar added
12/46 oz.	Grape	Juice	Concord	46 oz.		4 oz.	11½		Sugar added
12/46 oz.	Grape	Juice	Concord	46 oz.		4 oz.	11½		Unsweetened
12/46 oz.	Grapefruit	Juice	Texas or Florida	46 oz.		4 oz.	11½		Unsweetened
12/46 oz.	Orange	Juice	Florida Valencia	46 oz.		4 oz.	11½		Unsweetened
12/46 oz.	Orange and grapefruit	Juice	Florida	46 oz.		4 oz.	11½		Sugar added
12/46 oz.	Pineapple	Juice	Hawaiian	46 oz.		4 oz.	11½		Unsweetened
12/46 oz.	Prune	Juice		46 oz.		4 oz.	11½		Unsweetened juice of dried prunes
12/46 oz.	Tangarine	Juice	Florida	46 oz.		4 oz.	11½		Sugar added
6/10	Tomato	Juice	Eastern or California	3 qts.		4 oz.	24		
12/46 oz.	Tomato	Juice	Eastern or California	46 oz.		4 oz.	11½		
12/46 oz.	Vegetable	Juice	Eastern	46 oz.		4 oz.	11½		
12/46 oz.	Apricot	Nectar	California	46 oz.		4 oz.	11½		Sweetened
12/46 oz.	Boysenberry	Nectar	Northwest	46 oz.		4 oz.	11½		Sugar added
12/46 oz.	Loganberry	Nectar		46 oz.		4 oz.	11½		Sweetened
12/46 oz.	Peach	Nectar	California Elberta	46 oz.		4 oz.	11½		Sugar added
12/46 oz.	Pear	Nectar	California	46 oz.		4 oz.	11½		Sugar added
12/1 qt.	Punch	Beverage base	Oahu			8 oz.	27		Pineapple juice, orange juice, apricot nectar, loganberry nectar
4/1 gal.	Punch	Beverage base	Oahu			8 oz.	96		Pineapple juice, orange juice, apricot nectar, loganberry nectar
12/1 qt.	Syrup	Beverage base	Concord Grape			8 oz.	28¼		
12/1 qt.	Syrup	Beverage base	Lemonade			8 oz.	24		Sugar, water, corn syrup, concentrated lemon juice, lemon oil, ascorbic acid, certified artificial color, and 1/10 of 1 percent benzoate of soda
12/1 qt.	Syrup	Beverage base	Refresh-O-Orange Press			8 oz.	30		
				PICKLES					
6/10	Pickles	Sweet, circles	Kurley Kut (serrated)	3 qts.	360 to 400	3	120 to 133		1½-inch diameter
6/10	Pickles	Sweet	Miniature	3 qts.	425	2 to 3	130		About 1½-inch length
6/10	Pickles	Sweet	Tiny	3 qts.	230 to 240	2	125		About 1¾-inch length
6/10	Pickles	Sweet	Midget	3 qts.	160 to 165	2	80		About 2-inch length
6/10	Pickles	Sweet, chips	Twentieth-century cross cuts	3 qts.	461	3 to 4	150		Small-type pickle, 1¼-inch diameter
6/10	Pickles	Sweet	Quartered stix	3 qts.	170 to 180	2	75 to 80		
6/10	Pickles	Sweet	Tidbits	8 lbs.	315 to 320	1 oz.	88		Watermelon, cantaloupe, Burr gherkin halves, pickle rings, tiny sweet gherkins, diced red peppers
6/10	Pickles	Sweet	Mixed	3 qts.	357	1 oz.	70		70 percent cut mixed pickles, 20 percent cauliflower, 10 percent onions
6/10	Cucumber	Sweet, circles	Cross cut	3 qts.	225 to 235	2 to 3	110 to 120		
6/10	Pickles	Sweet	Whole No. 60	3 qts.	115 to 120	1 to 2	58 to 112		
6/10	Pickles	Sweet, whole	Small No. 36	3 qts.	55 to 60	1	55 to 60		About 3-inch length
6/10	Pickles	Home-style	Circles	3 qts.	390	4	95 to 98		Fresh cucumber pickles, bread-and-butter style

Table 9 (continued)

PICKLES (continued)

Cans per Case and Container Size	Food	Style	Type	Approximate Net Weight	Range in Contents per Container	Suggested Portion per Serving	Approximate Portions per Container	Approximate Drained Weight	Miscellaneous Information
6/10	Pickles	Home-style	Quartered, stix	3 qts	140 to 150	2	70 to 75		Bread-and-butter style
6/10	Pickles	Dill, sweet	Circles, cross cuts	3 qts	280 to 300	2 to 3	140 to 150		
6/10	Pickles	Dill, genuine	Circles	3 qts	225 to 235	2	110 to 115		
6/10	Pickles	Dill, genuine	Whole, No. 18	3 qts	32 to 35	½	75 to 80		About 3½-inch length
6/10	Pickles	Dill, genuine	Whole, No. 12	3 qts	20 to 24	¾	80 to 90		About 4-inch length
6/10	Pickles	Dill, genuine	Whole, No. 18, garlic-flavored	3 qts	30 to 35	¾	80 to 90		About 3½-inch length

OLIVES

Cans per Case and Container Size	Food	Style	Type	Approximate Net Weight	Range in Contents per Container	Suggested Portion per Serving	Approximate Portions per Container	Approximate Drained Weight	Miscellaneous Information
4/1 gal.	Olives	Colossal	Queen, plain	5 lbs 8 ozs	180 to 190	1	180 to 190		Imported Spain. Size: 60-60
4/1 gal.	Olives	Jumbo	Queen, plain	5 lbs 12 ozs	200	1	200		Size 70-80
4/1 gal.	Olives	Mammoth	Queen, plain	5 lbs 12 ozs	220	1	220		Imported Spain. Size: 80-100
4/1 gal.	Olives	Giant	Queen, plain	5 lbs 12 ozs	250	1	250		Size: 90-110
4/1 gal.	Olives	Large	Queen, plain	5 lbs 4 ozs	280	1 to 2	140 to 280		Imported Spain. Size: 100-110
4/1 gal.	Olives	Medium	Queen, plain	5 lbs	330	2 to 3	110 to 165		Size: 130-150
4/1 gal.	Olives	Fancy, pitted	Queen, plain	5 lbs 12 ozs	260	1	260		Size: 90-100
4/1 gal.	Olives	Colossal	Queen, stuffed	5 lbs 14 ozs	200	1	200		Imported Spain stuffed with bright red Spanish pimiento. Size: 70-80
4/1 gal.	Olives	Jumbo	Queen, stuffed	6 lbs	225	1	225		Size 80-90
4/1 gal.	Olives	Mammoth	Queen, stuffed	5 lbs 12 ozs	250	1	250		Imported Spain stuffed with bright red pimiento. Size: 90-100
4/1 gal.	Olives	Large	Queen, stuffed	5 lbs 12 ozs	300	1 to 2	150 to 200		Imported Spain stuffed with bright red pimiento. Size: 100-130
4/1 gal.	Olives	Medium	Queen, stuffed	5 lbs 4 ozs	330	2 to 3	110 to 165		Size: 130-150
4/1 gal.	Olives	Medium	Manzanilla, stuffed	5 lbs 12 ozs	700	3 to 4	175 to 233		Size: 240-260
4/1 gal.	Olives	Small	Manzanilla, stuffed	5 lbs 2 ozs	800 to 822	4 to 5	160 to 200		Imported Spain. Size: 300-320
6/10	Olives	Super colossal	Ripe	4 lbs	128	1	128		Seviliano variety
6/10	Olives	Colossal	Ripe	4 lbs	152	1	152		
6/10	Olives	Large	Ripe	4 lbs 2 ozs	404	1 to 2	202 to 404		Mission variety
6/10	Olives	Medium	Ripe. pitted		460	2 to 3	153 to 230		
6/10	Olives	Medium	Ripe. pitted	3 lbs 4 ozs	480	1 to 2	240 to 480		
24/5½ oz.	Olives	Medium		5½ oz.	50 to 52	1 to 2	26 to 52		

DESSERT POWDER BASES

Cans per Case and Container Size	Food	Style	Type	Approximate Net Weight	Range in Contents per Container	Suggested Portion per Serving	Approximate Portions per Container	Approximate Drained Weight	Miscellaneous Information
6/10	Dessert powder	Gelatin		5 lbs. 4 ozs.		4 oz.	128		Flavors: apple, wild cherry, citrus, grape, lemon, lime, melba, orange, black raspberry, red raspberry, strawberry. Dissolved in 3½ gals. of water
12/2½	Dessert powder	Gelatin		1 lb. 8 ozs.		4 oz.	32		Flavors: apple, wild cherry, citrus, grape, lemon, lime, melba, orange, black raspberry, red raspberry, strawberry. Dissolved in 1 gal. of water
6/10	Dessert powder			5 lbs.		4 oz.	70—⅛ C.		Flavors: butterscotch, chocolate, coconut, vanilla. Makes 6—9 in. pies. Used 2 gals. of water

6/10	Dessert powder		Lemon	5 lbs. 8 ozs.		4 oz.	70—½ C.		Makes 6—9 in. pies. Used 2 gals. of water
12/2½	Dessert powder			1 lb. 6 ozs.		4 oz.	20—½ C.		Flavors: butterscotch, chocolate, coconut, vanilla. Makes 2—9 in. pies Used 2¼ qts. of water
12/2½	Dessert powder		Lemon	1 lb. 8 ozs.		4 oz.	20—½ C.		Makes 2—9 in. pies. Used 2¼ qts. of water
12/2½	Dessert powder	Blancmange	Mix 'n serve	1 lb. 4 ozs.		4 oz.	30—½ C.		Flavors: chocolate, coconut. Used 2½ qts. of water
12/2½	Dessert powder	Blancmange	Mix 'n serve	1 lb. 8 ozs.		4 oz.	30—½ C.		Flavors: butterscotch, vanilla. Used 3 qts. of water

SEAFOODS

24/303	Clams	No. 1 Little Neck	Whole	1 lb. 4 ozs.	16 Whole 1¾ Cups			8 oz.	Liquor—1½ C.
24/2	Clams	No. 2 Little Neck	Whole	1 lb. 4 ozs.	66 Whole 1 Cup			10 oz.	Liquor— ½C.
12/5 Tall	Clams		Chopped or minced	3 lbs. 3 ozs.	4 Cups			1 lb. 7 ozs.	Liquor—3½ C.
24/1	Crab meat	King	Imported Japan	13 oz.	B & F—3½Cups C—2¾ Cups	2 oz. 4 oz.	6½ 3½	10 oz.	Liquor—½ C.
12/2½	Fish flakes	Pollack		2 lbs.	5¾ Cups				Liquor—1¼ C.
24/1	Lobster		Imported Canada	10 oz.	B & F—2½Cups C—2¼ Cups	2 oz. 4 oz.	5 2½		Liquor—½ C.
48/1	Salmon	Sockeye	Fancy Red Alaska	1 lb.	B & F—2¼ Cups C—2 Cups	2 oz. (⅓—½ C.) 4 oz. (⅔—¾ C.)	5 2½		Liquor—½C. Color—deep red. Small firm flakes

CONDENSED SOUPS

6/10	Chicken	Broth		3 qts.		8 oz. - 1C.	24+		Chicken broth, hydrolized wheat protein, chicken fat, and fresh vegetable flavoring
12/5	Chicken	Broth		3 lbs. 2 oz.		8 oz. - 1C.	12+		
12/5	Beef	Bouillon		3 lbs. 2 oz.		8 oz. - 1C.	12		Beef stock, parsnips, carrots, beef extract, onions, and seasonings
12/5	Tomato	Bouillon		3 lbs. 2 oz.		8 oz. - 1C.	12+		Tomato juice, sugar, salt, beef extract, vegetable oil, onion powder, and spices
12/5	Chicken	Chowder		3 lbs. 2 oz.		8 oz. - 1C.	12		Chicken broth, potatoes, carrots, chicken, celery, cornstarch, onions, peas, corn, tomatoes, red peppers, and seasonings
12/5	Clam	Chowder	Manhattan	3 lbs. 2 oz.		8 oz. - 1C.	12		Potatoes, clams, carrots, clam juice, tomato paste, red peppers, onions, celery, parsley flakes, and seasonings
12/5	Clam	Chowder	New England	3 lbs. 2 oz.		8 oz. - 1C.	12		Clams, potatoes, onions, and seasonings
12/5		Chowder	Red Snapper	3 lbs. 2 oz.		8 oz. - 1C.	12		Potatoes, red snappers, tomatoes, carrots, onions, clam juice, corn, celery, red peppers, rice
12/5	Asparagus, Bean, Beef, Celery, Chicken, Chicken-Rice, Mushroom, Pea, Pepper-Pot, Tomato, Vegetable	Soup		3 lbs. 2 oz.		8 oz. - 1C.	12		According to recipe

Table 9 (continued)

Cans per Case and Container Size	Food	Style	Approximate Net Weight	Suggested Portion Per Serving	Approx Portions Per Container	Miscellaneous Information
JAMS						
6/10	Apple	Butter	7 lbs 8 oz.	No. 45 souffle, 1 oz	120	Made from evaporated apples
6/4 3/4#	Cherry, Grape, Damson plum, Plum	Jam	4 lbs 12 oz	No. 45 souffle, 1 oz	76	Made from fresh fruits and juices
JELLIES						
6/4½#	Apple, Grape, Black Raspberry, Cherry, Currant, Elderberry, Mint, Plum, Quince, Strawberry	Jelly	4 lbs 8 oz	No. 45 souffle, 1 oz	72	Made from fresh fruits and juices
6/10	Apple, Grape	Jelly	8 lbs	No. 45 souffle, 1 oz	128	
PRESERVES						
6/10	Peach, Plum, Strawberry	Preserves	8 lbs 4 oz	No. 45 souffle, 1 oz	132	Made from fresh fruits and juices
6/4 3/4#	Apricot, Blackberry, Cherry, Grape, Elberta Peach, Orange, Pineapple, Pine Apricot, Plum, Raspberry, Strawberry	Preserves	4 lbs 12 oz	No. 45 souffle, 1 oz	76	

FROZEN FRUITS AND VEGETABLES

Frozen Fruits

There are not too many frozen fruits used directly by the hotel and restaurant trade, but in the large pastry shops in hotels and institutional kitchens, large quantities of a few items are used. The frozen fruit items used mostly in the pastry shop are apples, cherries, peaches, blueberries, and huckleberries, along with fresh fruit purees and some berry purees to be used in the making of fresh fruit sherbet and water ices. There are some frozen pineapple sections available in the market, and some operators buy frozen melon balls for topping fruit cups.

Most frozen raspberries and strawberries are packaged in 10-ounce containers. Pineapple sections are generally frozen in a #10 can, as are the exotic Ola Rosa peaches from California orchards. There are about forty peach halves in each #10 can, and there are 20 to 25 portions of pineapple chunks in a #10 can of frozen pineapple.

Frozen pie fruits are generally packed in 5-gallon tins with varying amounts of sugar added. The most popular are pie apples with a 6 to 1 sugar content, which means that there are six parts apple to one part sugar by weight. Some other pie fruits are more fragile, and the sugar content required may be increased to four parts of fruit to one part of sugar.

A 5-gallon tin of frozen pie fruits should produce about 20 to 25 8-inch by 1-inch pies.

CONVENIENCE FOODS

A leading dealer in convenience foods lists over six thousand items on his price sheets. His list has over one thousand ready-to-serve entree items with sauces, vegetables, potatoes, pastry, and practically any other food items necessary to back up a long and complicated menu. The packaging of these items varies from 6 to a package to 100 per package. Portion sizes vary from 1 ounce up to 10 ounces. Some are already combined with sauce, while others come with sauces to be added. Some include all of their ingredients, and others, like beef stew, require that cooked potatoes be added just before serving. Preparation methods vary from unwrapping and placing in a conventional oven to the use of more sophisticated equipment: convection ovens, crown-X ovens, and the K-5 and K-10 Re-con ovens put out by the Foster Refrigeration Manufacturing Company of Poughkeepsie, New York.

With such variety in packaging as well as portion sizes, it is impossible to offer a meaningful guide to the food buyer in this part of the table. Fortunately, for the buyer, almost all of the packages that are sold for convenience foods list not only the portion size but the weight of the package and the number of portions in the package. We refer the food buyer to the actual packaging information or to the dealers representing the convenience food supplier.

Appendix II

Calcumetric®: Anglo-Metric Converter

1. Temperature

Fahrenheit (F)		Centigrade (C)
212°	=	100°
32°	=	0°
0°	=	17.8°

°F · C

°F	°C
320°	160°
305°	150°
290°	140°
275°	130°
260°	
245°	120°
230°	110°
212°	100°
200°	90°
185°	
170°	80°
155°	70°
140°	60°
125°	50°
110°	40°
95°	
80°	30°
65°	20°
50°	10°
32°	0°
20°	−10°
5°	−20°
−10°	−30°
−25°	
−40°	−40

Source: Calcumetric® by SUCCESS Calendars, copyright 1975, by Columbian Art Works, Inc., Milwaukee, Wisconsin. Reprinted with permission.

2. Length

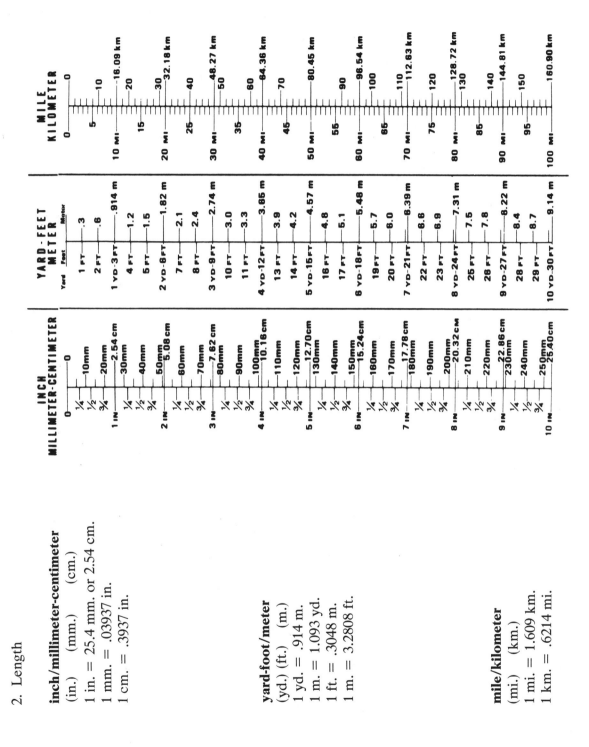

inch/millimeter-centimeter

(in.)   (mm.)   (cm.)

1 in. = 25.4 mm. or 2.54 cm.

1 mm. = .03937 in.

1 cm. = .3937 in.

yard-foot/meter

(yd.) (ft.)   (m.)

1 yd. = .914 m.

1 m. = 1.093 yd.

1 ft. = .3048 m.

1 m. = 3.2808 ft.

mile/kilometer

(mi.)   (km.)

1 mi. = 1.609 km.

1 km. = .6214 mi.

3. Area

square foot-square inch/square centimeter

(sq. ft.)   (sq. in.)   (sq. cm.)

1 sq. ft. = 144 sq. in. = 929.03 sq. cm.

1 sq. in. = 6.4516 sq. cm.

1 sq. cm. = .155 sq. in.

square yard-square foot/square meter

(sq. yd.)   (sq. ft.)   (sq. m.)

1 sq. yd. = 9 sq. ft. = .82 sq. m.

1 sq. ft. = .092 sq. m.

1 sq. m. = 10.8 sq. ft.

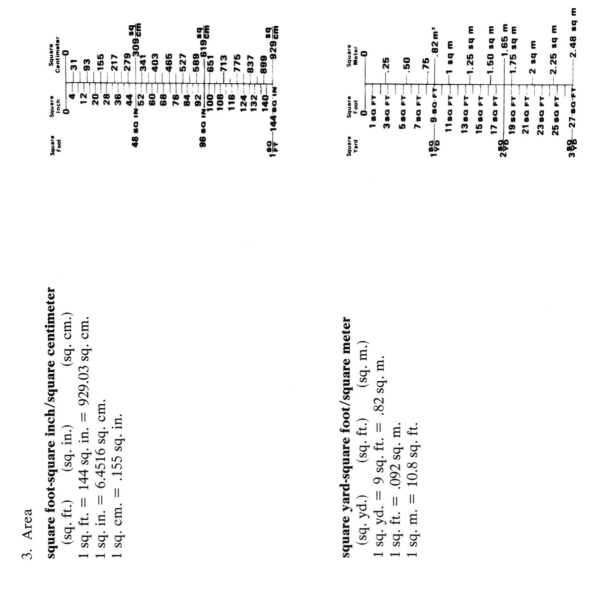

4. Capacity

| Unit | UNITED STATES | | | | | METRIC | |
	fluid ounce (fl. oz.)	liquid pint (liq. pt.)	liquid quart (liq. qt.)	cubic inch (c.i.)	cubic centimeter (c.c.)	deciliter (dl.)	liter (l.)
1 fl. oz.	1	.0625	.03125	1.8047	29.574	.2957	.0296
1 liq. pt.	16	1	.5	28.875	473.18	4.7316	.4732
1 liq. qt.	32	2	1	57.75	946.35	9.4633	.9463
1 c.i.	.5541	.3463	.01732	1	16.387	.1639	.0164
1 c.c.							
1 milliliter (ml.)	.0338	.00211	.00106	.06102	1	.01	.001
1 dl.	3.3815	.2113	.1057	6.1025	100	1	.1
1 l.	33.815	2.1134	1.0567	61.025	1,000	10	1

Note: The figures above have been rounded where full extension was impossible.

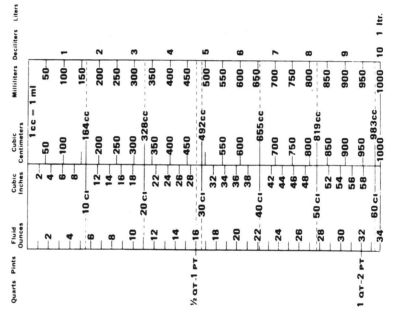

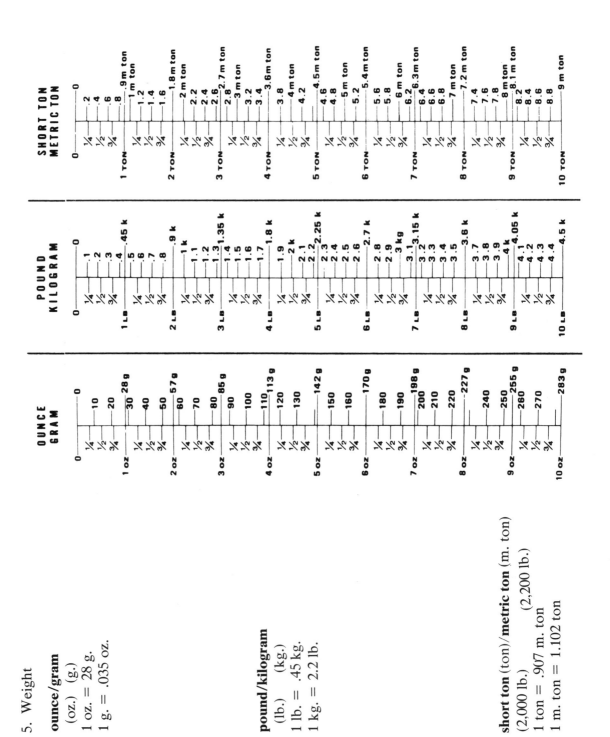

5. Weight

ounce/gram
  (oz.)   (g.)
1 oz. = 28 g.
1 g. = .035 oz.

pound/kilogram
  (lb.)   (kg.)
1 lb. = .45 kg.
1 kg. = 2.2 lb.

short ton (ton)/**metric ton** (m. ton)
(2,000 lb.)   (2,200 lb.)
1 ton = .907 m. ton
1 m. ton = 1.102 ton

Appendix III   The Big Four: Basic Complement Manual for a Hotel or Restaurant

Basic Complement Manual
For A Hotel/Restaurant

A. *Holloware Silver*
   1) Formal dining room
   2) Room service
   3) Banquet department

B. *Flatware*
   1) Main dining room
   2) Room service
   3) Coffee house
   4) Banquet department
   5) Employee cafeteria

C. *Chinaware*
   1) Main dining room
   2) Room service
   3) Banquet department
   4) Coffee house

D. *Beverage Glassware*
   Dining room and bars

E. *Food Glassware*
   Dining room and room service

F. *Food and Beverage Glassware—Banquets*

Silver Holloware Complement
Main Dining Room
Ratio to Total Seating Capacity

Item	Size	In-Service Par	One Year's Consumption
Boat, sauce	3 oz.	25%	
Boat, sauce	8 oz.	15%	
Bowl, ice and butter	128 oz.	5%	
Bowl, finger	5 in.	30%	For 100–200 seats
Bowl, finger (plate)	5¾ in	30%	
Bowl, sugar open	8 oz.	30%	
Caster, oil and vinegar	5–5½ in.	5%	
Chafing dish, one to two portions	8 in., 36 oz.	3%	1%
Chafing dish, three to four portions	10 in., 64 oz.	2%	1%
Cocktail set, oyster	7½ oz.	6%	1%
Compote	8 by 4 in.	3%	
Cover, oval meat platter	12 in.	10%	
Cover, oval meat platter	16 in.	3%	
Cover, vegetable dish, oblong, one to two portions	5½ in.	20%	3%
Cover vegetable dish, oblong, two to three portions	7 in.	10%	3%
Dish, vegetable, one to two portions	5½ in.	20%	6%
Dish, vegetable, three to four portions	7 in.	10%	3%
Pitcher, cream	3 oz.	30%	9%
Pitcher, cream	6 oz.	20%	6%
Pitcher, cream	8 oz.	6%	4%
Pitcher, water with lip	64 oz.	8%	1%
Platter, oval meat	12 in.	30%	5%
Platter, oval meat	16 in.	15%	1%
Platter, oval meat	18 in.	8%	
Pot, coffee (one portion)	10 oz.	30%	10%
Pot, coffee (two portions)		19%	%
Ravier, bread tray	13 oz.	25%	10%
Stand, ice cream	4¼–4 in.	25%	2%
Stand, parfait	4 oz.	15%	1%
Stand, supreme	5 in.	10%	2%
Stand, supreme liner		10%	2%
Stand, supreme ring		10%	2%
Top, salt and pepper		33%	20%
Tray, case plastic		10%	1%
Tray, waiter round	14 in.	4 each for every 150 seats	
Tureen, plate (small and large)		15%	7%
Tureen, soup (one to two portions)	20 oz.	12%	5%
Tureen, soup (two to four portions)	40 oz.	8%	2%
Wine cooler	8¼ in. high	6%	1%
Wine cooler, stand	24½ in.	3%	

Holloware Complement
Room Service

(In-service par ratio base figure is equal to 1/5 of the total number of rooms in the hotel for hotels over 1,000 rooms and ¼ for hotels with under 1,000 rooms.)

Item	Size	In-Service Par	One Year's Consumption
Caster, oil and vinegar	5½ in.	3%	
Chafing dish, food (one to two portions)	26 oz.	3%	1%
Chafing dish, food (three to four portions)	42 oz.	2%	1%
Cocktail set, oyster	7½ in.	6%	1%
Cover, meat platter	12 in.	7%	
Cover, meat platter	16 in.	3%	
Platter, oval meat (two portions)	12 in.	20%	5%
Pot, coffee (thermos-type stainless steel)	20 oz.	25%	3%
Salt and pepper		20%	20%
Supreme ring (stand)		10%	5%
Supreme stand	5 in.	10%	2%
Supreme stand		10%	15%
Tray, bread		5%	1%
Tureen, soup (one to two portions)	20 oz.	10%	5%
Tureen, soup (three to four portions)	40 oz.	6%	2%

Holloware Silver Complement
Banquet Department

(Based on ⅔ of the total seating capacity in function rooms)

Item	Size	In-Service Par	One Year's Consumption
Boat, sauce	12 oz.	10%	3%
Bowl, punch with underliner	4 gals.	Two for every 250 seats up to 1,000	
Bowl, sugar	8 oz.	10%	2%
Candlesticks, single (one per table)	11½ in.	10%	1%
Candelabras, three branch	18 in.	2%	
Caster, oil and vinegar		1%	
Chafing dish set	Legion	One set for every 500 covers (Limit of two)	
Cocktail set, oyster		1%	
Compote stand	8 in.	10%	4%
Cover, escoffier dish		10%	1%
Dish, vegetable (portions)	2 by 48 oz.	10%	1%
Escoffier dish	13 by 10¾ by 2½ in.	10%	1%
Pitcher, cream	8 oz.	10%	1%
Pitcher, water with lip	64 oz.	10%	1%
Platter, oval fish	25 in.	1%	
Platter, oval meat (ten portions) French service	18 in.	10%	1%
Pot, coffee (ten portions)	64 oz.	10%	2%

Holloware Silver Complement
Banquet Department *(continued)*

(Based on ⅔ of the total seating capacity in function rooms)

Item	Size	In-Service Par	One Year's Consumption
Stand, table no.	22 in.	10%	1%
Supreme stand	5 in.	75%	1%
Supreme stand ring		75%	5%
Supreme stand liner		75%	15%
Tea set, regent		One set for every 500 covers	
Top, salt and pepper	3–6 oz.	20%	20%
Tray, bread		10%	1%
Tray, ed. waiter s/s (French service)	14 in.	10%	1%
Tray, oblong waiter (buffet service)	22 in.	6 each for every 580 guests	
Tureen, soup	80 oz.	10%	
Tureen, underliner			
Urn, coffee	3 gals.	One for every 500 covers (Limit two)	

Flat Silverware Complement
(Also Stainless Steel)
Main Dining Room
Ratio to Total Seating

Item	In-Service Par	One Year's Consumption
Crumb scraper	6%	2%
Fork, dinner (med)	250%	60%
Fork, fish	10%	10%
Fork, oyster	75%	60%
Knife, dessert and butter	150%	70%
Knife, dinner	150%	40%
Knife, fish	10%	10%
Ladle, brule	1%	—
Ladle, soup, 8 oz.	20%	5%
Spoon, bouillon	50%	50%
Spoon, demitasse	50%	100%
Spoon, dessert or soup	50%	50%
Spoon, iced tea	35%	10%
Spoon, table and service	35%	10%
Spoon, tea	300%	150%
Tongs, ice	10%	1%

Flat Silverware Complement
(Also Stainless Steel)
Room Service

(In-service par ratio base figure is equal to 1/5 of the total number of rooms in the hotel over 1,000 rooms and ¼ for hotels with under 1,000 rooms)

Item	In-Service Par	One Year's Consumption
Fork, dinner and salad	200%	60%
Fork, oyster	25%	60%
Knife, dessert and butter	150%	70%
Knife, dinner	150%	40%
Spoon, dessert or soup	50%	50%
Spoon, iced tea	35%	10%
Spoon, table and service	25%	10%
Spoon, tea	300%	150%

Coffee House
Ratio to Total Seating

Item	In-Service Par	One Year's Consumption
Fork, dinner	200%	60%
Knife, dinner and butter	150%	40%
Spoon, dessert or soup	75%	50%
Spoon, iced tea	35%	10%
Spoon, table and service	25%	10%
Spoon, tea	300%	200%

Flat Silverware Complement
(Also Stainless Steel)
Banquet Department

(Ratio to ⅔ total seating of function rooms)

Item	In-Service Par	One Year's Consumption
Crumb scraper	2%	1%
Fork, dinner and salad	300%	60%
Fork, oyster	100%	60%
Knife, dessert and butter	125%	70%
Knife, dinner	125%	40%
Ladle, punch, long (3½ oz.)	One for every 250 covers	—
Ladle, soup (6 oz.)	10%	3%
Spoon, bouillon	80%	20%
Spoon, demitasse	100%	250%
Spoon, dessert or soup	50%	100%
Spoon, iced tea	25%	10%
Spoon, serving buffet	1%	1%
Spoon, table and service	50%	25%
Spoon, tea	300%	200%

Employees' Cafeteria
Ratio to Total Cafeteria Seating

Item	In-Service Par	
Fork, dinner and salad	300%	—
Knife, dinner and butter	200%	—
Spoon, dessert and soup	100%	—
Spoon, iced tea	50%	—
Spoon, tea	300%	—

Chinaware Complement
Main Dining Room
Ratio to Total Seating

Size	Item	In-Service Par	One Year's Consumption
10½ in.	Service plate	100%	10%
9¾ in.	Dinner plate	200%	75%
8 in.	Salad and underliner	300%	100%
6⅜ in.	Bread and butter	200%	125%
8⅞ in.	Soup plate	50%	25%
6¾ in.	Terrapin plate	25%	10%
5 in.	Vegetable dish	100%	50%
7 oz.	Coffee cup	300%	300%
6 in.	Saucer	200%	150%
10 oz.	Bouillion cup	80%	75%
3½ oz.	Demitasse cup	50%	50%
4⅝ in.	Demitasse saucer	50%	25%
11¼ in	Chop plate	25%	10%
7 in.	Salad bowl #1210 Hall China	75%	50%

Room Service
Ratio Per Complement Cover

(Based on 1/5 of total number of rooms [over 1,000 rooms]
1/4 of total number of rooms [under 1,000 rooms])

Size	Item	In-Service Par	One Year's Consumption
9¾ in.	Dinner plate	100%	Replace from dining room reserve
7⅜ in.	Salad and underliner	200%	"
6⅜ in	Bread and butter	150%	"
8⅞ in.	Soup plate	25%	"
5¼ in.	Vegetable dish	100%	"
7 oz.	Coffee cup	150%	"
6 in.	Coffee saucer	100%	"
6½ in.	Egg cup	10%	"
10 oz.	Bouillon cup	50%	"
7 in.	Salad bowl	25%	"
11¼ in.	Chop plate	25%	"

Banquet Department
(Based on 65% of total banquet seating)

Size	Item	In-Service Par	One Year's Consumption
9¾ in.	Dinner plate	150%	75%
8 in.	Salad and underliner	250%	100%
6⅜ in.	Bread and butter	125%	75%
8⅞ in.	Soup plate (French service)	125%	25%
5¼ in	Vegetable dish	25%	25%
7 oz.	Coffee cup	125%	200%
6 in.	Coffee saucer	100%	100%
10 oz.	Bouillon cup	50%	50%
3½ oz.	Demitasse cup	100%	50%
4⅝ in.	Demitasse saucer	75%	40%

Chinaware Complement
Coffee House
Ratio to Total Seating

Size	Item	In-Service Par	One Year's Consumption
9¾ in.	Dinner plate	150%	75%
8 in	Salad and underliner	200%	100%
6⅜ in	Bread and butter	150%	100%
6⅜ in.	Grapefruit and cereal	50%	20%
5¼ in.	Vegetable dish	50%	25%
9 in.	Meat platter	25%	10%
7 oz.	Coffee cup	300%	200%
6 in.	Coffee saucer	200%	75%
6 in.	Nappy bowl	10%	10%
6½ in.	Egg cup	10%	10%
7 in.	Salad bowl	50%	50%
6 oz.	Sugar bowl (com)	30%	10%

Beverage Glassware Complement—
Dining Room and Bars
Ratio to Total Seating

Size	Item	In-Service Par	One Year's Consumption
2 oz.	Whiskey glass—1¼ oz. line	25%	150%
8 oz.	Highball glass	133%	250%
12 oz.	Collins glass	25%	100%
9 oz.	Pilsner glass	10%	75%
4½ oz.	Whiskey sour	25%	75%
9 oz.	Old fashioned	33%	250%
12 oz.	Brandy snifter	5%	25%
2 oz.	Cordial glass	25%	25%
4 oz.	Brandy snifter	10%	25%
3 oz.	Sherry	30%	20%
6½ oz.	Still wine glass	50%	75%
8½ oz.	Spark lug wine	50%	75%
10½ oz.	Champagne wine	25%	75%
4 oz.	Cocktail glass	50%	150%
6 oz.	Cocktail carafe	25%	50%
5 in.	Nappy bowl	25%	50%
16 oz.	Bar water	10%	25%
9 oz.	Tulip champagne	20%	60%

Food Glassware Complement
Dining Rooms and Room Service

Size	Item	In-Service Par	One Year's Consumption
52 oz.	Water pitcher	10%	33%
5 oz.	Oil and vinegar	10%	16%
5 oz.	Delmonico glass	60%	100%
8 oz.	Highball—juices	25%	60%
5¼ oz.	Parfait glass	35%	5%
10 oz.	Water goblet	150%	200%
9 oz.	Water tumbler	50%	75%
12 oz.	Iced tea	30%	150%
3½ oz.	Oyster cocktail	25%	75%
4¾ oz.	Fruit nappy	25%	100%
7 oz.	Sherbet—Waterford style	60%	100%
8 oz.	Banana split	25%	25%

Food and Beverage Glassware—Banquets
Basic Complement

(Based on ⅔ total banquet seating)

Size	Item	In-Service Par	One Year's Consumption
64 oz.	Water pitcher	15%	
5½ oz.	Footed sherbet		
10 oz.	Water goblet	150%	150%
9 oz.	Tumbler	25%	25%
9 oz.	Highball	200%	200%
8 oz.	Old fashioned	20%	20%
4½ oz.	Cocktail—no line	25%	50%
6½ oz.	All-purpose wine (Can be used for sherry)	100%	200%
8 oz.	Round wine and champagne	100%	200%
2 oz.	Cordial—brandy	100%	200%

G Series refers to Edward Don-Chicago Catalogue—Does not include Specialty Glassware

Basic Complement
Rooms—Linen
Per Bed

Basic—
1 Fitted sheet
2 Top sheets
2 Pillow cases
2 Pillow covers
1 Underpad
1 Bedspread
1 Bed blanket
1 Throw blanket

Bathroom
2 Bath towels
2 Face towels
2 Washcloths

Minimum Per Required—five times
1. In room
2. In transit
3. In laundry
4. Resting
5. Reserve for replacement

Banquet and Dining Room Linen

	Per Table
Tablecloths	1
Table tops	2

	Per Seat
Napkins 17 x 17, 20 x 20, 21 x 21, 17 x 21	1½

Side towels	2 per waiter per shift

Uniforms—dining room	3 per waiter
Uniforms—banquet	1¼ per waiter

Minimum Per Required—five times
1. In use
2. In transit
3. In laundry
4. In linen room (resting)
5. In reserve for replacement

Note: Large banquet hotels usually carry a single set-up of two alternate colors of table linen for special events.

How To Determine Correct Tablecloth Size

Tablecloth Size, In. (approx.)	Fits Table Size, In.
40 square	24 square
46 square	30 square
49 square	33 square
52 square	36 square
58 square	42 square
64 square	48 square
40 x 46	24 x 30
40 x 52	24 x 36
40 x 58	24 x 42
46 x 52	30 x 36
46 x 58	30 x 42
46 x 61	30 x 45
46 x 64	30 x 48
46 x 88	30 x 72
46 x 112	30 x 96
52 x 88	36 x 72
52 x 112	36 x 96
36 round	20 round
40 round	24 round
46 round	30 round
52 round	36 round
58 round	42 round
64 round	48 round
67 round	51 round
70 round	54 round
76 round	60 round
88 round	72 round

Selected Bibliography

Efforts to compile the information in this volume were greatly aided by the cooperation of many organizations designed to aid people working with foods and in food operations. Many have already been mentioned, but a list of those especially likely to have information helpful to the buyer, along with their addresses, follows.

American Egg Board
205 Touhy Avenue
Park Ridge, IL 60068

California Raisin Advisory Board
P.O. Box 5335
Fresno, CA 93755

College of Agriculture Extension Service
Pennsylvania State University
University Park, PA 16801

Educational Department
Blue Goose, Inc.
P.O. Box 46
Fullerton, CA 92632

Florida Citrus Commission
Florida Department of Citrus
P.O. Box 148
Lakeland, FL 33802

Food and Nutrition Information and
    Educational Materials Center
National Agricultural Library, Room 304
Beltsville, MD 20705

Food and Wines from France, Inc.
Information and Promotion Center
1350 Avenue of the Americas
New York, NY 10019

Hotel, Restaurant, and Travel
    Administration
Flint Laboratory
University of Massachusetts
Amherst, MA 01003

Information Division
Canada Department of Agriculture
Ottawa K1A 0C7

Institute of Shortening and Edible Oils, Inc.
1750 New York Avenue, N.W.
Washington, DC 20006

Italian Trade Commission
One World Trade Center
Suite 2057
New York, NY 10048

National Association of Meat Purveyors
252 West Ina Road
Tucson, AZ 85704

National Consumer Educational Services
    Office
National Marine Fisheries Service
U.S. Department of Commerce
100 East Ohio Street
Room 526
Chicago, IL 60611

National Dairy Council
6300 North River Road
Rosemont, IL 60018

National Fisheries Institute
111 East Wacker Drive
Chicago, IL 60601

National Live Stock and Meat Board
444 North Michigan Avenue
Chicago, IL 60611

National Marine Fisheries Service
National Oceanic and Atmospheric
    Administration
U.S. Department of Commerce
Washington, DC 20235

National Marketing Services Office
National Marine Fisheries Service
100 East Ohio Street
Chicago, IL 60611

National Restaurant Association
One IBM Plaza
Suite 2600
Chicago, IL 60611

National Turkey Federation
Reston International Center
11800 Sunrise Valley Drive
Reston, VA 22091

Office of Communications
U.S. Department of Agriculture
Washington, D.C. 20250

Rice Council
P.O. Box 22802
Houston, TX 77027

Sunkist Growers, Inc.
14130 Riverside Drive
Sherman Oaks, CA 91423

Superintendent of Documents
U.S. Government Printing Office
Washington, DC 20402

Tea Council of the USA, Inc.
230 Park Avenue
New York, NY 10017

Texas Parks and Wildlife Department
4200 Smith School Road
Austin, TX 78744

United Fresh Fruit and Vegetable
    Association
1019 Nineteenth Street, N.W.
Washington, DC 20036

Wheat Flour Institute
1776 F Street, N.W.
Washington, DC 20006

A great many other firms and associations connected with the food industry have been helpful and courteous in responding to our requests for information and assistance. Among these, a special note of appreciation must go to the American Mushroom Institute, the American Spice Trade Association, the Cling Peach Advisory Board, Coldwater Seafood Corporation, the Dried Fruit Association of California, the Idaho Bean Commission, the International Apple Institute, the Louisiana Sweet Potato Commission, the National Canners Association, the National Coffee Association of the USA, the National Soybean Crop Improvement Council, the New Bedford Seafood Co-operative, the Olive Administrative Committee, the Pacific Coast Canned Pear Service, the Roquefort Cheese Association, S & W Fine Foods, Inc., Thomas Lipton, Inc., the Tri-Valley Growers, and the U.S. Trout Farmers Association. This by no means exhausts the names of the organizations that made an effort to help. There are hundreds of private and public organizations to assist the buyer, and libraries and librarians are helpful in locating them. The names and addresses of many trade associations and publishers can be found in: (1) the latest edition of the *Encyclopedia of Associations* (Detroit: Gale Research Co.); and (2) the annual bibliography in the August issues of the *Cornell Hotel and Restaurant Administration Quarterly*, which contains a section entitled "Addresses of Organizations and Publishers."

As for published sources, it is hoped that the following listing will also prove helpful. Once again, it is by no means exhaustive. The listing is divided into government publications and other publications.

U.S. GOVERNMENT PUBLICATIONS

Department of Agriculture

Beef and Veal in Family Meals: A Guide for Consumers. Revised ed. Home and Garden Bulletin No. 118. Washington, D.C., 1975.

Cheese in Family Meals: A Guide for Consumers. Revised ed. Home and Garden Bulletin No. 112. Washington, D.C., 1976.

Cheese Varieties and Descriptions. Agriculture Handbook No. 54. Washington, D.C., 1974.

Convenience Foods for the Hotel, Restaurant and Institutional Market: The Processor's View. Agriculture Economic Report No. 344. Washington, D.C., 1976.

Egg Grading Manual. Agriculture Handbook No. 75. Washington, D.C., 1977.

Eggs in Family Meals: A Guide for Consumers. Revised ed. Home and Garden Bulletin No. 103. Washington, D.C., 1974.

Federal and State Standards for Composition of Milk Products (and Certain Non-Milkfat Products), as of January 1, 1974. Compiled and edited by Roland S. Golden. Revised ed. Agriculture Handbook No. 51. Washington, D.C., 1974.

Food and Nutrition Information and Educational Materials Center Catalog. National Agricultural Library. Food and Nutrition Information and Educational Materials Center. Washington, D.C., 1974-77. Catalog and Supplements 1-5.

Food Purchasing Guide for Group Feeding. Prepared by Betty Peterkin and Beatrice Evans. Agriculture Handbook No. 284. Washington, D.C., 1965.

Fruits in Family Meals: A Guide for Consumers. Revised ed. Home and Garden Bulletin No. 125. Washington, D.C., 1975.

Grade Names Used in U.S. Standards for Farm Products. Revised ed. Agriculture Handbook No. 157. Washington, D.C., 1965.

How to Buy Beef Roasts. Home and Garden Bulletin No. 146. Washington, D.C., 1968.

How to Buy Beef Steaks. Revised ed. Home and Garden Bulletin No. 145. Washington, D.C., 1976.

How to Buy Canned and Frozen Fruits. Home and Garden Bulletin No. 191. Washington, D.C., 1971.

How to Buy Canned and Frozen Vegetables. Revised ed. Home and Garden Bulletin No. 167. Washington, D.C., 1975.

How to Buy Cheese. By F. E. Fenton. Home and Garden Bulletin No. 193. Washington, D.C., 1971.

How to Buy Dairy Products. Revised ed. Home and Garden Bulletin No. 201. Washington, D.C., 1974.

How to Buy Dry Beans, Peas, and Lentils. Home and Garden Bulletin No. 177. Washington, D.C., 1970.

How to Buy Eggs. Revised ed. Home and Garden Bulletin No. 144. Washington, D.C., 1975.

How to Buy Fresh Fruits. Home and Garden Bulletin No. 141. Washington, D.C., 1967.

How to Buy Fresh Vegetables. Home and Garden Bulletin No. 143. Washington, D.C., 1967; reprinted 1976.

How to Buy Lamb. By Sandra Brookover. Home and Garden Bulletin No. 195. Washington, D.C., 1971.

How to Buy Meat for Your Freezer. Home and Garden Bulletin No. 166. Washington, D.C., 1976.

How to Buy Potatoes. By Lawrence E. Ide. Home and Garden Bulletin No. 198. Washington, D.C., 1972.

How to Buy Poultry. Home and Garden

Bulletin No. 157. Washington, D.C., 1968.

How to Use USDA Grades in Buying Food. Revised ed. Home and Garden Bulletin No. 196. Washington, D.C., 1977.

Institutional Meat Purchase Specifications for Sausage Products Approved by USDA. Agricultural Marketing Service, Livestock Division. Washington, D.C., 1976.

Know the Eggs You Buy. Consumer and Marketing Service. Washington, D.C., 1967.

Lamb in Family Meals: A Guide for Consumers. Home and Garden Bulletin No. 124. Washington, D.C., 1974.

Marketing California Raisins. By Joseph C. Perrin and Richard P. Van Diest. Marketing Bulletin No. 58 [Washington, D.C.?], 1975.

Meat and Poultry: Labelled for You. Home and Garden Bulletin No. 172. Washington, D.C., 1969.

Meat and Poultry: Standards for You. Home and Garden Bulletin No. 171. Washington, D.C., 1973.

Meat and Poultry Inspection Program. Animal and Plant Health Inspection Service. Washington, D.C., 1974.

Milk in Family Meals: A Guide for Consumers. Home and Garden Bulletin No. 127. Washington, D.C., 1974.

Nutritive Value of Foods. Revised ed. Agriculture Handbook No. 8. Washington, D.C., 1963.

Nuts in Family Meals: A Guide for Consumers. Revised ed. Home and Garden Bulletin No. 176. Washington, D.C., 1971.

Official United States Standards for Grades of Carcass Beef. Agriculture Marketing Service. Washington, D.C., [1975?].

Pork in Family Meals: A Guide for Consumers. Home and Garden Bulletin No. 160. Washington, D.C., 1975.

Poultry in Family Meals: A Guide for Consumers. Revised ed. Home and Garden

Bulletin No. 110. Washington, D.C., 1974.

Regulations Governing the Grading and Inspection of Poultry and Edible Products Thereof and United States Classes, Standards, and Grades with Respect Thereof. Washington, D.C., 1971.

Regulations Governing the Grading of Shell Eggs and United States Standards, Grades, and Weight Classes for Shell Eggs [effective July 1, 1974]. Poultry Division. Washington, D.C., 1974.

Regulations Governing the Inspection of Eggs and Egg Products. Washington, D.C., 1972.

Seasoning with Spices and Herbs. Agricultural Research Service, Consumer and Food Economics Institute. Hyattsville, Md., 1972.

Shell Egg Grading and Inspection of Egg Products. Poultry Division, Agricultural Marketing Service. Washington, D.C., 1964.

Tips on Selecting Fruits and Vegetables. Marketing Bulletin No. 13. Washington, D.C., 1967.

USDA's Acceptance Service for Meat and Meat Products. Marketing Bulletin No. 47. Washington, D.C., 1970.

USDA's Acceptance Service for Poultry and Eggs. Marketing Bulletin No. 46. Washington, D.C., 1971.

USDA Grade Names for Food and Farm Products. Agriculture Handbook No. 157. Washington, D.C., 1967.

USDA Grades for Pork Carcasses. Marketing Bulletin No. 49. Washington, D.C., 1970.

USDA Grades for Slaughter Swine and Feeder Pigs. Marketing Bulletin No. 51. Washington, D.C., 1970.

USDA Standards for Food and Farm Products. Revised ed. Agriculture Handbook No. 341. Washington, D.C., 1976.

USDA Yield Grades for Beef. Revised ed. Marketing Bulletin No. 45. Washington, D.C., 1974.

USDA Yield Grades for Lamb. Marketing Bulletin No. 52. Washington, D.C., 1970.

Vegetables in Family Meals: A Guide for Consumers. Revised ed. Home and Garden Bulletin No. 105. Washington, D.C., 1975.

Your Money's Worth in Foods. By Betty Peterkin and Cynthia Cromwell. Revised ed. Home and Garden Bulletin No. 183. Washington, D.C., 1977.

Department of Commerce. National Marine Fisheries Service.

Food Fish Facts Nos. 1-56, 62. Developed at the National Consumer Educational Services Office, National Marine Fisheries Service. [Chicago?], undated.

How to Eye and Buy Seafood. Washington, D.C., 1976. "Institutional Purchasing Specification for the Purchasing of Fresh, Frozen, and Canned Fishery Products." By Jack B. Dougherty. [Washington, D.C.?], undated.

Let's Cook Fish! A Complete Guide to Fish Cookery. Fishery Market Development Series No. 8. Washington, D.C., 1976.

Protection through Inspection. Washington, D.C., 1974.

Department of Health, Education, and Welfare.

An Experimental Guide for Personnel Training Requirements of Technicians in Future Food Irradiation Technology Industries: Final Report. By Philip G. Stiles. Washington, D.C. Project No. OEG-1-8-08A007-0034-058.

Food Service Manual. Public Health Service. Washington, D.C., undated.

Department of the Interior. Fish and Wildlife Service.

Fishery Product Inspection. Bureau of Commercial Fisheries. Washington, D.C., 1965.

Guide to Buying Fresh and Frozen Fish and Shellfish. Revised ed. Bureau of Commercial Fisheries. Washington, D.C., 1965.

OTHER PUBLICATIONS*

Amendola, Joseph. *The Baker's Manual*. 3d rev. ed. Rochelle Park, N.J.: Hayden Book Co., Inc., 1972.

American Can Co. *Purchase and Use of Canned Foods: A Guide for Institutional Buyers and Meal Planners*. New York: American Can Co., undated.

American Hospital Association. *Food Service Manual for Health Care Institutions*. Chicago: American Hospital Association, 1966.

Armour and Co. *Convenience Concept for Food Service Systems*. Chicago: Armour Food Service Systems, 1972.

Axler, Bruce H. *Buying and Using Convenience Foods*. Indianapolis, Ind.: ITT Educational Publishing, 1974.

Baker, H. A. (ed.). *Canned Food Reference Manual*. New York: American Can Co., 1939.

Beals, Paul. "Distilled Spirits and the Beverage Operator," *Cornell Hotel and Restaurant Administration Quarterly*, 17 (November 1976), 76-85.

Beau, Francis N. *Quantity Food Purchasing Guide*. Rev. ed. Boston: Cahners Books International, 1974.

Bespaloff, Alexis. *The Signet Book of Wine: A Complete Introduction*. New York: New American Library, 1971.

"Best Buys in Fish and Seafood," *Good Housekeeping*, 181 (July 1975), 127-28.

Bloch, Jacques W. "What Makes a Successful Food Buyer?" *Hospitals: JAHA*, 40 (July 1966).

Bramah, Edward. *Tea and Coffee*. London: Hutchinson, 1972.

Brodner, Joseph, and others. *Profitable Food and Beverage Operation*. Rev. ed.

---

*References in text are keyed to last name of author and date of publication.

New York: Ahrens Publishing Co., Inc., 1962.

Broten, Paul R. "Progress in 'Ready Foods,'" *Cornell Hotel and Restaurant Administration Quarterly*, 15 (May 1974), 37-40.

Burns, Marjorie, and others. *Fish and Shellfish: Selection, Care, and Use.* Ithaca, N.Y.: Cornell University Press. 1962.

California Avocado Advisory Board. *All about the California Avocado.* Newport Beach, Calif.: California Avocado Advisory Board, 1974.

California Raisin Advisory Board. *A Raisin Is a Dried Grape.* Fresno, Calif.: California Raisin Advisory Board, undated.

"Canned Hams," *Consumer Reports*, 35 (October 1970), 581-85.

"Canned Sardines," *Consumer Reports*, 41 (February 1976), 71-75.

"Canned Tuna," *Consumer Reports*, 39 (November 1974), 816-19.

Carcione, Joe, and Bob Lucas. *The Greengrocer: The Consumer's Guide to Fruits and Vegetables.* New York: Pyramid Books, 1972.

Carpenter, Ross (ed.). *Make or Buy.* Boston: Cahners Books, for *Institutions/Volume Feeding Management*, 1970.

Chocolate Information Council. *Consumer's Guide to Cocoa and Chocolate.* New York: Chocolate Information Council, undated.

Chocolate Manufacturers Association. *The Story of Chocolate.* Washington, D.C.: Chocolate Manufacturers Association, 1960.

Clawson, Augusta H. *Equipment Maintenance Manual.* New York: Ahrens Publishing Co., 1951.

Coffee Brewing Center. *Facts about Coffee.* New York: Coffee Brewing Center, undated.

The Consumers Union Report on Wines and Spirits. Mount Vernon, N.Y.: Consumers Union, 1972.

"Cooking Oils and Fats," *Consumer Reports*, 38 (September 1973), 553-57.

Crosby, Marion W., and Katharine W. Harris. *Purchasing Food for 50 Servings.* Rev. ed. Cornell Extension Bulletin No. 803. Ithaca, N.Y.: Cornell University Press, 1963.

Davids, Kenneth. *Coffee: A Guide to Buying, Brewing, and Enjoying.* San Francisco: 101 Productions, 1976.

"Do Eggs Make the Grade?" *Consumer Reports*, 41 (February 1976), 71-75.

Economics Laboratory. *Food Equipment Sanitation Cleaning Procedures, Institutional Division.* New York: Economics Laboratory, Inc., 1965.

_____. *Food Service Operators Sanitation Checklist.* New York: Economics Laboratory, Inc., 1965.

Florida Department of Citrus. *Florida Citrus for Healthy Profits.* n.p.: State of Florida, Department of Citrus, 1975.

Food Grading in Canada. Revised ed. Publication No. 1283. [Ottawa]: Canada Department of Agriculture, 1973.

Gelatin Manufacturers Institute of America. *Standard Methods for the Sampling and Testing of Gelatins.* New York: Gelatin Manufacturers Institute of America, undated.

"Green Beans," *Consumer Reports*, 42 (July 1977), 392-95.

Griswold, Ruth M. *The Experimental Study of Foods.* Boston: Houghton Mifflin Co., 1962.

Grossman, Harold J. *Grossman's Guide to Wines, Spirits, and Beers.* 6th ed. Rev. by Harriet Lembeck. New York: Charles Scribner's Sons, 1977.

Guide to Food Grades. Publication No. 1500. Ottawa: Canada Department of Agriculture, 1972.

"A Guide to the Dairy Counter," *Consumer Reports*, 39 (January 1974), 74-75.

Hilton, Conrad N. *Be My Guest.* Englewood Cliffs, N.J.: Prentice-Hall, Inc., 1957.

Horwath, Ernest B., and others. *Hotel*

Accounting. Rev. ed. New York: Ronald Press, 1970.

"Ice Cream," *Consumer Reports*, 37 (August 1972), 495-502.

"Instant Potatoes," *Consumer Reports*, 36 (July 1971), 435-37.

Institute of Shortening and Edible Oils, Inc. *Food Fats and Oils.* 4th ed. Washington, D.C.: Institute of Shortening and Edible Oils, Inc., 1974.

Johnson, Hugh. *The World Atlas of Wine.* Fireside ed. New York: Simon and Schuster, 1971.

Johnson, Ogden C. "The Food and Drug Administration and Labeling," *Journal of the American Dietetic Association,* 64 (May 1974), 471-75.

Keeney, Philip G. *Commercial Ice Cream and Other Frozen Desserts.* University Park, Pa.: College of Agriculture, Pennsylvania State University, undated.

Keiser, James, and Elmer Kallio. *Controlling and Analyzing Costs in Food Service Operations.* New York: John Wiley and Sons, Inc., 1974, esp. pp. 108-109.

Keister, Douglas C. *Food and Beverage Control.* Englewood Cliffs, N.J.: Prentice-Hall, Inc., 1977.

Kotschevar, Lendal H. *Quantity Food Purchasing.* 2d ed. New York: John Wiley and Sons, Inc., 1976, esp. pp. 3-4.

———, and Margaret E. Terrell. *Food Service Planning: Layout and Equipment.* 2d ed. New York: John Wiley and Son, Inc., 1977.

Levie, Albert. *The Meat Handbook.* 3d ed. Westport, Conn.: Avi Publishing Co., 1970.

Lichine, Alex. *New Encyclopedia of Wines and Spirits.* New York: Alfred A. Knopf, 1974.

Maizel, Bruno. *Food and Beverage Purchasing.* New York: ITT Educational Services, Inc., 1971, esp. pp. 181-85.

Mead, Margaret. "The Changing Significance of Food," *American Scientist,* 58 (1970), 176.

Milner, Max (ed.). *Protein-Enriched Cereal Foods for World Needs.* St. Paul: American Association of Cereal Chemists, Inc., 1969.

Morgan, William J., Jr. *Supervision and Management of Quantity Food Preparation.* Berkeley, Calif.: McCutchan Publishing Corp., 1974, esp. p. 13.

National Association of Meat Purveyors. *Meat Buyer's Guide to Portion Control Meat Cuts.* Tucson, Ariz.: NAMP, 1967.

———. *Meat Buyer's Guide to Standardized Meat Cuts.* Tucson, Ariz.: NAMP, 1961.

National Canners Association. *Facts on Canned Foods.* Washington, D.C.: National Canners Association, 1966.

National Live Stock and Meat Board. *Beef Grading: What It Is; How It's Changed.* Chicago: National Live Stock and Meat Board, 1976.

———. *Facts about Beef.* Chicago: National Live Stock and Meat Board, undated.

———. *It's Beef for Food-Time USA.* Chicago: National Live Stock and Meat Board, undated.

———. *Lessons on Meat.* 4th ed. Chicago: National Live Stock and Meat Board, 1976.

———. *Meat Evaluation Handbook.* Chicago: National Live Stock and Meat Board, 1976.

———. *Meat Manual: Identification, Buying, Cooking.* 5th ed. Chicago: National Live Stock and Meat Board, 1952.

National Restaurant Association and American Spice Trade Association. *A Guide to Spices.* 2d rev. ed. Technical Bulletin 190. Chicago: National Restaurant Association, undated.

National Turkey Federation. *Turkey: A Dish a Day.* Mt. Morris, Ill.: National Turkey Federation, undated.

Nestlé Co., Inc. *The History of Chocolate and Cocoa*. White Plains, N.Y.: The Nestlé Co., Inc., undated.

"Orange Juice: Frozen, Canned, Bottled, Cartoned, and Fresh," *Consumer Reports*, 41 (August 1976), 435-42.

Pedderson, Raymond B. *Foodservice and Hotel Purchasing*. Boston: CBI Publishing Company, Inc., 1980.

Pedderson, Raymond B. *Specs: The Comprehensive Food Service Purchasing and Specification Manual*, ed. Jule Wilson (Boston: Cahners Books, 1977).

Pellegrini, Angelo M., and others. Chapter in *American Cooking: The Melting Pot*. Ed. James P. Shenton and others. New York: Time-Life Books, 1971.

Rausch, Alma G., and others (eds.). *The Guide to Convenience Foods*. Chicago: Patterson Publishing Co., Inc., 1968.

Sacharow, Stanley, and Roger C. Griffin, Jr. *Food Packaging*. Westport, Conn.: Avi Publishing Co., Inc., 1970.

Smith, Ora. *Potatoes: Production, Storing, Processing*. Westport, Conn.: Avi Publishing Co., Inc., 1968.

Stefanelli, John M. *Purchasing: Selection and Procurement for the Hospitality Industry*. New York: John Wiley and Sons, 1981.

Stokes, John W. *How to Manage a Restaurant or Institutional Food Service*. Dubuque, Iowa: Wm. C. Brown Co., 1967.

Sunkist Growers, Inc. *Sunkist Grower's "Sunkist/Fish N'Seafood."* Los Angeles: Institutional Division, Sunkist Growers, Inc., undated.

_____. *Fresh Citrus Quantity Service Handbook*. Los Angeles: Institutional Division, Sunkist Growers, Inc., undated.

_____. *Sunkist Fresh Citrus Buying Guide*. Sherman Oaks, Calif.: Sunkist Growers, Inc., 1975.

Wanderstock, J. J. "Meat Purchasing," *Cornell Hotel and Restaurant Administration Quarterly*, 11 (November 1970), 60-64.

Wenzel, George L. *How to Control Costs*. Austin, Texas: privately printed by George L. Wenzel, Sr. (403 Riley Road), 1971.

Wilkinson, Jule. *The Complete Book of Cooking Equipment*. Rev. ed. Boston: Cahners Books, 1975, esp. p. 72.

Woolrich, W. R., and E. R. Hallowell. *Cold and Freezer Storage Manual*. Westport, Conn.: Avi Publishing Co., 1970.

Index